Buddhahood Embodied

SUNY Series in Buddhist Studies

Matthew Kapstein, Editor

Buddhahood Embodied

Sources of Controversy in India and Tibet

JOHN J. MAKRANSKY

State University of New York Press

Quotations in Chapter 13 are taken from *A Treasury of Mahayana Sutras,* edited by Garma C. C. Chang (University Park: The Pennsylvania State University Press, 1983), pp. 16, 28, 31, 106, 109–10, 175, © 1983 by The Pennsylvania State University, and are reproduced by permission of the publisher.

Passages from *The Flower Ornament Sutra* translated by Thomas Cleary, © 1984, 1986, 1987, 1989, 1993, have been reprinted by arrangement with Shambhala Publications, Inc., Boston.

Published by
State University of New York Press

Printed in the United States of America

For information, address the State University of New York Press, State University Plaza, Albany, NY 12246

Production by Bernadine Dawes • Marketing by Hanna J. Hazen

Library of Congress Cataloging-in-Publication Data

Makransky, John J.
Buddhahood embodied : sources of controversy in India and Tibet / John J. Makransky.
p. cm. — (SUNY series in Buddhist studies)
Includes bibliographical references and index.
ISBN 0-7914-3431-1 (hc : acid free). — ISBN 0-7914-3432-X (pb : acid free)
1. Abhisamayālaṅkāra Criticism, interpretation, etc. 2. Buddhahood. I. Title. II. Series.
BQ1955.A83M33 1997
294.3'85—dc21 97-2682
CIP

This book is dedicated to

Barbara Rogers Makransky,

my wife,

who has blessed the life behind it

Contents

Preface

This book draws from the research of my doctoral dissertation, which examined disagreements over Buddhahood as it is taught in the *Abhisamayālaṃkāra,* a text much studied in Indian Mahāyāna and Tibetan Buddhism. This book, however, carries that research several more steps. It explains how disagreements over the *Abhisamayālaṃkāra*'s teaching of Buddhahood express alternative ways to engage a doctrinal tension at the very heart of systematic Mahāyāna thought. It thereby shows how long controversy over that text is systemically related to many other controversies over Buddhahood in India and Tibet, all of which express the same underlying tension. In the final chapter, the book identifies early Mahāyāna intuitions of practice that drove Mahāyāna doctrinal formation toward that tension. It argues that later controversies over the resolution of that tension represent a clash of alternative perspectives on Buddhahood, perspectives that differ in how they prioritize and systematize those intuitions of practice. Several such controversies over Buddhahood (in its relation to us and to our world) continue to the present day in living traditions of Asian Buddhist scholarship and praxis.

This book is written with three kinds of readers particularly in mind: (1) contemporary academic students and scholars who are interested in Mahāyāna Buddhist thought and practice; (2) traditionally trained Buddhist scholars in Asia and the West, whose knowledge of the texts under discussion here is continuous with their transmission in Asian Buddhist cultures over many centuries; (3) contemporary practitioners of Buddhism, most of whom are not scholars, but who desire clarification on reasons for the differing perspectives within Buddhist tradition on the doctrines they are now internalizing and the practices they are now performing. I am located somewhere within the intersection of all three of these groups, and therefore write not only as an academic scholar of Buddhism but as a Mahāyāna Buddhist.

The questions that led me into the studies behind this book are presented at the beginning of the first chapter. They are inspired by two basic practices transmitted to contemporary Mahāyāna Buddhists from long tradition: (1) Mahāyāna practice of refuge in the Buddha, and (2) cultivation of bodhicitta, the aspiration to attain enlightenment, to become Buddha, for the sake of beings. The questions are these: When we take refuge in the Buddha, what are we actually taking refuge in? When we aspire to become Buddha for the sake of beings, what are we actually aspiring to become, and how is our practice to fulfill that aspiration?

The precise answers to these questions have varied within Mahāyāna Buddhist traditions, even to the present day. Our authentic response to those questions must be based both on those traditions and on the realities of our individual and social practices as they continue to develop in new times and places. For contemporary Mahāyāna Buddhists, then, a first step toward finding our own response to such questions is to learn as much as we can about what Mahāyāna traditions, continuous with the ones we have inherited, have said about Buddhahood. Inasmuch as these traditions have sometimes disagreed in significant ways, we have to learn what the disagreements have most deeply involved, especially when viewed in their relation to Buddhist thought and practice as a whole. Only then can we begin to assess their possible implications for our own understanding and practice in the present.

That is the broad theological concern behind this book, which explores bases of disagreement over Buddhahood in some of the textual traditions of Indian and Tibetan Buddhism that are now part of our cultural inheritance in both Asia and the West. Because the book tries to dig rather deeply into ancient textual sources of disagreements on Buddhahood, and seeks to relate those disagreements to differing perspectives on Mahāyāna thought and practice as a whole, it should hold interest for scholars and students in Western universities and Asian Buddhist centers of higher learning. And because its underlying purpose is to clear a little more of the ground necessary for contemporary Mahāyāna Buddhists to discern what an authentic practice must become in our own place and time, it may be of some use to Mahāyāna practitioners of the present and future. At least that is my hope.

Without assuming that the reader knows Sanskrit, I do use Sanskrit terminology for many important terms throughout the book. I always provide the meaning in English for each context. But as the reader will soon appreciate, meanings of one Sanskrit term (like "dharmakāya") vary significantly in different contexts. A single standard translation applied to all contexts would erase potential meanings. The book is therefore written in a way that will enable the interested reader to pick up key Sanskrit terms without prior knowledge of Sanskrit.

Scholars and students may find the entire book useful. Contemporary practitioners of Buddhism who are interested in the overall concerns of the book, but not in all the details of textual analysis, need not read chapters 7 and 8 in their entirety. One can get the gist of them from their introductory and concluding sections. These chapters present literary-critical analysis of key texts. The full content of them is for scholars who want details of the evidence and for others who may wish to use this book to open up questions on the relevance of historical context and literary criticism for the understanding of sacred Buddhist texts.

In general, I have tried to write this book so that it may serve equally as a text for the university classroom, as a reference work on many of the key ideas and practices formative of Mahāyāna understandings of Buddhahood, or as a self-study manual for students of Dharma who want to dig more deeply into textual and doctrinal roots of Mahāyāna traditions in which they practice. If there is any merit in this book, karmic or otherwise, it comes from the Buddhas through all who have taught me. May it therefore come to fruition in the awakening of us all.

Acknowledgments

I am most deeply indebted to Geshe Lhundup Sopa, my mentor and advisor at the University of Wisconsin-Madison, who patiently provided me over many years the philological, philosophical, and theological background I have drawn upon for all subsequent work. Any errors there may be in my work, however, are not his fault!

I am extremely fortunate to work at Boston College in the Department of Theology, where I have received tremendous support. I must thank Donald Dietrich, the department chairman, for his encouragement and great help, and Francis Clooney, S.J., for his thoughtful responses to drafts of several of these chapters. I am continually inspired by the members of that department as a whole, brilliant theologians in the Roman Catholic tradition, who continually shed light for me on purposes for doing theology in any tradition, including Buddhism. In addition, I would like to thank the Boston College Research Grant Program for a summer 1993 grant that supported part of the research for this book, and the O'Neil library staff at Boston College for their great support. I also want to thank Wyatt Benner for his painstaking care and thoughtfulness in the copyediting of this book, and Bernadine Dawes, SUNY Production Editor, for her great help and efficiency in the completion of its production.

I am grateful for the fellowship of the following scholars, who have helped me in many ways over the period in which this book has formed, through their writing or correspondence, through discussions at crucial times in the formation of ideas, through critical responses and moral support: Roger Jackson, José Cabezón, David Germano, Jules Levinson, Ronald Davidson, Matthew Kapstein, Gregory Schopen, Raoul Birnbaum, Charles Hallisey, Masatoshi Nagatomi, M. David Eckel, William Bodiford, Leslie Kawamura, David Seyfort Ruegg, Hidenori Sakuma,

George Nickelsburg, Paul Griffiths, Yael Bentor, Dan Martin, David Patt, John Newman, William Waldron, Alex Naughton, John Keenan, John Dunne, and Sara McClintock.

I continue to draw upon the inspiration and help I received in India and Nepal from 1985 to 1987 while supported by a Fulbright-Hays research fellowship. I wish again to thank the Venerable Samdong Rinpoche, Director of the Institute of Higher Tibetan Studies in Sarnath, for his help as my advisor at that time; Ram Śāṇkar Tripāṭhī (of Varanasi Sanskrit University), Venerable Ngawang Samten, and Gen Sempa Dorje (Tibetan Institute) for their patient help with abstruse Sanskrit verses; Geshe Yeshe Tabkye, Geshe Jigme Dawa (Tibetan Institute), Kensur Lobsang (former abbot of Sera Je Monastic University), and Gyumay Kensur Lobsang Tenzin (former abbot of Gyumay Tantric College), who helped me read through many Tibetan and Indian texts relevant to the research.

I must express special gratitude to the late Ganden Geshe Thubten Tsering and to Sa skya Khenpo Migmar Tsering, brilliant scholars who spent many patient hours helping me study writings of Tsong kha pa and Go ram pa.

I am fortunate to have had contact with a number of other teachers, Tibetan, Indian and Western, from whose pool of inspiration and instruction I siphon every day in my thought and writing. I must therefore acknowledge them here with deep gratitude (in the order I met them): Ven. George Churinoff, Lama Zopa Rinpoche, Lama Thubten Yeshe, Serkong Rinpoche, Geshe Ngawang Dhargyey, Geshe Sonam Rinchen, Kyabje Trijang Rinpoche, His Holiness the Dalai Lama, Geshe Lhundup Sopa, Zong Rinpoche, Geshe Lobsang Donyo, Geshe Lobsang Namgyal, Mast Rām Bābā, Khenpo Tsultrim Gyamtso, Khenpo Jigme Phuntsog, Lama Surya Das, Nyoshul Khen Rinpoche, Khenpo Sonam Tobgyal Rinpoche, Lama Yeshe Gyamtso, Tulku Thondup Rinpoche, Drikung Kyabgon Chetsang Rinpoche, Chagdud Tulku, and Ayang Rinpoche.

Abbreviations

AA	*Abhisamayālaṃkāra*
Ashta	*Aṣṭasāhasrikā-prajñāpāramitā-sūtra*
DDV	*Dharmadharmatāvibhāga*
Kośa	*Abhidharmakośa*
Pk	Peking edition of the Tibetan Tripitaka (Tokyo and Kyoto: Tibetan Tripitaka Research Institute, 1956)
MAV	*Madhyāntavibhāga*
MHK	Bhāvaviveka, *Madhyamaka-hṛdaya-kārikā*
MSA	*Mahāyānasūtralaṃkāra*
Msg	*Mahāyānasaṃgraha*
PP	*Prajñāpāramitā*
RGV	*Ratnagotravibhāga*
RGVV	*Ratnagotravibhāga-vyākhyāna*
rP	Revised edition of the *Pañcaviṃśatisāhasrikā-prajñāpāramitā-sūtra*
sDe dge	sDe dge edition of the Tibetan Tripitaka
Toh	*Tohoku Catalogue of the Tibetan bKa' 'gyur and bsTan 'gyur*
Vṛttibhāṣya	*Sūtrālaṃkāravṛttibhāṣya*

1
Introduction

1.1
Basic Questions

> "I go to the Buddha as my refuge.
> I go to the Dharma as my refuge.
> I go to the Sangha as my refuge."

To repeat these words with sincerity after a preceptor in the proper ritual setting is to take Buddha (Teacher), Dharma (Practice of the Teaching), and Sangha (Spiritual Community) as one's ultimate refuge in this life and beyond, and thereby to enter into the ancient community of followers of the Buddha. This simple ritual has been an important marker of religious identity in each Asian Buddhist culture. Yet its implications are anything but simple.

Mahāyāna Buddhists in India and Tibet have carried into their practice of refuge their belief in numberless Buddhas whose attainment is unbounded in space and time. Mahāyāna practice of refuge in Buddha has been framed by authoritative texts that declare Buddhas completely freed from the suffering nature of our world, yet limitlessly active within it to the end of time, helping others to the same freedom. The Buddhas are those who have attained personal freedom from mental components that construct a deluded and suffering world, while remaining compassionately engaged within the world until all others are freed. It is by having seen through the nature of beings' delusions that Buddhas are said to have the wisdom to guide others to freedom.

These two qualities—freedom from the deluded world and compassionate participation within it—are a critical part of what has qualified Buddhas as worthy objects of ultimate refuge in Indo-Tibetan Mahāyāna traditions. Yet those very qualities, even as they provide a key doctrinal basis for Mahāyāna refuge practice, appear to be logically inconsistent. Don't each of the qualities preclude the other? If one's mind has stopped constructing a suffering world, hasn't one thereby stopped participating in such a world? In Indian and Tibetan Mahāyāna, to practice refuge in Buddha is to performatively answer this question with a resounding "No!," to affirm one's faith that the Buddhas will always appear and give guidance as one is karmically ready to perceive them, whether in meditative visions, dreams, in pure realms, or on earth. Yet how is one to make sense of this affirmation of faith?

In Mahāyāna literary and practice traditions of India and Tibet, practice of refuge in Buddha is associated with the impulse for enlightenment called *bodhicitta* (mind of enlightenment). In one of its principal senses, it refers to the powerful impulse that propels a person from entry into the Mahāyāna path to its completion: the intense aspiration to attain Buddhahood for the sake of all beings. The questions raised above return again in new form in connection with *bodhicitta:* What precisely does it mean for one to "seek Buddhahood for the sake of all beings," to commit oneself both to attain freedom from the world's delusions and to continue participating in that deluded world until all others are freed? How does the culmination of one's present practice fulfill that commitment?

Mahāyānists have looked to their scriptures and treatises for guidance. But the descriptions of Buddhahood in those sources express the logical tensions behind the questions. The mind of the Buddhas is said to abide in immovable equipoise on the emptiness of the entire cosmos, yet the Buddhas' activities are described as inconceivably vast. On the one hand, the Buddhas are entirely freed from the limitations of the dualistic world our minds construct. On the other hand, they pervade this world of our dualistic construction with cosmic power and activity. How can both be the case?

Such questions raise further questions at another level of inquiry: How significant is the autonomous exercise of human reason for determining the answers to such questions about Buddhahood? Or do human inferences about a Buddha's realization fall too far short of their mark? Are the logical tensions of Buddhahood inscribed in Mahāyāna scriptures resolvable only by attaining a Buddha's nonconceptual awareness for ourselves, like the morning mist dissolved by the rising sun? If so, should scriptural expressions of Buddhahood be received primarily as revelation, as revealing something that transcends thought and prodding us to realize in meditation what we cannot grasp conceptually? Or are logical tensions in scriptural descriptions of Buddhahood only apparent tensions, resolvable through careful analysis of the relevant concepts, so that scripture is to be received more primarily as a basis for reasoned and systematic reflection about Buddhahood?

These basic questions, flowing from the doctrinal underpinnings of basic Mahāyāna practices, are the implicit questions behind centuries of disagreement by Mahāyāna Buddhist scholars of India and Tibet over the proper interpretation of one of their most cherished texts: the *Abhisamayālaṃkāra.* Although non-Buddhist theistic religious traditions have engaged in systematic reflection through worldviews quite distant from those of Buddhism, they have struggled with parallel questions concerning the problem of the transcendence and immanence of God, and the capacity of human reason to comprehend God's relation to us. Some contemporary religious scholars have assumed that Buddhism, as a nontheistic religious tradition, has escaped the sorts of logical tensions that inhere in the theistic attempt to specify a relation between a transcendent being and the world. But for centuries Mahāyāna Buddhist scholars have wrestled with parallel questions about Buddhahood through their interpretations of the *Abhisamayālaṃkāra*, indicating that the problem of conceptualizing the transcendent may be more universal a religious phenomenon than has often been recognized.[1]

1.2
Long Controversy over the Abhisamayālaṃkāra on Buddhahood

The *Abhisamayālaṃkāra* (Ornament of realizations), an Indian Sanskrit commentary on the *Prajñāpāramitā* sūtras, was ascribed the highest authority by late Indian Buddhist scholars.[2] From the eighth century C.E., and perhaps earlier, they attributed it to the legendary figure Maitreya, the future Buddha. The *Abhisamayālaṃkāra* was probably composed sometime between the fourth and the early sixth centuries C.E.[3] It is a condensed, versified treatise that purports to summarize all of the practices and yogic realizations leading to the different types of Buddhist enlightenment implicitly taught in the *Prajñāpāramitā* sūtras.[4] The *Abhisamayālaṃkāra*'s eighth and final chapter (*AA* 8), entitled "Dharmakāya,"[5] describes the fullest and most complete form of enlightenment, *samyaksaṃbodhi*, Buddhahood, the final culmination of all the practices described in the prior seven chapters.[6] This chapter, like other Mahāyāna treatises of the period, explicates the *kāya*s (embodiments) of a Buddha: awakened awareness as embodied in its own experience and in its relations to others. With the Buddha *kāya*s, the same chapter elucidates pure mental and physical qualities of a Buddha and enumerates its activities *(buddhakarma)* that pervade the cosmos to guide living beings to spiritual freedom.

At the outset, it is worth noticing two special things about the *Abhisamayālaṃkāra:* first, its great popularity in late Indian and Tibetan scholarship, and second, the long controversy that its eighth chapter on Buddhahood has occasioned in India and Tibet.

On the first point, for reasons we can only speculate upon, the *Abhisamayālaṃkāra* (abbreviated *AA*) became one of the most popular and commented upon texts in late Indian and Tibetan Buddhism. Twenty-one Indian commentaries on this one text are extant (most now available only in Tibetan translation in the

Tibetan Tripitaka), and even more Indian commentaries may have been composed.[7] In Tibet, hundreds of commentaries upon it were written.[8] Perhaps because it lent itself better to Mādhyamika interpretation than other synoptic Indian texts on Buddhist practice (Mādhyamika thought having dominated Tibetan exegesis), the *AA* and its commentaries were chosen by Tibetan scholars as primary Indian sources for systematic description of all phases of praxis in nontantric Mahāyāna Buddhism. In fact, within the great monastic universities of Lhasa, commentaries upon the *AA* have comprised one of the fundamental subjects of monastic study.[9] In sum, the *Abhisamayālaṃkāra* and its commentaries have dominated exegesis in India and Tibet on the implicit meaning of the *Prajñāpāramitā* sūtras for the past fifteen hundred years (since the time of Ārya Vimuktisena, ca. early sixth century C.E.). This has meant that the *Abhisamayālaṃkāra*'s eighth chapter became one of the most important Indian textual sources for Tibetan thought on the nature of Buddhahood. Even up to the present day, if one asks a traditional Tibetan scholar about the qualities of a Buddha, often he will refer to the *Abhisamayālaṃkāra*'s eighth chapter (*AA* 8).

On the second point, at least twelve centuries ago in India, *AA* 8 gave rise to an ongoing controversy over the meaning of its verses on complete enlightenment, a controversy that has repeatedly renewed itself in Tibet and continues even to the present day among contemporary Tibetan scholars. The differing interpretations of the text, I argue in this book, are elicited less by the ambiguities of the text than by the differing frames of reference that its interpreters have brought to it. This means that disagreements purportedly concerned only with interpretation of textual passages have both expressed and masked deeper philosophical and theological differences that guided the interpretations. And these underlying differences involve different approaches to the very questions that begin this chapter, namely, How are we to make sense of the two seemingly contradictory qualities of Buddhahood which underpin Mahāyāna practice: a Buddha's simultaneous freedom from and engagement with the world?

Before we return to these larger questions, we must focus more specifically on *AA* 8 and the nature of the interpretive disagreements it occasioned. The eighth chapter, entitled "Dharmakāya," describes Buddhahood by reference to multiple Buddha *kāyas*. *Dharmakāya* is an exalted term, used with the deepest reverence for a Buddha's supramundane, nondual realization of reality as it is.

The fundamental sense of the Sanskrit word *kāya* is "body," meaning the physical body of a living being. The term *kāya* in *rūpakāya* in pre-Mahāyāna and Mahāyāna texts generally referred to a Buddha's *śarīra*, his "body" or "physical form" As with the English word "body," the term also came to possess several derivational meanings. *Kāya* often refers to a collection of things ("corpus"). It can refer to a substratum or a basis of qualities, or to the "embodiment" of those qualities in one's understanding and way of being. It can also be used to connote all such meanings at once. In Indian commentaries on the *Abhisamayālaṃkāra* (those by

Ārya Vimuktisena, Bhadanta Vimuktisena, Dharmamitra, Ratnākaraśānti, and Abhayākaragupta), and in various Indian Yogācāra commentaries, the word *kāya* in *dharmakāya* was generally etymologized in one or more of three ways:

1. *kāya* = "body" in the sense of *saṃcaya*, a collection of components or an accumulation of parts; *dharmakāya* = the collection *(kāya)* of Buddha's excellent qualities *(anāsravadharmāḥ);* in some pre-Mahāyāna texts and a few early Mahāyāna passages, it has also meant "collection *(kāya)* of the Buddha's teachings *(dharma)*";

2. *kāya* = "body" in the sense of *āśraya*, substratum or basis; *dharmakāya* = the substratum *(kāya)* of excellent qualities *(anāsravadharmāḥ)* or the basis *(kāya)* of sovereignty over all phenomena *(sarvadharmāh);*

3. *kāya* = "body" in the sense of embodiment; e.g., *dharmakāya* = that which embodies the real nature of things, the embodiment *(kāya)* of the real nature of things *(dharmatā)* in knowledge.

While *rūpakāya* has been a term of reverence for the physical form in which a Buddha appears to others, *dharmakāya* has often been a reverential term for a Buddha's own enlightened awareness.

Dharma, the first term in the compound *dharmakāya,* is a term with a very broad semantic range in Buddhist texts. *Dharma* refers to the real nature of things, reality as a Buddha knows it. It also refers to the nature and structure of reality as expressed in the Four Noble Truths or the two truths *(paramārtha satya* and *saṃvṛti satya),* and as realized in the direct experience of those truths *(adhigama)* through practice of the Buddha's path. It therefore also refers to the Buddha's teachings of those truths *(āgama)* and the practices to realize them. In its plural form *dharmāḥ* (dharmas), the term refers to the ultimate constituents of the psychophysical world of beings, subtle constituents of mind and body that gradually become perceptible through realization of the path (the *sarvadharmāḥ* of Abhidharma metaphysics). In some contexts, *dharmāḥ* may also refer to the pure constituents of a Buddha's mind or body: excellent qualities that derive from his or her completion of the path *(anāsravadharmāḥ).* When the term *dharma* appears in Mahāyāna texts as part of the compound *dharmakāya,* it can express many or all of these connotations at once, the diversity of its connotations reflecting the entire history of Buddhist doctrinal development from the earliest period of Buddhism through Mahāyāna. This makes the meaning of *dharmakāya* as a reverent designation of Buddhahood and the title of *AA* 8 enormously rich, complex, and difficult to interpret.

The disagreements of interpretation that *AA* 8 occasioned centered primarily upon the meanings of *dharmakāya* and *svābhāvikakāya* in their relation to each other and to other dimensions of Buddhahood. *Svābhāvikakāya* (as I argue in chapter 4 below) may be glossed "the embodiment [of Buddhahood] in its essence, in its real nature." The other dimensions of Buddhahood include *rūpakāya*s (embodiment in forms) and *buddhakarma* (Buddha activity for living beings). The *rūpakāya*s are the forms through which Buddhahood communicates with beings, categorized as *sāmbhogikakāya* (the glorious form through which a Buddha shares the dharma with great bodhisattvas) and *nairmāṇikakāya* (the limitless variety of forms through which a Buddha communicates dharma to the limitless varieties of other beings). *Buddhakarma* refers to Buddhahood's extensive activity for beings through those forms.

An exegete's interpretation of the meanings of *dharmakāya* and *svābhāvikakāya* in *AA* 8 automatically affects his understanding of the total number of *kāya*s taught there. In Tibetan commentaries, the interpretive controversy over *AA* 8 has therefore often been summarized as a debate over the number of *kāya*s. But the primary point of disagreement is not the numbers per se but the meanings of the key concepts, especially *dharmakāya* and *svābhāvikakāya.*

Ārya Vimuktisena (ca. early sixth century), the first *Abhisamayālaṃkāra* commentator whose work is extant, believed that *AA* 8 used the terms *dharmakāya* and *svābhāvikakāya* to refer to one thing, the essential nondual realization of Buddhahood, that appears to beings of different levels of purity as *sāmbhogikakāya* or *nairmāṇikakāya*. Hence, he wrote that the *AA* teaches three *kāya*s of a Buddha *(dharmakāya/svābhāvikakāya, sāmbhogikakāya, nairmāṇikakāya)*. Haribhadra (late eighth century) reinterpreted the *AA*'s eighth chapter, arguing that *dharmakāya* and *svābhāvikakāya* in its key verses refer to two distinct aspects of Buddhahood, which are *not* to be equated with each other, making a total of four Buddha *kāya*s in the text. It appears that Haribhadra's interpretation (and indeed his ascription of four *kāya*s to any such nontantric Buddhist text as the *Abhisamayālaṃkāra*) was initially controversial. Haribhadra's reputed disciple, Buddhajñānapāda (late eighth century), did not follow his four-*kāya* interpretation of *AA* 8 in his own commentary on the *AA*. Dharmamitra (late eighth century to early ninth century), author of the first subcommentary on Haribhadra's *Sphuṭārthā*, wrote that some Indian scholars rejected the four-*kāya* interpretation of *AA* 8 and found it impossible to believe that Haribhadra, already coming into recognition as a major authority, actually meant it as his own position. Gradually, however, Haribhadra's authority became more weighty, his interpretation of *AA* 8 being accepted as authoritative by a number of later Indian scholars, notably Prajñākaramati (ca. 950–1000 C.E.), Buddhaśrījñāna (ca. 1200 C.E.), and Kumāraśrībhadra (date unknown). Other well-known Indian scholars, however—Ratnākaraśānti (ca. 1000 C.E.) and Abhayākaragupta (ca. 1100 C.E.)—vehemently rejected Haribhadra's four-*kāya* interpretation of the *AA* and argued for a return to Ārya Vimuktisena's prior three-*kāya* view.[10] Several centuries later in Tibet some of the most influential interpreters of the *AA* came also to disagree with each other on the issue. Notably, the Sa skya scholar Go ram pa bsod nams senge ge (1429–89) supported Ārya Vimuktisena in asserting three *kāyas,* while Tsong kha pa blo bzang grags pa (1357–1419, father of the dGe lugs pa order) and his followers backed Haribhadra's assertion of four. Thus, taking Haribhadra as its initiator, the debate over the Buddha *kāya*s taught in the *Abhisamayālaṃkāra* has continued for over twelve hundred years, and Tibetan Sa skya and dGe lugs scholars of the present day continue to disagree on the issue.

What light this long disagreement may shed upon problematics in the development of Mahāyāna thought in India and Tibet has not been previously analyzed in depth. Until recently, most Western scholars, basing themselves on commentaries by Haribhadra and his Tibetan followers, have reported that the *AA* teaches four *kāyas* as if unaware of the controversy.[11] Japanese scholars have recently taken note of the controversy,[12] but leave some of the most fundamental questions unresolved: What did the *Abhisamayālaṃkāra* really teach? Looking beyond the surface level of discussion, what different doctrinal perspectives did scholars bring to the text, effecting their readings of it? What underlying problems in Mahāyāna thought were those scholars trying to address through their disagreements over the meaning of that text?

The long history of controversy over *AA* 8 raises for us at the outset some fundamental questions: historical, textual, philosophical, and theological.[13] In what follows, I will focus first on the historical and textual questions, then on the philosophical and theological ones.

1.3
Historical and Textual Issues behind the Controversy

The research presented in this book indicates that, while there is much the *Abhisamayālaṃkāra* shares with other classical Indian Mahāyāna treatises of its period (ca. fourth to early sixth centuries), there are also key features unique to the discussion of Buddahood in its eighth chapter. Those features gave the text sufficient ambiguity, at least by the late eighth century, that Haribhadra could plausibly interpret it in significantly new ways, and that later scholars could continue to disagree over his interpretation even to the present day. What are the sources of *AA* 8's unique features? What might they tell us about the author's intention in composing it?

This leads to more technical questions. What prior textual materials and traditions did the *AA*'s author draw from? How did he arrange those specific materials in his redaction of *AA* 8? What does this tell us about his purposes? Questions of this kind organize methods of textual analysis known as "source criticism" and "redaction criticism," literary-critical methods that have been developed in their application to the Bible. To apply these methods to *AA* 8 is to seek to uncover its textual sources (source criticism), to examine how those sources were put together and structured within its composition, and to analyze what that structure likely indicates about the intention of its author (redaction criticism). When source and redaction criticism are applied to *AA* 8, we find much evidence that its composition represents an attempt, probably for the first time in Indian Buddhism, to draw a clear and direct correspondence between two semiautonomous Mahāyāna descriptions of Buddhahood that had become normative: a *Prajñāpāramitāsūtra* description and a three-*kāya* description found in contemporary Yogācāra śāstras. In other words, *AA* 8 is neither an independent creation of its author nor a simple restatement of what was said in its sources or other texts of its period. Rather, it functions like a grid to map a Yogācāra model of enlightenment onto the *Prajñāpāramitā* sūtras. When seen in this light, the reasons for each of the unique features that made *AA* 8 ambiguous for later commentators become clear. At the same time, the likely original intention of its author also becomes evident.

The first part of this book, then, seeks the answer to all the textual questions above by analyzing the materials on Buddhahood from *Prajñāpāramitā* sūtras and Yogācāra treatises from which the *AA*'s author constructed its eighth chapter on *dharmakāya*. This analysis already goes beyond purely textual concerns, however, into the philosophical and theological. For it requires that we explore *Prajñāpāramitā* and Yogācāra concepts of *dharmakāya* from the unique perspective of their contribution to the *AA*. There are features of *Prajñāpāramitā* approaches to *dharmakāya* that stand out more vividly when seen in light of their role in the formation of the *Abhisamayālaṃkāra*. Similarly, there are aspects of Yogācāra buddhological analysis that gain unique significance when viewed in light of the later controversies over *AA* 8. Further, both of these literary traditions presume a background in preceding Abhidharma traditions that they both draw from and depart from.

Of the chapters that follow, chapter 2 focuses on selected aspects of Abhidharma buddhology that contributed to the *Prajñāpāramitā* sūtras and to Yogācāra buddhology, through them to the *AA*, and then to the controversy over its eighth chapter. Chapter 3 centers on *dharmakāya* in *Prajñāpāramitā* sūtras, focusing on aspects of special interest for their contribution to the *AA*. Chapters 4 and 5 explore classical Yogācāra buddhology, emphasizing new findings on the *kāyas* that emerge in light of Yogācāra contributions to the *AA*. Chapter 6 sets *AA* 8 within the *AA* as a whole, specifies the controversial passages, and delineates the philological disagreements over them in India. Chapters 7 and 8 draw upon the preceding chapters to seek answers to all the textual questions raised above, using source and redaction criticism of *AA* 8. The latter two chapters are quite technical.

Chapter 9 analyzes the commentary of Ārya Vimuktisena on *AA* 8. Among all extant commentaries, Ārya Vimuktisena's was composed closest to the time of the *Abhisamayālaṃkāra*. Steeped contemporaneously in the literary traditions from which the *AA*'s author drew, Ārya Vimuktisena read *AA* 8 as the Yogācāra-*Prajñāpāramitā* grid that it was, demonstrating how the *AA*'s author had matched the three Yogācāra *kāyas—svābhāvikakāya (= dharmakāya), sāmbhogikakāya*, and *nairmāṇikakāya*—to specific passages in the *Prajñāpāramitāsūtra*. In doing this, he reiterated an understanding of *dharmakāya* in *Prajñāpāramitā* and Yogācāra literature that had found expression in the *Abhisamayālaṃkāra:* dharmakāya = a Buddha's embodiment of dharma *(dharmakāya)* as his real nature, the embodiment of his real essence *(svābhāvikakāya),* i.e., a Buddha's own yogic realization, supramundane, beyond dualities of thought, undifferentiated, and inconceivable to others. Chapter 9 contextualizes this by showing how Ārya Vimuktisena's comments on a Buddha's realization resonate both with Yogācāra gnoseology and with that of Candrakīrti, a later Mādhyamika scholar.

Chapter 10 explores Haribhadra's interpretations of *AA* 8. Ārya Vimuktisena's interpretation was accepted as authoritative for more than two centuries. Then, according to our record of extant commentaries, Haribhadra formally rejected his reading of *dharmakāya* and *svābhāvikakāya* as synonyms in key passages, asserting that they must be distinguished as two distinct aspects of Buddhahood, two distinct *kāyas* (giving a total of four). We know *AA* 8 had unique features that could permit it to be reread in new ways in later centuries. But having established through literary criticism that the *AA* actually did teach three *kāyas*, and that Ārya Vimuktisena read it correctly, we are now confronted with a new question. What motivated Haribhadra to go against over two centuries of tradition and challenge the prior authoritative interpretation? This question leads us back to the philosophical and theological concerns with which this chapter began, questions concerning the Buddhas' relation to our world of delusion. For these concerns, it is argued here, are what implicitly motivated Haribhadra's new interpretation of *AA* 8.

1.4
Philosophical and Theological Concerns behind the Controversy

The fact that *AA* 8, read by itself in isolation, could plausibly be viewed in new ways in later centuries does not, in itself, explain Haribhadra's new interpretation. Given the semantic density of the *AA*'s verses, it is unlikely that any scholar, then as now, ever read the *AA* without consulting at least one major commentary. Further, we know Haribhadra was intimately familiar with the principal commentary of his time, Ārya Vimuktisena's, by his own references to it. Read through the lens of Ārya Vimuktisena's interpretations, *AA* 8 does not appear ambiguous. Haribhadra's perspective on the text must have been affected by concerns of his own place and time, concerns acute enough to motivate a new reading.[14]

Ample clues to Haribhadra's implicit concerns are provided in his commentaries on *AA* 8. One theme he repeatedly returns to (on five different occasions, in fact, in his comments on *AA* 8), is the importance of affirming a clear distinction between the ultimate, unconditioned aspect of a Buddha's awareness, on the one hand, and the conventional, conditioned aspect of it, on the other, to show particularly how the latter aspect becomes the basis for a Buddha's activity within this conventional, conditioned world. Clearly Haribhadra was troubled by what he viewed as the lack of a clear ontological basis within the three-*kāya* Yogācāra model for a Buddha's conditioned activity in the world. So he read *svābhāvikakāya* and *dharmakāya* in key verses of *AA* 8 not as synonyms for the Buddha's nondual ultimate realization, as Ārya Vimuktisena had done, but as designations for two distinct aspects of Buddha mind: the unconditioned aspect by which a Buddha transcends the conditioned world of delusion (*svābhāvikakāya*, essential body), and the conditioned aspect through which he appears to beings within their world of delusion to work for them (*[jñānātmaka] dharmakāya*, body of dharma-gnoses, conditioned forms of pure awareness). For this reason, Haribhadra makes explicit his concern that *AA* 8 teach four *kāya*s rather than three (*svābhāvikakāya, [jñānātmaka] dharmakāya, sāmbhogikakāya, nairmāṇikakāya*). All relevant passages of Haribhadra's commentary are translated and analyzed in chapter 10.

In Chapter 10, another reason for Haribhadra's interpretation is suggested that is closely related to the concern above: his interest as a Mādhyamika logician to critique an absolutism he saw in the Yogācāra, three-*kāya* model of enlightenment that he believed had become too generally embedded in late Indian Mahāyāna thought. Haribhadra seems to have felt that the Yogācāra model of *svābhāvikakāya* never properly distinguished the awareness of a Buddha per se (*buddhajñāna*, which Haribhadra asserted to be an impermanent, conventional existent) from the ultimate truth it knows (*śūnyatā*, unconditioned emptiness), thereby seeming to ascribe ultimate status to a conventional thing, an implicit absolutism he found unacceptable for Mādhyamikans. And because a Buddha's awareness and ultimate truth were never formally separated within the Yogācāra model of *svābhāvikakāya/dharmakāya*, which was characterized as permanent by nature, it appeared inexplicable to Haribhadra how the Yogācāras could have posited it as the foundation for a Buddha's activity in the conditioned world.

By creative interpretation of *AA* 8, then, Haribhadra, as an eighth-century Mādhyamika logician, sought to accomplish something which seemed long overdue to him. He sought to "Mādhyamika-ize" the Yogācāra model of Buddhahood that had been uncritically inherited by late Indian Mahāyāna, by making the multiple-*kāya* model of Buddhahood an object of logical analysis that would conform it more clearly to the two-truth ontology of Mādhyamika and account for its simultaneous participation in the unconditioned and the conditioned. Using analytical tools developed in the intervening centuries by Dignāga and Dharmakīrti, he thereby sought to resolve what he saw as the logical tension between unconditioned and conditioned aspects in the three-*kāya* model of Yogācāra.

This raises the next question. What is the source of the logical tension with which Haribhadra wrestled? It derives from something more basic in Mahāyāna thought than the particular model he encountered in *AA* 8. When we look at Yogācāra treatises that first formalized the three-*kāya* model expressed in *AA* 8, we find a deeper doctrinal source for the logical tension in that model. The source is a doctrine at the core of developed Mahāyāna soteriology: nonabiding nirvāṇa (*apratiṣṭhita nirvāṇa*). This is the doctrine, expressed in many ways throughout Indian Mahāyāna literature, that the nirvāṇa realized by a Buddha is *not* separate from saṃsāra.

Prior to the rise of Mahāyāna, early Buddhist and Abhidharma traditions had assumed a dualistic understanding of saṃsāra and nirvāṇa. The five *skandhas* (comprising the mind, body, and conditioned world of beings) were characterized as *duḥkha*, conditioned forms of dissatisfaction and suffering. The completion of the Buddha's path was said to culminate in the attainment of the unconditioned, nirvāṇa, by completely removing the causes of *duḥkha* which are the deepest generative causes of mind and body. Final nirvāṇa *(parinirvāṇa)*, then, the final attainment of the unconditioned upon physical death, involved the complete cessation of all conditioned states of mind and body, the cessation of all participation in this world: "Monks, there is an unborn, unbecome, unmade, unconditioned. Monks, if there were not an unborn, unbecome, unmade, unconditioned, then we could not here know any escape from the born, become, made, conditioned."[15] Logically, this posed no problems. The ultimate attainment of the unconditioned state entailed the abandonment of all conditioned states (the five *skandhas*, which comprise the conditioned world of saṃsāra).

Contributing to the rise of Mahāyāna traditions were several intuitions about further implications of the doctrines inherited from prior traditions. These intuitions gradually converged upon an important new understanding that eventually became dominant in Indian Mahāyāna (common to the *Abhisamayālaṃkāra*, its literary sources, and all its commentators): For a Buddha, saṃsāra is *not* apart from nirvāṇa; nirvāṇa is *not* apart from saṃsāra. With this, the prior dualistic understanding (that final attainment of the unconditioned entails abandonment of the conditioned world) was eradicated. Mahāyāna texts came to assert that a Buddha, upon fully attaining the unconditioned (nirvāṇa), *never* abandons the conditioned world (saṃsāra).

At the beginning of this chapter, *bodhicitta* was invoked as the raison d'être of praxis expressed in classical Indian Mahāyāna texts: the aspiration and strong commitment to attain enlightenment for the sake of all living beings. To attain nirvāṇa in the highest sense (Buddhahood), asserted these texts, is the way to fulfill this commitment, by remaining eternally active in the world as a force for the benefit of others. The Buddhas, through their experience of awakening, have removed the very root of their own conditioned existence, yet pervade the universe of beings with the power of their awareness and compassion, guiding others to awakening until all are freed.

This represented a sea change in the Buddhist worldview, the doctrinal repercussions from which reverberated through the long history of Indian and Tibetan Mahāyāna thought, instantiating in one particular way, I argue in this book, as the doctrinal tension underlying the long controversy over *AA* 8.[16] In classical Indian Mahāyāna texts, a Buddha's nirvāṇa was unconditioned (he was personally freed from the causes of the conditioned world) and at the same time, conditioned (manifesting pervasively in the conditioned world for others). It was given the name "nonabiding nirvāṇa" *(apratiṣṭhita nirvāṇa)*, because it was bound neither to the causal chain of conditioned existence, nor to the isolation of a quiescent (pre-Mahāyāna type) final nirvāṇa.[17] On the one hand, it was asserted, Buddhahood is highest nirvāṇa, free from all the dichotomous conceptualization *(vikalpa)* that constructs the phenomenological worlds of suffering beings. On the other hand, Buddhahood remains an active part of saṃsāra by appearing to beings within the phenomenological worlds of *their* conceptual construction.[18] A Buddha had, in some sense, to be both unconditioned and operative within conditions. This paradox is engendered by the enormous leap from pre-Mahāyāna to developed Mahāyāna understandings of nirvāṇa. The debates over *AA* 8 demonstrate one way in which this underlying paradox, without being explicitly invoked, has quietly functioned for centuries as a driving force behind a wide range of doctrinal disagreements over Buddhahood in India and Tibet.

The doctrine of nonabiding nirvāṇa was formalized and systematized in Yogācāra treatises from ca. fourth to fifth centuries C.E., which Indo-Tibetan traditions have ascribed to Maitreya, Asanga, and Vasubandhu. Formulations of Buddhahood in these texts (including the three-*kāya* model that became part of *AA* 8) developed out of several emergent Mahāyāna intuitions regarding enlightenment: ethical, ontological, gnoseological, soteriological, and theological, all of which found expression in the doctrine of nonabiding nirvāṇa.[19] Several of these texts and their commentaries note the logical tension within that doctrine (the paradox of Buddhahood being both unconditioned and active within the conditioned world), but they treat it as merely an apparent problem. It is to be resolved not by (futilely) trying to logically analyze a Buddha's realization, but by yogically realizing it for oneself. For this reason, Yogācāra texts really meant it when they claimed that Buddhahood, in essence, is inconceivable *(acintya),* to be known only through personal realization *(pratyātmavedanīya).* For the Yogācāras (and Mādhyamikas such as Candrakīrti prior to Haribhadra) a Buddha's gnosis was primarily an object of yogic realization, not of philosophical speculation. The realization of Buddhahood was referred to alternatively as *svābhāvikakāya* (embodiment of Buddhahood in its innermost essence) or *dharmakāya* (embodiment of dharma in its ultimate realization). Upon actual attainment of that, what had earlier appeared paradoxical about a Buddha would simply dissolve.[20]

The centuries intervening between these Yogācāra treatises and Haribhadra saw the rise of the Buddhist logico-epistemological tradition of Dignāga and Dharmakīrti. Haribhadra, like other eighth-century Mādhyamikas, was heavily influenced by that tradition. This gave him a different perspective on the apparent paradox of nonabiding nirvāṇa than that of earlier writers. The logical tension from that doctrine, which became inscribed in the Yogācāra three-*kāya* model embedded in *AA* 8, troubled Haribhadra enough to motivate his new interpretation of the text. But Haribhadra, confident in the new found power of Buddhist logic to solve such logical tensions, identified the source of the tension not in the doctrine of nonabiding nirvāṇa per se (normative for all the Mahāyāna schools of his time), but in the Yogācāra three-*kāya* formulation of it. That model, he believed, gave rise to the logical tension because it did not distinguish separate ontological bases in Buddhahood for its transcendence and immanence. So, as noted above, Haribhadra's comments on *AA* 8 revolve around his concern to divide the first of the three Yogācāra *kāyas*, *svābhāvikakāya/dharmakāya*, into two now distinct aspects: an unconditioned, transcendent aspect and a conditioned, immanent aspect. The unconditioned aspect, he argued, was what *Abhisamayālaṃkāra* 8 meant by *svābhāvikakāya* (referring to a Buddha's unconditioned purity), while the conditioned aspect must have been what it meant in key verses by *dharmakāya* (referring to a Buddha's conditioned awareness, *jñāna*). Reading this distinction into *Abhisamayālaṃkāra* 8, Haribhadra believed, by producing a four-*kāya* model, would give the doctrine of nonabiding nirvāṇa the logically coherent form that it ought to have, at least from his perspective as an eighth-century Mādhyamikan logician.

By doing this, however, he treated a Buddha's nonconceptual attainment as if it were far more accessible to autonomous logical analysis (apart from yogic experience) than earlier Mahāyāna traditions had believed.[21] *AA* 8 lists twenty-one types of a Buddha's mental qualities (undefiled dharmas), which largely derive from prior Abhidharma traditions that contributed to the *Prajñāpāramitā* sūtras and thence to the *AA*. Haribhadra, who was also an authority of Abhidharma, understood that list to refer to actual conditioned components of a Buddha's mind, analogous to (although purer than) the mental factors cultivated by bodhisattvas on their path to Buddhahood (described throughout the *AA* as elements of the path). Haribhadra's Abhidharmic reading of *AA* 8, then, made the awareness *(jñāna)* of a Buddha a conditioned, composite phenomenon, analogous enough to the minds of ordinary beings that inferences could be drawn about a Buddha's mind from the mental factors that ordinary beings cultivate on their path to Buddhahood. Haribhadra's comments reveal an implicit assumption on his part that the mind of a Buddha *can* be comprehended sufficiently by analogy to the human and that reason can arrive at a logically coherent and accurate model of it. His four-*kāya* reading of *AA* 8 represents an autonomous use of reason to infer that model. Since, in his view, he had arrived at that correct model through a valid inference, that must be the model intended by the author of the text, Maitreya.

This means that Haribhadra (and those, like Tsong kha pa in Tibet, who reaffirmed his interpretation of *AA* 8) understood the primary function of *AA* 8 to be something like systematic theology: to show how a received doctrine, even one that appears to contain logical tension, can be viewed as logically coherent and consistent with the entire system of inherited doctrine in which it is situated. Having read *AA* 8 as a systematic treatise, Haribhadra applied the logical procedures of his time to infer its systematic purpose. His four-*kāya* interpretation, then, implicitly represents a claim that the purpose of *AA* 8 was to present a model of Buddhahood that gave expression to the normative Mahāyāna doctrine of nonabiding nirvāṇa free from the logical tension with which the three-*kāya* model of it was burdened. All of this is explored in chapter 10 by reference to Haribhadra's commentaries.

Chapter 11 examines the views of Indian scholars who commented upon the *AA* after Haribhadra, some of whom were unfamiliar with or ignored his interpretation, some of whom supported it, and some of whom pointedly criticized it. Ratnākaraśānti and Abhayākaragupta directed strong criticism at Haribhadra's reading of *AA* 8, calling for a return to Ārya Vimuktisena's prior interpretation. Their reasons for this are not obvious, and have presented a puzzle for later scholars. One late Tibetan commentarial tradition, heavily influenced by Haribhadra's authority, even came to the conclusion that the interpretive difference between Ārya Vimuktisena and Haribhadra had been entirely philological; Ārya Vimuktisena, it said, had had the very same views on Buddhahood that Haribhadra had, and they differed only in their understanding of the Sanskrit grammar of key verses.[22] This viewpoint would make Ratnākaraśānti's call to return to Ārya Vimuktisena's interpretation a trivial matter. But as the research summarized above indicates, there was much more at stake. And a study of Ratnākaraśānti's writings, in particular, reveals deep differences between lineages of interpretation that go well beyond the philological.

Ratnākaraśānti's criticisms (echoed by Abhayākaragupta and Go ram pa in Tibet) concern two basic interrelated issues. The first issue is whether the nature of a Buddha's mind is as accessible to human thought as Haribhadra assumed, or is only made accessible by its own self revelation to us or by our own yogic attainment of it. The second issue, closely related to the first, is whether *AA* 8 should be read primarily as a reasoned systematization of doctrines concerning *dharmakāya* (as Haribhadra had read it) or as a revelation by *dharmakāya* of itself that points beyond the limits of reason.

On the first issue, Ratnākaraśānti sharply disagreed with Haribhadra's assumption that human thought could accurately represent the core realization of Buddhahood. He believed that logical inference, while important for other purposes, was extremely limited in its ability to ascertain the nature of a Buddha's awareness. He viewed the teaching of *svābhāvikakāya/dharmakāya* in *AA* 8 mainly from the perspective of yogic practice traditions, rather than from Haribhadra's Abhidharma *cum* Buddhist logic perspective.

We find a pattern of concerns in Ratnākaraśānti's corpus of writings on Mahāyāna praxis and Buddhahood that are reflected in his comments on *AA* 8. In Ratnākaraśānti's view, conceptual thought about *dharmakāya* never comes close to an adequate representation of it, precisely because *dharmakāya* is a nonconceptual and nondual yogic attainment, as unbounded as space. Haribhadra was therefore wrong to assume that logical tension in received models of Buddhahood constituted an anomaly to be solved by logical analysis.

Throughout his corpus and in his comments on *AA* 8, Ratnākaraśānti refers back to the textual tradition of Mahāyāna Buddhism viewed as a whole (sūtras and śāstras, Yogācāra and Mādhyamika). He frequently quotes Yogācāra treatises associated with the three-*kāya* model, several of which had explicitly noted the logical tension in their doctrine of nonabiding nirvāṇa. Some of these texts extolled that tension as an exalted quality of *dharmakāya*, an indication that it transcends the conceptual dichotomies through which ordinary beings try to think about it. The logical tension created by the attempt to conceptualize *dharmakāya* would disappear, it was believed, not through a more sophisticated conceptual analysis of *dharmakāya* (as Haribhadra had attempted), but by yogic practices that deconstruct all such conceptual frameworks, ultimately culminating in its nonconceptual realization.

In Ratnākaraśānti's view (later shared by Abhayākaragupta and Go ram pa in Tibet), the broad (and indeterminate descriptions) of nonabiding nirvāṇa found in earlier, *trikāya* (three-body) texts were quite sufficient for their purpose: to point practitioners toward Buddhahood, which, in the final analysis, would only be comprehensible when it was (yogically) accomplished. Ratnākaraśānti thought Haribhadra's imputation of conceptual dichotomy upon *dharmakāya* distorted its actual nonconceptual nature. In other words, he felt that the imprecision of the earlier three-*kāya* theory had the merit of leaving unexpressed what was, in fact, inexpressible.

This implies that Ratnākaraśānti (followed in this by Abhayākaragupta in India, and Go ram pa in Tibet) rejected not only Haribhadra's interpretation of verses in *AA* 8 but his understanding of the very status of the text. Haribhadra had read *AA* 8 as a systematic treatise whose purpose was to present a logically coherent model of Buddhahood. His perspective owed much to Buddhist logic and Abhidharma traditions that had sought such systematic coherence. Ratnākaraśānti, basing himself instead on the perspective of nondual yogic traditions, specifically understood the terms *svābhāvikakāya* and *dharmakāya* in *AA* 8 (and throughout Mahāyāna literature) to refer to a Buddha's *own* perspective on the nature of his attainment, *not* to a human perspective on it. Because *dharmakāya* is a nondual yogic attainment, light is shed on it by higher yogic practice. But human reason per se can only generate a human construct of *dharmakāya*, not actual knowledge of it. Therefore, implicit in Ratnākaraśānti's position is the assumption that in canonical and semicanonical texts such as the *Abhisamayālaṃkāra* the expressions of the core realization of Buddhahood through terms like *dharmakāya* are to be read not as systematic analyses but as revelation. *Dharmakāya* expresses itself through the teachings of Buddhas and high bodhisattvas in ways that do contain logical tension. But this is necessitated by the dualistic thought-world of those with whom it communicates. The logical tension itself thus serves to challenge trainees toward deconstructing the dichotomous world of their own conceptual construction which separates them from the attainment of *dharmakāya*. The term *dharmakāya*, then, must necessarily refer to something that transcends human thought or analysis, something that is known accurately only from a Buddha's own point of view. To analyze *dharmakāya* as a conceptual slot within a system of doctrines (as Ratnākaraśānti felt Haribhadra had done) is to reduce it to a projection of the limited conceptual schemes through which non-Buddhas try to think about Buddhahood. Because Ratnākaraśānti's views are of such interest and importance, much of chapter 11 is devoted to them.

Chapter 12 focuses upon the continuation of the controversy in Tibet by two important scholars of the *Abhisamayālaṃkāra*. Centuries after Indian Buddhist scholasticism had declined, Sa skya and dGe lugs scholars chose either Ārya Vimuktisena's or Haribhadra's interpretation of *AA* 8 as part of their project of creating a coherent system of thought and practice consistent with the thousands of sūtras, śāstras, and tantric texts Tibet had received from India. Within that project, Tibetan scholars perceived a number of problems as inter-related: problems concerning the two truths, the perfect knowledge of them which is *dharmakāya*, and the relation of that knowledge to the world that is expressed in the *rūpakāyas*. Go ram pa, a Sa skya scholar of great renown, and Tsong kha pa, the founder of the dGe lugs pa school, were two of Tibet's most influential commentators on the *AA*. Tsong kha pa, influenced by the logico-epistemological approach expressed in Haribhadra's work, supported his interpretation of *AA* 8. Go ram pa, drawing from a perspective framed by nondual yogic praxis, supported Ratnākaraśānti's call to return to the Ārya Vimuktisena's previous interpretation. Tsong kha pa's and Go ram pa's interpretations are closely related to their differing perspectives on a Buddha's awareness, which was an explicit topic of discussion in Candrakīrti's *Madhyamakāvatāra,* upon which they both commented. Their views on *AA* 8 in relation to their interpretations of Candrakīrti are explored in chapter 12.

We can begin to see that the ongoing disagreement over *Abhisamayālaṃkāra* chapter 8 has represented an ongoing clash between two fundamental perspectives on enlightenment in Indo-Tibetan Mahāyāna thought that have stood in tension through much of its history: a perspective that views Buddhahood primarily as a nondual yogic attainment beyond conceptual thought or inference, and a perspective that understands Buddhahood inferentially through conceptual thought. In what follows, I call the former perspective on Buddhahood the "nondual yogic-attainment perspective," and the latter the "analytic-inferential perspective." *AA* 8 provided a plausibly ambiguous enough textual basis for these perspectives to come into direct opposition over its interpretation. Haribhadra, and those in India and Tibet who followed his approach, read *AA* 8 as a basis for an analytic-inferential understanding of enlightenment, drawing upon Abhidharma elements of the text and analyzing them through logico-epistemological methods of late Indian Mādhyamika. Ratnākaraśānti, Abhayākaragupta, and those who followed their approach read the same text as one of many Mahāyāna sacred texts, taught by the Buddha or high bodhisattvas, that reveal their own nondual yogic perspective on enlightenment, which is inaccessible to autonomous inference.

The clash between these two perspectives transcends the usual distinctions between scholastic schools. It centers specifically on the core enlightenment experience itself, Buddhahood as Buddhas themselves realize and experience it. All the commentators discussed above from Haribhadra's time onward were familiar with procedures of Buddhist logic and theories of yogic praxis, and drew upon each within their corpus of writings. And all of them (including Ratnākaraśānti) understood their views to be consistent with the Mādhyamika tradition. No one chose one of these perspectives, nondual yogic attainment or analytic-inferential, exclusively over the other for all philosophical purposes. But in a specific context (such as *AA* 8) where a Buddha's own core realization comes under explicit discussion, a decisive choice was made as to the uses and limits of human reason and conceptual thought vis-à-vis Buddhahood. Ratnākaraśānti, Abhayākaragupta, and Go ram pa read the teaching of *dharmakāya* in *AA* 8 as part of the sacred Mahāyāna literature that reveals nonconceptual yogic attainment, while Haribhadra and Tsong kha pa read it as part of systematic Abhidharmic analysis informed by Buddhist logic.

From another angle, the two perspectives on enlightenment are distinguished by which of the two Mahāyāna truths each primarily looks to for understanding a Buddha's realization. Are we to understand *dharmakāya* primarily by logical inference, the perspective of conventional truth worked out in human thought? Haribhadra and his followers sought to resolve the logical tension in the underlying doctrine of nonabiding nirvāṇa by such analytic-inferential means. Or are we to understand *dharmakāya* exclusively by reference to the perspective of a Buddha, the perspective of ultimate truth fully realized in yogic praxis? Ratnākaraśānti and his followers thought the logical tension in Mahāyāna descriptions of Buddhahood inheres in dichotomous conceptualization itself. The tension should therefore resolve itself in yogic praxis that reveals ultimate truth directly as nondual reality beyond conceptual dichotomies (nondual yogic attainment).

1.5
Wider Implications for the History of Mahāyāna Thought

We may now sum up the wide range of issues, historical, textual, philosophical and theological, that have been at stake in the ongoing controversy over *Abhisamayālaṃkāra* chapter 8 and point out some of their wider implications for the history of Mahāyāna thought in India and Tibet.

Haribhadra, with whom the controversy over *AA* 8 begins in our written record, was also the first commentator to ascribe the *Abhisamayālaṃkāra* to Maitreya, the future Buddha. By Haribhadra's time, then, the *AA*'s authority approached (and exceeded in some cases) the authority of sūtras as an expression of enlightened awareness.[23] Literary analysis indicates that whoever the *AA*'s author may have been, his composition of *AA* 8 expresses a need of his own place and time: the need to draw new, specific correlations between two previously distinct literary expressions of

Buddhahood that had become normative: Yogācāra and *Prajñāpāramitā* expressions. Because *Prajñāpāramitā* textual sources of *AA* 8 also contained material from prior Abhidharma traditions, *AA* 8 formed a unique, composite product of all three literary sources. Later scholars of different centuries saw different messages in the text through the perspective of the differing traditions in which they situated themselves. The composite nature of *AA* 8 gave it the look of Abhidharmic analysis to Haribhadra and others who saw it through the lens of Buddhist logic *cum* Abhidharma tradition. Other components of *AA* 8 gave it the look of a yogic praxis perspective on *dharmakāya*, guiding the interpretation of Ratnākaraśānti and others. Source criticism of *AA* 8 helps expose the different lenses through which later commentators saw the text.

By making a new interpretation of the *Abhisamayālaṃkāra* (as Haribhadra did), or by calling for a return to prior authoritative interpretation (as Ratnākaraśānti did), scholars gave voice to concerns of their own time and place within the ongoing development of Mahāyāna thought and practice. And by voicing those concerns through their interpretation of a text now ascribed to Maitreya, their historically conditioned understandings appeared only to be clarifying what the future Buddha had intended, the eternal realization that all Buddhas have always had: *dharmakāya*. Philological arguments over *AA* 8, therefore, both express and mask the philosophical concerns behind them and the historical nature of those concerns. By doing philosophy and theology through interpretation of a received text of highest authority, scholars avoided giving the appearance of having a new perspective or making a personal innovation that might render their contributions unacceptable to conservative tradition. But embedded within the composition of *AA* 8 and the stages of debate over it is a history of great development and change in Buddhist thought that reveals itself upon closer scrutiny.

Yet also revealed in the corpus of *AA* 8 commentaries are great continuities, a continual reference back to long-established prior approaches to Buddhahood that transcend the usual distinctions between scholastic schools of Mahāyāna. Debates over *AA* 8 represent, in part, a recurrent collision between these two basic approaches: one approach drawing primarily upon Abhidharma-style analysis of Buddhahood in line with the logico-epistemological tradition and Mādhyamika thought; the other drawing primarily upon ancient traditions of nonconceptual yogic praxis as the main organizing principle behind the *dharmakāya* teaching of Mahāyāna as a whole.

The recurrent collision over *AA* 8 between these approaches reflects continuing disagreement over a wide range of related issues that center upon Buddhahood, and through that upon the nature of reality that a Buddha nondually knows and embodies. Specific disagreements have centered upon the following interrelated problems, couched here as questions:

1. In Mahāyāna tradition, how is the relationship between the unconditioned and conditioned aspects of a Buddha's attainment to be understood? How, in other

words, are the transcendent and immanent dimensions of a Buddha to be understood?

2. In more specific terms, within the inherited three-*kāya* model of Buddhahood, how is the unchanging *svābhāvikakāya* to function as the basis for the conditioned *rūpakāya*s? Given a Buddha's nondual attainment of the unconditioned, what is the basis for his or her continuing appearances and activities within our conditioned world? In gnoseological models of Buddhahood, what is the relation between a Buddha's nondual awareness of ultimate truth and his or her awareness of our conditioned world?

3. Is the logical tension in such inherited models the result of faulty model-making? Or does the logical tension itself communicate an important fact about Buddhahood: that it lies beyond dichotomous thought, thereby challenging the trainee to enter into the deconstructive yogic practices that attain it?

4. How important should conceptual analysis be in guiding our understanding of Buddhahood? How important should yogic practice be?

5. How accessible is Buddhahood to human thought and reason? Does the term *dharmakāya* in sacred texts refer to something that utterly transcends human analysis, known accurately only from a Buddha's own point of view? Or is the content of a Buddha's mind sufficiently analogous to that of a non-Buddha that valid inferences can be drawn about its nature based on Abhidharma analysis of mental components of the path? Should Mādhyamika philosophers base their understanding of Buddhahood primarily upon the perspective of conventional truth worked out in human thought, or upon the perspective of nondual awareness of ultimate truth, a Buddha's own perspective, as it has revealed itself in sacred texts and is realized in yogic practice?

6. Does *dharmakāya* have two aspects (conditioned and unconditioned, conventional truth and ultimate truth) that are distinguished as distinct from each other within a Buddha's own awareness? This would mean the conditioned and conventional is thoroughly real (confirmed by a Buddha's direct valid knowledge). Or is the conditioned and conventional thoroughly illusory, *dharmakāya* being precisely the ultimate awareness in which their utter deconstruction has culminated?

7. Where a sacred text teaches the *dharmakāya*, should we understand the text to be articulating a key component of a doctrinal system? Or should we view the text as the self-revelation of something that transcends systematic thought?

Differing responses to these questions guided recurrent disagreement over *AA* 8 for over a millennium. This book comprises a study of those responses over the history of Indian and Tibetan Mahāyāna thought, as they come into view through literary-historical analysis of *AA* 8 and by analyzing the writings of its interpreters in each historical period.

Below the surface of this set of interrelated concerns, and driving those concerns, has been a profound logical tension located in the core of classical Indian Mahāyāna thought: the paradox of nonabiding nirvāṇa. From a wider perspective, the long controversy over *AA* 8 provides just one complex example of the way in which this underlying paradox, without being explicitly invoked, has quietly functioned as a driving force behind a wide variety of doctrinal disagreements throughout the long history of Mahāyāna thought in India and Tibet.

Although this book specifically analyzes the controversy over *Abhisamayālaṃkāra* chapter 8, then, its implications go well beyond that text. The debates over *AA* 8 serve to illustrate subtle ways that surface discussions among Buddhist exegetes both express and hide their underlying purposes. They show us how scholars' historically conditioned perspectives on underlying philosophical problems implicitly guide their interpretations, even when their mode of expression gives the appearance of merely philological concern ("the verse doesn't say that; its says this"). The philosophical tension generated by the paradox of nonabiding nirvāṇa that drove the *AA* 8 debates has not previously been seen clearly, precisely because of the way the norms of Buddhist exegesis have hidden its own underlying purposes.

Our study of the *Abhisamayālaṃkāra* therefore sensitizes us to a dual function of traditional Buddhist interpretation that might appear paradoxical: (1) *to clarify* the religious issues of one's place and time through one's interpretation of a received text, and (2) *to hide* the role of historical-cultural change—in other words, to clarify the relevance of tradition to a new place and time, and to hide all signs of newness.

Appreciating this from our study of the *Abhisamayālaṃkāra* corpus affects our view of a wide range of other doctrinal problems in Indian and Tibetan texts outside of that corpus. In particular, when the tension in the paradox of nonabiding nirvāṇa that drove the *AA* 8 controversy is revealed, we begin to see how the same tension contributed to other disagreements over Buddhahood in other textual domains, whose modes of discourse have also tended to hide its implicit role. And those other disagreements have not been analyzed sufficiently in their relation to that underlying tension, to the *Abhisamayālaṃkāra* controversy, or to each other.

Those other disagreements over Buddhahood in India and Tibet share with the *Abhisamayālaṃkāra* controversy the concern to clarify the relations between the transcendent and immanent poles of nonabiding nirvāṇa: the relationship between Buddhahood as an attainment that transcends the world and the world as the sphere of its immanence and activity. Topics of disagreement have included: (1) the relation between a Buddha's knowledge of ultimate reality and knowledge of the world; (2) how Buddhahood, which has transcended the world, is salvifically active and accessible to beings in the world; (3) how to understand Buddhahood to be embodied in the world; (4) the precise ontological relation between Buddhahood and living beings, including the centrality or marginality of the doctrine of Buddha-nature *(tathāgatagarbha);* (5) the precise way in which enlightenment is made accessible to beings through the path (through the collection of enlightenment's causes, by eliminating what covers an intrinsic purity, simultaneist versus gradual models of awakening, etc.).

The broader purpose of this book, then, is to show how the tension that originated in the leap from pre-Mahāyāna to Mahāyāna concepts of nirvāṇa has functioned as a more significant force in the ongoing doctrinal development of Indian and Tibetan Mahāyāna than has generally been recognized. Chapter 13, the final chapter, suggests ways in which the leap from pre-Mahāyāna to Mahāyāna soteriology generated the ongoing doctrinal tension that continued to take new forms in the wide range of Indo-Tibetan disagreements over Buddhahood noted above. It examines early Mahāyāna intuitions (in relation to practices) concerning ontology, gnoseology, and soteriology which inspired Mahāyāna thinkers to develop new models of nirvāṇa, models that departed from pre-Mahāyāna understanding. When Mahāyāna texts came to redefine a Buddha's nirvāṇa as nonabiding (*apratiṣṭhita*, an attainment that transcends the dichotomy of nirvāṇa and saṃsāra), the new doctrine came into tension with other parts of the Four Noble Truths formula from pre-Mahāyāna tradition that Mahāyānists continued to accept unchanged as normative. Chapter 13 suggests, then, that many disagreements over Buddhahood in late Indian and Tibetan Buddhism express different perspectives on how to authentically reinterpret the Four Noble Truths formula consistent with basic intuitions of practice continuous from early Mahāyāna.

Chapter 13, then, seeks to shed light on the organizing principles behind alternative perspectives on Buddhahood that contributed to the disagreements above. If its suggestions have merit, the history of a wide range of disagreements over Buddhahood can be viewed, at least in part, as a long process of experimentation with different ways to make the doctrine of nonabiding nirvāṇa consistent with normative doctrines from pre-Mahāyāna Buddhism, so as to establish an authentic Mahāyāna way to resolve the logical tension that originated with the very rise of the Mahāyāna and the development of its patterns of systematic thought.

By showing how all the areas of doctrinal disagreement noted above represent, at least in part, differing transformations of an underlying tension from nonabiding nirvāṇa, each such area may come to shed new light upon the others. And by making explicit a deeper doctrinal problem that contributes to each, and that therefore must be engaged to find an adequate resolution for each, I hope that this study may also make a contribution to the ongoing analysis of these issues within living scholarly traditions of Buddhism in Asia and in the West.

Arcane as this study may appear to many theologians of Western religious traditions, it does comprise a modest contribution to comparative theology as well. The unique ways in which yogic praxis traditions and direct nonconceptual experience of reality have informed Mahāyāna Buddhist understandings of the transcendence and immanence of Buddhahood invite comparison with other theological traditions, particularly those that have put more emphasis on conceptual-analytic approaches to parallel problems.

2

The Buddha's Body of Dharmas *(Dharmakāya)* in Sarvāstivāda Abhidharma

The traditional mark of a Buddhist has been his or her formal taking of refuge in the Three Jewels *(triratna):* the Buddha, the Dharma, and the Sangha. Sarvāstivāda scholars posed the question: Precisely what is the Buddha refuge? When one takes refuge in the Buddha, what is one taking refuge in? The *Jñānaprasthāna*, a basic Abhidharma text of the Sarvāstivāda school, raises this question and gives a reply:

> One who takes refuge in the Buddha takes refuge in what? The real, true, qualities *(dharmāḥ),* which have as their name, appellation, designation, and expression the word "Buddha"; one is said to take refuge in the Buddha when he takes refuge in the fully accomplished qualities *(āśaikṣa dharmāḥ)* that constitute a Buddha.[1]

The dharmas referred to here are pure mental qualities. *Āśaikṣa dharmāḥ* are the purest mental qualities, those possessed by one who requires "no further training" *(āśaikṣa)*, one who has completed one of the supramundane yogic paths of Buddhism. In this context, they are the mental qualities that make a Buddha a Buddha, a fully enlightened being. The Sarvāstivāda *Mahāvibhāṣāśāstra* comments:

> Some say that to take refuge in the Buddha is to take refuge in the body constituted by the Tathāgata's head, neck, stomach, back, hands, and feet. It is explained, then, that that body, born of a father and the mother, is [composed of] defiled *(sāsrava)* constituents, and therefore not a source of refuge. The refuge is the Buddha's fully accomplished qualities *(aśaikṣa dharmāḥ)* which comprise enlightenment *(bodhi)*, i.e., [his], body of dharma(s) *(dharmakāya)*.[2]

The implication is that the fully accomplished qualities *(aśaikṣa dharmāḥ)* that comprise the Buddha refuge are undefiled *(anāsrava)*. The *Abhidharmakośa bhāṣya* comments further:

> One who goes to the Buddha for refuge goes for refuge to the fully accomplished qualities *(aśaikṣa dharmāḥ)* that make him a Buddha; [the qualities] principally because of which a person is called "Buddha"; [the qualities] by obtaining which he understands all, thereby becoming a Buddha. What are those qualities? *Kṣayajñāna* [knowledge of the destruction of the passions], etc., together with their attendants.[3]

The *Kośabhāṣya* goes on to say that one goes for refuge not to the Buddha's physical body, referred to as his *rūpakāya*, but to his *aśaikṣa dharmāḥ*, his special mental qualities that are beyond the need of further training. The reason is that those mental qualities are what actually constitute enlightenment. Their attainment is the attainment of enlightenment. They are the reason a person is called "Buddha." According to the Sarvāstivādins, a Buddha's physical body *(rūpakāya)* after enlightenment remains much the same as it was prior to enlightenment. Therefore, if that body were the source of refuge, a person would be able to go for refuge to a Buddha prior to his becoming a Buddha, which makes no sense. Furthermore, according to Sarvāstivādins, a Buddha's physical body is defiled *(sāsrava)*, while a Buddha's *aśaikṣa dharmāḥ* are undefiled.

In these formulations, the Sarvāstivādins were identifying the qualities that make a Buddha a Buddha, in other words, the qualities that comprise the defining essence of a Buddha. In the *Mahāvibhāṣā* passage above in particular, that essence of Buddhahood was referred to as *dharmakāya*. Dharma can mean the fundamental truths that the Buddha realized, the teachings of them he gave, the practice of those teachings, or the practice fully realized in the pure mental qualities discussed above. *Dharmakāya* in the *Mahāvibhāṣā* passage above therefore resonates with two prominent inter-connected meanings: "embodiment of dharma," and "body of dharmas," where to fully embody the dharma means to realize the pure mental qualities of a Buddha. In Sarvāstivāda understanding, then, it was the *dharmakāya*, a Buddha's undefiled mental qualities, as opposed to his *rūpakāya*, his defiled physical body, that was the defining essence of a Buddha and would constitute the Buddha refuge.[4]

It appears there were different traditions within Sarvāstivāda as to the precise identity of those Buddha dharmas that specifically comprised the Buddha refuge. In the *Kośabhāṣya* passage quoted above, Vasubandhu leaves it a bit open, saying just: "*Kṣayajñāna* [knowledge of the destruction of the passions], etc., together with their attendants." According to the Sarvāstivādins, *kṣayajñāna* and *anutpadajñāna* (knowledge of no further occurrence of the passions) are what comprise the enlightenment *(bodhi)* of a Buddha. But the same two knowledges are also what comprise the enlightenments *(bodhi)* of *śravaka*s and *pratyekabuddhas*.[5] If they alone were taken as the Buddha refuge, there would be nothing to distinguish taking refuge in a Buddha from taking refuge in *śravaka*s and *pratyekabuddha*s (arhats who are not Buddhas). Perhaps for this reason, as Vasubandhu notes, some scholars identified the Buddha refuge primarily with the eighteen *āveṇika dharmāḥ*, the mental qualities exclusive to a Buddha, which coexist with his other mental qualities (such as *kṣayajñāna* and *anutpadajñāna*).[6]

The *āveṇika dharmāḥ* are explained at length in chapter 7 of the *Kośabhāṣya*, where they are identified as the ten powers *(daśabala)*, four forms of fearlessness *(vaiśāradya)*, the three mindful equanimities *(smṛtyupasthāna)*, and the great compassion *(mahākaruṇā)*.[7] One passage of the *Mahāvibhāṣāśāstra* appears to include those qualities specifically within what it refers to as *dharmakāya*:

> The Buddhas are the same with respect to the *dharmakāya*. Just as one Buddha is filled with infinite qualities, beginning with the eighteen qualities exclusive to Buddhas: the ten powers, four forms of fearlessness, great compassion, and the three mindful equanimities, so are the other Buddhas.[8]

This passage appears to identify *dharmakāya* in a broad way with a Buddha's mental qualities in general, taking the qualities exclusive to Buddhas *(āveṇika dharmāḥ)* as primary. Here, again, *dharmakāya* means perfect embodiment *(kāya)* of dharma as the body *(kāya* = collection) of pure dharmas.

Whereas Vasubandhu's *Kośabhāṣya* (4.32, quoted above) says that a Buddha's *aśaikṣa dharmāḥ* (comprising the Buddha refuge) are: "*kṣayajñāna* [knowledge of the destruction of the passions], etc., together with their attendants," Yaśomitra's *Vyākhyā* says that the expression "etc." refers to *anutpādajñāna* (knowledge of no further occurrence of the passions) and *samyagdṛṣti* (right view), while the phrase "together with their attendants" refers to the five undefiled aggregates *(anāsravāḥ pancaskandhāḥ)*. According to Yaśomitra, then, the *Kośabhāṣya* identifies the Buddha refuge specifically with three types of undefiled Buddha knowledge *(kṣayajñāna, anutpadajñāna,* and *samyagdṛṣti)* together with the "five undefiled aggregates" *(anāsravāḥ pancaskandhāḥ)*.

This is a reasonable interpretation. The *Abhidharmakośa* (v. 7.1) and *bhāṣya* identify *kṣayajñāna* and *anutpādajñāna* (constitutive of *bodhi*, 6.67) as forms of undefiled *prajñā* (transcendental discernment). And the *Kośabhāṣya*, commenting on v. 1.2, identifies the five undefiled aggregates *(anāsravāḥ pancaskandhāḥ)* as the "attendants" of undefiled *prajñā*. It is reasonable to assume, then, that when Vasubandhu identified a Buddha's *aśaikṣa dharmāḥ* (i.e., the Buddha refuge) as "*kṣayajñāna* [knowledge of the destruction of the passions], etc., together with their attendants," he was including the five undefiled aggregates *(anāsravāḥ pancaskandhāḥ)* as the "attendants" of *kṣayajñāna* and *anutpādajñāna*. The five undefiled aggregates are listed in *Kośabhāṣya* 1.27, where they are given as: *śīla* (virtue), *samādhi* (concentration), *prajñā* (discernment), *vimukti* (liberation), and *vimuktijñānadarśana* (the vision of the knowledge of liberation).

Interestingly, the same set of five undefiled aggregates is found in other Nikāya literature as a formulaic description of enlightenment, and at some stage, this list came also to be identified in such literature as *dharmakāya*. The *Dīghanikāya*, *Saṃyuttanikāya*, and *Itivuttaka* of the Pali canon enumerated five undefiled *dhammakkhandas* constitutive of enlightenment: *sīla*, *samādhi*, *pañña*, *vimutti*, and *vimuttiñāṇadassana*.[9] The *Milindapañha* and Buddhaghoṣa's *Visuddhimagga* identified those five qualities as the *dhammakāya*.

Harivarman, a proponent of the Bahuśrutīya school and author of the *Satyasiddhiśāstra* (ca. third century C.E.), identified the same set of five undefiled aggregates with the *dharmakāya* of the Buddha. But because the five undefiled aggregates were not considered exclusive to a Buddha, but possessed by other types of arhat as well, he said that a Buddha's *dharmakāya* was distinguished by its inclusion of the eighteen *āveṇika dharmāḥ* (qualities exclusive to a Buddha), i.e., the ten powers, four forms of fearlessness, three mindful equanimities, and great compassion.[10] As mentioned above, those eighteen *āveṇika dharmāḥ* were also said by Vasubandhu (in his *Kośabhāṣya*) to have been identified as *dharmakāya* by some (presumably Sarvāstivādin) scholars.

In the seventh chapter of Vasubandhu's *Kośabhāṣya*, besides the eighteen *āveṇika dharmāḥ* exclusive to a Buddha, other mental qualities possessed by Buddhas are described which are said to be possessed by non-Buddhas as well: *araṇāsamādhi* (the meditative power preventing others' passions), *praṇidhijñāna* (the gnosis resulting from resolve), the four *pratisamvid* (analytical knowledges), the six *abhijñas* (supernatural knowledges), the four *dhyānas* (meditative absorptions), the four *ārūpyasamāpattis* (formless meditative states), the four *apramānas* (measureless thoughts), the eight *vimokṣas* (liberations), the eight *abhibhvāyatanas* (bases of overcoming), and the ten *kṛtsnāyatanas* (bases of meditative totality).[11] The thirty-seven *bodhipakṣas* (factors that foster enlightenment), which are realized by Buddhas and other arhats, are described in detail in *Kośabhāṣya* chapter 6.

This set of Buddha dharmas, taken as a whole, was understood in Sarvāstivādin Abhidharma to comprise the entire set of a Buddha's mental qualities (those shared with non-Buddhas as well as those unique to a Buddha). From what has been said above, it appears that various scholars of different Nikāya schools identified different sets of dharmas as the defining essence of Buddhahood that constituted the Buddha refuge or the Buddha's *dharmakāya*. It is important for us to note, however, that the entire set of Buddha dharmas delineated in the *Kośabhāṣya* above is taken up again in Mahāyāna literature where it is routinely presented as the formulaic list of a Buddha's mental qualities. Most notably the *Kośabhāṣya*'s set of Buddha dharmas given above, together with a few Mahāyāna additions, is formulaically presented throughout the *Prajñāpāramitā* sūtras as a description of a Buddha's qualities. The same set of dharmas also appears in many of the other Mahāyāna sūtras and śāstras for the same purpose, most importantly (for our purposes) in *AA* chapter 8, vv. 2–6.

Thus, the lists of Buddha dharmas (a Buddha's excellent mental qualities) found throughout the *Prajñāpāramitā* sūtras, and later in the *Abhisamayālaṃkāra,* are, for the most part, drawn from earlier proto-Abhidharma and Abhidharma traditions.[12] And, as noted above, in the Sarvāstivāda tradition, such a collection of dharmas, or various subsets of that collection, were identified as the Buddha refuge or *dharmakāya*, meaning "body, collection of pure dharmas."

Later in its seventh chapter, the *Kośabhāṣya* uses the term *dharmakāya* in a new way. It describes Buddhahood as the *phalasampad*, the "perfection of the result." In this context the term *dharmakāya* refers to Buddhahood in its entirety as the result of the yogic path, not just to its mental qualities. Vasubandhu explains that *dharmakāya*, meaning perfection of result *(phalasampad)*, includes four perfections: *jñānasampad* (the perfection of gnosis), *prahāṇasampad* (the perfection of elimination), *prabhāvasampad* (the perfection of power), and *rūpakāyasampad* (the perfection of the physical body).[13] If this concept of *dharmakāya phalasampad* was passed on to Vasubandhu from earlier strata of Sarvāstivāda thought, it may be a precursor of the *Abhisamayālaṃkāra*'s *dharmakāyaphalam* (*AA* v. 9.2), which also refers to the resultant state of Buddhahood as a whole. In such contexts, *dharmakāya* might be glossed as "embodiment *(kāya)* of dharma in its full realization and expression."

It is important to note that schools of Nikāya Buddhism in which Abhidharma became prominent, such as the Sarvāstivāda and Sthaviravāda, identified the ultimate result of the Buddhist paths—nirvāṇa—first and foremost as an immortal *(amṛta)* or unconditioned *(asaṃskṛta)* state, a state utterly freed from the conditions that generated a transitory world of profound suffering. According to Abhidharma schools, all Buddhist thought and practice was centered on the Four Noble Truths *(āryasatya)*: the truth of suffering *(duḥkhasatya)*, the truth of the origin of suffering *(samudayasatya)*, the truth of the cessation of suffering *(nirodhasatya)*, and the truth of path *(mārgasatya)*. Of these, the first and second truths concerned the intrinsically dissatisfying and painful nature of conditioned existence. The experiential world of beings was said to be caused by their own defiled actions *(karma)* and the passions *(kleśa)* that motivate them. Sentient existence for each individual constituted a beginningless cycle of rebirth and redeath referred to as saṃsāra. The Buddhist concept of saṃsāra represented a horrific vision of repeated immersion into various forms of sentient existence, followed by decay, disease, death, and rebirth.

According to the first two noble truths, then, conditioned sentient existence itself represented a profoundly disturbing existential problem that has to be solved. The defiled actions of sentient beings and the passions that drive them (the most basic passion being nescience, *avidyā*) constitute the fundamental conditions driving saṃsāra. Buddhist thought and practice as outlined in the various Abhidharmas was directed toward the extirpation of those conditions.

The fourth noble truth, the truth of the path, was the set of practices that would cut the chain of causes driving that cycle of birth and death. These were summarized as three spiritual trainings: moral conduct *(śīla)*, yogic concentration *(samādhi)*, and transcendental discernment *(prajñā)*.

The third noble truth, cessation *(nirodha)* or nirvāṇa, represented the ultimate aim of Buddhist practice in the Abhidharma traditions: the state freed from the conditions that created saṃsāra. Nirvāṇa was the ultimate and final state attained when the supramundane yogic path had been completed. It represented salvation from saṃsāra precisely because it was understood to comprise a state of complete freedom from the chain of saṃsāric causes and conditions, i.e., precisely because it was unconditioned *(asaṃskṛta)*.

Precise philosophical formulations of nirvāṇa varied between the Abhidharma schools, but in its primary description, nirvāṇa represented the cessation *(nirodha-satya)* of the *karma* (actions) and *kleśa* (passions) that give rise to the cycle of rebirth. Nirvāṇa was, most fundamentally, the state free from the conditions that produced the world and all experience of the world. As noted above, according to the *Kośabhāṣya* (at v. 6.67), the highest *bodhi* (enlightenment) of arhats (including Buddhas) consisted of two special knowledges: the knowledge of the destruction of the passions *(kṣayajñāna)* and the knowledge of no further occurrence of the passions *(anutpādajñāna)*. These knowledges were identified as enlightenment because they constituted a direct, personal verification that the fundamental causes for conditioned existence had been removed forever, i.e., that nirvāṇa had been attained.

Because an arhat who had attained such knowledges (whether a *śravaka*, *pratyekabuddha*, or Buddha arhat) still possessed embodied existence, he was said to have attained *sopadhiśeṣa nirvāṇa*, nirvāṇa with a residuum of conditioning. This meant that the arhat's physical body, and the mental components associated with it, comprised a residuum of conditioned existence (caused by the passions and actions of prior lives) that would continue until his physical death. But upon his physical death, because the root cause of future conditioned existence had been utterly removed, the arhat was said to pass into a state permanently free from further rebirth: *nirupadhiśeṣa nirvāṇa*, nirvāṇa beyond any further residual conditioning. The *nirupadhiśeṣa nirvāṇa* of arhats including Buddhas, then, represented an unconditioned state eternally liberated from the conditioned, mundane world of sentient beings.[14] And it was precisely because such a nirvāṇa was totally unconditioned *(asaṃskṛta)*, lacking any causal connection to the conditioned, mundane world, that it represented a final salvation from the suffering of that world.

3

The Buddhas' Embodiment of Dharma(tā) *(Dharmakāya)* in *Prajñāpāramitā* Sutras

The full enlightenment of a Buddha, *samyaksaṃbodhi*, is not treated as a separate, distinct topic or chapter within the *Prajñāpāramitā* sūtras (except in the revised version of the 25,000-verse *Prajñāpāramitā* sūtra to be discussed in chapter 7 below). In fact, reference to *dharmakāya* and *rupakāya* in the *Prajñāpāramitā* sūtras is rare. However, these sūtras do refer often indirectly to Buddhahood when they present formulaic lists of "all dharmas" *(sarvadharmāḥ)*. The "all dharmas" are understood to comprise all phenomena in the psychophysical universe of beings, as set forth in Abhidharma.[1] Included among all phenomena, of course, are a Buddha's mental qualities, his undefiled dharmas *(anāsrava dharmāḥ)*, much as they are listed in *Abhisamayālaṃkāra* chapter 8, verses 2–6. The undefiled dharmas are presented in extensive or abbreviated form throughout the *PP* sūtras. As the collection of a Buddha's mental qualities beyond the need of further training *(aśaikṣa dharmāḥ)* they correspond to what Sarvāstivādin Abhidharmikas referred to as a Buddha's *dharmakāya* his defining essence. The *PP* sūtras, however, do not identify a Buddha's undefiled dharmas per se as his defining essence. The reason for this lies in the difference between the ontologies of Sarvāstivāda Abhidharma and the *PP* sūtras.

Sarvāstivāda Abhidharmikas analyzed physical and mental phenomena into their ultimate components, all the dharmas that constitute mental and physical reality. Phenomenal things *(saṃvṛtisat)* could be physically or analytically broken down into ultimate constituents: physical atoms and moments of different types of awareness *(paramārthasat)*.[2] To develop transcendental wisdom *(prajñā)* required seeing through the apparent permanence and personal selfhood that was ordinarily associated with the phenomenal world and the minds and bodies of beings. By analyzing phenomena into their mental and physical constituents (the various dharmas) the illusions of permanence and an independent self were replaced with the realizations of the impermanence *(anityatā)* of all conditioned things and the selflessness of persons *(pudgalanairātmya)*. Such an analysis negated what was unreal (permanence in conditioned things, etc.), by affirming what was real (the various transitory dharmas that composed conditioned things). Consistent with this ontology, when seeking for what it was which comprised the Buddha refuge, Sarvāstivāda Abhidharma identified a Buddha's undefiled dharmas as the ultimate factors constituting his Buddhahood *(buddhakarakāḥ dharmāḥ)*. The undefiled dharmas ultimately defined what a Buddha was.[3]

The ontological position that emerged in the *Prajñāpāramitā* sūtras was quite different from that of the Abhidharmikas, defining itself, in fact, through frequent, direct contrast with the Abhidharma's ontology of dharmas. Abhidharma had negated the apparent permanence of phenomena by analytically reducing them to the dharmas that were their ultimate constituents. One key purpose of the *PP* sūtras was to negate the ultimacy of the very dharmas described in the Abhidharma, to deny the self-existence *(svabhāva)* of the dharmas themselves. The *PP* sūtras' formulaic repetition of the dharma lists, which were drawn mainly from Abhidharma or proto-Abhidharma sources, sets up a formulaic denial of the self-existence *(svabhāva)* of every one of the dharmas listed. The *PP*'s analysis leading to transcendental wisdom *(prajñā)* does not find dharmas. It finds only their emptiness of self-existence *(svabhāva-śūnyatā)*.[4] This realization is known as *prajñāparamitā* (often translated "perfection of wisdom"). It, conjoined with the aspiration to attain enlightenment for the sake of all beings *(bodhicitta)*, becomes the very heart of the Mahāyāna path, which when completed, issues in Buddhahood.

As in the Abhidharma, there are a few passages in *PP* sūtras that identify a Buddha's *dharmakāya*, not his *rupakāya* (his physical form), as the ultimate defining feature of a Buddha, his essence.[5] But they differ fundamentally as to what that essence is. The *PP* sūtras, despite their frequent enumeration of the undefiled dharmas, do not portray them as the ultimate defining principle of a Buddha. This is because the highest attainment in these sūtras is not a collection of dharmas, no matter how exalted, but the nondual realization of the real nature of all dharmas *(dharmatā)*, which is their emptiness *(śūnyatā)*. Since *dharmakāya* becomes one of the words to describe that nondual realization in several passages of the *PP* sūtras, it means something quite different in those passages from what it had meant in Abhidharma.

In this regard, two points should be made: (1) From the perspective of *prajñāpāramitā*, which is nondual realization of the real nature of dharmas *(dharmatā)* as empty *(śūnya)*, the Buddha dharmas, along with all other dharmas, are not perceived. What is not perceived by perfect wisdom can not be taken as the essential nature of a Buddha. (2) This means that unlike Abhidharma, the *PP* sūtras do not identify a Buddha's essential nature with any collection of Buddha dharmas per se.

They identify it instead with *śūnyatā*, the emptiness of all dharmas, and with *prajñā-pāramitā,* nondual knowledge of that emptiness.

Quoting from the *Aśṭasāhasrikā* (the *PP* sūtra in 8,000 verses):

> Bhagavan: If, Kauśika, on the one hand you were given this world filled to the top with relics of the Tathāgatas; and if, on the other hand, you could share in a written copy of this perfection of wisdom *(prajñā-pāramitā);* and if now you had to choose between the two, which one would you take?
>
> Śakra: I would take just this perfection of wisdom *(prajñāpāramitā).* Because of my respect for [it as] the guide of the Tathāgatas. Because it is the real relic/body of the Tathāgatas *(tathāgatānāṃ śarīraṃ).* As the Bhagavan has said: "The Buddhas, the Bhagavans, are those who have dharma as body *(dharmakāyā).* But, monks, you should not think that this [physical] body is my actual body. Monks, you should perceive me through the full realization of the body which is dharma *(dharmakāya).*" And one should see that this, the [actual] body of the Tathāgatas, is brought about *(prabhāvita)* by the limit of reality *(bhūtakoṭiḥ),* i.e., the perfection of wisdom *(prajñāpāramitā).*[6]

This passage from the 8,000-verse *PP* sūtra is important, being only one of a few such passages that specifically mention *dharmakāya* to intimate its special meaning in a *PP* context. Paul Harrison has suggested that the citation within the passage is from a pre-Mahāyāna canonical text: "As the Bhagavan has said: 'The Buddhas, the Bhagavans, are those who have dharma as body *(dharmakāyāḥ).* But, monks, you should not think that this [physical] body is my actual body. Monks, you should perceive me through the full realization of the body that is dharma *(dharmakāya).*'" This is indeed reminiscent of similar expressions in pre-Mahāyāna texts.[7] If so, how is the citation used in *this* context? The current passage uses it not just to parrot pre-Mahāyāna understanding of the term *dharmakāya*, but to redefine it. For the pre-Mahāyāna citation is intentionally set in the 8,000-verse *Prajñāpāramitā* sūtra as part of a passage that extols *prajñāpāramitā* itself as the preeminent principle of the path to awakening, the central defining principle of enlightenment, and therefore the true meaning of the term *dharmakāya.* The passage employs the citation to declare both that the term *dharmakāya* itself has been inherited from prior tradition and is therefore authoritative, and that the real meaning of the term is to be understood through the perfection of wisdom, *prajñā-pāramitā*, which is the subject of this sūtra and which is the actual defining principle of Buddhahood.

Thus, the passage identifies *prajñāpāramitā*, the perfection of wisdom, both as *dharmakāya* (embodiment of dharma in the ultimate sense = *tathāgatakāya*) and as the primary basis for attainment of *dharmakāya*. It is precisely this kind of relationship that *PP* sūtras frequently draw between *prajñāpāramitā,* on the one hand, and the various expressions for full enlightenment, on the other: *sarvākāra-jñatā* (omniscience), *anuttara-saṃyak-saṃbodhi* (complete, perfect enlightenment), *tathāgata* (thus gone or come), *tathāgatakāya* (body of the thus gone), and *dharma-kāya* (embodiment of dharma). *Prajñāpāramitā* is identified both as the primary cause of full enlightenment (however full enlightenment is designated), and as its very nature.[8]

A second key passage from the 8,000-verse *PP* sūtra also identifies the Buddha (referred to as the "Tathāgata") with *dharmakāya* as opposed to *rupakāya* (his physical form). But it does so in very subtle and uniquely informative ways. The Sanskrit term *tathāgata* can be etymologized equally as "thus come" *(tathā-āgata)* or "thus gone" *(tathā-gata)*. The passage begins with a subtle wordplay that identifies the true meaning of Tathāgata to be "thusness" *(tathatā)*, the real nature of things that is just "thus," as it is (free from extrinsic conceptual imputations upon it). But having thereby identified the Tathāgata as "thusness," the real nature of things that never changes, that is undifferentiated, and that is free from fixed points of reference, there can be no coming or going in reality for the "thus come" or the "thus gone." Through its punning wordplay around the meaning and etymology of "Tathāgata," a term of high reverence for the Buddha, the passage deconstructs all conceptual frames of reference for Buddhahood, implying that only a nonconceptual perspective on Buddhahood can actually know it, the perspective of thusness, which is the perspective of perfect wisdom *(prajñāpāramitā)*:

> 1. Dharmodgata: Son of the family, Tathāgatas (the "thus come" or "thus gone") certainly do not come from anywhere, nor do they go anywhere. For, indeed, thusness *(tathatā)* is unmoving, and the Tathāgata is thusness.[9] Nor, son of the family, does nonarising *(anutpāda)* come or go; the Tathāgata is nonarising. Nor is a coming or going of the limit of reality *(bhūtakoṭiḥ)* known; the Tathāgata is the limit of reality. Nor is a coming or going of emptiness *(śūnyatā)* known; the Tathāgata is emptiness. . . .
>
> 2. Nor, son of the family, is the Tathāgata other than the dharmas, for that which is the thusness of these dharmas *(dharmāṇāṃ tathatā)*, that which is the thusness of all dharmas, that which is the thusness of the Tathāgata, is just this one thusness. For thusness has no division. This thusness is just one, son of the family. Thusness is not two, not three. Thusness is beyond enumeration because it is not a being *(asattvāt)*.
>
> 3. [Dharmodgata gives a metaphor of a foolish man who mistakes a mirage of water for actual water. He asks Sadāprarudita whether the mirage water has come from anywhere or goes anywhere. Sadāprarudita replies that, since there is no water in the mirage, there is no coming or

going of water, and the man who believes there is water in the mirage is indeed foolish.]

4. Dharmodgata: In just the same way, son of the family, those who have fixed upon the Tathāgata by reference to his form or his voice imagine a coming or going of the Tathāgata. Like the person who conceives of water where there is none, they too would have to be called foolish and stupid. Because the Tathāgata is not to be perceived from his physical body *(rupakāya)*. The Tathāgatas are *dharmakāya*, and the real nature of dharmas *(dharmatā)* does not come or go. Precisely so, there is no coming or going of the Tathāgatas. . . .

5. The Bhagavan has said that all dharmas are like a dream. And those who do not know all dharmas to be like a dream as explained by the Tathāgata, they adhere to the Tathāgatas through [their] nominal body *(nāmakāya)* or physical body *(rupakāya)*, and imagine there is a coming or going of the Tathāgatas. . . . But those who know all dharmas to be like a dream as they really are, as explained by the Tathāgata, they do not imagine a coming or going of any dharma, . . . they know the Tathāgata by means of his real nature *(dharmatayā)*. . . . Those who know the real nature *(dharmatā)* of the Tathāgata, they practice close to full enlightenment; they practice the perfection of wisdom *(prajñāpāramitā)*.[10]

Having identified the Buddha with thusness *(tathatā)*, the first paragraph draws the implications of that.[11] For "thusness" does not refer to some ontological reality posited as distinct from the nature of things, but to the true nature of things itself, which is their emptiness *(śūnyatā)*. And to perceive emptiness is to see nothing substantial that arises within the arising of things *(anutpāda)*, and to break through cognitively to the point where reality as normally conceived comes to its end *(bhūtakoṭi)*.

The second paragraph develops further implications. The Buddha is not separate from all things, i.e., not separate from all the dharmas that constitute psychophysical reality, and this would include the mental and physical dharmas pre-Mahāyāna traditions ascribed to a Buddha. But neither is the Buddha to be directly identified with such dharmas. Rather, the Buddha is to be identified with the real, single, undifferentiated, nature of all dharmas: "the thusness of dharmas" *(dharmāṇāṃ tathatā)*, which is their emptiness.

The third paragraph of the extract quoted above further specifies the ontological status of all dharmas as empty, miragelike phenomena that, in their comings and goings, give the appearance of a real substantial core of arising and ceasing of which they are empty.

The fourth and fifth paragraphs then specify the ultimate defining principle of the Buddha, introducing the term *dharmakāya* in relation to the interplay of key terms and concepts from the prior paragraphs. *Dharmāḥ* (paragraphs 2 and 3) are the miragelike dharmas. But *dharmāṇāṃ tathatā* (paragraph 2) is the "thusness of dharmas," their actual nature, which is also to be called *dharmatā*, the "real nature of dharmas" (paragraph 4). And *dharmatā* (the real empty nature of dharmas) is the true identity of the Tathāgata, referred to now as *dharmakāya* (paragraphs 4 and 5).

Paragraphs 4 and 5 above, then, reject prior understanding of the term *dharmakāya* as it had been worked out in Abhidharma as "body [i.e., collection] of dharmas." The term is reinterpreted in line with the central themes of the *Prajñāpāramitā* sūtras. "Those who do not know all dharmas to be like a dream"—i.e., ordinary beings and Abhidharmikas—do not know the real essence of a Buddha. Mistaking the comings and goings of the Tathāgata's qualities *(dharmāḥ)* for the Tathāgata, they do not see the Tathāgata's real empty nature *(dharmatā),* which never comes or goes.

Dharmakāya as the ultimate defining principle of a Buddha, therefore, now means "embodiment of *dharmatā*" in knowledge. The etymology becomes: *dharmakāya = dharma[tā]kāya* = "*dharmatā* as body," i.e., *dharmatā* itself as one's true embodiment.

In connection with this, paragraphs 4 and 5 of the extract describe the way in which ordinary beings, who do not see the insubstantial nature of dreamlike dharmas, incorrectly identify the physical body *(rūpakāya)* of a Tathāgata, or the set of concepts *(nāmakāya)* they use to designate him, as his true identity. We usually identify persons with their bodies or through the concepts by which we label them. Here, then, the term *kāya,* in addition its usual basic meanings, refers broadly to the primary marker of a person's identity. Employing the term *kāya* in this way, the text contrasts the incorrect identity *(rūpakāya, nāmakāya)* with the correct one: *dharmakāya.*

The ancient understandings of *dharma* as the Buddha's teaching, the practice of that teaching, and its ultimate realization in the experience of awakening still hold. And they combine with the special etymology of *dharma[tā]kāya* in this passage to create further resonances of meaning for *dharmakāya. Dharmakāya* can still understood as the "embodiment of the dharma teaching" *(āgama),* which is the realization of the teaching in direct experience. *Dharmakāya* is therefore also still properly understood to be the "embodiment of the dharma as realization" *(adhigama).* But in the context of *Prajñāpāramitā*, the Buddha's realization is no longer to be adequately understood simply as an attainment of undefiled dharmas, impermanent mental qualities. More fundamentally, it is to be understood as the nondual realization of the unchanging, real empty nature of all such dharmas *(dharmatā)*, which is *prajñāpāramitā*, the perfection of wisdom.

Paragraph 5 of the extract makes this series of identities explicit by exposing the connection between all of the themes of the prior paragraphs and the central theme of the *PP* sūtras: to correctly perceive the Buddha's true embodiment, his true identity as *dharmatā*, requires practice of the perfection of wisdom, through which one comes closer and closer to seeing *dharmatā* (the real nature of things) as the Buddha does. In other words, there is only one way to perceive what the Buddha actually is, and that is to come to see everything as he does, to attain his realization of *prajñāpāramitā*.

In the last part of paragraph 4 of the extract, I left the term *dharmakāya* untranslated. The reason for this should now be clear. The larger passage in which *dharmakāya* is situated imbues the term with connotations difficult to capture simultaneously in any one English translation or gloss. The following connotations resonate simultaneously: "The Tathāgatas have *dharma[tā]* as body, and *dharmatā* does not come or go." "The Tathāgatas have *dharma* [knowledge of the real nature of dharmas] as body, and *dharmatā* [the real nature of dharmas] does not come or go."[12]

The *Vajracchedikā-prajñāpāramitā-sūtra* contains a relevant passage that seems closely related to the *Aṣṭāsahāsrikā* passage quoted above. One of the passages may have been modeled in part upon the other one. The *Vajracchedikā* passage, in succinct form, also denies the Buddha's phenomenal qualities any significance as a defining principle for him. In reality, the Buddha is not his phenomenal qualities, but the real nature of all phenomena *(dharmatā)* as he knows it. Furthermore, the real nature of things is not discernible from a phenomenal point of view, but only from the ultimate point of view:

> Those who saw me by my form,
> Those who followed me by my voice,
> Have been engaged in wrong practice,
> Me those beings will not see.
> From the dharma are Buddhas seen,
> Indeed the Guides are *dharmakāya.*
> But the real nature of things *(dharmatā)* cannot be discriminated,
> And so must not be discriminated.[13]

Similar to the earlier passage, there is a close interplay between key related terms: *dharma, dharmakāya,* and *dharmatā,* giving the term *dharmakāya* several rich, interrelated meanings: *dharmakāya* = the real nature of things *(dharmatā)* embodied *(kāya)* in nondiscriminating knowledge *(prajñāpāramitā)* = the ultimate embodiment *(kāya)* of the Buddha's teaching and practice *(dharma).* In fact, from the perspective of the perfection of wisdom, no phenomena are discerned, neither those which comprise a Buddha's physical form *(rūpakāya)* nor those identified by the Abhidharmikas as comprising his mind. As it says in the *Pañcaviṃśatisāhasrikā-prajñāpāramitā-sūtra* (the 25,000-verse *PP* sūtra):

> A bodhisattva who is endowed with that wisdom eye *(prājñācakṣuḥ)* does not know any dharma—be it conditioned or unconditioned, wholesome or unwholesome, faulty or faultless, defiled or undefiled, with or without passions, mundane or supramundane. With that wisdom eye he does not see any dharma, or hear, consider, or discern one. This is the perfectly pure wisdom eye of a bodhisattva.[14]

What is not seen by transcendental wisdom *(prajñā)* cannot be taken as defining a Buddha. What is not found under the scrutiny of the perfection of wisdom does not constitute what a Buddha really is, his actual nature: *dharmakāya*. In the *PP* sūtras, the undefiled dharmas of a Buddha *(anāsravadharmāḥ)* are presented repeatedly as a subset within lists of "all dharmas" *(sarvadharmāḥ)*, all the constituents of the psychophysical universe of beings. But along with all other dharmas, the self-existence *(svabhāva)* of a Buddha's undefiled dharmas is negated. Along with all other dharmas, those undefiled dharmas are not discerned by the bodhisattva engaging in the perfection of wisdom. To recognize *dharmakāya* as a Buddha's ultimate defining principle, then, is not to discern *any* collection of dharmas, no matter how exalted or free of fault. Instead, it is to realize the perfection of wisdom, which perceives the emptiness of all such dharmas. As it says in the 25,000-verse *PP* sūtra:

> Furthermore the Tathāgata, Arhat, Fully Enlightened One should not be attended to through the ten powers of a Tathāgata *(daśabala)*, the four forms of fearlessness *(vaiśāradya)*, the four analytical knowledges *(pratisamvid)*, great compassion *(mahākaruṇa)*, great love *(mahāmaitrī)*, or the eighteen dharmas exclusive to a Buddha *(āveṇikadharma)*. And why? Because they have no self-existence *(svabhāva)*, and that which has no self-existence is nonexistent. And why? Because the recollection of the Buddha *(buddhānusmṛti)* is a nonrecollection and a nonattention. . . . It is thus that the bodhisattva who engages in perfect wisdom *(prajñāpāramitā)* should attend to the recollection of the Buddha.[15]

The *Saptaśatikāprajñāpāramitāsūtra* (the 700-verse *PP* sūtra) develops this theme further:

> The Lord [Bhagavan]: Do you, Manjūśrī, reflect on the Buddha dharmas?
>
> Manjūśrī: No indeed, Lord. If I could see the specific accomplishment of Buddha dharmas, then I would reflect on the Buddha dharmas. But the development of perfect wisdom *(prajñāpāramitā)* is not set up through discriminating any dharma and saying, "these are the dharmas of ordinary people, these are the dharmas of disciples, these are the dharmas

> of *pratyekabuddhas*, these are the dharmas of fully enlightened Buddhas." . . . Just that, O Lord, is the development of perfect wisdom, where there is neither the stopping of the dharmas of an ordinary person, nor an acquisition of the Buddha dharmas."[16]

In sum, the *PP* sūtras above identify Buddhahood directly with perfect nondual knowledge (*prajñāpāramitā*, *abhisambodhi*, etc.), the object realized by that knowledge (*dharmatā:* the real nature of things, emptiness, thusness), and both undivided. In fact, it is because Buddhahood comprises nondual knowledge of the real nature of things that it is often equated directly with the real nature per se (*dharmatā*, thusness, emptiness), or with the knowledge per se, or with both at once.

> Subhuti: "Buddha" is spoken of, Bhagavan. For what is that a designation?
>
> Bhagavan: The true reality *(bhūta-artha)* is called "Buddha." Furthermore, when one has fully known *(abhisambuddha)* that real dharma, has realized that true reality, has fully known all phenomena as they really are, then he is called "Buddha."
>
> Subhuti: "Enlightenment" *(bodhi)* is spoken of, Bhagavan. For what is that a designation?
>
> The Bhagavan: "Enlightenment" is a designation for emptiness *(śūnyatā)*. It is a designation for thusness *(tathatā)*. It is a designation for the limit of reality *(bhūtakoṭi)*. It is a designation for the dharma realm *(dharmadhātu)*. . . . Moreover, Subhuti, because the Buddhas, the Bhagavans, have this enlightenment, it is called "enlightenment." Moreover, Subhuti, because it is fully known *(abhisambuddha)* by the Buddhas, the Bhagavans, it is called "enlightenment."[17]

> The Lord: How, Manjūśrī, should the Tathāgata be seen and honored?
>
> Manjūśrī: Through the mode of thusness *(tathatā)* do I see the Tathāgata, through the mode of nondiscrimination, in the manner of nonobservation.[18]

In spite of all that has been said, the *PP* sūtras ought not be construed simply to deny the existence of the undefiled dharmas that the Abhidharma understood to constitute full enlightenment. In several passages the *PP* sūtras affirm that these dharmas are indeed attained, but only by those who realize that they, like all other dharmas, are empty. In other words, only those who practice the perfection of wisdom accomplish the qualities (undefiled dharmas) that are understood from a phenomenal point of view to constitute full enlightenment. From a phenomenal point of view, the various psychophysical phenomena of the universe (including the pure mental qualities of a Buddha) are ontologically affirmed. For this reason, the bodhisattvas and Buddhas make various distinctions between the dharmas (those which are virtuous and those which are nonvirtuous, those which are to be attained and those which are to be abandoned, etc.) in order to teach beings the way to progress on the path to enlightenment. Such teaching is given precisely to lead trainees to the point at which they personally and directly realize the emptiness of all such distinctions (and to inculcate in them the compassion that impels them to teach others the same path). With the direct realization of emptiness, they too partake in the ultimate point of view *(prajñāpāramitā)* from which no phenomena (including a Buddha's qualities) are perceived.[19]

In the *PP* sūtras (in contrast to the Abhidharma), when the term *dharmakāya* refers to the essence of a Buddha's enlightenment, it *never refers* to the collection of undefiled dharmas per se.[20] Rather, the ultimate defining principle of a Buddha, whether referred to as "Tathāgata," *dharmakāya*, *tathāgatakāya*, "enlightenment," etc., is identified both with the perfection of wisdom and with the object it knows nondually (*dharmatā, śūnyatā, tathatā, bhūtakoṭi, dharmadhātu*, etc).

Prajñāpāramitā sūtras, like Abhidharma texts, occasionally also mention the *rūpakāya* of a Buddha. In the *PP* sūtras, the term refers to a Buddha's physical form. But it is apparently used for a broad range of manifestations. Various *PP* sūtras open with the familiar sūtra formula: "Thus have I heard at one time," and then identify an actual location in India where the sūtra is said to have been expounded, e.g., Rājagṛha. Because these texts declare themselves as taught by Śākyamuni Buddha in India at a particular time, the Buddha's occasional mentions of his *rūpakāya* seem to refer, for the most part, to his physical form as the teacher of the text.

In the larger versions of the *PP* sūtras, this physical form comes to be described in marvelous and extraordinary terms as gleaming with golden hue, emanating purifying light through all pores throughout the universe, illuminating the universe with the light of a smile, and so forth. The thirty-two marks and eighty signs of the legendary great person *(mahāpuruṣa)* of Indian legend are also ascribed to it. The form of Buddha as the teacher and central figure of the text is glorified in cosmic terms far exceeding descriptions found in pre-Mahāyāna sūtras. A number of passages also describe the Buddha emanating many other remarkable forms, including innumerable manifestations of his own body, into various realms of beings to assist them. Such vast manifestations, as physical forms, were also included in the semantic range of the term *rūpakāya*.[21] Within the larger versions of the *PP* sūtras, however, no terminology explicitly distinguishes the glorified central figure of Śākyamuni from the numberless forms that he manifests throughout the universe.

4

Embodiment of Buddhahood in its Own Realization: Yogācāra *Svābhāvikakāya* as Projection of Praxis and Gnoseology

4.1 Relevance of Yogācāra texts to the *Abhisamayālaṃkāra*'s Eighth Chapter

The eighth chapter of the *Abhisamayālaṃkāra* explains Buddhahood by reference to a set of five key terms: *svābhāvikakāya* (embodiment of a Buddha in his essence), *dharmakāya* (embodiment of dharma), *sāmbhogikakāya* (embodiment in communal enjoyment), *nairmāṇikakāya* (embodiment in created forms), and *karma* (or *kāritra*, Buddha's activity). These terms, particularly the terms for multiple Buddha *kāya*s, created an ambiguity for some later commentators, who disagreed over whether the text was teaching three or four *kāya*s. According to an introductory verse of the text, the *AA*'s eighth chapter contained four topics, but it was even unclear which of the five terms comprised those four topics.[1]

Haribhadra, in his *Āloka* and *Sphuṭārthā*, interpreted *AA* 8 as teaching four Buddha *kāya*s (comprising the four topics of the chapter) together with a Buddha's activity. Using a Madhyamaka style of analysis, he analytically separated the ultimate truth of a Buddha *(paramārtha satya)* from the conventional truth *(saṃvṛti satya)*. The former he identified as the *svābhāvikakāya*: the *śūnyatā* (emptiness) or *dharmatā* (ultimate reality) of a Buddha's mind. The latter he resolved into three conventional *kāya*s, distinguished according to the type of person to whom each appears. The *(jñānātmaka) dharmakāya* consists of a Buddha's undefiled dharmas, understood as his pure forms of awareness, his gnoses. They appear directly only to himself as conventional object.[2] The *sāmbhogikakāya* is the form in which a Buddha appears conventionally to *ārya* bodhisattvas, and the *nairmāṇikakāya* is the form in which he appears conventionally to other beings.[3] For Haribhadra, these four *kāyas*—the first *kāya* as ultimate truth *(paramārtha satya)* and the other three *kāyas* as conventional truth *(saṃvṛti satya)*—comprised the four topics of *AA* chapter 8. The other subject treated in detail in *AA* 8 is Buddha's activity *(buddha kāritra)*. Haribhadra treated this as a subsidiary item associated with the *(jñān-ātmaka) dharmakāya*.[4]

Within Haribhadra's delineation of the four *kāyas*, then, the first *(svābhāvika-kāya)* is the ultimate nature of a Buddha's gnosis, the second *(dharmakāya)* is the gnosis as it conventionally appears to Buddhas themselves, and the third and fourth are conventional appearances the gnosis manifests for others. Thus, Haribhadra's second *kāya* consisting of gnosis, the *(jñānātmaka) dharmakāya*, is central in his scheme, because he defines the other *kāyas* in terms of it. As the collection of undefiled Buddha dharmas (gnoses) that comprise the enlightened mind of a Buddha, the *(jñānātmaka) dharmakāya* is the conventional basis for the emptiness that Haribhadra defines as the *svābhāvikakāya*, and it is the dominant condition through which the two form *kāyas* manifest for others. This places it at the very heart of his four-*kāya* scheme. And it makes the collection of the undefiled Buddha dharmas the central defining principle of Buddhahood. In this Haribhadra hearkens back to the *Abhidharma* formulation that defined Buddhahood in terms of the Buddha dharmas, but he updates it by his application of Madhyamaka metaphysics distinguishing conventional and ultimate truths: the Buddha dharmas as conventional truth comprise the *(jñānātmaka) dharmakāya*, and their emptiness as ultimate truth is the *svābhāvikakāya*.

Although Haribhara's interpretation of *AA* 8 is brilliant, it is neither philologically nor historically accurate. A more accurate interpretation of *AA* 8 is reached by reading it more straightforwardly and literally than Haribhadra had done, by placing it in its historical context, and by examining it in relation to the main textual traditions upon which it drew; in this regard Ārya Vimuktisena set the standard. One of those textual traditions is that of the *Prajñāpāramitā* sūtras. The *AA* is primarily a commentary upon the 25,000-verse *Prajñāpāramitā* sūtra, and the expressions of Buddhahood in that sūtra (and the other *PP* sūtras closely related to it), as previously discussed, are therefore critical toward an understanding of the *AA*'s eighth chapter. But most of the *kāya* terminology that appears in *AA* 8 was developed in another textual tradition, the Yogācāra. And it is to that tradition that we must now turn.

It was in texts that appeared within (broadly) the same historical period as the *AA* (ca. the third to sixth centuries C.E.) that the theory of multiple Buddha *kāyas* (involving *svābhāvikakāya*, *sāmbhogikakāya*, and *nairmāṇikakāya*) was first formalized. These texts, like the *AA*, became traditionally associated with Maitreya/Asanga. All of them are either Yogācāra or closely related to the Yogācāra tradition. They represent the tradition of multiple-*kāya* terminology from which the *AA* drew. As mentioned above, in Haribhadra's interpretation of *AA* 8, the set of undefiled Buddha dharmas became the central defining characteristic of Buddhahood.

In the Yogācāra scheme, this was definitely not the case. In Haribhadra's interpretation of the *AA*, the set of undefiled Buddha dharmas formed a fourth *kāya,* the *(jñāna) dharmakāya*. In the Yogācāra scheme, it was inconceivable to posit such a fourth *kāya*.

The *AA* differed from the Yogācāra synoptic treatises of its period in purporting to serve not as a general commentary on numerous Mahāyāna sūtras, but as a direct commentary specifically on the 25,000-verse *PP* sūtra. *AA* 8's fundamental reliance on the latter gave its description of Buddhahood certain characteristics unique to it. Nevertheless, *AA* 8 also made specific use of the three-*kāya* names which were used only in Yogācāra and related texts of its period, not in the *PP* sūtras of its period.[5]

At the time the *AA* was composed, then, the multiple-*kāya* terminology that appears in its eighth chapter appeared elsewhere only within the Yogācāra related literature of the same general period. In fact, the terminology was developed in that literature. When the *AA* was composed, the only meanings the specific terms: *svābhāvikakāya, sāmbhogikakāya,* and *nairmāṇikakāya* had were the meanings they possessed in Yogācāra-related texts. And the term *dharmakāya* took on special meaning in relation to them. Conze has noted a number of places in the *AA* where it drew upon Yogācāra ideas in order to explicate the *PP* sūtras.[6] But nowhere is this more evident than in *AA* 8, where the terminology of multiple *kāya*s found in principle Yogācāra texts (*MSA*, *Msg*, etc.) is clearly superimposed onto *PP* material.

The *AA*'s eighth chapter may be better understood, then, by viewing it in relation to the other textual traditions of its time, particularly the Yogācāra traditions, than by seeking to interpret it in isolation as though it were merely an independent commentary on the *PP* sūtras. (The latter method was that of Haribhadra, and in modern times has been that of Obermiller, La Vallée Poussin, Dutt, and other scholars who followed Haribhadra in holding that the *AA* taught four *kāya*s).[7]

4.2
Defining Principle of Buddhahood in Classical Yogācāra: *Dharmakāya* as Realization of Thusness, not Buddha dharmas per se

In a number of early Mahāyāna sūtras, along with references to the formless *dharmakāya* of the Buddha, there are physical descriptions of Buddhas that go far beyond what is found in the Pali canon.[8] Attempts have been made by scholars to trace the historical development of these ideas in Buddhism prior to the full development of the Mahāyāna.[9] Here I will only note that certain treatises seminal for a newly emerging Yogācāra school reformulated earlier two-*kāya* descriptions in order to accommodate the new forms found in Mahāyāna sūtras. In the new model of three *kāyas*, *sāmbhogikakāya* was the term for exalted Buddhas of the Mahāyāna sūtras and *nairmāṇikakāya* referred to the limitless forms through which they enter into the realms of living beings to lead them to freedom.[10] Both of these *kāyas* were understood as subsets of the earlier, wider category of *rupakāya* (embodiments in form). The *svābhāvikakāya* corresponded broadly to what the Mahāyāna sūtras called *dharmakāya.*

It may be that the earliest textual material to set forth a clear and distinct terminology of three *kāyas* is found in the "Bodhi" chapter of the *Mahāyānasūtrālaṃkāra (MSA),* verses 9.56–66.[11] The *MSA* served as the basis for extensive discussion of the three *kāyas* in the *Mahāyānasaṃgraha (Msg),* which often quotes it. The *MSA* is especially significant for our study of *AA* 8, because it is the first śāstra we know of to attempt a systematic explanation of the three *kāyas,*[12] and because later proponents of three *kāyas* who commented on the *Abhisamayālaṃkāra* in India and Tibet followed and quoted this text more than any other in support of their views. The *MSA*, the *Msg,* and their commentaries seem to constitute a core Yogācāra literature that is closely related to the discussions of three *kāyas* that appear in numerous other texts: the *Abhisamayālaṃkāra, Ratnagotravibhāga (RGV), Kāyatrayasūtra, Kāyatrayastotra, Kāyatrayāvatāramukhaśāstra, Buddhabhūmivyākhyāna,*[13] etc. Brief mention of three *kāyas* is also made in the *Dharmadharmatāvibhāga (DDV)* and in the *Madhyantavibhāga (MAV) bhāṣya* and *ṭikā.*[14] The *MSA* and *Msg* were authored in the formative period of the Yogācāra school, the former perhaps in the third to fourth centuries, the latter in late fourth century C.E.[15] They and their commentaries give a good picture of the religio-philosophical context, primarily Yogācārin, in which the three-*kāya* theory developed. They present the three-*kāya* theory in relation to other Yogācāra models of enlightenment: *āśrayaparāvṛtti, dharmadhātu-viśuddhi, viśuddhā-tathatā, nirvikalpa-jñāna,* and *dharmakāya.*

As we saw earlier, various Abhidharmikas identified a Buddha's defining essence as his undefiled mental qualities *(anāsrava dharmāḥ),* such as his ten powers *(daśabala),* four forms of fearlessness *(vaiśāradya),* and great compassion *(mahākarunā).* And as noted above, Haribhadra's comments on *AA* 8 hearken back to them by defining what he called Buddha's "gnosis *dharmakāya*" *(jñānātmaka dharmakāya)* as the collection of the twenty-one types of undefiled Buddha dharmas, and then understanding the other *kāyas* primarily in relation to it.[16]

The Yogācāra school of Mahāyāna Buddhism arose prior to and during the period that the *AA* was presumably composed. The names that *AA* 8 used for the Buddha *kāyas (svābhāvikakāya, sāmbhogikakāya,* and *nairmāṇikakāya)* were presented and explained in detail for the first time in fundamental Yogācāra treatises such as the *MSA* and *Msg.* And these treatises presented their three-*kāya* theory in such a way as to make it explicit that Buddhahood was not to be defined in terms of the Buddha dharmas *(anāsrava dharmāḥ).* Yogācāra texts, in line with the *Prajñāpāramitā* sūtras, acknowledged the undefiled Buddha dharmas to be the pure qualities of a Buddha as they are taught or conceptualized from a phenomenal point of view. But these texts did not understand them to be a Buddha's defining essence *(svabhāva)*. We saw earlier that the *PP* sūtras identified Buddhahood's ultimate defining principle, not as any collection of dharmas per se, but as the emptiness of all dharmas and the nondual realization of that emptiness *(prajñāpāramitā)*, referred to with terms such as *tathāgatakāya*, *dharmakāya*, the (real) "Tathāgata," etc. The *MSA*, *Msg*, and other Yogācāra texts, basing themselves on the *PP* and other early Mahāyāna sūtras, follow their lead.

The *MSA* and its commentaries agree with the *PP* sūtras that while the undefiled dharmas are acknowledged to be qualities of a Buddha, they are not to be taken as his defining essence *(svabhāva)*. The *MSA*'s ninth chapter focuses on the state of Buddhahood. The *MSA bhāṣya* calls it *bodhyadhikāraḥ* (the chapter on enlightenment). Near the beginning of this chapter, *MSA* 9.4 and its *bhāṣya* say:

> On the nondual character of Buddhahood, and its power:[17]
>
> All phenomena are Buddhahood,
> But there is no phenomenon at all.
> It consists of excellent qualities,
> But it is not defined by them.
>
> (*MSA* 9.4)
>
> All phenomena are Buddhahood, because thusness has no differentiation, and because [Buddhahood] consists of the purity of that [thusness]. But in Buddhahood there is no phenomena whatsoever existing in terms of the imagined nature of phenomena. And Buddhahood consists of excellent qualities, because there is transformation of virtues like the perfections by its presence. But it is not defined by them, because the perfections, etc. have no perfect establishment by nature as perfections, etc. This is its nondual identity.[18]

This states explicitly that Buddhahood is not to be defined in terms of its excellent qualities per se (the set of Buddha dharmas). Rather, its true identity is to be found in its nondual nature, referred to in the *bhāṣya* as "the purity of thusness" *(tathatāviśuddhi)*.

The ultimate nature of things—thusness *(tathatā)* or emptiness *(śūnyatā)*—is hidden from the view of ordinary beings by their own mental obstructions *(āvaraṇa)*. Thusness, as the real, ultimate nature of things, has always been there. But beings have not seen it because the impurity of their own minds obstructs it from view. According to Yogācāra texts such as the *MSA*, the Mahāyāna yogic path cultivates an awareness, a gnosis, that directly realizes thusness. Gradually it removes all the mental obstructions until, at full enlightenment, it realizes thusness in an inseparable, uninterrupted way. A Buddha, as *dharmakāya*, takes appearance in the world in many ways to teach beings; but a Buddha's mind never wavers from undistracted concentration on thusness. *MSA 9.4* and its *bhāṣya* deny that Buddhahood is to be defined by its excellent qualities *(śukladharmāḥ)*, because its real defining principle, its real identity, is the purity of thusness *(tathatāviśuddhi)*. And this claim is supported by a paradox: that all phenomena are both to be identified with Buddhahood and to be negated.

All phenomena, in their real nature as thusness, "are Buddhahood" (the purity of thusness) when the mental obstructions hiding their real nature are removed. As the *bhāṣyakāra* notes, within thusness there is no differentiation (differentiation, as a product of conceptual thought, is not a quality of the real nature of things in itself). Since Buddhahood is the nondual realization of thusness, there is no thusness separate or apart from it. Therefore, all phenomena, seen in their real nature through the pure, unobstructed perspective of enlightenment, are Buddhahood, are the purity of thusness *(tathatāviśuddhi)*. However, according to the *MSA* and other texts, the nature of phenomena imagined by unenlightened beings—e.g., conceptualized in terms of an ultimately distinct subject and object of cognition—does not exist. The realization of Buddhahood is also the realization of the nonexistence of that imagined nature of duality *(parikalpita svabhāva)*. According to the *bhāṣya*, the line "there is no phenomenon at all" carries this sense.

All phenomena, then, are said to exist as Buddhahood (in their thusness), and yet not to exist (in their imagined nature of duality). In a parallel way, the verse's last two lines assert that the excellent qualities which a yogi cultivates to attain enlightenment (the undefiled Buddha dharmas) make up Buddhahood, but do not "define" it *(na ca tais tan nirupyate)*, i.e., do not comprise its defining essence. The undefiled dharmas, as a set of excellent mental qualities, are defined and distinguished from each other through conceptual categories ("six perfections," "ten powers," etc.), "imagined" *(parikalpita)* by the conceptual minds of non-Buddhas. The text affirms that they are cultivated up to the attainment of Buddhahood. But as conceptually constructed qualities, they are the products of discursive thought, not ultimately real. The *bhāṣya* says that the excellent mental qualities ordinarily ascribed to the Buddha, such as the perfections *(pāramitās)*, "have no perfect establishment by nature as perfections, etc." *(pāramitādi bhāvenāpariniṣpatti)*. Because of this, it says, they do not define *(nirdiśyate)* Buddhahood. This implies that what does define Buddhahood, unlike this set of mental qualities, *is* perfectly established by nature *(bhāvena pariniṣpatti)*, is ultimately real, and is not merely a conceptual construct. It is this which the *bhāṣya* identified in its first sentence as the purity of thusness *(tathatāviśuddhi)*.

Sthiramati's *Vṛttibhāṣya* on *MSA* 9.4 comments:

> Buddha[hood] is characterized by nonduality. How so? Duality concerns subject and object [of cognition]. At the time of enlightenment, the duality [of] subject and object is removed, hence it is "nondual." In an-

other way, duality concerns the pair: existence and nonexistence. When enlightened, there is neither existence nor nonexistence. Therefore it is "nondual." How is there not existence? At enlightenment, the imagined characteristic that imagines a subject and object does not exist. How is there not nonexistence? [At enlightenment,] the characteristic of perfected existence exists [Tib., *yong su grub pa yod pa'i mtshan nyid yod pa*]. . . .

"All phenomena are Buddha[hood]."[19] [Here,] "Buddha[hood]" refers to the selflessness of persons, the selflessness of phenomena, and to phenomena as nonarising and nonceasing. Amongst all phenomena, there is none which is without the two selflessnesses, or is not nonarising and nonceasing. And as for Buddha's *dharmakāya,* being the nature of the two selflessnesses, the nature of nonarising and nonceasing, there is not even the slightest bit of it which is other than in the nature of the two selflessnesses of all phenomena, of nonarising and of nonceasing. Therefore, all phenomena are called "Buddha[hood]." For this reason the *Ārya-Vajracchedikā-sūtra* says:

> Whoever sees me as [my] form,
> Whoever knows me as [my] voice,
> By having engaged in wrong practice,
> Me those beings do not see.
>
> As thusness *(tathatā)* are Buddhas seen,
> The guides have *dharma[tā]* as body *(dharmakāya),*
> [But] the real nature of things *(dharmatā)* being unknowable,
> They are not to be discerned.[20]

[Someone] may ask, "If all phenomena are Buddha[hood], then all phenomena would have the nature of enlightened existence [in line with the statement above that at enlightenment, "the characteristic of perfected existence exists"]. So do [all] phenomena, like Buddhahood, have that nature of existence?" [To answer that, the second line of the verse] says: "But there is no phenomenon at all." This means that phenomena having the characteristics imagined by childish common people, of subject and object, and of "vase," "blanket," etc., do not exist at all.

[The next line of the verse] says: "It consists of excellent qualities." [This is said because] Buddha[hood] is first achieved through accomplishing the stages *(bhūmi*s*)*, perfections *(pāramitā*s*)*, the factors that foster enlightenment *(bodhipakṣa*s*)*. So at the time of enlightenment also, it continues to abide in the nature of the stages, perfections, factors that foster enlightenment, powers, forms of fearlessness, etc. In this sense it consists of excellent qualities. [Someone] may ask: "In that case is Buddha[hood]

> just the nature of those perfections *(pāramitās)?*" [To respond to this, the final line of the verse] says: "But it is not defined by them." Perfections *(pāramitās)* of imagined characteristic that are perceived under three aspects, e.g. a giver, a receiver and a gift, do not exist by their own intrinsic nature [Skt., *svabhāvataḥ nāsti;* Tib., *rang bzhin gyis yod pa ma yin*]. Therefore it can not be said with respect to a perfection *(pāramitā)* of imagined characteristic that its nature is Buddha[hood]. Why? Because Buddha [hood] is not an imagined phenomena. The [lines of verse] up to here have explained the nondual character [of Buddhahood].[21]

Here, Sthiramati explores further the ontological aspect of Buddhahood. When one is enlightened, he says, the imagined characteristic *(parikalpita lakṣaṇa)*, which conceptually separates a subject and object of cognition, no longer exists. But the perfected characteristic *(pariniṣpanna lakṣaṇa)* very much exists.[22] The *MSA* 9.4 *bhāṣya* implied that what "defines" Buddhahood is "perfectly established by nature," i.e., ultimately real, not merely a conceptual construct *(parikalpita)*. What defines Buddhahood, according to Sthiramati, is not something found not to exist at enlightenment (the imagined characteristic, *parikalpita lakṣaṇa*), but something found to exist (the perfected characteristic, *pariniṣpanna lakṣaṇa*). In line with this he later comments that the perfections *(pāramitās)*, as conceptual constructions *(parikalpita)*, do not define Buddhahood, because they "do not exist by their own intrinsic nature" (Skt., *svabhāvataḥ nāsti;* Tib. *rang bzhin gyis yod pa ma yin*).

Sthiramati understands the statement "all phenomena are Buddhahood" to mean that all phenomena are without self *(nairātmya)*, and that Buddha's *dharmakāya* is entirely that same nature. But since he has just said that all phenomena have the nature of selflessness, it would be trivial for him to say that the *dharmakāya* also has that nature, unless he means something special by it.[23] His vehemence in stating that "not even the slightest bit of [the *dharmakāya*] is other than in the nature of the two selflessnesses of phenomena" indicates that for him, a Buddha is identified with selflessness (emptiness, thusness) in a very special way that distinguishes him from other beings. Only a Buddha's awareness realizes selflessness nondualistically in a way which is inseparable, uninterrupted, and unceasing. It is only a Buddha's mind that in this sense so utterly identifies itself with ultimate reality.

It is significant that Sthiramati employs the term *dharmakāya* precisely at this point. The *dharmakāya* is the Buddha's perfect, nondual gnosis of selflessness. Using Yogācāra ontological categories of the three natures of phenomena (the imagined nature, dependent nature, and perfected nature), Buddhahood is free of the imagined nature *(parikalpita svabhāva)* and identified with the perfected nature *(pariniṣpanna svabhāva)*. Sthiramati's quote from the *Vajracchedikāsūtra* reiterates this by identifying the Buddha not with his appearance or voice but with the *dharmakāya* as thusness (*tathatā* = *pariniṣpanna svabhāva* in Yogācāra ontology).

Sthiramati acknowledges that Buddhahood is understood to consist of a set of excellent qualities from a phenomenal point of view (i.e., the undefiled Buddha dharmas). But, at the same time, he reaffirms the *MSA*'s statement that those qualities do not "define" Buddhahood *(tais tan na nirupyate)*. His reason is that qualities such as the six perfections, insofar as they are conceived through the imagined characteristic as involving a subject and object do not apply to Buddhahood. When nonenlightened beings use terms like "the six perfections," "the ten powers," etc., they understand them to refer to subjects and objects, givers and receivers, which exist by their own intrinsic nature *(svabhāvato 'sti, rang bzhin gyis yod pa)*, independent of the conceptual process that labels them as such. But in reality, according to Yogācāra philosophy, such categories are our own conceptual constructions, and in this sense, products of our own imagination (Skt., *parikalpita;* Tib., *kun brtags)*.

At enlightenment, nonduality is realized. This is the realization that subjects and objects of cognition, although appearing as separate entities, are actually separated only through the conceptual construction of the categories "subject" and "object." Realization of nonduality is also the realization that no other conceptually constructed things (such as vases or blankets) exist by their own nature, apart from our conceptual construction *(parikalpita)* of them. According to Sthiramati, the very essence of Buddhahood is the realization of this nonduality. If it is the essence of a thing that defines it; it is this nondual realization, fully attained at enlightenment, that "defines" Buddhahood. The collection of Buddha dharmas, a conceptually differentiated set of mental qualities, although descriptive of Buddhahood from a phenomenal point of view, is not adequate to define Buddhahood, to capture its essence. *MSA* 9.4 and Sthiramati's commentary on it are reminiscent of the *PP* sūtras, where the ultimate defining principle of Buddhahood as *dharmakāya* is identified with thusness and its realization, not with the collection of undefiled Buddha dharmas per se.

Near the end of this same chapter of the *MSA*—chapter 9 concerning enlightenment—verses 78–79 return to the question raised above in verse 4 regarding what exists and does not exist in enlightenment. But they also frame the question epistemologically in terms of what is and is not perceived. Looked at in their logical relation to 9.4, these verses also concern the question of what defines (comprises the essence of) Buddhahood and what does not. *MSA* 9.78–9.79 and their *bhāṣya* say:

Concerning the method of entry into Buddhahood:[24]

> Nonexistence itself is supreme existence,
> Utter nonperception is the highest perception.
>
> (*MSA* 9.78)

> Nonexistence of the imagined nature is itself the supreme existence of the perfected nature. Utter nonperception of the imagined nature is itself the supreme perception of the perfected nature.
>
> Those who do not see any meditation,
> Have the supreme meditation.
> Those who do not see any attainment,
> Have the highest attainment.
>
> (*MSA* 9.79)
>
> Nonperception of meditation is itself the supreme meditation. Nonperception of any attainment is itself the supreme attainment.[25]

Sthiramati's *Vṛttibhāṣya* comments:

> [Quoting the first line of *MSA* verse 9.78:] "Total nonexistence is itself supreme existence." Upon [attaining] the first stage *(bhūmi)*, one realizes the nonexistence of the imagined nature. The imagined subject-object nature has become nonexistent for the first [time], and that itself is named "the supreme existence." Why? Because it is the existence of the perfected characteristic that is free of subject-object [duality]. [Quoting the second line of *MSA* verse 9.78:] "Utter nonperception is the supreme perception." Upon [attaining] the first stage *(bhūmi)*, one does not perceive the imagined nature, does not perceive what is conceptualized as a self, a "mine," a phenomena. That nonseeing itself is called "the supreme perception." Why? Because at that time one perceives, one sees, the perfected characteristic that is free of subject-object [duality].[26]

Sthiramati relates the verses to the stages of yogic realization of reality up to the attainment of full enlightenment. Here he says that when a bodhisattva first enters into a direct yogic realization of emptiness (which in Yogācāra soteriology occurs at the attainment of the first stage), the subject-object duality "imagined" by his own mind ceases to appear, revealing the ultimate nonexistence of any such duality. What then appears is what does ultimately exist, the absence of duality, the "perfected nature." The "perfected nature," then, is precisely the nonexistence of the "imagined nature," the nature falsely imagined to exist. Similarly, when the yogi does not see any real subject-object duality, i.e., when he "sees through" the imagined nature, he sees clearly; he has the truest perception, that of the perfected nature. Realization of the nonexistence of the one reveals the existence of the other. Sthiramati continues:

> [Quoting the first line of *MSA* verse 9.79:] "Not seeing meditations is the supreme meditation." From the second stage *(bhūmi)* up to the tenth stage, the conceptions of subject-object [duality], of "I," and of "mine," are abandoned. Making this one's meditation repeatedly without seeing duality is the highest meditation. Why? Because it is meditation on the characteristic of nonperception. [Quoting the second line of *MSA* 9.79:] "Not seeing any attainment is the supreme attainment." Upon reaching the Buddha stage there is the highest attainment: the not seeing of any attainment of *sāmbhogikakāya*, of *nairmāṇikakāya*, or of [Buddha] dharmas such as the [ten] powers and the [four] fearlessnesses. Why is that? Because it is the supreme attainment, the highest of all dharmas, the *dharmakāya*.[27]

Sthiramati continues to describe the rest of the stages of yogic realization prior to Buddhahood (second to tenth stages) as repeated meditation on nonduality and selflessness, on the nonperception of the imagined nature referred to above as the "supreme perception." Finally, the attainment of Buddhahood is described as the extension of this same process. It is a yogic realization that does not see any of the attainments conceptually ascribed to Buddhahood. Those aspects of Buddhahood which appear dualistically to other beings (the form *kāyas*) or are dualistically conceptualized and labeled by other beings (the undefiled Buddha dharmas) are not seen at the attainment of Buddhahood. Buddhahood in itself does not involve any such conceptual construction. It is the "supreme attainment." And as the culmination of the yogic process thus far described, it is the final "supreme perception" of "supreme existence"—i.e., the final realization of the perfected nature: *dharmakāya*.

MSA 9.78–79 and their commentaries clarify further the statement at the beginning of the same chapter (v. 9.4) that Buddhahood is not "defined" by the collection of his mental qualities, the Buddha dharmas. The defining essence of Buddhahood is not a set of conceptually differentiated qualities, no matter how exalted their status in Buddhist tradition. Rather Buddhahood's essence is its nondual realization of reality *(śūnyatā, tathatā, pariniṣpanna)*, its realization of the emptiness of all phenomena, including all phenomena traditionally ascribed to Buddhahood. It is this essence that is referred to as *dharmakāya*. The Yogācāra formulation recapitulates the structure of the *PP* sūtras' teaching on *dharmakāya*. Commentators such as Sthiramati explicitly placed this teaching within a classical Yogācāra framework, emphasizing the nonduality of subject and object and the realization of *pariniṣpanna*. Similar accounts of *dharmakāya* and Buddhahood can be found throughout classical Yogācāra literature.[28]

4.3
Yogācāra Sixfold Analysis of Buddhahood: "Essence" *(Svabhāva)* Corresponds to *Svābhāvikakāya*

A number of key themes emerge in the *Mahāyānasūtrālaṃkāra* verses and commentaries above, and we will have reason to return to several of them again. One such theme is the distinction drawn between the very essence of Buddhahood, its intrinsic nature *(svabhāva)*, on the one hand, and the set of phenomenal qualities prior traditions had ascribed to it, on the other (the undefiled Buddha dharmas, exalted physical marks of the *rūpakāya*s, etc.). As we have seen, according to Yogācāra texts under examination here, the various qualities *(dharmāḥ)* traditionally ascribed to Buddhahood do not define it. What does define it is its very essence, identified as the purity of thusness *(tathatā viśuddhi)*, as the perfected nature *(pariniśpanna)*, and as the nondual realization of thusness that comprises the real embodiment of dharma *(dharmakāya)*.

Buddhahood's essence and its adjunct qualities comprise two of the six categories set forth in an analysis of Buddhahood distinctive of the Yogācāra school. According to this Yogācāra scheme, Buddhahood is described through the following six categories: (1) its essence, its own real nature *(svabhāva),* (2) its cause *(hetu)*, (3) its result *(phala)*, (4) its activity *(karma)*, (5) its endowment *(yoga)*, and (6) its functional modes *(vṛtti)*.[29] Among these, Buddhahood's essence *(svabhāva)* is the first category, and its adjunct qualities comprise the fifth category, "endowment" (*yoga*, meaning the qualities with which Buddhahood is endowed). *MSA* 21.60–61 and the *bhāṣya* say:

> You have accomplished the ultimate,
> You have issued from all the stages *(bhūmis)*
> You have obtained preeminence among all beings,
> You are the liberator of all beings.
>
> (*MSA* 21.60)
>
> Endowed with inexhaustible, unequaled excellences,
> You are beheld in the worlds and in the assemblies,
> Yet are entirely invisible to gods and men.
>
> (*MSA* 21.61)

> *bhāṣya:* Here Buddha's characteristics are explained through six topics: essence, cause, result, activity, endowment, and functional modes. Purified thusness *(viśuddhā tathatā)* is the ultimate that is accomplished *(niṣpannaḥ paramārthaḥ)*. And it is the very essence *(svabhāva)* of the Buddhas. Their cause *(hetu)* is their issuance from all the bodhisattva

> stages. Their result *(phala)* is the attainment of preeminence among all beings. Their activity *(karma)* is the liberating of all beings. Their endowment *(yoga)* is [their] possession of inexhaustible, incomparable qualities. Their mode of function *(vṛtti)* is threefold: showing [themselves] in various world realms through embodiment in created forms *(nirmāṇakāya)*, showing [themselves] among the assemblies through embodiment in communal enjoyment *(sāmbhogikakāya)*, and being utterly invisible with respect to their embodiment of dharma *(dharmakāya)*.[30]

In this sixfold analysis, the qualities of a Buddha, such as the undefiled dharmas, are classified as his "endowment," *not* his essence. His essence is purified thusness *(viśuddhā tathatā)*. A Buddha, though "endowed with" undefiled qualities, is not to be identified with them. Although conceptualized by ordinary beings as possessed of many things ("inexhaustible excellences"), a Buddha in his own essence, which they do not see, is a simple, undifferentiated thing: purified thusness *(viśuddhā tathatā)*.

According to the *bhāṣya*, a Buddha's functional modes *(vṛtti)* are threefold: embodiment in created forms *(nairmāṇikakāya)* to teach limitless beings, embodiment in communal enjoyment *(sāmbhogikakāya)* to share the dharma with assemblies of great bodhisattvas, and embodiment of the dharma *(dharmakāya)* in his own inmost realization. Among these, *dharmakāya*, being "entirely invisible to gods and men," is equivalent to the essence of Buddhahood *(svabhāva)*, the accomplishment of the ultimate *(niṣpannaḥ paramārthaḥ)*. When showing themselves to others as *nairmāṇikakāya* or *sāmbhogikakāya*, the Buddhas appear endowed with many excellences But *dharmakāya*, their own inmost realization of purified thusness, cannot be shown to others.

Mahāyānasūtrālaṃkāra 9.56–9.59 employ a distinctive and important term to refer to enlightenment: *dharmadhātu-viśuddha* (purified dharma realm).[31] These verses apply the same sixfold analysis to it, according to which the purified dharma realm *(dharmadhātu-viśuddha)* encompasses the thusness *(tathatā)* of all phenomena unobstructed within the nondual awareness *(jñāna)* of enlightenment, the vast activities of enlightenment, all of enlightenment's qualities, and all three of its *kāyas*. This makes it quite clear that the term "purified dharma realm" *(dharmadhātu-viśuddha)* refers to Buddhahood in its entirety, although the connotations of the name emphasize Buddhahood's purity, where all of its aspects are understood as expressions of that basic purity (the name for Buddhahood in the earlier portion of the same chapter—*anāsrava-dhātu* [undefiled realm]—possesses very much the same connotations).

Under the first category of the sixfold analysis, *MSA* 9.56 and *bhāṣya* specify the defining essence *(svabhāva)*, the very identity *(lakṣaṇa)* of the "purified realm of dharma" that is Buddhahood.

> *MSA bhāṣya*: Four verses [follow] on the purified realm of dharma *(dharmadhātu-viśuddha)*:
>
> Its identity is the thusness of all phenomena, purified of the two obstructions.
> Its identity is the undiminishing power of the awareness of phenomena that rests upon that [thusness].
>
> (*MSA* 9.56)
>
> *MSA bhāṣya*: The topic of this first verse is the essence *(svabhāva)* [of the purified realm of dharma]. Its identity is the thusness of all phenomena purified of the two obstructions: the affective and the cognitive. And its identity is the undiminishing power of two [aspects of its] awareness: awareness that rests upon [thusness] and awareness of phenomena.

This provides a working definition for "purified dharma realm," *dharmadhātu-viśuddha*. Its defining essence *(svabhāva)* is thusness purified of all that had obscured it from awareness, hence it is inclusive of thusness and awareness together *(tathatā-viśuddhi* and *jñāna)*. The purified dharma realm is the nature of all phenomena as embraced by the unobstructed nondual awareness, the gnosis, of a Buddha *(jñāna)*. It is Buddhahood in its fullest, cosmic dimension: the totality of all phenomena as viewed through a Buddha's nondual awareness of their true nature.

Verses 9.57–58 elaborate the second through fifth categories analytical of the purified dharma realm of Buddhahood: cause, result, activity, and endowment. Verse 9.59 then explains the sixth category, vṛtti, functional modes of the purified dharma realm, which are its three embodiments *(kāyas)*. Significantly, this verse with *bhāṣya* uses the very term for the defining essence of the purified dharma realm, *svabhāva*, to construct the name of its first "embodiment" *(kāya): svābhāvikakāya*. This would seem to imply that the first of the three *kāyas* is the very essence of Buddhahood, a Buddha's own inmost realization. *Svābhāvikakāya* would therefore mean "the embodiment [of Buddhahood] in its essence," where Buddhahood's "essence" *(svabhāva)* is understood just as defined above—as nondual awareness of purified thusness.[32]

The verses on the six categories of Buddhahood (*MSA* 21.60–61) are also quoted in the last chapter of the *Mahāyānasaṃgraha*, "Resultant Awareness" (Tib., "Bras bu ye shes," section 10.27 on *dharmakāya*), the chapter on a Buddha's realization as the result of completing the path. The *Mahāyānasaṃgraha (Msg)* quotes *MSA* 21.60–21.61 as above, analyzing Buddhahood in terms of its six categories. The *Msg*'s brief preface to these two verses says:

> Furthermore, *[dharmakāya]* has the following qualities: essence, cause, result, activity, endowment, and functional modes. Thus the qualities of the Buddhas are to be known as unsurpassed.[33]

Asvabhāva's commentary says:

> Explanatory of these verses [*MSA* 21.60–21.61] is [the *Msg*'s statement:] "Furthermore, the embodiment of dharma *(dharmakāya)* has the following six qualities: essence, etc." The verse "You have accomplished the ultimate" means that with respect to its own essence *(svabhāva)* the embodiment of dharma *(dharmakāya)* is completely perfected, because it consists of purified thusness *(viśuddhā tathatā)*."[34]

According to Asvabhāva, a Buddha's enlightenment as the embodiment of dharma *(dharmakāya)*, in its very essence *(svabhāva)*, is purified thusness. A distinctive semantic relation between the Sanskrit terms *svabhāva* and *dharmakāya* is drawn here, expressing an understanding that may have contributed to the usage of two closely related terms in classical Yogācāra texts: *dharmakāya* and *svābhāvikakāya*. These texts often treat these terms as synonyms to designate just the first of the three *kāya*s. This would make sense if the latter term, among its other connotations, was also viewed as a specification of the former term, i.e., *svābhāvikakāya* = *dharmakāya svābhāvikaḥ*: embodiment *(kāya)* of the dharma in its essence *(svābhāvikaḥ)*, meaning awareness of dharma as the Buddhas know it in their own inmost realization.[35]

In any case, the first analytical category of Buddhahood in classical Yogācāra, *svabhāva* (essence of enlightenment), directly corresponds to *svābhāvikakāya* (embodiment of enlightenment in its essence), which is the first of the embodiments of enlightenment *(kāyas)* that comprise its sixth analytical category (functional modes of enlightenment, *vṛtti*). It looks like *svābhāvikakāya* as part of the sixth analytical category derived its name from the name of the first category *(svabhāva)*. It would therefore appear that the six-category scheme and the three-*kāya* model were closely connected theoretical developments in Yogācāra circles. The logic of the sixth category is consistent with this, for it borrows not only the name of the first category but also its sense, in defining *svābhāvikakāya* and distinguishing it from the other two *kāya*s. *Svābhāvikakāya* is precisely the essence of Buddhahood *(svabhāva)* in inmost realization that comprises the first *kāya*; its relations and manifestations to others comprise the other two *kāya*s.

The listing of the undefiled Buddha dharmas in classical Yogācāra texts, therefore, represents the preservation of an older, pre-Yogācāra description of Buddhahood, while the six-category analysis and three-*kāya* model appear to be distinctive

Yogācāra developments. We saw how prior Abhidharma traditions presented the list of Buddha dharmas as the defining essence of Buddhahood. Largely the same list of dharmas is retained in the Yogācāra system, where it is now understood as a phenomenal description of Buddhahood, not a defining essence. It is for this reason that the list is slotted within the six-category scheme as *yoga,* (endowment) rather than as *svabhāva* (essence).

The six-category scheme, in effect, separates out the pre-Yogācāra model of Buddhahood, the list of Buddha dharmas, from the distinctively Yogācāra models. The Buddha dharmas are analytically segregated through the six-category scheme from what Yogācāras understood to comprise the real defining essence of enlightenment *(svabhāva)*, and therefore also from their distinctive model of three *kāya*s (the functional modes or "embodiments" of that defining essence).

Because the Buddha dharmas are a traditional pre-Mahāyāna and Abhidharma description of enlightenment, a place is kept for them within this scheme, as an understanding that retains validity from a phenomenal perspective, while no longer adequate to serve as Buddhahood's defining principle. In the Yogācāra scheme, the defining essence of Buddhahood *(svabhāva)* must be presented from an ultimate perspective, conforming to the Yogācāra concept of enlightenment as a nondual realization of reality: pure awareness, gnosis *(jñāna)* of purified thusness *(viśuddhā tathatā)*, corresponding to *svābhāvikakāya.*

4.4
Meanings Implicit in *Kāya* Name Morphologies: Embodiment of Buddhahood in its Essence *(Svābhāvika),* in its Communal Enjoyment of Dharma *(Sāmbhogika),* in its Manifestations *(Nairmāṇika)*

As just noted, *Mahāyānasūtrālaṃkāra* verses 9.56–9.59 analyze Buddhahood as the "purified realm of dharma" *(dharmadhātu-viśuddha),* under six distinctive topics: essence *(svabhāva)*, cause *(hetu)*, result *(phala)*, activity *(karma)*, endowment *(yoga)*, and functional modes *(vṛtti)*. Verse 9.59 explains the sixth topic, according to which there are three basic functional modes *(vṛtti)* of Buddhahood, which comprise what it calls a threefold *kāya*. *MSA* verses 9.60–9.66 further elaborate upon that threefold *kāya.* This section of the *MSA* comprises its core teaching of the three-*kāya* model. As possibly the earliest systematic explanation of the three-*kāya do*ctrine in Yogācāra literature (third century to fourth century C.E.), it exerted tremendous influence upon later developments in India and Tibet. *MSA* verses 9.59–9.60 open the section and define its content. We will examine them closely in the Sanskrit, together with their earliest commentary, the *MSA bhāṣya.*[36]

Verse 9.59 introduces the topic in which the *kāya* model is situated:

svabhāvadharmasambhoganirmāṇairbhinnavṛttikaḥ
dharmadhāturviśuddho 'yam buddhānāṃ samudāhṛtaḥ

(*MSA* 9.59)

[This is declared as the Buddhas' purified realm of dharma *(dharmadhātu-viśuddha),* whose mode of function varies as to essence, communal enjoyment of dharma, and manifestation.]

eṣa vṛttyarthamārabhya caturthaḥ ślokaḥ svābhāvikasāṃbhogikanairmāṇikakāyavṛttyā bhinnavṛttikaḥ

(*MSA* 9.59 *bhāṣya)*

[The fourth of the verses {on the six topics} concerns the {sixth} topic: functional mode *(vṛtti).* The function {of the purified realm of dharma} varies according to its mode of embodiment: in its own essence, in its communal enjoyment, in its manifestation(s).][37]

The threefold *kāya* is introduced as the threefold function *(vṛtti)* of the "purified dharma realm" *(dharmadhātu-viśuddha)*, the latter term referring, as we have seen, to the gnosis of unobstructed thusness that all Buddhas share, i.e., to Buddhahood in its fullest cosmic dimension.

The fact that the *MSA* introduces its three-*kāya* model within this final topic of the Yogācāra sixfold analysis has great significance. It reveals the three-kāya model's systematic purpose: to relate the nature of Buddhahood (topic 1: essence, *svabhāva*) to its functions (topic 6: functions, *vṛtti*). The three-*kāya* model delineates how the very essence of Buddhahood (nondual gnosis of thusness) can be understood to function for itself and for others by the ways in which it "embodies" its realization. Buddhahood embodies its realization:

1. In its own knowledge of the thusness of all phenomena, which is its own innermost essence *(svābhāvika)*

2. In the sharing of that knowledge with its closest communities of disciples (great bodhisattvas) in communal enjoyment *(sāmbhogika)*

3. In its communication of that knowledge to limitless beings through diverse manifestations *(nairmāṇika)*

Note the specific way that the *MSA bhāṣya* derives the morphology of the three *kāya* names that later became characteristic of Yogācāra literature. *MSA* 9.59 presents the three terms from which the three compound names are made in primary derivative form *(kṛt)*, as nouns in a copulative compound in instrumental case: *(svabhāva) . . . (saṃbhoga) (nirmānaiḥ).*[38] The terms are in nominal form, naming three contexts in which Buddhahood is understood to function with respect to itself and others: its own "essence," its "communal enjoyment" of dharma, and its "manifestation(s)."

The *bhāṣya* to 9.59 then converts these three nouns into the secondary derivative form *(taddhita)* as adjectives modifying the noun phrase *kāya-vṛtti:* "svābhāvika sāṃbhogika nairmāṇika kāya-vṛttyā bhinna-vṛttikaḥ" [The function {of the purified dharma realm} varies according to its mode of embodiment *(kāya):* in its own essence *(svābhāvika)*, in its communal enjoyment *(sāṃbhogika)*, and in its manifestation(s) *(nairmāṇika)*]. The adjectival morphology of the first terms in the compound names for the *kāyas* *is* the very morphology most often possessed by those terms throughout the earliest extant Sanskrit literature in which they appear.[39]

The *MSA bhāṣya*'s way of deriving the morphologies of the *kāya* names within the context of this sixth topic (functional modes of Buddhahood) gives the three terms *svābhāvika*, *sāmbhogika*, and *nairmāṇika* a special adjectival usage: to specify three kinds of function that one "thing" (the purified dharma realm) has, three ways that one "thing" is embodied in its own experience and in relation to the experience of others ("this, this, and this kind" of embodiment).

The word *kāya* takes on a special meaning here, closely related to but not identical with meanings from pre-Mahāyāna Buddhist traditions. In this context, *kāya* does not mean physical "body" (a common meaning of *rūpakāya* in pre-Mahāyāna texts). It does not mean "collection of components" (as in some pre-Mahāyāna texts where *dharmakāya* refers to a "collection of dharma teachings" or "collection of pure qualities"). Here *kāya* refers to the way in which a Buddha's ineffable realization of thusness is *embodied* within his own being and within his relations to the suffering beings of the universe.

Strictly speaking, then, in what may be the earliest systematized formulation of the three-*kāya* theory, there are not three different things called *kāyas* (e.g., three "bodies" of a Buddha, as the term has often been translated with reference to the Yogācāra *trikāya* model). There is one insubstantial, unlimited, and undivided "thing," the purified dharma realm, the realization of reality that all Buddhas share, which is "embodied" in three ways. The purified dharma realm is the nondual awareness of thusness in its full scope, within which there are no ontological divisions.[40] Distinctions among its *kāyas* can be made only with reference to the distinct ways in which that undivided realization functions *(vṛtti)* for those who have it (the Buddhas) and for those who do not (non-Buddhas).[41]

Hence, I chose not to translate *kāya* above as "body," since three *kāyas* would then connote three "bodies," which in ordinary English usage would refer to three distinct ontological entities. Instead, *kāya* is translated here as "embodiment," three *kāyas* connoting three "embodiments," referring to three functional expressions of *one* ontic reality: the purified dharma realm that all Buddhas realize.[42]

MSA 9.60 and its *bhāṣya* further clarify and reiterate the purpose behind the distinctive morphology of the *kāya* names:

svābhāviko 'tha sāṃbhogyaḥ kāyo nairmāṇiko 'paraḥ
kāyabhedā hi buddhānām prathamastu dvayāśrayaḥ

(*MSA* 9.60)

[The varieties of embodiment of the Buddhas are: embodiment in their own essence, in communal enjoyment, and in manifestation(s) as well. But the first is the basis of the {other} two.]

trividhaḥ kāyo buddhānām
svābhāviko dharmakāya āśraya-parāvṛtti-lakṣaṇaḥ
sāṃbhogiko yena parṣanmaṇḍaleṣu dharma-saṃbhogaṃ karoti
nairmāṇiko yena nirmāṇena sattvārthaṃ karoti

(*MSA* 9.60 *bhāṣya*)

[Embodiment of the Buddhas is threefold, {being}:

1. in essence *(svābhāvika)*, the embodiment of dharma *(dharmakāya)*, whose identity is fundamental transformation.
2. in communal enjoyment *(sāṃbhogika)*, that which creates enjoyment of dharma within the circles of assembly.
3. in manifestation *(nairmāṇika)*, manifestation(s) that work for the benefit of beings.]

The expression "embodiment of the Buddhas" *(kāya . . . buddhānām)* in verse 9.60 substitutes for the expression "purified dharma realm of the Buddhas" *(dharmadhātu-viśuddha . . . buddhānām)* of verse 9.59, indicating that 9.60's "embodiment of the Buddhas" refers to the Buddhas' embodiment of the purified dharma realm *(dharmadhātu-viśuddha)*, the realization of thusness all Buddhas share.

The first half of verse 9.60 puts the word *kāya* in the singular: a singular noun modified by three adjectives: *svābhāvika, sāmbhogika, nairmāṇika.* The *bhāṣya* clarifies the adjectival function of the latter three terms. *The embodiment (kāya)* of the purified dharma realm of the Buddhas, *with respect to its own nature (svābhāvika)*, is the embodiment of the dharma in its fullest realization *(dharmakāya),* the fruit of ultimate transformation *(āśraya-parāvṛtti)*. Enjoying the dharma through its fullest realization, Buddhahood shares its enjoyment with its closest communities of disciples, the great bodhisattvas. *With respect to the sharing of its enjoyment (sāmbhogika),* it takes form within those communities ("the circles of assembly"). Finally, *with respect to its widest scope of manifestation (nairmāṇika),* it manifests in manifold ways to teach vast numbers of beings. From the adjectival meanings italicized above come the distinctive morphologies of the names: *svābhāvikakāya, sāmbhogikakāya, nairmāṇikakāya.* In this fundamental Yogācāra formulation of the three-*kāya* theory, enlightenment functions in its own essence *(svābhāvika)* simply as nondual knowledge, unmanifest to others. But that knowledge functions for the world in two ways: in communal enjoyment *(sāmbhogika)*, and in diverse forms of manifestation *(nairmāṇika)*.[43] Enlightenment as one undivided realization, functioning in those three ways, is the "threefold *kāya*."

The author(s) of the *MSA* and *bhāṣya* passages above seem to have used their language very consciously and precisely to specify, as clearly as it can be specified in Sanskrit, that what was intended by the "threefold *kāya*" was not three distinct ontological entities (three "bodies"), but the embodiment of one undifferentiated realization in three ways. In line with that, if *MSA* verse 9.60 *bhāṣya* (line 1) were to be translated "The body of the Buddhas is threefold," it would make little sense. What precisely, in this context, would "body" mean? And how is a body supposed to be threefold? But the line readily makes sense in its fuller context translated as above: "Embodiment is threefold."[44]

After it is established that what is under discussion is the embodiment *(kāya*, singular) of one insubstantial "thing" in three ways, the terminology becomes looser and the expression "three *kāya*s" in the plural form begins occasionally to appear (e.g., *MSA* 9.65: "Know that [all] embodiments of the Buddhas are included within these three embodiments").[45] Still, the basic formulation, that there is one undifferentiated realization of enlightenment that functionally expresses itself in three ways, is preserved both in the usage of the terms and in the adjectival forms of the three *kāya* names. In Mahāyāna literature, even when the *kāya*s are discussed in the plural, they are most often referred to as *svābhāvikakāya*, embodiment (of Buddhahood) in its essence, *sāmbhogikakāya*, embodiment (of Buddhahood) in communal enjoyment, and *nairmāṇikakāya*, embodiment (of Buddhahood) in its manifestations. Each term refers to the embodiment of one insubstantial "thing," the purified dharma realm, in one of three ways. The terms do not generally appear in the primary derivative forms: *svabhāvakāya*, *sambhogakāya*, and *nirmāṇakāya*, morphologies that might lend themselves more easily to misunderstanding the *kāya*s as three distinct ontological entities, three "bodies."

The *Buddhabhūmivyākhyāna*, commenting[46] on the verse in the *Buddhabhūmisūtra* that is the exact equivalent of *MSA* 9.59, also explains Buddhahood as one undifferentiated realization *(dharmadhātu-viśuddha)* whose "embodiment" *(*Tib., *sku;* Skt., *kāya*) is qualified by three terms in adjectival form to signify its three functional modes: embodiment of Buddhahood in its own essence (Tib., *rang bshin pa* = Skt., *svābhāvika*), in enjoyment (Tib., *longs spyod pa pa* = Skt., *sāmbhogika*), and in manifestation (Tib., *sprul pa pa* = Skt., *nairmāṇika*). The Tibetan translators of the text took great care to express the secondary derivative (adjectival) forms of the Sanskrit terms when translating them into Tibetan, a language that ordinarily does not have such forms.

What is the broader significance of this? We noted earlier how Sarvāstivāda Abhidharma identified a Buddha's pure mental qualities, his collection of Buddha dharmas, as his defining essence. In section 1 of this chapter, we noted how

Haribhadra seemed to refer back to Abhidharma tradition in his comments upon the *Abhisamayālaṃkāra*, by making the collection of undefiled Buddha dharmas the central defining principle of Buddhahood, in terms of which all *kāya*s are understood. But the Yogācāra three-*kāya* understanding enunciated here, whose distinctive terminology the *Abhisamayālaṃkāra* employed, fundamentally differs both from pre-Mahāyāna Abhidharma and from Haribhadra.

The Yogācāras identified the defining essence of Buddhahood *(svabhāva) not* as a set of dharmas, but as an unobstructed nondual gnosis of the thusness of dharmas, which in its own essence *(svābhāvika)* embodies the very being of a Buddha *(svābhāvikakāya)*, and in its communal enjoyment of dharma and vast manifestation, embodies a Buddha's outreach to beings *(sāmbhogikakāya* or *nairmāṇikakāya)*. Contrary to Abhidharma and Haribhadra, then, the Yogācāras did not define Buddhahood in terms of a collection of many mental qualities, but as a single, undifferentiated realization. And the unobstructed and undivided nature of enlightenment receives subtle expression throughout the earliest *trikāya* literature in the usage and morphology of the three *kāya* names, which indicate the embodiment of one intrinsically undivided realization in three functional ways.

The portion of the *Abhisamayālaṃkāra*'s table of contents that outlines the entire content of its chapter on Buddhahood (verse 1.17 on chapter 8) also uses secondary derivative forms for the names of the three *kāya*s, and makes use of them adjectivally in a way recognizably similar to their usage in *MSA* v. 9.60. In all likelihood, this is because the *Abhisamayālaṃkāra*'s author wanted the terms to carry much the same meaning in his text that they carried in other texts of his time. This is an important consideration for interpreting the *Abhisamayālaṃkāra*'s eighth chapter.[47]

In what follows, then, my glosses and translations of the three *kāya* names will be based upon their etymology and explanations in *MSA* vv. 9.59–9.60 with *bhāṣya*. This leaves room for a number of alternative expressions. As a noun, *svābhāvikakāya* could be glossed as "embodiment of Buddhahood *in* its own essence" (i.e., in its own real nature, which is nondual gnosis of the thusness of all phenomena).[48] It could also be glossed as "embodiment of Buddhahood *as* the essence of all phenomena" (i.e., as the thusness of things from which a Buddha's nondual gnosis is inseparable).[49] Or in a more condensed way, it could be translated as "essential embodiment," "intrinsic embodiment." *Sāmbhogikakāya* could be glossed as "embodiment of Buddhahood *in* communal enjoyment of dharma" or "embodiment *for* communal enjoyment of dharma."[50] Finally, *nairmāṇikakāya* could be glossed: "embodiment of Buddhahood in its manifestation(s)" or "embodiment of Buddhahood as diverse manifestation."

The derivation, morphologies, and usage of the *kāya* names, set within the context of the Yogācāra sixfold analysis of Buddhahood, harmonize with the findings of the previous two sections of this chapter. Retained in the morphology of the Sanskrit names (which derive from Yogācāra analysis of Buddhahood's functional modes) and retained also in the sense of the terms is the idea that the defining principle of Buddhahood is not a dualistically conceptualized set of qualities (such as the Buddha dharmas), but an indivisible, nondual realization of undivided thusness that is functionally embodied in three ways. That defining principle is the "essence" *(svabhāva)* of Buddhahood in the sixfold analysis, identified as the "embodiment of dharma" in its ultimate realization *(dharmakāya)*.[51] As an ontologically undivided reality, it functions for different kinds of beings in three different ways: embodied within the Buddhas' own knowledge *(svābhāvikakāya)*, and embodied in the fundamental ways Buddhas share their knowledge with great bodhisattvas *(sāmbhogikakāya)* and ordinary beings *(nairmāṇikakāya)*.

4.5
Two Meanings of *Dharmakāya* in Yogācāra, with the Term *Svābhāvikakāya* Mediating between Them

In the previous chapter, we examined *Prajñāpāramitāsūtra* passages that identified *dharmakāya* as thusness *(tathatā, śūnyatā, dharmatā)* together with its realization in nondual knowledge *(prajñāpāramitā)*. In sections 2 and 3 of this chapter we saw how Buddhahood in classical Yogācāra texts was identified in its essence not as a set of conceptually differentiated Buddha dharmas but as purified thusness *(tathatā-viśuddhi)* and nonconceptual gnosis *(nirvikalpa-jñāna)*. Together these two—purified thusness and nonconceptual gnosis *(tathatāviśuddhi* and *nirvikalpa-jñāna)*—were understood to comprise *dharmakāya*, the embodiment of dharma in its fullest realization, which is a Buddha's realization. Sthiramati explicitly equated this Yogācāra understanding of *dharmakāya* with that of the *PP* sūtras by inserting into his comments the famous quote from the *Vajracchedikā-prajñāpāramitā-sūtra*:

> Whoever sees me as [my] form,
> Whoever knows me as [my] voice,
> By having engaged in wrong practice,
> Me those beings do not see.
> As thusness *(tathatā)* are Buddhas seen,
> The guides have *dharma[tā]* as body *(dharmakāya)*. . . .

We noted in section 3 of this chapter the close relation between this notion of the *dharmakāya* and the first of the six Yogācāra categories analytical of Buddhahood: *svabhāva* (essence), the essence of Buddhahood being *dharmakāya*, a realization that is invisible to gods and men.

MSA 9.60 *bhāṣya* (quoted in section 4 above) weaves these themes into its etymological definition for the first of the three *kāyas*. It says: "The embodiment *(kāya)* of the Buddhas . . . in its essence *(svābhāvika)* is the embodiment of dharma *(dharmakāya)*, whose identity is fundamental transformation *(āśrayaparāvṛtti)*." Fundamental transformation *(āśrayaparāvṛtti)* will be discussed in the following section. According to this early etymological explanation of the term, *svābhāvikakāya* derives its very name from the notion that it is the *dharmakāya* specified as the very essence *(svābhāvika)* of Buddhahood. The very meaning of the term *svābhāvikakāya* is constructed by reference to the meaning of *dharmakāya* as it had been understood in Mahāyāna sūtras such as the *PP*, where it referred to the ultimate awareness of a Buddha inseparable from thusness.

The new Yogācāra designation, *svābhāvikakāya*, specifically distinguishes *dharmakāya*, a Buddha's own nondual knowledge, from the other two *kāyas*, which are the ways *dharmakāya* embodies its knowledge to communicate with non-Buddhas. Because *svābhāvikakāya* is simply *dharmakāya* (i.e., nondual gnosis) specified as the very essence of a Buddha, it became common in classical Yogācāra literature to refer to the first of the three *kāyas* alternatively either as *svābhāvikakāya* or as *dharmakāya*, i.e., to treat the two terms in many contexts as synonyms. In earlier texts the common name for the first *kāya* was *svābhāvikakāya;* but this term was increasingly supplanted by *dharmakāya* in later commentaries, making it quite standard to call the three *dharmakāya*, *sāmbhogikakāya*, and *nairmāṇikakāya*.[52]

At the same time, as noted in the previous section, the formulation of three-*kāya* theory in the *MSA* and its commentaries actually asserted only one undivided ontological reality of enlightenment: the perfected, nondual realization of universal thusness, whose functions are distinguished as threefold. That undivided reality was understood as the unique ontological foundation of all enlightened qualities and *kāyas*. As we have seen, it was commonly referred to in Yogācāra literature as *dharmadhātu-viśuddha* (purified dharma realm) or *anāsravadhātu* (undefiled realm). And it was also frequently referred to as *dharmakāya*. Thus, it was also quite common in Yogācāra texts to use the term *dharmakāya* in a much more inclusive sense than that explained above, referring not just to the first of three *kāyas*, but to the entire state of Buddhahood as a whole, including all enlightened qualities and all three *kāyas*.[53]

In sum, the term *dharmakāya* had two basic meanings in Yogācāra literature: (1) an exclusive sense as the first of three Buddha *kāyas*, and (2) an inclusive sense as the state of Buddhahood in its entirety (including all three *kāyas*). This did not involve a contradiction. As noted, the three *kāyas* were never conceived as three separate entities. They were understood ontologically as one "thing" (simply enlightenment) as it came under the purview of and functioned for three kinds of beings: Buddhas, *ārya* bodhisattvas, and other beings. All three *kāyas*, then, were understood to be functional expressions of one ontologically undivided attainment, characterized both as the first of three *kāyas* and the basis upon which all three are designated.

When the term *svābhāvikakāya* was first introduced in texts such as the *MSA*, it was employed to differentiate these two meanings. *Dharmakāya* in its own nature, *svābhāvika*, was designated *svābhāvikakāya*. *Dharmakāya* as the nondual realization that is the basis of all enlightened qualities and *kāyas* was designated simply *dharmakāya*. But as later commentaries began to drop the differentiating term *svābhāvikakāya*, the term *dharmakāya* was given double semantic duty. Thus, the term *dharmakāya* came to be used in Yogācāra literature either with an exclusive sense (meaning *svābhāvikakāya* alone out of the three *kāyas*), or with an inclusive sense (meaning all of Buddhahood inclusive of all three *kāyas*).

We saw in chapter 2 above that the *Abhidharmakośa*, in verse 7.34, used the term *dharmakāya* in a special inclusive sense to designate the state of Buddhahood in its entirety as *phalasampad*, "the perfection of the result," the perfect fruition of the path. The Yogācāra usage of the term *dharmakāya* in its inclusive sense may bear some historical relation to this. In any case, the Abhisamayālaṃkāra refers to the entire subject matter of its eighth chapter as *dharmakāya-phalam*, "resultant *dharmakāya*," meaning the entire state of Buddhahood as the result of the Mahāyāna path. And this inclusive usage of the term probably derives from the Yogācāra usage.

4.6
Svābhāvikakāya as a Direct Extrapolation from Yogācāra Meditational Praxis and Gnoseology

Mahāyānasūtrālaṃkāra 9.60 *bhāṣya* is a seminal source of three-*kāya* theory. It was analyzed earlier in section 4, but we must turn to it again for further information on *svābhāvikakāya*:

> Embodiment of the Buddhas is threefold, [being]: (1) In its own essence *(svābhāvika)*, the embodiment of dharma *(dharmakāya)*, whose identity is fundamental transformation *(āśrayaparāvṛtti)*; (2) in communal enjoyment *(sāṃbhogika)*, that which creates enjoyment of dharma within the circles of assembly; (3) in manifestation *(nairmāṇika)*, manifestation(s) that work for the benefit of beings. *(MSA* 9.60 *bhāṣya)*

This text, in succinct form, gives one defining characteristic for the embodiment of Buddhahood in its essence *(svābhāvikakāya): āśrayaparāvṛtti*, translated "fundamental transformation," or the "transformation of the basis."[54]

Like *MSA* chapter 9, the *Mahāyānasaṃgraha*'s two final chapters concern the enlightenment of a Buddha as the result of the Mahāyāna path. At the beginning of these chapters, a Buddha's enlightenment as nonabiding nirvāṇa *(apratiṣṭhita-nirvāṇa)*, and *svābhāvikakāya/dharmakāya* is defined first in terms of fundamental transformation *(āśrayaparāvṛtti)*.[55] The *Buddhabhūmivyākhyāna* in its treatment of *svābhāvikakāya* appears to follow the *MSA bhāṣya,* equating *svābhāvikakāya* with *dharmakāya* and identifying fundamental transformation *(āśrayaparivṛtti)* as its defining characteristic.[56]

The concept of "fundamental transformation" *(āśrayaparāvṛtti* or *āśraya-parivṛtti)* in classical Yogācāra texts is a model of full enlightenment in which the basis of ordinary existence is transformed into the enlightenment of a Buddha through the process of yogic realization. This model puts its focus on enlightenment as the result of a transformative yogic process, the process through which the yogi's total being in its impure state is transformed into the pure state of Buddhahood. The impure state is the "basis," *āśraya.* This is the psychophysical organism, the mental and physical composite that comprises a sentient being prior to enlightenment. Yogācāra literature contains many different models for the basis *(āśraya),* some inherited from early Buddhism (the *skandhas*, *dhātus*, *āyatanas*), and some that are Mahāyāna or specifically Yogācāra concepts *(samalā-tathatā, alaya-vijñāna, saṃkleśa-bhāga paratantra-svabhāva).* Through the practice of the Mahāyāna path, the basis is utterly transformed *(parāvṛtti/parivṛtti)* into one of the Mahāyāna models of enlightenment: the purified dharma realm *(dharmadhātu-viśuddha),* the undefiled realm *(anāsrava-dhātu),* purified thusness *(tathatā-viśuddhā),* nonconceptual gnosis *(nirvikalpa-jñāna),* embodiment of dharma *(dharmakāya),* the perfect nature *(parinispanna).* At the stage of the literature at which the three *kāyas* appear, all such models are considered equivalent to each other *(dharmadhātu-viśuddha = anāsrava-dhātu = tathatā-viśuddhi = dharmakāya).*[57]

Because fundamental transformation *(āśrayaparāvṛtti)* is an essential defining feature of the embodiment of Buddhahood in its essence *(svābhāvikakāya),* we will examine its place in the *MSA*, *Msg*, and commentaries (which are our earliest detailed sources for the three-*kāya* theory) and other early Yogācāra texts that treat it as a principal topic.

MSA 9.12 and *bhāṣya* explain Buddhahood as *āśrayaparivṛtti*, complete transformation of the basis, attained when all affective and cognitive obstructions *(kleśa-jñeyāvaraṇa)* are eliminated.[58] Sthiramati's commentary says that *āśraya* refers to the five defiled aggregates (the *skandhas*, the psychophysical constituents of living beings: physical form, consciousness, feeling, recognition, and mental formations). They are the basis. The affective and cognitive obstructions within those aggregates are removed by practice of the Mahāyāna path, from whose completion the aggregates are replaced by the purified dharma realm *(dharmadhātu-viśuddha)* and nonconceptual gnosis *(nirvikalpajñāna)* of Buddhahood. That constitutes the completed transformation *(parāvṛtti/parivṛtti)* of the impure basis into perfect purity.[59] Buddhahood then, as fundamental transformation, is characterized by two key terms: *dharmadhātu-viśuddha* (purified dharma realm) and *nirvikalpa-jñāna* (nonconceptual gnosis).

The term *dharmadhātu* (dharma realm) in Yogācāra literature refers to ultimate reality as it is understood in that tradition. As such, it is equated with the terms *tathatā* (thusness, the unchanging reality of things that is "ever thus"), *paramārtha* (the ultimate, the object of ultimate gnosis), *dharmatā* (thinghood, the ultimate nature of things) and *śūnyatā* (emptiness, the nonexistence of inherent duality).[60] The term *dharmadhātu-viśuddha* (purified dharma realm) is thus equivalent to the terms *tathatā-viśuddhi* (purity of thusness) and *viśuddhā-tathatā* (purified thusness), terms that Yogācāra texts use as a definition of Buddhahood (as we saw in sections 2 and 3 above). The term *nirvikalpa-jñāna* (nonconceptual gnosis) also frequently appears together with the term *tathatā-viśuddhi* or its equivalents as a pair to characterize the essence of Buddhahood.[61]

In Yogācāra literature, *nirvikalpa-jñāna* and *tathatā-viśuddhi* or their equivalents often appear as a pair because together they designate an important Yogācāra model of enlightenment as a transformative cognitive process: what is unreal disappears from view as what is real appears clearly. Enlightenment is at once a nonperception of what is unreal and a perception of what is real.[62] Within the compound *tathatā-viśuddhi*, *tathatā* refers to thusness, reality as it is. *Viśuddhi* (purity, purification) means that the thusness of things is purified of all the affective and cognitive obstructions that would prevent its being known.[63] Within the term *nirvikalpa-jñāna*, *nirvikalpa* means "nonconceptual, free from dualistic conceptualizing." *Jñāna* means "profound awareness, gnosis."[64]

Thus, purified thusness *(tathatā-viśuddhi)* is reality as it really is, free of all obstructions that would prevent its being known, while nonconceptual gnosis *(nirvikalpajñāna)* is awareness free of all the dualistic conceptualization that would prevent its knowing reality. The two terms are mutually implicative. And together they point to a nondual realization of reality in which epistemological subject and object *(grāhaka* and *grāhya)* are no longer conceptually constructed, and hence no longer distinguished. Purified thusness *(tathatā-viśuddhi)* means reality is unobstructed from view, while nonconceptual gnosis *(nirvikalpa-jñāna)* means that the viewer is no longer obstructed from reality. From within the perspective of yogic realization, highest knowledge and the reality it knows are no longer "subject" and "object." They are experientially undivided. It is the state of utter identification between nonconceptual gnosis and universal thusness that comprises the very essence of Buddhahood: *svābhāvika-kāya*.

In the state of enlightenment, there is no purified thusness *(tathatā-viśuddhi)* apart from nonconceptual gnosis *(nirvikalpajñāna)*, and no nonconceptual gnosis apart from purified thusness. Because both terms refer to one nondual realization and mutually imply each other, often just one of the two terms suffices as the defining principle for Buddhahood as a whole. This was noted in sections 2 and 3 above, where purified thusness *(tathatā-viśuddhi)* was taken as the defining principle of full enlightenment, comprising its essence *(svabhāva)*. The equivalent concepts—purified dharma realm *(dharmadhātu-viśuddha)* and undefiled realm *(anāsravadhātu)*—are used similarly throughout *MSA*, chapter 9, to refer to Buddhahood as a whole.[65] The final chapter of the *Msg* is entitled "Phala-Jñāna," (Resultant gnosis), referring to the entire state of Buddhahood as gnosis *(jñāna)*. And the *Dharmadharmatāvibhāga (DDV)* with its *vṛtti* describes the entire gradual process of attaining enlightenment as "entry into nonconceptual gnosis" *(nirvikalpa-jñāna praveśa)*.

The *DDV* is an important source of information on the Yogācāra theory of fundamental transformation *(āśrayaparāvṛtti)*. Its title can be translated: "The distinction between phenomena *(dharma)* and their real nature *(dharmatā)*." Its yogic and philosophical models are closely related to those found in the *Mahāyāna-sūtrālaṃkāra (MSA)*, *Madhyānta-vibhāga (MAV)*, *Abhisamayālaṃkāra (AA)*, and *Ratnagotravibhāga (RGV)*, all of which are ascribed by the Tibetan tradition to Maitreya, in part, undoubtedly, because of the apparent close relationship between these texts. Even though the primary focus of each of the five texts differs in important ways from the others, they significantly overlap. The *DDV* and *MAV* are seminal articulations of fundamental Yogācāra yogic and philosophical theory. The *MSA* is a giant compendium of the entire spectrum of Mahāyāna (primarily Yogācāra) practice and theory. The *AA* is an enigmatic interpretation of the *PP* sūtras in terms of Mahāyāna paths and stages. And the *RGV* is the most detailed Indian commentary on the theory of Buddha-nature *(tathāgatagarbha)*. In a number of places these texts draw on a common substratum of ideas, primarily Yogācāran ideas (such as *āśrayaparāvṛtti*, the fivefold model of the yogic path, the four *samādhis* of the *prayoga mārga* leading to *nirvikalpa-jñāna*, *citta-prakṛti-viśuddhi*, and *trikāya* terminology). Although many images and concepts are shared among these treatises, they sometimes differ in their formulation and use of them.

More than half of the *Dharma-dharmatā-vibhāga (DDV)* is devoted to the explanation of fundamental transformation *(āśrayaparivṛtti)*.[66] It and its closest commentary (the *vṛtti* ascribed to Vasubandhu) explain fundamental transformation as the process of yogic realization that leads to full enlightenment, describing the stages of its development through the Mahāyāna paths *(mārga)*. In what follows, quotations will be translated from relevant portions of the *DDV* and *vṛtti* to build a wider Yogācāra context for this important model of enlightenment. We will then translate related quotes from other Yogācāra texts. The *DDV* says:

> Entry into reality *(dharmatā)* by six modes is supreme: entry (1) into its characteristic *(lakṣana)*, (2) into its basis *(sthiti)* (3) into analytical penetration of it *(nirvedha)*, (4) into contact with it *(sparśa)*, (5) into its recollection *(anusmṛti)*, and (6) into the arrival at its very nature *(tadātmakopagata)*. (1) Its characteristic is as in sūtras. (2) Its basis is all phenomena and all collections of scriptures. (3) Analytical penetration of it is all paths of preliminary yogic practice *(prayoga mārga)* comprising correct attention *(yoniśa-manasikāra)* in reliance upon the Mahāyāna scriptures. (4) Contact occurs through attaining the accurate view. [Contact] is the obtainment and

direct experience of thusness *(tathatā)* by the path of direct seeing *(darśana mārga)*. (5) Recollection is the path of meditation *(bhāvanā mārga)* upon the object seen by knowledge. Comprising the factors that foster enlightenment *(bodhipakṣa)*, it serves to clear away impurity. (6) Finally, there is arrival at the very nature of reality *(dharmatā)*. When thusness *(tathatā)* has become free of impurity, all appears only as thusness: that is the establishment of fundamental transformation *(āśrayaparivṛtti)*.[67]

Note how the *DDV* organizes the stages of the Mahāyāna path (path of preliminary yogic practice, path of direct seeing, path of meditation, path beyond further training) around the central notion of purification of thusness. Thusness *(tathatā)*, ultimate reality, which does not appear to beings whose minds are covered by impurity, is gradually uncovered through stages of yogic penetration, until, at full enlightenment, it shines forth without obstruction. The process is one of fundamental transformation *(āśrayaparivṛtti)*, developed in stages, completed at Buddhahood. We will look at the *DDV vṛtti* commentary on the latter portion of the *DDV* passage above, concerning the latter part of the Mahāyāna path, the modes of entry into reality numbered (5) and (6). The terms "thusness" *(tathatā)* and "reality" (or "real nature of things," *dharmatā*) are used as synonyms:

> The *[Dharmadharmatāvibhāga]* teaches: "Recollection consists of the path of meditation *(bhāvanā mārga)* comprising all the factors that foster enlightenment, that focuses on what was seen [by the prior path of direct seeing] in order to totally eliminate the impurities." "Recollection" refers to the path of meditation that immediately follows the path of direct seeing. Recollection that reconfirms the path just attained brings one near [to the very nature of reality *(dharmatā)*]. What is its purpose? It is for the purpose of utterly eliminating the impurities [that cover thusness *(tathatā)*]; for the purpose of removing the remaining impurities that are to be eliminated, by meditating on thusness *(tathatā)*.
>
> Immediately following recollection comes arrival at the very nature of [reality *(dharmatā)*] . Therefore the [*DDV* root text] instructs: "Arrival at the very nature of [reality]: when thusness has become free of impurity, all appears only as thusness." When the remaining impurity has been eliminated by the path of meditation *(bhāvanā mārga)* so that thusness is free of impurity, then with the final path [i.e., the path beyond further training, Buddhahood] everything appears only as thusness. This is because, by elimination of all impurities, [all] has become merely thusness. That alone has become the cognitive object. That is called "arrival at the very nature of [reality *(dharmatā)*]." It is the complete establishment of fundamental transformation *(āśrayaparivṛtti)*, being the very nature of

> [reality]. On the [earlier] stages, the path of direct seeing, etc. there was also transformation *(parivṛtti)*. But this [final transformation] is said to be completely established, because all the impurities have been eliminated.[68]

The *DDV* root text continues with a more detailed discussion of the modes of entering into this realization of fundamental transformation:

> Entry into fundamental transformation *(āśrayaparivṛtti)* by ten modes is supreme: (1) essence *(svabhāva)*, (2) objects *(vastu)*, (3) persons *(pudgala)*, (4) distinctiveness *(viśeṣa)*, (5) purpose *(prayojana)*, (6) foundation *(āśraya)*, (7) attention *(manasikāra)*, (8) yogic practice *(prayoga)*, (9) faults *(ādinava)*, (10). benefits *(anuśaṃsa)*.
>
> (1) Entry into the essence *(svabhāva)* is thusness's *[tathatā's]* freedom from impurity, so that adventitious impurity does not appear, and thusness does appear.[69]

The *vṛtti*, commenting on this, says:

> So that adventitious impurity no longer appears and thusness alone appears, thusness has become free of impurity. As such it is the essence *(svabhāva)* of fundamental transformation *(āśrayaparivṛtti)*. Such thorough knowledge *(parijñāna)* is called "supreme entry into the essence" [of fundamental transformation].[70]

Note how the text specifically equates purified thusness *(tathatā-viśuddhi)* with thorough knowledge *(parijñāna)*, which is nonconceptual gnosis *(nirvikalpa-jñāna)*. "Purifying thusness" means removing what covers reality so that it is permitted to appear just as it is. "Thusness appearing" implies an awareness to which it appears. And that awareness is the most "thorough" kind of knowledge *(parijñāna)*.

Mahāyānasūtrālaṃkāra verses 19.53–19.54 express the same theme. The essential meditation practice leading to enlightenment *(āśrayaparāvṛtti)* is the development of the gnosis *(jñāna)* that uncovers thusness, permitting it to appear, while ordinary beings see only the impurity that covers it:

> For fools, reality *(tattvaṃ)* is covered and it is unreality *(atatvaṃ)* that completely appears.
> But for bodhisattvas, having removed that [covering], reality completely appears.
>
> (*MSA* 19.53)

> The nonappearance of the nonexistent and the appearance of the existent
> are to be realized *(jñeya)*.
> This is liberation, fundamental transformation *(āśrayaparāvṛtti)*, because
> one proceeds freely.
>
> (*MSA* 19.54)

> *MSA* 19.54 *bhāṣya*: The nonappearance of the [dualistic] sign *(nimitta)*, the nonexistent object, and the appearance of thusness *(tathatā)*, the existent object, are to be known as fundamental transformation *(āśrayaparāvṛtti)*. For through it the one does not appear and the other appears. And precisely that is to be known as liberation. . . .[71]

Thusness free from all the impurity that has covered it *(vimalā tathatā)* is the essence of full enlightenment. Gradual purification of thusness occurs through development of more and more powerful forms of gnosis realizing thusness, referred to as "nonconceptual gnosis" *(nirvikalpa-jñāna)* or "thorough knowledge" *(parijñāna)*. The complete purification of thusness is accomplished by and realized by that gnosis. The essence of enlightenment being purified thusness, nonconceptual gnosis is both entrance into that essence and inseparable from it.

Where cognitive subject and object are no longer separated through conceptual construction, nonconceptual knowledge *(jñāna)* and its "object" (thusness) are not distinguishable. It is for this reason that Buddhahood's essence *(svabhāva)* is designated in Yogācāra literature through an abstract terminology uniquely designed to point to a nondual realization that does not fit into our usual epistemological categories of subject and object, while including what we ordinarily call "subject" and "object" within that realization. Hence, Buddhahood is fundamental, ultimate transformation *(āśrayaparāvṛtti)*, which is defined as purified thusness-nonconceptual gnosis *(tathatāviśuddhi-nirvikalpajñāna)*, which can be equated with the purified realm of dharma *(dharmadhātu-viśuddha)*, the undefiled realm *(anāsravadhātu)*, the embodiment of dharma/*dharmatā* in ultimate realization *(dharmakāya)* and the embodiment of Buddhahood in its own essence *(svābhāvika-kāya)*.

These themes are further developed in the *DDV vṛtti*'s explanation of "the foundation" *(āśraya)* of fundamental transformation:

> The foundation *(āśraya)* of fundamental transformation *(āśrayaparāvṛtti)* is nonconceptual gnosis *(nirvikalpajñāna)*, because [fundamental transformation] is attained on that foundation. How does one enter into [that foundation]? [The root text] says: "through six aspects of entry into nonconceptual gnosis *(nirvikalpajñāna praveśa)*." The six aspects of entry are: (1) the support *(ālambana)*, (2) elimination of signs *(nimittaparivarjana)*, (3) correct practice *(saṃyakprayoga)*, (4) characteristics *(lakṣaṇa)*, (5) benefits *(anuśaṃsa)*, and (6) thorough knowledge *(parijñāna)*.[72]

This is not the place to enter into a complete study of this passage. We will focus on a point of particular relevance to the present discussion, "correct practice" (*saṃyakprayoga*, number 3 above), the third aspect of entry into nonconceptual gnosis *(nirvikalpajñāna praveśa)*. The *DDV* says:

> Entry into correct practice is fourfold through practice of (1) perception *(upalambha)*, (2) nonperception *(anupalambha)*, (3) nonperception of perception *(upalambhānupalambha)*, and (4) perception of nonperception *(nopalambhopalambha)*.[73]

The *DDV vṛtti* comments:

> (1) Practice of perception is practice of the perception of cognition-only *(vijnaptimātra)*. (2) Practice of nonperception is nonperception of an object. (3) Practice of the nonperception of perception is as follows: there being no object, cognition-only is not perceived, because if there is no object to be cognized, there can not be any cognizing [of it]. (4) Practice of the perception of nonperception is as follows: by not perceiving both [cognizer and cognized], the lack of both, nonduality, is perceived.[74]

The *DDV* expands on this in its later discussion of entry into fundamental transformation through attention *(manasikāra)*:

> Entry into attention *(manasikāra)*: The bodhisattva who wishes to enter into nonconceptual gnosis *(nirvikalpajñāna)* mentally attends as follows: Because of not knowing thusness *(tathatā)*, there has been the abode of all seeds *(sarvabījaka)* of false conceptualization *(abhūtaparikalpita)*, the cause of the appearance of nonexistent duality, and the other causes [of that appearance, i.e., the sense consciousnesses] which are based upon it. Thus, although the cause with its result [nonexistent duality] has appeared, it does not exist. By its appearing, reality *(dharmatā)* does not appear. And by its not appearing, reality appears. The bodhisattva who attends correctly in this way is at the entry into nonconceptual gnosis *(nirvikalpa-jñāna)*.
>
> From perceiving thus, he enters into the perception of cognition-only *(vijñaptimātropalambha)*. From the perception of cognition-only, he enters into the nonperception of objects *(arthānupalambha)*. From the nonperception of objects, he enters into the nonperception of cognition-only *(vijñaptimātrānupalambha)*. From the nonperception of that, he enters into the perception that lacks dual distinctions. That is nonperception of dual distinctions. And that is nonconceptual gnosis, because it lacks an object *(viṣaya)*, a cognitive support *(ālambana)*, being characterized by the nonperception of all cognitive objects *(nimitta)*.[75]

These passages describe four basic stages of yogic realization fundamental to early Yogācāra Buddhism. The *vṛtti* comments:

> [The *DDV*] says: "Although the cause with its result [nonexistent duality] has appeared, it does not exist." This means that although what is falsely conceptualized [i.e., duality] has always appeared in awareness, it simply does not exist. "By its appearing, reality *(dharmatā)* does not appear." This means thusness *(tathatā)* does not appear. "By its not appearing, reality appears." This is because it [reality] consists of the nonexistence of that [duality]. "A bodhisattva by zealously attending in this way is at entry into nonconceptual gnosis *(nirvikalpa-jñāna)*." This means that [what is being described] is within the path of preliminary yogic practice *(prayoga mārga)*.[76]

This explains the entrance into the first of the four stages that comprise the Yogācāra path of preliminary yogic practice *(prayoga mārga)* as it culminates in the path of direct seeing *(darśana mārga)*. The path of preliminary yogic practice leads to an unmediated experience of thusness on the path of direct seeing *(darśana mārga)* by generating the nonconceptual gnosis *(nirvikalpa-jñāna)* that directly "sees" thusness. The yogic process gradually eliminates the false conceptualization of duality that hides reality. The false conceptualization *(abhuta-parikalpita)* hiding reality has to be purified away. When what hides reality no longer appears, reality itself *(dharmatā, tathatā)* appears for gnosis. Therefore, to say that false conceptualization *(abhuta-parikalpita)*, which hides reality *(tathatā)*, is purified away *(viśuddhā)* is just to say that one enters into a gnosis free from such conceptualization *(nirvikalpa jñāna)*. The *vṛtti* describes the four yogic stages involved:

> [The *DDV*] says: "Through that perception. . . ." This means that although what is falsely conceptualized *(abhūta-parikalpita)* is seen to appear, one perceives that it does not exist. Such perceptions "enter into the perception of cognition-only *(vijñaptimātra)*" because it is [just] cognition which is appearing dualistically. "From the perception of cognition-only, he enters into the nonperception of all objects." This means that because it is cognition itself which appears as object, there is no external object. "From the nonperception of all objects, he enters into the nonperception of cognition-only." This means that the cognizing itself can not be established as a "cognizing," because if an object to be cognized does not exist then there cannot be a cognizing [of it]. "From the nonperception of that. . . ." This means from the nonperception of subject [cognizing] and object [cognized]. ". . . he enters into the perception which lacks dual distinctions." By the very lack of duality itself, there are no

> dual distinctions. "Dual" refers to perception in the dual nature of subject and object. This is to be known as a perception free from distinctions, because the distinction is that of duality, which, were it to exist, would here be known. "That is nonperception of duality," being perception of the lack of subject and object. "And that is nonconceptual gnosis *(nirvikalpa-jñāna)*." This shows the subject matter [of the passage]. As it said [at the beginning of the passage], the bodhisattva who wishes to enter into nonconceptual gnosis mentally attends in this way. And one who attends in this way enters into nonconceptual gnosis *(nirvikalpa-jñāna)*.[77]

These passages delineate a fundamental gnoseological model of classical Yogācāra literature. The four stages of entry into gnosis are as follows: First, the bodhisattva attends to the way in which phenomena ordinarily appear. She notes the appearance of duality: a subject and object of cognition which appear to exist independently as separate entities, apart from any conceptual construction of "subject" and "object." In fact "subject" and "object" as they appear to awareness are conceptual constructions, mental designations. But false conceptualization *(abhūta-parikalpana)* constructs them and then adheres to them as if they existed independent of any such process. The independent subject and object conceived by false conceptualization is a duality, which, while not existing, appears to exist. When phenomena *(dharmāḥ)* appear under this aspect of nonexistent duality, their reality *(dharmatā, tathatā)*, which is the lack of such duality, cannot appear. And by the appearance of nonexistent duality ceasing, reality can appear.

Comprehending this, the bodhisattva enters into the perception of cognition-only *(vijñaptimātra)*, the understanding that "subject" and "object" are both aspects of cognition. This is the first stage. From that, she enters into "the nonperception of objects," a more vivid awareness that the epistemological object, which appears to be external to consciousness, is not. This is the second stage. But "cognition," consciousness, itself can only be designated and distinguished in relation to what is not consciousness, an object external to it. The external object having been negated, "consciousness" as subject can no longer be distinguished in relation to it. At this point she enters the third stage, the nonperception even of "cognition-only" *(vijñaptimātra = cittamātra*, mind-only). Both "subject" and "object" having been deconstructed, she now enters the fourth stage, perception of reality *(dharmatā)* lacking dual distinctions. At this point gnosis passes beyond all conceptual construction to know reality directly, with no further distinction between knower and known.

During the course of this process, not only has the mistaken conception of an independent subject and object been negated but all conceptual constructions including the concepts "subject" and "object" have utterly disappeared in the nonconceptual realization *(nirvikalpajñāna)* of thusness *(tathatā)*. The *DDV* says specifically that entry into nonconceptual gnosis requires the total elimination of all cognitive objects *(nimitta)*, and all discursive distinctions, even the distinctions "gnosis" *(jñāna)* and "thusness" *(tathatā)*.[78]

These four stages comprise the path of preliminary yogic practice *(prayoga-mārga)* as it culminates in the nonconceptual realization of thusness (*sparśa*, "contact"), which is the path of direct seeing *(darśanamārga)*. This nonconceptual realization is repeatedly recalled (*anusmṛti*, "recollected") on the path of meditation *(bhāvanamārga)*, purifying further and further the obstructions that have obscured thusness. The process finally culminates in the total purification of thusness, complete fundamental transformation *(āśrayaparivṛtti)*, i.e., Buddhahood, at which point gnosis *(nirvikalpajñāna)* and thusness *(tathatāviśuddhi)* remain ever epistemologically one.[79]

In preceding sections of this chapter we noted how the essence *(svabhāva)* of Buddhahood in the Yogācāra tradition, consistent with the *Prajñāpāramitā* tradition, was identified not as a set of varied mental qualities (as had been the case in Abhidharma tradition), but as a single undifferentiated principle: a Buddha's gnosis of ultimate reality *(tathatāviśuddhi/nirvikalpajñāna)*. And this comprised the first and fundamental embodiment of the Buddha, the *svābhāvikakāya*, the embodiment of Buddhahood in its own intrinsic nature. The *DDV* passages discussed above explain the yogic practices that naturally unfold into the attainment of *svābhāvikakāya*. The way the Yogācāras understood *svābhāvikakāya* conformed to their understanding of their core meditation practices and realizations. *Svābhāvikakāya* is a direct extrapolation from Yogācāra praxis and gnoseology.

The Yogācāra tradition received its name from its focus on meditation practice ("those who practice yoga," i.e., specific forms of meditation). One clear purpose of its early literature was to explain methods of yogic practice that its adherents actually engaged in, to describe the content of their meditation experience, and to construct doctrinal systems that would systematically relate their actual practices and gnoseological findings to the doctrinal traditions that they had inherited. The *DDV* was quoted above at some length because it provides such a vivid and eloquent example of the synergy of meditational praxis and doctrinal system-building that characterized classical Yogācāra literature on Buddhahood. In particular, it eloquently unpacks the notion of fundamental transformation *(āśrayaparāvṛtti)* with which we began this section, having found it at the center of Yogācāra understanding of *svābhāvikakāya*. The *DDV* also teaches the three *kāyas* in brief. But more important for our purposes is the basic structure of its meditational and gnoseological theory, which is found throughout classical Yogācāra literature, including the *Mahāyānasūtrālaṃkāra*, the *Mahāyānasaṃgraha,* and their commentaries, which are among the first to systematically explain the theory of three *kāyas*.

The *Mahāyānasūtrālaṃkāra*'s sixth chapter concerns the realization of "thatness," *tattvam*, a Yogācāra synonym for *tathatā* (thusness) and *dharmadhātu* (realm of reality), i.e., reality unobscured by false conceptualization. *MSA* verses 6.6 through 6.9 explain the *MSA*'s yogic praxis and gnoseology, which parallels that of the *DDV:*

> A bodhisattva, having gathered merit and gnosis collections limitless to complete, has a well-considered ascertainment of phenomena. Through this, he realizes that their objective mode derives from verbalization. (*MSA* 6.6)
>
> Discerning that objects are merely verbalization, he abides in mind alone appearing as them. From that, the realm of dharma *(dharmadhātu)* becomes manifest, free of dual character. (*MSA* 6.7)
>
> Realizing with discerning intelligence that there is nothing other than mind, he then understands the nonexistence of mind. Understanding the nonexistence of duality, the sage abides in the realm of dharma, which is free of it. (*MSA* 6.8)
>
> The force of the sage's nonconceptual gnosis, always and everywhere gone to sameness, purges the impenetrable host of faults, his [impure] base, like a powerful antidote dispels poison. (*MSA* 6.9) [80]

According to the *bhāṣya* and Sthiramati's commentary, these four verses summarize the five Mahāyāna paths to enlightenment by describing entrance into and gradual perfection of the "ultimate gnosis" (*pāramārthika jñāna* = *nirvikalpa-jñāna*, nonconceptual gnosis) that realizes the realm of *dharma* (*dharmadhātu* = *tathatā*, thusness). Again, the *MSA*'s summation of yogic praxis centers upon the two key concepts we have been discussing: thusness and nonconceptual gnosis as progressively realized until Buddhahood.

Sthiramati carefully divides the verses into parts, identifying the correspondence of each part to each of the five Mahāyāna paths *(mārga)*. Of special importance are the four stages of the path of preliminary yogic practice *(prayoga mārga)* that culminate in the path of direct seeing *(darśana mārga)*. They are equivalent to the four stages of yogic realization we noted earlier in the *DDV*. Sthiramati draws the correlations, consistent with the *MSA bhāṣya*, as follows:

Path of Vast Collection

MSA 6.6, first three feet: "A bodhisattva, having gathered merit and gnosis collections limitless to complete, has a well-considered ascertainment of phenomena."

Vast collections of karmic merit and gnosis *(jñāna)* on the path of accumulation *(saṃbhāra mārga)* empower the bodhisattva in his meditations on the fundamental characteristics of all phenomena of saṃsāra: suffering, impermanence, selflessness, etc., until he becomes free of doubt regarding them.

Path of Preliminary Yogic Practice: Heat – Appearance Obtained

MSA 6.6, fourth foot: "Through this, he realizes that their objective mode derives from verbalization."

Following this, the bodhisattva comes to understand that what appear as objects in his cognition are distinguished as such through mental "verbalization," i.e., conceptual construction, which distinguishes, names, and thinks of them. He realizes that cognitive objects do not stand outside his cognition, and hence are not separate from his mind. This is called the "meditative concentration of appearance obtained" *(ālokalabdha samādhi)* because he now understands how the appearance of cognitive objectivity occurs through mental verbalization. This occurs in the heat stage *(uṣman)* of the path of preliminary yogic practice *(prayoga mārga).*

Path of Preliminary Yogic Practice: Summit – Appearance Increased

MSA 6.7, first foot: "Discerning that objects are merely verbalization. . . ."

On the heat stage above, the practitioner *understood* the way cognitive objects appeared from his own mind. Now, he actually *sees* how cognitive objects appear from his own mind, how the mind takes on the appearance of objects. This is the meditative concentration of increased appearance *(ālokavṛddhi samādhi)* that occurs on the summit stage *(mūrdhan)* of the path of preliminary yogic practice *(prayoga mārga).*

Path of Preliminary Yogic Practice: Patience – Partial Entry into Reality

MSA 6.7, second foot: ". . . he abides in mind alone appearing as them."

"As them" means "as objects." Having removed his belief that the objects in cognition stand outside of cognition, he abides in "mind alone," aware that everything that appears is a cognitive appearance not external to mind. This is the meditative concentration of partial entry into reality *(tattvaikadeśānupraviṣṭa samādhi)* that occurs on the patience stage *(kṣānti)* of the path of preliminary yogic practice.

According to Sthiramati, then, the last foot of v. 6.6 through the second foot of verse 6.7 above concern the first three stages of the path of preliminary yogic practice (heat, summit, patience). The final two feet of verse 6.7 describe the path of direct seeing *(darśana mārga),* by saying: "From that, the realm of dharma *(dharmadhātu)* becomes manifest, free of dual character." Sthiramati says this refers to the nonconceptual gnosis *(nirvikalpa-jñāna)* of the path of direct seeing that makes manifest the *dharmadhātu*. On the path of direct seeing, the bodhisattva abides in the *dharmadhātu* free of characteristics of both object and subject, hence "free of dual character." Sthiramati says that the next verse, 6.8, returns to the path of preliminary practice to unpack its final stage, the highest mundane realization that brings about the manifestation of *dharmadhātu* at the path of direct seeing.

Path of Preliminary Yogic Practice: Highest Mundane Realization – Uninterrupted Concentration

MSA 6.8, first three feet: "Realizing with discerning intelligence that there is nothing other than mind, he then understands the nonexistence of mind. Understanding the nonexistence of duality. . . ."

"Realizing intellectually that there is nothing other than mind, he then understands the nonexistence of mind." In the patience stage the bodhisattva has removed the obstruction of adhering to cognitive objects as independent of cognition, and has abided in mind alone. Now he reaches the stage of highest mundane realization *(laukikāgradharma*, still on the path of preliminary yogic practice), where he realizes that in the absence of any independent cognitive object, there can be no cognitive subject. Put another way, in the patience stage, he realized that the objects in his cognition were actually aspects of cognition, and hence aspects of the cognizing subject, mind alone. Now, in the stage of highest mundane realization, he realizes that the very notion of "subject" depends on the notion of a separate "object" that is cognized by it. Since he no longer adheres to such an "object," there is no longer any basis to adhere to a "subject" cognizing it. Thus, he "understands the nonexistence of mind," "mind" being cognitive subjectivity.

"Understanding the nonexistence of duality. . . ." The bodhisattva, having comprehended the nonexistence of both the object and subject of cognition, releases the obstruction of subject-object duality. As soon as this occurs, the realm of dharma *(dharmadhātu)*—that is, reality per se—becomes manifest to nonconceptual gnosis *(nirvikalpajñāna)*, which means that the bodhisattva attains the path of direct seeing *(darśana mārga)*, the direct seeing of reality as it is. The stage of mundane realization just prior to this attainment is called the "uninterrupted meditative concentration" *(ānantaryasamādhi)* because it leads into the path of direct seeing without interruption.

Path of Direct Seeing

MSA 6.8, last foot: " . . . the sage abides in the realm of dharma *(dharmadhātu)* that is free of [duality]."

When the path of direct seeing *(darśana mārga)* occurs, the bodhisattva's nonconceptual gnosis abides in the realm of dharma free of subject-object duality.

This direct seeing of reality purifies one level of delusion adhering to duality *(darśana-prahātavya kleśa)*.

Path of Higher Meditation Culminating in Buddhahood

MSA 6.9: "The force of the sage's nonconceptual gnosis, always and everywhere gone to sameness, purges the impenetrable host of faults, his [impure] base, like a powerful antidote dispels poison."

On the path of higher meditation *(bhāvanā mārga)*, the bodhisattva repeatedly recalls and familiarizes himself with that gnosis until the force of it becomes so powerful that it dispels the poison of affective and cognitive obstructions *(āvaraṇa)* like a powerful antidote. His gnosis *(jñāna)* is nonconceptual *(nirvikalpa)* because it does not conceptualize object or a subject. The word "his" in "his base" refers to the bodhisattva on the path of higher meditation. The "base" is his basal consciousness *(ālayavijñāna)*. The "faults" are the affective obstructions *(kleśāvaraṇa)* and propensities for subject-object duality *(grāhyagrāhaka vāsanā)* that are embedded in his basal consciousness. Just as a powerful antidote dispels poison, the nonconceptual gnosis *(nirvikalpajñāna)* strengthened on the path of meditation utterly eliminates all affective and cognitive obstructions, even the subtlest, thereby bringing about the complete transformation of the basis *(āśrayaparāvṛtti)* in which the nonconceptual gnosis of the Buddha stage *(buddhabhūmi)* manifests.[81]

According to this description, and similar descriptions throughout Yogācāra literature, the four meditative concentrations *(samādhis)* that traverse the four stages of the path of preliminary yogic practice *(prayoga mārga)* provide the entrance into nonconceptual gnosis *(nirvikalpajñāna)* at the path of direct seeing *(darśana mārga)*. This nonconceptual gnosis is strengthened and perfected through the path of higher meditation *(bhāvanā mārga)* until it culminates in Buddhahood. The "object" of that gnosis is universal thusness, the realm of dharma (*tathatā*, *dharmadhātu*). But because the epistemological distinction between subject and object is precisely what is removed by entrance into that gnosis, its fullest fruition, Buddhahood, cannot be appropriately described as involving a "knower" of reality. The conceptual construction of "knower" and "known" is a fabrication, not a part of a Buddha's realization. It is for this reason that Buddhahood, as complete ultimate transformation *(āśrayaparāvṛtti)*, is expressed through either one, or both, of the terms under discussion throughout this chapter: nonconceptual gnosis *(nirvikalpajñāna)* and purified thusness (*tathatā-viśuddhi*, *dharmadhātu-viśuddhi*, or their equivalents). The meaning of "nonconceptual gnosis" is weighted more toward the cognitive subject, connoting an unobstructed realization *(nirvikalpajñāna)*, while the sense of "purified thusness" or "purified dharma realm" is weighted more toward the cognitive object, connoting a reality free from obstruction *(tathatā-viśuddhi)*. Both point to a nondual knowledge-reality not adequately captured by the epistemological terms we ordinarily use, since such terms presuppose the dualistic, subject-object frame of reference we unreflectively share.[82]

The four meditative concentrations *(samādhis)* of the path of preliminary yogic practice are what are said to lead to that nondual, direct seeing. Let's look again at them in simple, phenomenological terms:

1. Appearance Obtained *(Ālokalabdha samādhi)*. Yogācāras characterize our everyday awareness something like this. Even though a cognitive object (such as "tree") appearing within awareness is, in fact, an aspect of that awareness, we unreflectively apprehend it as though it existed outside of awareness. The image of a tree within our cognition is the product of a complex process of sensory integration and conceptual construction. That complex image of "tree," as the product of our own sensory and cognitive apparatus, is not an external object, an object standing fully formed as "tree" outside of cognition. But on the prereflective and behavioral level, we adhere to our own cognitive image of "tree" as if it existed fully formed and conceptually structured as "tree" before it ever entered our awareness. That is to say that on the prereflective level, we are all naive realists. In the first concentration, from the force of much prior accumulation of karmic merit and meditation on the aspects of the Four Noble Truths, the yogi intellectually negates his adherence to his own prereflective notion that cognitive objects such as "trees" exist external to consciousness. He thereby begins to understand experientially that such objects are constructed by his own mind, his own cognitive apparatus, even though they appear to stand outside of his mind through his own conceptualization *(manojalpa*, "mental verbalization").

2. Appearance Increased *(Ālokavṛddhi samādhi)*. Through continued practice, the yogi's experience of the nonobjectivity of cognitive objects increases *(vṛddhi)* and he now actually sees them as aspects of awareness (Sthiramati uses the term *paśyati,* "he sees").

3. Partial Entry into Reality *(Tattvaikadeśānupraviṣṭa samādhi)*.Through continued practice, even the appearance of cognitive objects as distinct from mind ceases. Phenomenologically, the yogi feels that he abides in "mind alone" *(cittamātra)*.

4. Uninterrupted Concentration *(Ānantarya samādhi)*. This meditative concentration begins on the last level of the path of preliminary yogic practice and leads the yogi into unmediated perception of nondual reality, the nonconceptual gnosis of the path of direct seeing. Here the very notion and feeling of "mind only" deconstruct, as deeper implications of his prior practice now dawn. Subjectivity is only distinguishable in relation to the objectivity that he does not find. Realizing vividly now the mutual nonexistence of "object" and "subject," dualistic conception is abandoned, nonconceptual gnosis emerges, the nondual realm of reality *(dharmadhātu)* appears, and he attains the path that sees it directly *(darśana mārga)*.

It is this realization which the bodhisattva repeatedly recalls and familiarizes himself with through the path of higher meditation *(bhāvanā mārga)*, and which, fully purified and perfected, becomes the very essence of full enlightenment, the "embodiment of Buddhahood in its own actual nature," i.e., *svābhāvikakāya*.[83]

Mahāyānasūtrālaṃkāra vv. 14.28–14.29 describe the culmination of these four yogic stages in the direct seeing of reality *(darśana mārga)*. These verses are noteworthy for their emphasis on the idea that the gnosis reached through these very steps comprises the fundamental transformation *(āśrayaparāvṛtti)* that, when perfected, is Buddhahood in all its purity:

> Then he obtains nonconceptual gnosis *(nirvikalpajñāna),* which is free from perception of duality, supramundane, supreme, stainless. (*MSA* 14.28)
>
> *MSA bhāṣya*: From here onwards is the stage of the path of direct seeing *(darśana mārgāvasthā)*. It is free from perception of duality because it is liberated from the perceptions of subject and object. It is supreme by the supremacy of the [Mahāyāna] vehicle. It is nonconceptual *(nirvikalpaṃ)* because it is free from the conceptualization of subject and object. It is stainless because passions removable by the [path of] seeing are eliminated. Through this it is said to be pure and stainless.
>
> This is the [bodhisattva's] fundamental transformation *(āśrayaparāvṛtti)*, accepted as the first bodhisattva stage *(bhūmi)*. It takes measureless aeons for it to become perfectly pure.[84] (*MSA* 14.29)

The bodhisattva's attainment of nonconceptual gnosis *(nirvikalpajñāna)* at his first direct seeing of reality permanently removes one level of cognitive obstruction (the "passions removable by the path of seeing"). This comprises a fundamental transformation of his mind, which is the first of the ten stages *(bhūmis)* of bodhisattva realization leading to full enlightenment. "It takes measureless aeons for it to become perfectly pure" means that it is this process of fundamental transformation and this gnosis which eventually transform into Buddhahood, but only after many more eons of practice.

The four stages of meditation we have been discussing, the four meditative concentrations *(samādhis)* culminating in nonconceptual gnosis *(nirvikalpajñāna)*, are the essential yogic practice described in the principle synoptic treatises of early Yogācāra. Their descriptions in the *Dharmadharmatāvibhāga* and *Mahāyānasūtrālaṃkāra,* chapter 6, were quoted above. The same basic stages are described at length in *MSA* vv. 14.23–14.26 and *bhāṣya* (preceding the passages quoted just above). They are a crucial part of the meditation practice explained in the third chapter of the *Mahāyānasaṃgraha* (especially *Msg* 3.8, 3.9 and 3.13). They find expression in *Madhyāntavibhāga* vv. 1.6–1.7 and are delineated in detail in Sthiramati's commentary on that text. They are expressed in condensed form in *MSA* vv. 11.47–11.48, *Msg* 8.20ff. (Lamotte's numbering), *Trisvabhāvanirdeśa* vv. 36–37, and *Triṃśika* v. 28.[85]

Yogācāra Buddhism has sometimes been described in modern scholarly works as an ontological idealism that speculatively reduces all phenomena to the nature of consciousness alone. But we can see from the descriptions of the meditation practice stages above that the yogic process itself does not comprise a speculative philosophy of any kind, let alone a speculative ontology. In Western philosophical terms, it correlates better with the project of phenomenology; that is, it involves a careful observation and analysis of the structure of what appears to awareness. But it also goes far beyond Western phenomenology insofar as the four yogic stages lead the practitioner into deeper and deeper strata of consciousness, through an analytical and meditative process that permanently alters, at its most fundamental level, the affective and cognitive structures of consciousness itself; hence, the importance of the concept "fundamental transformation" *(āśrayaparāvṛtti)*, the distinguishing feature of *svābhāvikakāya.*

Texts quoted above indicated that the attainment of nonconceptual gnosis and direct seeing of reality comprised a fundamental transformation *(āśrayaparāvṛtti)* that, when perfected, became Buddhahood. Thus, the attainment of nonconceptual gnosis in itself could be viewed as a commencement of enlightenment, *svābhāvikakāya/dharmakāya* (and through that all three *kāyas*) in a germinal form. This idea is expressed in portions of the *Mahāyānasaṃgraha (Msg)* and its commentaries.

In the *Msg*, the practice of the four meditational stages culminating in nonconceptual gnosis is termed "entry into cognition-only" *(vijñaptimātratā praveśa)*. This is explained in passages 3.7–3.9 and 3.13. Passage 3.12 explains the reason for the practice of "entry into cognition-only," i.e., the four meditative concentrations culminating in the path of direct seeing:

> What, then, is the purpose of entering into cognition-only? By the supramundane gnosis of concentration and insight (*śamathavipaśyanājñāna)* viewing [the nature of] accumulated phenomena, and by the gnosis that follows from it *(pṛṣṭhalabdhajñāna)* [viewing] the varied ideations, the [bodhisattva] eliminates the seeds of the basal consciousness *(alayavijñāna)* with their causes and develops a germ of contact with *dharmakāya (dharmakāyasparśabija)*, i.e. he undergoes fundamental transformation *(āśrayaparāvṛtta)*. Then, by accomplishing all excellent qualities of a Buddha, he obtains omniscience. It is for this purpose that he enters [cognition-only].[86]

Msg, chapter 8, is dedicated to nonconceptual gnosis *(nirvikalpajñāna)*. Passage 8.13 and its commentaries discuss the outcome of perfecting it:

> Culmination *(niṣṭhā)* of the bodhisattvas' nonconceptual gnosis is for the purpose of obtaining the three *kāyas* in pure form, and supreme mastery.[87]

Vasubandhu comments:

> "In pure form" is said because here the three *kāyas* are obtained on the very first bodhisattva stage [the first *bhūmi*, equivalent to the path of direct seeing] but it is on the tenth bodhisattva stage [just before Buddhahood] that they become extremely pure.[88]

In other words, with the first attainment of nonconceptual gnosis at the path of direct seeing *(darśana mārga)*, Buddhahood is already obtained in a germinal form. The final form is reached through the gradual perfection of that very gnosis through the ten stages *(bhūmis)* of bodhisattva practice.

We noted earlier that the concept of *svābhāvikakāya/dharmakāya*, as the undivided essence of Buddhahood, was characterized in the *MSA* and its commentaries as a fundamental transformation *(āśrayaparāvṛtti)*, understood in Yogācāra literature as the culmination of a yogic process that attains purified thusness and nonconceptual gnosis *(tathatāviśuddhi* and *nirvikalpajñāna)*. The *Msg*, another major source of Yogācāra three-*kāya* theory, also characterized Buddhahood and *svābhāvikakāya/dharmakāya* as fundamental transformation with that understanding. Because the *Msg* centered its discussion of the yogic path on the Yogācāra theory of three natures *(trisvabhāva)* or "three identities" *(trilakṣaṇa)*, its explanation of fundamental transformation *(āśrayaparāvṛtti)* was couched in those terms. Taking that into account, its explanation is similar to the explanations of fundamental transformation we have seen above.[89]

The three natures *(trisvabhāva)* are the imagined nature *(parikalpita)*, the dependent nature *(paratantra)*, and the perfected nature *(pariniṣpanna)*. All things experienced by sentient beings possess these three natures. In general, the imagined nature *(parikalpita-svabhāva)* is that aspect of things which is conceptually constructed and designated. In the *Msg* it is identified in particular as conceptually constructed duality, that is, the appearance and adherence to an independent subject and object of cognition that exist separate from each other, independent of conceptualization and of the designations "subject" and "object."[90] The dependent nature *(paratantra-svabhāva)* comprises the entire content of conditioned cognition, that is, all data of the senses, the process of conceptual construction and its contents. It is called "dependent" because it comprises all that exists in dependence upon causes and conditions. The perfected nature *(pariniṣpanna-svabhāva)* is the actual reality of things. It is the lack of the duality that is ordinarily imagined and adhered to within the dependent nature.

For example, a "tree" appearing in awareness as a cognitive object is a product both of sense data and of the conceptual structuring that integrates the data of the senses and applies the designation "tree." But the "tree" as an object within cognition appears to stand apart from the cognizer, as if independent of that constructive process. The appearance of and adherence to such a "tree" is the imagined nature that is false. The sense data, the process of conceptual construction, and its content are the dependent nature, which in fact exists. The nonexistence of the imagined nature within the dependent nature, as well as the gnosis realizing that nonexistence, is the perfected nature.[91]

Metaphors are often used in Yogācāra literature to explain the three natures. One is the metaphor of a mirage of water in the desert. When such a mirage occurs, a person sees and believes there to be real water present in the distance. This corresponds to the imagined nature. Still, the appearance of water in the distance, and all the factors that condition such an appearance, do exist. This corresponds to the dependent nature. The lack of any real water within that appearance corresponds to the perfected nature.[92]

Chapters 9 and 10 of the *Msg* are its final chapters. They describe Buddhahood as the result of the yogic praxis of the bodhisattva explained in earlier chapters. Chapter 9 describes Buddhahood as the complete elimination of mental afflictions and defilements *(phalaprahāṇa)* by nonconceptual gnosis. Chapter 10 describes Buddhahood as the gnosis itself, the result of the yogic path *(phalajñāna)*. Turning first to chapter 9, *Msg* 9.1 says:

> The bodhisattvas' elimination *(prahāṇa)* is a nonabiding nirvāṇa *(apratiṣṭhita-nirvāṇa)*. Its identity is fundamental transformation *(āśraya-parāvṛtti)*, [transformation into] a foundation *(āśraya)* that has eliminated affliction *(kleśa)* without rejecting cyclic existence *(saṃsāra)*.
>
> Cyclic existence *(saṃsāra)* comprises the afflicted portion *(saṃkleśa-bhāga)* of the dependent nature *(paratantra-svabhāva)*.
>
> Nirvāṇa comprises the purified portion *(vyavadāna-bhāga)* of it.
>
> The foundation *(āśraya)* is the dependent nature, comprising both [afflicted and purified portions].
>
> Transformation *(parāvṛtti)* is the dependent nature when its antidote [for affliction] has occurred and has purged its afflicted portion, reducing it to its purified portion.[93]

Asvabhāva's commentary on this explains:

> What is the foundation of transformation? [The *Msg*] says "Cyclic existence *(saṃsāra)* comprises [the afflicted portion] of the dependent nature *(paratantra-svabhāva)*." Cyclic existence consists of the mistaken mentalities and mental factors that relentlessly drag one by the rope of recurrent birth and death. The "afflicted portion" is the portion [of the

> dependent nature] that is the imagined aspect *(parikalpitākara)*. Nirvāṇa comprises [the dependent nature's] purified portion, i.e., it comprises the portion lacking the imagined entity. The foundation *(āśraya)* comprises both. It is the dependent nature.
>
> Of what is it the foundation? It is the foundation of transformation. . . . How does that transformation occur? "[Transformation] is the dependent nature when its antidote [for affliction] has arisen . . . ," i.e., when nonconceptual gnosis *(nirvikalpajñāna)* has arisen. ". . . and has purged the afflicted portion, . . ." "Afflicted portion" refers to the mistaken portion: subject-object duality; "purged" means there is total transformation. ". . . reducing it to its purified portion," i.e., reducing it to the real *(vastu),* which is free of subject-object duality. That lack of subject-object duality, being inexpressible, is to be personally experienced.[94]

These passages explain Buddhahood as fundamental transformation *(āśraya-parāvṛtti/parivṛtti),* which might be better translated here: "foundational transformation," where the "foundation" is the dependent nature *(paratantra-svabhāva)*. By the force of nonconceptual gnosis *(nirvikalpajñāna)*, the defiled portion of the dependent nature, the falsely imagined duality, is expelled. In other words, nonconceptual gnosis removes the imagined nature *(parikalpita-svabhāva)* that previously hid reality. This reduces the dependent nature to its pure essence, free of imagined duality. That is the perfected nature *(pariniṣpanna-svabhāva)*, equivalent to purified thusness *(tathatāviśuddhi)*.[95]

Msg passage 10.3, explaining *svābhāvikakāya/dharmakāya* as foundational transformation *(āśrayaparāvṛtti),* gives the same account. These descriptions, although couched in terms of the Yogācāra model of three natures, closely parallel the descriptions of fundamental transformation quoted earlier from the *MSA* and *DDV*. In the *Msg* as in those texts, the yogic praxis culminating in Buddhahood as fundamental transformation involves two basic principles that comprise an undivided, nondual realization of reality: nonconceptual gnosis and purified thusness.[96]

In fact, at one point the author of the *Msg* explicitly equates his explanations of fundamental transformation *(āśrayaparāvṛtti)* with those of the *MSA*. At *Msg* 9.2.4 it is said that a bodhisattva's fundamental transformation is the disappearance of all signs, all that is unreal, with the appearance of the real. This is close to the expression of *MSA* verses 19.53–19.54 that were quoted earlier. And the *Msg*'s author, seeing that similarity, quotes those same verses as a summary of his own account:[97]

> *Msg* 9.3 = *MSA* 19.53–19.54:
>
> For fools, reality *(tattvaṃ)* is covered and it is unreality *(atattvaṃ)* which completely appears.

But for bodhisattvas, having removed that [covering], reality completely appears.
The nonappearance of the nonexistent and the appearance of the existent are to be realized *(jñeya).*
This is liberation, fundamental transformation *(āśrayaparāvṛtti)*, because one proceeds freely.

4.7 Summary

We previously noted how Sarvāstivāda Abhidharma identified a Buddha's pure mental qualities, the Buddha dharmas (four fearlessnesses, ten powers, etc.) as his defining essence. In the Yogācāra tradition, on the contrary, those qualities were categorized as adjunct qualities of Buddhahood *(yoga)*, not its defining essence *(svabhāva)*. The list of Buddha dharmas was kept as a phenomenal description of Buddhahood understood to retain validity from a phenomenal point of view. Functionally a historical survival from prior tradition, it held a place within the Yogācāra scholastic treatment of enlightenment, but not at its center. At the center of the Yogācāra understanding of Buddhahood was the concept of purified thusness-nonconceptual gnosis, the Buddha's nondual awareness of ultimate reality, undivided and unlimited in scope. That nondual reality-gnosis is what Yogācāra literature identified as the defining essence *(svabhāva)* of Buddhahood. And the Buddhas' embodiment of that defining essence within their own direct experience is what was meant by *svābhāvikakāya*. This was identified directly with *dharmakāya*, understanding *dharmakāya* much as it was taught in the *Prajñāpāramitā* passages quoted in chapter 3: *dharmakāya* = embodiment of *dharmatā* (the real nature of things, thusness) in perfect, nondual knowledge *(prajñāpāramitā)*.

Svābhāvikakāya/dharmakāya was further specified by reference to Yogācāra understanding of fundamental transformation *(āśrayaparāvṛtti)*. This was a model of enlightenment involving the ultimate transformation of the entire psychophysical makeup of the practitioner into the state of Buddhahood through yogic praxis. In Yogācāra texts, it involved the notion of the disappearance of the unreal (duality) with the appearance of the real (nonduality), the gradual purification of thusness *(tathatāviśuddhi)* by entry into nonconceptual gnosis *(nirvikalpajñāna)* through stages of meditative concentration. The reason that purified thusness/nonconceptual gnosis was central in Yogācāra buddhology is therefore quite clear. Yogācāra understanding of Buddhahood was strongly conditioned by its understanding of meditational praxis and the accompanying gnoseology. Buddhahood understood as purified thusness, nonconceptual gnosis, *svābhāvikakāya/dharmakāya*, i.e., as a nondual, undivided reality-gnosis, was conceived as the natural result of the yogic praxis described in principal Yogācāra texts.

5

Enlightenment's Paradox: Nondual Awareness of the Unconditioned *(Svābhāvikakāya)* Embodied in Conditioned Activity for Beings *(Sāmbhogikakāya, Nairmāṇikakāya)*

5.1
Buddhahood as Nonabiding Nirvāṇa *(Apratiṣṭhita Nirvāṇa)*

If one looks at the principal schools of Indian religious thought that have endured, it appears to be a requirement of Indian soteriology that the ultimate result of religious discipline be unconditioned *(asaṃskṛta)*, a state eternally free from the control of worldly conditions. This requirement held true for all schools of Buddhism.[1] As noted in chapter 2, the attainment of nirvāṇa in early and Abhidharma Buddhism was understood as the attainment of an unconditioned state, permanently liberated from the conditions of saṃsāra. In Mahāyāna soteriology, this feature of nirvāṇa was preserved. But perhaps the most important distinguishing feature of classical Mahāyāna was its paradoxical notion that nirvāṇa, although an unconditioned state, was to be attained for the purpose of acting within the conditioned world for others. The bodhisattva aimed for a nirvāṇa not subject to the controlling conditions of saṃsāra *(karma* and *kleśa)* in order to be free to act effectively within saṃsāra for others.[2]

Buddhahood, the result of the Mahāyāna path, is therefore understood as a state at once unconditioned *(asaṃskṛta)* and conditioned *(saṃskṛta)*: a Buddha is personally free from the conditions of *karma* and *kleśa* but pervasively active within the conditioned world on behalf of others. A common term for Buddhahood in classical Mahāyāna literature is *apratiṣṭhita nirvāṇa* (nonabiding nirvāṇa) meaning that a Buddha is restricted neither by the uncontrolled suffering of saṃsāra nor by a quiescent state of liberation that would leave him powerless to help beings in saṃsāra. Buddhahood is a state that is free from the power of worldly conditions *(karma* and *kleśa)* without standing apart from the world.[3] A Buddha's gnosis was understood to pervade the world, not only in nondual knowledge of its ultimate reality (thusness) but also in active relations to all the world's suffering beings.

Understood in relation to this doctrine, the ultimate purpose of Mahāyāna practice is twofold. For oneself, its ultimate purpose is total freedom from the control of the saṃsāric conditions of *karma* and *kleśa*. For others, its ultimate purpose is unrestricted immersion in saṃsāra to teach and help beings. The Mahāyāna path involves two basic modes of practice to achieve those purposes: the cultivation of supramundane wisdom *(prajñā)* and the application of methods in skillful service to others *(upāya)*. These practices generate the collections of gnosis and merit *(jñānapuṇyasambhāra)*, which result in ultimate benefit for self as *svābhāvikakāya* (= *dharmakāya)* and ultimate benefit for others as *rūpakāya* (embodiment in forms = *sāmbhogikakāya*, *nairmāṇikakāya*).

In chapter 4 we focused on the yogic development of the gnosis that ultimately issues in Buddhahood as embodied within its own realization *(svābhāvikakāya)*. At the path of direct seeing, the bodhisattva experiences a direct, nondual realization of thusness for the first time. When this realization is perfected at Buddhahood, it never ceases. We saw that permanent cognitive identification of gnosis and thusness *(nirvikalpajñāna/tathatāviśuddhi)*, as the essence *(svabhāva)* of Buddhahood, is *svābhāvikakāya* (Buddhahood as it is embodied in its own essence). Thusness is unconditioned (the real nature of all phenomena is, always was, and always will be just thus). Therefore, its perfect nondual realization, which is *svābhāvikakāya,* constitutes nondual attainment of the unconditioned: nirvāṇa. *Svābhāvikakāya* is also unconditioned in the sense that its attainment proffers complete freedom from the power of *karma* and *kleśa*, i.e., total freedom from the controlling conditions of saṃsāra. *Svābhāvikakāya*, then, constitutes the unconditioned aspect of nonabiding nirvāṇa.

But, as noted above, Buddhahood is the outcome not only of practice of supramundane wisdom or gnosis *(prajñā/jñāna)* but also of cultivation of compassion in skillful service to others *(upāya)*. Just as the practice of wisdom issues at final enlightenment in *svābhāvikakāya*, the practice of skillful service naturally issues in the *svābhāvikakāya*'s manifestation of forms *(rūpa)* for compassionate engagement in the world. In Mahāyāna sūtras and treatises, these forms are referred to as *rūpakāya* (embodiment of Buddhahood in form[s])." They include all manifestations of *sāmbhogikakāya* and *nairmāṇikakāya*, thus constituting the aspect of nonabiding nirvāṇa that operates within the conditioned worlds of beings.[4] *Rūpakāya*, although the manifestation of the unconditioned *svābhāvikakāya*, is subject to the conditions of the world insofar as it functions within the world. Hence, its diverse manifestations are encountered or recognized only by those who have created the appropriate karmic conditions to do so—bodhisattvas and other beings with sufficient spiritual merit.

The doctrine of nonabiding nirvāṇa therefore, has involved the notion of an attainment that is somehow both unconditioned and operative within conditions, corresponding to *svābhāvikakāya,* on the one hand, and *sāmbhogikakāya/nairmāṇikakāya,* on the other.

5.2
Svābhāvikakāya as Ontological Foundation of the *Rūpakāyas*, Epistemologically Exclusive to Buddhas

In the earliest literature that formally taught three *kāya*s, the three are distinguished not by reference to an ontological division within the realization of Buddhahood itself, but by reference to the different ways its undivided realization functions for those who have it (Buddhas) and those who do not (non-Buddhas). According to the texts we examined in chapter 4, Buddhahood is ontologically a simple, undifferentiated realization: purified thusness/nonconceptual gnosis, the embodiment of dharma in its ultimate realization *(dharmakāya).* This, as the embodiment of enlightenment in its own essence *(svabhāva)*, is *svābhāvikakāya.* But while *svābhāvikakāya* is "invisible to gods and men," the other two *kāya*s *do* become visible to "gods and men" in order to come into relation with them (chapter 4, sections 3 and 4). Thus while ontologically one, Buddhahood is both functionally and epistemologically divided into three: *dharmakāya* as only Buddhas know it *(= svābhāvikakāya)*, and *dharmakāya* in its twofold manifestation to others (as *sāmbhogikakāya* and *nairmāṇikakāya*).

We turn again to *Mahāyānasūtrālaṃkāra,* verse 9.60, with *bhāṣya* as a principal source of three-*kāya* theory within classical Yogācāra. As previously discussed, *MSA* 9.59 explains the three embodiments *(kāya*s*)* as functional modes *(vṛtti)* of the purified realm of dharma (*dharmadhātu-viśuddha* = Buddhahood). The text continues:

> svābhāviko 'tha sāṃbhogyaḥ kāyo nairmāṇiko 'paraḥ
> kāyabhedā hi buddhānām prathamastu dvayāśrayaḥ
>
> (*MSA* 9.60)

[Varieties of embodiment of the Buddhas are: embodiment in their own essence, in communal enjoyment, and in manifestation(s) as well. But the first is the basis of the {other} two.]

> trividhaḥ kāyo buddhānām
> svābhāviko dharmakāya āśrayaparāvṛttilakṣaṇaḥ
> sāṃbhogiko yena parṣanmaṇḍaleṣu dharmasaṃbhogaṃ karoti
> nairmāṇiko yena nirmāṇena sattvārthaṃ karoti
>
> (*MSA* 9.60 *bhāṣya*)

> [Embodiment of the Buddhas is threefold, {being}:
> 1. in essence *(svābhāvika)*, the embodiment of dharma *(dharmakāya)*, whose identity is fundamental transformation.
> 2. in communal enjoyment *(sāṃbhogika)*, that which creates enjoyment of dharma within the circles of assembly.
> 3. in manifestation *(nairmāṇika)*, manifestation(s) that work for the benefit of beings.]

The *Buddhabhūmivyākhyāna* by Śīlabhadra, basing itself on the *MSA*, clarifies its notion that the three *kāyas* are distinguished not ontologically but functionally, and therefore epistemologically, in terms of how and for whom they appear. The *Buddhabhūmivyākhyāna* says, "The *kāya* of the Tathāgatas *(= dharmakāya)*, which is the purified dharma realm *(dharmadhātuviśuddhi)*, is undivided. However, because it functions as distinguished into three *kāyas*, it is said to have functional divisions."[5] In other words, the division into three *kāyas* distinguishes different functional aspects of the *dharmakāya (= dharmadhātuviśuddhi)*, while its ontological oneness is affirmed. It is in this sense that the latter two *kāyas* are said to be "based" on the first. The *svābhāvikakāya/dharmakāya* is the insubstantial ontological essence of which all other qualities of Buddhahood are composed.[6]

The *Buddhabhūmivyākhyāna* then draws the distinctions between the *kāyas* epistemologically, with reference to the type of being for whom each appears. *Svābhāvikakāya*, the Buddhas' own ultimate realization, is subtle, difficult to fathom, directly known only to Buddhas. *Sāmbhogikakāya* is the form under which that realization manifests to share the enjoyment of dharma with communities of *ārya* bodhisattvas in pure realms.[7] *Nairmāṇikakāya* comprises its diverse forms of manifestation throughout the universe, assisting beings less spiritually mature than great bodhisattvas. Thus, the functional distinctions that define the three *kāyas* serve equally as epistemological distinctions between them.[8] Ontologically the realization of Buddhahood is one *(svābhāvikakāya, dharmakāya, dharmadhātuviśuddhi)*. To benefit non-Buddhas it must participate with them in their cognitive worlds. This means that, epistemologically, the Buddhas' realization becomes part of the cognitive worlds of different kinds of beings in different ways. For the unenlightened or not yet fully enlightened, it manifests as *rūpakāyas* (*sāmbhogikakāya, nairmāṇikakāya)*. When it expresses itself to the unenlightened, it is comprehensible only within their forms of thought, through which it is conventionally understood as a set of pure qualities, such as the Buddha dharmas extrapolated from the excellent qualities of the path to Buddhahood. Sthiramati's explanation of *MSA* 9.60–9.62 is very close on these points to that of the *Buddhabhūmivyākhyāna*.[9]

In classical Yogācāra literature, the precise content of Buddha's awareness is explicitly held to be a mystery to non-Buddhas. A basic characteristic of *svābhāvikakāya* in these texts is its epistemological exclusivity. *Svābhāvikakāya* is characterized as *pratyātma-vedanīya*, knowable only through personal realization. In chapter 4 I quoted *Mahāyānasūtrālaṃkāra* 21.61, which said: "You [Buddha] are beheld in the worlds and in the assemblies, yet are entirely invisible to gods and men." The *MSA bhāṣya* identifies Buddha's appearance "in the worlds" as *nairmāṇikakāya* and his appearance "in the assemblies" as *sāmbhogikakāya*, while his very being, "invisible to gods and men," is *dharmakāya (= svābhāvikakāya)*. Asvabhāva, commenting on this, says: "Because *dharmakāya* is knowable only through personal realization *(pratyātma-vedanīya)*, it is characterized as inconceivable *(acintya)*. As it is not an object of inference, there is nothing in the world that could serve as an example for it."[10] *MSA* 9.62 says that *svābhāvikakāya* is "the same" *(sama)* and "subtle" *(sūkśma)*. The *MSA bhāṣya* says these terms mean, respectively, that the *svābhāvikakāya* is undifferentiated and difficult to know. The *Buddhabhūmi-vyākhyāna*, commenting on this, says: "It *(svābhāvikakāya)* is the same for all Tathāgatas, subtle, and difficult to know. For this reason it is said to be inaccessible to speculative investigation; and is not an object of inference, being beyond ascertainment by reason."[11] The *Mahāyānasaṃgraha* says: "It *(dharmakāya)* has the characteristic of inconceivability *(acintyalakṣaṇa)*, because as purified thusness *(tathatā-viśuddhi)* it must be realized personally, is without compare in the world, and is not an object of inference."[12]

Such frequent expressions of the *svābhāvikakāya*'s epistemological exclusivity were probably intended to limit speculation concerning the precise content of Buddha's awareness, on the grounds that its content was too different from an ordinary being's awareness to be understood by extrapolating from the epistemological structures of ordinary awareness.[13] The texts delimit the range of discussion of Buddha's gnosis to very general and often metaphorical discussions that hearken back to earlier scriptures. Precisely what it means for a person's mind (which in our experience is an impermanent) to have a nondual realization of thusness (a permanent) is not detailed. Nor is it explained precisely how a Buddha's nondual realization of undifferentiated thusness cognizes the differentiated world so as to take action within it to teach and help beings.

It is not just that these issues were not fully explained. Rather, they were explicitly characterized as impossible for ordinary persons to understand or explain with precision. The precise content of a Buddha's enlightenment was understood as quite literally inconceivable *(acintya)*, meaning, as the texts explicitly say, that it is beyond the range of inference and beyond precise extrapolation from ordinary, limited experience, and therefore beyond precise description in language.[14]

Yogācāra tradition, then, makes it quite explicit that there are severe limitations on our comprehension of Buddhahood, and in particular, on our comprehension of the relation between the aspects of Buddhahood that are unconditioned *(asaṃskṛta)* and concern thusness or emptiness *(tathatā, śūnyatā)*, and those which conform to the conditioned *(saṃskṛta)* world and concern phenomena.[15] But certain principles of the relation between Buddhahood and the world are broadly described, often metaphorically, and they warrant investigation. Each could serve as the subject of extensive future research. For our purpose, we will look briefly at certain fundamental correlations between conditioned and unconditioned aspects of Buddhahood as regards gnosis, action, and embodiment.

5.3
The Paradox of Buddhahood as Nonabiding Nirvāṇa: Unconditioned Basis of Pervasive Activity in a Conditioned World

In chapter 4 we noted the identification of *svābhāvikakāya* with purified thusness *(tathatā-viśuddhi),* the nondual realization of ultimate reality purified of all cognitive obstructions. The term *tathatā-viśuddhi* has two semantic components, each of which connotes an aspect of Buddhahood that is unconditioned *(asaṃskṛta)* and permanent *(nitya):* (1) *tathatā*: cognitive identification with thusness, the nondual nature of things that is ever "thus," never changes; (2) *viśuddhi*: complete purification, the permanent cessation of the affective and cognitive obstructions *(kleśajñeyāvaraṇa)* that obscure thusness for ordinary beings. As purified thusness *(tathatā-viśuddhi), svābhāvikakāya* is unconditioned and permanent, both in its cognitive identification with thusness as unconditioned and in its permanent cessation of the obscurations that had covered thusness prior to enlightenment.[16]

Other themes in early Mahāyāna and Yogācāra literature also contribute to the notion of *svābhāvikakāya/dharmakāya* as unconditioned and permanent. The attainment of *svābhāvikakāya* is the final realization of thusness *(tathatā).* But thusness is not newly created or subject to any particular conditions.The attainment of *svābhāvikakāya,* then, is not the creation of something new, but the complete revelation of what had always been the case.[17] As discussed in the previous chapter, the *svābhāvikakāya*'s realization of thusness is nondual, so that from the perspective of realization, subject and object are no longer distinguished. The nondual realization of thusness, then, may be understood to entail an identification with its unconditioned nature.[18]

A related idea prominent in the Yogācāra texts under discussion is the doctrine of the innate, luminous purity of mind *(cittam prakṛtiprabhāsvaram, citta-prakṛtiviśuddhi).* This doctrine, too, contributes to the notion of enlightenment as unconditioned *(asaṃskṛta)* and permanent. It holds that the mind of each sentient being is essentially pure, luminous awareness, while the affective and cognitive impurities that cover the mind, being adventitious to it, are not part of its very nature. All mental impurities, passions *(kleśa)* and cognitive obstructions, are therefore removable through practice of the yogic path and, when removed, leave just the pure, luminous essence of the mind that constitutes enlightenment. In this theory too, the real, the primordial purity, is unconditioned. It does not need to be created.

The practice of the yogic path just removes what has covered it, revealing the pure essence of mind that has always been present and has never changed.[19]

Since the doctrine of innate pure mind appears throughout Yogācāra literature we should look at a vivid textual example of it. The *Dharmadharmatāvibhāga*'s final words sum up its doctrine of complete fundamental transformation (*āśraya-parivṛtti* = full enlightenment), as follows: "Analogies for fundamental transformation are the sky, gold, water, etc."[20] The *DDV vṛtti*, commenting on this, says:

> Although there has been a fundamental transformation *(āśrayaparivṛtti)* [at full enlightenment], nothing has undergone an actual change. How this is so is demonstrated by the analogies [in the root text]. . . .
>
> For example, intrinsically, the sky is just pure. But it is not considered so when it is beclouded by fog, etc., which are adventitious to it. When it is free of the [fog, etc.], it is then [considered] pure. . . . The purity is not originated. Rather, the purity is just [newly] seen, when it has become free of what prevented it from being seen. The fact that the sky is [newly] perceived to be pure does not mean that it should be taken as something which has undergone change. Likewise, gold exists simply in its own splendor. But when its luster is hidden by adventitious stain, one does not perceive [the splendor], and when it is freed from the stain, its [splendor] is perceived. That is all. By perceiving [the splendor of gold], one is not creating it. Similarly, water exists simply in its own sparkling clarity. But the water, through its association with mud, is not perceived as [clear]. And when freed from the mud, it is perceived [as such]. That is all. Perceiving it as such does not cause the substance of the water, which has been continually present, to generate [clarity], nor is that [clarity] created. One should not take the water to be something that has undergone a change just because one [newly] perceives its clarity.
>
> In the same way, the innate luminosity *(prakṛti prabhāsvaraṃ)* in fundamental transformation *(āśrayaparivṛtti)* is not previously nonexistent. Rather, through the appearance of adventitious obstructions, it did not appear, just like the impurity [in the analogy of the sky], the lack of splendor [in the analogy of the gold], and the lack of clarity [in the analogy of the water]. That is all. When the [innate luminosity] is freed from those [obstructions], it appears. From this, through that transformation, the real nature of things *(dharmatā)* comes to appear; but by its appearing it is not [newly] generated, nor is it created. Because there is no [creation] of it, the real nature of things *(dharmatā)* and the fundamental transformation consisting of it *(tadprabhāvitāśrayaparivṛtti)* are permanent *(nitya)*.[21]

Although *svābhāvikakāya/dharmakāya* is characterized as unconditioned and permanent for all the reasons above, it has another important, and apparently contradictory, characteristic: It gives rise to pervasive activity throughout the universe to assist living beings still trapped there. An unconditioned thing, then, is the source of conditioned activity. This paradox is entailed by the doctrine of nonabiding nirvāṇa *(apratiṣṭhita nirvāṇa)* that became normative for classical Indian Mahāyāna and fundamental to it, frequently invoked as the means to distinguish Mahāyāna from non-Mahāyāna Buddhism.[22]

MSA 9.14 *bhāṣya* shows how the Mahāyāna doctrine of nonabiding nirvāṇa gives rise to the paradox of Buddhahood as both unconditioned and conditioned. Describing Buddhahood as fundamental transformation *(āśrayaparivṛtti)*, it says:

> Its operation is nondual *(advayā vṛtti)* because of its abiding neither in saṃsāra nor in nirvāṇa *(saṃsāra-nirvāṇa-apratiṣṭhitatvāt)*, through its being both conditioned and unconditioned *(saṃskṛta-asaṃskṛtatvena)*.[23]

Implicit here is an etymology: *apratiṣṭhita nirvāṇa*: = *saṃsāra-nirvāṇa-apratiṣṭhitatvam*—nonabiding nirvāṇa is an attainment of nirvāṇa that abides neither in saṃsāra nor in [quiescent] nirvāṇa. *Svābhāvikakāya/dharmakāya*, although itself freed from the suffering conditions of the world *(karma* and *kleśa)*, does not remain in a quiescent state separate from the world.[24] It gives rise to extensive activity throughout the world. Thus, even though *dharmakāya* is free from worldly conditions, its activity on behalf of others must take part in worldly conditions. Its activity, as mentioned above, is the natural fruition of the method *(upāya)* aspect of the path to enlightenment, the expression of aeons of bodhisattva activity for beings prior to the attainment of full enlightenment. Because a Buddha's activity operates in the visible world, it must take visible expression. This is *rūpakāya*, embodiments of Buddhahood in various forms *(sāmbhogikakāya* and *nairmāṇikakāya)*, *dharmakāya*'s manifestations in the world.

The logical implications of the nonabiding-nirvāṇa doctrine take various expressions in the literature. As developed in chapter 4, Buddhahood (as *svābhāvikakāya/dharmakāya*) is a nondual realization of ultimate reality in which cognitive subject and object are no longer distinguished. *Svābhāvikakāya,* as the final cognitive identification with ultimate reality, is referred to as purified thusness, purified realm of dharma, undefiled realm, etc. *(tathatā-viśuddhi, dharmadhātuviśuddhi, anāsravadhātu,* etc.). As such, Buddhahood is described as "unmoving," (Skt., *acalaṃ;* Tib., *mi gyo ba*), meaning that it is always cognitively inseparable from ultimate reality *(tathatā, dharmadhātu),* which is unconditioned and permanent. Yet it is the source of activities that, like the world in which they manifest, are ever changing.

MSA 9.51 says that a Buddha manifests activities throughout the universe: taking birth, teaching, demonstrating the attainment of enlightenment, etc., over and over again. It then adds: "He never moves from that place, and yet he carries it all out." The *MSA bhāṣya* identifies "that place" as the undefiled realm *(anāsrava-dhātu*, synonymous in the *MSA bhāṣya* with *dharmadhātuviśuddha* and *tathatā-viśuddhi).* Sthiramati explains this to mean that "although [Buddha] does not move, does not budge, does not waver from the undefiled realm, he carries out all the activities whose characteristic is movement."[25]

The *Buddhabhūmisūtra* says: "In space, there appear the arising and ceasing of diverse forms. Yet space neither arises nor ceases. Likewise, within the purified dharma realm *(dharmadhātuviśuddha)* of the Tathāgatas, there appear the arising and ceasing of awareness, manifestation, and performance of all the activities for sentient beings. Yet the purified dharma realm has neither arising nor ceasing."[26] The commentary explains: "Forms and so forth, ultimately, are the nature of thusness *(tathatā)*. Therefore, [in the purified dharma realm of the Buddhas] there is no arising, etc., though [arising, etc.] is posited conventionally. For that very reason, 'there appear' is the terminology used [in the sūtra], meaning that conventionally there are [arising and ceasing], but ultimately there are not. The manifestations of [the Buddhas'] gnosis *(jñāna)* and so forth are all like that."[27]

This indicates that a Buddha's gnosis is inseparably fixed upon ultimate reality *(tathatā*, *dharmadhātu*, etc.) without change. Yet somehow through that, it manifests and acts pervasively within the transactional, changing world of sentient beings. The purified dharma realm per se *(dharmadhātuviśuddha)* is thusness and the nondual gnosis of it, the ultimate perspective. But because thusness is the real nature of the entire phenomenal world, the gnosis knowing it pervades the entire world. And because a Buddha's gnosis of thusness is fully perfected, it is transactionally operative within the entire phenomenal world that it pervades. Its activity, then, is simply the forms it manifests within the conventional perspective of ordinary beings. Conventionally, in the phenomenal world of beings, its activities "appear," while ultimately within the purified realm of dharma, there is no activity, no change.

The pervasiveness of Buddha's activity, then, is related to the fact that Buddha's gnosis is conjoined with thusness in a nondual way, where thusness is pervasive, i.e., is the ultimate nature of the entire universe. The *Buddhabhūmisūtra* says: "Because the purified dharma realm is utterly limitless, within the purified dharma realm of the Tathāgatas, in all ten directions, activities individually establishing help and happiness for all sentient beings are utterly limitless. Yet the purified dharma realm does not come or go, does not move or shift."[28]

In other words, a Buddha's activity is available to each and every being, because his gnosis pervades the entire universe of beings. And his gnosis pervades the entire universe, because it is cognitively conjoined with thusness, the undivided ultimate nature of everything in the universe. This is expressed in the *Buddhabhūmisūtra* with the notion that the purified dharma realm pervades all things in "one taste" *(ekarasa)*, just as space pervades all forms: "For example, space is omnipresent in all types of varied forms, but neither can it be expressed by them nor is it varied, because it is one taste. Likewise, the purified dharma realm *(dharmadhātuviśuddha)* of the Tathāgatas is omnipresent in all types of all the varied things to be known. But neither can it be expressed by them nor is it varied, because it is one taste *(ekarasa)*."[29] Asvabhāva's commentary on *Msg* 3.12 expresses a similar idea when it explains that nonconceptual gnosis (i.e., *nirvikalpa-jñāna*) perceives everything taught in the Mahāyāna, because everything taught shares the single nature of thusness *(tathatā)*.[30] A related idea appears in *MSA* 9.6, which says "Buddhahood includes all phenomena." Sthiramati glosses this as saying, "Because there is no phenomena which is not included within emptiness, so Buddhahood includes all phenomena."[31] In other words, ontologically, all things are one in their ultimate nature (emptiness, thusness). And therefore epistemologically, a Buddha knows all things through that one nature. A Buddha perceives all things through the one taste *(ekarasa)* that all things share.[32]

But if a Buddha's mind is epistemologically one with the dharma realm *(dharmadhātu)* whose content is undifferentiated thusness, it does not conceptualize. Therefore, it does not conceptualize what it should do to assist beings. Then how can a Buddha act in our conceptually constructed, transactional world? Although this problem is raised in Yogācāra commentaries, we get the sense that it is subsumed, at least in part, under Buddhahood's inconceivability *(acintyalakṣaṇa)*. A full answer would require a detailed analysis of the content and mechanism of a Buddha's awareness. But as noted in section 2 above, all texts, invoking the epistemological exclusivity of Buddhahood, studiously avoid such an analysis. Instead they address the problem with a very broad, metaphorical discussion.

The *Mahāyānasūtrālaṃkāra,* vv. 9.18–9.19, uses two metaphors to explain Buddha's activity as a spontaneous reflex of the enlightened state. Verse 9.18 compares Buddha's activity in the world to the sounds that come forth from the heavenly gongs (of Indian legend), which automatically sound without being struck. Verse 9.19 compares Buddha's activity to a jewel automatically radiating light. In the metaphors, neither the gongs nor the jewel exert any effort or require premeditation for their actions. They perform their functions automatically. Sthiramati comments: "Like the [gongs] in the analogy, the Tathāgatas, dwelling in the undefiled realm *(anāsravadhātu)* carry out the various explanations of dharma for sentient beings, without any premeditated thought, 'I will teach the dharma,' and without any effort or striving on their part. Rather the teaching of the dharma arises in utter spontaneity."[33] In other words, the Buddhas dwell in the unconditioned state of cognitive identification with thusness (referred to in the *MSA* alternatively as *anāsravadhātu*, *dharmadhātuviśuddhi*, or *dharmakāya*), from which arises activities for beings which are an automatic reflex of that state and the natural result of prior merit.

Msg 8.17 says: "Just as the respective functions of jewels and gongs occur without any premeditation, so the various activities of the Buddhas arise, always without any premeditation."[34] The *Msg bhāṣya* and Asvabhāva's commentary say this statement is a response to the following problem: Since Buddhahood consists of nonconceptual gnosis *(nirvikalpa-jñāna)*, how can it carry out activities for sentient beings when it is entirely free of the conceptualization characteristic of those beings? Asvabhāva comments:

> The analogies of the jewels and the [heavenly] gongs demonstrate how the activity [of Buddhahood] is automatic.... The [jewels and gongs] have no thought process that thinks, "We will radiate," or "We will emit sound." And yet, the wish granting jewel radiates light and the heavenly gongs emit sound without anyone striking them, just by the power of the sentient beings who are born there [i.e. through the force of their own karma]. Similarly, even though the Buddhas, the Bhagavans, lack the dichotomous conceptualization *(vikalpa)* of sentient beings, etc., their various activities arise, helping [beings] in precise accord with the needs of their training.[35]

Such analogies do not prescribe precisely how a Buddha's gnosis can be fixed on universal thusness, free of conceptualization, and still give rise to actions to assist sentient beings who operate in a world of their own conceptual construction. Rather the analogies provide the reader with a mental image through which such an ability might be accepted, if not really understood.[36] According to the explanation, *dharmakāya*, Buddha's unlimited nonconceptual gnosis, is not an intentional agent of activity, since an intentional agent requires discursive thought considering options and intending to do something. Rather, intransitive verbs are used to express the passivity and automatic nature of the *dharmakāya*'s actions. The actions "arise" or "come forth" *('byung ba, sambhava)* in dependence upon the various karmic capacities and conditions of sentient beings. In accord with the individual karma of different beings (the cognitive propensities left by their own previous actions), *dharmakāya* naturally and automatically gives rise to activities appropriate to the spiritual training of each. Somehow, the *dharmakāya* is the basis of automatic activity in the conditioned world of beings, while free of the conceptualizing and discursive thought processes that constitute and drive those beings.[37]

Chapter 4 of the *Ratnagotravibhāga* and its commentary provide nine analogies for the activities of Buddhahood.[38] Two of those analogies are the same as those above: the wish granting jewel and the heavenly gongs that sound without being struck. The R*GV*'s explanation of Buddha's activities describes their lack of premeditation and automaticity, and emphasizes the fact that the activities occur as reflections within the minds of sentient beings, in accord with their own cognitive capacities (*RGV* 4.25: "svacittapratibhāso 'yamiti naivaṃ pṛthagjanāḥ / jānantyatha ca tatteṣāmavandhyaṃ bimbadarśanam" [Ordinary beings do not know that it {the Buddha's form} is just an appearance within their own minds, but their seeing of the {Buddha's} reflection is purposeful for them]). The forms that carry out the *dharmakāya*'s activities *(rūpakāya)* are reflections of the *dharmakāya* within the cognitive world of sentient beings. *Dharmakāya*, itself nonconceptual, is refracted through the conceptual cognitions of sentient beings to manifest as *rūpakāya.*[39]

RGV 1.145 and its commentary describe *dharmakāya* in two aspects: (1) the perfect purity of the dharma realm *(dharmadhātu)* realized in nonconceptual gnosis, i.e., the personal realization of a Buddha *(pratyātmādhigama dharma)*, and (2) its natural outflow *(suviśuddha-dharmadhātu niṣyandaḥ)*, the source of cognitive appearances *(vijñapti)* among sentient beings that accord with the needs of their spiritual training, i.e., the teaching of dharma as it is communicated to sentient beings *(deśanā dharma)*.[40] The first aspect corresponds to *svābhāvikakāya*, i.e., the *dharmakāya* as it is personally realized by a Buddha. The second aspect is the natural outflow *(niṣyandaḥ)* of the *dharmakāya*. This corresponds to the *rūpakāyas (sāmbhogikakāya* and *nairmāṇikakāya)*, which are the modes under which the *dharmakāya* appears to teach beings. In this model, again, the need to distinguish the *dharmakāya* as it is personally realized from the *dharmakāya*'s automatic outflow of activity in the world is the raison d'être for distinguishing *dharmakāya* as *svābhāvikakāya* from the other two *kāyas*.[41]

The concept of nonabiding nirvāṇa, then, requires that Buddhahood reconcile within itself unconditioned and conditioned aspects. The unconditioned part of Buddhahood is its unchanging, nondual realization of ultimate reality and its permanent elimination of affective and cognitive obstructions. The conditioned part of Buddhahood is its active expression of compassion for beings in their conditioned world. This entails that Buddhahood reconcile the duality of the unconditioned and the conditioned with respect to a whole set of dichotomies, where the first term of each dichotomous pair corresponds to the unconditioned, the second to the conditioned: *svābhāvikakāya* and *rūpakāya*, ultimate reality and phenomenal reality, unmanifest and manifest, formlessness and form, the permanent and the impermanent, support and supported, the infinite and the finite.

Still, the precise mechanism whereby Buddhahood reconciles within itself the unconditioned with the conditioned, gnosis of ultimate reality with phenomenal activity, etc., is left unspecified except for the metaphors and broad discussions of the sort given above. Yogācāra texts are not embarrassed by their inability to present a more detailed answer. As we have seen, they clearly state that Buddhahood, being beyond ordinary linguistic and conceptual categories, cannot be specified more precisely. With that understanding, the apparent contradictoriness of *svābhāvikakāya/dharmakāya* is taken as a further indication of a Buddha's greatness. The fact that a Buddha's nondual realization can reconcile within itself what appear to dualistic minds as irreconcilable properties is another indication of its profundity, to be comprehended through disciplines of the path (such as those summarized in chapter 4), never through conceptual thought alone.[42]

5.4
Paradox of a Buddha's Awareness: Inseparable from Unconditioned Thusness, yet Operative in the Conditioned World

In classical Yogācāra descriptions of the practice of ārya bodhisattvas (bodhisattvas who have directly realized thusness), the yogi alternates between periods of single-pointed meditative equipoise on thusness, which contributes to his accumulation of gnosis *(jñānasambhāra)*, and periods of altruistic activity, which contributes to his accumulation of merit *(puṇyasambhāra)*. The gnosis that nondualistically realizes thusness in meditative equipoise is referred to as "nonconceptual gnosis," *nirvikalpajñāna*. During periods of altruistic activity subsequent to those meditation sessions, the yogi's cognitions are fundamentally altered by the nonconceptual gnosis realized during the sessions. Whereas during the session he perceives thusness, in the period following the session he again sees the world of dualistic appearances. But whereas ordinary beings adhere to that dualism, the yogi no longer feels such adherence. The force of the nonconceptual gnosis from his prior meditation session makes all dualistic appearances appear as illusions or dreams. The apparent independence and separateness of cognitive subject and object seem as unreal to the yogi as a magician's illusion. This kind of cognition, which, following from the force of nonconceptual gnosis during prior meditation, sees phenomena as an illusion or dream, is referred to as *pṛṣṭhalabdhajñāna* (subsequent gnosis). Whereas nonconceptual gnosis *(nirvikalpajñāna)* perceives thusness, ultimate truth *(paramārtha satya)*, the "gnosis subsequent to it" *(pṛṣṭhalabdhajñāna)* perceives the phenomenal world, conventional truth *(saṃvṛti satya)*, as an illusion. On the bodhisattva path prior to attainment of Buddhahood, the yogi alternates between nonconceptual gnosis, *nirvikalpajñāna,* during meditation sessions, and subsequent gnosis, *pṛṣṭhalabdhajñāna,* during the rest of his day. In short, the yogi's subsequent gnosis is precisely his perception of the phenomenal world as effected by prior realization of nonconceptual gnosis *(nirvikalpajñāna)*.[43]

Unlike the bodhisattva who alternates between periods of meditation on thusness and periods of activity in the world, a Buddha can never leave his "meditation session" on thusness. That a Buddha has attained a permanent nondual realization of universal thusness is the mark of having attained full enlightenment. That realization, in fact, comprises *svābhāvikakāya,* which is specified as unconditioned and eternal by nature. A Buddha's nonconceptual gnosis *(nirvikalpajñāna)* conjoined with thusness would never cease, just as thusness never ceases. It is therefore impossible for a Buddha to have a second kind of gnosis (like the "subsequent gnosis" of the bodhisattva) that would arise after nonconceptual gnosis *(nirvikalpa-jñāna)* receded.

Does this mean that a Buddha possesses only nonconceptual gnosis *(nirvikalpajñāna)* and *nothing* analogous to the bodhisattva's subsequent gnosis *(pṛṣṭhalabdhajñāna)?* Not entirely. Texts do explicitly ascribe both *nirvikalpajñāna* and *pṛṣṭhalabdhajñāna* to a Buddha.[44] But in the case of a bodhisattva, these comprise two distinct gnoses, only one of which is operative at a time. In the case of a Buddha, nonconceptual gnosis and what is called "subsequent gnosis" now become two aspects of a *single* gnosis (since nonconceptual gnosis per se never ceases). When Buddhahood is attained, through the complete elimination of all cognitive obstructions *(jñeyāvaraṇa-prahāṇa),* what had been the bodhisattva's subsequent gnosis now becomes a capacity of Buddha's nonconceptual gnosis to cognize and function within the phenomenal world. The elimination of all cognitive obstructions gives a Buddha the unique capacity to realize thusness directly and unceasingly *(nirvikalpajñāna)* while simultaneously cognizing and operating within the phenomenal world *(pṛṣṭhalabdhajñāna).*

For the bodhisattva, then, "nonconceptual gnosis" and "subsequent gnosis" designate two kinds of awareness. But after attaining Buddhahood, they designate two capacities of a single awareness. A Buddha's gnosis is called *nirvikalpajñāna* insofar as it nondually realizes thusness. It is called *pṛṣṭhalabdhajñāna* insofar as it cognizes and is operative within the phenomenal world. In the section 3 of this chapter, we noted how the pervasiveness of a Buddha's activity was related to the pervasiveness of his gnosis conjoined with thusness, since thusness is the nature of the entire universe. Ontologically all things are one in their ultimate nature (thusness). Therefore epistemologically, a Buddha (having removed all cognitive obstructions) knows all things through that ultimate nature, perceives all through the one taste *(ekarasa)* which they share. The Buddha's perception of the one ultimate nature is his nonconceptual gnosis *(nirvikalpajñāna).* His knowing of all things through that perception is called his "subsequent gnosis" *(pṛṣṭhalabdhajñāna).* In a Buddha's case, perhaps it could be said that the latter gnosis logically follows from the first (and hence is "subsequent"), rather than sequentially following it.

The latter perception, then, is based on the former perception, just as the *rūpakāya*s are understood to be based upon the *svābhāvikakāya* (*MSA* 9.60, quoted in section 2 above). Nonconceptual gnosis is a Buddha's nondual awareness of unconditioned thusness. Subsequent gnosis for a Buddha is the way he cognizes the conditioned world based upon his cognition of its thusness. For a Buddha, a single awareness is distinguished as "nonconceptual" or "subsequent" by reference to its perception of the unconditioned *(paramārtha satya)* and the conditioned *(saṃvṛti satya)* respectively. As might be expected, then, our textual sources draw a direct correspondence between nonconceptual gnosis and *svābhāvikakāya* (identified earlier as the unconditioned *kāya*) and a direct correspondence between subsequent gnosis and the *rūpakāya*s (the *kāya*s based on *svābhāvikakāya* which manifest in the world subject to its conditions).

Mahāyānasaṃgraha 10.28.10, discussing the profundity of the *dharmakāya*, says: "They [the Buddhas] examine all, without examining anything at all. They appear every place, yet are not objects of the six senses."[45] Asvabhāva comments that the subsequent gnosis *(pṛṣṭhalabdhajñāna)* of the *dharmakāya* inspects every knowable thing in existence. Yet, at the same time, the *dharmakāya* is said to inspect nothing at all, because as nonconceptual gnosis *(nirvikalpajñāna)*, it is free of discrimination *(vicārarahita)* (again, precisely how the *dharmakāya*'s awareness knows each distinct thing conventionally while ultimately knowing only indivisible thusness is not explained). Asvabhāva says the *Msg* phrase "they appear every place" refers to the embodiment of Buddhahood in its manifestations *(nairmāṇikakāya)*, which manifest everywhere. He says the statement "yet [they] are not objects of the six senses" means that ultimately the Buddhas are *dharmakāya*, which is not cognizable by sentient beings, whose cognition is restricted to the objects of the sense organs. In this account, nonconceptual gnosis and *dharmakāya* are the realization of ultimate reality *(paramārtha satya)*, the unconditioned, while subsequent gnosis and *nairmāṇikakāya* are the *dharmakāya*'s cognitive and transactional relation to the conditioned world.[46]

Mahāyānasūtrālaṃkāra 9.62 says that the *svābhāvikakāya* is connected with the *sāmbhogikakāya*, since it is the "cause of mastery over communal enjoyment" *(saṃbhoga)*.[47] Sthiramati comments:

> How is the [*svābhāvikakāya/dharmakāya*] the cause of the [*sāmbhogikakāya*]? The *sāmbhogikakāya* arises as the natural outflow *(niṣyanda)* of the *dharmakāya* to share the enjoyment of the unique, Mahāyāna dharma with the bodhisattva *mahāsattva*s who have entered the *bhūmi*s. Or, put another way, the *pṛṣṭhalabdhajñāna*, the pure worldly gnosis, is referred to as *sāmbhogikakāya*. Since the pure worldly gnosis *(pṛṣṭhalabdhajñāna)* emerges from the *nirvikalpajñāna* (nonconceptual gnosis), the *dharmakāya* is said to be connected with the *[sāmbhogikakāya]*.[48]

Here, the *sāmbhogikakāya* as a manifestation of *svābhāvikakāya (= dharmakāya)* is explicitly equated with subsequent gnosis *(pṛṣṭhalabdhajñāna)* as the way in which a Buddha's nonconceptual gnosis *(= svābhāvikakāya)* interacts with the phenomenal world.

The *Buddhabhūmivyākhyāna* presents a similar analysis. It identifies the *sāmbhogikakāya* as subsequent gnosis *(pṛṣṭhalabdhajñāna)*, i.e., an expression of the nonconceptual gnosis *(nirvikalpajñāna)* of the *svābhāvika-kāya*. A Buddha's subsequent gnosis, as *sāmbhogikakāya*, is what brings about the sharing of his enjoyment of dharma with the great bodhisattvas. But subsequent gnosis is identified not only with *sāmbhogikakāya,* but also with all of a Buddha's varied manifestations for beings throughout the universe, i.e., *nairmāṇikakāya.*[49] In the *Buddhabhūmivyākhyāna*, then, nonconceptual gnosis again corresponds to *svābhāvikakāya;* while subsequent gnosis *(pṛṣṭhalabdhajñāna)* is identified with both *sāmbhogikakāya* and *nairmāṇikakāya.*

Verses 14.42–14.49 of the *Mahāyānasūtrālaṃkāra* describe the practices of the path of higher meditation *(bhāvanā mārga)* that culminate in Buddhahood as fundamental transformation (*āśrayaparāvṛtti*, cf. chapter 4 section 6 above). Identified as a principal practice is the cultivation of the two types of gnosis, nonconceptual gnosis realizing thusness *(nirvikalpajñāna)* and subsequent gnosis perceiving phenomena as illusory *(pṛṣṭhalabdhajñāna)*. The former is said to perfect the bodhisattva's own qualities of Buddhahood, while the latter is said to bring about the spiritual development of other beings. Nonconceptual gnosis then, is identified as the cause of enlightenment, while subsequent gnosis is the cause of enlightenment's manifestation to help others.[50]

The *Ratnagotravibhāga* echoes this analysis in its second and third chapters on Buddhahood and its qualities. *RGV* vv. 3.1–3.3 and 3.37–3.38 identify the *paramārthakāya* (ultimate embodiment) as "one's own purpose" *(svārtha),* which is *svābhāvikakāya/dharmakāya*, and the *saṃvṛtikāya* (conventional embodiment) as the "purpose of others" *(parārtha),* which is the *rūpakāyas*. *RGV*'s second chapter identifies nonconceptual gnosis and subsequent gnosis as the primary causes of Buddhahood. These give rise to Buddhahood per se and Buddhahood in its manifestation to others, respectively (*RGV* vv. 2.8, 2.10–2.11). The attainment of Buddhahood, the result of nonconceptual gnosis, is *svābhāvikakāya/dharmakāya*, which fulfills one's own purpose. The manifestation of Buddhahood to help other beings, the result of subsequent gnosis, is the two *rūpakāyas*, which fulfill the purpose of others (*RGV vyākhyāna* introductory to *RGV* vv. 2.18–2.20). Here correspondences are explicitly drawn between nonconceptual gnosis, *svābhāvikakāya,* one's own purpose, and the ultimate *(paramārtha),* on the one hand, and between subsequent gnosis, the two *rūpakāyas*, others' benefit, and the phenomenal *(saṃvṛti),* on the other.[51]

A different but equally important theory of a Buddha's gnosis in Yogācāra texts, particularly the *MSA*, the *Buddhabhūmisūtra,* and their commentaries, is the theory of the four Buddha gnoses *(jñānas)*. The reader should not be misled by the plural form "gnoses," because like a Buddha's nonconceptual and subsequent gnoses, the four "gnoses" were not understood as temporally distinct gnoses, but as four capacities of a single awareness. The first is mirror gnosis *(ādarśajñāna)*, which is described as unmoving *(acalaṃ)*. The other three are the gnosis of sameness *(samatājñāna)*, the gnosis that thoroughly inspects *(pratyavekṣājñāna)*, and the gnosis that accomplishes activities *(kṛtyānuṣṭhānajñāna)*. These three are said to be based upon the mirror gnosis *(ādarśajñāna)*. And while mirror gnosis is described as "unmoving," the latter three are said to be "moving" *(cala)*.[52]

According to both Sthiramati and Śīlabhadra (author of the *Buddhabhūmivyākhyāna*), the mirror gnosis *(ādarśajñāna)* is fixed or unmoving because it is always cognitively conjoined with the *dharmadhātu*, universal thusness. This makes it equivalent to nonconceptual gnosis *(nirvikalpajñāna)*, and Sthiramati explicitly identifies it as such. The other three gnoses, as "moving," correspond to different aspects of a Buddha's subsequent gnosis *(pṛṣṭhalabdhajñāna)*. They "move" in that they are cognizant of and operative within the conditioned world of changing phenomena. A cognition of an impermanent object cannot begin until the object comes into existence, and must cease when the object ceases. Mirror gnosis, once achieved, never changes, since it is fixed on universal thusness, an "object" that never changes. But the other three gnoses, being cognizant of a changing world, shift with it.[53]

The qualities ascribed to the four Buddha gnoses in *MSA* 9.67–9.76 have correspondence to those of the three *kāyas*, and the commentators make the correspondences even more explicit. We noted in the previous section the statement in *MSA* 9.51: "He [a Buddha] never moves from that place, and yet he carries it all out." The unmoving aspect of Buddhahood is its nondual cognition of thusness, i.e., *svābhāvikakāya* (which includes nonconceptual gnosis = mirror gnosis), while the aspects of Buddhahood that "carry it all out" (carry out all Buddha's activities in the world) are the *rūpakāyas* and the "moving" gnoses associated with them (gnosis of sameness, gnosis that thoroughly inspects, and gnosis that accomplishes activities). And just as the *svābhāvikakāya* is said to be the basis of the *rūpakāyas* (*MSA* 9.60, 9.65), the mirror gnosis *(ādarśajñāna)* is said to be the fundamental gnosis upon which all others are based (*MSA* 9.67, 9.69).

Sthiramati says the mirror gnosis is nonconceptual gnosis, which perceives everything as the same because it perceives all phenomena through its perception of the *dharmadhātu*, universal thusness. In his account, mirror gnosis *(ādarśajñāna)* also nonjudgmentally perceives the phenomena whose thusness it is, like a clear mirror that reflects what is put before it.[54] The other three gnoses, then, comprise different aspects of a Buddha's perception of phenomena, all of which derive from the mirror gnosis's perception of their thusness.[55] Just as the *rūpakāyas* are reflections of *svābhāvikakāya* in the conceptually constructed world of sentient beings, so the latter three gnoses comprise aspects of the mirror gnosis *(ādarśajñāna)* as it is cognitively and transactionally related to the phenomenal world. In line with this parallelism, the commentators explicitly identify mirror gnosis as *svābhāvikakāya (= dharmakāya)*.[56]

The gnosis of sameness (*samatājñāna*, *MSA* 9.70–9.71) perceives all phenomena while cognizant of their sameness in the ultimate nature they share: thusness, emptiness. According to the text and commentaries, the gnosis of sameness focuses upon the essential sameness of all other beings and oneself. When the bodhisattva first gains direct realization of emptiness *(śūnyatā)* on the first bodhisattva stage (the path of direct seeing), he gains the gnosis of sameness, because through his perception of emptiness, he realizes how on the ultimate level there is no distinction whatsoever between himself and all others. Based on that perception, the previous mental force of concern for self (directed by ignorance) transforms into a powerful concern for all others (directed by his first direct sight of emptiness). When this gnosis is fully perfected through meditation on the rest of the bodhisattva stages *(bhūmis)* it becomes a Buddha's gnosis of sameness *(samatājñāna),* through which he identifies with the needs and sufferings of sentient beings, feeling love and compassion for them.[57] This love and compassion takes expression through a Buddha's manifestations, which appear to sentient beings according to their capacities.

The gnosis that thoroughly inspects (*pratyavekṣājñāna*, *MSA* 9.72–9.73) views all specific and general characteristics of phenomena, and in particular all the aspects of what must be taught to sentient beings for their spiritual development. This, together with the gnosis of sameness *(samatājñāna)*, is identified in commentaries with the *sāmbhogikakāya*. As aspects of a Buddha's awareness, they are called "gnosis of thorough inspection" and "gnosis of sameness." As a Buddha's form of interaction with his closest communities of disciples, the great bodhisattvas of the pure realms, those very gnoses are said to manifest as *sāmbhogikakāya* (embodiment of Buddhahood for communal enjoyment) of the dharma.[58]

The gnosis that accomplishes activities *(kṛtyānuṣṭhānajñāna*, *MSA* 9.74–9.75) is the aspect of a Buddha's awareness that is actively engaged in working for sentient beings throughout the universe. It does this by taking form in limitless ways, appearing, for example, as any sort of sentient being that would be appropriate for any particular set of circumstances, place, or time, in accord with the mentalities *(karma)* of beings to be taught. This aspect of a Buddha's gnosis takes form in limitless manifestations throughout the universe, one of which is identified as the Śākyamuni Buddha of our world's history, but most of which ordinary beings do not even recognize as manifestations of Buddhahood. As such, the gnosis that accomplishes activities is identified by commentators with *nairmāṇikakāya:* embodiment of Buddhahood in its limitless manifestations.[59]

This identification of the four Buddha *jñāna*s with the three *kāya*s (mirror gnosis = *svābhāvikakāya/dharmakāya*, gnoses of sameness and of thorough inspection = *sāmbhogikakāya*, gnosis that accomplishes activities = *nairmāṇikakāya*) became widespread in Mahāyāna literature. It is found in germinal form in the *MSA*, and made explicit in Sthiramati's commentary on the *MSA* and Śīlabhadra's commentary on the *Buddhabhūmisūtra,* as noted above. It also occurs in the *Kāyatrayasūtra* (Pk 949, vol. 37, 108.3.4–6), Buddhajñānapāda's commentary on the *Abhisamayālaṃkāra* (*Saṃcayagāthāpañjikā*, Pk 5196, vol. 91, 152.5.7–153.1.4), Atiśa's short commentary on the *Abhisamayālaṃkāra* (*Prajñāpāramitāpiṇḍārthapradīpa*, Pk 5201, vol. 92, 106.5.1–2), and a text ascribed to Candragomin that is quoted by Tsong kha pa in his commentary on the *Abhisamayālaṃkāra* (*Legs bshad gser phreng*, fols. 230a4–b2).

In line with this is the *MSA*'s descriptions of the functions of the four Buddha gnoses. Mirror gnosis is the only one of the four that is described primarily in terms of its cognitive functions. When describing the other three gnoses, the *MSA* puts greater emphasis on their modes of function and manifestation in the world for the benefit of beings than on their specific cognitive functions. The mirror gnosis *(ādarśajñāna)* is described as free of dualistic conceptual construction; it is spatially and temporally limitless in its cognition, knowing all phenomena without adhering to them through its cognition of universal thusness (*MSA* 9.69 and Sthiramati's commentary). The commentaries identify this gnosis with *svābhāvika-kāya (= dharmakāya).* The gnosis of sameness *(samatājñāna)* manifests an image of the Buddha for beings that accords with their faith (*MSA* 9.71). The thoroughly inspecting gnosis *(pratyavekṣājñāna)* shows its powers in the circle of assemblies (*MSA* 9.73). The commentaries identify these gnoses with the *sāmbhogikakāya*, taking the "circle of assemblies" to be the great bodhisattvas. The gnosis that accomplishes activities *(kṛtyānuṣṭhānajñāna)* works for all beings through limitless types of manifestations. The commentaries identify this with *nairmāṇikakāya.*

One gets the impression from the *MSA* and its commentaries that the mirror gnosis is Buddha's fundamental cognition, a nondual cognition of universal thusness through which, somehow (again not specified), all phenomena are known and limitless sentient beings can be engaged. The other three gnoses, cognitively, are just different aspects of mirror gnosis (*MSA* 9.67, 9.69). In their descriptions, therefore, the emphasis is not as much on their modes of cognition as on the forms they manifest in the world to help beings (*MSA* 9.70–9.75). This, again, accords with the logic of the three *kāya*s, where the first *kāya* is simply Buddhahood in its essence, the fundamental nondual awareness of thusness, while the other two *kāya*s are ways that awareness becomes actively embodied in communication with beings, within their conceptually constructed worlds and in accord with their differing mentalities.

In the previous chapter we showed how the defining essence *(svabhāva)* of Buddhahood was identified as nondual awareness of universal thusness, referred to as *svābhāvikakāya.* We noted how all other qualities and manifestations attributed to the Buddhas were understood as reflections of that defining essence within the cognitive worlds of sentient beings. The defining essence of Buddhahood is an unconditioned attainment, which is not subject to worldly conditions. But the manifestations of Buddhahood are part of the cognitive world of sentient beings, which is subject to worldly conditions. Therefore the appearance and disappearance of those manifestations conforms to the mentalities of beings. Yogācāra analyses of a Buddha's awareness also follow this fundamental structure. A Buddha's fundamental awareness, whether described as nonconceptual gnosis *(nirvikalpajñāna)* or mirror gnosis *(adarśajñāna)*, is perfect realization of universal thusness, through which cognition of all phenomena and awareness of all beings is possible. The aspects of that fundamental gnosis that reach outward to all beings, aware of their condition and active in their aid, are conditioned by the world.

The key point here is that the various qualities ascribed to a Buddha from a phenomenal point of view, whether expressed in terms of different types of gnosis, different forms of embodiment *(rūpakāya*s*),* or different pure mental qualities *(buddhadharmāḥ),* were all understood as phenomenal expressions of Buddhahood's undivided, defining essence. And that undivided essence was referred to as *svābhāvikakāya* (embodiment of Buddhahood in its essence), *dharmakāya* (embodiment of dharma in its ultimate realization) *nirvikalpajñāna* (nonconceptual gnosis), *tathatā-viśuddhi* (purified thusness), *dharmadhātuviśuddhi* (purified realm of dharma), and *anāsravadhātu* (undefiled realm), all of which were understood as ontologically equivalent.

This means that throughout the entire literature in which the three *kāyas* were first systematically delineated, *svābhāvikakāya* (or its ontological equivalent) is understood as the foundation and ontological ground of all aspects of Buddhahood. The undefiled Buddha dharmas, *rūpakāyas*, and gnoses associated with the world, etc., as phenomenal categories of Buddhahood were not thought to comprise its defining essence. Rather, they were thought to express that essence, which is *svābhāvikakāya (= dharmakāya)*, as it comes into relation to us, our world, and our limited understanding.

5.5
Sāmbhogikakāya as Embodiment in Communal Enjoyment: *Nairmāṇikakāya* as Manifold Manifestations for Limitless Activity

In chapter 4, section 2 , we noted that the Mahāyāna sūtras contain physical descriptions of Buddhas that far exceed what is ordinarily found in the Pali canon.[60] These descriptions came to be viewed as of two basic types: (1) descriptions of a glorious, luminous Buddha form, often radiating voluminous light, who may appear in a pure realm and is surrounded by a retinue of numerous lofty disciples, foremost among whom are great bodhisattvas who receive from that Buddha the Mahāyāna teaching contained in the sūtra; (2) limitless manifestations of innumerable kinds that pervade the universe, assisting beings of many types and teaching them the dharma in the form most suitable to their own mentalities. The Mahāyāna commentaries we have been discussing, in formalizing the doctrine of three *kāyas*, distinguished these two basic types of descriptions, thereby dividing into two types what had previously been referred to in the *Prajñāpāramitā* sūtras as *rūpakāya* (embodiment in forms). They identified the first type of Buddha form as *sāmbhogikakāya*, embodiment of Buddhahood for communal enjoyment of dharma, which could appear only to great beings (*ārya* bodhisattvas) who had purified their minds enough through direct realization of thusness to have contact with such an embodiment. The latter type of Buddha form, comprising limitless types of expression and form, was identified as *nairmāṇikakāya,* embodiment of Buddhahood in manifestations. This mode of embodiment appeared to anyone who had created positive karmic conditions for contact with Buddhahood, but had not yet realized thusness directly.

Because the glorious forms identified as *sāmbhogikakāya* were described in various Mahāyāna sūtras in terms of their blissful sharing of the dharma with their retinues of bodhisattvas, they were characterized particularly in terms of their *sambhoga*, "enjoyment" or "bliss," from which was derived the name. When our earliest commentarial sources describe *sāmbhogikakāya*, they do not describe it by reference to its *own* experience of enjoyment, but by reference to its *sharing* of the enjoyment of dharma with its retinue of disciples. Again *MSA* 9.60 and *bhāṣya* are seminal:

> svābhāviko 'tha sāṃbhogyaḥ kāyo nairmāṇiko 'paraḥ
> kāyabhedā hi buddhānām prathamastu dvayāśrayaḥ
>
> (*MSA* 9.60)

> [The varieties of embodiment of the Buddhas are: embodiment in their own essence, in communal enjoyment, and in manifestation(s) as well. But the first is the basis of the {other} two.]

> trividhaḥ kāyo buddhānām
> svābhāviko dharmakāya āśraya-parāvṛtti-lakṣaṇaḥ
> sāṃbhogiko yena parṣanmaṇḍaleṣu dharma-saṃbhogaṃ karoti
> nairmāṇiko yena nirmāṇena sattvārthaṃ karoti
>
> (*MSA* 9.60 *bhāṣya*)

> [Embodiment of the Buddhas is threefold, {being}:
> 1. in essence *(svābhāvika)*, embodiment of dharma *(dharmakāya)*, whose identity is fundamental transformation.
> 2. in communal enjoyment *(sāṃbhogika)*, that which brings enjoyment of dharma to the circles of assembly.
> 3. in manifestation *(nairmāṇika)*, manifestation(s) that work for the benefit of beings.]

Here we see *sāmbhogikakāya* defined as that which "brings enjoyment of dharma to the circles of assembly," not that which only enjoys dharma for itself. The same basic definition, involving an enjoyment of dharma that a Buddha shares mutually with his retinue of bodhisattva disciples, appears throughout the commentarial literature that followed the *MSA*.[61]

The Sanskrit term *bhoga* generally means "enjoyment." However, I have not seen previous discussions in contemporary scholarship on the semantic purpose of the prefix *saṃ-* added to *bhoga* to construct the name *sāmbhogikakāya*. Tibetan translators rendered *sāmbhogikakāya* as *longs spyod rdzogs pa'i sku*, where *longs spyod*, meant enjoyment *(bhogika)*, *sku* meant embodiment *(kāya)*, and *rdzogs pa* stood for the prefix *sam-*. In Tibetan, *rdzogs pa* means "complete," "finished,." But the Sanskrit prefix *sam-* carries the primary meaning "with" or "together with," and connotes completeness only in a derivative sense.[62] Since etymological definitions of *sāmbhogikakāya* in the literature stress its reference to the Buddhas' enjoyment of dharma specifically through the mutual sharing of it with communities of bodhisattva disciples, I would propose that the Sanskrit prefix *sam-* means "together with," "mutual," and by extension in these literary contexts: "communal." I believe the Tibetan *rdzogs pa* (meaning "complete") was a mistranslation of the Sanskrit prefix *sam-*. The term *sāmbhogikakāya* as derived in these texts, then, ought to be translated "embodiment [of Buddhahood] in communal enjoyment of dharma," or "embodiment for communal enjoyment of dharma."[63]

One way of defining *sāmbhogikakāya* that became widespread in Tibet, at least from the fourteenth century, was by reference to "five definites" *(nges pa lnga).* Bu ston, a fourteenth-century Tibetan scholar, presented them as follows:

1. Definite place. *Sāmbhogikakāya* manifests only in the pure realm known as "Akaniṣṭha." (Bu ston quotes the *Lankāvatārasūtra* to support this. Other Tibetan commentators did the same, quoting Candrakīrti's *Madhyamakāvatāra.*)

2. Definite form. Possessing the thirty-two marks and eighty signs of a *mahāpuruṣa*, a great being.

3. Definite retinue. Bu ston identifies the retinue, i.e., closest community of disciples, as bodhisattvas of the tenth *bhūmi* (the final stage prior to Buddhahood). Other commentators identify it as bodhisattvas from the first *bhūmi* up to the tenth.[64]

4. Definite type of dharma shared and enjoyed. Mahāyāna teaching alone.

5. Definite duration. Lasting eternally, or until the end of saṃsāra.[65]

This compilation of five "definite" characteristics for *sāmbhogikakāya* is unknown in the early and classical Yogācāra literature to which we have been referring. The first list of definite characteristics for the *sāmbhogikakāya* that I am aware of in Indian literature appears in Atiśa's condensed commentary on the *Abhisamayālaṃkāra,* a commentary that was written in the eleventh century (*Prajñāpāramitāpiṇḍārthapradīpa*, Pk 5201, vol. 92, fol. 106.5.4). There just four "definites" are given, "definite duration" being left out. *MSA* 9.61 and its commentaries explicitly characterize different *sāmbhogikakāyas* as differing in regard to their retinues, pure realms, names, forms, types of dharma enjoyed, and activities. Sthiramati, commenting on the different names and pure realms of *sāmbhogikakāyas*, identifies Vairocana, Amitābha, and Samantabhadra in their different pure realms as *sāmbhogikakāyas*. This, of course, contradicts the notion of "definite place" that is first in Bu ston's list above.[66]

The ascription of the thirty-two marks and eighty signs of a *mahāpuruṣa* (great being) to *sāmbhogikakāya* was probably done for the first time in the *Abhisamayālaṃkāra*'s eighth chapter. The thirty-two marks and eighty signs were not specifically attributed to the *sāmbhogikakāya* in the *MSA*, *Msg,* or *RGV* (where they were listed among the set of Buddha dharmas without attribution to a specific *kāya*, or were attributed just to *rūpakāya* in general). The *Abhisamayālaṃkāra* probably attributed the marks and signs to the *sāmbhogikakāya* as part of its overall project of matching Yogācāra *kāya*s to *Prajñāpāramitāsūtra* descriptions of Buddhahood.[67] I suspect, then, that the notion of "definite form" in Bu ston's list was passed on to Tibet through Indian commentaries on the *Abhisamayālaṃkāra*. It did not play a part in other Indian Mahāyāna textual traditions.

Because limitless manifestations of Buddhahood in Mahāyāna sūtras represented the vast unrestricted activity of a Buddha throughout the universe, our sources characteristically identified *nairmāṇikakāya* closely with the activity of Buddhahood. Although both *sāmbhogikakāya* and *nairmāṇikakāya* are manifestations of Buddhahood to share its knowledge and liberation with beings, in Yogācāra literature *nairmāṇikakāya* was more often directly identified with Buddha's activity, probably because of the tremendous range of its activities.

In the previous chapter we discussed the six-category analysis of Buddhahood in Yogācāra texts. The fourth of these categories was *karma*, the activity of Buddhahood. *Mahāyānasūtrālaṃkāra*, verse 9.58, explicitly identifies the activity *(karma)* of Buddhahood with its *nirmāṇa*s of body, speech, and mind, i.e., its diverse manifestations. These are identified in *MSA* 9.59 and 9.63 as components of the *nairmāṇikakāya*, the embodiment of Buddhahood in its limitless variety of manifestations. *MSA* 9.66 *bhāṣya* says the *kāya*s of all Buddhas are indistinguishable in basis *(āśraya)* (referring to *svābhāvikakāya*), in aspiration *(āśaya)* (referring to *sāmbhogikakāya*), and in activity *(karma)* (referring to *nairmāṇikakāya*). At *MSA* 9.74–9.75 a Buddha's gnosis of accomplishing activities *(kṛtyānuṣṭhāna-jñāna)* is uniquely identified with *nairmāṇikakāya* alone. *MSA* 11.43 *bhāṣya* explicitly identifies a Buddha's "excellence of activity" *(karma-viśeṣa)* with *nairmāṇikakāya*, while his "excellence of communal enjoyment" *(sambhoga-viśeṣa)* is identified with the *sāmbhogikakāya*. The *bhāṣya* on *Madhyāntavibhāga* 4.14, in its only mention of the three *kāya*s, specifically identifies *nairmāṇikakāya* as the activity of a Buddha. The *bhāṣya* on the *Dharmadharmatāvibhāga* identifies *nairmāṇikakāya* as the support for accomplishing a Buddha's activities for living beings. Identification of *nairmāṇikakāya* with the limitless scope of Buddhahood's activity *(karma, kriya)* is characteristic of *trikāya* literature.[68]

One further point needs to be made on the permanence of a Buddha as regards the *sāmbhogikakāya* and *nairmāṇikakāya*. The Tathāgata or *tathāgatakāya* is routinely described in Mahāyāna sūtras as permanent or eternal *(nitya)*, which gives the impression that Buddhahood as a whole is permanent in some sense. Therefore, Yogācāra treatises have also tried to show how permanence can be ascribed to Buddhahood as a whole, in spite of the fact that it possesses both conditioned (impermanent) and unconditioned (permanent) aspects. Formulas to address this appear in the *Mahāyānasūtrālaṃkāra*, the *Mahāyānasaṃgraha,* and their commentaries. According to the *MSA* and its commentaries, *dharmakāya (= svābhāvikakāya)* is permanent by its very nature *(svabhāvena nityatvam)*. *Sāmbhogikakāya* and *nairmāṇikakāya* are designated "permanent" in a secondary sense, the former because of its uninterrupted communal enjoyment of the dharma, the latter because manifestations of Buddhahood appear again and again without cease to communicate with beings.[69] The *Msg* and its commentaries echo the *MSA*, and add the further observation that *sāmbhogikakāya* and *nairmāṇikakāya* are designated "permanent" in a derivative sense since *dharmakāya*, which is intrinsically permanent, is their foundation.[70]

6

The *Abhisamayālaṃkāra* and its Eighth Chapter on Buddhahood

There are many *Prajñāpāramitā* sūtras of varying lengths and historical periods of composition. Edward Conze identified three of the most important of these—the *Prajñāpāramitā* sūtras in 18,000, 25,000, and 100,000 verses—as three versions of one basic sūtra, which he referred to as the *Large Prajñāpāramitā*.[1] These three versions differ mainly in the extent to which they repeat the same *PP* formulas regarding the emptiness of all dharmas. The *Abhisamayālaṃkāra-prajñāpāramitā-upadeśa-śāstra* (abbreviated *AA*) is a condensed, versified commentary on the *Large Prajñāpāramitā Sūtra*. It was most probably composed as a commentary on the *Large Prajñāpāramitā Sūtra* in its 25,000-verse version, the *Pañcaviṃśati-sāhasrikā-prajñāpāramitā-sūtra* (evidence for this will be presented in the next chapter).

In chapter 3 we saw that the *Prajñāpāramitā* sūtras present lists of "all dharmas," *sarva-dharmāḥ*, the mental and physical constituents thought to comprise the phenomenological universes of living beings, as earlier elaborated in Abhidharma literature. Unlike Sārvāstivāda Abhidharma, which took the dharmas (at least on their atomic or momentary level) as ultimate reals, the *Prajñāpāramitā* sūtras explicitly negate the ultimacy of all dharmas, declaring them to be empty *(śūnya)* of self-existence *(svabhāva)*. The *Prajñāpāramitā*'s analysis leading to liberating wisdom *(prajñā)* does not find dharmas. It finds only their emptiness of self-existence *(svabhāva-śūnyatā)*, the direct, unmediated realization of which is known as *prajñāpāramitā*, the perfection of wisdom. The explicit theme of the *Prajñāpāramitā* sūtras, then, is the emptiness of all phenomena *(dharma śūnyatā)* and the nondual realization of that emptiness *(prajñāpāramitā)*. It is this theme which was explicated in detail in commentaries by Nāgārjuna, a father of Mahāyāna Buddhism and founder of the Mādhyamika school.

To declare all phenomena "empty," however, required the delineation of all the phenomena that were understood to be empty. Therefore, in order to teach their theme of universal emptiness, *Prajñāpāramitā* sūtras delineated all dharmas that comprise both the entire physical universe and all aspects of the minds of beings. These included not only the mental constituents of ordinary beings, but also the constituents of yogic realization, the components of the path *(mārga)* gradually accomplished by Buddhist practitioners in their progress to enlightenment. Thus, in order to teach emptiness as their explicit message, *Prajñāpāramitā* sūtras also taught the various Buddhist paths, practices, and stages of realization as their implicit message.

It is this latter, implicit message of the *Prajñāpāramitā* sūtras that the *Abhisamayālaṃkāra* explained, doing so in an extremely terse, versified form. The *Abhisamayālaṃkāra* served as a table of contents for the entire *Large Prajñāpāramitā Sūtra*, as a condensed summary of all the practices, paths and stages of realization to Buddhahood understood to be implicit in that sūtra. Each portion of the *Large Prajñāpāramitā Sūtra* was interpreted as a specific teaching on one of the paths and stages to enlightenment. The *Abhisamayālaṃkāra* and its corpus of commentaries, therefore, provide some of the most detailed analyses of pre-Mahāyāna and Mahāyāna yogic practices in Indian Buddhist literature. This corpus became a central resource for scholastic understanding of Buddhist practice in relation to systematic doctrine in late Indian and Tibetan Buddhism.

Thus, the *Abhisamayālaṃkāra* and its commentaries have continuously dominated exegesis in India and Tibet on the implicit meaning of the *PP* sūtras, i.e., the detailed contents of practice and realization, for the past fifteen hundred years.[2] And in Tibetan centers of scholastic learning even up to the present time they remain one of the primary bases for study of Mahāyāna practice, the paths and stages of realization *(abhisamaya)*. As fundamental as the *Abhisamayālaṃkāra* became to late Indian and Tibetan Buddhism, it was never studied in China. It is likely that some of the differences between Sino-Japanese Buddhism, on the one hand, and Indo-Tibetan Buddhism, on the other, stem in part from that fact.[3]

Although the *Abhisamayālaṃkāra* purports to be a commentary on the *Large Prajñāpāramitā Sūtra*, and therefore expresses the content of that sūtra, it also employs schemata of the spiritual path and its ultimate result (Buddhahood) that were not found in the *Prajñāpāramitā* sūtras. Some of these schemata developed in Yogācāra circles and were superimposed onto the textual material of the *PP* sūtras by the author of the *AA*.[4] This is especially true of *AA* chapter 8, which centers on Buddhahood, and which employs specific terms for Buddhahood with which we are now familiar: *svābhāvikakāya*, *sāmbhogikakāya*, and *nairmāṇikakāya*; terms not found in the *PP* sūtras but developed, as we have seen, in texts associated with the Yogācāra tradition.

As previously mentioned, the *Abhisamayālaṃkāra*, like other texts discussed in the previous two chapters (the *Mahāyānasūtrālaṃkāra*, *Dharmadharmatāvibhāga*,

Madhyāntavibhāga, and *Ratnagotravibhāga*), has been associated in Indo-Tibetan traditions with Maitreya.[5] Many of the *AA*'s ideas, and a number of its Sanskrit verses, are very close to those in the other "Maitreya" texts. There is a substratum of concepts shared by all these texts. But whereas the other texts traditionally associated with Maitreya are synoptic commentaries, summarizing and explicating the content of many different Mahāyāna sūtras in the form of independent commentary, the *AA* was based section by section upon corresponding sections of the *Large Prajñāpāramitā Sūtra*. Therefore, where it employs Yogācāra terminology foreign to the *Large PP Sūtra* itself, it always relates that terminology directly to *PP* textual material. Unlike the *MSA*, *Msg,* or *DDV* (which we often quoted in the previous two chapters), the *AA* was not an independent commentary on Mahāyāna practice and philosophy, but a commentary always directed to and anchored in *PP* sūtra textual material. For this reason, the *AA* can not be properly understood unless read in close consultation with the corresponding sections of the *Large Prajñāpāramitā Sūtra*. At the same time, it must be read in relation to the textual traditions of its time, from which it draws terminology not in the *Large Prajñāpāramitā Sūtra*. This is especially important with regard to its eighth chapter, which is structured through Yogācāra terminology.

From the perspective of modern scholarship, the date and authorship of the *Abhisamayālaṃkāra* are still unknown. Haribhadra (ca. 770–810 C.E.), in his *Abhisamayālaṃkāra Āloka* and *Sphuṭārthā*, ascribed the *AA*'s authorship to Maitreya.[6] But the late eighth century is a late time to ascribe such authorship (Maitreya, Asanga's teacher, allegedly having lived between the third and fourth centuries C.E.) and the attribution may well have been used just as a means to ascribe greater authority to the text. Haribhadra also claimed that Asanga (ca. fourth century C.E.) and Vasubandhu (ca. fourth to fifth century C.E.) wrote commentaries on the *AA*.[7] If this is true, the *AA* was composed by the fourth century C.E. It is hard to imagine its having been composed earlier than that, since as mentioned above, it employs terminology specific to Yogācāra textual traditions that developed from the third to fourth centuries C.E. (traditions that produced the *MSA*, *Msg*, and other works). The first *AA* commentary extant in any language is that of Ārya Vimuktisena (extant in Sanskrit and Tibetan, although only the first chapter of the Sanskrit has been published).[8] Ārya Vimuktisena has been dated in modern scholarship to the early sixth century C.E. If his was the *AA*'s first commentary, it would put the *AA*'s terminus ad quem in the fifth century or early sixth century. To be safe, then, we will assume here that the *AA* was composed sometime between the fourth century and the early sixth century C.E.[9]

Among the texts traditionally associated with Maitreya, the *Abhisamayālaṃkāra* is unique in being an explicit commentary on the *PP* sūtras, whose thought is a principal basis of the Mādhyamika school. This may be the reason that most of the Indian commentaries on the *AA* that have come down to us (a few in Sanskrit manuscript, most in Tibetan translation in the Tibetan canon) are ascribed by Tibetan doxographers to Mādhyamikas, who are usually assigned to the "Yogācāra-Madhyamaka" school of Indo-Tibetan Buddhism. A total of twenty-one Indian commentaries on the *AA* have been preserved in the Tibetan canon.[10]

Ārya Vimuktisena's commentary aligned each verse of the *AA* with the section of the 25,000-verse *Prajñāpāramitā* sūtra that he took to correspond to it. Because the focus of this book is the eighth chapter of the *Abhisamayālaṃkāra,* a chapter that concerns Buddhahood, Ārya Vimuktisena's commentary is especially important, because his interpretation of that chapter as a teaching of three Buddha *kāya*s appears to have been normative for several centuries in India and was followed by several influential commentators in India and Tibet. Of special note among these commentators were Bhadanta Vimuktisena, Ratnākaraśānti, and Abhayākaragupta in India, and the Sa skya scholar Go ram pa bsod nams seng ge and his followers in Tibet.

The other Indian commentator of special importance to us is Haribhadra, who presented a new interpretation of the Abhisamayālaṃkāra's eighth chapter, claiming that it taught four Buddha *kāyas*. This was the first time in the extant literature (as far as I know) that any scholar had claimed that a nontantric Buddhist text explicitly taught four Buddha *kāya*s. Following Haribhadra in this view were Prajñākaramati, Kumāraśrībhadra, and Buddhaśrījñāna in India, and later in Tibet, Tsong kha pa and the entire scholastic tradition of the dGe lugs pa school that he founded.[11] Haribhadra became the most influential Indian interpreter of *AA* doctrine to Tibetans, with virtually every major *AA* commentator in medieval Tibet writing a subcommentary on his *Sphuṭārthā* (even those like Go ram pa who did not agree with all of Haribhadra's views still wrote subcommentaries on his work).

In sum, then, interpretations of the *AA*'s eighth chapter in late Indian and Tibetan Buddhism tended to follow either Ārya Vimuktisena's or Haribhadra's view. And in Tibet, leading scholars of the Sa skya school (those who followed Go ram pa bsod nams seng ge) chose Ārya Vimuktisena's interpretation, while all commentators of the dGe lugs pa sect that I am aware of, following Tsong kha pa's lead, chose Haribhadra's interpretation. This disagreement over *AA* 8 continues to the present day among scholars of the Sa skya and dGe lugs schools.

The Abhisamayālaṃkāra contains eight chapters of subject matter *(aṣṭa-padārthāḥ)* with a brief synopsis of them as its ninth chapter. The subjects of the eight substantive chapters are the eight fundamental realizations *(abhisamayāḥ, abhisambodhāḥ).*

The subjects of the first three chapters of the *Abhisamayālaṃkāra* are, respectively, the three knowledges *(jñātāḥ)* conforming to the capacities of three types of *ārya* (an *ārya* being a person who has had direct realization of emptiness on the path of direct seeing, *darśana mārga*). *Sarvākāra-jñatā* (total omniscience, the realization of a Buddha) is the subject matter of *AA* 1; *mārga-jñatā* (knowledge of the paths, the realization of *ārya* bodhisattvas) is the subject matter of *AA* 2; and *sarva-jñatā* (all-knowledge, the realization conforming to the insight of a *śrāvaka* or *pratyekabuddha ārya*) is the subject matter of *AA* chapter 3. These three knowledges are the aims of yogic practice (*viṣaya*, *AA* 9.2).

The subjects of the next four chapters of the *Abhisamayālaṃkāra* are, respectively, the four yogic practices (*prayogāḥ*, *AA* 9.2) that take those three knowledges as their aim. *Sarvākāra-abhisaṃbodha* (full realization of all aspects) is the subject matter of *AA* 4; *mūrdha-abhisamaya* (realization at its summit) is the subject matter of *AA* 5; *anupūrva-abhisamaya* (progressive realization) is the subject matter of *AA* 6; and *ekakṣaṇa-abhisamaya* (realization in a single moment) is the subject matter of *AA* 7.

The subject of the eighth chapter of the *Abhisamayālaṃkāra* is the final result of the Mahāyāna path (*phalaṃ*, *AA* 9.2), the culmination of all the practices described in the prior chapters: *dharmakāya-abhisaṃbodha* (realization of *dharmakāya*, Buddhahood).

After two introductory verses, the *Abhisamayālaṃkāra* presents a versified table of contents (consisting of verses 1.3 through 1.17) that summarizes its entire content with reference to these eight basic subjects *(aṣṭau padārthāḥ;* Tib. *dngos po brgyad)* and the seventy topics they encompass *(artha saptatiḥ*, Tib. *don bdun cu).*[12] Ārya Vimuktisena, the earliest commentator, identifies these fifteen verses as "the setting forth of the subject matter of the corpus" (Skt., *padārtha śarīra vyavasthānam;* Tib., *dngos po lus rnam bzhag*), i.e., the table of contents for the *Abhisamayālaṃkāra* as a whole.[13] The first two of these fifteen verses, verses 1.3–1.4, present the eight fundamental subjects that comprise the *AA*'s eight substantive chapters:

> prajñāpāramitāṣṭābhiḥ padārthaiḥ samudīritā
> sarvākārajñatā mārgajñatā sarvajñatā tataḥ
>
> (*AA* 1.3)
>
> sarvākārābhisambodho mūrdhaprāpto 'nupūrvikaḥ
> ekakṣaṇābhisambodho dharmakāyaś ca te'ṣṭadhā
>
> (*AA* 1.4)
>
> [The perfection of wisdom *(prajñāpāramitā)* is proclaimed through eight subjects, these eight being: total omniscience, knowledge of the paths, and then all-knowledge, the full realization of all aspects, the [realization] that has attained the summit, the progressive [realization], the realization in a single moment, and the embodiment of dharma *(dharmakāya).*][14]

In the commentaries, these eight subjects serve as titles for the *Abhisamayālaṃkāra*'s eight substantive chapters. Note that the subject and title of the eighth chapter is identified simply as *dharmakāya* (embodiment of dharma). All commentators understood this term, as employed in this particular verse, to refer to Buddhahood as a whole, the ultimate attainment achieved from complete accomplishment of all paths and practices described in the *AA*'s earlier chapters. Tibetan commentators therefore refer to the *AA's* eighth chapter as "Resultant *Dharmakāya*" ("'bras bu chos sku," probably basing themselves on *AA* 9.2, which uses the expression *dharmakāya-phalaṃ* with this meaning).[15]

In the body of the *Abhisamayālaṃkāra*, each of the eight subjects above is explained by reference to a number of topics *(artha;* Tib. *don).*[16] The first subject, *sarvākāra-jñatā* (total omniscience), is explained by reference to ten topics; the second subject, *mārga-jñatā* (knowledge of the paths), is explained by reference to eleven topics; the third subject, *sarva-jñatā* (all-knowledge), by reference to nine topics; the fourth subject, *sarvākāra-abhisambodha* (full realization of all aspects), by reference to eleven topics; the fifth subject, *mūrdha-abhisamaya* (realization at its summit), by reference to eight topics; the sixth subject, *anupūrva-abhisamaya* (progressive realization), by reference to thirteen topics; the seventh subject, *ekakṣaṇa-abhisamaya* (realization in a single moment), by reference to four topics; and the eighth and final subject, *dharmakāya* (embodiment of dharma in its ultimate realization), by reference to four topics. The explanation of all eight subjects, then, involves a total of seventy topics *(artha saptatiḥ;* Tib., *don bdun cu)* that comprise the eight substantive chapters of the *AA*.

The *Abhisamayālaṃkāra*'s table of contents continues with verses 1.5–1.17, which again name each of the eight substantive chapters and list in order (often in abbreviated form) the topics contained in each of them. As our focus is the *AA*'s eighth chapter on Buddhahood, *AA* v. 1.17 is of particular importance, being the final verse of the *AA*'s table of contents, which serves as the table of contents specifically for the *AA*'s eighth chapter:

> svābhāvikaḥ sasāmbhogo nairmāṇiko 'paras tathā
> dharmakāyaḥ sakāritraś caturdhā samudīritaḥ[17]
>
> (*AA* 1.17)

We will not attempt a translation of this verse yet, as it stands at the very heart of the disagreement by later commentators over the meaning of *AA* chapter 8. Our own analysis and translation of this controversial verse will be made in chapter 8, section 2, of this book below. The terms *caturdhā samudīritaḥ* that appear in it mean "proclaimed to be fourfold," i.e., that the chapter is explained through four topics. But the commentators disagreed over what the four topics were.

Ārya Vimuktisena's commentary says the verse teaches three Buddha *kāyas*, represented by the terms *svābhāvikaḥ*, *sasāmbhogo*, and *nairmāṇiko*. These are the first three topics of the chapter. The term *dharmakāya,* he says, designates the subject and the title of the chapter, Buddhahood as a whole, *dharmakāya* as the total result of the path (*dharmakāya-phalaṃ*, Pk 5185, fol. 98-5-1). *Sakāritraḥ* refers to the *nairmāṇikakāya*'s activity, which he identifies as the chapter's fourth topic. According to Ārya Vimuktisena, then, the four topics of the eighth chapter are the three Buddha *kāya*s and the activity of enlightenment *(kāritraḥ, karma)* associated with *nairmāṇikakāya*.[18]

Over two centuries later, Haribhadra read the verse quite differently. His commentaries say the term *dharmakāya* designates a fourth *kāya*, a *kāya* consisting of a Buddha's gnosis *(jñānātmaka dharmakāyaḥ)*. He therefore claims that *AA* chapter 8 is describing Buddhahood through four *kāyas (svābhāvikakāya, [jñānā] dharmakāya, sāmbhogikakāya,* and *nairmāṇikakāya)*, and that these four *kāya*s comprise the four topics of that chapter (a Buddha's activity, *kāritraḥ*, being an adjunct quality of the *[jñāna] dharmakāya*).[19]

Having glanced at *AA 1.17*, the table of contents for *AA* chapter 8, we now turn to the verses of the chapter itself. *AA* chapter 8, verse 1, describes a Buddha's *svābhāvikakāya* (embodiment of a Buddha in his own nature):

> sarvākārāṃ viśuddhiṃ ye dharmāḥ prāptā nirāsravāḥ
> svābhāviko muneḥ kāyas teṣāṃ prakṛti-lakṣaṇaḥ
>
> (*AA* 8.1)

> [The embodiment of the Sage in his essence: Its identity is the primordial nature of the undefiled dharmas that are obtained in utter purity.][20]

Both Ārya Vimuktisena's and Haribhadra's commentaries agree that this verse teaches the first *kāya* of a Buddha, *svābhāvikakāya*, the embodiment of a Buddha in his essence, understood as the primordial nature *(prakṛti)* of the undefiled dharmas (a Buddha's pure mental qualities). They did not agree precisely on what "primordial nature" *(prakṛti)* refers to. This will be discussed in chapters 9 and 10 of this book.

Verses 8.2 through 8.6 list these undefiled dharmas, divided into twenty-one types, and then relate them to the word *dharmakāya*, embodiment of dharma:

> bodhipakṣāpramāṇāni vimokṣā anupūrvaśaḥ
> navātmikā samāpattiḥ kṛtsnaṃ daśavidhātmakam
>
> (*AA* 8.2)

> abhibhvāyatanāny aṣṭa prakārāṇi prabhedataḥ
> araṇā praṇidhijñānam abhijñāḥ pratisamvidaḥ
>
> (*AA* 8.3)

> sarvākārāś catasro 'tha śuddhayo vaśitā daśa
> balāni daśa catvāri vaiśāradyāny arakṣaṇam
>
> (*AA* 8.4)

trividhaṃ smṛtyupasthānaṃ tridhāsaṃmoṣa-dharmatā
vasanāyāḥ samudghāto mahatī karuṇā jane

(*AA* 8.5)

āveṇikā muner eva dharmā ye 'ṣṭadaśeritāḥ
sarvākārajñatā ceti dharmakāyo 'bhidhīyate

(*AA* 8.6)

["The factors that foster enlightenment, the measureless thoughts, the liberations, the nine meditative attainments, the ten meditative totalities, the bases of overpowering divided into eight kinds, the meditative power freeing from passions, the gnosis resulting from resolve, the supernatural knowledges, the analytical knowledges, the four total purities, the ten sovereignties, the ten powers, the four forms of fearlessness, the three ways in which [a Buddha] has nothing to hide, the threefold mindful equanimity, the nature of never forgetting, the complete destruction of [negative] propensities, the great compassion for living beings, the qualities unique to the Sage that are proclaimed as eighteen, and total omniscience": thus is *dharmakāya* denominated.][21]

Ārya Vimuktisena understood *AA* 8's first six verses to teach one *kāya* of a Buddha, which is called *svābhāvikakāya* (embodiment of the Sage in his essence) in verse 1, and *dharmakāya* (embodiment of dharma) in verse 6. For him the two terms are synonyms.[22] Haribhadra, arguing that Ārya Vimuktisena had been mistaken in his understanding of these two key terms, reinterpreted the verses. According to Haribhadra, *svābhāvikakāya* of verse 1 and *dharmakāya* of verse 6 are *not* synonyms. They refer to two different aspects of Buddhahood identified in the text as two different *kāyas*. *Svābhāvikakāya* in verse 1, Haribhadra claimed, refers to the ultimate nature of the undefiled dharmas, their *dharmatā* or *śūnyatā*. The term *dharmakāya* in verse 6, he wrote, refers to a Buddha's undefiled dharmas, the pure qualities of his mind, his gnoses as conventional phenomena ("body of pure dharmas"). The latter term, therefore, is to be understood as "*dharmakāya* consisting of gnosis" *(jñānātmaka dharmakāya)*. For Haribhadra, the emptiness of a Buddha's mind (its ultimate nature, *paramārtha*) and the gnosis itself (as a conventional, conditioned phenomenon, *saṃvṛti*) were specifically designated in the *AA* by two terms specifying two distinct *kāyas*: *svābhāvikakāya* (of verse 1) and *(jñānātmaka) dharmakāya* (of verse 6) respectively.[23] Of course, Ārya Vimuktisena's and Haribhadra's interpretations of *AA* 8 vv. 1–6 are closely related to their interpretations of *AA* 1.17, the table of contents for the *AA*'s eighth chapter that I left untranslated above.

The *AA*'s eighth chapter continues with two verses that show the superiority of the Buddha's gnosis over that of *śrāvakas* (accomplished disciples of the Buddha on non-Mahāyāna paths) and other lesser saints:

śrāvakasyāraṇā dṛṣṭer nṛkleśaparihāritā
tatkleśasrota-ucchittyai grāmādiṣu jināraṇā

(*AA* 8.7)

anābhogam anāsaṇgam avyāghātaṃ sadā sthitaṃ
sarvapraśnāpanud bauddhaṃ praṇidhijñānam iṣyate

(*AA* 8.8)

[A disciple's meditative power freeing from passions is the avoidance of men's passions {arising} from seeing {that disciple}. The Victor's {Buddha's} meditative power freeing from passions is for cutting off the stream of their passions in towns, etc. It is accepted that the Buddha gnosis {resulting from} resolve is automatic, unattached, unobstructed, forever operative, and answers all questions.][24]

The *araṇā samādhi* (meditative power freeing from passions, literally the "non-passion samādhi") and *praṇidhi-jñāna* (gnosis resulting from resolve) of these verses, like most of the other undefiled dharmas listed in *AA* verses 8.2–8.6, are discussed in Abhidharma literature, where they are ascribed not only to Buddhas but also to saints of lesser attainment: *śrāvakas*, *pratyekabuddhas*, etc.[25] The *AA*'s author appears to have selected these two from among the twenty-one undefiled dharmas of verses 8.2–8.6 as examples to demonstrate how *all* of a Buddha's dharmas (gnoses and mental qualities) are superior to those of all other beings, including those dharmas that bear the same names as those ascribed in earlier Abhidharma literature to lesser saints.[26]

The commentaries on *AA* 8.7 explain that a *śrāvaka*'s meditative power freeing from passions *(araṇā)* is a meditative concentration through which the *śrāvaka* knows how to avoid coming into contact with others whose passions would be aroused by seeing him. The yogic quality of the same name ascribed to a Buddha is said to be far superior. A Buddha avoids contact with no one. He freely enters crowded and populous areas such as towns, because, by the force of his yogic power, contact with him actually stops passions from arising in whomever he approaches.

The commentaries on *AA* 8.8 say that a Buddha's gnosis is distinguished from that of any lesser being by the five qualities listed in the verse. In Abhidharma texts, all the various types of Buddhist yogi are said to cultivate what is referred to as *praṇidhi-jñāna* (gnosis resulting from resolve). It involves first a resolve to know something, and then the accomplishment of the capacity to know that thing through yogic practice. A bodhisattva's resolve for knowledge, however, is unique. It is a resolve to know everything necessary to assist all living beings to liberation. According to the *AA* commentaries, such a resolve results in the unique properties of a Buddha's gnosis: its spontaneity, freedom from personal concern, knowledge of all things in all times, uninterrupted operation to the end of saṃsāra, and ability to help beings according to each one's need. The gnosis of the same name ascribed to *śrāvaka*s and other lesser yogis is said to lack those five properties.[27]

These verses have close parallels in Yogācāra texts. *Abhisamayālaṃkāra* verse 8.8, for example, is almost identical to *Mahāyānasaṃgraha* 10.13 (which is a quotation of *Mahāyānasūtrālaṃkāra* verse 21.46), and *Abhisamayālaṃkāra* verse 8.7 is very close to *Mahāyānasaṃgraha* 10.12 (= *Mahāyānasūtrālaṃkāra* 21.45). In fact, most of the verses comprising *AA* 8 closely parallel the concepts and expressions of the *MSA, Msg*, and *RGV*.

We continue with *AA* verses 8.9 and 8.10:

> paripākaṃ gate hetau yasyayasya yadāyadā
> hitaṃ bhavati kartavyaṃ prathate tasyatasya saḥ
>
> (*AA* 8.9)
>
> varṣaty api hi parjanye naivābījaṃ parohati
> samutpāde 'pi buddhānāṃ nābhavyo bhadram aśnute
>
> (*AA* 8.10)
>
> [When the cause has reached fruition, whenever and for whomever there is benefit to be accomplished, then and there he appears. But even when the god of rain pours down rain, an infertile seed does not sprout. So even when Buddhas arise, one who is unfit does not obtain the blessing.][28]

AA verse 8.8 had given the impression that a Buddha's gnosis, and therefore his capacity to manifest and help beings, was limitless and always operative. It is natural to wonder, then, why more suffering persons do not have some sort of recognizable, direct contact with a Buddha. Verses 8.9 and 8.10 address this by reference to the Buddhist worldview framed by karmic causality. According to the doctrine of karma, whatever a person experiences is utterly conditioned by his own past mental, verbal, and physical actions. Although a Buddha's gnosis is universally pervasive (*AA* 8.8) and able to manifest to teach a being anywhere at any time, each individual can perceive a Buddha or his teaching only in accord with his or her own karma. In other words, the Buddhas per se are always universally accessible. But whether a particular person has contact with a Buddha's manifestation is entirely dependent on the purity of that individual's own mind. Even though Buddhas manifest without restriction in space or time, an individual whose mind is unprepared (i.e., lacks enough virtue) is incapable of coming into contact with such a manifestation, much as a burnt or rotten seed cannot sprout no matter how much it may rain.[29]

AA verse 8.11 concerns the pervasiveness *(vyāpitvaṃ)* and permanence *(nityatā)* that the Mahāyāna sūtras ascribe to Buddhahood:[30]

iti kāritra vaipulyād buddho vyāpī nirucyate
akṣayatvāc ca tasyaiva nitya ity api kathyate

(*AA* 8.11)

[Because of such extensiveness of activity, Buddha is declared to be pervasive. And because of his inexhaustibility, he is called "permanent."][31]

Because a Buddha's manifest activity is universal in the sense explained in the previous two verses, he is often declared "pervasive" in the Mahāyāna texts.[32] And because a Buddha's gnosis, as mentioned in verse 8.8, is "forever operative," forever and "inexhaustibly" engaged in the world to help beings through such activity, he is declared "permanent" or "eternal" *(nitya)*. We may note that this way of interpreting a Buddha's permanence applies equally to all of the *kāya*s discussed in chapters 4 and 5 of this book, since none of the *kāya*s cease functioning, appearing, or reappearing until the end of saṃsāra. It conforms to the descriptions of a Buddha's permanence, understood as applicable to all of Buddhahood, as given in Yogācāra texts mentioned in chapter 5, section 5 above.[33]

Ārya Vimuktisena interprets all the preceding verses of *AA* 8, verses 8.1 through 8.11, as concerning *svābhāvikakāya*.[34] Haribhadra says only the first verse concerns *svābhāvikakāya,* and verses 8.2 through 8.11 concern what he identified as a second *kāya:* the *dharmakāya* consisting of gnosis *(jñānātmaka-dharmakāya)*.[35] All commentators agree, however, that the next verse, *AA* verse 8.12, describes the *sāmbhogikakāya* (embodiment of the Buddha in his communal enjoyment).

dvātriṃśallakṣaṇāśītivyañjanātmā muner ayam
sāmbhogiko mataḥ kāyo mahāyānopabhogataḥ

(*AA* 8.12)

[This form of the Sage with thirty-two marks and eighty signs is to be understood as his embodiment in communal enjoyment *(sāmbhogikakāya)*, from its enjoyment of the great vehicle *(mahāyāna)*.][36]

This verse refers to the thirty-two marks and eighty signs characteristic of a great being *(mahāpuruṣa)* in Indian legend, exalted physical characteristics that came to be associated with Śākyamuni Buddha as the physical manifestation of his long prior practice of virtue. Here the *Abhisamayālaṃkāra* specifically assigns these marks and signs to the glorious Buddha form that the *Mahāyānasūtrālaṃkāra*, *Mahāyānasaṃgraha*, and their commentaries referred to as *sāmbhogikakāya*.

The thirty-two marks and eighty signs are discussed in detail in the various versions of the *Large Prajñāpāramitā Sūtra*.[37] As noted in chapter 3 above, *PP* sūtras knew only the *kāya* categories *rūpakāya* (a Buddha's physical forms) and *dharmakāya* (embodiment of *dharma[tā]*, a Buddha's nondual realization of the real nature of things). Śākyamuni Buddha as the central character and teacher of those sūtras was described as a glorious physical presence possessed of those wonderful marks and signs. That physical presence was designated *rūpakāya* (physical form or embodiment of Buddhahood in form). Further specification of types of *rūpakāya* as *sāmbhogikakāya* or *nairmāṇikakāya* was a Yogācāra development not found in the *Prajñāpāramitā* sūtras themselves.

Prior to the *Abhisamayālaṃkāra*, Yogācāra texts teaching *sāmbhogikakāya* (the *MSA*, *Msg*, etc.) did not specifically identify the thirty-two marks and eighty signs with *sāmbhogikakāya*, and certainly did not define that *kāya* in terms of those marks and signs. Like the *Prajñāpāramitā* sūtras, Yogācāra traditions ascribed the marks and signs to *rūpakāya* in general, meaning that they were present equally on *nairmāṇikakāya*, at least in certain forms (e.g., Śākyamuni) and on *sāmbhogikakāya*. The *AA*'s eighth chapter may represent the first time in Indian Mahāyāna Buddhist literature that the *sāmbhogikakāya* (in contradistinction to *nairmāṇikakāya*) was singled out as the possessor of the marks and signs. It is also the only place in this historical stage of the literature that the primary definition of *sāmbhogikakāya* is made by reference to the marks and signs. This provides a good indication of what the author of the *AA* viewed as his primary task in composing his eighth chapter: to match Yogācāra concepts of Buddhahood (e.g., *sāmbhogikakāya*) with the expressions of Buddhahood that he found in the *Large Prajñāpāramitā Sūtra* (e.g., the list of the marks and signs).

Verses 8.13–8.32 of the *Abhisamayālaṃkāra* can be summarized as follows: Verses 8.13 through 8.17 simply list the thirty-two marks of the *mahāpuruṣa* that were ascribed to the *sāmbhogikakāya* in verse 8.12—marks of wheels on his hands and feet, an *uṣṇiṣa* (crown protuberance), firm feet like a tortoise, webbing between the fingers and toes, a heavenly voice, and so forth. This replicates the list of the thirty-two marks provided in the *Large Prajñāpāramitā Sūtra.*[38] Verses 8.18 through 8.20 then provide a partial list of the virtuous bodhisattva practices on the path to Buddhahood that karmically produce the thirty-two marks upon attainment of Buddhahood. This is also drawn from the *Large Prajñāpāramitā Sūtra*, particularly the version in 25,000 verses, which lists the virtuous practices that cause each of the thirty-two marks, practices such as proper reliance upon spiritual mentors, proper maintenance of vows, introducing others to the teaching, and giving gifts.[39] Verses 8.21 through 8.32 then list the eighty signs ascribed to the *sāmbhogikakāya* in verse 8.12.

Because *Abhisamayālaṃkāra* verses 8.13–8.32 concern the specifics of the marks and signs beyond what is of importance to this book, I refer the reader to the Sanskrit text and Edward Conze's translation of those verses.[40] We will focus on verses of particular relevance to our concerns: the fundamental understandings of multiple Buddha *kāya*s in the *AA* corpus.

We continue then with *AA* verses 8.33 through 8.40, which concern the *nairmāṇikakāya* and karma (or *kāritra*, activity) of Buddhahood. Verse 8.40, it should be noted, is the final verse of the *AA*'s eighth chapter:

karoti yena citrāṇi hitāni jagataḥ samaṃ
ā bhavāt so 'nupacchinnaḥ kāyo nairmāṇiko muneḥ
(*AA* 8.33)

tathā karmāpy anucchinnam asyā saṃsāram iṣyate
(*AA* 8.34a)
gatīnāṃ śamanaṃ karma saṃgrahe ca caturvidhe
(*AA* 8.34b)

niveśanaṃ sasaṃkleśe vyavadānāvabodhane
sattvānām arthayāthātmye ṣaṭsu pāramitāsu ca
(*AA* 8.35)

buddhamārge prakṛtyaiva śūnyatāyāṃ dvayakṣaye
saṃkete 'nupalambhe ca paripāke ca dehināṃ
(*AA* 8.36)

bodhisattvasya mārge 'bhiniveśasya nivāraṇe
bodhiprāptau jinakṣetraviśuddhau niyatiṃ prati
(*AA* 8.37)

aprameye ca sattvārthe buddhasevādike guṇe
bodher aṅgeṣv anāśe ca karmaṇāṃ satyadarśane
(*AA* 8.38)

viparyāsaprahāṇe ca tadavastukatānaye
vyavadāne sasambhāre saṃskṛtāsaṃskṛte prati
(*AA* 8.39)

vyatibhedāparijñāne nirvāṇe ca niveśanaṃ
(*AA* 8.40a)
dharmakāyasya karmedam saptaviṃśatidhā matam
(*AA* 8.40b)

[The embodiment of the Sage in his manifestation(s) *(nairmāṇikakāya)* is that through which he impartially carries out diverse benefits for the world. It is uninterrupted for as long as the existence {of the world}. (*AA* 8.33)

> Likewise, it is agreed, its activity *(karma)* is uninterrupted for as long as cyclic existence lasts: (*AA* 8.34a)
>
> activity *(karma)* that pacifies the states of rebirth, that establishes {beings} in the fourfold means of collecting {disciples}, (*AA* 8.34b)
>
> that establishes *(niveśanaṃ)* them in the comprehension of affliction and purification, in the proper nature of the welfare of beings, and in the six perfections, (*AA* 8.35)
>
> that establishes them in the Buddha path, in emptiness with respect to the primordial nature, in nonduality, in conventional symbolization *(saṃkete)*, in nonperception, and in the maturing of embodied beings, (*AA* 8.36)
>
> that establishes them in the bodhisattva path, in preventing adherence {to things}, in the attainment of enlightenment *(bodhi)*, in the purity of a Buddha's realm, in definite destiny, (*AA* 8.37)
>
> that establishes them in the welfare of limitless beings, in the excellence of attending upon and devoting oneself to the Buddhas, in the limbs of enlightenment, in the nonwastefulness of deeds *(karma)*, and in the vision of the truths, (*AA* 8.38)
>
> that establishes them in the elimination of false views, in the method of {ascertaining} the baselessness of those {views}, in purification and its accompanying accumulation, in the knowledge of nondistinction between conditioned and unconditioned, and that establishes them {finally} in nirvāṇa. (*AA* 8.39–8.40a)
>
> This is regarded as the twenty-seven-fold activity of the embodiment of dharma *(dharmakāya)*. (*AA* 8.40b)][41]

Ārya Vimuktisena's commentary interprets these verses straightforwardly as follows. First, he reads verse 8.33 as conjoined in meaning to verse 8.34a (the first half of 8.34):

> The embodiment of the Sage in his manifestation(s) *(nairmāṇikakāya)* is that with which he impartially carries out diverse benefits for the world. It is uninterrupted for as long as the existence [of the world]. (*AA* 8.33)
>
> Likewise, it is agreed, its activity is uninterrupted for as long as cyclic existence lasts. . . . *(AA* 8.34a)

He therefore understands the phrase "its activity" *(karma . . . asya)* in 8.34a to refer to the activity of the *nairmāṇikakāya*, the embodiment of the Sage in his manifestations. Verses 8.34b through 8.40a name the twenty-seven types of activity that the *AA* ascribes to Buddhahood. According to the author of the *AA*, these are the active means through which a Buddha works for the welfare of beings, ultimately establishing them in enlightenment itself. Because Ārya Vimuktisena reads verses 33 and 34a together, he understands all the activities to which they refer to be *nairmāṇikakāya*'s. But he also takes note of the fact that this entire section of *AA* 8, from verse 8.33 through 8.40, ends with the following half-verse:

> This is regarded as the twenty-seven-fold activity of the embodiment of dharma *(dharmakāya)*. (*AA* 8.40b)

According to Ārya Vimuktisena, the term "embodiment of dharma" *(dharmakāya)* here refers to Buddhahood as a whole, *dharmakāya* as the total result of the path *(dharmakāya phalam)*. He understands the term *dharmakāya* here to have the same inclusive meaning that he understood it to have in verse *AA* 1.17, i.e., the entire resultant state of Buddhahood. Thus, for Ārya Vimuktisena, *AA* verses 8.33 through 8.40 explain the way in which Buddhahood, as resultant *dharmakāya*, engages in activity for sentient beings through its manifestations as *nairmāṇikakāya*.[42]

Therefore, we may note, it is only at verse 8.6 that Ārya Vimuktisena interprets the term *dharmakāya* in an exclusive sense, i.e., as synonymous with the term *svābhāvikakāya*, referring just to the first of the three Buddha *kāyas*. At verses 1.17 and 8.40, he interprets it in an inclusive sense, as resultant *dharmakāya*, which includes all *kāyas* and all qualities of Buddhahood.[43]

Haribhadra, in keeping with his reading of *AA* 1.17, which is very different from Ārya Vimuktisena's, gives a very different interpretation of *AA* verses 8.33–8.40. We present *AA* 1.17 again for reference:

> svābhāvikaḥ sasāmbhogo nairmāṇiko 'paras tathā
> dharmakāyaḥ sakāritraś caturdhā samudīritaḥ
>
> (*AA* 1.17)

As noted above, Haribhadra interpreted the term *dharmakāya* in this verse as a *(jñānātmaka) dharmakāya*, a "*dharmakāya* consisting of gnosis," which he said comprised a fourth Buddha *kāya*.[44] For him, then, the terms *svābhāvikaḥ*, *sasāmbhogo*, *nairmāṇiko*, and *dharmakāya* in verse 1.17 designated four different *kāyas*. And the term *kāritraḥ*, meaning activity, was placed just after the term *dharmakāya* to show that the Buddha's activity was attributable specifically to his *(jñānātmaka) dharmakāya*, his "*dharmakāya* consisting of gnoses" (not to his *svābhāvikakāya*, which for Haribhadra signified only the unconditioned aspect of Buddhahood, its emptiness and cessation of impurity, a permanent that cannot be the basis of activity).

In line with his interpretation of *AA* 1.17, Haribhadra isolates verse 8.33 as the only verse in the eighth chapter to teach *nairmāṇikakāya*. He understands 8.34 through 8.40 inclusive to be teaching the twenty-seven activities that are to be specifically associated with the *(jñānātmaka) dharmakāya*, the Buddha's set of gnoses. The activities listed in those verses are to be ascribed to the *(jñānātmaka) dharmakāya* alone, he says, because it is that *kāya* alone, as a set of pure, impermanent gnoses, which serves as the substantial cause to generate a Buddha's activities through various manifestations. Because Haribhadra interprets *svābhāvikakāya* as a permanent, it cannot be identified in his scheme as the basis of activity, an impermanent. Since *sāmbhogikakāya* and *nairmāṇikakāya* are the manifestations through which activity is carried out, they also cannot be identified as the cause of the activity. In Haribhadra's scheme, then, only the gnosis itself can be so identified. Thus, Haribhadra interprets the term *dharmakāya* of verse 8.40b to mean *(jñānātmaka) dharmakāya*, the *dharmakāya* consisting of gnosis, which he takes as semantically equivalent to the same term in verse 1.17.[45]

In order to make this interpretation of verses 8.33–8.40, Haribhadra has to perform some hermeneutic gymnastics with the important half-verse 8.34a. Again verses 8.33–8.34a read as follows:

> karoti yena citrāṇi hitāni jagataḥ samaṃ
> ā bhavāt so 'nupacchinnaḥ kāyo nairmāṇiko muneḥ
>
> (*AA* 8.33)
>
> tathā karmāpy anucchinnam asyā saṃsāram iṣyate
>
> (*AA* 8.34a)

> [The embodiment of the Sage in his manifestation(s) *(nairmāṇikakāya)* is that through which he impartially carries out diverse benefits for the world. It is uninterrupted for as long as the existence {of the world}. (*AA* 8.33)
>
> Likewise, it is agreed, its activity *(karma)* is uninterrupted for as long as cyclic existence lasts. . . . (*AA* 8.34a)]

Haribhadra interprets the phrase "its activity" *(karma . . . asya)* to mean the activity of the *(jñānātmaka) dharmakāya*. This requires the assumption that verse 8.34a is continuing a train of thought, not from the immediately preceding verse 8.33 (on *nairmāṇikakāya*), but from the much earlier verse 8.11. As mentioned above, Haribhadra interpreted all of verses 8.2 through 8.11 as concerning the *(jñānātmaka) dharmakāya*. In particular, he took half-verse 8.11b to be a discussion of the eternality of the *(jñānātmaka) dharmakāya*. In one of his final remarks on *AA* 8, he draws the subject matter of the set of verses 8.34a–8.40 and that of verse 8.11

together by applying the key phrase *ā saṃsāram* (for as long as cyclic existence lasts) identically to both. He says: "Thus, it is agreed, like the *[jñānātmaka] dharmakāya* [of verse 8.11], its twenty-seven-fold activity [of verses 8.34a to 8.40] lasts as long as cyclic existence."[46]

Finally, there is one other verse of great importance for interpretation of *AA* 8. That is the final verse of the entire *Abhisamayālaṃkāra*, verse 9.2. This verse summarizes the content of the entire text in terms of three basic topics: the aim of yogic practice, the yogic practice itself, and the ultimate result of the practice:

> viṣayas tritayo hetuḥ prayogaś caturātmakaḥ
> dharmakāyaphalaṃ karmety anyas tredhārthasaṃgraha
>
> (*AA* 9.2)

> [The threefold aim, as cause, the fourfold practice, the embodiment of dharma {with its} activity as result, thus in another way is {the entire subject matter} summarized in three topics.][47]

In brief, the "threefold" aim is the subject of the *AA*'s first three chapters: total omniscience *(sarvākārajñatā)*, knowledge of the paths *(mārgajñatā)*, and all-knowledge *(sarvajñatā)*, the knowledges realized through the fourfold practice. The fourfold practice is the subject of the *AA*'s next four chapters, comprising full realization of all aspects *(sarvākāra-abhisambodha)*, realization at its summit *(mūrdha-abhisamaya)*, gradual realization *(anupūrva-abhisamaya)*, and realization in a single moment *(ekakṣaṇābhisamaya)*. "The result" is the subject matter of the *AA*'s eighth chapter: embodiment of dharma, *dharmakāya* in its inclusive sense, the entire state of Buddhahood including its activity on behalf of beings *(karma)*.[48]

Notice how *AA* verse 9.2 identifies the entire subject matter of chapter 8 as *phalaṃ* (result) of the practice, expressed as *dharmakāya karma*, which clearly refers to the whole state of Buddhahood (including all *kāya*s) together with its activity.

Ārya Vimuktisena's and Haribhadra's analyses of *AA* 8 will be discussed in further detail in chapters 9 and 10 below.

7

Literary-Critical Analysis of *Abhisamayālaṃkāra*, Chapter 8: A Map that Projects the Three *Kāyas* of Yogācāra onto the *Large Prajñāpāramitā Sūtra*

7.1 Introduction

As mentioned in the preface, this chapter and chapter 8 are written for scholars and others who are interested in details of literary-critical analysis of Buddhist sacred texts such as the *Abhisamayālaṃkāra*. Those readers who are interested only in the doctrinal and practical concerns of such an analysis, not all the details, may wish to read only the introductory and concluding sections of chapters 7 and 8, and the translations of *Prajñāpāramitāsūtra* and *Abhisamayālaṃkāra* passages that appear in the body of these chapters. That would be enough to proceed on to chapter 9 if so desired.

As we have noted, the explicit theme of the *Prajñāpāramitā* sūtras is the emptiness of all phenomena *(sarvadharma-śūnyatā)* in nondual awareness *(prajñāpāramitā)*, explicated in the commentaries of Nāgārjuna, while the implicit theme of those sūtras is the set of yogic practices and realizations called "paths" *(mārgāḥ)* to enlightenment. The latter, implicit theme of the *Prajñāpāramitā* sūtras is the subject matter of the *Abhisamayālaṃkāra (AA)*, which relates each section of the 25,000-verse version of the *Large Prajñāpāramitā Sūtra* to the schema of the paths, as those schema were understood at the time of its composition.

Some of the path schema were expressed directly in the *Large PP Sūtra* itself, as it drew upon ideas from earlier scriptural and Abhidharma sources. There are *Prajñāpāramitāsūtra* passages, for example, which clearly explain the "five eyes" *(pañcacakṣuh)* and "six superknowledges" *(ṣaḍabhijña);*[1] and these form the textual basis for their mention in *Abhisamayālaṃkāra* verse 1.22 among the subtopics of "instruction" (*avavāda*, the second topic of *AA* chapter 1).[2]

There are significant portions of the *Abhisamayālaṃkāra*, however, that superimpose a path-system scheme onto *Prajñāpāramitāsūtra* passages that do not have any such order themselves. *AA* chapter 1, topic 4 (verses 1.37–1.39), for example, identifies *gotra* as the basis or support for thirteen different constituents of the bodhisattva's path. But these constituents are not mentioned in the corresponding passage in the *PP* and can only be read into it in the most artificial way.[3] The *AA*, then, sometimes makes explicit what is already expressed in the *Large PP Sūtra*, and other times superimposes path schema onto the *PP* that were accepted at the time of the *AA*'s composition, but were either not yet developed or not yet widely accepted at the time of the *PP* sūtra's composition. *AA*'s chapter 8, concerning Buddhahood as result of the Mahāyāna path, performs both of these functions: It relates the Yogācāra theory of multiple Buddha *kāyas* (which was extrinsic to the *PP*) to the *PP* sūtras' own central ways of expressing Buddhahood (the undefiled dharmas, *dharmakāya*, the thirty-two marks and eighty signs of the great being, etc.).

But this is already anticipating some of our conclusions. To make a precise inference concerning the author's intention in composing *Abhisamayālaṃkāra,* chapter 8, we must first determine the following: (1) Which version of the *Prajñāpāramitāsūtra*, and precisely which passages within it, did the author of the *Abhisamayālaṃkāra* comment upon in composing *AA* chapter 8? (2) Which terms and concepts did he draw from Yogācāra textual tradition extrinsic to the *PP*? These two questions frame the discussion of this chapter.

To address the first question above, we need to answer two textual questions. Which *Prajñāpāramitā* sūtra is the *AA* based upon? Which portion of that sūtra served as text basis for the *AA's* eighth chapter on Buddhahood?

7.2
Abhisamayālaṃkāra Chapter 8's Textual Basis in the 25,000-verse *Prajñāpāramitā* Sūtra

a. Late Indian and Tibetan commentators identify *rP* passages 8.1–8.3 as the textual basis of *AA* chapter 8's teaching on the Buddha *kāyas*

The earliest extant commentaries on the *Abhisamayālaṃkāra* are Ārya Vimuktisena's *Abhisamayālaṃkāra-vṛtti* (ca. early sixth century C.E.) and Bhadanta Vimuktisena's *Abhisamayālaṃkārakārikā-vārttika* (sixth or seventh century C.E.).[4] Ārya Vimuktisena's commentary was fundamental for all the centuries of commentary that followed him in India and Tibet, for his was the first to establish the textual basis in the 25,000-verse *PP* sūtra for each portion of the *AA*. In fact, his own explications are generally brief, the primary purpose of his commentary being to establish the precise textual correspondence between the passages of the 25,000-verse *PP* sūtra and the seventy topics of the *AA* that comprise its eight substantive chapters. Bhadanta Vimuktisena's commentary, for the most part, is a repetition or rephrasing of Ārya Vimuktisena's correlations and comments. It is Ārya Vimuktisena's *Abhisamayālaṃkāra-vṛtti* that established the textual foundation for fourteen hundred years of commentary and discussion on the *AA* in the Indo-Tibetan tradition up to the present day.

The earliest extant commentaries on the *Abhisamayālaṃkāra*, then, related it to the 25,000-verse *PP* sūtra alone. In the late eighth century, more than two hundred years after Ārya Vimuktisena, Haribhadra wrote his influential treatise, the *AA Āloka*, which related the *AA* for the first time to the 8,000-verse *PP* sūtra. Indian commentators after Haribhadra related the *AA* not only to the 25,000- and 8,000-verse *PP*, but also to the 100,000-verse *PP*, the 18,000-verse *PP*, and to the *Ratnaguṇasaṃcaya-gāthā* (an abbreviated version of the 8,000-verse *PP*).[5]

Conze's research on the *PP* literature has shown that the 25,000-verse *PP*, the 100,000-verse *PP*, and the 18,000-verse *PP* are all different versions of one sūtra, which he calls the *Large Prajñāpāramitā* or *Large Sūtra on Perfect Wisdom*. Conze noted that this *Large PP Sūtra* (in any of its three versions), when divided into three parts, can be related to the 8,000-verse *PP*, which he believed to be the oldest *PP* sūtra. The *Large PP*'s first part is an expansion of the 8,000-verse *PP*'s first chapter. The *Large PP*'s second part closely follows chapters 2–28 of the 8,000-verse *PP*, usually expanding the text, sometimes abbreviating it. The third part of the *Large PP Sūtra* is independent of the 8,000-verse *PP*.[6]

If we were to choose from among all *PP* sūtras known to us, we would choose the *Large PP Sūtra*, especially in its 25,000-verse version, as the one most likely to have served as textual basis for the *AA*. There are two principal reasons for inferring this. First, upon examination, the 8,000-verse *PP* sūtra does not provide an adequate textual basis for the last three-and-a-half chapters of the *AA*, while the *Large PP Sūtra* does. Indeed, it is the third part of the *Large PP Sūtra* that serves as that textual basis, the part missing from the 8,000-verse *PP* sūtra. So only the *Large PP* could have been the textual basis for the *AA* in its entirety. Secondly, as far as we know, in the earliest centuries of commentary on the *AA*, the 25,000-verse *PP* was the only *PP* sūtra identified as the *AA*'s textual basis, and convincingly so, by its earliest commentator. It took more than two hundred years before any other *PP* sūtra (the 8,000-verse *PP*) was so identified.[7]

From among all *PP* sūtras, it is the 25,000-verse *PP* sūtra that Ārya Vimuktisena identified as the textual basis for the *AA*, and he did so carefully and convincingly, by quoting from or paraphrasing from all of the sūtra passages that correlate with each of the *AA*'s seventy topics. As far as we know, no other textual basis for the *AA* was assumed prior to or during his time. The influence of Ārya Vimuktisena on the work of all later *AA* scholars cannot be overemphasized, as he established the basic pattern of relationships between the *AA* and the *PP* to which all the scholars who came after him referred, even when they later attempted to establish relationships between the *AA* and *PP* sūtras other than the 25,000-verse version. It must also be noted in this regard that among all the *PP* sūtras, it is only the 25,000-verse *PP* into which the topic titles of the *AA* were inserted, resulting in a revised recension of the sūtra showing its connection to the *AA*.

The *Abhisamayālaṃkāra*'s association with the 8,000-verse *PP* has become particularly renowned in traditional and modern scholarship through the work of Haribhadra, whose *Āloka* first made that association. But it is quite clear that *Abhisamayālaṃkāra* chapters 6, 7, and 8 were written as commentary on corresponding portions of the *Large PP Sūtra*, particularly its 25,000-verse version, *not* as commentary on the 8,000-verse *PP*. Conze has shown that the *Large PP* (including its versions in 100,000, 25,000, and 18,000 verses) corresponds closely to the 8,000-verse *PP* up to the latter's chapter 28. According to Ārya Vimuktisena and Haribhadra, this would correspond to the middle of *AA* 5.[8] Beyond that point, the *Large PP* continues to serve as a reasonable textual basis for the rest of *AA*'s chapters 5, 6, 7 and 8. But the portion of the 8,000-verse *PP* taken as the textual basis for the *AA* comes to an end very abruptly after its twenty-eighth chapter, forcing Haribhadra in his *Āloka* to identify just one verse of that sūtra as the textual basis for all of *AA* 6, just one more verse as the basis for all of *AA* 7, and a very brief passage (which obviously has little or no relation to *AA* 8) as the basis for *AA* 8.

Even a brief glance at Ārya Vimuktisena's *Vṛtti* is sufficient to see that relevant portions of the 25,000-verse *PP* are extensive enough and correspond well enough to the concepts in the corresponding portions of the *AA* to have served as the textual basis for *AA* chapters 6, 7, and 8. The corresponding sūtra passages identified by Ārya Vimuktisena take up over one hundred pages in English translation.[9] But the part of the 8,000-verse *PP* that Haribhadra's *Āloka* identifies as the textual basis for *AA* chapters 6, 7, and 8 is not even remotely related to them conceptually, and is far too brief. It takes up less than one page of English translation.[10] This forces Haribhadra to give long independent explanations of *AA* chapters 6, 7, and 8 with only cursory reference to the 8,000-verse *PP* sūtra that they are supposed to be explicating.[11]

To illustrate the point, we can compare the 25,000-verse *PP* passages that Ārya Vimuktisena identified as textual basis for *AA* 6 in his Vṛtti, and the 8,000-verse *PP* passages that Haribhadra identified in his *Āloka*. *AA* chapter 6's subject matter is the "progressive realization" *(anupūrva-abhisamaya)*. This refers to the progressive or gradual realization of all the aspects of the three types of knowledge that are the subject of the *AA*'s first three chapters *(sarvākāra-jñatā, mārgā-jñatā,* and *sarva-jñatā)*. The progressive realization (*anupūrva-abhisamaya)* is analyzed into thirteen types: the six perfections of bodhisattva practice *(pāramitās)*, the six types of recollection *(anusmṛti)*, and lastly, the realization of the nonsubstantiality of all dharmas. *AA* 6 consists of just one verse; but that single verse refers to all thirteen types of progressive realization.[12] We would expect the portion of the *PP* sūtra that was the textual basis for *AA* 6 to discuss, or at least to mention, those thirteen types of realization.

The portion of the 25,000-verse *PP* that Ārya Vimuktisena identified as the textual basis for *AA* 6 does indeed discuss each of the thirteen types of realization, in order and at length.[13] First, Subhuti asks the Buddha to explain how the bodhisattva can be understood to progressively realize full enlightenment. The Buddha explains the progressive training of the bodhisattva through his or her perfections of generosity, virtue, patience, enthusiastic perseverance, meditative concentration and wisdom (the six perfections). He then explains the bodhisattva's progressive training through recollections of Buddha, Dharma, Saṃgha, virtue, renunciation, and the deities *(buddha, dharma, saṃgha anusmṛti, śīla anusmṛti, tyāga anusmṛti, devatā anusmṛti)*. Finally he explains the bodhisattva's thirteenth progressive training and realization: gnosis of the nonsubstantial nature of all phenomena *(sarva-dharmā-abhāva-svabhāva-jñāna)*. *AA* 6 consists of one verse that lists those thirteen progressive realizations:

> dānena prajñayā yāvad buddhādau smṛtibhiś ca sā dharmābhāva-
> svabhāvenetyanupūrvakriyā matā
>
> (*AA* 6.1)

> [Progressive activity {includes the practices from} generosity through wisdom, the mindfulnesses of Buddha etc., up to the nonsubstantial nature of phenomena.]

The *AA*'s term *anupūrvakriyā* here is precisely the term used in the 25,000-verse *PP* sūtra passage summarized above. It literally means "progressive activity." Ārya Vimuktisena was quite reasonable to identify that very *PP* passage as the textual basis for that *AA* verse.

The 8,000-verse *PP* passage that Haribhadra's *Āloka* identifies as the textual basis for *AA* chapter 6 is only the following verse: "siṃha nāda nadanatayā prajñāpāramitā nadanatā 'nugantavyā."[14] Conze translates this: "One should approach the resounding declaration of the perfection of wisdom through the [analogy of the] roaring of the lion's roar."[15] Haribhadra identifies that single, metaphorical verse as the entire textual basis in the 8,000-verse *PP* for *AA* 6. The verse makes no mention of thirteen progressive realizations. The word "progressive" *(anupūrva)* does not even appear in it. There is no relationship whatsoever between this verse and *AA* 6. Wisely, Haribhadra makes no attempt to expose one. He just designates the *PP* verse as the textual basis for *AA* chapter 6 and proceeds to explicate the chapter independently of it.[16]

Like *AA* 6, *AA* 7 and 8 are closely related to the corresponding sections of the 25,000-verse *PP* identified by Ārya Vimuktisena, and totally unrelated to the sections of the 8,000-verse *PP* identified by Haribhadra. If we are to choose from *PP* sūtras known to us, we can only conclude that the *AA*'s last three chapters were originally written as commentary on the *Large PP Sūtra* (most probably its version in 25,000 verses) and not on the 8,000-verse *PP* sūtra.

There is a special revised version of the 25,000-verse *PP sūtra* that is extant in Sanskrit and, in its Tibetan translation, is ascribed to Haribhadra as redactor.[17] Conze calls this the "recast version of the *Pañcaviṃśati-sāhasrikā Prajñāpāramitā sūtra*," or "the version in 25,000 lines that has been adjusted to conform to the divisions of the *Abhisamayālaṃkāra*." It is a revised version of the 25,000-verse *PP* sūtra that, in all likelihood, was redacted some time after Ārya Vimuktisena, because it reflects precisely the correspondences he drew between the *PP* sūtra and the *AA*.[18] In this revised version of the sūtra, each sūtra passage is labeled with the name of the *AA* topic or subtopic for which that portion of the sūtra was thought to be the textual basis. Apart from the insertion of *AA* topic titles into the sūtra after their corresponding passages, no appearance is given of any explicit commentary or explication. The textual material is all in the style characteristic of *Prajñāpāramitā* sūtras, with dialogues between the Buddha and his disciples in question-and-answer form. In what follows, I will refer to this special redaction of the 25,000-verse *PP* sūtra as "the revised version of the 25,000-verse *PP* sūtra," and abbreviate it *"rP."*

The *rP* gives the appearance of containing no explicit commentary or exegesis. Nevertheless, it is included in the Tibetan canon within the bsTan 'gyur (Collection of commentaries) rather than within the bKa' 'gyur (Collection of sūtras), as if it were a commentary *(śāstra)*. This may seem a bit strange, because, as noted above, *rP* gives the appearance of just being the 25,000-verse sūtra with *AA* topic titles inserted for ease of cross-reference. Late Indian and Tibetan *AA* commentators quote *rP* as their reference for the 25,000-verse *PP* sūtra, referring to it as the *Large PP Sūtra*, not as a commentary upon that sūtra. *rP* was used in the commentarial tradition of late Indian and Tibetan Buddhism as a ready reference version of the 25,000-verse *PP* sūtra, the version in which passages corresponding to *AA* topics were easy to find.

Bu ston (1290–1364 C.E.), the initial compiler of the Tibetan Buddhist canon, may have grouped *rP* with commentaries in the bsTan 'gyur because *rP* obviously had a redactor who had inserted *AA* topic titles into the sūtra (the redactor is not mentioned in the Sanskrit manuscripts, but is identified in the colophon of the Tibetan translation as Haribhadra). Bu ston may have considered this enough to preclude classifying the text with sūtras in the bKa' 'gyur, since sūtras were traditionally understood to be the word of the Buddha taken verbatim and without redaction. There is another, unrevised version of the same 25,000-verse *PP* sūtra in the bKa' 'gyur of the Tibetan canon (Pk 731). The texts of the unrevised version and the revised version *(rP)* of the 25,000-verse *PP* sūtra are close in content. However, there are a few of places in the revised version *(rP)* where the sūtra has been altered by addition or transposition of passages, evidently in order to make it conform a little better to the structure of the *AA*.[19]

As noted above, the 25,000-verse *PP* is the version of the *Large PP Sūtra* upon which the *AA* was probably based, and in its revised version *(rP)* each sūtra passage bears the name of the *AA* section to which it was thought to correspond. The *rP* is divided into eight chapters that correspond to and bear the names of the *AA*'s eight chapters. The *rP's* eighth chapter, called "Realization of *Dharmakāya*" *(dharmakāya-abhisamaya)* is divided into five sections, which are labeled as the textual bases for five corresponding sections of *AA* chapter 8. *rP* chapter 8's first section (8.1) is labeled *svābhāvikaḥ kāyaḥ*. Its second section (8.2) is labeled *sāmbhogikaḥ kāyaḥ*. Its third section (8.3) is labeled *nairmāṇikaḥ kāyaḥ*. Its fourth section (8.4) is labeled *sāmānyena nirmāṇakāyadvārena dharmakāyasya karma* (the activity of the *dharmakāya* in general by means of the *nairmāṇika-kāya*). And its fifth section (8.5) is labeled simply *karmāni* ("activities" of Buddhahood).[20] *rP* passages 8.1–8.5 inclusive are found in *all* extant editions of *rP* in Sanskrit manuscripts and in Tibetan translation.

The revised 25,000-verse *PP (rP)* plays an important role in late Indian *PP* literature and in the major *PP* commentaries of Tibet. In India, Ratnākaraśānti (ca. 1000 C.E.) and Abhayākaragupta (early twelfth century) quoted its passages to identify the *PP* textual basis for the *AA*.[21] Later, the most influential *PP* commentators in Tibet, such as Bu ston rin chen grub (1290–1364 C.E.), gYag ston sangs rgyas dpal (ca.1350–1414), Rong ston smra ba'i seng ge (1367–1449), Tsong kha pa blo bzang grags pa (1357–1419), rGyal tshab dar ma rin chen (1364–1432), and Go ram pa bsod nams seng ge (1429–89) cited *rP* passages as the textual bases for each *AA* section they commented upon. Ratnākaraśānti, Abhayākaragupta, and the major Tibetan scholars identified *rP* 8 as the textual basis for *AA* chapter 8, and *rP* sections 8.1–8.3 as the primary textual basis for *AA* 8's explanation of the Buddha *kāya*s (as delineated in the paragraph above).

Notice should be taken of the fact that when Ratnākaraśānti and Abhayākaragupta quoted the *PP* textual basis for *AA* 8's teaching on the Buddha *kāya*s, they wrote, "As it was said in the two large *Prajñāpāramitā* sūtras" (literally: "As it was said in the two great *Bhagavatī*s [uktam mahatyorbhagavatyoḥ]"). By this they meant that the quote they were giving was found in the large versions of the *PP* sūtra, presumably the two largest versions, the 100,000-verse *PP* and the 25,000-verse *PP*. But the quote that they then provided was invariably a quote from the *revised* version of the 25,000-verse *PP*, *rP* 8.1–8.3.[22] It appears that by the time of Ratnākaraśānti (ca. 1000 C.E.), and perhaps somewhat earlier, Indian *Prajñāpāramitā* scholars found the revised 25,000-verse *PP* sūtra *(rP)* the most convenient version of the sūtra to use when composing commentary on the *AA*, since only this version of the sūtra had its passages marked with the *AA's* topic names for ready reference. Tibetan commentators followed the Indians in using *rP* as their ready reference version of the 25,000-verse *PP* sūtra. Tibetan scholars, before quoting the textual basis for *AA* chapter 8's *kāya* teachings, wrote *mdo las*, meaning "from the *[PP]* sūtra(s)." They, too, assumed that their quote was to be found in *PP* sūtras in general, at least in their large versions. But the actual quote they gave was invariably from the revised 25,000-verse *PP* (*rP* 8.1–8.3).[23]

The *rP*, then, was used in the commentarial tradition of late Indian and Tibetan Buddhism as the ready reference edition of the 25,000-verse *PP* sūtra in correspondence with the *AA*. Because they relied so heavily on *rP* as their textual source for *AA* chapter 8 in this way, Ratnākaraśānti, Abhayākaragupta, and all the Tibetan *PP* scholars I know of thought that passages 8.1–8.3 of *rP* were the *PP* textual bases for the *AA*'s teaching on the Buddha *kāyas*.[24] Quoting *rP* as scripture, they assumed passages 8.1–8.3 within it, like all other *PP* sūtra passages accepted as authoritative, were the words of the Buddha, and were therefore to be found generally in the major recensions of the *Large PP Sūtra* that preserved those words.

rP 8.1–8.3 are translated below from the Sanskrit.[25] The Tibetan translation in the bsTan 'gyur (Pk 5188) differs slightly from the Sanskrit manuscripts, but not in ways that affect the discussion here. In the Sanskrit and Tibetan texts of *rP* 8.1–8.3 the names of the three *kāyas* are presented as the titles of their respective sūtra passages, just as presented here:[26]

rP 8.1:

> *Svābhāvikaḥ kāyaḥ*
> Moreover, Subhuti, of all the undefiled [Buddha] dharmas, which are like a dream, which are nonentities, whose self-existence *(svabhāva)* is nonexistent, which are empty of self-identity *(svalakṣaṇa-śūnya)*, which are fully purified through omniscient knowledge, of them the primordial nature *(prakṛti)*, which has only one identity, i.e., no identity, is to be known as the Tathāgata, the Arhat, the Fully Enlightened One. It is thus that the bodhisattva, the great being, should train in the perfection of wisdom.
> *Subhuti:* What again, Blessed One *(Bhagavan)*, are all the undefiled [Buddha] dharmas?
> *The Blessed One:* The thirty-seven factors that foster enlightenment, the four measureless thoughts, the eight liberations, the nine meditative attainments, the ten meditative totalities, the bases of overpowering divided into eight kinds, the meditative power freeing from passions, the gnosis resulting from resolve, the six supernatural knowledges, the four analytical knowledges, the four total purities, the ten sovereignties, the ten powers, the four forms of fearlessness, the three ways in which a Buddha has nothing to hide, the threefold mindful equanimity, the nature of never forgetting, the complete destruction of [negative] propensities, the great compassion, the eighteen qualities unique to a Buddha, total omniscience, path knowledge and all knowledge: These are indeed, Subhuti, all the

undefiled [Buddha] dharmas. It is thus, Subhuti, that the bodhisattva, the great being, should train in the perfection of wisdom.[27]

rP 8.2:

Sāmbhogikaḥ kāyaḥ

Moreover, Subhuti, when he has trained in perfect wisdom, when by the full attainment of just these dharmas he has realized highest complete enlightenment, his body always and everywhere entirely adorned with the thirty-two marks of the great being *(mahāpuruṣa)* and the eighty associated signs, the Tathāgata, the Arhat, the Fully Enlightened One demonstrates for the bodhisattvas, the great beings, the supreme Mahāyāna dharma in order to bring them unsurpassed pleasure and satisfaction, joy and happiness. It is thus that the bodhisattva, the great being, should train in the perfection of wisdom.[28]

rP 8.3:

Nairmāṇikaḥ kāyaḥ

Moreover, Subhuti, when he has trained in perfect wisdom, when by the full attainment of just these dharmas he has realized highest, complete enlightenment, the Tathāgata, the Arhat, the Fully Enlightened One, in endless and limitless world systems in the ten directions, during the whole of time, by means of a cloud of multiform manifestations *(nirmāṇa-meghena)*, carries out the benefit of all beings. It is thus that the bodhisattva, the great being, should train in the perfection of wisdom.[29]

Ratnākaraśānti, Abhayākaragupta, and the major *PP* commentators of Tibet believed that *AA* chapter 8, which teaches multiple Buddha *kāyas*, constituted a commentary on *rP* 8.1–8.3 quoted above. Therefore, they reasoned, the number of *kāyas* taught in *rP* 8.1–8.3 must be the number taught in the *AA*.

Ratnākaraśānti, Abhayākaragupta, and, in Tibet, Go ram pa bsod nams seng ge backed Ārya Vimuktisena's claim that the *AA* taught three *kāyas*. In part, this was because they believed that *rP* 8.1–8.3 clearly taught three *kāyas*.[30] Looking at the passages above, it is easy to appreciate their perspective. The "primordial nature" *(prakṛti)* of the perfectly pure dharmas would be the first *kāya*: *svābhāvikakāya* (embodiment of Buddhahood in its own nature). The Buddha in the glorious form of the sūtra's teacher, bearing the marks and signs of a great being and sharing his enjoyment of dharma with his closest community of bodhisattvas, would be the second *kāya: sāmbhogikakāya* (embodiment of Buddhahood in communal enjoyment of dharma). And the Buddha's extensive manifestations would comprise the third *kāya: nairmāṇikakāya* (embodiment of Buddhahood in manifestations).

Furthermore, there is a clear relation between key terms within sūtra passages *rP* 8.1–8.3 above and the names of the three *kāyas*. In *rP* 8.1, the key term is *prakṛti*, which I translate "primordial nature." This term can be synonymous in Buddhist philosophical Sanskrit with *svabhāva* (essence, self-existence, own-being), the adjectival form of which forms the name *svābhāvikaḥ kāyaḥ* (embodiment of Buddhahood in its essence). In *rP* 8.2 there are numerous terms for enjoyment, which is the central connotation of *sāmbhogikaḥ* in *sāmbhogikaḥ kāyaḥ*. And in *rP* 8.3, limitless benefit to beings is created by a cloud of manifestations *(nirmāṇa)*, *nirmāṇa* being the term that, in secondary derivative form, gives the name *nairmāṇikaḥ kāyaḥ*.[31] *rP* passages 8.1–8.3, then, certainly give the appearance of a clear basis within the *PP* sūtra for interpreting *AA* 8 as a teaching of the three kāyas.

The two commentaries in which Haribhadra set forth his four-*kāya* interpretation of the *AA* are his *Āloka* and *Sphuṭārthā*. The former commentary relates the *AA* to the 8000-verse *PP* sūtra; the latter commentary explicates the *AA* independently, without specific reference to sūtras. Neither commentary directly relates the *AA* to the 25,000-verse *PP* sūtra.

However, it appeared clear to later Tibetan scholars from Haribhadra's comments on *AA* verses 8.1–8.6, which are very close in expression to *rP* passage 8.1 above, that Haribhadra read two Buddha *kāyas* into that passage.[32] Therefore, the major commentators in Tibet believed Haribhadra found textual support for his theory of four Buddha *kāyas* in *rP* passages 8.1–8.3.[33] According to Tibetan commentators, Haribhadra agreed with Ārya Vimuktisena that *rP* 8.2 and 8.3 taught *sāmbhogikakāya* and the *nairmāṇikakāya*, but believed that *rP* 8.1, divided into two parts, was to be understood to teach *two* other *kāyas*: *svābhāvikakāya* (embodiment of Buddhahood in its essence) and *jñānātmaka dharmakāya* (*dharmakāya* consisting of gnosis). With the latter term Haribhadra referred to a Buddha's gnoses as conventional phenomena to be distinguished, so he claimed, from their ultimate, empty nature, which is *svābhāvikakāya.* In line with this understanding, Tibetan commentators on Haribhadra believed he understood the first paragraph of *rP* 8.1 to teach *svābhāvikakāya* and the rest of *rP* 8.1 to teach *jñānātmaka dharmakāya* (*dharmakāya* consisting of gnosis) as follows:[34]

rP 8.1a. The *PP* passage expressing *svābhāvikakāya* in Haribhadra's interpretation (according to Tibetan commentators):

> Moreover, Subhuti, of all the undefiled [Buddha] dharmas, which are like a dream, which are nonentities, whose self-existence *(svabhāva)* is nonexistent, which are empty of self-identity *(svalakṣaṇa-śūnya)*, which are fully purified through omniscient knowledge, of them the primordial nature *(prakṛti)*, which has only one identity, i.e., no identity, is to be known as the Tathāgata, the Arhat, the Fully Enlightened One. It is thus that the bodhisattva, the great being, should train in the perfection of wisdom.

rP 8.1b. The *PP* passage expressing *Jñānātmaka Dharmakāya* in Haribhadra's interpretation (according to Tibetan commentators):

> *Subhuti:* What again, Blessed One *(Bhagavan)*, are all the undefiled [Buddha] dharmas?
> *The Blessed One:* The thirty-seven factors that foster enlightenment, the four measureless thoughts, the eight liberations, the nine meditative attainments, the ten meditative totalities, the bases of overpowering divided into eight kinds, the meditative power freeing from passions, the gnosis resulting from resolve, the six supernatural knowledges, the four analytical knowledges, the four total purities, the ten sovereignties, the ten powers, the four forms of fearlessness, the three ways in which a Buddha has nothing to hide, the threefold mindful equanimity, the nature of never forgetting, the complete destruction of [negative] propensities, the great compassion, the eighteen qualities unique to a Buddha, total omniscience, path knowledge and all knowledge: these are indeed, Subhuti, all the undefiled [Buddha] dharmas. It is thus, Subhuti, that the bodhisattva, the great being, should train in the perfection of wisdom.

The term *jñānātmaka dharmakāya (dharmakāya* consisting of gnosis) is of Haribhadra's making, and is not actually found in either *rP* or the *AA*. However, as we see here, *rP* 8.1–8.3 can be understood semantically to serve as a textual basis for the *AA*'s teaching of four *kāyas* if one seeks to do so.

The important point is that if one believes *AA* 8's teaching on the *kāyas* to be based on the *rP* passages quoted above, the ambiguity of passage 8.1 in particular can be used to support a four-*kāya* reading of *AA* 8.

In fact, however, *rP* passages 8.1–8.3 are unique to the revised version of the 25,000-verse *PP;* these passages are not found in any version of the *PP* sūtras other than that one (not even in the unrevised version of the 25,000-verse *PP*). This, together with evidence from Chinese editions of the *PP* sūtras and from Ārya Vimuktisena's commentary, indicates that *rP* 8.1–8.3 did not exist at the time the *AA* was composed. The evidence indicates that *rP* passages 8.1–8.3 were inserted into the 25,000-verse *PP* sūtra sometime after Ārya Vimuktisena made his commentary on the *AA* (ca. early sixth century), which was necessarily after the *AA* was composed. This means that *AA* 8 could not have been commenting on *rP* passages 8.1–8.3, and should not be read as if it were. This fact is crucial for evaluating the *AA*'s teaching on the Buddha *kāyas*. If *AA* chapter 8 did not comment upon *rP* 8.1–8.3, then its comments are based upon another portion of the 25,000-verse *PP* sūtra, the identification of which would shed much light on its meaning.[35]

As it happens, Ārya Vimuktisena's commentary identifies that portion of the

PP sūtra for us. Upon examining that portion of sūtra, one finds, surprisingly, that its primary subject matter is not Buddhahood! Rather, its primary concern is to explain four traditional bodhisattva methods to collect disciples *(catvāri saṃgraha-vastūni)*, in relation to which a discussion of a Buddha's qualities is included as supplementary material. Several of the central terms and concepts used in *AA* 8 (such as *svābhāvikakāya*, *sāmbhogikakāya*, and *nairmāṇikakāya*) were never specified in the *PP* text basis for *AA* 8.

The obvious conclusion is that the *AA*'s author drew those terms and concepts from Buddhist textual sources other than the *PP*, probably Yogācāra sources. And this suggests that the purpose of the *AA*'s author in composing *AA* 8 was to draw a clear correlation, perhaps for the first time in Indian Buddhism, between the Yogācāra descriptions of Buddhahood (as *svābhāvikakāya*, *sāmbhogikakāya*, *nairmāṇikakāya*) and the descriptions found in the *PP* sūtras (Buddhahood as *dharmakāya*, as undefiled dharmas, as *rūpakāya* with marks and signs, etc.).

b. Evidence that *rP* passages 8.1–8.3 were composed after the *Abhisamayālaṃkāra*, and thus could not have been the textual basis for *Abhisamayālaṃkāra* Chapter 8

1. *rP* passages 8.1–8.3 are missing in all Chinese translations of the 25,000-verse *Prajñāpāramitā* sūtra

The revised version of the 25,000-verse *PP* sūtra *(rP)* is extant in Sanskrit and in Tibetan translation. The Sanskrit manuscripts are from eighteenth- and nineteenth-century Nepal, and do not give the compiler's name. The Tibetan translation occasionally departs from the Sanskrit texts. Its colophon names Haribhadra as the compiler. In *rP* passages 8.1–8.3, of particular concern here, the Tibetan translation is close to the Sanskrit, departing from it in only minor ways that do not affect our discussion.

The unrevised version of the 25,000-verse *PP* sūtra was translated into Chinese four times. The earliest of these translations, by Dharmarakṣa, ca. 286 C.E., is incomplete, covering only the first portions of the sūtra, and therefore is not relevant here. The three other translations cover the 25,000-verse *PP* in its entirety. These are Mokṣala's in 291 C.E., Kumārajīva's in 403–4 C.E., and Hsuan Tsang's in 659–63 C.E. The revised version of this sūtra was never translated into Chinese. Hsuan Tsang, although he brought to China many *PP* manuscripts and translated several of them, never mentioned the revised version of the 25,000-verse *PP*. This is one indication that it may postdate him.[36]

Nancy Lethcoe, in her 1976 paper, studied the relationships between the *AA*, the revised version of the 25,000-verse *PP* sūtra in Sanskrit, and the three Chinese translations of the unrevised 25,000-verse *PP* sūtra. She wanted to determine to what extent the redactor of the *rP* might have altered the sūtra in order to make it conform better to the divisions of the *AA*. The Chinese translations all represent versions of the sūtra prior to the revised version. She compared the passages of the three Chinese translations to each other and to the Sanskrit of the revised version. She found that most of the passages in the Sanskrit revised version do occur in all three Chinese translations, but that a number of its passages are missing in one or more of the Chinese translations. For example, out of two hundred twenty-two sections in *rP* corresponding to the first *abhisamaya* (the first chapter of the *AA*), thirty-seven are missing in one or more of the Chinese translations. The vast majority of sections missing in one or more Chinese translation occur in the first and eighth *abhisamayas* (corresponding to the first and eighth chapters of the *AA*). Very few are missing in the other six *abhisamayas*.[37]

Some passages of *rP* missing in the earliest Chinese translation do appear in later Chinese translations. This indicates that they may have been added to the 25,000-verse *PP* text some time after 291 C.E. (the time of Mokṣala's earliest translation) but before the final redaction of the revised version. Besides such additions, Lethcoe found a number of passages in *rP* that had been transposed from other parts of the unrevised *PP* in order to make it conform better to the *AA*. Importantly, she found that out of approximately twelve hundred sections of *rP* corresponding to subtopics in the *AA*, fifty-five sections do not occur in any Chinese version. They include both additions and transpositions, and most of them bear a very close relationship to their corresponding *AA* headings.[38] Such passages were probably added to or transposed within the *PP* sūtra in order to better align it to the *AA*.[39] In other words, even though the *AA* is a commentary on the *PP* sūtra, portions of the *rP* represent changes written into the sūtra in order to make it conform better to its commentary. The commentary was a force, over time, in the transformation of the sūtra upon which it had been based.

Among the passages that appear to have been added to the 25,000-verse *PP* sūtra for this purpose are *rP* 8.1–8.3.[40] They are not found in any portion of any of the Chinese translations of the 25,000-verse *PP*. They are only found in the *rP*, a version that was unknown in China.

The fact that *rP* passages 8.1–8.3 are missing in all Chinese translations likely means that they were a late addition to the 25,000-verse *PP*, an addition not known to any Chinese translator. And the fact that these passages align so clearly with *AA* 8 suggests that they were added to the *PP* sūtra precisely to give the appearance that they were the original textual basis within that sūtra for *AA* 8. These observations do not constitute a proof of their addition to the sūtra after the *AA* was composed. But they are suggestive, and fit further patterns of evidence to be presented below.

Hsuan Tsang was a prodigious Chinese scholar who traveled to India in the seventh century and studied for several years at Nālandā Monastic University under its abbot, Śīlabhadra. He carried to China and later translated the 100,000-verse *PP*, the 25,000-verse *PP*, the 18,000-verse *PP*, and two versions of the 8,000-verse

PP sūtras.[41] We would expect him to have known about any version of the *PP* sūtra available at Nālandā. The fact that he did not even make mention of the revised 25,000-verse *PP* does raise the distinct possibility that it was not yet composed in his time.[42] We have conservatively dated the *AA* to the period from the fourth century to the early sixth century C.E. Hsuan Tsang went to India in the middle of the seventh century. If *rP* passages 8.1-8.3 were added to the 25,000-verse *PP* after Hsuan Tsang, it would mean that those sūtra passages were written at least a century and a half after the *AA* was composed.

2. rP passages 8.1–8.3 are missing in all *Prajñāpāramitā* sūtras extant in Sanskrit and Tibetan except *rP*

As mentioned above, the *Large PP Sūtra* is represented by three different texts: the 100,000-verse *PP*, the 25,000-verse *PP*, and the 18,000-verse *PP*. As Conze notes: "These three texts are really one and the same book. They only differ in the extent to which the 'repetitions' are copied out."[43]

Checking all extant Sanskrit and Tibetan editions of the *Large PP Sūtra*,[44] we find that *rP* passages 8.1–8.3 do not occur in the Sanskrit manuscripts of the 100,000-verse *PP*.[45] They do not occur in the Tibetan translation of that sūtra.[46] They do not occur in the Tibetan translations of the unrevised 25,000-verse *PP*.[47] They do not occur in the Sanskrit Gilgit manuscript of the 18,000-verse *PP*.[48] Nor do they occur in the Tibetan translations of the 18,000-verse *PP*.[49] In short, *rP* passages 8.1–8.3 are missing in all extant Sanskrit and Tibetan editions of the *Large PP Sūtra* except *rP*.

No translator is named in the Tibetan bKa' 'gyur for the 100,000-verse, the unrevised 25,000-verse, and the 18,000-verse *PP* sūtras.[50] However, all of these sūtras are listed in the lDan kar catalog, which was compiled in the latter part of the eighth century during the reign of the Tibetan king Khri srong lde brtsan (ca. 740–98 C.E.).[51] The Sanskrit manuscripts from which the first Tibetan translations of these sūtras were made, then, were presumably eighth-century manuscripts.

All of this tends to indicate that the passages in question (*rP* 8.1–8.3) were added to the *Large PP Sūtra* after all three of its recensions were well established. And because the passages occur only in the revised version of the 25,000-verse *PP* (in its Sanskrit manuscripts and Tibetan translation), and, to my knowledge, are not found in any other version of any *PP* sūtra in any language, it is not unreasonable to assume that they were inserted into the revised *PP* at the time of its redaction.[52]

The translators into Tibetan of *rP* are identified in its colophon as Tshul khrims rgyal ba and Śāntibhadra, both of whom can be dated to the middle part of the eleventh century.[53] Thus, *rP*, the revised version of the 25,000-verse *PP* sūtra was transmitted to Tibet about two-and-a-half centuries after all the other versions of the *Large PP Sūtra*. This may indicate that *rP* was not redacted until after the other versions of the *Large PP* had already been transmitted to Tibet, i.e., not until at least the latter part of the eighth century. In the postscript of the Tibetan translation of *rP*, the redactor identifies himself as Haribhadra (Pk 5188, fols. 61-3-1 to 61-3-2). Because Haribhadra lived from the end of the eighth century to the beginning of the ninth century, it is not unreasonable to believe that postscript and accept that he was *rP*'s redactor.[54] Further, the first Indian scholars to my knowledge to quote from *rP* are Ratnākaraśānti (ca. 1000 C.E.) and Abhayākaragupta (early twelfth century), both of whom wrote after Haribhadra's time.[55] From that time onward, Tibetan scholars routinely quoted *rP* in their commentaries on the *AA*.

3. *rP* passages 8.1–8.3 were not part of the *Prajñāpāramitāsūtra* in Ārya Vimuktisena's time

A central purpose of Ārya Vimuktisena's commentary (the *Abhisamayālaṃkāra-vṛtti)*, was to identify the textual basis in the 25,000-verse *PP* sūtra for each of the *AA*'s topics and subtopics. The *AA* consists of eight substantive chapters, each of which explicates one of the eight realizations of the path and its fruition (*abhisamaya*s, summarized in chapter 6 of this book). The explanation of the eight realizations in the eight chapters occurs by reference to seventy topics. And the seventy topics divide into some twelve hundred subtopics. Although it is beyond the scope of this book to examine Ārya Vimuktisena's treatment of each of the twelve hundred subtopics, I have examined how he introduces each of the seventy topics and a great many of the subtopics.

Throughout Ārya Vimuktisena's commentary, whenever he introduces a new *AA* topic he uses a standard procedure to identify the *PP* sūtra passage upon which he believes that topic to be based. First, he names the *AA* topic. He gives a brief explanation of it (often breaking it into its subtopics). He quotes the *AA* verse or verses that teach that topic. And he either quotes or explicitly paraphrases the corresponding 25,000-verse *PP* sūtra passage upon which he believes the *AA* verses to be based. Using this procedure, he identifies explicitly, by quote or paraphrase, the 25,000-verse *PP* sūtra passages that he thought to be the textual bases for all of the first sixty-six of the seventy topics in the *AA*, i.e., for every single one of the topics in the *AA*'s first seven chapters.

How can we be sure that he is quoting or paraphrasing the *PP* sūtra for each of topics in the *AA*'s first seven chapters? Couldn't he be giving his own explanations, using concepts and expressions similar to those of the *PP* sūtras? In fact, Ārya Vimuktisena gives explicit indication in his Sanskrit syntax that he is quoting or paraphrasing the *PP* sūtra rather than presenting his own explanations. He always uses one of the expressions standardly employed in Sanskrit to indicate direct quotes and paraphrases: *yad āha . . . iti* (as is said [in the *PP* sūtra]), *yad āha . . . ityādi* (as [the *PP* sūtra] said, etc.), *yathā* (as it is [in the sūtra]), or *iti,* indicating a direct quote. Only the first chapter of Ārya Vimuktisena's *AA* commentary is presently available in Sanskrit,[56] but that is a lengthy chapter; and it can be used to find the correlative Tibetan terms in the Tibetan translation of the rest of the commentary, available in the Tibetan Tripitaka (Pk 5185, pp. 45–102). The Tibetan equivalents are, respectively: *zhes gang gsungs pa yin no*, *zhes bya ba la sogs pa gang gsungs pa yin no*, *ji skad du*, and *zhes bya ba*. For all sixty-six topics in the *AA*'s first seven chapters Ārya Vimuktisena uses one or more of these expressions to indicate that he is quoting or directly paraphrasing the 25,000-verse *PP* sūtra. For all the topics in the *AA*'s first seven chapters, he quotes the *AA* verses that teach the topic and, soon thereafter, quotes or directly paraphrases the *PP* sūtra passages upon which he thinks those *AA* verses were based.

In most of these cases (fifty-one out of the sixty-six topics), he uses the vocative case for the name of a person in the *PP* sūtra. The *PP* sūtra, like other Buddhist sūtras, is in the form of dialogues between the Buddha and various disciples and deities. In these dialogues, one person is always addressing another, and therefore, generally begins his speech by calling out to the person he is addressing, using the vocative form of the person's name. Thus, the vocatives of "Bhagavan," "Subhuti," "Śāriputra," etc. appear in almost every *PP* passage, e.g.:

> [The Bhagavan says:] Śāriputra [vocative], a bodhisattva, a great being, who wants to fully know all dharmas in all respects should make endeavors in the perfection of wisdom.
> [Śāriputra replies:] Bhagavan [vocative], how should he make such endeavors?]

The appearance of these names in the vocative case in Ārya Vimuktisena's commentary again shows that he is directly quoting the *PP* sūtra. For fifty-one of the sixty-six topics of the *AA*'s first seven chapters, he gives the vocative forms of the names of the participants in the dialogues of the corresponding *PP* sūtra passages. Even for the fifteen of the sixty-six topics where he does not quote the names of the speakers, he clearly signals that he is quoting or directly paraphrasing their words from the sūtra through his use of the Sanskrit markers mentioned above.

Given Ārya Vimuktisena's invariable procedure of identifying *PP* sūtra passages for each *AA* topic upon introducing the topic, it is significant that he stops doing this when he begins commenting on *AA* 8. All commentators agreed that *AA* 8 taught Buddhahood through four topics. Ārya Vimuktisena identified the four topics of *AA* 8 as *svābhāvikakāya*, *sāmbhogikakāya*, *nairmāṇikakāya*, and Buddha *karma* (a Buddha's activity).[57] If Ārya Vimuktisena thought the first three topics of *AA* 8 (the three *kāyas*) were based upon *PP* sūtra passages *rP* 8.1–8.3, as later Indian and Tibetan commentators thought, we would expect him to quote or paraphrase those sūtra passages, just as he did for every single one of the sixty-six topics in the *AA*'s first seven chapters. But he does not. Unusually, when he introduces the first two topics of *AA* 8, *svābhāvikakāya* and *sāmbhogikakāya*, he quotes the *AA* verses that teach them, but makes no direct reference to the *PP* sūtra. Instead, he presents only his own autonomous explanations of these *kāyas*. We can tell he is giving his own explanation of the topics, not quoting or paraphrasing the *PP* sūtra, because he does not use any of the necessary Sanskrit markers, nor does he give the names of the *PP* characters in the vocative.[58]

But when he introduces the third topic of *AA* 8, *nairmāṇikakāya*, he reverts to his usual procedure of quoting the *PP* passage that teaches the topic, marking the quote with the usual Sanskrit markers (*iti;* in the Tibetan text, *zhes bya ba*) and quoting the names of the *PP* characters in the vocative.[59] Interestingly, the *PP* passage he quotes as the textual basis for the topic *nairmāṇikakāya* is not *rP* 8.3, the one identified as such by late Indian and Tibetan commentators. It is the *PP* passage immediately following *rP* 8.3, the *PP* passage numbered 8.4 in Conze's numbering system for the *Large PP Sūtra*.[60]

Ārya Vimuktisena again employs his usual modus operandi when he introduces the fourth topic of *AA* chapter 8: [Buddha] *karma*. He quotes the *PP* text basis for the topic, marking the quote with the usual Sanskrit markers. And the *PP* passage he quotes as the basis for the fourth topic, [Buddha] *karma*, is the *PP* passage numbered 8.5 in Conze's numbering system.[61] In short, Ārya Vimuktisena makes no mention whatsoever of *rP* 8.1–8.3. If he had known of those passages, we would expect him to have referred to them directly as the text bases of their corresponding topics in the *AA*, as he had done for all other *PP* passages corresponding to all other topics of the *AA*.

It is useful to recall here that *rP* 8.1–8.3, of which Ārya Vimuktisena was unaware, are not found in any version of the *Large PP Sūtra* except *rP*, while *PP* passages 8.4 and 8.5, which Ārya Vimuktisena presented as the entire text basis for *AA* chapter 8, are found in every version of the *Large PP Sūtra* available to us in Sanskrit, Chinese and Tibetan. This is strong evidence that *rP* passages 8.1–8.3 were added to the *Large PP Sūtra* sometime after Ārya Vimuktisena, and that *rP* passages 8.4–8.5 were indeed the sūtra text basis for *AA* 8.

Besides the negative evidence that Ārya Vimuktisena did not refer to *rP* 8.1–8.3, he also provides us with important positive evidence to support the hypothesis that the *Large PP Sūtra* of his time did not contain passages *rP* 8.1–8.3, but only passages 8.4–8.5. Although, as noted, he does not quote the *PP* sūtra when he introduces the first two topics of *AA* chapter 8—*svābhāvikakāya* and *sāmbhogikakāya*—he does quote from the *PP* sūtra when dealing with a few of their subtopics. And these quotations, too, come not from *rP* 8.1–8.3, but from the passages that follow them.

According to Ārya Vimuktisena's commentary, the first verse of *AA* 8 teaches its first topic, *svābhāvikakāya*, while verses 8.2–8.6 explicate the set of twenty-one undefiled Buddha dharmas, which are included within that first topic as a phenomenal description of the *svābhāvikakāya*'s nondual gnosis.[62] According to Ārya Vimuktisena's commentary, then, the twenty-one types of undefiled dharma comprise twenty-one subtopics of *svābhāvikakāya*. Ārya Vimuktisena explains several of the undefiled dharmas in some detail, probably basing himself upon Abhidharma sources.[63] When he comes to the last of the dharmas listed in *AA* v. 8.6, total omniscience *(sarvākārajñatā)* he quotes the *PP* sūtra as the textual basis.[64] The passage he quotes is found in section 8.5 of the unrevised 25,000-verse *PP* in the versions extant in Tibetan translation and in Kumarajiva's and Hsuan Tsang's Chinese translations.[65] Thus, although Ārya Vimuktisena does not quote the *PP* sūtra when introducing the *AA* topic *svābhāvikakāya*, he does give one direct quote when explaining the last of its subtopics, total omniscience *(sarvākāra-jñatā)*. And that quote is drawn from *PP* passage 8.5 (in Conze's number system).

Similarly, although he does not quote the *PP* sūtra when introducing *AA* 8's second topic, *sāmbhogikakāya* (*AA* v. 8.12), he does quote the *PP* sūtra on several of its subtopics: the thirty-two marks and eighty signs (*AA* vv. 8.13–8.32). All of these sūtra quotes are from the *Large PP* passage 8.5. When explaining the causes of the *sāmbhogikakāya's* thirty-two major marks, he simply gives *PP* section 8.5's account of them, indicating that he is quoting sūtra by saying: *yathā sūtram* (Tib., *ji skad du mdo las*, "as in the sūtra").[66] He also quotes from *PP* passage 8.5 extensively on the eighty signs.[67]

Finally, after completing his explanations of *svābhāvikakāya* and *sāmbhogikakāya*, Ārya Vimuktisena gives us the most convincing positive evidence of all that he based his entire commentary of *AA* 8 on *PP* sūtra passages 8.4 and 8.5. Immediately after finishing his comments on *svābhāvikakāya* and *sāmbhogikakāya*, he says: "As for the teaching of these two *[kāyas]*, they are taught in the section of the *[PP]* sūtra that teaches the *nairmāṇikakāya*'s activity, [in the section on] the means of gathering disciples that is the giving of supramundane dharma. Therefore they were not taught earlier."[68] Ārya Vimuktisena's statement: "the teaching of these two" *('di gnyis kyi bshad pa ni)* can only refer to the teaching of *svābhāvikakāya* and *sāmbhogikakāya*, the two topics he has just finished explaining. Ārya Vimuktisena is saying that the *PP* sūtra does not contain any distinct or separate sections concerning *svābhāvikakāya* and *sāmbhogikakāya*. Rather, he finds a sūtra textual basis for these *kāya* topics within the *PP* sūtra passage that he understands to be teaching *nairmāṇikakāya*, specifically within the passage that explains a bodhisattva's four methods of collecting disciples *(catvāri saṃgrahavastūni)*. That passage is a portion of *Large PP* passage 8.5. In it, the Buddha explains to Subhuti a Buddha's undefiled dharmas, thirty-two marks, and eighty signs.[69] It is the very same passage from which Ārya Vimuktisena drew all of his quotes for his explanations of the subtopics under *svābhāvikakāya* and *sāmbhogikakāya* discussed just above.

Upon introducing the third topic of *AA* 8, *nairmāṇikakāya*, Ārya Vimuktisena resumes his procedure of quoting the *Large PP Sūtra,* but not the passage we would have expected if *PP* passages *rP* 8.1–8.3 were contained in the sūtra of his time. According to Ārya Vimuktisena, the *nairmāṇikakāya* is the means through which resultant *dharmakāya* (*dharmakāyaphalaṃ*, meaning Buddhahood as a whole) carries out its vast, uninterrupted activity for living beings. He quotes *AA* 8's verses 33–34a as teaching *nairmāṇikakāya*, and then quotes *PP* sūtra passage 8.4 as the textual source of those verses.[70]

As mentioned earlier, Ratnākaraśānti, Abhayākaragupta and Tibetan commentators identified *rP* 8.3 as the sole textual basis for the *AA*'s teaching of *nairmāṇikakāya*. If the *PP* sūtra available to Ārya Vimuktisena contained that passage, we would have expected him to have quoted it, rather than *PP* passage 8.4. After all, *rP* passage 8.3 (translated above in section 2.a) is a clear description of a Buddha's vast manifestations *(nirmāṇa)*, which comprise his *nairmāṇikakāya*. But Ārya Vimuktisena writes as if there were no passage 8.3. Again, the simplest explanation for this is that the *PP* sūtra of his time did not contain it. He then identifies the rest of *AA* chapter 8's verses, 8.34b–8.40, with the fourth topic: [Buddha] *karma*, the activity of Buddhahood carried out by *nairmāṇikakāya*. And he quotes *PP* passage 8.5 as the textual source for those verses.[71]

To recapitulate, immediately following Ārya Vimuktisena's explanation of what he identified as *AA* chapter 8's first two topics, *svābhāvikakāya* and *sāmbhogikakāya*, he tells us directly that the textual basis of those topics in the *PP* sūtra is to be found solely in passage 8.5, and not to be found any earlier within the *PP* sūtra. This, he says, is because the *PP* sūtra implicitly teaches *svābhāvikakāya* and *sāmbhogikakāya* in the course of its explanation of the *nairmāṇikakāya*'s activity, in *PP* passage 8.5. He then goes on to explain the third and fourth topics of *AA* 8 as *nairmāṇikakāya* and [Buddha] *karma*.[72] He identifies the textual bases for these two topics as *PP* passages 8.4 and 8.5 respectively, quoting them extensively. Ārya Vimuktisena, then, tells us straightforwardly that the sole textual bases in the *PP* sūtra of his time for all four topics of *AA* chapter 8, the three Buddha *kāyas* and Buddha's activity, are to be found in *Large PP Sūtra* passages 8.4 and 8.5. This proves that the *PP* sūtra that Ārya Vimuktisena knew did not contain *PP* passages *rP* 8.1–8.3.

It would appear, then, that Edward Conze, one of the greatest pioneers of *Prajñāpāramitā* studies, inadvertently obscured some of the textual history of the *Large PP Sūtra* by devising a numbering system for its passages based on its revised version, *rP*. *rP* passages 8.1–8.3 were added to the *Large PP Sūtra* some time after Ārya Vimuktisena's commentary was composed. *PP* passages 8.4 and 8.5 were the only passages Ārya Vimuktisena knew that could correspond to *AA* chapter 8. If Conze had devised his numbering system for *PP* sūtra passages based on the unrevised *Large PP* available in Ārya Vimuktisena's time (ca. early sixth century) together with Ārya Vimuktisena's commentary, rather than basing his numbering system on *rP*, the *PP* sūtra passages he numbered 8.4 and 8.5 might have been designated simply "8," signifying the section of the *Large PP Sūtra* upon which *AA* 8 in its entirety was based.

4. *Large Prajñāpāramitā Sūtra* passages 8.4–8.5 were the actual textual basis for *Abhisamayālaṃkāra* chapter 8

Ārya Vimuktisena was the foremost *Prajñāpāramitā* scholar of his day. The fact that he had no knowledge of *rP* 8.1–8.3 is strong evidence that they were simply not part of the *PP* sūtra during his time. This means that they were probably added to the *PP* sūtra after him. If we may assume that the *AA* was composed earlier than any of its commentaries, *rP* passages 8.1–8.3 were not part of the *PP* sūtra at the time the *AA* was composed.[73] Therefore, even though Ratnākaraśānti, Abhayākaragupta, and leading Tibetan *PP* scholars thought *AA* chapter 8 was based in large part upon *PP* passages *rP* 8.1–8.3, in fact it was not.

Why did such prodigious late Indian and Tibetan scholars not realize this? One reason is that Ārya Vimuktisena's introductory comments on each of the three *kāyas* are quite similar to the descriptions of them found in *rP* 8.1–8.3. Traditional scholars made the seemingly reasonable assumption that this similarity occurred because he had based his remarks on those *PP* sūtra passages. They assumed that his comments were in fact paraphrases of those sūtra passages. But we have demonstrated that those passages were almost certainly added after Ārya Vimuktisena's commentary was written. It is likely, therefore, that the actual situation is the exact reverse of what later scholars assumed: somebody composed *rP* passages 8.1–8.3 and inserted them into the *Large PP Sūtra* using Ārya Vimuktisena's comments as basis. Ārya Vimuktisena's remarks were not based on *rP* passages 8.1–8.3; rather, *rP* passages 8.1–8.3 were probably based upon his remarks.[74]

As we have noted, Ārya Vimuktisena identifies *PP* passages 8.4 and 8.5 as the textual bases for all of *AA* chapter 8. And this does appear reasonable. While *rP* passages 8.1–8.3 are late additions, found only in the revised version of the *Large PP*, *PP* passages 8.4–8.5 are found in all extant recensions and translations of the *Large PP Sūtra* in Sanskrit, Chinese and Tibetan. *PP* passages 8.4–8.5 are found in the Gilgit manuscript of the 18,000-verse *PP*, which is dated to the fifth or sixth century C.E., and in Mokṣala's Chinese translation of the 25,000-verse *PP*, dated to 291 C.E. It is likely, then, that they were generally included within the *Large PP Sūtra* at the time the *AA* was composed, ca. fourth century to early sixth centuries C.E. Within the *Large PP*, passages 8.4–8.5 comprise the last part of the sūtra, and immediately follow the passages identified by Ārya Vimuktisena and other commentators as the textual basis for *AA* chapter 7. It is natural that 8.4–8.5 would be the textual basis for *AA* chapter 8. Furthermore, *AA* 8, if read side by side with *PP* passages 8.4–8.5, clearly does, in fact, comprise a brief synopsis of the content of those very sūtra passages (particularly with reference to the undefiled dharmas, the thirty-two marks and eighty signs, and the various bodhisattva activities).[75] It is therefore likely, as Ārya Vimuktisena claimed, that the *AA*'s author based *AA* 8 on *PP* passages 8.4–8.5.[76]

5. Textual history of *rP*, and evidence that Haribhadra was its redactor

Some comments were made above concerning the possible date of redaction of *rP* and the probability that Haribhadra was its redactor. Those comments need to be updated with reference to the evidence of Ārya Vimuktisena's commentary just above, and in light of a few other observations.

Nancy Lethcoe's 1976 paper aligned the topics and subtopics of the *AA* with corresponding passages in three different Chinese translations of the unrevised 25,000-verse *PP* sūtra (translations made in three different periods in China: 291 C.E., 403–4 C.E., and 659–63 C.E.), and the Sanskrit manuscript of the revised 25,000-verse *PP*. Lethcoe's findings indicate that the 25,000-verse *PP* sūtra went through several stages of development in India, involving additions of passages, transpositions, and in some cases omissions, culminating in the redaction of the revised version, *rP*.[77]

On pages 503–4 of her paper, Lethcoe notes a number of *AA* subtopics for which, in all three Chinese translations of the 25,000-verse *PP* sūtra, there are no corresponding sūtra passages, but in the revised version of the sūtra *(rP)* there are corresponding passages. Of course, among these are *rP* passages 8.1–8.3, which are missing in all Chinese translations of the sūtra. Certain *AA* subtopics, according to Lethcoe's study, have no corresponding sections in all Chinese translations of the sūtra but do have corresponding sections in *rP* (numbered according to Conze's numbering system for *AA* topics and subtopics): 1.1e.7–10, 1.10.8.c–d, 3.1–3, and 3.5.[78] Without question, these passages of *rP*, together with *rP* passages 8.1–8.3, missing in all Chinese translations of the 25,000-verse *PP* sūtra up to the middle of the seventh century, are late additions to that sūtra .

I have checked Lethcoe's findings against the unrevised 25,000-verse *PP* sūtra (Peking edition) in the Tibetan canon (Pk 731) and against Ārya Vimuktisena's commentary, which aligns the passages of the 25,000-verse *PP* sūtra with corresponding sections of the *AA*.[79] I found that of the passages noted that are missing in all Chinese translations of the unrevised 25,000-verse *PP* sūtra, passages 1.1e.7–10 are also missing in the Tibetan translation of that sūtra but are directly quoted in Ārya Vimuktisena's commentary (Pk 5185, fols. 10-3-8 to 10-4-8); passages 1.10.8.c–d are also missing in the Tibetan translation and are *not* quoted or referred to in Ārya Vimuktisena's commentary (Pk 5185, fols. 44-5-5ff. is where they should have appeared); and passages 3.1–3.3 and 3.5 are found in the Tibetan translation and are quoted in Ārya Vimuktisena's commentary (Pk 5185, fols. 54-5-6 to 55-2-1). Passages 8.1–8.3 are also missing in the Tibetan translation of that sūtra, and are not quoted or referred to in Ārya Vimuktisena's commentary.

All of this tends to support Lethcoe's contention that the 25,000-verse *PP* sūtra went through stages of development in India. It also indicates that passages were added to and transposed within certain recensions of the sūtra gradually over time to make it align better with the *AA*. This appears to have been gradual process of change, which finally culminated with the insertion of the *AA*'s topic and subtopic titles into corresponding portions of the sūtra together with the addition of passages corresponding to *AA* topics 8.1–8.3.[80] This could mean that a special edition of the 25,000-verse *PP* sūtra developed in *AA* cult circles over time, eventually becoming redacted as the revised edition, *rP*.

The evidence discussed earlier indicates that *rP* passages 8.1–8.3 were written and inserted into the sūtra based upon Ārya Vimuktisena's commentary. In fact, the correspondences made in *rP* between *PP* sūtra passages and the sections of the *AA* seem to follow precisely Ārya Vimuktisena's alignment of those correspondences, and the *AA* topic titles inserted into *rP* reflect Ārya Vimuktisena's titles and synopses. Since *rP* as a whole, then, was apparently redacted based upon Ārya Vimuktisena's commentary, it is not surprising for us to have found that *rP* passages 8.1–8.3 were written and newly inserted into the sūtra based upon Ārya Vimuktisena's own remarks.

What was the *rP* redactor's motivation for writing new passages into the *PP* sūtra, a text that was traditionally accepted as scripture? Actually, the redactor of *rP* may not have noticed that Ārya Vimuktisena, at the point corresponding to *AA* 8 in his commentary, suddenly stopped quoting the *PP* sūtra. He may have been so accustomed to Ārya Vimuktisena's usual procedure of quoting the sūtra for each *AA* topic and subtopic that he simply presumed that the remarks Ārya Vimuktisena made on the first few topics of *AA* chapter 8 were paraphrases of passages found in some version of the sūtra the redactor did not have. And based on such considerations, he may have written Ārya Vimuktisena's remarks into the sūtra as passages 8.1–8.3 without realizing that he was making a new addition to the sūtra. The irony in this case would be that the redactor may have thought that he was restoring the sūtra to a form closer to what it was in Ārya Vimuktisena's time. He did not, of course, have available to him all the editions of the 25,000-verse *PP* sūtra in its various translations in Chinese and Tibetan that are now available to us in modern research libraries.

rP passages 8.1–8.3, then, are a distinguishing trait of *rP*, found only in that version of the sūtra, and apparently added to the sūtra close to or at the time of its redaction in the form of *rP*. We know that *rP*, as we have it, was redacted some time after Ārya Vimuktisena (ca. early sixth century) and before Ratnākaraśānti (ca. 1000 C.E.), because Ratnākaraśānti quoted *rP* passages 8.1–8.3. Although the large versions of the *PP* sūtra in 100,000 verses, 25,000 verses and 18,000 verses are all listed in the lDan kar catalog, compiled during the reign of Tibetan king Khri srong lde brtsan (ca. 740–98 c.e.), *rP* is not listed in the catalog. This may indicate it was not redacted until at least the end of the eighth century. As mentioned above, the redactor of *rP* identifies himself in the postscript of its Tibetan translation as Haribhadra.[81] Haribhadra lived near the end of the eighth and beginning of the ninth centuries C.E., the earliest time we could accept for the redaction of *rP*. I see no reason to doubt that he was the redactor.

Basing himself on a report by the Tibetan scholar Taranatha (sixteenth to seventeenth centuries) that said that Ārya Vimuktisena (ca. early sixth century) consulted a revised version of the *PP*, Conze surmised that at least the Sanskrit edition of *rP* belonged to the fifth century, while perhaps the Tibetan translation represents a later redaction by Haribhadra.[82] But passages 8.1–8.3 are found in both the Sanskrit manuscripts and in the Tibetan translation of *rP*, and the textual evidence presented above strongly suggests that any text of *rP* containing those passages was redacted in the late eighth century at the earliest, supporting its attribution to Haribhadra. In any case, we have proven that *rP* came after, not before, Ārya Vimuktisena, Taranatha's remark (made a thousand years after the fact) notwithstanding.

There is also evidence that Haribhadra himself knew of *rP* and referred to it. If true, this would make Haribhadra himself the first Indian scholar to refer directly to *rP*, which lends some further support to his having been its redactor. At the close of his remarks in the *Sphuṭārthā* on *AA* verses 8.2–8.6 concerning the set of undefiled Buddha dharmas, Haribhadra makes an important remark concerning the use of the word "and" *(ca)* in *AA* v. 8.6. *AA* verses 8.2–8.5 (the reader may recall from the previous chapter) list the various undefiled Buddha dharmas up to great compassion *(mahatī karuṇā)*. *AA* verse 8.6 lists the final two undefiled dharmas, the eighteen unique qualities, and total omniscience, and then ends the whole list of dharmas with the term *ca:*

> āveṇikā muner eva dharmā ye 'ṣṭadaśeritāḥ
> sarvākārajñatā ceti dharmakāyo s'bhidhīyate
>
> (*AA* 8.6)

> ["the eighteen qualities unique to the Sage, and total omniscience": thus is *dharmakāya* denominated.]

The Sanskrit term *ca*, placed at the end of a list, generally connects the last term to all previous terms in the list. In English, we say, "the dog, the cat, and the parrot." In Sanskrit, this list would be structured: "dog, cat, parrot *ca*," with the same sense. In *AA* v. 8.6, the list of twenty-one types of undefiled Buddha dharmas ends with the twenty-first term, *sarvākārajñatā* (total omniscience), followed by the terms *ca* and *iti;* the two latter terms are modified by external *saṃdhi* to make *ceti*. *AA* vv. 8.2–8.6, then, are most straightforwardly translated: " 'The factors that foster enlightenment, the measureless thoughts, the liberations, . . . the great compassion for living beings, the eighteen qualities unique to the Muni, and *(ca)* total omniscience': thus *(iti)* is *dharmakāya* denominated."

In his *Sphuṭārthā*, Haribhadra makes an unusual remark concerning the word *ca.* He says, "Included within the expression *ca* is the path knowledge *(mārgajñatā)*, etc., which have already been explained earlier [in previous chapters]."[83] Haribhadra is saying that the term *ca* following the term *sarvākārajñatā* (total omniscience) is used to designate the inclusion of path knowledge *(mārgajñatā)* and (we are safe to assume) all-knowledge *(sarvajñatā)*, which as a threesome comprise the three realizations *(abhisamayas)* that are the subject matter of the *Abhisamayālaṃkāra*'s first three chapters. But this is an unusual interpretation for the meaning of the Sanskrit term *ca*. Haribhadra goes out of his way to stretch the meaning of the term so that all three principal knowledges (total omniscience, path knowledge, and all-knowledge) forming the subject matter of the *AA* will be semantically included in *AA* verses 8.2–8.6.[84] Haribhadra's unusual interpretation of the Sanskrit indicates that the semantic inclusion of all three knowledges *(jñatās)* at this juncture in the *AA* was important to him for some reason.

As noted in chapter 3 of this book, the lists of undefiled Buddha dharmas *(anāsravadharmāḥ)* are repeatedly presented throughout the *Prajñāpāramitā* sūtras as phenomenal expressions of a Buddha's gnosis. The lists of undefiled dharmas, more or less complete, appear in the various editions of the *Large PP Sūtra* in the passages corresponding to *AA* subtopics 1.5.5, 1.5.7, 1.5,11, 1.9.14, 4.1.3, and 8.5.2.[85] These lists are presented throughout all the editions of the *Large PP Sūtra* available in Sanskrit and Tibetan. I have examined all editions available to me of the *Large PP* Sūtra in Sanskrit and Tibetan, and have found that wherever the list of undefiled Buddha dharmas is presented, the term "total omniscience" *(sarvākārajñatā)* is never accompanied by the terms "path knowledge" *(mārgajñatā)* or all-knowledge *(sarvajñatā)* with only one exception. That exception is (you guessed it) *rP* passage 8.1, which is, to my knowledge, unique among all *Large PP Sūtra* passages in ending its list of the undefiled dharmas with all three *jñātās* listed together: "The thirty-seven factors that foster enlightenment, (etc. to) . . . total omniscience, path knowledge and all knowledge: these indeed, Subhuti, are all the undefiled dharmas."[86]

What does this mean? One possibility is that Haribhadra had *rP* before him and referred to *rP* passage 8.1 when he made his remarks on *AA* vv. 8.2–8.6. He would therefore have felt it necessary to interpret the ending of *AA* verses 8.1–8.6 in a way parallel to what he saw at the end of *rP* passage 8.1 (the set of three *jñātās* listed together). Another very distinct possibility, however, is that Haribhadra himself, for sake of completion, wanted the three *jñatās* listed together in the list of undefiled dharmas, and therefore wrote them himself into *rP* passage 8.1 and into his remarks on *AA* vv. 8.2–8.6. In other words, Haribhadra at least knew of *rP*. And when we combine these observations with all those above, it is not unreasonable to hypothesize that he made *rP*, that he was its redactor and the author of *rP* passages 8.1–8.3.

There is further evidence that Haribhadra was indeed the redactor of *rP*.

Dharmamitra, thought to be an immediate successor of Haribhadra, wrote an important subcommentary to Haribhadra's *Sphuṭārthā:* the *Prasphuṭapadā.*[87] Dharmamitra, with reference to the controversy apparently created by Haribhadra's having newly interpreted *AA* 8 to be teaching four *kāyas*, wrote that some scholars thought Haribhadra personally held to only three *kāyas*, but that he taught four in some of his commentaries to please his guru, Vairocana. This is indicated, said these scholars, by the fact that Haribhadra taught three *kāyas* in another of his texts.[88] The only text ascribed to Haribhadra that explicitly delineates three *kāyas* is *rP* itself (which distinguishes three *kāyas* in its titles for *rP* passages 8.1–8.3). Although Haribhadra makes a formalized prayer "for the attainment of the three *kāyas*" at the end of his *Āloka*, he clearly delineates four *kāyas* at length in his remarks earlier in that same text.[89] His formalized prayer at the end of his *Āloka* follows a standard, traditional form that does not constitute a teaching or commentary on his part. His *Sphuṭārthā* also clearly delineates four *kāyas*, as does his very brief commentary, the *Saṃcaya-gāthā-pañjikā subhodinī.*[90] Therefore, Dharmamitra's remark that some Indian scholars of his time ascribed a text to Haribhadra that delineated three *kāyas* probably refers to *rP*, the revised version of the 25,000-verse *PP* sūtra, and to its redaction by Haribhadra.

Why would Haribhadra make a redaction of the *rP*—the 25,000-verse *PP* sūtra that delineates three *kāyas*, naming the three in its inserted titles—and then write two substantial commentaries in which he rejects the interpretation of *AA* 8 as a three-*kāya* teaching, asserting instead that it teaches four *kāyas*? In fact this makes more sense than it might appear. Haribhadra was the first scholar to take on the prodigious task of writing extensive commentaries on the *AA* since the time of the Vimuktisenas. There would be nothing more logical to do, as preparation for such a task, than to make for oneself a working copy of the *Large PP Sūtra* that would contain all the topics and subtopics of the *AA* inserted as titles after their corresponding sūtra passages—in other words, to begin by making a reference guide to correspondences between the *AA* and the *Large PP Sūtra*. The logical way to proceed was to base the redaction of this "reference guide" on Ārya Vimuktisena's commentary, which identified all the correspondences between the *AA* and the *Large PP Sūtra,* and which delineated three *kāyas*.

Haribhadra may well have written *rP* passages 8.1–8.3 into the sūtra to "restore it" to the form he thought it had when Ārya Vimuktisena had composed his commentary. It would provide a sūtra basis for the Ārya's remarks on *svābhāvikakāya*, *sāmbhogikakāya*, and *nairmāṇikakāya* (he may not have noticed Ārya Vimuktisena's brief statement that there is no sūtra basis for *svābhāvikakāya* and *sāmbhogikakāya* prior to *PP* passage 8.5; see section 2.b.3 above). Having redacted *rP* as his reference manual, Haribhadra would then be prepared to compose his own commentaries (the *Āloka* and *Sphuṭārthā*) in which he introduced his own four-*kāya* interpretation.

6. Terms and concepts in *Abhisamayālaṃkāra* chapter 8 not found in *Prajñāpāramitā* passages 8.4–8.5

We have concluded that the *Abhisamayālaṃkāra*'s author based the eighth chapter of his work on *PP* passages 8.4–8.5.[91] We have therefore identified the actual scriptural basis for *AA* 8 in those passages. Now we can examine the relation between *AA* 8 and the *PP* passages upon which it was based to see what light may be shed on its meaning. *AA* 8 both names and explains *svābhāvikakāya*, *sāmbhogikakāya*, *nairmāṇikakāya*, and Buddha *karma* (activity of a Buddha for beings). And it mentions *dharmakāya*. What do *PP* passages 8.4 and 8.5 teach? Surprisingly, they do not center on Buddhahood per se, and do not specifically refer to the Buddha *kāyas*.

PP passage 8.4 explains how bodhisattvas use skill in means *(upāyakauśalya)* to lead living beings from their suffering to enlightenment. This passage describes the paradox presented by a bodhisattva's skill in means. The bodhisattva, realizing the emptiness of all phenomena *(dharmāḥ),* does not perceive any phenomena. Yet he uses his skill in means, his ability to teach living beings in ways appropriate to their own capacities, in order to lead them toward enlightenment. And that involves making the distinctions between virtuous and nonvirtuous dharmas, levels of practice, etc., necessary for disciples to progress on the spiritual path. Thus, although established in emptiness free from discrimination of phenomena, the bodhisattva makes distinctions between phenomena necessary to teach others.[92] While this is relevant to Buddhahood as a core practice leading to it, it is not a description of Buddhahood in any systematic sense such as we saw in the Yogācāra texts of chapters 4 and 5 above or in the *Abhisamayālaṃkāra*'s eighth chapter (translated in chapter 6 above).

Similarly, Buddhahood is not the focus of *PP* passage 8.5, although qualities of Buddhahood do come up as an important part of the discussion. The primary teaching of *PP* 8.5 concerns the four ways in which bodhisattvas gather disciples to themselves *(catvāri saṃgrahavastūni).*[93] The first of these four ways is the giving of gifts. According to *PP* 8.5, bodhisattvas gather disciples by giving them material gifts and the gift of dharma. The latter includes the gift of mundane dharma and the gift of supramundane dharma. A bodhisattva gives the gift of mundane dharma when he teaches all the practices and realizations shared by both Buddhists and non-Buddhists. He gives the gift of supramundane dharma when he teaches all the practices and realizations distinctive of the Buddhist path, which culminate in the achievement of all the undefiled dharmas of a Buddha (pure mental qualities, *anāsravadharmāḥ*), as well as the thirty-two marks and eighty signs that distinguish a Buddha's body as that of an eminent person *(mahāpuruṣa).*

The passage gives an inventory of all the practices and realizations of the Buddhist paths transmitted by bodhisattvas to persons. And within that inventory, included among many other practices and realizations, are the realizations and qualities of Buddhahood itself. There is no mention of the *kāyas* of a Buddha, nor even specifically of a Buddha's activity. The numerous activities mentioned in the passage are carried out by bodhisattvas, the Buddha merely observing and describing what they do: "Here, Subhuti, surveying the world with my Buddha-eye, I have seen in all directions in world systems countless like the sands of the Ganges, bodhisattvas who help men with the four means of gathering disciples. . . ."[94] Consistent with much of the rest of the *PP* sūtra, *PP* passage 8.5 describes the activities of bodhisattvas who are engaged in the practice of the perfection of wisdom *(prajñāpāramitā)* conjoined with skill in means.

PP passage 8.5's mention of a Buddha's qualities, then, is ancillary to its teaching of bodhisattva practice, Buddha qualities being among the many qualities a bodhisattva helps people to obtain. This material provided a limited textual basis for the author of the *Abhisamayālaṃkāra* to use in his composition of chapter 8. He had systematically explained the entire Mahāyāna path to enlightenment in the *AA*'s first seven chapters. What remained was to provide a systematic explanation of the fruit of that path, Buddhahood. This was the purpose of his eighth chapter. But after he had used most of the *Large PP Sūtra* as textual basis for his first seven chapters, the only passages that remained, *PP* 8.4 and 8.5, did not take Buddhahood per se as their central focus.

Still, contained within those passages was the list of undefiled Buddha dharmas found throughout the *PP* sūtras as a phenomenal expression of a Buddha's pure cognitive qualities. Also contained in those passages was a list of the thirty-two marks and eighty signs of the *mahāpuruṣa*, ascribed to the form of a Buddha.[95] Such lists of undefiled dharmas and marks and signs were common *PP* sūtra expressions of Buddhahood as understood on the phenomenal or conventional level.[96] Therefore, the author of the *AA* found in passages 8.4 and 8.5 standard *PP* sūtra conventional expressions of Buddhahood, the undefiled dharmas and the marks and signs. Those, combined with a reinterpretation in passage 8.5 of the bodhisattvas' activities as activities of Buddhahood in its manifestations, provided a sufficient *PP* textual basis for a discussion of Buddhahood in *AA* chapter 8.

7.3
Conclusion: *Abhisamayālaṃkāra* Chapter 8 as a Yogācāra-*Prajñāpāramitā* Mapping

If *AA* 8 were based on *rP* passages 8.1–8.3, which explicitly delineate multiple *kāyas*, we would follow late Indian and Tibetan scholars in concluding that *AA* 8 must be teaching whatever kāyas those passages taught. But *AA* 8 was not based on them. It was based on *PP* passages 8.4 and 8.5. And these passages present the same lists of Buddha dharmas and physical marks and signs that are to be found repeatedly throughout the *PP* sūtras. In explicating them, *AA* 8 was explicating the

PP sūtras' most common way of describing Buddhahood in phenomenal terms. Importantly, *AA* chapter 8, without any basis within the *PP* sūtra, employed the specific technical terms *svābhāvikakāya*, *sāmbhogikakāya*, and *nairmāṇikakāya* to structure its entire exposition of Buddhahood. These terms and concepts, which do not appear in the *PP* sūtras at all, were drawn from other sources. We have dated the *AA* from the late fourth century to the early sixth century C.E. The only contemporaneous sources from which it could have drawn such terminology are Yogācāra.

The doctrines of *svābhāvikakāya*, *sāmbhogikakāya*, and *nairmāṇikakāya* were systematized in the Yogācāra texts that we explored in chapters 4 and 5 of this book. As we noted there, the three-*kāya* doctrine formed within a Yogācāra milieu of thought and praxis, finding systematic expression for the first time in *śā*stras such as the *MSA*, *Msg, Buddhabhūmivyākhyāna*, etc., which appeared from the third to the sixth centuries C.E. The three-*kāya* model was constructed in organic relation to other Yogācāra models of enlightenment: fundamental transformation *(āśrayaparāvṛtti)*, purified dharma realm *(dharmadhātuviśuddha)*, purified thusness/nonconceptual gnosis *(tathatāviśuddhi/nirvikalpajñāna)*, as they informed and were informed by Yogācāra meditational praxis and gnoseology.

In the Yogācāra presentation of the three-*kāya* doctrine explored in earlier chapters, *svābhāvikakāya* is identified with *dharmakāya* as the very essence of Buddhahood (nondual, nonconceptual realization of thusness gnosis). *Dharmakāya* is described in Yogācāra texts, from a phenomenal point of view, in terms of the undefiled Buddha dharmas, but is not "defined" by them, i.e., is not identified *as* them, the reason being that *dharmakāya* is not captured by any such set of conceptually differentiated terms and concepts, but is the nondual realization of the emptiness of all such terms and concepts.

Abhisamayālaṃkāra verses 8.1–8.6 fully reflect that basic Yogācāra structure of thought. But because the *AA* author's task required his commentary to be grounded within the textual material of the *Large PP Sūtra* itself, his exposition of *svābhāvikakāya* required him to give the list of undefiled dharmas (from *PP* passages 8.4 and 8.5) greater prominence than it had received in Yogācāra texts where *svābhāvikakāya* had originally been formulated.

Along similar lines, the *AA*'s author, in *AA* v. 8.12, specifically links the Yogācāra term and concept *sāmbhogikakāya* to the *PP* textual material in passage 8.5, which lists the thirty-two marks and eighty signs of a Buddha's physical body.[97] He then expounds the *PP* material on the marks and signs at greater length in vv. 8.13 to 8.32. Similarly, at *AA* v. 8.33, the author links the Yogācāra term *nairmāṇikakāya* to the *PP* textual material in passages 8.4 and 8.5 describing how bodhisattvas carry out extensive activity for beings.[98] Then he expounds the *PP* textual material on those activities at greater length from vv. 8.34 to 8.40.

The structure and pattern of *AA* 8, then, is quite clear. The *AA*'s author first makes an explicit linkage between each *kāya* term of the Yogācāra tradition and the textual material of a corresponding *PP* passage. He does this with one verse (v. 8.1, v. 8.12, v. 8.33, v. 8.34). Then he details the content of the *PP* passage with a further set of verses.[99] *AA* v. 8.1 links the Yogācāra *svābhāvikakāya* with the undefiled Buddha dharmas of *PP* passage 8.5. Then, vv. 8.2-8.6 specify the Buddha dharmas, as taught in the *PP* passage. *AA* v. 8.12 links the Yogācāra *sāmbhogikakāya* with the glorious physical form of the Buddha described in *PP* passage 8.5, qualified by the marks and signs of eminence. Then, vv. 8.13–8.32 detail those marks and signs as they are described in the *PP* passage. *AA* v. 8.33 links the Yogācāra *nairmāṇikakāya* with the bodhisattvas carrying out activities for beings in *PP* passages 8.4-8.5. Then, vv. 8.34-8.40 detail those activities as described in those passages.[100] It is quite clear that the *AA*'s author either drew his *kāya* terminology from Yogācāra texts (such as the *MSA*), or he drew it from the substratum of ideas that gave rise to such texts.[101]

The author of *AA* 8, then, by explicating *PP* passages 8.4 and 8.5's lists of Buddha qualities, was explaining the way the *PP* sūtras *generally* talked about Buddhahood. And, simultaneously, he was linking this to the way Yogācāra texts generally talked about Buddhahood. What he was seeking to explain, then, was not just the meaning of a few short *PP* passages (such as *rP* passages 8.1-8.3), but rather the relationship between the different ways Buddhahood was generally described in two of the main Mahāyāna textual traditions of his time, the *PP* sūtras and the Yogācāra śāstras.

This presents us with a basic question. Why did the *AA*'s author feel called upon to include in the eighth chapter of his work both *PP* and Yogācāra terminology? Why wasn't he content, in composing that chapter, to write a few verses describing the Buddha qualities as they are presented in the *PP* sūtra, and to leave it at that? The only way to approach such questions, its seems to me, is to look at the *AA* in its historical context, to try to see, at least in part, what role it may have played in the development of Buddhist thought during the period in history in which it was composed.

Let us look at what the author of the *AA* was faced with as he sat down to compose his eighth chapter. Having versified the entire Mahāyāna path, it was time to write his verses on the ultimate fruit of that path, Buddhahood. He was presumably very much aware that, by his time, two influential ways to articulate enlightenment had emerged within textual traditions of Mahāyāna Buddhism. One was the doctrine of three *kāya*s articulated in Yogācāra treatises (also closely connected to the doctrine of Buddha-nature, *tathāgatagarbha*, as it took expression in textual sources for the *Ratnagotravibhāga*). The other was an older corpus of buddhological teachings found in Abhidharma and *PP* sūtras, which included lists of undefiled dharmas *(anāsravadharmāḥ)*, thirty-two marks and eighty signs of the *mahāpuruṣa*, and occasional references to *dharmakāya* or *rupakāya*. The Yogācāra three-*kāya* doctrine was gaining prominence in this period, appearing as it does in the *MSA*, *Msg*, *Buddhabhūmisūtra*, *MAV*, *RGV*, and related commentaries that are thought to have been composed prior to, within, or near the same period as the *AA*. Within the history of Indian Mahāyāna Buddhism to this point, nobody had explicitly related the buddhology of the *Prajñāpāramitā* sūtras to the increasingly influential Yogācāra descriptions. Were the *PP* sūtras and the Yogācāras talking about the same state of enlightenment, or not? Surely the author of the *AA* would want to say that they were. The *PP* comprised perhaps the most fundamental and, in Mahāyāna circles, the most universally accepted collection of sūtras. As far as we know, no established Mahāyāna school thought of its buddhology as divorced from or in conflict with that of the *PP* sūtras. But this would mean that what the *PP* referred to in terms of "undefiled Buddha dharmas," "marks and signs," *dharmakāya*, and *rupakāya* must be the same thing that Yogācāras referred to in terms of *svābhāvikakāya*, *sāmbhogikakāya*, and *nairmāṇikakāya*. The obvious question would then be: Precisely how do the two descriptions correspond? Which items in the *PP* expressions of Buddhahood correspond to each of the three *kāya*s? At the time that the *AA* was composed, it is this question that its author would have wanted to address.

A number of modern scholars, Conze, Dutt, La Vallée Poussin, Obermiller and others have reported that *AA* 8 teaches four *kāya*s.[102] Conze, Dutt, and La Vallée Poussin probably based their remarks on the pioneering work of Obermiller, who himself relied on Tibetan commentators who followed Haribhadra's interpretation of *AA* 8. But Haribhadra and his followers in India and Tibet looked at the *AA* from a perspective many centuries removed from the time of its composition. If the *AA* did teach four *kāya*s, it would have been proposing a new theory, one that had not yet been worked out in either Yogācāra or *PP* sources.[103] But it is doubtful that that kind of new development would occur so abruptly. As far as we can tell, never before in the history of Buddhist thought had a *PP* commentator explicitly related the buddhology of the *PP* sūtras to that of the Yogācāras in a major commentary. Would he begin by making a new theory? It is much more likely that he would begin by seeking to find the correspondence between the two theories already at hand. If this line of reasoning is correct, then the author's intention in *AA* chapter 8 was to explain which of the terms and concepts in the *PP* sūtras corresponded to each of the three *kāya*s of Yogācāra, i.e., to show how they matched up. His task was to map Yogācāra terms and concepts onto *PP* terms and concepts. This would mean that the *AA* was indeed a three-*kāya* text, mapping the three *kāya*s of Yogācāra onto the *Large PP Sūtra*.

Is there support for this conclusion among any of the *AA*'s commentators? Do any of them understand *AA* chapter 8 to constitute such a mapping? In fact, this is precisely how Ārya Vimuktisena understood the text. He specified the *AA*'s textual basis for *svābhāvikakāya* as *PP* passage 8.5's listing of the undefiled Buddha dharmas, the *AA*'s textual basis for *sāmbhogikakāya* as *PP* 8.5's listing of the marks and signs, the *AA's* textual basis for *nairmāṇikakāya* in *PP* 8.5's descriptions of limitless bodhisattvas pervading the universe, and the *AA*'s textual basis for Buddha activity *(karma)* in the activities carried out by those bodhisattvas. In sum, Ārya Vimuktisena's commentary identifies the *svābhāvikakāya* of Yogācāra with the *dharmakāya* of the *PP* sūtras (expressed in *PP* passage 8.5 in terms of the list of Buddha dharmas); the *sāmbhogikakāya* of Yogācāra with the Buddha's glorious form possessed of marks and signs in *PP* passage 8.5; and the *nairmāṇikakāya* of Yogācāra with the infinite bodhisattvas in *PP* passage 8.5 (understood as manifestations of enlightenment working for beings).[104] In Ārya Vimuktisena's view, *AA* chapter 8 is precisely a mapping of the three Yogācāra *kāyas* onto corresponding passages of the *Large PP Sūtra.*

Our conclusion that *AA* chapter 8 constitutes an attempt to map the three kāyas of Yogācāra onto the *Large PP Sūtra* is based on literary-critical and historical considerations, and is therefore necessarily somewhat speculative. But, as it happens, it is supported by Ārya Vimuktisena, the first and quite possibly the greatest *AA* commentator whose work is extant. And his interpretation continued to be the standard one in India for several hundred years after his time.[105]

We conclude, then, that *Abhisamayālaṃkāra* chapter 8 was not newly presenting a theory of four *kāyas*, as many have claimed, but was instead performing a far more pressing task at the time it was composed: to show, for the first time, the relation between the *PP* descriptions of Buddhahood and the Yogācāra descriptions. According to this hypothesis, the *Abhisamayālaṃkāra* teaches three *kāyas*. But it does so quite differently from other texts of its time, because rather than expounding the three-*kāya* doctrine as embedded within the systematic framework of Yogācāra praxis and theory (as in the *MSA*, *Msg*, etc.), it tries to show how the three *kāyas* of Yogācāra are tacitly expressed in *PP* passages that make no explicit mention of them. If this hypothesis is correct, we might expect to find more evidence within the structure and language of the *Abhisamayālaṃkāra* itself to support our claim that it represents a mapping of Yogācāra concepts onto the *Large PP Sūtra*, and therefore teaches three rather than four *kāyas*. In fact, there is a tremendous amount of evidence for this within the overall structure and Sanskrit terminology of the *AA*, and we will take it up in the next chapter.

8
Internal Evidence that *Abhisamayālaṃkāra* Chapter 8 Teaches the Three Yogācāra *Kāyas*

8.1
Introduction: *Prajñāpāramitā* and Yogācāra Patterns of Thought Relevant to Analysis of *Abhisamayālaṃkāra* Chapter 8

Based on literary-critical and historical considerations, we suggested in the last chapter that *Abhisamayālaṃkāra* chapter 8 represented an attempt, quite possibly for the first time in Indian Buddhism, to correlate directly the Yogācāra doctrine of three *kāyas* with standard expressions of enlightenment found in the *Prajñāpāramitā* sūtras. In this chapter, we will analyze in detail the structure and Sanskrit terminology of the *AA* to show how it provides corroboration for this conclusion.

We identified *AA* chapter 8's textual basis in the passages of the *Large Prajñāpāramitā Sūtra* (particularly the version in 25,000 verses) that are numbered 8.4 and 8.5 by Conze in his various editions of that text.[1] And we found that *AA* chapter 8 was structured around key *kāya* terms drawn from Yogācāra traditions contemporary to the *AA*'s period of composition in India. Since *AA* chapter 8 represents a conjoining of two textual traditions (the *PP* and the Yogācāra), we must begin by briefly reviewing our findings thus far on the pattern of buddhological concepts found in those two traditions. Then we can examine *AA*'s eighth chapter in the light of those patterns.

In chapter 3 above, we found that the *PP* sūtras' most frequent way of expressing Buddhahood is through their frequent listing of the all-dharmas (the constituents of the psychophysical universe of beings), included amongst which are the undefiled Buddha dharmas (the ten powers, four fearlessnesses, etc., which are the pure noetic qualities of a Buddha). Within the *PP* sūtras, this sort of listing does not usually center upon Buddhahood, and is never intended as an ultimate definition of Buddhahood. In fact, it was often employed for the purpose of denying the self-existence *(svabhāva)* of every dharma listed, including the Buddha dharmas.

All dharmas are declared "empty" of self-existence *(svabhāva-śūnya)*, since they arise in dependence upon causes, conditions, etc., and are distinguished only through conceptual construction. It is this emptiness *(śūnyatā)*, frequently called "thusness" *(tathatā)* or the "real nature of dharmas" *(dharmatā)*, together with the nondual realization of it *(prajñāpāramitā)*, which *PP* sūtras identify as the defining principle of Buddhahood. They occasionally refer to that defining principle as *dharmakāya*. For this reason, where *PP*-sūtra passages designate a Buddha's defining principle *dharmakāya*, the term never refers to the collection of Buddha dharmas per se. Rather *dharmakāya* is precisely the emptiness of all such dharmas nondually known *(prajñāpāramitā)*.[2]

The list of Buddha dharmas in *PP* sūtras, then, as a conceptually differentiated set of phenomena, represents a conventional or phenomenal expression of Buddhahood whose defining essence, *dharmakāya*, is as undivided as the thusness it nondually knows. The *dharmakāya* of the *PP* sūtras, as it is expressed for the discursive consideration of non-Buddhas, is described as a set of pure dharmas (the ten powers, four fearlessnesses, etc.), but as actually realized by a Buddha, is entirely nonconceptual. Therefore, although *dharmakāya* is described or denominated in terms of the undefiled dharmas, it is never simply identified with them.

As noted in the previous chapter, *PP* passage 8.5, like many other *PP* passages, lists the undefiled Buddha dharmas. It presents them amongst a large set of other dharmas (qualities) that bodhisattvas impart to beings through their teaching.[3] There is no specific reference to *dharmakāya* in passage 8.5, although the usage of the term as noted above is established in other parts of the *PP* sūtra corpus (cf. chapter 3 of this book).

Identified in the introductory passages of the *Large PP Sūtra* is its expounder, Śākyamuni Buddha. He appears in the *Large PP* in an especially glorious form, radiating light throughout the universe, preaching to countless throngs of disciples, and, in some passages, radiating limitless manifestations of Buddha forms that preach in all realms of sentient beings.[4] In *PP* sūtras, all such forms, including both the glorious central expounder of the sūtra and his limitless manifestations, are occasionally referred to by the term *rūpakāya*, the Buddha's "physical body" or "embodiment in form(s)."

In *Large PP* passage 8.5, an especially exalted quality of a Buddha's form is the set of thirty-two marks and eighty signs signifying a preeminent person *(mahāpuruṣa)*. These marks and signs are included in passage 8.5 among the all inclusive list of Buddha dharmas.[5] Within the *PP*, the marks and signs would be associated with *rūpakāya* (no formal distinction of *sāmbhogikakāya* and *nairmāṇikakāya* was yet made). Also described at great length in *PP* passage 8.5 are limitless activities of bodhisattvas, whom the Buddha observes as they enter into all realms of beings to teach and assist them.[6]

In chapters 4 and 5 above, we discussed Yogācāra patterns of buddhological doctrine. The Yogācāra framework of buddhology builds on that of the *PP* and other Mahāyāna sūtras, but also draws from specific Yogācāra understandings of gnoseology related to meditational praxis. In the Yogācāra sixfold scheme of buddhological categories, the defining essence of Buddhahood is the first category: *svabhāva* ("defining essence"), which is purified thusness *(tathatāviśuddhi)* and nonconceptual gnosis *(nirvikalpa-jñāna)*. This is identified as *dharmakāya*, which is the embodiment of the Buddhas in their defining essence *(svābhāvika)* and is therefore also referred to as *svābhāvikakāya* with that meaning (chapter 4, sections 3 and 4 above). Yogācāra treatises explicitly state, however, that Buddhahood, (which in its own nature is *svābhāvikakāya/dharmakāya*), cannot be "defined" in terms of the set of Buddha dharmas (the set frequently listed in the *PP* sūtras). The reason is that the defining quality of Buddhahood, its defining essence *(= svābhāvikakāya/ dharmakāya)*, is its nondual awareness of the emptiness of all phenomena, including all those phenomena that have been traditionally ascribed to Buddhahood (chapter 4 section 2). The set of Buddha dharmas, then, comprises only a phenomenal description of Buddhahood, and for that reason is categorized in the Yogācāra sixfold scheme as *yoga* (phenomenal qualities "associated" with Buddhahood), not as *svabhāva* (defining essence = *svābhāvikakāya*). Thus, consistent with the *PP* sūtras, Yogācāra texts acknowledge the set of Buddha dharmas as a conventional description of enlightenment that denominates *dharmakāya* from a phenomenal point of view. But *dharmakāya (= svābhāvikakāya)* is not to be defined by that set, being a nonconceptual realization uncontainable within any such conceptual boundaries.

We also noted that Yogācāras frequently use the term *dharmakāya* in two senses: one exclusive, the other inclusive. The exclusive sense is that noted just above, with *dharmakāya* specifically identified as *svābhāvikakāya*, i.e., where *dharmakāya* is identified exclusively as the first of the three Yogācāra *kāya*s. The inclusive sense of the term *dharmakāya* refers to Buddhahood inclusive of all its discernible features, including all *kāya*s, all of a Buddha's activities, and so forth. The inclusive sense of the word may hearken back to Abhidharma descriptions of *dharmakāya* as "perfection of the result" *(phala-sampad)*, i.e., the final attainment of the path in its totality, Buddhahood inclusive of all its features (chapter 2 of this book). It is the inclusive sense of *dharmakāya* that appears in the expression of *AA* v. 9.2, *dharmakāya phalam*, referring to Buddhahood as the final and total result of the paths, including all *kāya*s, activities, etc. It is also the inclusive sense that appears in *AA* v. 1.4 where "Dharmakāya" is the title for the *AA*'s entire eighth chapter.

Yogācāra tradition, then, identifies *dharmakāya* in the exclusive sense with *svābhāvikakāya,* which, though describable phenomenally in terms of the undefiled Buddha dharmas, is not to be identified with them. It identifies *dharmakāya* in the inclusive sense with Buddhahood in its totality, equivalent to the set of all three *kāya*s with all their qualities (chapter 4, section 5 above).

We noted in chapters 4 and 5 that Yogācāra texts formally distinguished, for the first time, the glorious, cosmic Buddha figures of Mahāyāna sūtras from the infinite manifestations that such figures emanate into the realms of beings. The glorious, central figures in the sūtras are designated *sāmbhogikakāya* (embodiment of Buddhahood in its communal enjoyment of the dharma with great bodhisattvas; chapter 5, section 5 above). The infinite manifestations throughout the cosmos are designated *nairmāṇikakāya* (embodiment of Buddhahood in its limitless manifestations). From among the three *kāyas*, it is *nairmāṇikakāya* that came to be identified in Yogācāra texts formally with the activity *(karma)* of Buddhahood, presumably because such an infinite range of activity was ascribed to it: spanning the whole universe through eternity, reaching all realms of beings (chapter 5, section 5).

Finally, we noted in chapter 4, section 4 a special purpose of the secondary derivative morphology of the three *kāya* names. The secondary derivative forms are *svābhāvika*, *sāmbhogika,* and *nairmāṇika.*[7] These morphologies make the terms adjectives, designating three ways that one insubstantial and indivisible "thing" (the purified dharma realm, Buddhahood) embodies its knowledge and its participation in the world. The undifferentiated realization of enlightenment is functionally "embodied" for itself within its own awareness *(svābhāvikakāya)*, for its closest communities of disciples in its purest appearance *(sāmbhogikakāya)*, and for all other beings in its limitless manifestations *(nairmāṇikakāya)*. The distinctive morphology of the three *kāya* names emphasizes the ontological oneness of Buddhahood, undifferentiated in its actual realization, even while distinguishing its functions for different kinds of beings whose conceptual worlds do not yet permit them to see it that way.

The important point to keep in mind when interpreting *AA* chapter 8 is this: In the Yogācāra textual tradition from which the *AA* drew its *kāya* terminology, Buddhahood is not to be defined as any collection or set of diverse qualities (including the undefiled Buddha dharmas), but as a single, undifferentiated ultimate awareness. *Svābhāvikakāya/dharmakāya*, as that defining essence of Buddhahood, is therefore never identified as the set of differentiated Buddha dharmas per se, which serve merely as a phenomenal expression of it for beings restricted to conceptual understanding. We can understand this in the same way that we can understand that *svābhāvikakāya/dharmakāya* is not *rūpakāyas*. Rather, *rūpakāya*s are the forms in which beings encounter *svābhāvikakāya/dharmakāya* prior to their own nondual realization of it.

These patterns of buddhological thought in *PP* sūtras and Yogācāra literature must inform interpretation of *AA* chapter 8. And it is to that interpretation that we now turn.

8.2
Abhisamayālaṃkāra Chapter 8's Table of Contents: *AA* verse 1.17

We begin by examining the table of contents for *Abhisamayālaṃkāra* chapter 8, *AA* v. 1.17:

> svābhāvikaḥ sasāmbhogo nairmāṇiko 'paras tathā
> dharmakāyaḥ sakāritraś caturdhā samudīritaḥ[8]
>
> (*AA* 1.17)

We noted in chapter 6 that Ārya Vimuktisena had interpreted this verse to teach three Buddha *kāya*s (represented by the terms *svābhāvikaḥ*, *sasāmbhogo*, and *nairmāṇiko*) while Haribhadra interpreted it to teach four *kāya*s (three designated by those three terms, plus a fourth *kāya* designated by the term *dharmakāyaḥ*, referring to a *dharmakāya* consisting of gnosis, which Haribhadra called *jñānātmaka dharmakāya*). Let us proceed with our own analysis, and then give a translation for the verse.[9]

Note that the first three terms are adjectival in form. *Svābhāvikaḥ* and *nairmāṇikaḥ* are in the familiar secondary derivative (adjectival) form, while *sa,* as a possessive prefix attached to *sāmbhogaḥ*, also gives that term a broadly adjectival function (*sasāmbhogaḥ,* meaning "with enjoyment," should modify something possessing the enjoyment). As noted above, putting key *kāya* terms into secondary derivative form, giving them a broad adjectival function, is characteristic of their usage in Yogācāra texts that first developed the terminology. The term *sakāritraḥ* is also in a possessive, adjectival form. All four terms—*svābhāvikaḥ*, *sasāmbhogo*, *nairmāṇikaḥ*, and *sakāritraḥ*—are in adjectival form, indicating that they modify a noun in the verse. The fifth key term, *dharmakāyaḥ*, is the only simple noun in the verse. It is a singular, in nominative case. Taken together, in the simplest and most straightforward reading, the five terms translate something like this: "*Dharmakāya*, in its essence *(svābhāvikaḥ)*, with its enjoyment *(sasāmbhogo)*, in its manifestation *(nairmāṇiko)*, [and] with its activity *(sakāritraś)*. . . ."

The verb of the verse, *samudīritaḥ*, is a past passive participle, which can be translated "is proclaimed." This verb is singular in number, not plural. It should modify a singular noun. Again, *dharmakāya* is the only simple, singular noun within the verse it could modify ("The *dharmakāya* . . . is proclaimed"). The term *caturdhā* is an adverb, meaning "fourfold." The phrase *aparas tathā* means "and also the other," "the other as well," etc. If we take the Sanskrit itself as our basis (apart from any commentaries), the simplest, most direct reading of the verse would be this:

> svābhāvikaḥ sasāmbhogo nairmāṇiko 'paras tathā
> dharmakāyaḥ sakāritraś caturdhā samudīritaḥ
>
> (*AA* 1.17)

> [In its essence, with its enjoyment, and in its manifestation(s) as well, embodiment of dharma *(dharmakāya)*, with its activity, is proclaimed as fourfold.]

Such an understanding makes sense if the term *dharmakāya* is understood in its inclusive sense (as resultant *dharmakāya*, *dharmakāya phalam*, of *AA* vv. 9.2 and 1.4), i.e., as the total result of the Mahāyāna path, inclusive of all *kāya*s, enlightened activity, and so forth. Then in this verse, *dharmakāya*, referring to Buddhahood in its totality, distinguished by its three functional modes *(svābhāvika, sāmbhogika*, and *nairmāṇika)* and its enlightened activity, is proclaimed "as fourfold."

We interpret *AA* v. 1.17, then, as another expression of the three-*kāya* doctrine prominent in other texts of its period (as discussed in chapters 4 and 5 of this book). The Sanskrit appears quite precise. But Sanskrit is a flexible language. Other interpretations are usually possible (as Haribhadra discerned). Nevertheless, there are many other pieces of textual evidence to support the interpretation given here.

Let us compare *Mahāyānasūtrālaṃkāra* vv. 9.59, 9.60 and *bhāṣya* to *AA* v. 1.17 above (the reader may want to refer again to chapter 4, section 4 of this book):

> svabhāvadharmasambhoganirmāṇairbhinnavṛttikaḥ
> dharmadhāturviśuddho 'yam buddhānāṃ samudāhṛtaḥ
>
> (*MSA* 9.59)

> [This is declared to be the Buddhas' purified realm of dharma *(dharmadhātuviśuddhaḥ)*, whose mode of function varies as to essence, communal enjoyment of dharma, and manifestation.]

> eṣa vṛttyarthamārabhya caturthaḥ ślokaḥ
> svābhāvikasāṃbhogikanairmāṇikakāyavṛttyā bhinnavṛttikaḥ
>
> (*MSA* 9.59 *bhāṣya*)

> [The fourth of the verses {on the six topics of the purified dharma realm} concerns the {sixth} topic: functional mode(s) *(vṛtti)*. The function {of

the purified dharma realm} varies according to its mode of embodiment: in its own essence, in its communal enjoyment, in its manifestation(s).]

svābhāviko 'tha sāṃbhogyaḥ kāyo nairmāṇiko 'paraḥ
kāyabhedā hi buddhānām prathamastu dvayāśrayaḥ

(*MSA* 9.60)

[The varieties of embodiment of the Buddhas are: embodiment in their own essence, in communal enjoyment, and in manifestation(s) as well. But the first is the basis of the {other} two.]

trividhaḥ kāyo buddhānām
svābhāviko dharmakāya āśraya-parāvṛtti-lakṣaṇaḥ
sāṃbhogiko yena parṣanmaṇḍaleṣu dharma-saṃbhogaṃ karoti
nairmāṇiko yena nirmāṇena sattvārthaṃ karoti

(*MSA* 9.60 *bhāṣya*)

[Embodiment of the Buddhas is threefold, {being}:

1. in essence *(svābhāvika)*, the embodiment of dharma *(dharmakāya)*, whose identity is fundamental transformation;

2. in communal enjoyment *(sāṃbhogika)*, that which creates enjoyment of dharma within the circles of assembly;

3. in manifestation *(nairmāṇika)*, manifestation(s) which work for the benefit of beings]

According to these passages, the purified dharma realm (= Buddhahood) is embodied in three functions *(vṛtti)* that are designated through the adjectival (secondary derivative) forms of the three *kāya* names: this, this, and this kind of embodiment.

Let us look again at *AA* v. 1.17 as it compares to *MSA* v. 9.60 above:

svābhāviko 'tha sāṃbhogyaḥ kāyo nairmāṇiko 'paraḥ
kāyabhedā hi buddhānām prathamastu dvayāśrayaḥ

(*MSA* 9.60)

svābhāvikaḥ sasāmbhogo nairmāṇiko 'paras tathā
dharmakāyaḥ sakāritraś caturdhā samudīritaḥ

(*AA* 1.17)

In *AA* v. 1.17, the term *dharmakāya* stands in place of the *MSA* 9.60 expression *kāya buddhānām* (embodiment of the Buddhas), which stands in place of the *MSA* 9.59 expression *dharmadhātuviśuddha* (purified realm of dharma). In *MSA*

9.60, the adjectival morphology of the three key terms *(svābhāvika, sāmbhogika, nairmāṇika)* enable them to modify the noun *kāya* (embodiment) so as to designate three types of embodiment of one undifferentiated realization: the purified realm of dharma, the realization of Buddhahood. In *AA* v. 1.17, adjectival morphologies for the same three terms now modify the noun *dharmakāya*. The parallelism is evident: adjectival forms again designate three kinds of embodiment of one ontologically undivided realization, this time referred to as *dharmakāya*.

The phrase *aparas tathā* in *AA* v. 1.17 parallels the phrase *atha . . . aparaḥ* in *MSA* 9.60. In both cases the term *aparaḥ* (as well, also) serves to mark off the three *kāya* terms as a complete set ("in its essence, in its shared enjoyment, and in its manifestation[s] *as well*"). Sthiramati, in his comments on *MSA* v. 9.60, discusses the function of the term *aparaḥ* in the verse. He notes that the term is intended to designate inclusion of the *nairmāṇikakāya* with the first two *kāyas* to complete the set of three.[10]

The phrase *aparas tathā* also appears in a similar half-verse at the beginning of the *Kāyatrayāvatāra-mukha-śāstra*, a text extant in the Tibetan canon which explicitly teaches three *kāyas* in some detail (Pk 5290, ascribed to a Nāgamitra).[11] This text names the first of the three *kāyas*: *dharmakāya* (rather than *svābhāvikakāya*), a usage not uncommon in classical Yogācāra texts (see chapter 4, section 5, above). It opens with a half-verse similar to *MSA* 9.60 and *AA* 1.17: "sprul dang longs spyod rdzogs pa dang / de bzhin gzhan ni chos sku ste," which might be reconstructed into Sanskrit as: "nairmāṇikaśca sāmbhogyo dharmakāyo 'paras tathā," translated: "In its manifestation(s), its communal enjoyment, and *dharmakāya* [per se] as well." In all the verses under discussion, the term *aparaḥ* is used to mark off the three *kāya* terms as a closed set, i.e., to indicate that there are precisely three, no less and no more.

In verse *MSA* 9.60 and the verse from the *Kāyatrayāvatāra-mukha-śāstra*, then, we see terms designating the three *kāyas* arranged in a characteristic way within the space of a half-verse. This may represent an established Yogācāra syntactical pattern to specify the three *kāyas* as a closed set. *AA* v. 1.17 follows the very same pattern.

Before proceeding further, let us entertain for a moment the principal alternative interpretation of *AA* v. 1.17 that has been prominent in Indo-Tibetan tradition, that of Haribhadra. In Haribhadra's interpretation, the terms: *svābhāvikaḥ, sasāmbhogo, nairmāṇikaḥ*, and *dharmakāyaḥ* designate four Buddha *kāyas. Dharmakāya* of verse 1.17 is an abbreviation for *jñānātmaka dharmakāya* (a *dharmakāya* consisting of gnosis, to be distinguished from *svābhāvikakāya,* which is emptiness per se). And *sakāritraḥ* is semantically linked to *(jñānātmaka) dharmakāya*.[12] The translation according to Haribhadra would be something like this:

> svābhāvikaḥ sasāmbhogo nairmāṇiko 'paras tathā
> dharmakāyaḥ sakāritraś caturdhā samudīritaḥ
>
> (*AA* 1.17)

[The essence {body}, with the communal enjoyment {body}, the manifestation {body}, and the body of dharmas *(dharmakāya)* with its activity as well: as fourfold are {they} proclaimed.]

According to this (Haribhadra's) interpretation, the first three terms of the verse have to be interpreted as simple nouns; their adjectival morphologies are left unexplained and without any distinct adjectival function. If they fulfilled their adjectival morphology, the only noun they could modify would be *kāyaḥ* taken as semantically separate from *dharma* within the term *dharmakāyaḥ*. But then we might expect the term *dharma* also to have an adjectival morphology in the verse, such as the secondary derivative *dhārmika*, which it does not have. In any case, under this four-*kāya* mode of interpretation, the verb *samudīritaḥ* modifies all four *kāya* terms ("as fourfold are *they* proclaimed"). But then we might expect the verb to be plural, not singular. If the singular verb *samudīritaḥ* modifies one thing, and that is not the term *dharmakāya*, then what would it modify? *AA* v. 1.17 is the table of contents for the *AA*'s eighth chapter, and whatever is "proclaimed" in that verse is precisely the overall subject of that chapter. Would the author have left the overall subject of the chapter unnamed? Would he end verse 1.17 with the statement: "it is proclaimed as fourfold" (where "it" is the entire subject of chapter 8) and then not even identify what "it" is?

We presented *AA* vv. 1.3–1.4 in chapter 6 above. In those verses, the eight basic subjects of the *AA*'s eight substantive chapters are named. The eight subjects are the eight *abhisamaya*s (fundamental realizations), presented in those verses as follows:

prajñāpāramitāṣṭābhiḥ padārthaiḥ samudīritā
sarvākārajñatā mārgajñatā sarvajñatā tataḥ

(*AA* 1.3)

sarvākārābhisambodho mūrdhaprāpto 'nupūrvikaḥ
ekakṣaṇābhisambodho dharmakāyaś ca te'ṣṭadhā

(*AA* 1.4)

[The perfection of wisdom *(prajñāpāramitā)* is proclaimed through eight subjects, these eight being: total omniscience, knowledge of the paths, and then all-knowledge, the full realization of all aspects, the {realization} that has attained the summit, the progressive {realization}, the realization in a single moment, and the embodiment of dharma *(dharmakāya)*.][13]

The overall subject of the *AA*'s eighth chapter is clearly identified and named here. It is *dharmakāya* that is the final attainment of the path. As the subject title of *AA* chapter 8, it is precisely what should be "proclaimed as fourfold" in verse 1.17, the table of contents for that chapter. Our *trikāya* interpretation of verse 1.17 above accords with this finding, since in that verse we understand *dharmakāya* in its inclusive sense as the subject title of chapter 8, and the three *kāyas*, together with enlightened activity *(kāritra)* as the four topics of that subject matter.

Furthermore, *AA* verses 1.5 through 1.16 serve as the table of contents for the first seven chapters of the *AA*, just as verse 1.17 is the table of contents for the eighth chapter. In vv. 1.5–1.16, the subject titles for every one of the seven chapters prior to chapter 8 are presented; and they are precisely the same as those given above in vv. 1.3–1.4.[14] According to our interpretation, verse 1.17 follows suit by presenting the term *dharmakāya* as the title of chapter 8 (the very same term that appears as the title of chapter 8 in verse 1.4 above). According to Haribhadra's four-*kāya* interpretation, verse 1.17 is the only portion of the *AA*'s table of contents which fails to give the subject title for its chapter. In his interpretation of verse 1.17, the meaning of the term *dharmakāya* is not the subject title of chapter 8, but just one out of the four *kāyas* he posits (which he designates *[jñānātmaka] dharmakāya*, a *dharmakāya* consisting of gnosis, i.e., the Buddha dharmas per se).

In vv. 1.5–1.15, topics comprising *AA* chapters 1 through 5 are listed in the precise order that they are discussed in their respective chapters of the *AA*. Verse 1.16 mentions the number of topics in chapters 6 and 7 without giving their names. Then, v. 1.17 again lists the topics comprising its chapter, the four topics of chapter 8.[15] If the term *dharmakāya* in v. 1.17 is understood as the subject title of chapter 8, as in our interpretation, the four topics in the verse occur in precisely the same order that they appear in chapter 8: first *svābhāvikakāya*, then *sāmbhogikakāya*, then *nairmāṇikakāya*, then *kāritra* (activity). This would conform to the pattern found through the rest of the *AA*'s table of contents (vv. 1.5–1.17). But if v. 1.17's *dharmakāya* is interpreted as Haribhadra does (as merely one of the four topics of chapter 8, not its title), the order of topics in the verse no longer corresponds to their order within chapter 8. According to Haribhadra's analysis, the order of topics in v. 1.17 is: *svābhāvikakāya, sāmbhogikakāya, nairmāṇikakāya, (jñānātmaka) dharmakāya*; but the order of their explanation in *AA* chapter 8 is: *svābhāvikakāya, (jñānātmaka) dharmakāya, sāmbhogikakāya, nairmāṇikakāya*. According to Haribhadra, then, v. 1.17 is the only part of the *AA*'s table of contents that presents the topics of its corresponding chapter in the wrong order.

According to our three-*kāya* interpretation of *AA* 1.17, then, the pattern of naming the chapter title, and, when listing chapter topics, presenting them in correct order, is strictly followed throughout vv. 1.5 through 1.17, the *AA*'s entire table of contents. According to Haribhadra's four-*kāya* interpretation, v. 1.17 becomes an anomaly. It would be the only part of the *AA*'s table of contents that leaves out its chapter title and that lists the chapter's topics in the wrong order.

AA v. 9.2, the final verse of the entire *Abhisamayālaṃkāra*, provides further internal evidence to support our interpretation of v. 1.17. Verse 9.2, as we mentioned in chapter 6 of this book, presents an abbreviated, final summation of the *AA*'s eight basic subjects by means of three concepts: the aim *(viṣaya)* of yogic practice (i.e., the three knowledges that are the subjects of the *AA*'s first three chapters), the yogic practice itself (the four realizations, *abhisamaya*s, which are the subjects of the next four chapters), and the final result of the practice (resultant *dharmakāya*, the subject of the eighth chapter).

> viṣayas tritayo hetuḥ prayogaś caturātmakaḥ
> dharmakāyaphalaṃ karmety anyas tredhārthasaṃgraha
>
> (*AA* 9.2)

> [The threefold aim, as cause, the fourfold practice, the embodiment of dharma [with its] activity as result *(dharmakāya phalaṃ karma)*, thus in another way is {the entire content} summarized in three topics.][16]

This verse identifies the complete subject matter of *AA* chapter 8 as *phalaṃ*, the final result of practice, expressed by two terms: *dharmakāya karma*, where these terms must refer to the whole state of Buddhahood (including all *kāya*s) together with its activity, since that is what constitutes the total content of chapter 8. *AA* v. 1.17 contains a functionally identical expression: *dharmakāya sakāritraḥ* (the *dharmakāya* with its activity). The simplest explanation is this: the phrase in v. 9.2 and the phrase in v. 1.17 both designate the total content of *AA* chapter 8 as a whole, resultant *dharmakāya* (Buddhahood inclusive of the threefold *kāya*) together with its activity. This means the term *dharmakāya* in v. 1.17 is used in its inclusive sense, referring to *dharmakāya phalaṃ*, Buddhahood as the total result of the path. And that means *dharmakāya* in v. 1.17 indeed constitutes the title of *AA* chapter 8, with the terms: *svābhāvikaḥ*, *sasāmbhogo*, *nairmāṇiko*, and *sakāritraḥ*, in their proper order, designating the four aspects of resultant *dharmakāya* as the four topics that are explained in chapter 8.

In sum, the term *dharmakāya* is used with precisely the same inclusive sense in *AA* vv. 1.4, 1.17 and 9.2. It designates the total subject matter and the title of *AA* chapter 8.[17] *AA* v. 1.17's other four key terms *(svābhāvikaḥ, sasāmbhogo, nairmāṇiko,* and *sakāritraḥ)*, then, are in adjectival form for good reason. They modify the noun *dharmakāya* as its four functional modes. As such, they comprise the four topics of the "Dharmakāya" chapter, *AA* chapter 8.

We have done a grammatical analysis of *AA* v. 1.17, analyzed it in relation to the structure of the *AA* as a whole, and pointed out correlations to other texts of its period (texts of the Yogācāra tradition that developed the multiple-*kāya* terminology the *AA* uses). The evidence is substantial: *AA* v. 1.17 explicates three (not four) *kāyas*. Since v. 1.17 comprises the table of contents for *AA* chapter 8, we have already established that chapter 8 teaches three *kāyas* (as Ārya Vimuktisena thought), not four *kāyas* (as Haribhadra thought). As we analyze the key verses in chapter 8 below, we will find much further evidence for this conclusion.

Haribhadra's interpretation of *AA* v. 1.17 is permitted within the rules of Sanskrit grammar. But he ignored a number of fairly obvious ways that the verse is specifically situated within the text, and the resonances the verse would have for a scholar steeped in the textual traditions of its own period of composition. Haribhadra's interpretation of four *kāyas* in the *AA*, while technically permitted by Sanskrit grammar, expresses a perspective quite alien to the text and the period of its composition, the perspective of a different time and a different philosophical concern.

8.3
Svābhāvikakāya/dharmakāya: Abhisamayālaṃkāra verses 8.1–8.6

The eighth chapter of the *Abhisamayālaṃkāra* begins with a set of six verses that, like verse 1.17, became a source of interpretive controversy among Indian and Tibetan commentators of succeeding centuries. The verses are as follows:

> sarvākārāṃ viśuddhiṃ ye dharmāḥ prāptā nirāsravāḥ
> svābhāviko muneḥ kāyas teṣāṃ prakṛti-lakṣaṇaḥ
>
> (*AA* 8.1)
>
> bodhipakṣāpramāṇāni vimokṣā anupūrvaśaḥ
> navātmikā samāpattiḥ kṛtsnaṃ daśavidhātmakam
>
> (*AA* 8.2)
>
> abhibhvāyatanāny aṣṭa prakārāṇi prabhedataḥ
> araṇā praṇidhijñānam abhijñāḥ pratisamvidaḥ
>
> (*AA* 8.3)
>
> sarvākārāś catasro 'tha śuddhayo vaśitā daśa
> balāni daśa catvāri vaiśāradyāny arakṣaṇam
>
> (*AA* 8.4)
>
> trividhaṃ smṛtyupasthānaṃ tridhāsaṃmoṣa-dharmatā
> vasanāyāḥ samudghāto mahatī karuṇā jane
>
> (*AA* 8.5)
>
> āveṇikā muner eva dharmā ye 'ṣṭadaśeritāḥ
> sarvākārajñatā ceti dharmakāyo 'bhidhīyate
>
> (*AA* 8.6)

[The embodiment of the Sage in his essence *(svābhāvikakāya):* Its identity is the primordial nature of the undefiled dharmas which are obtained in utter purity.[18] "The factors that foster enlightenment, the measureless thoughts, the liberations, the nine meditative attainments, the ten meditative totalities, the bases of overpowering divided into eight kinds, the meditative power freeing from passions, the gnosis resulting from resolve, the supernatural knowledges, the analytical knowledges, the four total purities, the ten sovereignties, the ten powers, the four forms of fearlessness, the three ways in which [a Buddha] has nothing to hide, the threefold mindful equanimity, the nature of never forgetting, the complete destruction of [negative] propensities, the great compassion for living beings, the qualities unique to the Sage that are proclaimed as eighteen, and total omniscience": thus is *dharmakāya* denominated.][19]

The definition of *svābhāvikakāya* is presented in verse 8.1. It is defined as the primordial nature *(prakṛti)* of the undefiled Buddha dharmas. The list of those dharmas is then presented in verses 8.2-8.6. Importantly, at the very end of v. 8.6 appears the expression *iti dharmakāyo 'bhidhīyate* (thus is the *dharmakāya* denominated). Other possible translations are "thus is the *dharmakāya* named," "thus is the *dharmakāya* indicated," and "thus is the *dharmakāya* described."

In the first section of this chapter, we noted that *PP* sūtras make frequent reference to Buddhahood through their listing of the undefiled Buddha dharmas. However, they do not identify *dharmakāya as* the set of undefiled dharmas. The undefiled dharmas comprise a conventional description of *dharmakāya* from a phenomenal point of view, not *dharmakāya* itself, which is the nondual realization of their emptiness *(prajñāpāramitā).*

When *Abhisamayālaṃkāra* vv. 8.2–8.6 are viewed in light of this *PP*-sūtra understanding, the likely meaning emerges. The *AA*, after presenting the set of undefiled dharmas as they are listed in its scriptural source (*Large PP* passage 8.5), says: "thus is *dharmakāya* denominated." It does not say the *dharmakāya is* the collection of undefiled dharmas. It says *dharmakāya* is conventionally *denominated* in terms of those dharmas. This would echo the *PP* sūtras.

What about *AA* v. 8.1? The term *svābhāvikakāya* does not appear in the textual basis for *AA* chapter 8 (*Large PP Sūtra* passage 8.5). Clearly, the author of the *AA* drew the term from Yogācāra tradition. But *AA* v. 8.1 is very unusual in its usage of the Yogācāra term *svābhāvikakāya*, for it defines the term in specific relation to the undefiled Buddha dharmas, as their "primordial nature" *(prakṛti)*, and nowhere in classical Yogācāra texts is *svābhāvikakāya* defined in that way. Yogācāra texts formulate *svābhāvikakāya* as the defining essence *(svabhāva)* of Buddhahood embodied *(kāya)* in a nondual, undivided realization (thusness/gnosis), free from any conceptual boundaries such as "dharma" qualities. And Yogācāra texts explicitly state that the undefiled dharmas are not to be taken as Buddhahood's defining essence.[20]

Light is shed on this problem by recalling the unique commentarial purposes of the *Abhisamayālaṃkāra* suggested in the last chapter. The task of the Yogācāra treatises discussed in chapters 4 and 5 was to formulate and systematize Mahāyāna doctrines based upon a wide spectrum of Mahāyāna sūtras. This was *not* the *AA*'s task. The *AA*'s purpose was to comment upon Mahāyāna thought and practice as it was expressed explicitly or implicitly just within the *Large PP Sūtra*, while occasionally relating Yogācāra terms and concepts to that particular scripture. Therefore, the *AA*'s author had to base his eighth chapter upon the specific *PP* sūtra material he had before him. As noted in the previous chapter, the scriptural material before him was *Large PP Sūtra* passages 8.4–8.5, which presented a list of Buddha dharmas, the marks and signs of a Buddha's exalted body, and a plethora of bodhisattva activities that the Buddha observes and describes. This was the only scriptural material available to the *AA*'s author upon which to map Yogācāra concepts of Buddhahood.

Returning our attention to *AA* vv. 8.1–8.6, then, the *AA*'s author had to specify the Yogācāra *svābhāvikakāya* by specific reference just to what he found in *PP* passages 8.4 and 8.5. And within those passages, all that might reasonably be seen to correspond to *svābhāvikakāya* was the list of Buddha dharmas of *PP* passage 8.5. At least the Buddha dharmas comprised a phenomenal description of a Buddha's nondual gnosis, which, as a Buddha experiences it, is indeed *svābhāvikakāya*. The Buddha dharmas are listed among the numerous qualities imparted by bodhisattvas to beings, being the highest such qualities any being could attain from their teaching.[21] In sum, the *AA*'s author, seeking to draw direct correspondences between Yogācāra terms and *PP* passages, was required by the constraints of his scriptural basis to define *svābhāvikakāya* (apparently for the first time in Indian Buddhist literature) solely by reference to the Buddha dharmas.

Given the *AA* author's concern to map key Yogācāra concepts onto *PP sūtra* understandings, it was reasonable to take that list of dharmas as textual basis for the Yogācāra *svābhāvikakāya*. The collection of Buddha dharmas does, after all, comprise a phenomenal description of the *PP* sūtras*' dharmakāya*. As noted above, *AA* vv. 8.2–8.6 transmit that *PP* understanding ("thus is *dharmakāya* denominated"). By putting those verses immediately after v. 8.1, the *AA*'s author also transmits the understanding of Yogācāra treatises that had identified their *svābhāvikakāya* with the *PP dharmakāya*. Thus, the Buddha dharmas of *PP* passage 8.5, understood in *PP* tradition as a phenomenal description of *dharmakāya*, become in *AA* vv. 8.1–8.6 a phenomenal description of *svābhāvikakāya* as well.

In *AA* v. 8.1, then, the *AA*'s author defines *svābhāvikakāya* in direct relation to the Buddha dharmas. But consistent with *PP* understanding of *dharmakāya*, he does not define *svābhāvikakāya* itself *(= PP dharmakāya) as* the set of dharmas. Rather, he defines it as the "primordial nature" *(prakṛti)* of those dharmas, i.e., the nonconceptual nature of Buddhahood that is prior to any such differentiation, that is denominated in terms of differentiated dharmas for the discursive understanding of non-Buddhas.[22]

This indicates how *AA* vv. 8.1–8.6 express the patterns we found in *PP* textual tradition. What about the Yogācāra tradition? The genius of the *AA*'s author is that, with the exception of the prominent role he gives to the Buddha dharmas in vv. 8.1–8.6 (necessitated by his scriptural source), the same verses are fully consistent with Yogācāra patterns of thought on Buddhahood.

As noted in chapter 4, sections 4 and 5, Yogācāra texts that formulated the theory of *svābhāvikakāya* identify it with *dharmakāya,* understood in its exclusive sense as the defining essence of Buddhahood, the nondual realization of thusness.[23] Yogācāra texts, probably basing themselves in part upon the *PP* sūtras, state explicitly that *svābhāvikakāya/dharmakāya* cannot be "defined" in terms of the collection of undefiled dharmas, since it is beyond such conceptualization. Nevertheless, Yogācāra texts retained the list of undefiled dharmas as a phenomenal description of *svābhāvikakāya/dharmakāya.* Looked at, then, in light of these Yogācāra patterns, *AA* vv. 8.1–8.6 would read as follows: the *svābhāvikakāya* of verse 8.1 is identified as *dharmakāya* in verse 8.6, where *dharmakāya* is understood in its exclusive sense as the very essence of Buddhahood, the first of the three *kāya*s. That *svābhāvikakāya/dharmakāya*, the subject of all six verses 8.1–8.6, is denominated from a phenomenal perspective in terms of the undefiled dharmas.

We noted in section 2 of this chapter that the term *dharmakāya* is used with its inclusive sense in *AA* vv. 1.4, 1.17, and 9.2 to designate the whole subject matter of *AA* chapter 8, Buddhahood as a whole. But *AA* v. 8.6 appears to use the term *dharmakāya* in its exclusive sense to refer to the first of the three *kāya*s alone, *svābhāvikakāya.* Both usages, of course, fully conform to established Yogācāra patterns contemporaneous to the composition of the *AA*.

If, then, we take seriously both of the textual roots of *AA* 8, *AA* vv. 8.1–8.6 read straightforwardly as follows: The *svābhāvikakāya* (of Yogācāra) is the very essence, the primordial nature of Buddhahood, described (in *PP* passage 8.5) in terms of the undefiled dharmas. *Svābhāvikakāya is* the *dharmakāya* of the *PP* sūtras (and in its exclusive sense, of Yogācāra tradition), conventionally denominated in *PP* passage 8.5 in terms of those undefiled dharmas.

A straightforward reading of the Sanskrit verses (as presented above) supports this interpretation, which also accords simultaneously with the patterns of thought found in the *PP* and Yogācāra textual roots of *AA* 8.

Did any of the *AA* commentators see it this way? As it happens, our interpretation, although based on many literary-historical considerations presented above, is in complete conformity with that of the first great *AA* commentator whose work is extant: Ārya Vimuktisena. Ārya Vimuktisena, too, wrote that *svābhāvikakāya* of verse 8.1 and *dharmakāya* of verse 8.6 were intended as synonyms, referring to a nondual realization that was described in terms of the Buddha dharmas but not to be identified with any such conceptually differentiated collection.[24] Ārya Vimuktisena, living in the early sixth century, close to the time of the *AA*'s composition, and steeped in the two textual traditions upon which it drew (the *PP* and the Yogācāra) apparently assumed the sort of literary critical analysis that has here been made explicit.

Haribhadra, a Mādhyamika who wrote more than two centuries after Ārya Vimuktisena, made a new interpretation (new for our extant written record, anyway). He wrote that *AA* verse 8.1 defines *svābhāvikakāya* as the *dharmatā*, the emptiness, of the undefiled dharmas that are the gnoses of a Buddha. As emptiness (ultimate truth), then, *svābhāvikakāya* cannot be understood to include a Buddha's gnoses (conventional truth). Haribhadra therefore interpreted *dharmakāya* in verse 8.6 as a reference to the collection of gnoses. But in his view, this would be a Buddha *kāya* distinct from *svābhāvikakāya.* As such, he gave this distinct *kāya* the name *jñānātmaka dharmakāya* (*dharmakāya* consisting of gnosis). This gnosis *dharmakāya*, as the set of undefiled dharmas, he understood as the phenomenal basis in Buddhahood of the emptiness that is *svābhāvikakāya.* In Haribhadra's view, then, *AA* verses 8.2–8.6 list the set of undefiled dharmas in order to identify that set directly as a second Buddha *kāya*, *(jñānātmaka) dharmakāya*, a Buddha's conventionally existent gnoses.[25] *AA* verses 8.1–8.6, he concluded, teach two distinct Buddha *kāyas*: *svābhāvikakāya* and *jñānātmaka dharmakāya* (which, with *sāmbhogikakāya* and *nairmāṇikakāya,* makes a total of four *kāya*s taught in the *AA*).

Although Haribhadra's interpretation presents an intriguing independent analysis of Buddhahood (owing much to developments in Buddhist logic and Mādhyamika thought in the centuries following the *AA*) there is reason to question its accuracy as an interpretation of *AA* chapter 8. If Haribhadra were correct, *AA* verse 8.6 would be identifying the set of undefiled dharmas per se as *dharmakāya.* But this is not the normative understanding of either the *Prajñāpāramitā* sūtras or the Yogācāra textual tradition upon which *AA* chapter 8 was based. According to Haribhadra's interpretation, *AA* verses 8.2–8.6 should say that the set of undefiled dharmas *is dharmakāya*, or that the set of undefiled dharmas is called *dharmakāya.* But that is not precisely what the Sanskrit says. The Sanskrit literally says: "'The factors that foster enlightenment, the measureless thoughts, the liberations, . . . and total omniscience': *thus is dharmakāya denominated*" (emphasis mine). In other words, the verses do not say that *dharmakāya* is the set of undefiled dharmas. They say that *dharmakāya* is [conventionally] denominated in terms of those dharmas. This is a subtle but important distinction. For the literal reading of the verses simultaneously accords with patterns of thought found in the *PP* sūtras and the Yogācāra texts upon which *AA* 8 was based. Haribhadra's reading does not.[26]

Section 2 of this chapter demonstrated that *AA* v. 1.17, the table of contents for *AA* chapter 8, explicates three *kāya*s, not four. If *AA* vv. 8.1–8.6 are interpreted as we and Ārya Vimuktisena have done, that finding is confirmed, for vv. 8.1–8.6

are then understood to teach one *kāya: svābhāvikakāya* of 8.1 = *dharmakāya* of v. 8.6. Since all commentators agreed that *AA* vv. 8.12 and 8.33 teach two more *kāyas (sāmbhogikakāya* and *nairmāṇikakāya)* there would indeed be three in all. Not only does Haribhadra's interpretation conflict with the patterns of buddhological thought in both of the textual bases of *AA* 8 (*PP* and Yogācāra), but it conflicts with all the evidence presented in the previous section of this chapter, by making *AA* 8 a teaching of four *kāyas*.

We have dated the *AA* to sometime between the fourth and the early sixth centuries. Ārya Vimuktisena is dated to the early sixth century, and Haribhadra from the late eighth to early ninth centuries. As we have seen, *AA* vv. 8.1–8.6 comprise a unique expression of buddhological concepts for its period, a new way to associate the concepts of *svābhāvikakāya, dharmakāya,* and Buddha dharmas that was necessitated by the *AA*'s special project of mapping Yogācāra concepts onto *PP* passages. Closer to the time of the *AA*'s composition, it would appear, it was more clearly seen as the Yogācāra-*PP* mapping that it was, hence Ārya Vimuktisena's precise and elegant interpretation of it as such (discussed in chapter 9 below). Centuries after the period of the *AA*'s composition, however, with Buddhist logic and Mādhyamika concerns having developed considerably in the intervening period, the *AA* was seen through a different lens, resulting in a new interpretation by Haribhadra.

8.4
Abhisamayālaṃkāra verses 8.7–8.11

We conclude that *AA* vv. 8.1–8.6 in their entirety teach *svābhāvikakāya* (= the *PP dharmakāya* and the Yogācāra *dharmakāya* in its exclusive sense). Verses 8.7–8.11 then continue that discussion by explaining several of the *svābhāvikakāya/dharmakāya*'s unique qualities: its gnosis, eternality, pervasive activity, etc. I refer the reader to chapter 5 above for a discussion of these aspects of *svābhāvikakāya*, and to chapter 6 for their expression in *AA* vv. 8.7–8.11.

As we might expect, in line with the *AA* author's concern to map Yogācāra concepts onto the *Prajñāpāramitāsūtra, AA* vv. 8.7–8.11 have specific parallels in Yogācāra texts. *AA* v. 8.7, concerning a Buddha's meditative concentration that frees others from passions *(araṇāsamādhi)*, parallels the *bhāṣya* on *Mahāyāna-sūtra-alaṃkāra* 21.45 and Asvabhava's comments on *Mahāyānasaṃgraha* 10.12.[27] *AA* v. 8.8 on a Buddha's gnosis resulting from resolve *(praṇidhijñāna)* is almost identical to *Msg* 10.13 and *MSA* 21.46.[28] *AA* vv. 8.9–8.10, which explain why Buddhahood does not manifest to those lacking the karmic merit through the metaphor of rain and rotten seed, have parallels in *MSA* vv. 9.16 and 9.34, and to the *Ratnagotravibhāga*'s comparison of Buddha's activity to a shower of rain.[29] The discussion of Buddhahood's pervasiveness *(vyāpi)* and permanence or eternality *(nitya)* in *AA* v. 8.11 has parallels to *MSA* vv. 9.15, 9.17, 9.20, and 9.66 with their *bhāṣya* and to *Msg* 10.3.4.[30]

All of this further corroborates our understanding of the central project of *AA* chapter 8: to draw upon the Yogācāra textual tradition in its explication of its *PP* text basis. *AA* vv. 8.7–8.11 base themselves, for the most part, upon established Yogācāra characterizations of *svābhāvikakāya/dharmakāya*.

8.5
Sāmbhogikakāya: Abhisamayālaṃkāra verses 8.12–8.32

AA v. 8.12 introduces and defines the second of the three *kāyas*, *sāmbhogika-kāya:*

> dvātriṃśallakṣaṇāśītivyañjanātmā muner ayam
> sāmbhogiko mataḥ kāyo mahāyānopabhogataḥ
>
> (*AA* 8.12)

> [This form of the Sage, with thirty-two marks and eighty signs, is to be understood as his embodiment in communal enjoyment *(sāmbhogikakāya)*, from its enjoyment of the great vehicle *(mahāyāna)*.][31]

This verse provides strong corroboration for our understanding of *AA* 8 as a mapping of three Yogācāra *kāyas* onto the textual material of the *Large PP Sūtra*. The reasoning is as follows.

Neither the term *sāmbhogikakāya* nor the term *nairmāṇikakāya* is found in the *PP* sūtras. These sūtras employ the more general term *rūpakāya* (physical body, embodiment in form) to refer to a Buddha's physical body or manifestations in general.[32]

Sāmbhogikakāya is a term employed by Yogācāra texts to designate the exalted, often central Buddha figures of early Mahāyāna sūtras, while *nairmāṇikakāya* was specified in Yogācāra texts to refer to their countless manifestations in the worlds of beings (chapters 4 and 5 above).

Interestingly, throughout the entire Yogācāra and Yogācāra-related literature discussed in chapters 4 and 5 above, the thirty-two marks and eighty signs were never specifically assigned to either the *sāmbhogikakāya* or the *nairmāṇikakāya*. Rather, they were ascribed simply to *rūpakāya* in general. Even though these Yogācāra texts (third to sixth centuries C.E.) often explicate *sāmbhogikakāya* and *nairmāṇikakāya* at length, clearly distinguishing between them, they do not distinguish between them in the ascription of the thirty-two marks and eighty signs. This is because they mention the marks and signs only when listing or describing the qualities (dharmas) of a Buddha in general, without ascribing them to one type of embodiment or another. In this they are much like the *PP* sūtras, which had never formally distinguished *sāmbhogikakāya* from *nairmāṇikakāya* and therefore could only ascribe the marks and signs to *rūpakāya* in general.

The marks and signs are mentioned in *Mahāyānasūtrālaṃkāra* vv. 21–49 *bhāṣya,* where they form a part of the list of undefiled Buddha dharmas discussed in *MSA* chapter 21.[33] Although as we have seen, the *MSA*'s ninth chapter explains the *kāyas* in detail, no choice is made between *sāmbhogikakāya* and *nairmāṇikakāya* as to the possessor of those marks and signs.

Mahāyāna-saṃgraha 10.16 quotes *Mahāyānasūtra-alaṃkāra* verse 21.49, and the commentary by Asvabhāva identifies the verse as a teaching of a Buddha's marks and signs.[34] But again, no specific mention is made of *sāmbhogikakāya* or *nairmāṇikakāya.*

Similarly, the *Ratnagotravibhāga*'s third chapter describes the thirty-two marks of a preeminent person within a general discussion of Buddha qualities. Verses 3.1–3.3 assign the thirty-two marks to the *saṃvṛti-kāya* (conventional embodiment of a Buddha) as opposed to the *paramārtha-kāya* (ultimate embodiment), where *saṃvṛti-kāya* designates *rūpakāya* in general (a Buddha's embodiment in forms, inclusive of *sāmbhogikakāya* and *nairmāṇikakāya*).[35] Then, in verse 3.38, the *RGV* explicitly assigns the thirty-two marks to *both* the *sāmbhogikakāya* and *nairmāṇikakāya,* taken together.[36]

In short, as far as we know, prior to the composition of the *Abhisamayālaṃkāra*, no Indian Buddhist text specifically assigned the thirty-two marks and eighty signs to *sāmbhogikakāya* taken as distinct from *nairmāṇikakāya*. And nowhere in Yogācāra-related literature that developed the *trikāya* theory do the marks and signs enter into the definitions or formulative explanations of either *sāmbhogikakāya* or *nairmāṇikakāya*.[37] Yet the *Abhisamayālaṃkāra*'s eighth chapter assigns the marks and signs specifically to *sāmbhogikakāya*, and defines *sāmbhogikakāya* specifically in terms of them for the first time. Why? The reason becomes clear when *AA* chapter 8 is viewed as a mapping of Yogācāra *trikāya* terms onto specific passages of the *Large PP Sūtra.*

Recall that *AA* 8 is based on *Large PP* passages 8.4–8.5. *PP* passage 8.5 lists the thirty-two marks and eighty signs. They are ascribed to the glorious physical form of the sūtra's central figure, the Bhagavan Buddha.[38] The passage extols the marks and signs as remarkable qualities of Buddha's physical form. The *AA*'s author found in the *PP* passage's list of marks and signs the only textual material available to him for correlation to the Yogācāra concept of *sāmbhogikakāya*. Since the thirty-two marks and eighty signs are extolled in the *PP* passage as especially exalted qualities of Buddha's form, they were the only reasonable place in the *PP* sūtra to apply the Yogācāra label *sāmbhogikakāya*, which was meant to designate the glorious and exalted Buddha figures of Mahāyāna sūtras.

This was a natural match. The constraints of the *PP* text basis, and the guiding concern to map Yogācāra *kāyas* onto *PP* passages, required the *AA*'s author to specify the *sāmbhogikakāya* (of Yogācāra) as the possessor of the marks and signs (taught in *PP* passage 8.5) for the first time in Indian Buddhist literature.

Look again at *AA* verse 8.12:

> This form of the Sage, with thirty-two marks and eighty signs, is to be understood as his embodiment in communal enjoyment *(sāmbhogikakāya)*, by its enjoyment of the great vehicle *(mahāyāna)*. (*AA* 8.12)

The two textual sources for this are clear. The first is the *PP* sūtra, whose passage 8.5 lists the thirty-two marks and eighty signs. The second is the Yogācāra textual tradition, which defines *sāmbhogikakāya* in terms of its communal enjoyment of the Mahāyāna dharma.[39]

AA verses 8.13–8.32 list and further discuss the marks and signs alluded to in verse 8.12.[40] They add nothing further to the present analysis.

As we noted in chapter 5, section 5 above, *Mahāyānasūtrālaṃkāra* v. 9.61 and its commentaries explicitly characterize different forms of *sāmbhogikakāya* as different with respect to their retinues, pure realms, names, forms, sūtra teachings, and activities. Sthiramati (ca. 510–70 C.E.), commenting on the different teachings given by different *sāmbhogikakāya*s, identifies the *Prajñāpāramitāsūtra*, along with the *Daśabhūmikasūtra* and the *Laṅkāvatārasūtra*, as examples of different sūtras taught by different *sāmbhogikakāyas*.[41] This indicates that at least some Yogācāras by the sixth century C.E. had specifically identified the central figure of the *Prajñāpāramitā* sūtras as one example of the *sāmbhogikakāya* of their *trikāya* scheme.

It is possible that Sthiramati's identification of the central figure of the *Prajñāpāramitāsūtra* as *sāmbhogikakāya* may have been based upon the pattern that was first established by the *AA*. The marks and signs mentioned in the *PP* sūtras are ascribable to the form of the Bhagavan Buddha, the central figure and expounder of those sūtras. *AA* v. 8.12 identifies the *sāmbhogikakāya* as the possessor of the marks and signs in the *PP*. Could that have inspired Sthiramati's inclusion of the *PP* sūtra among the teachings of different *sāmbhogikakāyas*? It is also possible, of course, that *AA* v. 8.12 and Sthiramati's comment express a general understanding of the period, or are independent developments. In any case, *AA* v. 8.12 appears to be the first Indian Mahāyāna specification of the marks and signs to *sāmbhogikakāya* per se, and the first time *sāmbhogikakāya* is defined primarily in terms of them.

Having drawn the correspondence in *AA* v. 8.12 between *sāmbhogikakāya* (of Yogācāra) and the marks and signs (listed in *PP* passage 8.5), the author then details those marks and signs individually, together with some of their causes, in *AA* vv. 8.13–8.32. He does so precisely in accordance with their presentation in *PP* passage 8.5.[42] As a set, then, *AA* vv. 8.12 through 8.32 provide further corroboration for our view that the *AA* is a mapping of Yogācāra categories onto the *Large*

PP Sūtra. And this, in turn, provides further corroboration for our interpretation of the *AA* as a three-*kāya* text in general.

8.6
Nairmāṇikakāya and its Activity: *Abhisamayālaṃkāra* vv. 8.33–8.40

The *AA*'s author establishes a distinctive pattern above. First he presents one verse to draw a direct correspondence between one of the Yogācāra *kāya*s and a textual passage from the *Large PP Sūtra* (v. 8.1 for *svābhāvikakāya*, v. 8.12 for *sāmbhogikakāya*). Then, in a number of subsequent verses, he details the content of the *PP* passage (vv. 8.2–8.6 detailing the Buddha dharmas, vv. 8.13–8.32 detailing the marks and signs). The same pattern is followed in his presentation of *nairmāṇikakāya*. In verse 8.33, the *AA*'s author draws a correspondence between the Yogācāra *nairmāṇikakāya* and the extensive textual material in *PP* passages 8.4 and 8.5 which describe the many kinds of activities bodhisattvas do for the liberation of beings. *AA* vv. 8.34–8.40 then detail those activities as they are presented in that *PP* passage.

PP passage 8.4 discusses general ways bodhisattvas use skill in means *(upāya-kauśalya)* to lead beings out of their suffering to enlightenment. Then, in passage 8.5, the Buddha explains the activities of bodhisattvas in detail. He describes what he sees as he surveys the universe: countless bodhisattvas manifesting in all realms of beings. By means of their extraordinary abilities, bodhisattvas lead beings step by step from lower realms into higher realms, and then through each stage of the Buddhist paths to nirvāṇa and full enlightenment.[43]

Besides working to assist hell beings, ravenous ghostlike beings *(preta*s*)*, and animals, the bodhisattvas also enter into the realms of humans to assist them. They do so primarily through four means of gathering and teaching disciples *(catvāri saṃgrahavastūni)*: giving, kind words, beneficial action, and consistency of action. The passage devotes most of its discussion to the first of these means: giving *(dāna)*. Things that bodhisattvas impart to humans include material gifts, excellent qualities of a mundane kind *(laukika-dharmāḥ)*, and excellent qualities of a supramundane kind *(lokkotara-dharmāḥ)*. Included among the supramundane qualities is the collection of undefiled Buddha dharmas and marks and signs of a preeminent person. As noted earlier, this portion of *PP* passage 8.5 provides the scriptural basis for *AA* vv. 8.1–8.32 on *svābhāvikakāya* and *sāmbhogikakāya*.[44] But this is only a small portion of the total passage.

In the rest of passage 8.5, bodhisattvas (having engaged in the four means of gathering disciples) employ many methods of teaching their disciples the Buddhist path, all of which involve comprehension of the emptiness of own-being, the non-perception of things, etc.: the *PP*'s central theme. Bodhisattvas train their disciples in the comprehension of defilement and purification, in accomplishing the benefit of beings even while not perceiving any real beings, in the six perfections, in the ten virtuous practices of the Buddha path, in nonduality, in the use of conventional expressions, etc., and finally in the nature of nirvāṇa.[45] There are a total of twenty-seven such types of bodhisattva activity described in this long and detailed *PP* passage. *AA* v. 8.33 formally links the *nairmāṇikakāya* of the Yogācāra tradition to the entire content of *PP* passages 8.4 and 8.5. *AA* vv. 8.34–8.40 then name the twenty-seven activities described at length in *PP* passage 8.5:

> karoti yena citrāṇi hitāni jagataḥ samaṃ
> ā bhavāt so 'nupacchinnaḥ kāyo nairmāṇiko muneḥ
>
> (*AA* 8.33)

[The embodiment of the Sage in his manifestation(s) *(nairmāṇikakāya)* is that with which he impartially carries out diverse benefits for the world. It is uninterrupted for as long as the existence {of the world}.]

> tathā karmāpy anucchinnam asyā saṃsāram iṣyate
> gatīnāṃ śamanaṃ karma saṃgrahe ca caturvidhe
>
> (*AA* 8.34)

[Likewise, it is agreed, its activity (karma) is uninterrupted for as long as cyclic existence lasts: activity (karma) that pacifies the states of rebirth, that establishes [beings] in the fourfold means of collecting {disciples},]

> niveśanaṃ sasaṃkleśe vyavadānāvabodhane
> sattvānām arthayāthātmye ṣaṭsu pāramitāsu ca
>
> (*AA* 8.35)

[that establishes *(niveśanaṃ)* them in the comprehension of affliction and purification, in the proper nature of the welfare of beings, and in the six perfections,]

> buddhamārge prakṛtyaiva śūnyatāyāṃ dvayakṣaye
> saṃkete 'nupalambhe ca paripāke ca dehināṃ
>
> (*AA* 8.36)

[that establishes them in the Buddha path, in the emptiness of intrinsic nature, in nonduality, in conventional symbolization *(saṃkete)*, in nonperception, and in the maturing of embodied beings,]

bodhisattvasya mārge 'bhiniveśasya nivāraṇe
bodhiprāptau jinakṣetraviśuddhau niyatiṃ prati

(*AA* 8.37)

[that establishes them in the bodhisattva path, in preventing adherence {to things}, in the attainment of enlightenment *(bodhi)*, in the purity of a Buddha's realm, in definite destiny,]

aprameye ca sattvārthe buddhasevādike guṇe
bodher aṅgeṣv anāśe ca karmaṇāṃ satyadarśane

(*AA* 8.38)

[that establishes them in the welfare of limitless beings, in the excellence of attending upon and devoting oneself to the Buddhas, in the limbs of enlightenment, in the nonwastefulness of deeds *(karma)*, and in the vision of the truths,]

viparyāsaprahāṇe ca tadavastukatānaye
vyavadāne sasambhāre saṃskṛtāsaṃskṛte prati
vyatibhedāparijñāne nirvāṇe ca niveśanaṃ

(*AA* 8.39–8.40a)

[that establishes them in the elimination of false views, in the method of {ascertaining} the baselessness of those {views}, in purification and its accompanying accumulation, in the knowledge of nondistinction between conditioned and unconditioned, and that establishes them {finally} in nirvāṇa.]

dharmakāyasya karmedam saptaviṃśatidhā matam

(*AA* 8.40b)

[This is regarded as the twenty-seven-fold activity of the embodiment of dharma *(dharmakāya)*.][46]

These verses function neatly as a complete set. Verse 8.33 defines *nairmāṇikakāya* as the means through which the Sage (*muni*, i.e., Buddha) carries out his extensive activities for the world. Then verses 8.34–8.40 detail those activities in accord with *PP* passage 8.5. In particular, the logical linkage between *nairmāṇikakāya* (as the agent of activity) and the activity it carries out is made explicit through the parallelism of Sanskrit expression in verses 8.33 and 8.34. The second half of verse 8.33 (which leads into verse 8.34) characterizes *nairmāṇikakāya* with two specific expressions: it is uninterrupted *(anupacchinnaḥ)* for as long as the existence (of the world) *(ā bhavāt)*. The first half of verse 8.34 then specifically echoes those characteristics : "likewise, . . . its activity is uninterrupted *(anucchinnaḥ)* for as long as cyclic existence lasts *(ā saṃsāram)*." Verse 8.34's term *asya* (its) should refer back to the subject of the preceding verse 8.33, which is *nairmāṇikakāya*. The term *asya*, together with the parallelism in expression between v. 8.33b and 8.34a (which is obviously intentional), draws the two verses close together semantically. Clearly, verse 8.33 functions together with verses 8.34–8.40 as a block to describe the *nairmāṇikakāya* together with its activities.[47]

The second half of verse 8.40 might surprise the reader at first, because it concludes the entire set of verses 8.34–8.40 by ascribing all activities listed in them to the *dharmakāya*. This seems strange at first reading, because vv. 8.33–8.39 seemed to read so smoothly as a discussion of the *nairmāṇikakāya* and *its* activities. Why then would there be a final ascription of all activities to *dharmakāya* at the very end of the verses? In fact, if v. 8.40 is read not in isolation, but in its relation to the overall structure of the *AA*, its mode of expression makes sense and further supports our interpretation of *AA* chapter 8.

In section 2 of this chapter we pointed out the parallelism between *AA* v. 1.17 (the table of contents for *AA* chapter 8) and *AA* v. 9.2 (the conclusion of the book) in their use of the expressions *dharmakāya sakāritraḥ* (v. 1.17) and *dharmakāya-phalaṃ karma* (v. 9.2). Given their place in the overall structure of the *AA*, both expressions must denote *dharmakāya* as the overall subject matter and title of the *AA*'s eighth chapter, *dharmakāya* understood as the total result of the path *(dharmakāya-phalaṃ)*, together with its activity *(kāritra, karma)*. The second half of verse 8.40 employs an equivalent phrase, *dharmakāyasya karma* (the activity of *dharmakāya*). In doing so, the verse parallels vv. 1.17 and 9.2, and like them, appears to employ that phrase to denote the *dharmakāya* in its inclusive sense, inclusive of all three *kāya*s together with its activity *(karma)*.

This becomes clearer when we notice that v. 8.40 is the *final verse* of the *AA*'s eighth chapter. As such, it is not surprising that the author would "wrap everything up" by using the expression at the closing of his chapter that semantically includes within it the entire content of that chapter: *dharmakāyasya karma*, the "activity" (*karma,* which is the content of the final seven verses of the chapter) of resultant *dharmakāya* (which, in its inclusive sense, comprises all three *kāya*s explained in the chapter). This, then, is why the author chose the phrase *dharmakāyasya karma* for the final verse of chapter 8.

Another aspect of the *AA* that is puzzling at first is the prominence of enlightened "activity" as a buddhological category in its eighth chapter. As we saw in v. 1.17 (section 2 of this chapter above), four aspects of resultant *dharmakāya* are formally distinguished as the four topics of the *AA*'s 8th chapter: three *kāya*s and enlightened activity *(karma, kāritra)*.

Yogācāra *trikāya* texts discussed enlightened activity *(karma)* as a separate buddhological category in their sixfold analysis of Buddhahood.[48] In this sixfold scheme, Buddhahood is described by reference to: (1) its essence *(svabhāva)*,[49] (2) its causes *(hetu)*, (3) its status as a result *(phala)*, (4) its activity *(karma)*, (5) its endowment *(yoga*, the set of Buddha dharmas), and (6) its functional modes *(vṛtti)*. Activity *(karma)* is the fourth of the six categories, while the three *kāya*s together constitute the sixth category, the functional modes *(vṛtti)* of Buddhahood (in its own knowledge and its manifestations for others).[50] But nowhere in these texts is Buddhahood analyzed specifically through the fourfold scheme which *AA* chapter 8 introduced: three *kāya*s with activity as fourth. Instead, as noted in chapter 5 section 5 above, Yogācāra texts often formally identified the activity of Buddhahood with *nairmāṇikakāya*. Yet in the *AA*'s eighth chapter, Buddhahood is formally analyzed as fourfold: three *kāya*s plus activity as a new, fourth member of the set. Why did the *AA* introduce this formulation?

The explanation is simple when we recall both textual traditions upon which the *AA* 8 is based. Although the terminology of three *kāya*s comes from the Yogācāra tradition, the *PP* sūtra passages that are the scriptural basis for the *AA*'s eighth chapter are 8.4 and 8.5 as described above. Those passages devote comparatively little space to discussions of Buddha dharmas, marks, and signs. The vast majority of those passages comprise a long description of numerous bodhisattva activities for beings. In those passages, it is worth noting, the activities are not directly ascribed to the Buddha himself. Rather, the Buddha observes limitless bodhisattvas as they manifest in all realms, and he describes their activities. Those PP passages may have seemed to the *AA*'s author a meager textual basis upon which to construct his entire eighth chapter on Buddhahood.

On the other hand, if all the activities described in those passages were viewed as activities of the Buddha himself, through his manifestations *(nirmāṇāḥ)* taking the form of limitless bodhisattvas, the *PP* material then becomes a plausible textual basis for an entire *AA* chapter on Buddhahood, but a chapter on Buddhahood which would need to make a prominent place in its exposition for a Buddha's activity. Although *PP* passages 8.4–8.5 do not specifically say the bodhisattvas they describe are manifestations of Buddhahood, other passages in the *PP* sūtras do describe countless emanations created by the Buddha, the central teacher of the sūtra. This is especially notable throughout the introductory portion of the *Large PP Sūtra,* which sets the stage for its discourse and dialogues by describing numerous extraordinary emanations by the Buddha, which fill his audience of disciples with awe.[51]

This, then, is precisely the interpretation of *PP* passages 8.4–8.5 that the *AA*'s author made. He took the *PP* passages that describe bodhisattva activities as descriptions of a Buddha's manifestations *(nirmāṇāḥ)*. The twenty-seven kinds of activity in those passages, then, become the activities of a Buddha by means of his *nairmāṇikakāya*. Because *nairmāṇikakāya* was already formally identified in Yogācāra tradition with a Buddha's activity (as noted in chapter 5, section 5 above), the entire content of passages 8.4 and 8.5 then becomes a suitable textual basis for *nairmāṇikakāya*. A purchase for correspondence between the Yogācāra *trikāya* scheme and the *PP* text basis was found there.

Embedded within a small portion of that same *PP* passage (8.5) are lists of a Buddha's undefiled dharmas and marks and signs. The *AA*'s author fell upon this as the meager but sufficient textual anchor for discussions of the Yogācāra *svābhāvikakāya* and *sāmbhogikakāya* (*AA* vv. 8.1–8.32).

However, because the vast majority of textual content in *PP* passages 8.4–8.5 is devoted to bodhisattva activities, *activity itself is the central focus of the entire PP sūtra section upon which AA chapter 8 was based.* The *AA*'s author felt compelled to acknowledge the prominence of activity in his *PP* text basis by making "activity" *(karma, kāritra)* a fourth category of Buddhahood alongside the three *kāyas* of Yogācāra. This, then, is why the *AA*'s author introduced a fourfold analysis of Buddhahood as a set of three *kāyas* plus activity, making a new contribution to the Indian Buddhist literature of his time.

The Yogācāra tradition identified enlightened activity with *nairmāṇikakāya*. The *AA* replicated this pattern by associating activity specifically with *nairmāṇikakāya* (in *AA* verses 8.33–8.34). But the *PP* text basis for *AA* 8 also required the *AA* to distinguish activity as a fourth category of Buddhahood equal in importance to the three Yogācāra *kāyas*. And this is how it appears in *AA* verses 1.17, 8.40 and 9.2.

In *AA* verses 8.33–8.40, then, the *AA*'s author once again draws upon both his literary sources (Yogācāra and *PP*) at once, following the same characteristic pattern: the first verse of the set makes a linkage between the two textual sources; subsequent verses detail the content of the *PP* sūtra. Following this pattern, he makes the explicit linkage in verse 8.33 between the Yogācāra concept of *nairmāṇikakāya* and the *PP* textual material which teaches the altruistic activities of bodhisattvas (passages 8.4 and 8.5 taken as a whole). Then, in verses 8.34–8.40, he details the content of the twenty-seven activities as described in PP passage 8.5. Again, the genius of the *AA*'s author lay in his ability to conform to the buddhological patterns of both his literary sources, while also making special correspondences between those sources for the first time in Indian Buddhist literature.

Haribhadra, in his interpretation, identifies the *dharmakāya* of *AA* v. 8.40 with the fourth *kāya* he posited: gnosis *dharmakāya (jñānātmaka dharmakāya)*. He then ascribes all the activities of verses 8.34–8.40 to that fourth *kāya*. For him, verse 8.33 by itself is the entire teaching of *nairmāṇikakāya*.[52] Contrary to Haribhadra, and in agreement with Ārya Vimuktisena, we earlier concluded that *dharmakāya* in verse 8.40 carries the same inclusive sense the term carries in vv. 1.17 and 9.2 (the *AA*'s table of contents and verse of summation), both of which use the same term to refer to resultant Buddhahood as the total subject matter of *AA* chapter 8, inclusive of all three *kāyas*. Haribhadra ignores the position of verse 8.40 within the overall structure of the *AA*. He ignores the ways Yogācāra and *PP* textual sources are drawn into correspondence throughout *AA* 8 (including vv. 8.33–8.40). And he crudely misreads the close semantic linkage between verses 8.33 and 8.34 that was noted above. Haribhadra's alternative reading of these verses, and of the entire 8th chapter of the *AA*, was clearly motivated by reasons external to the text itself.

8.7
Conclusion

Evidence from literary-historical criticism indicates that the author of the *Abhisamayālaṃkāra* constructed his eighth chapter as a map, to draw explicit correspondences between Yogācāra *trikāya* concepts and *Large Prajñāpāramitā Sūtra* passages 8.4 and 8.5 (based upon Conze's numbering system). He was brilliant at this syncretic project. At the same time, however, the syncretic product of his work, *AA* chapter 8, created problems of interpretation which gave rise to an enduring controversy over its meaning, the resolution for which has never been agreed upon by leading *Prajñāpāramitā* scholars of India or Tibet.[53] In each portion of the eighth chapter, the author found a compromise of expression that elegantly communicated the buddhological patterns of both of his literary sources simultaneously (Yogācāra and *Prajñāpāramitā*). But the result was an idiosyncratic product which could no longer be read easily as the simple expression of either tradition. *Abhisamayālaṃkāra* verses 1.17, 8.1-8.6, 8.12, and 8.33–8.40 all created problems of interpretation for commentators centuries after Ārya Vimuktisena.[54]

Apparently, scholars closest to the period of the *Abhisamayālaṃkāra*'s composition, most notably Ārya Vimuktisena, saw the eighth chapter clearly for the *trikāya-Prajñāpāramitā* mapping that it was. In fact, Ārya Vimuktisena's interpretation of the *AA*'s eighth chapter is so accurate, elegant, and incisive that one has to wonder whether he might indeed have been the author of the *AA* himself. By the time Haribhadra composed his commentaries on the *Abhisamayālaṃkāra*, Mādhyamika thought, Buddhist logic, and tantric (four-*kāya*) doctrine had developed much in the interim, affecting his view of the text.[55]

9
Ārya Vimuktisena on Gnoseology and Buddhology in the *Abhisamayālaṃkāra*

9.1
Introduction

As we noted in chapter 7 above, Ārya Vimuktisena's *Abhisamayālaṃkāra-vṛtti* is the earliest extant commentary on the *Abhisamayālaṃkāra*.[1] We have little reliable historical data on its author. Most of our information derives from the history of Buddhism by the Tibetan scholar Taranatha (late sixteenth to early seventeenth centuries), which was written too many centuries removed from Ārya Vimuktisena to be accepted at face value. Taranatha reports that Ārya Vimuktisena was a contemporary of both Dignāga (ca. 440–520 C.E.) and Bhāvaviveka (ca. 500–570? C.E.), which leads some modern scholars to date Ārya Vimuktisena to the early sixth century; but this may well be revised if new historical evidence appears.[2] Although Haribhadra (late eighth century) refers in his *Āloka* to commentaries on the *Abhisamayālaṃkāra* by Asanga and Vasubandhu,[3] he never quotes them. They are not extant in any language, and Ārya Vimuktisena never mentions them. It is quite possible, then, that Ārya Vimuktisena's commentary is not only the oldest available commentary on the *Abhisamayālaṃkāra* but also the first. As we have said, it is also quite possible that Ārya Vimuktisena himself was the author of the *AA*.

Ārya Vimuktisena's comments upon the *Abhisamayālaṃkāra* correlate all of its sections with corresponding passages in the 25,000-verse *Prajñāpāramitā* sūtra. He quotes each section of the *AA* and quotes or cites each corresponding passage of the sūtra. But when quoting the *AA*, is he quoting a prior author? Or is he presenting the *AA* in that form as his own composition? If he himself composed the *AA*, he was certainly in a position to know its correspondence to the sūtra. His own independent comments on the meaning of the *AA*'s verses are generally terse.

Whoever its author may have been, literary-critical evidence and historical considerations presented in chapter 7 showed that *AA* 8 is a mapping of Yogācāra buddhological categories upon specific passages of the *Large PP Sūtra*, from which we concluded that it teaches the three *kāya*s of Yogācāra. The previous chapter presented further evidence for this. There we reviewed the overall patterns of buddhological thought in both the *PP* and Yogācāra traditions, examined the place of the eighth chapter in the *AA*'s overall structure, examined the Sanskrit of relevant verses, and drew correspondences between *AA* 8 and patterns of thought found in Yogācāra and *PP* textual traditions. In this chapter, we look for further insight from the first eminent scholar of the *AA* whose work has come down to us: Ārya Vimuktisena.

9.2
Correspondence between Ārya Vimuktisena's Gnoseology and the *Svābhāvikakāya* of Yogācāra

Earlier we noted that the Yogācāra doctrine of *svābhāvikakāya* was not merely speculative, but constructed within a matrix of interrelated Yogācāra understandings of yogic praxis, gnoseology, and enlightenment (cf. chapter 4, section 6, above).

AA chapter 7 (which immediately precedes the exposition of Buddhahood in *AA* 8) is a condensed exposition of Mahāyāna gnoseology based on passages of the *Large Prajñāpāramitā Sūtra*. The subject of the chapter is referred to as *ekakṣaṇa abhisambodha* (one-moment comprehension) and as *ekakṣaṇa abhisamaya* (one-moment realization).[4] According to Haribhadra's commentaries, the bodhisattva who has reached the very end of the Mahāyāna path has a special flash of profound insight an instant before the attainment of Buddhahood. It is this instant of gnosis through which the bodhisattva, in the very next moment, attains full enlightenment, resultant *dharmakāya*. "One-Moment Comprehension" is the title of *AA* chapter 7. Such an understanding of *AA* 7 has been the dominant understanding in modern scholarship because most modern scholars have based their understanding either on Haribhadra or on commentaries by his Tibetan followers.[5]

Unlike Haribhadra, Ārya Vimuktisena's commentary on *AA* chapter 7 nowhere identifies the "one-moment comprehension" *(ekakṣaṇa abhisambodha)* as the gnosis of a bodhisattva the moment before enlightenment. In fact, as we shall see, near the end of his comments on *AA* 7 he specifically identifies the "one-moment comprehension" as the gnosis of a Buddha, the gnosis of enlightenment itself. It would appear that Haribhadra understood the expression "one-moment comprehension," at least in part, to refer to a gnosis that lasts just a moment prior to enlightenment, while Ārya Vimuktisena understood the term to refer to the capacity of a Buddha's gnosis to comprehend all phenomena in each moment. This requires further study. But in any case, Ārya Vimuktisena's remarks on *AA* chapter 7 comprise an important preliminary to his remarks on *AA* chapter 8. We saw that the theory of *svābhāvikakāya* was based on Yogācāra gnoseology and yogic praxis. Similarly, Ārya Vimuktisena's gnoseology (in his comments on *AA* 7) frames his understanding of *svābhāvikakāya/dharmakāya* (in his comments on *AA* 8). Before examining his comments on *AA* 8, then, we present below most of his commentary on *AA* 7 (leaving out a few quotations and adjunct remarks).

The seventh chapter of the *AA* is very short, consisting of only five verses. The one-moment comprehension is said to have four aspects, which comprise the four topics of the chapter. Ārya Vimuktisena identifies the four aspects as follows: (1) The quality of including in one moment of comprehension all the undefiled dharmas, such as the perfection of giving, etc., (2) the one-moment comprehension of all undefiled dharmas in the state of matured *dharmatā*, (3) the one-moment comprehension of all dharmas as identityless *(alakṣaṇa)*, (4) the one-moment comprehension of all dharmas in their character of nonduality.[6] According to Ārya Vimuktisena's commentary, the first two verses of the chapter describe the first aspect of the one-moment comprehension, while each of the remaining three verses describes, respectively, each of the three remaining aspects. His comments follow:

> Now the comprehension of one mind moment is to be explained. The [following question from the *PP* sūtra] is asked so the one-moment comprehension *(ekakṣaṇa abhisamaya)* would be set forth: "Oh Bhagavan, when a bodhisattva, a great being, practices the perfection of wisdom *(prajñāpāramitā)*, how does just one moment of his mind possess all six perfections, . . . ?"[7] The one-moment comprehension *(ekakṣaṇa abhisamaya)* has four aspects, [the first of which] is the quality of including in one moment [of comprehension] all the undefiled dharmas, giving, etc. Concerning this, [*Abhisamayālaṃkāra* v. 7.1 says:]
>
> "It should be known that the comprehension of the Sage is of a single moment, because of the inclusion by [this] single [awareness] of all undefiled dharmas through giving, etc."[8] (*AA* v. 7.1)
>
> Because the perfections of giving and so forth are possessed by the perfection of wisdom *(prajñāpāramitā)*, [and all undefiled dharmas] all the way up to the eighty excellent signs are possessed by it, this nondual cognition, this one-moment comprehension itself includes in its comprehension all virtuous qualities. Situated within this undefiled mind, giving is performed without perceiving any sign of who gives what to whom. This is precisely the one-moment comprehension in which there is no perception of any dharma.[9]

Here in his comments on *AA* v. 7.1, Ārya Vimuktisena identifies the one-moment comprehension with the perfection of wisdom *(prajñāpāramitā)*. As noted in chapter 3 above, the perfection of wisdom of the *PP* sūtras is a nondual gnosis of thusness *(tathatā)*, a direct realization of the emptiness of self-existence of all dharmas *(sarva-dharma-svabhāva śūnyatā)*. As such, it is often described as the "nonperception" of any dharma. Following these remarks, Ārya Vimuktisena paraphrases the corresponding *PP* sūtra passage that advocates the accomplishment of all perfections and other virtues by "dedicating them through 'nonperception.'"[10] Then he explicates *AA* v. 7.2:

> But how, when one has entered into a meditation cognizant of just one undefiled dharma [i.e., the perfection of wisdom], are all undefiled dharmas included? In response to this problem, [*AA* v. 7.2] presents an example taken from everyday life: "Just as a person, with a single kick, moves the whole water wheel at once, so is the one-moment gnosis."[11] In other words, the [one-moment comprehension] occurs from the propulsive force of previous [virtue].[12]

This completes Ārya Vimuktisena's comments on the first topic of *AA* chapter 7: "the quality of including in one-moment [of comprehension] all the undefiled dharmas." Next, he comments on *AA* v. 7.3, concerning the second topic of *AA* chapter 7:

> On the one-moment comprehension of all undefiled dharmas in the state of matured *dharmatā*, [*AA* v. 7.3] says: "When the matured state of *dharmatā*—the perfection of wisdom *(prajñāpāramitā)* that comprises all virtues—occurs, then there is gnosis in a single moment."[13]

This verse, too, identifies the one-moment comprehension or gnosis *(ekakṣaṇe jñānam)* with the perfection of wisdom *(prajñāpāramitā)*. Ārya Vimuktisena next quotes the *PP* sūtra passage that corresponds to this verse. He then comments on the third topic of *AA* chapter 7:

> On comprehension in one moment of all dharmas as identityless, [*AA* v. 7.4] says: "Having become situated in dharmas as dreamlike in one's practice of giving, etc., one obtains the identitylessness of dharmas in a single moment."[14] [The objection might be raised that] it seems that the identities of the dharmas that are so different from each other could not be included in the comprehension of one dharma [i.e., in the perfection of wisdom alone]. In that case, it would follow that there could be no one-moment comprehension. As answer to this the [*PP* sūtra passage] is taught

> that begins: "Subhuti, when the bodhisattva great being practices the perfection of wisdom, abiding in the five aggregates that are like a dream" and goes up to "he knows all dharmas in their extensiveness to be identityless." This teaches the one-moment comprehension of the identitylessness of all dharmas.[15]

Ārya Vimuktisena, basing himself upon the *Prajñāpāramitāsūtra*, is saying that all phenomena, although conceptually distinct from each other, can be included within the perfection of wisdom's one-moment comprehension through its perception of the single identitylessness that they all share.[16] He briefly glosses a few terms from the sūtra passage and then continues:

> When engaging in giving, etc., whether interferences occur or not, by functioning within emptiness the practice becomes supreme. Having experienced the collection [of virtuous practices] as serviceable, when the [one-moment] comprehension [of all dharmas as identityless] occurs, there is no differentiation of dharmas that are just one taste. Through that [understanding], the essential point is made.[17]

Ārya Vimuktisena is saying that although many different phenomena are conceptualized, all can be comprehended in a single moment through the perception of the one "identity" they all share, their identitylessness *(alakṣaṇatvam)*, i.e., their emptiness of self-existence.[18] This single-moment comprehension is the perfection of wisdom *(prajñāpāramitā),* which knows all phenomena through their one flavor *(ekarasa)* of emptiness, thusness. Ārya Vimuktisena makes some adjunct remarks upon the sūtra, then comments on *AA* v. 7.5, which teaches the fourth topic of *AA* 7:

> On the one-moment comprehension of all dharmas in their character of nonduality, [*AA* v. 7.5] says: "One does not even see the dream and its seer in a dual way. In one moment, one sees the nondual thatness *(tattvam)* of dharmas."

Ārya Vimuktisena quotes the corresponding *PP* sūtra passage, which says that when a bodhisattva practices the perfection of wisdom, he does not see the dream, nor does he see the experiencer of the dream. The dreamlike dharmas and the perfection of wisdom are not separate. They are utterly nondual. The sūtra passage he quotes goes on to say: "He [the bodhisattva] sees all dharmas as included within the perfection of wisdom *(prajñāpāramitā)*, but he does not perceive those dharmas. Why? Because those very dharmas and that perfection of wisdom are nondual and undivided. Why? Because there is no differentiation of dharmas. All dharmas are undifferentiated through their identification with the dharma realm *(dharmadhātu)* with thusness *(tathatā)*, with the limit of reality *(bhūtakoṭi)*."[19] Ārya Vimuktisena continues:

> But if all dharmas are undifferentiated, there should be no teaching of virtuous and nonvirtuous dharmas, etc. [which differentiates them as "virtuous," "nonvirtuous," etc.]. And yet there is an expression of them as such [taught in the sūtra]. Therefore [the *PP* sūtra] describes [Subhuti] seeking the reason why they are expressed as [differentiated], and then discusses the inexpressibility of all dharmas in their real nature *(dharmatā)*. And likewise [the *PP* sūtra] discusses the skill in the essence of all dharmas *(sarvadharma-svabhāva-kuśalaḥ)*, perfect accomplishment of which is referred to as *dharmakāya*. Understood in that way, the [synopsis of *AA* chapter 7 in v. 1.16 that says] "the one-moment comprehension *(ekakṣaṇa abhisambodha)* is fourfold in its character" should be seen in its relation to the latter subject, [*dharmakāya*, the subject of *AA* chapter 8 and v. 1.17].
>
> [The objection could be raised that] it is said in the sūtra: "The *śravaka āryas* attend to suffering as suffering, attend to the source [of suffering] as the source, and attend to the path as the path. Through their undefiled attention, they distinguish the associated dharmas." Doesn't the theory of the one-moment comprehension contradict this? No, there is no such contradiction, because such statements explicitly refer to *ārya śrāvakas*, whereas this [the one-moment comprehension] is the comprehension of a Buddha.[20]

In the first paragraph above, Ārya Vimuktisena refers to the *PP* sūtra at the end of the passage corresponding to *AA* chapter 7.[21] In that passage, Subhuti asks how it is, if all dharmas are undifferentiated, that they are distinguished as virtuous and nonvirtuous, etc. (precisely as they are taught throughout the sūtra). The Bhagavan (Buddha) replies by asking whether there is, within the *dharmatā* (the real nature) of the dharmas, any expression of those dharmas. Subhuti says no. The Bhagavan then describes how the bodhisattva, practicing perfect wisdom that does not perceive any dharma, through his "skill in the essence of dharmas" *(sarva-dharma-svabhāva-kuśalaḥ)*, completes the path to enlightenment in order to purify his Buddha realm and to mature other beings. Ārya Vimuktisena says the perfected accomplishment of "skill in the essence of dharmas" (i.e., the perfection of wisdom discussed throughout the passage) is *dharmakāya*. He therefore considers this section of the sūtra (upon which *AA* chapter 7 is based) to be integrally related to the next section of sūtra (upon which *AA* chapter 8's discussion of *dharma-kāya* is based).

Ārya Vimuktisena's comments are packed with implications for his buddhology. His prior discussion leading into the quotation above concerned both the ultimate nature of all dharmas and the perfection of wisdom *(prajñāpāramitā),* which knows that nature in a nondual way and, through that, knows all dharmas at once ("one-moment comprehension"). It is this, the "skill" in the essence of all phenomena (the perfection of wisdom), that Ārya Vimuktisena explicitly identifies with *dharmakāya*. In addition, his final remark above identifies the one-moment comprehension *(ekakṣaṇa abhisambodha)*, the entire subject matter of *AA* chapter 7, as the gnosis of a Buddha.[22]

According to Ārya Vimuktisena, then, the single-moment comprehension is a Buddha's nondual knowledge of all phenomena at once through the emptiness that is their undivided nature. His discussion of *AA* chapter 7, mirroring the *PP* sūtra, centers on the problem of how one moment of knowledge can know all things, which are so extensive and so different from each other. The answer, repeated again and again in different ways both in the sūtra and Ārya Vimuktisena's commentary, is that the perfection of wisdom knows all things by knowing the one undivided essence they all share, emptiness. This is "skill in the essence of all dharmas." It is expressed in *PP* sūtra expressions of the "nonperception" of all dharmas and the comprehension of their "identitylessness." It is expressed by Ārya Vimuktisena in his assertion that all is known in "one taste" *(ekarasa)*.

He specifies it further in his response to the hypothetical objections at the end of his comments. A hypothetical objector says that *śrāvaka āryas* are said in scripture to "attend to suffering *as suffering*, to attend to the source of suffering *as the source*," etc. He asks whether this doesn't contradict the explanation of one-moment comprehension *(ekakṣaṇa abhisambodha)*, according to which all phenomenal things are known not through their different phenomenal natures (such as "suffering"), but through their "identitylessness," their essential nature of emptiness.

In chapter 5, section 3 of this book, we discussed the paradox in the Yogācāra tradition that lay implicit in the Mahāyāna theory of nonabiding nirvāṇa *(apratiṣṭhita nirvāṇa):* a Buddha is both unconditioned and conditioned, cognitively one with universal emptiness (an unconditioned dimension), yet spontaneously active in the conditioned world to help beings (a conditioned function). According to several Yogācāra texts we explored, the pervasiveness of a Buddha's activity was explained by the fact that a Buddha's gnosis pervades the universe. And his gnosis pervades the universe because it is cognitively conjoined with the one ultimate nature of everything in the universe: thusness, the realm of dharma *(dharmadhātu)*. The *Buddhabhūmisūtra* expressed this by saying that the purified dharma realm *(dharmadhātuviśuddhi)* pervades all things in "one taste" *(ekarasa)*, just as space pervades all forms.[23]

Ārya Vimuktisena's remarks on a Buddha's gnosis follow this pattern of thought. They point to a single, undifferentiated gnosis that knows all things in one taste through their undivided emptiness. For Ārya Vimuktisena, as for the Yogācāras, the essential principle of enlightenment is a nonconceptual gnosis of thusness, through which all else is known and all other qualities informed and fulfilled.

This, again, is utterly opposed to the notion, promulgated by Abhidharmikas, that the defining essence of Buddhahood is a differentiated collection of mental qualities, the undefiled dharmas. It also therefore differs most fundamentally from Haribhadra's postulation of a fourth *kāya* as a defining feature of Buddhahood, *jñānātmaka dharmakāya* (*dharmakāya* consisting of gnoses), understood as a collection of conceptually differentiated Buddha dharmas.

In line with both the *PP* sūtras and Yogācāra tradition, Ārya Vimuktisena finds the defining essence of enlightenment in a single undifferentiated principle, nondual gnosis of thusness, based upon which all else, including omniscience, follows. This becomes a natural basis for his acceptance of the three-*kāya* theory of Yogācāra. For it is precisely the nondual, undifferentiated realization of thusness that the Yogācāras identified as *svābhāvikakāya*, the defining essence of Buddhahood. *Sāmbhogikakāya* and *nairmāṇikakāya* (and the set of Buddha dharmas) were then understood as phenomenal expressions of *svābhāvikakāya* as it comes under the conceptually constructed purview of sentient beings.[24]

In the last section of his comments, Ārya Vimuktisena identifies "skill *(kuśala)* in the essence *(svabhāva)* of all dharmas" as *dharmakāya*. "Skill in the essence of all dharmas" is a *PP sūtra* expression for *prajñāpāramitā,* perfection of wisdom of emptiness. As noted in chapter 3 above, it is the thusness of all phenomena, and the nondual realization of it *(prajñāpāramitā),* that the *PP* sūtras identified as the defining essence of Buddhahood. Similarly, as noted in chapters 4 and 5 above, Yogācāra tradition identified purified thusness and nonconceptual gnosis as the defining essence of Buddhahood: *svābhāvikakāya*, which is also referred to as *dharmakāya* in the exclusive sense. Ārya Vimuktisena's identification of *dharmakāya* in his final comments above accords well with both traditions.

By making these observations, it should be noted, we are not assigning Ārya Vimuktisena in any formal sense to the "Yogācāra school" of Indian Buddhism as opposed to the "Madhyamaka school." Haribhadra refers to Ārya Vimuktisena as a Mādhyamika in the introduction to his *Sphuṭārthā*,[25] and Tibetan doxographers have come to characterize him as "Yogācāra Madhyamaka," but any such characterization on our part would require further research.[26] Even then we may find it is impossible to specify his school. Rather, our observations are intended to show how his acceptance of the three-*kāya* buddhology from Yogācāra (in his comments on *AA* chapter 8) naturally follows from his gnoseology (in his comments on *AA* chapter 7). It is worth noting that Candrakīrti, the eminent seventh-century philosopher, in the final chapter of his *Madhyamakāvatāra* on Buddhahood, ascribes a "one-moment comprehension" to the Buddha through which he comprehends all things "in one taste." The second verse of the chapter says:

> Just as space is not divided by the divisions of containers [that enclose it], so there is no division in reality made by phenomena. Through rightly

> comprehending with excellent knowledge that [all] is the same in one taste *(ekarasa)*, you comprehend all things in one instant.[27]

Candrakīrti, who was of course a Mādhyamika, attributes a "one-moment comprehension" to the Buddha that is very much like what Ārya Vimuktisena described. And like Ārya Vimuktisena, Candrakīrti, in the rest of his *Madhyamakāvatāra*, proceeds to delineate three *kāyas*.[28]

Ārya Vimuktisena's comments on related sections of the *Abhisamayālaṃkāra* conform to his remarks above, and provide further insight into his buddhology. *AA* chapter 1, subtopic 2.3 is called "Instruction on the Three Jewels" *(ratnatraya avavāda)*. Concerning the Buddha Jewel *(buddharatna)*, Ārya Vimuktisena quotes the *PP* sūtra and then comments: "This teaches that the gnosis *(jñāna)* of the sameness of subject and object is Buddha."[29] This identifies the nondual perfection of wisdom itself as Buddha. *AA* chapter 6, topic 7 is the "Recollection of the Buddha" *(buddhānusmṛti)*. Echoing the *PP* sūtra, Ārya Vimuktisena declares that the Buddha is to be recollected precisely by *not* attending to his physical form, since form is without self-existence and is unreal. Similarly, he says, one is to recollect the Buddha by *not* attending to his marks and signs, ten powers, etc.—i.e., by not attending to any of the undefiled dharmas ascribed to Buddhas.[30] For Ārya Vimuktisena, to recollect Buddha is to become aware of the emptiness of all his qualities, and thereby to enter into the Buddha's own perfection of wisdom.

In chapter 4, section 2 of this book, we saw how Yogācāra texts characterized the list of undefiled dharmas as a phenomenal description of Buddhahood, inadequate to capture its defining essence. They specified a Buddha's defining essence *(svabhāva)* to be his unobstructed, nondual gnosis of thusness. That gnosis, as a Buddha's own knowledge that is not under the purview of non-Buddhas, was also named *svābhāvikakāya*. (embodiment of Buddhahood in its own innermost essence), and was thereby distinguished from its embodiments in functional relations to others that were named *sāmbhogikakāya* (embodiment in communal enjoyment of dharma) and *nairmāṇikakāya* (embodiment in countless manifestations).[31] Ārya Vimuktisena's gnoseology in the seventh chapter of his work, which is based upon his reading of the *Prajñāpāramitāsūtra*, also parallels that of the Yogācāras, predisposing him to understand the *AA*'s buddhology in its eighth chapter as well through the thought forms of both of its textual sources.

9.3
Ārya Vimuktisena on *Svābhāvikakāya/Dharmakāya*

At the outset, Ārya Vimuktisena identifies the subject matter of *Abhisamayālaṃkāra* chapter 8 to be *dharmakāya*, understood in its inclusive sense as the complete fruition of the bodhisattva path: *dharmakāya-phalam*, resultant Buddhahood.[32] Resultant Buddhahood is threefold: *svābhāvikakāya*, *sāmbhogikakāya*, and *nairmāṇikakāya*. Concerning *svābhāvikakāya*, he quotes *AA* v. 8.1:

> The embodiment of the Sage in his essence *(svābhāvikakāya):* Its identity is the primordial nature of the undefiled dharmas that are obtained in utter purity.

We noted in chapter 8, section 3, of this book that the *AA*'s author was constrained by his *PP* sūtra basis to define *svābhāvikakāya* of Yogācāra tradition in an unusual way, by reference to the undefiled dharmas as presented in *PP* sūtra passage 8.5.2.[33] Ārya Vimuktisena's discussion of this verse reveals his awareness that *AA* 8 expresses Yogācāra intuitions read in and through *PP* sources:

> Of the utterly purified, undefiled all-dharmas, possessed of the dharma realm *(dharmadhātu)*, the primordial nature (Tib., *rang bzhin;* Skt., *prakṛti*), the essence (Tib., *ngo bo nyid;* Skt., *svabhāva*), should be known as the embodiment of the Bhagavan in his essence *(svābhāvikakāya)*, [where "essence"] means it is uncreated. It is well known in the world that an "essence" *(svabhāva)* is that which is not created. The supramundane path obtains that [essence]; it is not its creator.[34]

At the start, Ārya Vimuktisena specifies that the undefiled dharmas, utterly purified, are "possessed of the dharma realm" *(dharmadhātu)*. Notice how he takes the *PP* sūtra talk of "undefiled dharmas," which is reflected in *AA* verse 8.1, and contextualizes it so as to recapitulate Yogācāra understanding of Buddhahood as *dharmadhātuviśuddha*, purified dharma realm. And this, in turn, aligns naturally with the Yogācāra model of *svābhāvikakāya* that is the primary subject of the verse.

As discussed in chapter 4, sections 3 and 4, of this book, "purified dharma realm" refers to the Buddhas' unobstructed awareness of the thusness of all phenomena: Buddhahood in its fullest cosmic dimension. And *svābhāvikakāya* is specified as the first functional mode *(vṛtti)* of that "purified dharma realm": a Buddha's nondual realization as it is embodied in its own knowledge, prior to specification in its functional relations to non-Buddhas. Since the principal subject of *AA* verse 8.1, of course, is *svābhāvikakāya*, the verse must be understood to replicate the meaning of *dharmadhātuviśuddha* (purified dharma realm) even through the constraint of its *PP* source (8.5.2), which lists only the "all dharmas" of a Buddha. Therefore Ārya Vimuktisena says that to understand *AA* verse 8.1, one must understand how the teaching of undefiled "all dharmas" in the *PP* sūtra reveals *dharmadhātuviśuddha* (of Yogācāra). He therefore glosses the phrase as such: "utterly purified all-dharmas, possessed of the dharma realm *(dharmadhātu)*." The expression "possessed of the dharma realm," then, refers to a Buddha's awareness in its capacity of nondually cognizing the *dharmadhātu*, the realm of dharma, the cosmos in its thusness. Ārya Vimuktisena's use of the phrase "utterly purified" both echoes the phrase "utter purity" from *AA* 8.1 and replicates the term *viśuddha* (purified) within *dharmadhātuviśuddha* (purified dharma realm). Thus, Ārya Vimuktisena says, the undefiled dharmas listed in the *PP* text basis are taken into *AA* verse 8.1 as a designation for the purified dharma realm *(dharmadhātuviśuddha)* as unobstructed (purified) nondual awareness of the thusness of all phenomena.

Ārya Vimuktisena's reading of *AA* 8.1 also readily follows from his reading of *AA* chapter 7's "one-moment comprehension," explained in the prior section. Recall what he wrote on *AA* v. 7.1:

> Because the perfections of giving and so forth are possessed by the perfection of wisdom *(prajñāpāramitā)*, [and all undefiled dharmas] all the way up to the eighty excellent signs are possessed by it, this nondual cognition, this one-moment comprehension itself includes in its comprehension all virtuous qualities.

The comprehension of all virtuous dharmas in one essential principle, *prajñāpāramitā*, is extended in v. 7.4 to all dharmas, all phenomena, without exception:

> "Having become situated in dharmas as dream-like in one's practice of giving, etc., one obtains the identitylessness of dharmas in a single moment." (*AA* v. 7.4)
>
> [I]t seems that the identities of the dharmas that are so different from each other could not be included in the comprehension of one dharma [i.e., in the perfection of wisdom alone]. In that case, it would follow that there could be no one-moment comprehension. As answer to this the [*PP* sūtra passage] is taught that begins: "Subhuti, when the bodhisattva great being practices the perfection of wisdom, abiding in the five aggregates that are like a dream" and goes up to "he knows all dharmas in their extensiveness to be identityless." This teaches the one-moment comprehension of the identitylessness of all dharmas.

Thus the *AA*'s seventh chapter leading into *AA* v. 8.1 above has already established a single, quintessential awareness that includes within it all the undefiled dharmas of a Buddha, and in its nondual knowledge of emptiness, includes all dharmas. Recall in his comments on v. 7.5, Ārya Vimuktisena quoted the *PP* sūtra as follows:

> He [the bodhisattva] sees all dharmas as included within the perfection of wisdom *(prajñāpāramitā)*, but he does not perceive those dharmas. Why? Because those very dharmas and that perfection of wisdom are nondual

> and undivided. Why? Because there is no differentiation of dharmas. All dharmas are undifferentiated through their identification with the dharma realm *(dharmadhātu)* with thusness *(tathatā)*, with the limit of reality *(bhūtakoṭi)*.

That single, essential awareness includes all dharmas by seeing them in their identity with the dharma realm, with unobstructed thusness. Ārya Vimuktisena goes on, as we saw, to identify this one moment comprehension as *dharmakāya* itself, the perfection of wisdom as it has been fully realized by a Buddha.

His comments on v. 8.1 above replicate these very understandings: *svābhāvikakāya* is another name for that one moment comprehension, *dharmakāya*, the enlightened awareness that includes within it all Buddha dharmas, indeed all dharmas, through its "possession" of all within the *dharmadhātu*.

In *AA* verse 8.1, Ārya Vimuktisena says, this core awareness of enlightenment, *dharmakāya*, is appropriately given the specific designation *svābhāvikakāya*, meaning the *embodiment* of the *very essence* of the Buddha's attainment. The term "essence" *(svabhāva)*, he says, is employed for its connotation of uncreatedness. In the common parlance of the world, the "essence" of water, for example, is its wetness. The heat of hot water or the cold of cold water must be added to the water, generated or created within it. But the wetness of water is not something that needs to be added to or created in the water. It is intrinsic to it. Similarly, the "embodiment of the very essence of Buddhahood" is called "essence" because it too is never created or made out of something else. It is a nondual awareness *obtained* by the supramundane paths of seeing, meditation, etc., but not constructed out of them: "The supramundane path obtains that [essence]; it is not its creator."

For Ārya Vimuktisena, Yogācāra intuitions illuminate the *Prajñāpāramitā* sūtra in its refraction through *Abhisamayālaṃkāra* verses. His comments on *AA* 8.1 flow simultaneously from the *Prajñāpāramitā* gnoseology reflected in *AA* chapter 7 and from Yogācāra understanding of *svābhāvikakāya*. In chapter 5, section 3, of this book, we noted several ways *svābhāvikakāya/dharmakāya* is characterized in Yogācāra texts as unconditioned, permanent, and uncreated. Thusness *(tathatā)*, the real nature of all things, is unconditioned. When all cognitive obstructions obscuring it have been purified, a Buddha becomes nondually identified with it as "purified thusness" *(tathatāviśuddhi)*, which is therefore unconditioned both by its very nature and in terms of its permanent cessation of all obscuration. Thusness itself is primordial, never newly created. It has always been the case. What is attained through the yogic path is just the nondual awareness of it, *dharmakāya*, referred to as *svābhāvikakāya* to emphasize its identification with that primordial essence *(svabhāva, prakṛti)* which is also the very "essence" of Buddhahood.[35]

In addition, many Yogācāra texts explicitly or implicitly express the idea of an innate, luminous purity of mind *(citta-prakṛti-viśuddhi)*, which, at the attainment of enlightenment, becomes fully manifest. In resonance with this, *svābhāvikakāya*, as the final removal of all obscurations that had covered innate purity of mind, is also not a new creation. It is a revealing of what has always been. Such understandings of the permanence and uncreatedness of *svābhāvikakāya/dharmakāya* are common to Yogācāra texts that first formulated and developed the doctrine of *svābhāvikakāya/dharmakāya*.[36]

According to Ārya Vimuktisena, *Abhisamayālaṃkāra* vv. 8.2–8.6 continue the explanation of *svābhāvikakāya* that verse 8.1 began. In his view, verse 8.1 would naturally raise a question for its readers, which verses 8.2–8.6 are supposed to answer: "What are the undefiled dharmas whose completely purified essence *(svabhāva)* is *dharmakāya?*"

He then quotes *AA* vv. 8.2–8.6 as the *AA*'s answer to that question:

> "The factors that foster enlightenment, the measureless thoughts, the liberations, the nine meditative attainments, the ten meditative totalities, the bases of overpowering divided into eight kinds, the meditative power freeing from passions, the gnosis resulting from resolve, the supernatural knowledges, the analytical knowledges, the four total purities, the ten sovereignties, the ten powers, the four forms of fearlessness, the three ways in which [a Buddha] has nothing to hide, the threefold mindful equanimity, the nature of never forgetting, the complete destruction of [negative] propensities, the great compassion for living beings, the qualities unique to the Sage proclaimed as eighteen, and total omniscience": thus is *dharmakāya* denominated.[37]

Note the specific form of Ārya Vimuktisena's question: "What are the undefiled dharmas [alluded to in verse 8.1] whose completely purified essence is *dharmakāya?*" In his hypothetical question, Ārya Vimuktisena already replaces *svābhāvikakāya* of verse 8.1 with *dharmakāya* of v. 8.6, making explicit their synonymy. In conformity with *PP* gnoseology (refracted through *AA* chapter 7) and with Yogācāra tradition, he understands both terms to refer to the quintessential realization of enlightenment: *dharmakāya* of the *PP* sūtras = *svābhāvikakāya* of Yogācāra (situating *dharmakāya* here in its exclusive sense as the first of the three Yogācāra *kāyas*).

AA vv. 8.2–8.5 list the first nineteen types of undefiled dharma. Verse 8.6 finishes that list and then declares *dharmakāya* to be denominated through it: "'the qualities unique to the Sage proclaimed as eighteen, and total omniscience': thus is *dharmakāya* denominated."

After quoting the verses, Ārya Vimuktisena comments on the term *dharmakāya* of v. 8.6:

> The particle *[tā]* has been elided. Thus it is *dharmatā-kāya* that is referred to [by the term *dharmakāya*]. Because otherwise, *dharmakāya*

> would become a *kāya* (body, collection) of dharmas. But that would negate the *svabhāva* (essence) [of *svābhāvikakāya*, essence embodiment] and make of it a fluctuating phenomenon *(caryārtha)*. And the fault of being conditioned would then follow. As for calling it a *kāya*, it is designated as such in accordance with the state prior [to Buddhahood].[38]

This short passage is packed with meaning, so we will analyze it a portion at a time. Recall Ārya Vimuktisena's comment quoted in the prior section of this chapter on *AA* verse 7.3, concerning a Buddha's "one-moment comprehension in the state of matured *dharmatā*":

> On the one-moment comprehension of all undefiled dharmas in the state of matured *dharmatā* , [*AA* v. 7.3] says: "When the matured state of *dharmatā*—the perfection of wisdom *(prajñāpāramitā)* that comprises all virtues—occurs, then there is gnosis in a single moment."[39]

This identifies the one moment awareness of a Buddha as the perfection of wisdom in the "matured state of *dharmatā*." It is the realization of the enlightened one who is mature in the real nature of all dharmas *(dharmatā)*. As Ārya Vimuktisena further elaborates in comments on v. 7.4, it is a realization that knows all dharmas in their identitylessness, which therefore knows them all in one "taste," without differentiation. In his comments on v. 7.5, Ārya Vimuktisena, echoes the *PP* sūtra, raising the question as to why the various virtuous and nonvirtuous dharmas are taught when, in their real nature, they are just undifferentiated. The sūtra implies the teaching of them is necessary in order for the bodhisattva to fulfil the path, mature other beings, etc. Yet, the sūtra says, in order for that path to be effective, the bodhisattva must become accomplished "in the essence of all dharmas" *(sarva-dharma-svabhāva-kuśalaḥ)*, in their actual undifferentiated, identityless and uncreated nature. According to Ārya Vimuktisena, perfect accomplishment in that "essence" is *dharmakāya*, which knows all phenomena in their real nature *(dharmatā)*. It is therefore natural for him to identify the *dharmakāya* of verse 8.6 with knowledge of *dharmatā* (the real nature of dharmas), which he had explained in his just prior comments on *AA* chapter 7.

As discussed in chapter 2 of this book, Abhidharmikas used the term *dharmakāya* to designate the defining essence of a Buddha as the *body* (i.e., collection) of a Buddha's pure *dharmāḥ* (pure qualities). In chapter 3 we examined *PP*-sūtra passages that reinterpret *dharmakāya* to identify the defining essence of a Buddha in a different way. *Dharmakāya* was implicitly etymologized in the 8,000 verse and *Vajracchedikā PP* sūtras through the term *dharmatā*. *Dharmakāya* (a Buddha's defining principle) say these scriptures, cannot be understood by reference to the conceptually constructed dharmas through which non-Buddhas understand Buddhahood. Rather, *dharmakāya* is *dharmatā*, the undifferentiated real nature of dharmas, as it is embodied *(kāya)* in the nondual knowledge of the Buddhas *(prajñā-pāramitā)*.[40]

The meaning of Ārya Vimuktisena's first comments on *AA* 8.6 now becomes clear:

> "[T]he qualities unique to the Sage proclaimed as eighteen, and total omniscience": thus is *dharmakāya* denominated. (*AA* v. 8.6)

[In this verse,] the particle [*tā*] has been elided. Thus it is *dharmatākāya* that is referred to [by the term *dharmakāya*]. Because otherwise, *dharmakāya* would become a *kāya* (body, collection) of dharmas.

Ārya Vimuktisena is saying that, according to the *PP* tradition upon which the *Abhisamayālaṃkāra* is based, a Buddha's defining realization is *not* a collection of dharmas, even though such has been the understanding of many Abhidharmikas. Rather, the defining principle of a Buddha is his realization of the *real nature* of all dharmas *(dharmatā)* that, as embodied in a Buddha's knowledge, is to be designated *dharmakāya (dharma[tā]kāya)*.

What problems would be created if *dharmakāya* of verse 8.6 were mistakenly interpreted in line with Abhidharma understanding, rather than through the understanding of the *PP* sūtras?

> [O]therwise [i.e., if understood as in Abhidharma rather than in *PP* tradition], *dharmakāya* would become a *kāya* (body, collection) of dharmas. But that would negate the *svabhāva* (essence) [of *svābhāvikakāya*, essence embodiment] and make of it a fluctuating phenomenon *(caryārtha)*.[41] And the fault of being conditioned would then follow. As for calling it a *kāya*, it is designated as such in accordance with the state prior [to Buddhahood].

The Sanskrit term *kāya* in its primary meaning is "body," from which derives the common secondary meaning "a collection" (since a body is a collection of parts).[42] If the term *dharmakāya* is understood, as in Abhidharma, to mean the collection *(kāya)* of undefiled dharmas, the whole sense of the term *svabhāva* (essence) in *svābhāvikakāya* (essence embodiment) would be lost. Just previously, Ārya Vimuktisena explained that the term "essence" in "essence embodiment" means that a Buddha's nondual realization is uncreated, not something constructed out of conditioned things. If *dharmakāya* of v. 8.6 were mistakenly understood to refer to a collection of dharmas, *svābhāvikakāya/dharmakāya* would have to be something created by the accumulation of conditioned phenomena, such as the components of the path. And this, he says, would negate the sense of "essence" in "essence embodiment" *(svābhāvikakāya)*. Obtainment of *svābhāvikakāya/dharmakāya* is the unobstructed coming aware of what had always been the case.

Ārya Vimuktisena goes on: "[T]hat would negate the essence *(svabhāva)*, and make of it *(svābhāvikakāya/dharmakāya)* a fluctuating phenomenon. And the fault of being conditioned would follow." If *AA* 8.6's *dharmakāya* were interpreted Abhidharmically as a collection of dharmas, it would be an accumulation of fluctuating, conditioned phenomena, however pure or virtuous they may be. Such an understanding would be far from *Prajñāpāramitā* tradition, according to which *dharmakāya* is precisely that awareness which has broken through the self-existent appearance of "miragelike" dharmas that "come and go" to the unconditioned nature of dharmas *(dharmatā)* beyond coming and going. The *PP dharmakāya*, as we explored in chapter 3 of this book, is the embodiment of the real nature *(dharmatā)* of dharmas: *dharma[tā]kāya*. It is nondual knowledge *(prajñāpāramitā)* of the empty, unconditioned essence of all dharmas, not a conditioned construct created from the dharmas of the path.

Ārya Vimuktisena's remarks also mirror Yogācāra understanding. According to Yogācāra texts, the activity of a Buddha is available to every being because a Buddha's awareness pervades the universe of beings. And his awareness pervades the universe because it is cognitively conjoined with thusness *(tathatā)*, the dharma realm *(dharmadhātu)*, the one ultimate nature *(dharmatā)* all things share (see chapter 5, section 3, above). This nondual, nonconceptual gnosis of universal thusness is described as "unmoving" *(acala)*. *MSA* v. 9.51 says: "He [a Buddha] never moves from that place, and yet he carries it all out." "That place," according to the commentaries, is the dharma realm *(dharmadhātu)*, universal thusness. The Buddhas' nonconceptual gnosis of thusness itself is the essence of Buddhahood, *svābhāvikakāya*, while its manifestations as *sāmbhogikakāya* and *nairmāṇikakāya* to guide beings to liberation are the way it appears under the conceptual purview of those beings (see chapter 5 above, sections 3 and 4).

Such Yogācāra understandings, in addition to the *Prajñāpāramitā* considerations just noted, also come to expression in Ārya Vimuktisena's remarks above: "[O]therwise [i.e., if *dharmakāya* were understood as in Abhidharma rather than *PP* tradition], *dharmakāya* would become a *kāya* (body, collection) of dharmas. But that would negate the *svabhāva* (essence) [of *svābhāvikakāya*] *and make of it a fluctuating phenomenon (caryārtha). And the fault of being conditioned would then follow*" (emphasis mine). If *dharmakāya (= svābhāvikakāya)* were mistakenly understood as a collection of undefiled dharmas (conditioned virtues and consciousnesses), it would not be, as it is understood in Yogācāra tradition, a nondual, nonconceptual gnosis of the dharma realm *(dharmadhātu)*. It would not be cognitively inseparable from the "unmoving," unconditioned nature of all things, a knowledge of all things through their real nature, thusness. Rather, *svābhāvika-*

kāya/dharmakāya would become a collection of many conditioned awarenesses, including knowledges of numerous phenomenal things per se. And knowledges of phenomenal things are "moving" *(cala),* i.e., they begin and end entirely with the appearance and disappearance, the "coming and going," of conditioned phenomena.[43] Phenomenal knowledge "fluctuates" *(caryā)* with the fluctuating phenomena of the conditioned world. As such, it too would be conditioned by that world. If that were the essential nature of a Buddha's knowledge, Ārya Vimuktisena implies, a Buddha would not be liberated from saṃsāra. A Buddha's awareness would not see the shifting world through its unfluctuating insubstantial essence (thusness, emptiness), but would be as conditioned by the fluctuating appearances of the world as that of ordinary beings.

Ārya Vimuktisena adds: "As for calling it a *kāya*, it is designated as such in accordance with the state prior [to Buddhahood.]" Although the *Prajñāpāramitā* sūtras had given the term *dharma* in *dharmakāya* a new etymology as *dharmatā* (in contradistinction to the Abhidharma etymology "dharmas"), the term *kāya* by itself still carried earlier connotations of "body" in the sense of "collection," 'set of parts," etc. Ārya Vimuktisena feels called upon to account for that older connotation within the newer *PP* understanding.[44] He says "it" *(svābhāvikakāya/dharmakāya)* is designated as *kāya* (body in the sense of collection) in accord with the "prior state" (Tib., *sngon gyi gnas skabs*; Skt., *pūrva-avasthā*[?]). The most direct way to understand this statement is as a reference to the bodhisattva on the path prior to attainment of Buddhahood. The collection of virtuous qualities that compose the bodhisattva path and lead to attainment of *dharmakāya* have informed the construction of the latter term, *kāya*, through earlier Buddhist and Abhidharma usage (where *dharmakāya* means "body," in the sense of "collection," of dharmas). But the dharmas of the path are conditioned attainments of beings prior to Buddhahood; they do not define Buddhahood from a *Prajñāpāramitā* perspective (according to which the "one-moment comprehension" of a Buddha knows all things at once through nondual knowledge of their undifferentiated nature, *dharmatā*). Though the undefiled dharmas, as conditioned, differentiated modes of awareness, compose a bodhisattva's mind prior to Buddhahood (not a Buddha's nondual, undifferentiated awareness per se) their use to denominate *dharmakāya* in *PP* sūtras and the *Abhisamayālaṃkāra* retains validity, as a description of Buddhahood in terms understandable to those who do not know Buddhahood directly, who can only conceptualize it by extrapolation from what they know of the path.[45]

Ārya Vimuktisena's remark, "as for calling it a *kāya*, it is designated as such in accord with the prior state," probably means that the term *kāya* in *dharmakāya* can be understood in its earlier meaning of "collection [of dharmas]" to refer to the mind of a Buddha (which is undifferentiated, not a collection) insofar it is in continuity with the bodhisattva on the path prior to full enlightenment, whose mind had been composed of conditioned dharmas. Ārya Vimuktisena's remark is brief, but the interpretation proposed here fits his fuller textual context. And it accords with the interpretation of Ratnākaraśānti, a later exponent of Ārya Vimuktisena's views on *AA* 8 who took special note of that remark.[46]

Ārya Vimuktisena, then, points out two problems entailed by identifying *svābhāvikakāya/dharmakāya* with the collection of undefiled dharmas, the first being that *svābhāvikakāya/dharmakāya* would no longer be an uncreated "essence," and the second being that it would become a "fluctuating phenomenon." And then he presents the underlying fault of both: *svābhāvikakāya/dharmakāya* would be conditioned. As something made from a collection of things, and as something cognitively conditioned by the phenomenal world, it would be a conditioned phenomenon. And as noted, Yogācāra tradition explicitly formulated *svābhāvikakāya* within its model of nonabiding nirvāṇa *(apratiṣṭhita nirvāṇa)* as a complete personal liberation from saṃsāric conditions, so as to be in the best possible position to liberate others still trapped by saṃsāric conditions (see chapter 5, sections 1 and 3). In addition, then, to the *Prajñāpāramitā* considerations always in the forefront of his mind, Ārya Vimuktisena refers us back to the basic formulation of *svābhāvikakāya/dharmakāya* of Yogācāra tradition.[47]

Taken as a whole, then, Ārya Vimuktisena's comments on *svābhāvikakāya/dharmakāya* (*AA* chapter 8 vv. 1–6) reflect Yogācāra patterns of thought, even as they continue his prior reflections on "one-moment comprehension" (from *AA* chapter 7) that reflect the gnoseology of the *PP* sūtra. Although the undefiled dharmas listed in verses 8.1–8.6, according to him, do not define *svābhāvikakāya/dharmakāya*, they are, nevertheless, an important and useful description of it from a phenomenal point of view (from our point of view, not the Buddha's). Therefore, Ārya Vimuktisena continues his commentary by explaining each of the twenty-one types of undefiled dharma that are listed in *AA* vv. 8.2–8.6, occasionally referring the reader to earlier parts of his commentary where some are discussed, and drawing from Abhidharma descriptions for others.[48]

The last of the undefiled dharmas listed in *AA* v. 8.6 is *sarvākāra-jñatā*, the total omniscience of a Buddha. Ārya Vimuktisena's comments on this are revealing.[49] The Sanskrit term *sarvākārajñatā* literally means "knowledge of all aspects." Ārya Vimuktisena presents the opinions of scholars who differ on the meaning of the term, defining it differently according to how they interpret the semantic component *ākāra* (aspect). According to some scholars, he says, "the knowledge of all aspects" *(sarvākārajñatā)* is the knowledge perceiving the Four Noble Truths *(catvāri āryasatyāni)*, which includes knowledge of all sixteen of their aspects (impermanence, suffering, selflessness, etc.). According to others, it is the gnosis *(jñāna)* that realizes the ultimate aspects of phenomena: their lack of self-existence, their nonorigination, noncessation, primordial peace, etc. According to others, he says, the "knowledge of all aspects" refers to Buddha's capacity, based on his gnosis, to fulfill the highest aspirations of sentient beings [in all their aspects], like the wish-fulfilling jewel of Indian legend. According to others, it is called "knowledge of all aspects" because it is the gnosis that has eliminated the obscurations in all their aspects (emotional and cognitive obscurations and their propensities).

Ārya Vimuktisena says that all these interpretations of a Buddha's knowledge of all aspects have merit, but he likes best the interpretation put forth by Ācaryā Bhadrapāla *(slob dpon bzang skyong)*. I am not familiar with this scholar and have not seen reference to him before. But Ārya Vimuktisena quotes Bhadrapāla as follows:

> It is the quintessence (Tib., *snying po;* Skt., *sāra*) contained in [all] objects of knowledge in their ten aspects: basal consciousness *(ālayavijñāna)*, etc.. Therefore, it is called "the knowledge of all aspects" *(sarvākārajñatā)*.

Ārya Vimuktisena then comments: "This is the very best [interpretation of *sarvākāra-jñatā*], because it [knowledge of all aspects] perceives the perfected *(parinișpanna)*."[50]

I am not sure what the "ten aspects" are to which Bhadrapāla refers. He names only one: *ālayavijñāna*, one of the eight types of consciousness distinctively set forth in the Yogācāra school. The term *ālayavijñāna* is so distinctively Yogācāra, that it is likely Bhadrapāla was an *ācaryā* of that school. And his comments above, if accurately quoted by Ārya Vimuktisena, may indicate that he understood *sarvākāra-jñatā* (knowledge of all aspects) primarily as the Buddha's *citta-prakṛti-viśuddhi*, the primordial, quintessential purity of mind at the stage of enlightenment. The theory of such an innate, quintessential purity, as we have seen, was prevalent in Yogācāra tradition.[51]

Ārya Vimuktisena's only comment expressing his personal opinion is the one at the very end. He likes Bhadrapāla's interpretation best, he says, because a Buddha's knowledge of all aspects "perceives the perfected." The term "the perfected" *(parinișpanna)* sometimes appears in the *Large PP Sūtra* as a synonym for *śūnyatā, tathatā, bhūtakoti*, etc., another term for the nature of things seen as it really is. But probably its most popular usage in the period when Ārya Vimuktisena wrote (ca. early sixth century) was Yogācāra. *Parinișpanna* designated one of the three natures of phenomena described in Yogācāra śāstras (the *Mahāyānasūtrālaṃkāra, Mahāyānasaṃgraha, Madhyāntavibhāga, Dharmadharmatāvibhāga, Trimsika*, etc.). In Yogācāra doctrine, the three natures are the imaginary *(parikalpita)*, the dependent *(paratantra)*, and the perfected *(parinișpanna)*. The "imaginary" is the unreal duality conceptually constructed and superimposed onto reality by sentient beings. The "dependent" is the actual content of conditioned cognition, which exists, but is structured in that illusory, dualistic way. The "perfected" *(parinișpanna)* refers to the emptiness of the duality imagined within the dependent and to the gnosis that realizes that emptiness.[52]

It is worth noting, then, that Ārya Vimuktisena's favorite interpretation for *sarvākāra-jñatā*, Buddha's omniscience, was apparently made by a Yogācāra ācaryā (Bhadrapāla), and that Ārya Vimuktisena's only personal comment on *sarvākāra-jñatā* describes it in characteristically Yogācāra terminology as *pariniṣpanna*. Furthermore, his understanding of *sarvākāra-jñatā* as "the perception of *pariniṣpanna*" makes of it (in accord with Yogācāra gnoseology) a nondual, undifferentiated gnosis of thusness. Again, then, Ārya Vimuktisena understands Buddha's omniscience ("knowledge of all aspects") primarily as a nondual knowledge of the one ultimate nature that all knowables ("all aspects") share. That Ārya Vimuktisena draws upon Yogācāra concepts here should not surprise us, since his entire commentary on *AA* 8 understands it to be teaching the three *kāya*s of Yogācāra tradition as a teaching implicit within the *Large Prajñāpāramitā Sūtra*.

Following the comments above, Ārya Vimuktisena then quotes the portion of the 25,000-verse *PP* sūtra that teaches *sarvākāra-jñatā*, total omniscience. It is noteworthy that this is the first time in his comments on *AA* chapter 8 that he quotes the *PP* sūtra. In the rest of his commentary on all chapters prior to chapter 8, he had quoted the *PP sūtra* soon after introducing every one of the *AA*'s topics (for all sixty-six of the *AA* topics prior to *svābhāvikakāya*). In chapter 8, rather than quoting the *PP sūtra* upon introducing *svābhāvikakāya* (the first topic of the chapter), he waits until his discussion of *sarvākāra-jñatā* (which is not a principal topic but a subtopic of *svābhāvikakāya*). Significantly, the portion of the *PP sūtra* that he quotes as the textual basis for *sarvākāra-jñatā* is in passage 8.5.2 (in Conze's numbering system), the passage in which the Bhagavan explains the list of undefiled dharmas (one of which is *sarvākāra-jñatā*).[53] As shown in chapter 7 above, *Prajñāpāramitāsūtra* passages 8.1–8.3 were composed after Ārya Vimuktisena's time. The only *PP* textual basis that Ārya Vimuktisena found for the *AA*'s teaching of *svābhāvikakāya* (*AA* vv. 8.1–8.6) was the listing of undefiled dharmas in *PP* passage 8.5.2.[54]

Ārya Vimuktisena's comments on *AA* vv. 8.7–8.11 are brief and do not add anything new to our analysis.[55] He understands these verses to continue the explanation of *svābhāvikakāya/dharmakāya* that was begun in vv. 8.1–8.6. I refer the reader to the translation and explanation of vv. 8.7–8.11 presented in chapter 6 above. Ārya Vimuktisena's brief comments accord with what was said there.

9.4 Ārya Vimuktisena on *Sāmbhogikakāya* and *Nairmāṇikakāya*

Ārya Vimuktisena next quotes *AA* v. 8.12, the verse that first describes *sāmbhogikakāya*, the second topic of *AA* chapter 8, the embodiment of the Buddha in his communal enjoyment of dharma. His own comments characterize *sāmbhogikakāya* as the form in which the Bhagavan (Buddha) shares the enjoyment of the Mahāyāna dharma with his retinue of bodhisattvas, i.e., his close disciples. The content of his comments parallels Yogācāra definitions of *sāmbhogikakāya* in the *MSA*, *Msg*, *Buddhabhūmivyākhyāna*, etc., while his style of expression parallels the style of the *PP* sūtras.[56] Recognizing the *AA*'s eighth chapter for what it was—a mapping of Yogācāra *kāyas* onto the *PP* sūtra—his comments again harmonize both textual traditions.

After his own brief explanation of *sāmbhogikakāya*, he spends many folios detailing the thirty-two marks and eighty signs ascribed to it in *AA* vv. 8.13–8.32. He does so in conjunction with quotes and paraphrases from the 25,000-verse *PP* sūtra. All his quotes and paraphrases on the marks and signs come from *PP* passage 8.5.2, the section that lists the marks and signs right after the list of undefiled dharmas.[57]

Thus, in Ārya Vimuktisena's discussion of *svābhāvikakāya* and *sāmbhogikakāya* (the first two topics of *AA* chapter 8), all *PP*-sūtra quotes and paraphrases are taken from *PP* passage 8.5.2 (the passage that lists the undefiled dharmas and the marks and signs of a preeminent person). At the end of his remarks on *svābhāvikakāya* and *sāmbhogikakāya*, Ārya Vimuktisena explicitly identifies passage 8.5.2 as the *PP*-sūtra basis for the *AA*'s teaching of those two *kāyas*. He says:

> As for the teaching of these two *[kāyas]*, they are taught in the section of the *[PP]* sūtra that teaches the *nairmāṇikakāya*'s activity, [in the section on] the method of gathering disciples that is the giving of supramundane dharma. Therefore they were not taught earlier [in the sūtra].[58]

PP passage 8.5.2 teaches the four methods of gathering disciples, the first of which is giving. The undefiled dharmas and marks and signs are listed examples of the supramundane dharma proffered by bodhisattvas to beings. Ārya Vimuktisena's remark explictly identifies this very passage as the sole textual basis for the *AA*'s teaching of *svābhāvikakāya* and *sāmbhogikakāya*.[59]

Ārya Vimuktisena's commentary on *AA* vv. 8.33–8.40 concerns *nairmāṇikakāya* (embodiment of Buddhahood in limitless manifestations) and its activity. This has been discussed in the latter part of chapter 6 of this book.[60] Ārya Vimuktisena reads verse 8.33, the *AA*'s synoptic description of *nairmāṇikakāya*, as grammatically connected to the first half of verse 8.34, which concerns the *nairmāṇikakāya*'s activity:

> The embodiment of the Sage in his manifestation(s) *(nairmāṇikakāya)* is that through which he impartially carries out diverse benefits for the world. It is uninterrupted for as long as the existence [of the world]. Likewise, it is agreed, its activity is uninterrupted for as long as cyclic existence lasts. . . . *(AA* 8.33–8.34a)

Commenting upon this verse, Ārya Vimuktisena defines *nairmāṇikakāya* as the vast manifestations of Buddhahood that pervade the universe to carry out activities for beings until the end of saṃsāra (i.e., until every being has been liberated).[61] He believed that *AA* vv. 8.33–8.40 as a whole teach the activity of resultant *dharmakāya* (Buddhahood) by means of its *nairmāṇikakāya*. *AA* vv. 8.33–8.34a, in his view, describe *nairmāṇikakāya* in general as the agent of enlightened activity, while vv. 8.34b–8.40 detail the twenty-seven different types of activity that *nairmāṇikakāya* (as agent of resultant *dharmakāya*) carries out.[62]

Ārya Vimuktisena quotes *PP* sūtra passage 8.4 as the textual basis for *AA* v. 8.33–8.34a concerning *nairmāṇikakāya* with its activity in general. And he quotes extensively from *PP* sūtra passage 8.5 as the textual basis for the detailed description of the *nairmāṇikakāya*'s activities in *AA* vv. 8.34b to 8.40.[63] He understood the *AA*'s author to have taken the activities described in *PP* passage 8.5 (enacted by numberless bodhisattvas) as activities of Buddhahood itself, carried out through its manifestations *(nirmāṇā)*, i.e., by *nairmāṇikakāya*. As noted in chapter 8 above, *AA* v. 8.40b says: "This is regarded as the twenty-seven-fold activity of *dharmakāya*." Ārya Vimuktisena understood the term *dharmakāya* here to refer to *dharmakāya-phalam*, the resultant state of Buddhahood as a whole, whose activities are enacted through its limitless manifestations as *nairmāṇikakāya*.[64]

According to Ārya Vimuktisena, then, the *Abhisamayālaṃkāra* used the term *dharmakāya* in its inclusive sense (as inclusive of all three *kāyas*) in *AA* v. 8.40 (as well as in v. 1.17 and v. 9.2; see chapter 6 above).[65] It used the term *dharmakāya* in its exclusive sense (as a synonym for *svābhāvikakāya* alone) only in *AA* v. 8.6 (discussed above).

In chapter 5, section 5 of this book, we noticed many Yogācāra texts that formally identified *nairmāṇikakāya* with Buddhahood's extensive activity. This identification was apparently well known to Ārya Vimuktisena. He assumed that the *AA*'s author constructed *AA* vv. 8.33–8.40 in accord with it, taking *nairmāṇikakāya* as the primary vehicle of enlightened activity.[66]

In sum, Ārya Vimuktisena's commentary reads *AA* chapter 8 as a direct mapping of the three Yogācāra *kāyas* onto specific passages of the *Large PP Sūtra* that he clearly identifies for us (passages 8.4 and 8.5 in Conze's numbering system). According to Ārya Vimuktisena, *AA* v. 8.1 links the Yogācāra *svābhāvikakāya* (synonymous with *Prajñāpāramitā dharmakāya*) with the undefiled dharmas listed in *PP* passage 8.5.2. He understands those dharmas to be a phenomenal description of *svābhāvikakāya/dharmakāya*. *AA* vv. 8.2–8.6 then detail the *PP* content at greater length, listing each of the undefiled dharmas. *AA* v. 8.12 links the Yogācāra *sāmbhogikakāya* with a Buddha's marks and signs as listed in *PP* passage 8.5.2. Then *AA* vv. 8.13–8.32 detail the content of that *PP* passage, presenting the marks and signs with some of their causes. *AA* vv. 8.33–8.34a link the Yogācāra *nairmāṇikakāya* with the limitless activities of *PP* passage 8.4 that are described in detail in *PP* passage 8.5. *AA* vv. 8.34b–8.40 then detail the content of *PP* passage 8.5, listing all twenty-seven types of activity described therein.

9.5 Conclusion

Our earlier finding that the *AA*'s eighth chapter is a mapping of Yogācāra concepts onto *PP sūtra* content, and is therefore a three-*kāya* text, was based on many textual-historical considerations. To reach our conclusion, we had to use literary-critical and historical methods to project ourselves back into the period when the *AA* was composed (chapters 7 and 8 of this book). Ārya Vimuktisena lived at a time much closer to when the *AA* was composed. He reached the same conclusions we did. But he probably did so because he was living in a time when both of the textual traditions that structured the *AA*'s eighth chapter were still very much alive. For a scholar such as Ārya Vimuktisena, who was immersed in the Yogācāra and *Prajñāpāramitā* traditions of his time, it likely seemed self-evident that the purpose of *AA* 8 was to draw an explicit correlation between those two traditions, both with respect to their gnoseologies and with respect to their buddhologies.

One key point made by Ārya Vimuktisena is worth remembering as we go forward. Both of the textual traditions from which *AA* 8 was redacted, *Prajñāpāramitā* and Yogācāra, understood a Buddha's defining realization *not* as a differentiated collection of conditioned phenomena produced by the path, but as a nondual cognitive identification with the *unconditioned, undifferentiated* nature of all things, through which the phenomena of the conditioned world are known. This is expressed in the interrelated gnoseologies and buddhologies of both those textual traditions. Through his comments on *AA* 8, Ārya Vimuktisena reiterates this prominent Mahāyāna understanding of the way in which the unconditioned nature of a Buddha's attainment relates to the conditioned worlds of beings whom it guides to liberation.

10
Haribhadra's Analytic-Inferential Perspective on Buddhahood: Buddha Dharmas as Fourth "Body"

10.1
Haribhadra's Eighth-Century Lens on *Abhisamayālaṃkāra* 8

At the conclusion of the last chapter, we noted that Ārya Vimuktisena read *Abhisamayālaṃkāra* chapter 8 steeped in both of the textual traditions from which it was constructed: Yogācāra and *Prajñāpāramitā*. More than two centuries later, Haribhadra, the Madhyamaka scholar who was to become the most influential of all *AA* commentators, saw the *Abhisamayālaṃkāra* through a very different lens.

The quarter of a millennium that separated Haribhadra from Ārya Vimuktisena was a period of tremendous development in Indian Buddhist thought. Two such developments in eighth-century Madhyamaka thought contributed heavily to Haribhadra's perspective on Buddhahood, which, in turn, contributed to controversies over enlightenment from his period to the present day. To understand the implicit reasons for these controversies, the two developments in question need to be specified.

First, India in the eighth century was a period when Madhyamaka writers felt responsible to critique elements of Yogācāra thought viewed as incompatible with Madhyamaka understanding. Sharp Madhyamaka criticism of Yogācāra ontology was prominent in the writings of Bhāvaviveka (ca. 500–570) and Candrakīrti (ca. 600–650), and continued in the writings of influential eighth-century Mādhyamikas, including Śāntideva, Jñānagarbha, Śāntarakṣita, Kamalaśīla, and Haribhadra. The latter three scholars qualified their criticism of Yogācāra by accepting key elements of Yogācāra ontology and praxis as useful intermediary understandings for gradual realization of ultimate truth in the Madhyamaka sense. For this reason, Śāntarakṣita, Kamalaśīla, and Haribhadra were later classified by Tibetan scholars as "Yogācāra-Mādhyamikas"; they were critical of Yogācāra ontology and relativized it, but then reappropriated elements of it into praxis as stepping-stones to the Madhyamaka realization of ultimate truth.[1] These Mādhyamikas appropriated Yogācāra analyses of the conceptual construction of duality, the bodhisattva path with its stages of meditation, fundamental transformation, and Buddhahood as embodied in multiple *kāyas*.[2]

The second development decisive in Haribhadra's intellectual formation was the Buddhist tradition of logic and epistemology that came into greater and greater prominence during the centuries between Ārya Vimuktisena and Haribhadra. Dignāga (ca. 440–520), a Yogācāra scholar following upon Vasubandhu, helped initiate a logical and epistemological school that Dharmakīrti (ca. 650) developed. The methods of this logical tradition heavily influenced Mādhyamikas of the eighth century, through which they treated conventional objects of Buddhist understanding *(saṃvṛti satya)* from the perspective of Dharmakīrtian logical inference.[3]

The tradition of Buddhist logic exerted tremendous influence upon Haribhadra's Madhyamaka scholarship. He was not unique in this. Jñānagarbha, Śāntarakṣita's teacher, and Śāntarakṣita were Mādhyamika exponents of the Buddhist logic tradition.[4] What appears to be new in Haribhadra's writing is his specific application of the logic tradition's principles of inferential understanding to the core realization of Buddhahood itself, as if a Buddha's realization was accessible to such procedures of inference.

Malcolm David Eckel in his excellent book on the eighth-century scholar Jñānagarbha notes the great influence of Dharmakīrti's logical tradition upon Jñānagarbha's Madhyamaka views. Many of Eckel's observations also apply to Haribhadra. Eckel raises an important issue: "What we need is . . . a principle that will make clear how far Jñānagarbha can go in adopting Dharmakīrti's point of view without compromising the integrity of his own Madhyamaka method." Eckel goes on to describe the way in which Jñānagarbha critiques elements of Dharmakīrti's ontology, relativizes them, and thereby reappropriates them for Mādhyamika use.[5] But Eckel does not mention any Buddhist scholars after Jñānagarbha who may have criticized him for "compromising the integrity" of Mādhyamika in his use of Dharmakīrti's logic.

As we shall see below, Haribhadra's application of logical inference not just to phenomena in general, but to the core realization of Buddhahood itself, drew intense criticism from some later Mahāyāna scholars for the very reason Eckel raised, although Haribhadra's critics frame their critical concern more broadly: Has Haribhadra compromised the integrity of Mahāyāna Buddhism as a whole by assuming that human reason per se can comprehend an object that is beyond its capacity to know? In the view of Haribhadra's critics, whose work we will study in chapters 11 and 12, the answer is an emphatic yes. Eckel's question, which he left unanswered with reference to Jñānagarbha, becomes helpful to us toward understanding why Haribhadra's writing on Buddhahood has given rise to such a long controversy, continuing even to the present day.

A few words about Śāntarakṣita, one of Haribhadra's teachers, will help us to further contextualize Haribhadra's work. Śāntarakṣita was instrumental in the transmission of Buddhism to Tibet. He wrote commentaries on Dharmakīrti's logic and epistemology and drew heavily from Yogācāra thought while reinterpreting it to fit a Mādhyamika perspective. As noted above, he established what came to be known in Tibet as a "Yogācāra-Madhyamaka" tradition (in Tibetan doxography, *rnal 'byor spyod pa'i dbu ma*), formalizing a synthesis of Yogācāra and Madhyamaka thought and praxis. He adopted the Yogācāra view of cognitive subject-object duality as a mere conceptual construct.[6] In so doing, however, he accepted the Yogācāra discernment of external objects as cognitive appearances only as a discernment of the phenomenal level of reality, conventional truth *(saṃvṛti satya)*, not as a discernment of the ultimate level of reality *(paramārtha satya)*.

According to Śāntarakṣita, Yogācāra analysis of nonduality cannot actually specify ultimate truth because it does not go far enough. In his view, it still permitted a possible adherence to the substantiality (*svabhāva*, self-existence) of cognition itself, which the Mādhyamika, critiquing all forms of self-existence, denies. But in Śāntarakṣita's system, the Yogācāra theory of nonduality formed a useful *first* step toward the graded realization of ultimate truth *(paramārtha satya)* which was to be understood more precisely in line with Madhyamaka analysis. His explanation of ultimate truth, then, employs a characteristic eighth-century Madhyamaka form of analysis, analytically penetrating the appearance of self-existence *(svabhāva)* in phenomena to arrive at their emptiness: the argument of "neither one nor many."

> In reality the things that we and others talk about are empty, because they are neither one nor many, like a reflection.[7]

Whereas Yogācāras had identified *parinispanna* as ultimate truth (the perfected nature, thusness known in nondual knowledge: *MAV* 3.10–3.11, 3.13 *bhāṣya*), and later Yogācāra scholars such as Sthiramati had affirmed the self-existence of consciousness itself,[8] Śāntarakṣita, as a Mādhyamika, denied the self-existence of all phenomena, including consciousness, including even nondual gnosis itself.[9]

Haribhadra is reported in the Tibetan tradition to have been Śāntarakṣita's disciple.[10] Haribhadra's writings indicate that, to a significant degree, he followed the "Yogācāra-Madhyamaka" principles that Śāntarakṣita had elucidated.[11] He was an accomplished scholar of the logico-epistemological school that had flowered in the centuries prior to him, was thoroughly familiar with Abhidharma, and was a rigorous proponent of Madhyamaka thought.[12] He wrote two key commentaries on the *Abhisamayālaṃkāra* which exerted a profound influence on the history of all further such commentary in India and Tibet. His *Abhisamayālaṃkāra-Āloka* related the *Abhisamayālaṃkāra* to the *Prajñāpāramitā* sūtra in 8,000 verses. This was the first time such a relationship had been established, for, as we noted in chapter 7 above, the *Abhisamayālaṃkāra* was composed based upon the *Prajñāpāramitā* sūtra in 25,000 verses, and was commented on only in relation to that version of the sūtra until Haribhadra. Haribhadra's *Abhisamayālaṃkāra-śāstra-vṛtti* (also known as the *Sphuṭārthā*) served as a summary of his *Āloka*, containing its comments on the *Abhisamayālaṃkāra* without including its extensive quotations from the 8,000-verse *PP* sūtra.

Living a quarter of a millennium after Ārya Vimuktisena, Haribhadra owed much to the intervening developments in Madhyamaka thought sketched above, particularly the Buddhist logical tradition, and his interpretation of *Abhisamayālaṃkāra* chapter 8 reveals those influences. Two principal interrelated concerns appear to order his exegesis of Buddhahood in *AA* 8.

First and foremost, he was concerned to specify the precise way in which the unconditioned nature of a Buddha's attainment could be viewed as consistent with a Buddha's vast activity for beings within the conditioned world. In other words, Haribhadra wanted to logically resolve the ancient Mahāyāna paradox of nonabiding nirvāṇa, the problem of how a Buddha can be personally free from the cognitive conditions that imprison beings in saṃsāra, yet actively participate within *their* cognitively conditioned realms of suffering until all are freed. As discussed earlier, prior Mahāyāna traditions had intentionally left this paradox unresolved, understanding it to point to a Buddha's nonconceptual realization of saṃsāra and nirvāṇa as nondual, a realization inaccessible to the conceptual, dualistic thought of non-Buddhas. Apparently Haribhadra, dissatisfied with this long-held assumption, believed it was time for the procedures of Buddhist logic to be applied to Buddhahood, to show how unconditioned and conditioned aspects of enlightenment could be consistently affirmed, and thereby to demonstrate that the ancient Mahāyāna paradox of Buddhahood had been merely a problem of poor reasoning.[13] The apparent problem of nonabiding nirvāṇa, in Haribhadra's view, was not necessitated by an unbridgeable gap between perspectives of ordinary beings and Buddhas. It was logically resolvable through procedures of Buddhist logic that earlier Mahāyāna traditions had not had available or had not applied.

Secondly, and related to that first concern, Haribhadra apparently thought that the time had finally come to extend the Madhyamaka critique of Yogācāra ontology to the Yogācāra ontology of Buddhahood. By identifying the very essence of Buddhahood as an inseparable unity of gnosis and unconditioned emptiness *(svābhāvikakāya/dharmakāya)*, Yogācāra tradition, in his view, had collapsed conventional truth (conditioned appearances) and ultimate truth (their unconditioned emptiness) into each other, thereby making it impossible to distinguish the conditioned basis in Buddhahood for its participation in the world from its unconditioned, ultimate reality. The Yogācāra *trikāya* doctrine of Buddhahood in particular, Haribhadra apparently believed, had created this very problem, by declaring the first of the three *kāyas (svābhāvikakāya/dharmakāya)* to be an undifferentiated, unconditioned essence of Buddhahood, gnosis-thusness inseparable, and yet that Buddhahood's activity in the conditioned world (through *sāmbhogikakāya* and *nairmāṇikakāya*) is somehow based upon that unconditioned essence.[14] This, in Haribhadra's view, was simply incoherent.

The paradox of nonabiding nirvāṇa, and how it took expression in the three-*kāya* doctrine of classical Yogācāra treatises, was discussed at length in chapters 4 and 5 of this book. In order to further understand the poignancy of Haribhadra's concern as an eighth-century Madhyamaka scholar, we should also note that several important Mādhyamikas during the centuries intervening between those Yogācāra treatises and Haribhadra also adopted and reaffirmed three-*kāya* models consonant with what the Yogācāra had promulgated. We noted in the previous chapter that Ārya Vimuktisena, whom Haribhadra characterized as a Mādhyamika and was later so classified by Tibetans, accepted the three-*kāya* doctrine as normative and interpreted *Abhisamayālaṃkāra* chapter 8 in line with that.[15] The *Tarkajvālā*, ascribed to the great sixth-century Mādhyamika Bhāvaviveka, although critical of Yogācāra ontology in other specifics, continued to promulgate the Yogācāra model of Buddhahood in three *kāyas*.[16] And Candrakīrti, an influential Mādhyamika of the seventh century, also taught a three-*kāya* paradigm of Buddhahood in the "Buddhabhūmi" section of his magnum opus, the *Madhyamakāvatāra*, modeling himself upon expressions of Buddhahood in the *Dasabhūmikasūtra,* which had served as a formative resource for Yogācāra buddhology.[17] Also important to later Indian Buddhism was a short treatise called the *Trikāyastotra* (Praise to the three *kāyas*), which gives the appearance of a Madhyamaka, three-*kāya* text.[18]

Thus, within our extant written record up to the time of Haribhadra, not only did Yogācāra writings repeatedly reaffirm the three-*kāya* doctrine of Buddhahood that inscribed within itself the paradox of nonabiding nirvāṇa, but Mādhyamikas had also adopted and repeatedly reaffirmed such a three-*kāya* paradigm. Precisely how Buddhahood might be understood to participate simultaneously in the ultimate reality that is unconditioned, and in the constructed reality of living beings that is conditioned, remained unspecified and, at least in human terms, was unresolved.

Discomfort with the Yogācāra formulation of Buddhahood, which previous Mādhyamikas had uncritically accepted, may have developed gradually in certain Mādhyamika milieus of the eighth century. Haribhadra's teacher Vairocana (to whom he pays respect in his *Āloka* and *Sphuṭārthā*) may have been part of a movement within the Madhyamaka school to reevaluate the *trikāya* buddhology that Mādhyamikas had inherited from Yogācāra.[19] It appears, then, that Haribhadra's late-eighth-century exegesis of Buddhahood as represented in *Abhisamayālaṃkāra* 8 may represent the first textual expression of a concern among some (not all) Mādhyamikas to correct perceived problems that Yogācāra buddhology had created.

Haribhadra, through his exegesis of Buddhahood in *Abhisamayālaṃkāra* 8, reveals himself to be a Mādhyamika with a mission. He was keen to critique the last bastion of Yogācāra ontology, Buddhahood itself, by applying Buddhist logic toward a Madhyamaka purpose: to distinguish the unconditioned from the conditioned within Buddhahood, the ultimate truth from the conventional truth. In Haribhadra's view, the tradition of Buddhist logic that he had inherited for this task had developed considerably in the centuries since the three-*kāya* model had been formulated. The time was now ripe to demonstrate, through analytic-inferential procedures, that the paradox of nonabiding nirvāṇa had always been only an apparent paradox, and was now resolvable through logic consistent with Madhyamaka philosophy.

Haribhadra's concern, then, was to distinguish and logically separate the poles of Buddhahood that had previously been kept undivided and had thereby contributed to the paradox: unconditioned/conditioned; ultimate truth/conventional truth; nirvāṇa/saṃsāra; eternal/temporal. Yogācāra philosophy, as we earlier noted, extrapolated meditational praxis and gnoseology to Buddhahood as, in its own essence *(svābhāvikakāya)*, a complete deconstruction of subject-object duality, hence, a realization of ultimate truth as the inseparability of universal thusness and nondual awareness (chapter 4, section 6). Based upon its unconditioned, indivisible realization of ultimate truth, so it was declared, Buddhahood manifests as conditioned, conventional appearances to beings: *sāmbhogikakāya*, *nairmāṇikakāya*.

Haribhadra, applying himself as a Madhyamaka logician, reasoned that the paradox of Buddhahood as something simultaneously unconditioned and conditioned would disappear if a Buddha's own realization were analyzed into two distinct, separable aspects: ultimate truth and conventional truth, the emptiness of Buddhahood and the conventional nature of Buddhahood, the unconditioned aspect that transcends the world and the conditioned aspect that participates in the world. The purity of a Buddha's realization, its permanent cessation of all obscuration and defilement, was also to be included within the unconditioned aspect. Haribhadra used *Abhisamayālaṃkāra* chapter 8 as the textual authority to separate and distinguish these two poles of Buddhahood, which, making use of the textual material of that chapter, became *svābhāvikakāya* (emptiness-purity, ultimate truth, unconditioned) and *(jñāna) dharmakāya* (Buddha dharma-gnoses, conventional truth, characterized by Haribhadra as pure forms of conditioned consciousness).

Toward this, Haribhadra interpreted *dharmakāya* of *AA* v. 8.6 as a "body of Buddha dharmas," a collection of gnoses comprising a *conditioned* basis within Buddhahood for its ongoing connection to the world through manifestations of *sāmbhogikakāya* and *nairmāṇikakāya*. And this conditioned aspect of a Buddha's attainment was to be distinguished, now as a fourth *kāya*, from the unconditioned *svābhāvikakāya*, thus providing a discernible conditioned source within a Buddha's own core realization for uninterrupted activity in the conditioned world.

By this mode of exegesis of *AA* 8, Haribhadra radically altered the previous prevailing methods of buddhological inquiry. As we explored in chapters 4 and 5 of this book, Yogācāra tradition understood a Buddha's realization primarily as extrapolated from its yogic praxis and gnoseology. Buddhahood, in its own essential knowledge (as *svābhāvikakāya/dharmakāya*), was said to be knowable *only* through personal realization, because it sees through and utterly deconstructs the epistemological categories of ordinary beings (chapter 5, section 2). The paradox of nonabiding nirvāṇa was thus viewed as the necessary consequence of the enormous epistemological distance between dualistic human knowledge and nondualistic Buddha knowledge. Such a huge epistemological gap, it was believed, made it impossible for human reason alone, basing itself upon ordinary epistemological assumptions, to comprehend Buddhahood (chapter 5, section 3).

Haribhadra, confident in the power of the eighth-century tradition of Buddhist logic *cum* Mādhyamika analysis to solve previously unsolved problems, felt that it was the Yogācāra scheme itself that had engendered the apparent paradox, and that it could be solved by subjecting Buddhahood to the same sort of logical analysis that any other phenomenon ought to be subject to. *Abhisamayālaṃkāra* 8 lists twenty-one types of a Buddha's gnosis, in large part Buddha dharmas drawn from prior Abhidharma tradition as refracted through the *Prajñāpāramitā* sūtras and thence the *AA*. Haribhadra, an authority of Abhidharma and in line with its understanding, interpreted that list of Buddha dharmas to be actual conditioned components of a Buddha's mind, analogous to (although purer than) the mental factors cultivated by bodhisattvas on their path to Buddhahood. Haribhadra's Abhidharmic reading of *AA* 8, then, made the gnoses *(jñāna)* of a Buddha a conditioned, composite phenomenon, analogous enough to the minds of ordinary beings that inferences could be drawn about a Buddha's mind from Abhidharma understanding of the mental factors that ordinary beings cultivate on their path to Buddhahood. Haribhadra's comments reveal an implicit assumption on his part that the mind of a Buddha *can* be comprehended sufficiently by analogy to the human that reason can arrive at a logically coherent and accurate model of it. His four-*kāya* reading of *AA* 8 represents an autonomous use of reason to infer that model. Since, he reasoned, he had arrived at that correct model through a valid inference, that must be the model that the author of the text had intended.

In short, whereas Yogācāra tradition had formulated *svābhāvikakāya/dharmakāya* as an extrapolation of its yogic praxis and nondual gnoseology, Haribhadra's perspective on *AA* 8 was framed by analytic-inferential procedures of eighth-century Madhyamaka logic and Abhidharma.

We noted in chapter 6 above that the *Abhisamayālaṃkāra*'s unique project of mapping Yogācāra categories onto the *Prajñāpāramitāsūtra* created a number of possible ambiguities in its Sanskrit verses. We found that these ambiguities were resolvable, however, by reading the Sanskrit with close attention to the structure of the *Abhisamayālaṃkāra* text as a whole contextualized by historical and literary-critical analysis (chapters 7 and 8 above). But if a scholar's primary concern in his exegesis of the *Abhisamayālaṃkāra* was not philological accuracy, but a new clarification of buddhological theory, the *AA*'s ambiguities serve not as a source of consternation but as a blessing: They permit corrective work to be read into the text. The *AA* provided Haribhadra with an ambiguous enough text in versified Sanskrit to make a new formulation of buddhological theory (a theory of four *kāyas* in nontantric Buddhism), while permitting ascription of his theory to a sacred, authoritative text, thereby avoiding the criticism that he had innovated and departed from tradition. It is in Haribhadra's *Āloka* and *Sphuṭārthā* that we find the first ascription of the *AA*'s authorship to Maitreya, a bodhisattva-Buddha figure of the highest traditional authority.

10.2
Translation of Haribhadra's Commentary on the Four *Kāyas*

Haribhadra's *Sphuṭārthā* on *Abhisamayālaṃkāra* chapter 8 constitutes a complete treatise on the Buddha *kāyas* presented without being structured around quotations from the *Prajñāpāramitāsūtra* (his *Āloka* is structured around quotations from the 8,000-verse *PP* sūtra). As such, the *Sphuṭārthā* presents Haribhadra's exegesis on Buddhahood straightforwardly, without the *Āloka*'s somewhat more awkward structuring. Here translated is Haribhadra's *Sphuṭārthā* on all the verses of *AA* chapter 8 relevant to our understanding of his fundamental four-*kāya* formulation. I have left out his individual explanations of each of the thirty-two marks, eighty signs, and twenty-seven types of activity, which are lengthy and not directly relevant to our discussion. Contained here is an English translation of Haribhadra's presentation of the four *kāyas* in his comments on *Abhisamayālaṃkāra* verses 8.1–8.12, on verse 8.33, his prologue to verses 8.34–40, and his concluding comment.[20]

The translation is first given here in its entirety for ease of reference. Then, in the following sections of this chapter, Haribhadra's remarks on each of his four *kāyas* will be presented passage by passage, with my own comments for clarification.

Essence Body *(Svābhāvikakāya)*

> In the next moment after the completion of the one-moment comprehension, there occurs the realization of [resultant] *dharmakāya*. The [resultant *dharmakāya*] is fourfold, by its division into essence body *(svābhāvikakāya)*, etc.[21] First the essence body *(svābhāvikakāya)* is declared:
>
> "The essence body of the Sage *(svābhāvikakāya)*: Its identity is the primordial nature *(prakṛti)* of the undefiled dharmas which are obtained in utter purity" [*AA* 8.1].
>
> The mindfulnesses and other [Buddha dharmas], consisting of supramundane gnosis, are undefiled. Because of the adventitiousness of [former]

impurities *(malānām āgantukatvena)*, [these dharmas] are obtained in utter purity [from adventitious stain]. And because [they] are by nature universal emptiness *(dharmadhātu)*, they are characterized by freedom from intrinsic existence *(prakṛti vivikti lakṣaṇaṃ)*. Their actual intrinsic nature *(prakṛti)*, their real essence *(svabhāva)*, which is their nonarising nature, is this: the essence body *(svābhāvikakāya)* of the Sage, the Buddha, the Bhagavan. It is obtained by the supramundane path, not created. Thus, with that meaning of being uncreated, it is essence body *(svābhāvikakāya)*, which is obtained through the realization that consciousness and all phenomena are like illusion.[22]

The remaining three *kāyas* (bodies), appearing with respect to true [worldly] convention *(tathyasaṃvṛtyā)*, are ultimately in the nature of reality *(dharmatā)*. Distinguished in accordance with [differing] mentalities, they are established by their being cognitive objects for [three different types of person]: Buddhas, bodhisattvas, and *śrāvaka*s, etc.

To indicate this, tradition *(nyāya)* says: "For the nonseparateness of what is discerned from the discernment is accepted," which means that even though it *[svābhāvikakāya]* is not separate from them [the conventional *kāya*s], it is posited as separate.[23]

Body of Dharmas Consisting of Gnosis *(Jñāna-ātmaka Dharmakāya)*

Having thus explained the first *kāya (svābhāvikakāya)*, the second *[kāya]* is declared, the body of dharmas consisting of gnosis free from discursive conceptualization *(jñāna-ātmaka dharmakāya)*, which is composed of undefiled [Buddha dharmas] such as the mindfulnesses, etc.:

"'The factors which foster enlightenment, the measureless thoughts, the liberations, the nine meditative attainments, the ten meditative totalities, the bases of overpowering divided into eight kinds, the meditative power freeing from passions, the gnosis resulting from resolve, the supernatural knowledges, the analytical knowledges, the four total purities, the ten sovereignties, the ten powers, the four forms of fearlessness, the three ways in which [a Buddha] has nothing to hide, the threefold mindful equanimity, the nature of never forgetting, the complete destruction of [negative] propensities, the great compassion for living beings, the qualities unique to the Sage proclaimed as eighteen, and total omniscience': thus is the body of [Buddha] dharmas *(dharmakāya)* denominated" [*AA* vv. 8.2–8.6].

[These verses set forth:] (1) the factors that foster enlightenment beginning with the mindfulnesses and ending with the eightfold path; (2)

the measureless thoughts: love, etc., that are the four heavenly abodes, as earlier [explained]; (3) the eight liberations: two in which [the yogi], himself possessing form or not possessing form, beholds external forms; one in which [the yogi] manifests with his form the liberation of beauty, and fully obtaining it, abides [in it]; the four [formless] meditative attainments of space, consciousness, nothingness, and neither discrimination nor nondiscrimination; and the [attainment] of the cessation of discrimination and feeling; (4) the nine meditative states: the four concentrations of the form realm, the four formless meditative states, and the attainment of cessation; (5) the ten types of meditative totality: earth, water, fire, air, blue, yellow, red, white, consciousness, and space; (6) the eight kinds of bases of overpowering: four in which a person, [first] with the cognition that he himself has form, [then] with the cognition that he himself has no form, focuses upon external objects, [first] those of small size, [then] those of large size, and overpowering them, knows them; and four in which a person, just with the cognition that he himself has no form, overpowering blue, yellow, red and white, perceives them; (7) the meditative power which suppresses passions by eradicating the continuum of passions and delusions contained in others' mental continua; (8) the knowledge resulting from resolve, utterly free of all signs, all attachment eliminated, which continues for as long as saṃsāra and liberation exist, through its fulfillment of the resolution to remove the doubts [of all beings]; (9) the six supernatural knowledges; (10) the four analytical knowledges that were explained earlier; (11) the four purities: complete purity with respect to one's basis, objects, mind and gnosis; (12) the ten sovereignties: dominion over life, mind, requisites, action, birth, [whatever one is] interested in, [whatever one] has resolved, supernatural power, gnosis, and truth; (13) the ten powers and (14) the four forms of fearlessness explained earlier; (15) the three ways in which [Buddha] has nothing to hide: the Tathāgata, having utterly pure conduct of body, speech, and mind, has no wrong conduct he would think to conceal out of fear that others may discover it; (16) the threefold mindful equanimity: toward those who like listening to his teaching, those who do not like to listen, and [a group of] those [which includes] both, [he is] free of attachment, aversion and both; equanimous only he abides, possessed of mindfulness; (17) the nature of never forgetting, such that he never disregards when it is time to carry out the benefit of others; (18) the complete destruction of all negative propensities by having destroyed the seeds, the predispositions, of the affective and cognitive obstructions *(kleśa-jñeya-āvaraṇa);* (19) the great compassion for living beings that is the resolute intention to help all beings; (20) the eighteen qualities unique to a Buddha; (21) total omniscience *(sarvākāra-jñatā).*

Included in the word "and" [in the expression "and total omniscience" of *AA* v. 8.6] is the knowledge of the path *(mārga-jñatā)* and so forth, which were explained earlier.

According to some, the body of dharmas [*dharmakāya* of v. 8.6] is explained to consist of all those [undefiled] dharmas, the factors fostering enlightenment, etc., the gnoses free from discursive conceptualization which are the transformed [result] of fundamental transformation *(āśraya-parāvṛtti)*.[24]

But, others explain as follows:

AA v. 8.1: "The essence body *(svābhāvikakāya)* of the Sage: Its identity is the primordial nature *(prakṛti)* of the undefiled dharmas that are obtained in utter purity," literally means that, having accepted the supramundane undefiled dharmas [of the Buddha], the essence body's identity is their actual intrinsic nature *(prakṛti):* nonarisingness *(anutpādatā)*. And that [essence body] is also *dharmatākāya* (body of reality), which is indicated by [the concluding word of v. 8.6]: *dharmakāya*, through the elision of the particle that indicates abstract nouns *(-tā)*.

Then they [raise this hypothetical] question: "What are the undefiled [Buddha] dharmas, the intrinsic nature of which is the *dharma[tā]kāya*'s identity?" And they understand *[AA]* verses [8.2–8.6] [as the answer to that]: "The factors that foster enlightenment. . . . " etc.

Others [reply that] [Buddha's] nondual primary consciousnesses and mental factors *(citta-caittā)*, which are the transformed [result] of fundamental transformation *(āśrayaparāvṛtti)*, are what carry out [his] effective actions *(artha-kriyā)* of teaching the dharma, etc. by generating appearances that have specific purposes in conformance to the conventional [perspectives] of yogi [trainees]. How, according to those [whose assertion is immediately above], are those [primary consciousnesses and mental factors] which must surely be accepted, included [within the *kāyas*]?[25]

Some, [criticizing] the four-*kāya* explanation, cite [*AA* v. 1.17, the table of contents for *AA* chapter 8]: "*svābhāvika*, *sasāmbhoga*, and *nairmāṇika* as well, / *dharmakāya*, with activity, is proclaimed as fourfold."

In [this] verse, [they claim,] since the word *dharmakāya* does not follow immediately after the word *svābhāvika* there are only three *kāyas*.[26]

But others [reply] that, on the strength of the intention just demonstrated, for felicity in the construction of the verse, and for the sake of associating activity with the gnosis alone, it was stated thusly. Therefore [the *AA*] is consistent with all the statements in other quarters *(pradeś-āntara)*[27] that the *kāyas* are fourfold.[28]

That being so, in order to show the superiority of a Buddha's meditative power freeing from passions *(araṇā-samādhi)* over that of the disciples *(śrāvaka*s), etc., the following verse [*AA* v. 8.7] is said:

"A disciple's meditative power freeing from passions is the avoidance of men's passions [arising] from seeing [that disciple]. The Victor's [Buddha's] meditative power freeing from passions is for cutting off the stream of their passions in towns, etc."

Having thought, "May there be no arising of passions in anyone because of seeing me," the arising of passions in people is avoided. [This is] the meditative power of the disciples *(śrāvaka*s), etc. that frees from passions. But the Tathāgata's meditative power freeing from passions eradicates the continua of passions of all beings in [entire] towns, etc.

In order to explain the superiority of a Buddha's gnosis [resulting from] resolve *(praṇidhijñāna)* over that of the disciples, etc., the following verse [*AA* v. 8.8] is said:

"It is accepted that the Buddha gnosis [resulting from] resolve is automatic, unattached, unobstructed, forever operative, and answers all questions."

Through its freedom from signs *(nimitta)*, it operates of its own accord. Because it does not adhere to things, it is free from attachment to forms, etc. Because it has abandoned the affective and cognitive obstructions *(kleśajñeyāvaraṇa)* together with their propensities, it is unobstructed with reference to all objects of knowledge. Because it remains for as long as cyclic existence lasts *(saṃsāra)*, it is forever operative. Because it has obtained the analytical knowledges, it provides the answers for questions. Such is accepted for the Tathāgata's gnosis [resulting from] resolve. Since that of the disciples, etc. is just the reverse, it is not like [a Buddha's].[29]

If [a Buddha] always abides as *dharmakāya* with a nature of great compassion, why isn't the welfare [of beings] always being accomplished? In order to respond to this, the following verse [*AA* v. 8.9] is said:

"When the cause has reached fruition, whenever and for whomever there is benefit to be accomplished, then and there he appears."

With Buddha, etc. as a basis,[30] through meeting one's spiritual guide, etc., the cause, i.e., the seed, the root of virtue planted in the past, reaches maturity. Then, any time the teaching of dharma, etc., would have long-term benefit for any such being, in order to benefit that being, the Bhagavan, through the fulfillment of his previous resolutions, accomplishes beneficial activity through a manifestation appropriate for that [very being at that very time]. So, even though he abides always nearby in the manner of a wish-fulfilling gem, [if] due to one's own karmic faults, the causes [for his manifestation to oneself] are incomplete, then [Buddha], who bestows their result, does not manifest. That is the purport [of the verse].

How is that so? An example is given by the following verse [*AA* v. 8.10]:

"But even when the god of rain pours down rain, an infertile seed does not sprout. So even when Buddhas arise, one who is unfit does not obtain the blessing."

Even when the king of gods is showering down rain, a seed such as a sesame that, being rotten, is infertile, does not sprout forth. Likewise, even when Buddhas arise who are expert at fulfilling all wishes, one without [karmic] fortune does not obtain the blessing, i.e., the hearing of the holy dharma, etc.

How can the *dharmakāya* consisting of gnosis *(jñānātmaka dharmakāya)* be called "pervasive" *(vyāpī)* and "permanent" *(nitya)* when it exists within the mental continuum of each yogi [Buddha] individually, and is produced *(utpadyamānaḥ)* moment by moment? [An answer is provided] by the following verse [*AA* v. 8.11]:

"Because of such extensiveness of activity, Buddha is declared to be pervasive. And because of his inexhaustibility *(akṣayatvāt)*, he is called permanent."

In the manner just indicated [in *AA* verses 8.8–8.10 above], Buddha is called "pervasive" *(vyāpī)* because of the extensiveness of the activity that he carries out through his universal manifestations, and he is called "permanent" *(nitya)* because the Bhagavan has no diminution, his continuity remaining for as long as cyclic existence lasts.[31]

Body of Communal Enjoyment *(Sāmbhogikakāya)*

Having thus presented the second *kāya (jñānātmaka dharmakāya)*, the third [*kāya*] is taught, the body of communal enjoyment *(sāmbhogikakāya)*, which blazes with the marks and signs, and which is by nature a body of form:

"This form of the Sage with thirty-two marks and eighty signs is to be understood as his embodiment in communal enjoyment *(sāmbhogikakāya)*, from its enjoyment of the great vehicle *(mahāyāna)*" [*AA* v. 8.12].

Because it partakes in the pleasure and happiness of sharing the enjoyment of the impeccable Mahāyāna dharma in company with the great bodhisattvas who have entered into the ten stages *(bhūmis)*, it is the communal enjoyment body *(sāmbhogikakāya)* of the Buddha, the Bhagavan, whose nature is the thirty-two marks and eighty signs.[32]

Body of Manifestation(s) *(Nairmāṇikakāya)*

Having thus presented the third *kāya [sāmbhogikakāya]*, the fourth *(kāya)* is taught, the body of manifestation(s) *(nairmāṇikakāya)*, which [appears] in common to all ordinary beings:

"The embodiment of the Sage in his manifestation(s) *(nairmāṇikakāya)* is that through which he impartially carries out diverse benefits for the world. It is uninterrupted for as long as the existence [of the world]" [*AA* v. 8.33].

That which, through forms such as Śākyamuni's, carries out the desired benefit of beings in all realms of the universe equally for as long as cyclic existence *(saṃsāra)* lasts, is the manifestation body of the Buddha, the Bhagavan. It is uninterrupted because of its continuousness.[33]

All Activities Ascribed to the Body of Dharmas Consisting of Gnosis

Thus have the three [conventional] *kāya*s been presented, which are produced from the force of meditational practice, whose [ultimate] nature is the essence body *(svābhāvikakāya)*, and which, by being [different] cognitive objects for Buddhas, [bodhisattvas, *śrāvaka*s], etc., are designated in dependence on [Buddha's] gnosis *(jñānam)*, etc. Conventionally the gnosis alone carries out the activities through its generation of manifestations as *sāmbhogikakāya*, etc. Thus, the activities for trainees through [those] manifestations, which occur based upon the power of that [gnosis], belong to the *dharmakāya* [consisting of gnosis]. With this sense, it is said [*AA* vv. 8.34–8.40]:

"Likewise, it is agreed, its activity *(karma)* is uninterrupted for as long as cyclic existence lasts: the activity that pacifies the states of rebirth, that establishes [beings] in the fourfold means of collecting [disciples], that establishes *(niveśanaṃ)* them in the comprehension of affliction and purification, in the proper nature of the welfare of beings, and in the six perfections, that establishes them in the Buddha path, in emptiness with respect to the primordial nature, in nonduality, in conventional symbolization *(saṃkete)*, in nonperception, and in the maturing of embodied beings, that establishes them in the bodhisattva path, in preventing adherence [to things], in the attainment of enlightenment *(bodhi)*, in the purity of a Buddha's realm, in definite destiny, that establishes them in the welfare of limitless beings, in the excellence of attending upon and devoting oneself to the Buddhas, in the limbs of enlightenment, in the nonwastefulness of deeds *(karma)*, and in the vision of the truths, that

> establishes them in the elimination of false views, in the method of [ascertaining] the baselessness of those [views], in purification and its accompanying accumulation, in the knowledge of nondistinction between conditioned and unconditioned, and that establishes them [finally] in nirvāṇa. This is regarded as the twenty-seven-fold activity of the *dharmakāya*."[34]

Haribhadra concludes the section:

> Thus, it is agreed, like the *dharmakāya*, its twenty-seven-fold activity [operates] for as long as cyclic existence lasts.[35]

10.3 Haribhadra's Reinterpretation of Essence Body *(Svābhāvikakāya)*

In this and the following sections of this chapter, I comment upon portions of Haribhadra's *Sphuṭārthā* that are crucial in understanding the underlying purposes of his interpretation. This section focuses upon Haribhadra's remarks on *svābhāvikakāya;* the following sections focus on his *dharmakāya* consisting of gnosis, his attempt to refute the previous three-*kāya* interpretation of *AA* 8, and the way he reads four *kāya*s into the remainder of *AA* 8, respectively.

Essence Body *(Svābhāvikakāya)*

> In the next moment after the completion of the one-moment comprehension, there occurs the realization of [resultant] *dharmakāya*. The [resultant *dharmakāya*] is fourfold, by its division into essence body *(svābhāvikakāya)*, etc. First the essence body *(svābhāvikakāya)* is declared:
>
> "The essence body of the Sage *(svābhāvikakāya):* Its identity is the primordial nature *(prakṛti)* of the undefiled dharmas that are obtained in utter purity" [*AA* 8.1]
>
> The mindfulnesses and other [Buddha dharmas], consisting of supramundane gnosis, are undefiled. Because of the adventitiousness of [former] impurities *(malānām āgantukatvena)*, [these dharmas] are obtained in utter purity [from adventitious stain]. And because [they] are by nature universal emptiness *(dharmadhātu)*, they are characterized by freedom from intrinsic existence *(prakṛti vivikti lakṣaṇaṃ)*. Their actual intrinsic nature *(prakṛti)*, their real essence *(svabhāva)*, which is their nonarising nature, is this: the essence body *(svābhāvikakāya)* of the Sage, the Buddha, the Bhagavan. It is obtained by the supramundane path, not created. Thus,

> with that meaning of being uncreated, it is essence body *(svābhāvikakāya)*, which is obtained through the realization that consciousness and all phenomena are like illusion.[36]

In this passage, Haribhadra identifies the essence body, *svābhāvikakāya*, as the "nonarising nature" of the undefiled dharmas that are "obtained in utter purity." This formulation may appear peculiar at first, but it has special significance. First, Haribhadra carefully avoids identifying *svābhāvikakāya* with the Buddha's gnosis per se. Rather he explicitly identifies it with the "nonarising," *dharmadhātu* nature of the gnoses, i.e., their ultimate, unconditioned nature, their emptiness of intrinsic existence *(prakṛti)*. It is only their emptiness itself, he says, that is correctly understood as their actual nature or essence *(prakṛti, svabhāva)*. Thus, Haribhadra's primary formulation of a Buddha's essence body, *svābhāvikakāya*, identifies it as the emptiness of the Buddha's mind. The undefiled dharmas being Buddha's mental qualities or gnoses, *svābhāvikakāya* is precisely the emptiness of those dharmas.

At the same time, however, Haribhadra also emphasizes the purity of the Buddha's mind. The undefiled dharmas are said to be utterly pure in two senses. The first sense refers to their purity from "adventitious" stain. This means that all affective and cognitive obstructions that polluted the mind prior to enlightenment have been entirely removed by completion of the Mahāyāna path. Those obstructive impurities were adventitious to the mind because they were removable from it. Their removal, then, constitutes a change in an accidental feature of the mind, not a change in its very essence.

The second sense of "purity" refers to what Haribhadra identifies as the very essence of the mind. That is the mind's primordial freedom from intrinsic existence *(prakṛti vivikti lakṣaṇaṃ)* because of its being, in essence, *dharmadhātu* (emptiness). In other words, Haribhadra identifies the very essence of the mind with its emptiness (its freedom from self-existence) as one with the *dharmadhātu* (the "realm of dharma" that is universal emptiness). The expression *vivikta* in Sanskrit connotes "separation from," "freedom from," "isolation from," and as a secondary connotation, it also refers to purity (purity being a freedom from pollution or stain).[37] By using the expression *prakṛti vivikti lakṣaṇaṃ*, Haribhadra identifies the mind's primordial emptiness as a kind of innate purity (since it is primordially free from, "purified of," self-existence). In fact, it is quite possible to translate his expression *prakṛti vivikti lakṣaṇaṃ* in two equally valid ways: "the character of freedom from intrinsic existence" (as in the translation above) or "the character of primordial purity." Haribhadra has identified emptiness itself, in its Madhyamaka understanding, as the innate purity of the mind, the mind being empty by nature of self-existence both prior to and after attaining enlightenment.

In sum, Haribhadra identifies *svābhāvikakāya* as two types of purity: first and most fundamental is the innate purity that is the emptiness of the Buddha's mind.

Associated with that is the adventitious purity that is its cessation of every type of mental obstruction. In section 1 of this chapter, I presented some reasons for Haribhadra's desire to identify *svābhāvikakāya* primarily as the Buddha's emptiness. This followed from Madhyamaka analysis, which seeks the apparent self-existent essence of any phenomenon, and, analytically deconstructing it, finds only its emptiness of such self-existence *(svabhāva-śūnyatā)*. That very procedure, directed toward Buddhahood, finds only its emptiness. Hence, emptiness itself constitutes the only "essence" *(svabhāva)* of a Buddha that is actually found upon analysis. So it is emptiness, says Haribhadra, that constitutes a Buddha's defining essence, and is therefore properly his "essence body" *(svābhāvikakāya)*.

But why, then, does Haribhadra also specifically distinguish the adventitious purity of the Buddha's mind as another distinct aspect of *svābhāvikakāya?* One reason probably concerns the etymology of the term *svābhāvikakāya* that Ārya Vimuktisena had presented in his commentary centuries earlier. Ārya Vimuktisena had said that the *svābhāvikkāya* was designated "essence" precisely because it was something that was not made or created. An essence in everyday life is understood as a property of something that is intrinsic to it. Similarly, wrote Ārya Vimuktisena, *svābhāvikakāya* is obtained by the supramundane path, but not created out of it.[38] His comment is abstruse, but, as we have seen, the notion of *svābhāvikakāya* as uncreated was an old one in Yogācāra buddhology, deriving from the identification of *svābhāvikakāya* as purified, uncreated thusness *(tathatāviśuddhi)*, and in some texts, also as an intrinsic purity of mind that is uncovered by the path, not made by it *(citta-prakṛti-viśuddhi*, see chapter 5, section 3 above). But in Ārya Vimuktisena's buddhology, as in Yogācāra tradition, the *svābhāvikakāya*'s uncreatedness did not preclude its being identified also with a Buddha's gnosis, for a Buddha's gnosis was understood to be undivided from the uncreated thusness it knows nondually.

As delineated in section 1 above, Haribhadra made a new interpretation of *AA* 8 designed to more clearly distinguish the ultimate or unconditioned aspect of Buddhahood from its conventional or conditioned aspect, thereby attempting to resolve the apparent paradox of nonabiding nirvāṇa by separating its dichotomous poles. For that purpose, he wanted to identify *svābhāvikakāya* with the unconditioned emptiness of the Buddha's gnosis, thereby distinguishing it from the second *kāya* he would posit, a *dharmakāya* consisting of conditioned gnosis *(jñānātmaka dharmakāya)* that would serve as Buddhahood's connection to the conditioned world.

But Haribhadra also had to account for the traditional etymology of the term *svābhāvikakāya,* which had appeared in Ārya Vimuktisena's comments: a Buddha's essence body was referred to as "essence" *(svābhāvika)* precisely because it was "obtained, but not created" (obtained by the path, not constructed out of it). But if *svābhāvikakāya*, as Haribhadra wanted to characterize it, was just the emptiness of a Buddha's mind, it would never need to be newly "obtained." For everyone's mind, including a Buddha's, has always been empty of self-existence by nature. For *svābhāvikakāya* to be something that is newly obtained at Buddhahood, it must be something more than just emptiness per se ("innate purity"); it must include something else that is a new acquisition. A Buddha's cessation of mental obstructions and impurities is newly acquired upon completion of the bodhisattva path. This is what Haribhadra distinguishes above as a Buddha's "adventitious" purity. And this "adventitious purity," a Buddha's cessation of mental obstructions, although it is newly obtained at Buddhahood, is also never "created" out of causes. It is a permanent destruction of defilement rather than a conditioned construction. Thus, in Haribhadra's understanding, a Buddha's newly obtained, permanent freedom from adventitious defilement had to be specified as part of the defining nature of *svābhāvikakāya* in order for his new definition of the term to continue to conform to the traditional etymology: "[newly] obtained, not created."

Two "purities," then, comprised *svābhāvikakāya* for Haribhadra: the innate purity, a Buddha's emptiness, which is the only "essence" of Buddhahood *(svabhāva)* to be found upon Madhyamaka analysis, and adventitious purity, a Buddha's cessation of mental obstructions, which justified the traditional etymology of *svābhāvikakāya* (essence body) as something obtained but not created. Both of these types of "purity" were understood as permanent, unconditioned aspects of Buddhahood that would correspond to many other traditional accounts of *svābhāvikakāya/dharmakāya/tathāgatakāya* as unconditioned and permanent by nature.[39]

Thus, Haribhadra's comments on *svābhāvikakāya*, reveal a fundamental concern: a concern to wrest the concept of *svābhāvikakāya* from the Yogācāras, to radically redefine it in Madhyamaka terms, but to do so without doing violence to long-accepted, now normative descriptions of it as something both newly obtained and, in some sense, not new at all.

As noted in chapter 5, section 3, above, classical Yogācāra texts characterized *svābhāvikakāya* variously as the continuation of something that has never changed, and, at the same time, as the obtainment of something new. Several Yogācāra texts formulative of *trikāya* doctrine explained that universal thusness, the dharma realm *(dharmadhātu)* that has always been the nature of all phenomena, never changes; it is discovered through the path, not created by it. A number of texts also specify that an intrinsic quality of pure luminosity *(citta-prakṛti-prabhāsvara)* has always been the essence of every being's mind, and as such, also never changes. In each of these Yogācāra formulations, an unchanging continuity of something is posited (thusness or innate purity of mind) that, at enlightenment, is *svābhāvikakāya*. But upon attaining full enlightenment, universal thusness (which has never changed) is now known nondually, completely free from obstruction. Or, alternatively, the innate purity of mind (which has never changed) is now fully uncovered to shine forth.[40]

Thus, *svābhāvikakāya* represents an unchanging continuation, but it equally represents a new attainment: the removal of all that had hidden thusness or all that had covered innate purity of mind. It is this removal of accidental obstructions from the essential purity of the mind that was understood to comprise the new attainment of *svābhāvikakāya* in Yogācāra texts.

As discussed in chapters 4 and 5 above, Yogācāra formulations of *svābhāvikakāya/dharmakāya* from the fourth to fifth centuries characterized it as a Buddha's nondual and indivisible awareness of universal thusness. Since Yogācāras understood the "subject" and "object" of cognition to be just the constructions of conceptual imagination *(parikalpita)*, projections of ignorance, it was precisely the subject-object duality that had to be utterly deconstructed at Buddhahood. Hence, Yogācāra texts that formulated *svābhāvikakāya* described it through terms pointing to an indivisibility of the knower and the known: *tathatāviśuddhi* (thusness purified for awareness) *nirvikalpa-jñāna* (awareness free from conceptions that obstruct thusness), etc. (see chapter 4 section 6, above).

Haribhadra, seeing the Yogācāra *svābhāvikakāya* refracted through the plausibly ambiguous text of *Abhisamayālaṃkāra* 8, and viewing it through the lens of his late-eighth-century Madhyamaka perspective, wanted to reject what he saw as an implicit absolutism in the Yogācāra formulation. The Yogācāras, in his view, by identifying the very essence of Buddhahood as an indivisible unity of gnosis and unconditioned emptiness *(svābhāvikakāya/dharmakāya)*, had collapsed conventional truth (conditioned appearances) and ultimate truth (their unconditioned emptiness) into each other, thereby making it impossible to distinguish the conditioned basis in Buddhahood for its participation in the world from its unconditioned, ultimate reality. As a Mādhyamika, Haribhadra wanted instead to assert that the only essence of Buddhahood findable on ultimate analysis was its emptiness, and that only this was therefore properly *svābhāvikakāya* (essence body). But at the same time, he had to maintain the long-accepted understanding of *svābhāvikakāya* as something that was both the continuation of an unchanged intrinsic purity prior to Buddhahood and the new obtainment of a newfound purity at Buddhahood.

Thus, in his comments above, Haribhadra reinterprets *svābhāvikakāya* as just an unconditioned "purity" of two types: an "intrinsic purity" (which is a Buddha's own emptiness) and an "adventitious purity" (which is a Buddha's newly obtained freedom from obstructions). In this way, Haribhadra reaffirms the traditional understanding of *svābhāvikakāya*, while simultaneously redefining it in explicitly Mādhyamika terms. Rejecting Yogācāra formulations of *svābhāvikakāya* as nondual gnosis-emptiness, Haribhadra separates out the gnosis (for his second *kāya*, a body of dharmas consisting of conditioned gnosis), and reinterprets *svābhāvikakāya* primarily as the emptiness of Buddhahood, which is all that a Mādhyamika finds upon ultimate analysis to be the "essence" of any thing, including Buddhahood.[41]

Haribhadra's statement that the *svābhāvikakāya* is obtained through "the realization that consciousness and all phenomena are like illusions" *(mayopamavijñānasarvadharmapratipatti)* may also constitute a subtle Madhyamaka criticism of those late Yogācāra philosophers who had asserted consciousness itself to be a self-existent independent.[42]

Haribhadra then continues his remarks on *svābhāvikakāya*, discussing its logical relation to the other *kāya*s, which for Haribhadra are the body of dharmas consisting of conditioned gnoses *(jñānātmaka dharmakāya)*, the body of communal enjoyment *(sāmbhogikakāya)*, and the body of manifestations *(nairmāṇikakāya)*:

> The remaining three bodies *(kāyas)*, appearing with respect to true [worldly] convention *(tathyasaṃvṛtyā)*, are ultimately in the nature of reality *(dharmatā)*. Distinguished in accordance with [differing] mentalities, they are established by their being cognitive objects for [three different types of person]: Buddhas, bodhisattvas, and *śrāvaka*s, etc.
>
> To indicate this, tradition *(nyāya)* says: "For the nonseparateness of what is discerned from the discernment is accepted," which means that even though it *[svābhāvikakāya]* is not separate from them [the conventional *kāya*s], it is posited as separate.[43]

This is Haribhadra's opening salvo in his attempt to solve the paradox of nonabiding nirvāṇa through logic. Reaffirming his view that *svābhāvikakāya* is to be understood primarily as the (unconditioned) emptiness of Buddhahood, he takes his logical analysis one crucial step further: he logically distinguishes from *svābhāvikakāya* a separate conditioned aspect of a Buddha's own realization (a *dharmakāya* consisting of gnoses) that he takes as the basis for a Buddha's conditioned appearances to beings as *sāmbhogikakāya* and *nairmāṇikakāya* .

In Haribhadra's comments below on *AA* vv. 8.2–8.6, he distinguishes the undefiled dharmas (a Buddha's set of gnoses) as a second *kāya*, which he calls "*dharmakāya* consisting of gnosis" *(jñānātmaka dharmakāya)*. That is a new interpretation. But then in line with previous *AA* commentators, he interprets *AA* vv. 8.12 and 8.33 to be teaching *sāmbhogikakāya* and *nairmāṇikakāya,* respectively. Thus, in his exegesis of *AA* 8, he posits a total of four *kāya*s. Of these four *kāya*s, he says, three *(dharmakāya* consisting of gnosis, *sāmbhogikakāya*, and *nairmāṇikakāya)* are conventionally established just by their phenomenal appearance to three different types of person. Buddhas conventionally perceive their own gnoses as the set of undefiled dharmas (the *dharmakāya* consisting of gnoses). *Ārya* bodhisattvas, not yet having experienced the gnosis of Buddhahood directly, are karmically pure enough to perceive the *sāmbhogikakāya* form of Buddhas in pure realms. *Śrāvaka*s—i.e., arhats and others spiritually less developed than *ārya* bodhisattvas—perceive, at best, *nairmāṇikakāya* manifestations of Buddhahood.

Haribhadra refers to these three *kāya*s as appearances with respect to "true [worldly] convention" *(tathya-saṃvṛti)*. "True worldly convention" is a technical expression employed by Haribhadra's eighth-century Madhyamaka predecessors Śāntarakṣita and Jñānagarbha. Śāntarakṣita defines the term as follows:

> One should understand that [true] convention is in essence (1) that which is agreeable and tacitly accepted only as long as it is not investigated critically; (2) that which is characterized by arising and decay; and (3) whatever has causal efficiency.[44]

By referring to the three latter *kāya*s as *tathya-saṃvṛti* (true convention), then, Haribhadra explicitly distinguishes those three as a set from *svābhāvikakāya*, ascribing a conditioned, causal nature to them that contrasts with the *svābhāvikakāya*'s unconditioned nature. To a knowledgeable reader of his time, Haribhadra's description of his second *kāya* in particular (*dharmakāya* of gnosis) as "true worldly convention" distinguishes a conditioned aspect of a Buddha's very own realization from the unconditioned aspect, separating out the gnosis half of the Yogācāras' nondual *svābhāvikakāya*, thereby newly providing a distinct, conditioned basis within the very core of a Buddha's attainment for its connection to the conditioned world.

Previously we noted how classical Yogācāra formulations of multiple-*kāya* theory distinguished three *kāya*s from each other epistemologically with respect to how and for whom each appeared. In those formulations, *svābhāvikakāya* was the very essence of a Buddha's own realization, directly known only to Buddhas. *Sāmbhogikakāya* and *nairmāṇikakāya* appear to *ārya* bodhisattvas and to other, less spiritually developed beings, respectively (chapter 5, section 2, above). Haribhadra reaffirms the epistemological criterion for distinguishing multiple *kāya*s, but he does so in such a way as to make *kāya* theory now conform specifically to Mādhyamika dialectic.

What distinguishes Haribhadra's formulation from the Yogācāra is that he separates out the Buddha's gnosis to place it explicitly on the phenomenal, conventional level. This would have been inconceivable for prior formulators of three-*kāya* theory. For, in line with Yogācāra meditational praxis and gnoseology, it is precisely the apparent duality between cognitive object and subject that must utterly collapse at Buddhahood, making its awareness and its "object" ultimate reality (thusness, emptiness) inseparable. For Haribhadra, on the other hand, this old understanding collapses the Madhyamaka distinction between conventional and ultimate truth, collapsing whatever conditioned aspect of a Buddha's attainment there may be into the unconditioned, which thereby makes it impossible to understand how a Buddha's attainment could be related to our conditioned world. This, in Haribhadra's view, is what created the paradox of nonabiding nirvāṇa.

Thus, Haribhadra seeks to avoid the Yogācāra tendency to conceptually collapse a Buddha's gnosis into the thusness it knows as an undivided ultimate reality *(paramārtha satya)*. For Mādhyamikas, ultimate truth is only what is found upon ultimate analysis, as set forth in the treatises of Nāgārjuna and later Mādhyamikas such as Śāntarakṣita. But upon ultimate analysis of any thing, including a Buddha's gnosis, only emptiness is found. For Haribhadra, then, *just* the emptiness of

Buddhahood is its analytically findable "essence" *(svabhāva)*, which alone is to be understood as *svābhāvikakāya* (essence body), *not* the gnosis. The gnosis, if distinguished as phenomenal, conditioned, conventional truth, then provides a clear basis within a Buddha's own attainment for his active connection to the conditioned world. This is the source of Haribhadra's concern to interpret *AA* 8 so as to distinguish in a new, clearer way a fourth Buddha *kāya:* the body of conditioned dharmas consisting of gnosis *(jñānātmaka dharmakāya)*.

In support of his analysis above, Haribhadra quotes a half-verse from prior tradition: "For the nonseparateness of what is discerned from the discernment is accepted" [viviktāvyatirekitvaṃ vivekasya yato matam]. This half-verse appears in a quotation given by the scholar Triratnadāsa (ca. fifth to sixth centuries C.E.) in his commentary on Dignāga's *Prajñāpāramitā-piṇḍārtha*.[45] Triratnadāsa does not identify the original source from which he quoted. But the fuller quotation he gives (in which the half-verse quoted by Haribhadra is imbedded) and his own remarks indicate that the quote comes from a Yogācāra text that establishes the nonseparateness of thusness *(tathatā)* from the perfection of wisdom *(prajñāpāramitā)* that nondually knows it.

Prior to the half-verse quotation in question, Triratnadāsa says: "As it is declared, the perfection of wisdom *(prajñāpāramitā)* is not other than thusness *(tathatā)*, it is not at all separate from it. Rather it is like the lamp and its light." He then gives the quotation in which is embedded the half-verse that Haribhadra quotes above: "Emptiness is not at all separate from the knowledge [of it]. *For the nonseparateness of what is discerned from the discernment [of it] is accepted.* If this were not the case, it would imply that consciousness was not empty of duality. And this would constitute the opposite of nonduality, which would imply there is a dual self. That being the case, it is taught that the nature of thusness is precisely the Bhagavan. For both the knower and the known are supported in consciousness itself" (emphasis added).[46]

If Haribhadra drew his quote from Triratnadāsa, his quotation of the half-verse represents an explicitly Mādhyamika reinterpretation of that Yogācāra expression. In the Yogācāra formula, nonseparateness is asserted with reference to an epistemological subject and object. In Haribhadra's interpretation, however, nonseparateness is now asserted with reference to conventional phenomena and their own ultimate nature which is emptiness. Instead of focusing on the nonduality of gnosis as subject *(grāhya)* and thusness as object *(grāhaka)* as in Yogācāra, Haribhadra identifies a nonseparateness between a Buddha's gnosis (as a conventional phenomenon) and its own ultimate nature, emptiness. In other words, Haribhadra substitutes a Madhyamaka formulation of *dharmī* (conventional substratum) and *dharmatā* (emptiness, the ultimate nature of the substratum) for the Yogācāra structure of *grāhya* (cognitive object) and *grāhaka* (cognitive subject). For Yogācāras, *svābhāvikakāya* is the nondual realization in which gnosis and thusness as subject and object are inseparable. Haribhadra reinterprets *svābhāvikakāya* as the emptiness *(dharmatā) of* gnosis (rather than as a nonduality of gnosis and emptiness). Therefore, when Haribhadra quotes the half-verse that says that the discerned and the discernment are not separate, he means that the emptiness of a Buddha's gnosis (which Buddha discerns), and the gnosis itself (the discernment), are not separate things. The emptiness of the gnosis is a quality of the gnosis itself, not something apart from it. But, implies Haribhadra, the emptiness of the gnosis (and of the form *kāya*s designated to it), which is *svābhāvikakāya*, is appropriately posited as separate for thought (in order to distinguish, for example, conditioned and unconditioned aspects of Buddhahood).[47]

This completes Haribhadra's Mādhyamika reinterpretation of *svābhāvikakāya*, the first of the four *kāya*s he discerned in *Abhisamayālaṃkāra* chapter 8.

10.4 Haribhadra's Body of Conditioned Dharmas Consisting of Gnosis *(Jñānātmaka Dharmakāya)*

Haribhadra continues his commentary by quoting *AA* vv. 8.2–8.6, which, he says, delineate a second *kāya*, which he designates "the body of dharmas consisting of gnosis" *(jñānātmaka dharmakāya):*

Body of Dharmas Consisting of Gnosis *(Jñāna-Ātmaka Dharmakāya)*

> Having thus explained the first *kāya (svābhāvikakāya)*, the second *[kāya]* is declared, the body of dharmas consisting of gnosis free from discursive conceptualization *(jñāna-ātmaka dharmakāya)*, which is composed of undefiled [Buddha dharmas] such as the mindfulnesses, etc.:
>
> "'The factors which foster enlightenment, the measureless thoughts, the liberations, the nine meditative attainments, the ten meditative totalities, the bases of overpowering divided into eight kinds, the meditative power freeing from passions, the gnosis resulting from resolve, the supernatural knowledges, the analytical knowledges, the four total purities, the ten sovereignties, the ten powers, the four forms of fearlessness, the three ways in which [a Buddha] has nothing to hide, the threefold mindful equanimity, the nature of never forgetting, the complete destruction of [negative] propensities, the great compassion for living beings, the qualities unique to the Sage proclaimed as eighteen, and total omniscience': thus is the body of [Buddha] dharmas (*dharmakāya)* denominated" [*AA* vv. 8.2–8.6]
>
> [These verses set forth:] (1) the factors that foster enlightenment beginning with the mindfulnesses and ending with the eightfold path; (2) the measureless thoughts: love, etc., which are the four heavenly abodes,

as earlier [explained]; (3) the eight liberations: two in which [the yogi], himself possessing form or not possessing form, beholds external forms; one in which [the yogi] manifests with his form the liberation of beauty, and fully obtaining it, abides [in it]; the four [formless] meditative attainments of space, consciousness, nothingness, and neither discrimination nor nondiscrimination; and the [attainment] of the cessation of discrimination and feeling; (4) the nine meditative states: the four concentrations of the form realm, the four formless meditative states, and the attainment of cessation; (5) the ten types of meditative totality: earth, water, fire, air, blue, yellow, red, white, consciousness, and space; (6) the eight kinds of bases of overpowering: four in which a person, [first] with the cognition that he himself has form, [then] with the cognition that he himself has no form, focuses upon external objects, [first] those of small size, [then] those of large size, and overpowering them, knows them; and four in which a person, just with the cognition that he himself has no form, overpowering blue, yellow, red and white, perceives them; (7) the meditative power that suppresses passions by eradicating the continuum of passions and delusions contained in others' mental continua; (8) the knowledge resulting from resolve, utterly free of all signs, all attachment eliminated, which continues for as long as saṃsāra and liberation exist, through its fulfillment of the resolution to remove the doubts [of all beings]; (9) the six supernatural knowledges and (10) the four analytical knowledges which were explained earlier; (11) the four purities: complete purity with respect to one's basis, objects, mind, and gnosis; (12) the ten sovereignties: dominion over life, mind, requisites, action, birth, [whatever one is] interested in, [whatever one] has resolved, supernatural power, gnosis, and truth; (13) the ten powers and (14) the four forms of fearlessness explained earlier; (15) the three ways in which [Buddha] has nothing to hide: the Tathāgata, having utterly pure conduct of body, speech, and mind, has no wrong conduct he would think to conceal out of fear that others may discover it; (16) the threefold mindful equanimity: toward those who like listening to his teaching, those who do not like to listen, and [a group of] those [which includes] both, [he is] free of attachment, aversion and both; equanimous only he abides, possessed of mindfulness; (17) the nature of never forgetting, such that he never disregards when it is time to carry out the benefit of others; (18) the complete destruction of all negative propensities by having destroyed the seeds, the predispositions, of the affective and cognitive obstructions *(kleśa-jñeya-āvaraṇa);* (19) the great compassion for living beings that is the resolute intention to help all beings; (20) the eighteen qualities unique to a Buddha; (21) total omniscience *(sarvākāra-jñatā).*

Included in the word "and" [in the expression "and total omniscience" of *AA* v. 8.6] is the knowledge of the path *(mārga-jñatā)* and so forth, which were explained earlier.

According to some, the body of dharmas [*dharmakāya* of v. 8.6] is explained to consist of all those [undefiled] dharmas, the factors fostering enlightenment, etc., the gnoses free from discursive conceptualization that are the transformed [result] of fundamental transformation *(āśraya-parāvṛtti)*.[48]

Haribhadra's prologue above is important: "Having thus explained the first *kāya*, the second *[kāya]* is declared: the body of dharmas consisting of gnosis . . . , which is composed of undefiled [Buddha dharmas] such as the mindfulnesses, etc." Haribhadra says *AA* vv. 8.2–8.6 identify the collection of Buddha dharmas directly as a second *kāya* called "body of dharmas" *(dharmakāya)*. In his view, *AA* v. 8.1 explained the first *kāya (svābhāvikakāya)* as the emptiness of a Buddha's gnoses. And vv. 8.2–8.6 set forth the second *kāya (dharmakāya* in v. 8.6), which comprises the Buddha's set of gnoses per se. This second *kāya* is what he calls *jñānātmaka dharmakāya* (body of dharmas consisting of gnosis), which as a phenomenal product of causes and conditions, is impermanent and conditioned.

According to prior Yogācāra formulations, the three *kāya*s were distinguished epistemologically according to who perceived them: Buddhas, *ārya* bodhisattvas, and less-developed beings directly perceived the *svābhāvikakāya*, *sāmbhogikakāya*, and *nairmāṇikakāya* respectively. In Haribhadra's new Madhyamaka formulation, *svābhāvikakāya* is separated out from the others not epistemologically (as in Yogācāra understanding) but logically: as the empty nature, the *dharmatā*, of the other *kāya*s. This leaves Buddha's gnosis, the set of undefiled dharmas, logically separate from *svābhāvikakāya,* on the one hand, and epistemologically distinct from *sāmbhogikakāya* and *nairmāṇikakāya,* on the other.

The Yogācāra criterion for distinguishing *kāya*s epistemologically was shifted in Haribhadra's analysis to the conventional level alone. Three conventionally existent *kāya*s, says Haribhadra, are still to be distinguished according to those who perceive them: Buddhas, aware of their own gnosis, perceive the collection of undefiled dharmas *(jñānātmaka dharmakāya)*, *ārya* bodhisattvas perceive *sāmbhogikakāya*, and others perceive *nairmāṇikakāya*. Conventionally, then, three *kāya*s are distinguished by Haribhadra according to the traditional epistemological criterion. But *svābhāvikakāya* is now distinguished from all the others logically (not epistemologically) according to Madhyamaka principles. On the ultimate level, there is only the *dharmatā*, the emptiness of all three conventional *kāya*s. And that, says Haribhadra, is what should be designated "essence body" *(svābhāvikakāya)*, since it is the only essence of Buddhahood findable under Madhyamaka analysis.

We may recall from our discussion in chapter 2 above, that Sarvāstivādin Abhidharmikas had identified a Buddha's collection of pure mental qualities (undefiled dharmas) as the defining essence of Buddhahood, which they referred to as *dharmakāya* (body of pure dharmas). In chapters 3 and 4 above, we saw how *PP* sūtras and Yogācāra treatises, as a critique of the Abhidharma understanding, explicitly avoided identifying the undefiled dharmas as a Buddha's defining essence *(dharmakāya)*, since they were now understood to comprise a phenomenal description of Buddhahood, not its essence. As the defining principal of Buddhahood, *dharmakāya* (also designated *svābhāvikakāya* in Yogācāra texts, the embodiment of the Buddhas' essence) was characterized as undifferentiated, nondual knowledge of thusness.

Haribhadra's Madhyamaka mission, ironically, resurrected the Abhidharma formulation by reidentifying the set of undefiled dharmas (of *AA* vv. 8.2–8.6) as a *dharmakāya*, and in such a way as to make that concept of *dharmakāya* the defining center of Buddhahood (with *svābhāvikakāya* now understood as its ultimate nature, emptiness; *sāmbhogikakāya* and *nairmāṇikakāya* as its conditioned appearances). In Haribhadra's Madhyamaka formulation, however, the Abhidharma-like identification of *dharmakāya* as a body of dharmas is made only with reference to the conventional level of reality. Ultimately, in Haribhadra's understanding, it is emptiness alone that comprises a Buddha's essence *(svābhāvikakāya)*.

In prior Yogācāra formulations, *svābhāvikakāya* was a Buddha's realization of ultimate truth (thusness), in the yogic experience of which gnosis and thusness (subject and object) are not distinguishable. *Svābhāvikakāya* (synonymous with *dharmakāya* in its exclusive sense) is closely identified with ultimate truth as a Buddha has realized it, while *sāmbhogikakāya* and *nairmāṇikakāya* are conventional appearances for others. In line with this, the undefiled dharmas, as a discursively conceptualized collection, were also relegated to the conventional level. It constituted a historical survival in Mahāyāna texts from earlier Buddhism, but was understood by Yogācāras as a description of Buddhahood merely from a phenomenal point of view that no longer captured its essence (see chapter 4, section 3, above).

Ārya Vimuktisena saw in *AA* vv. 8.1–8.6 the traditional Yogācāra pattern of using *svābhāvikakāya* and *dharmakāya* as synonyms. He understood the verses to be saying that the *svābhāvikakāya*, which is *dharmakāya*, is the very essence of Buddhahood, which is denominated in the *PP* sūtras in terms of undefiled dharmas, though not actually to be identified with such differentiation. Haribhadra, on the other hand, ignoring this pattern, reached back instead to another traditional pattern, that of Abhidharma, to declare the *dharmakāya* of verse 8.6 a separate *kāya* composed of differentiated undefiled dharmas. In his concern to distinguish the ultimate from the conventional, the unconditioned from the conditioned aspects of a Buddha's attainment, Haribhadra broke with the long-established pattern of the *PP* sūtras and Yogācāra tradition that never identified a Buddha's own core realization, *dharmakāya*, as any mere collection of conventional phenomena, no matter how exalted a collection (cf. chapter 3 and chapter 4, section 2, above).

Haribhadra's final comments on *AA* v. 8.1 quoted earlier[49] distinguish three conventional *kāyas* according to the persons who perceive them on the conventional level. Haribhadra says: "The remaining three *kāyas* [*dharmakāya* consisting of gnosis, *sāmbhogikakāya*, and *nairmāṇikakāya*], appearing with respect to true [worldly] convention, are ultimately in the nature of reality *(dharmatā)*. Distinguished in accordance with [differing] mentalities, they are established by being the cognitive objects for Buddhas, bodhisattvas, and *śrāvakas*, etc." This means that the undefiled dharmas (Buddha's gnoses) are perceived by the Buddha himself as a conventional existent, and that this is precisely what distinguishes them as a distinct *kāya (jñānātmaka dharmakāya)*. In prior formulations, a Buddha's gnosis was understood as a nondual awareness of thusness, epistemologically inseparable from ultimate reality (see chapters 4 and 5, above). In Haribhadra's scheme, a Buddha's gnosis is now explicitly distinguished as an appearance of conventional truth *(saṃvṛti satya)*, perceived by a Buddha as distinct from ultimate truth within his own awareness.

It is not clear whether Haribhadra realized how radical a departure this was from prior Mahāyāna buddhology. According to *PP* sūtras, Yogācāra treatises, and prior Madhyamaka texts such as Ārya Vimuktisena's *AA* commentary, Candrakīrti's *Madhyamakāvatāra*, and the *Trikāyastotra*, a Buddha's gnostic realization is epistemologically one with the *dharmadhātu*, the dharma realm of universal thusness, undifferentiated emptiness. Ontologically, all things are one in their ultimate nature of thusness. Therefore, epistemologically, a Buddha is understood to be "omniscient," to know all phenomena (in some sense) through the ultimate nature they all share, to perceive all phenomena in the "one taste" *(ekarasa)* of their final nature.[50]

In this long-established prior understanding, which took expression in the three-*kāya* paradigm, a Buddha's own nondual realization, referred to as *svābhāvikakāya* or *dharmakāya*, is itself epistemologically one with the ultimate realm of undifferentiated emptiness *(dharmadhātu)*. Somehow based upon that realization, manifestations appear in the phenomenal realm of living beings, the realm of conventional appearance *(saṃvṛti)*, to carry out enlightened activity. *Svābhāvikakāya/dharmakāya* is the realization of the realm of ultimate truth, while *sāmbhogikakāya* and *nairmāṇikakāya* are merely appearances for others within *their* realm of conventional truth.[51] In other words, a Buddha's awareness was understood to "inhabit" the realm of universal thusness, emptiness *(dharmadhātu)*, *not* to inhabit our phenomenal world per se. Rather a Buddha was understood in some sense to know the phenomenal world, and to give rise to action within it, based upon his nondual cognition of its ultimate nature.

In the three-*kāya* formulation, then, the essential realization of Buddhahood *(svābhāvikakāya/dharmakāya)* was entirely beyond conceptual construction and differentiation. The list of undefiled dharmas was understood just as a phenomenal description of a Buddha's gnosis, a description for *our* point of view, not a Buddha's.

But according to Haribhadra's four-*kāya* formulation, Buddha perceives his own realization in terms of those dharmas. For Haribhadra, the list of undefiled dharmas becomes not just a description of Buddha's gnosis from our phenomenal point of view, but a description from a Buddha's own point of view. And this means that, in Haribhadra's understanding, a Buddha's gnostic realization is no longer understood to inhabit primarily the realm of ultimate truth *(paramārtha)*. A Buddha himself distinguishes, within his own awareness, an aspect of conventional truth and an aspect of ultimate truth.[52]

In Haribhadra's formulation of *kāya* theory, the set of undefiled dharmas is distinguished as a separate *kāya (jñānātmaka dharmakāya)* precisely because it is an appearance, within the realm of conventional truth, for Buddhas themselves. Since conventional truth and ultimate truth can only be differentiated by conceptual thought, Haribhadra's theory entails that a Buddha's own gnostic realization contains conceptual differentiation within it. Haribhadra may not have intended this implication, but it is inescapable. This, in turn, would imply that conventional truth is not just the conceptually constructed world of ordinary beings (non-Buddhas), but that Buddhas themselves conceptually construct conventional truth within their own experience. This constitutes a very different understanding of a Buddha's gnosis, and of conventional truth itself, than we have seen in Mahāyāna traditions under study in prior chapters.

Implicit in Haribhadra's buddhology, then, lurks what appears to be a new understanding of Buddhahood: the understanding that a Buddha's realization inhabits not just the ultimate realm of emptiness but also, and equally, the phenomenal realm of conventional appearances. Since, according to Haribhadra, a Buddha's own awareness discursively distinguishes between conventional and ultimate truth, it would follow that a Buddha similarly discursively distinguishes other conventionalities as well. And this would imply that a Buddha's gnosis validates conventionalities as much as it validates their emptiness. In that case Buddha's awareness of the phenomenal world is not merely an expression of his nondual gnosis of its emptiness, but is on equal terms with it. A Buddha does not cognize phenomena based upon or through his gnosis of their ultimate nature. He cognizes phenomena qua phenomena, just like he cognizes their emptiness. Then conventional appearances per se, like their emptiness, would be equally validated by a Buddha's direct cognition. And this would grant to conventionalities an ontological status equal to their emptiness.[53]

All of these issues lay implicit in Haribhadra's buddhology (whether or not he was fully aware of it). Although not explicitly worked out in his writings, they were discerned by later Indian and Tibetan scholars, some of whom, for that very reason, forcefully rejected Haribhadra's four-*kāya* interpretation of the *AA*, while others, for the same reason, defended his position. According to Ratnākaraśānti and Abhayākaragupta of India and Go ram pa bsod nams seng ge of Tibet, Haribhadra, by ignoring prior understanding of Buddhahood as a nondual realization inaccessible to non-Buddhas, and by formulating his understanding of it based on independent inferences, projected his own logical constructions onto Buddhahood, mistaking them for Buddhahood itself. Other Indian and Tibetan scholars, however (notably Tsong kha pa blo bzang grags pa in Tibet), defended Haribhadra, appreciating the logical distinctions he made and/or embracing their implications for the improved ontological status of conventional truth. This will be explored in chapters 11 and 12 below.[54]

At the end of Haribhadra's remarks quoted above, he says that "some" scholars identify the *dharmakāya* (of v. 8.6) as the collection of undefiled dharmas (thus distinct from *svābhāvikakāya*). In fact, this represents his own view, as he makes clear in his prologue to vv. 8.2–8.6 above and throughout his commentary on *AA* 8 (having introduced *svābhāvikakāya* and the *dharmakāya* consisting of those dharmas respectively as his first and second *kāyas*). It is quite possible that Haribhadra's view conformed to that of his teacher Vairocana, to whom he pays respect in the closing verses of his *Āloka*.[55] This may also have been the view of some other Mādhyamikas of his time.

In his comments on vv. 8.2–8.6, Haribhadra briefly glosses each of the undefiled dharmas listed in the verses. In several places he refers his readers back to earlier portions of his commentary, especially on the *AA*'s first two chapters, where several such dharmas were already discussed. The list of undefiled dharmas, of course, is very old in Buddhism. The list that appears in *AA* 8 was drawn from the 25,000-verse *PP* sūtra (passage 8.5 as noted in chapters 7 and 8 of this book). The list is employed in that scripture as a phenomenal expression of Buddhahood that, for the most part, was drawn from earlier Abhidharma sources (see chapters 2 and 3 above). Haribhadra's glosses on several of the undefiled dharmas, therefore, are drawn from Abhidharma descriptions (mainly the *Abhidharma-kośa-bhāṣya*, which is one of his reference texts for the *Āloka*). Some merely repeat what Ārya Vimuktisena had already said. Many Indian and Tibetan commentators on the *AA* after Haribhadra also gave extensive commentary on each of the undefiled dharmas. Virtually the same list of dharmas also appears in Yogācāra texts such as the *Mahāyānasūtrālaṃkāra*. and *Mahāyānasaṃgraha*, and their commentaries also include extensive discussion of each of them.[56] On *sarvākārajñatā* (a Buddha's "total omniscience"), Ārya Vimuktisena's commentary presented a range of the opinions of his period (see chapter 9, section 3) that Haribhadra does not repeat.

In chapters 4 and 5 above, we described the Mahāyāna buddhology that was taking shape in the fourth to the sixth centuries in India, particularly in Yogācāra circles. The descriptions of Buddhahood we found in those texts were infinite in scope. A Buddha's gnosis and activity were said to pervade the universe. The *dharmadhātu* being utterly limitless and undivided, Buddha's nondual gnosis of it was equally limitless, pervading all. Through this, his spontaneous activity was said to be operative at all times and places. Since this understanding of Buddhahood had become more and more prevalent in textual Mahāyāna Buddhism by the time the *AA* was composed (ca. the fourth to the early sixth centuries C.E.), it is a bit startling to read the list of undefiled dharmas in *AA* chapter 8 as a primary description of a Buddha's gnostic qualities. Many of the items in that list of dharmas appear trivial in light of the buddhology of the time. Included in the list, for example, are the "three ways in which a Buddha has nothing to hide": i.e., a Buddha does not misbehave in any way that would cause him to hide the fact from others' disapproval. Also included is the "threefold mindful equanimity," according to which a Buddha does not get angry with people who do not like to listen to him. How remarkable are these qualities for one whose mind literally pervades the universe?

Much of the list was obviously compiled at a time when the conception of a Buddha focused more on human qualities and less on infinitely pervasive powers. As such, the list is in some ways embarrassingly unsuited to the task of describing the gnostic qualities of Buddhahood during the period of the flowering of more all-encompassing buddhological conceptions. As we noted in chapters 7 and 8 above, however, the author of the Abhisamayālaṃkāra was constrained by his textual basis in the *Large Prajñāpāramitā Sūtra* to place the list of undefiled dharmas at the center of his description of *svābhāvikakāya*. *AA* verses 8.7 through 8.11, in fact, appear to constitute the author's attempt to update that list of undefiled dharmas, to interpret it in such a way as to bring it up to the standards of contemporary Mahāyāna buddhology.

For reasons we can only speculate on, the Abhisamayālaṃkāra became an enormously popular text in later Indian Buddhism and then in Tibet. This may have occurred with the rise in influence of the Madhyamaka school, since the *AA* lent itself more easily to strict Madhyamaka interpretation than most other principal texts on Mahāyāna praxis, paths, and stages that had developed primarily in Yogācāra circles (such as the *Mahāyāna-sūtrālaṃkāra* and *Mahāyāna-saṃgraha*). In fact, in Tibet, the *AA* gradually eclipsed texts such as the *Mahāyāna-sūtrālaṃkāra* and became the central treatise for Tibetan scholars on the nontantric Mahāyāna paths and stages.[57] With the rise in popularity of the *AA* in late Indian and Tibetan Buddhism, the list of undefiled dharmas found in its eighth chapter was resurrected as a primary description of Buddhahood for Mahāyāna tradition. The irony is that the gnoseology and buddhology of Indian Mahāyāna textual traditions had already outgrown that list of undefiled dharmas at the time the *AA* was composed.

10.5
Haribhadra's "Refutation" of the Traditional Three-*Kāya* Interpretation

Haribhadra's commentary on *AA* chapter 8 now enters into direct debate with those who adhere to the prior three-*kāya* interpretation of the text. He presents further reasons for rejecting such a view and adopting the four-*kāya* interpretation that he offers. He begins by paraphrasing part of Ārya Vimuktisena's commentary and then rebutting it:

> But, others explain as follows:
>
> *AA* v. 8.1: "The essence body *(svābhāvikakāya)* of the Sage: Its identity is the primordial nature of the undefiled dharmas that are obtained in utter purity," literally means that, having accepted the supramundane undefiled dharmas [of the Buddha], the essence body's identity is their actual intrinsic nature *(prakṛti):* nonarisingness *(anutpādatā).* And that [essence body] is also *dharmatākāya* (body of reality), which is indicated by [the concluding word of v. 8.6]: *dharmakāya*, through the elision of the particle that indicates abstract nouns *(-tā).*
>
> Then they [raise this hypothetical] question: "What are the undefiled [Buddha] dharmas, the intrinsic nature of which is the *dharma[tā]kāya*'s identity?" And they understand *[AA]* verses [8.2–8.6] [as the answer to that]: "The factors that foster enlightenment. . . . ," etc.
>
> Others [reply that] [Buddha's] nondual primary consciousnesses and mental factors *(citta-caittā)*, which are the transformed [result] of fundamental transformation *(āśrayaparāvṛtti)*, are what carry out [his] effective actions *(artha-kriyā)* of teaching the dharma, etc. by generating appearances which have specific purposes in conformance to the conventional [perspectives] of yogi [trainees]. How, according to those [whose assertion is immediately above], are those [primary consciousnesses and mental factors] that must surely be accepted, included [within the *kāya*s]?[58]

The first paragraph above is Haribhadra's paraphrase of Ārya Vimuktisena's comments on *AA* vv. 8.1–8.6. The second paragraph is Haribhadra's own response. However, Haribhadra, perhaps without realizing it, subtly misrepresents Ārya Vimuktisena. Concerning *AA* v. 8.1, Ārya Vimuktisena wrote:

> Of the utterly purified, undefiled all-dharmas, possessed of the dharma realm *(dharmadhātu)*, the primordial nature (Tib., *rang bzhin;* Skt., *prakṛti*), the essence (Tib., *ngo bo nyid;* Skt., *svabhāva*), should be known as the embodiment of the Bhagavan in his essence *(svābhāvikakāya)*, [where "essence"] means it is uncreated. It is well known in the world that an "essence" *(svabhāva)* is that which is not created. The supramundane path obtains that [essence], it is not its creator.[59]

As previously noted, Ārya Vimuktisena identified *svābhāvikakāya*, as the "primordial nature" of the undefiled dharmas, meaning a Buddha's nondual awareness of universal emptiness *(dharmadhātu)*, *not* just emptiness alone. He characterized

Buddha's gnosis as "possessed of the *dharmadhātu*," meaning not just that it is empty (all things are empty in Mahāyāna metaphysics), but that it has taken possession *in knowledge* of the *dharmadhātu*.

But as Haribhadra's comments above reveal, he assumed that Ārya Vimuktisena, like himself, had identified *just* emptiness per se as *svābhāvikakāya*. His comments subtly alter Ārya Vimuktisena's meaning by putting the term "nonarisingness" *(anutpādatā)* into his mouth as the primary understanding of *svābhāvikakāya*, a term used here as a Madhyamaka buzzword for emptiness. Haribhadra believed Ārya Vimuktisena to have been a Mādhyamika.[60] But Haribhadra was steeped in the logico-Mādhyamika traditions that had become increasingly prominent in the centuries between Ārya Vimuktisena and himself. He therefore interpreted Ārya Vimuktisena's remarks from his own late-eighth-century perspective, projecting back onto Ārya Vimuktisena his own understanding that *svābhāvikakāya* is unconditioned, uncreated, and "nonarising" because it is just emptiness, an emptiness logically separate from gnosis. In fact, Ārya Vimuktisena had made no such logical distinction.

Rather, Ārya Vimuktisena had followed the Yogācāra pattern of understanding *svābhāvikakāya* through gnoseology (not logic), characterizing it as nondual gnosis of *dharmadhātu*, based upon which *sāmbhogikakāya*, *nairmāṇikakāya*, and the set of undefiled dharmas are mere imputations from a phenomenal point of view. It never occurred to Ārya Vimuktisena to logically separate the emptiness and awareness of Buddhahood, since *svābhāvikakāya* had always been understood as precisely that attainment in which the appearance of separate cognitive subject and object was entirely removed, eliminating any apparent separation between emptiness and knower of emptiness.

But Haribhadra, having projected back onto Ārya Vimuktisena the logical separation between emptiness and awareness that he himself had made (within the logical discourse of his own place and time), now finds no logical place within the three-*kāya* model for a Buddha's awareness or gnosis (described in *AA* 8.2–8.6 in terms of the undefiled dharmas). Haribhadra's central argument for positing a fourth *kāya* consisting of gnosis now logically follows in the second of his paragraphs quoted above:

> Others [reply that] [Buddha's] nondual primary consciousnesses and mental factors *(citta-caittā)*, which are the transformed [result] of fundamental transformation *(āśrayaparāvṛtti)*, are what carry out [his] effective actions *(artha-kriyā)* of teaching the dharma, etc., by generating appearances that have specific purposes in conformance to the conventional [perspectives] of yogi [trainees]. How, according to those [whose assertion is immediately above], are those [primary consciousnesses and mental factors], which must surely be accepted, included [within the *kāya*s]?

This paragraph also makes clear Haribhadra's overarching concern to solve the paradox of nonabiding nirvāṇa by sorting out the unconditioned and conditioned aspects of Buddhahood. In his view, *svābhāvikakāya* is just emptiness, unconditioned. But a Buddha's activities in the world are carried out through conditioned appearances for trainees: *sāmbhogikakāya* and *nairmāṇikakāya*. The undefiled dharmas, reasons Haribhadra, must comprise the conditioned basis within a Buddha's mind for those conditioned appearances. But they are not *svābhāvikakāya*, which is just emptiness, unconditioned. And they can not be identified with *sāmbhogikakāya* or *nairmāṇikakāya*, being their conditioned cause. So they have to comprise a distinct, fourth *kāya*—a "body of dharmas consisting of gnosis"—and this must be what *AA* v. 8.6 means by *dharmakāya*. In line with this, Haribhadra ignores the implicit *Prajñāpāramitāsūtra* etymology of *dharmakāya* as *dharma[tā] kāya* (embodiment of dharma[tā], embodiment of reality in nondual knowledge) that Ārya Vimuktisena had picked up on, returning instead to the prior Abhidharma understanding of *dharmakāya* as "body of [pure Buddha] dharmas."

Logically distinguishing the unconditioned from the conditioned in Buddhahood, Haribhadra also borrows from Abhidharma analysis of the human mind, in which the sense consciousnesses are referred to as "primary consciousnesses" *(citta)* that are structured through "mental factors" *(caitta)* such as attention, memory, feeling, discernment, and the emotions. Extrapolating this Abhidharma analysis of the ordinary minds of beings to Buddhahood, Haribhadra takes the *AA*'s list of undefiled dharmas as an accurate description of the actual contents of a Buddha's mind, divided into sense consciousnesses and mental factors just like the minds of ordinary beings, although purer. This, of course, contrasts sharply with the prior *Prajñāpāramitāsūtra* and Yogācāra understandings that Ārya Vimuktisena followed, in which a Buddha's awareness is characterized as just nondual gnosis-thusness, entirely undifferentiated, with the list of undefiled dharmas downgraded as a mere phenomenal description for the sake of non-Buddhas.[61]

Earlier Mahāyāna writings agreed that a Buddha manifests various appearances in the world to work for beings. In order to do this, Haribhadra reasoned, a Buddha must possess all the sense consciousnesses and mental factors necessary to perceive what needs to be done and to take specific actions in the world for the right persons at the right time through the proper manifestation. This, he says, "must surely be accepted." Then if *svābhāvikakāya* is understood as just the emptiness of a Buddha's consciousnesses and mental factors, the consciousnesses and mental factors themselves become unassignable to any of the three traditional *kāya*s, for the reasons above. The logical conclusion, Haribhadra argues, is a fourth *kāya*.

This reasoning is at the very center of Haribhadra's analysis of Buddhahood in four *kāya*s, and is repeated in various forms throughout his comments on *AA* 8.[62] By using eighth-century-Mādhyamika logic to distinguish in a new way the ultimate truth from the conventional truth within a Buddha's own core realization, he believed he had logically distinguished the unconditioned aspect of that realization (*svābhāvikakāya*, emptiness, ultimate truth) from the conditioned aspect upon which enlightened activity and manifestation depend (Buddha dharma-gnoses, conventional truth, *jñānātmaka dharmakāya*). His use of such logico-Mādhyamika inference becomes his hermeneutic for interpretation of *AA* 8. For, in his view, given ambiguities in the *AA* verses, one must fall back upon autonomous reasoning to infer what the author must have intended. Then, since Maitreya composed the *AA*, one could assume that the true doctrine was the one that Maitreya espoused.[63] To read *AA* vv. 8.2–8.6 as a teaching of a separate "body of dharmas consisting of gnosis" *(jñānātmaka dharmakāya)* was logical, hence true, hence surely Maitreya's intended message.

Haribhadra's extrapolation of Abhidharma mental analysis to Buddhahood distinguishes him from Mahāyāna traditions of Buddhahood discussed in prior chapters of this book. He argued that a Buddha "surely" required a set of primary sense consciousnesses and mental factors *(citta-caitta)* to carry out activity in the conditioned world. But in Yogācāra texts that formulated three-*kāya* doctrine, precisely the opposite was assumed: A Buddha's activity was said to be entirely spontaneous and free of any conditioned forethought (chapter 5, section 3 above). No primary consciousnesses or mental factors, as in Abhidharma analysis of mind, were explicitly ascribed to a Buddha in such texts. Rather, it was asserted that through a Buddha's nondual realization of universal thusness, and from the force of his previous vows and collection of merit, conjoined with the karmic readiness of disciples, a Buddha's activity manifested spontaneously within the conditioned world. Common metaphors used to illustrate this were the wish-fulfilling gem and heavenly drums of Indian legend, which performed their functions without any consciousnesses or mental factors. To claim that phenomenal consciousnesses and mental factors are required for such spontaneous enlightened activity is to run counter to the Yogācāra tradition from which the *AA* drew its *kāya* terminology (chapter 5, section 4), and thence to contradict Ārya Vimuktisena's understanding.

Haribhadra's division of a Buddha's awareness into consciousnesses and mental factors also runs counter to Candrakīrti, a leading Mādhyamika of the seventh century. Candrakīrti explicitly states in the "Buddhabhūmi" chapter of his *Madhyamakāvatāra* that the gnosis of a Buddha is free of conditioned consciousnesses and mental factors. Candrakīrti raises the problem of how a Buddha can teach about the realization of thatness (*tattvam*, emptiness) when his own gnosis has become epistemologically one with its nonarising nature, which would mean that Buddha's awareness itself is also "nonarising," unconditioned. Candrakīrti says that the manifestation of *rūpakāya*s and the words they teach are spontaneous, arising from the force of previous merit and by the Buddha's blessing. He compares the Buddha's activity to the wish-fulfilling gem of Indian folklore, because the Buddha, "without moving from the *dharmadhātu* for even a moment," spontaneously carries out the welfare of sentient beings in precise accord with their needs.

This is through the force of the Buddha's prior vows and the karmic merit of the disciples. Candrakīrti then discusses *dharmakāya*. This is his term for the nondual gnosis of thatness which is the first of the three *kāyas* (corresponding to *svābhāvika-kāya* of Yogācāra tradition). He says that the *dharmakāya* "burns up the dry firewood of [all] objects of knowledge," from which there is the "nonarising of objects of knowledge," and through that the *dharmakāya* "comes to [cognitively] possess that nonarising" (to become epistemologically one with it). He concludes that, because the gnosis of *dharmakāya* is utterly focused on thatness *(tattvam)*, there are no conditioned consciousnesses *(citta)* or mental factors *(caitta)* operative in it.[64]

Haribhadra's assumption, then, that primary consciousnesses and mental factors make up a Buddha's mind was based more on extrapolation of Abhidharma to Buddhahood than on prior Mahāyāna buddhology. Haribhadra's reliance upon Abhidharma thought would also explain why he ignored prior Mahāyāna understanding to retrieve the list of undefiled dharmas as a defining center of Buddhahood. In Sarvāstivāda Abhidharma, the undefiled dharmas were identified as a Buddha's defining essence: *dharmakāya*. In both the *Prajñāpāramitā* and Yogācāra traditions, they were downgraded to a phenomenal description of *dharmakāya* (from our point of view, not a Buddha's), and hence inadequate to capture its real essence. Haribhadra resurrects the list of undefiled dharmas to identify it as a fourth *kāya* because (he says) it appears conventionally to Buddha himself, thereby taking that list as an accurate conventional description of the way a Buddha's gnosis appears from the Buddha's *own* point of view.[65]

Haribhadra, relying much on inference and less on philology, was evidently aware that his interpretation of *AA* 8 was especially vulnerable to attack on linguistic and textual grounds.[66] Next in his commentary, then, he presents the objection of a hypothetical three-*kāya* proponent, who attacks Haribhadra's four-*kāya* interpretation on textual grounds. Haribhadra then attempts to rebut the objection:

> Some, [criticizing] the four-*kāya* explanation, [quote *AA* v. 1.17, the table of contents of *AA* chapter 8]: "*svābhāvika*, *sasāmbhoga*, and *nairmāṇika* as well, / *dharmakāya*, with activity, proclaimed as fourfold."[67]
>
> In [this] verse, [they claim,] since the word *dharmakāya* is not said immediately after the word *svābhāvika*, there are only three *kāyas*.
>
> But others [reply] that, on the strength of the intention just demonstrated, for felicity in the construction of the verse, and for the sake of associating activity with the gnosis alone, it was stated thusly. Therefore [the *AA*] is consistent with all the statements in other quarters *(pradeś-āntara)* that the *kāyas* are fourfold.[68]

In the first paragraph above, the proponent of the three-*kāya* interpretation puts his objection. The terms that Haribhadra understood to designate four separate *kāyas* in *AA* chapter 8 appear in that chapter in the following order: *svābhāvikakāya* (*AA* v. 8.1), *dharmakāya* (meaning "body of dharmas consisting of gnosis," v. 8.6), *sāmbhogikakāya* (v. 8.12), *nairmāṇikakāya* (v. 8.33). But the corresponding terms in *AA* verse 1.17, the table of contents for chapter 8, appear in a different order: *svābhāvikakāya, sāmbhogikakāya, nairmāṇikakāya, dharmakāya.* This, Haribhadra has his opponents say, indicates that only three *kāyas* are taught in the *AA*. For if the term *dharmakāya* of v. 8.6 designated a separate *kāya* (rather than serving as a synonym for *svābhāvikakāya* of v. 8.1), then it should have appeared after the term *svābhāvikakāya* in v. 1.17, the verse that sets forth the order of topics for chapter 8. In a three-*kāya* interpretation of the text, the fact that *dharmakāya* appears last in v. 1.17 indicates that it serves there as the title of the chapter, not as the name of a fourth *kāya.*[69]

In Haribhadra's interpretation, *AA* v. 1.17 specifies four separate *kāyas* by those four key terms. He therefore had to give reasons why the four *kāya* terms were presented in a different order in v. 1.17 than in chapter 8. He gives three reasons. The first is "the strength of the intention just demonstrated" *(upadarśita-prayojana-sāmarthyāt)*. Just prior to his remarks above, Haribhadra had presented his central argument for his four-*kāya* interpretation of the *AA* (fols. 25a4–a6 quoted earlier). There he argued from the acknowledgment of a Buddha's manifestations and activities in the world to the acceptance of his having a collection of mental factors, which, logically separate from *svābhāvikakāya* and epistemologically separate from *sāmbhogikakāya* and *nairmāṇikakāya*, had to be posited as a fourth *kāya*. Given the assumption that the *AA* was teaching whatever was most reasonable, its ambiguities were to be resolved by reliance on this valid inference of four *kāyas*. This is the intention *(prayojana)* of the *AA* according to Haribhadra that he has just demonstrated by inference. On "the strength" of that demonstrated (four-*kāya*) intention behind the text, *AA* v. 1.17 is to be interpreted as follows.

First the verse: "*svābhāvika, sasāmbhoga,* and *nairmāṇika* as well, / *dharmakāya*, with activity, proclaimed as fourfold" (*AA* v. 1.17). Haribhadra's interpretation: The *svābhāvika[kāya]* is the empty nature, the *dharmatā*, of Buddhahood, the ultimate nature of the three other *kāyas*, hence it is presented first in the verse. The *sāmbhogikakāya* and *nairmāṇikakāya* are a Buddha's manifestations, the evidence of his activities in the world. Therefore they appear next in the verse. All acknowledge that they appear in order to carry out a Buddha's activities. Based on that, all should acknowledge that a Buddha possesses the consciousnesses and mental factors necessary to generate such manifestations and act through them, i.e., the conventionally existent gnoses, the undefiled dharmas. Given that collection of gnoses, a fourth *kāya*, a body of dharmas consisting of gnosis *(jñānātmaka dharmakāya)*, must be posited. Therefore, the term *dharmakāya* appears next in the verse. According to Haribhadra, the *AA*'s author set forth the terms for the four *kāyas* in *AA* v. 1.17 in the order he did precisely to indicate the rationale behind the teaching of four *kāyas*. But within the text of chapter 8 itself, the *AA*'s author had to present the *dharmakāya* consisting of gnosis just after his presentation of *svābhāvikakāya,* since the latter is defined precisely as the intrinsic nature of the undefiled dharmas which comprise the former. All this is contained in the first of Haribhadra's three reasons above for the disparate order of terms in v. 1.17: "on the strength of the intention just demonstrated."[70]

His second reason is "for felicity in the construction of the verse." This means that the *AA*'s author did not put the term *dharmakāya* immediately after the term *svābhāvika* in v. 1.17 because the numerous requirements of meter and syntax in the construction of Sanskrit verse precluded it. This sort of argument is very commonly used by Indian philosophers who want to propose an interpretation of a text that requires an unusual reading of it. It often has some merit, for the exigencies of Sanskrit meter do sometimes require ambiguous modes of expression that would not have occurred in prose. But the better composers of Sanskrit verse were remarkably adept at communicating their intentions and meanings clearly in spite of the difficulties. For this reason, any argument for a nonstraightforward interpretation of a verse on the grounds that it had to be composed awkwardly is prima facie a suspicious argument, often signaling a hidden agenda on the part of the interpreter. This is not always the case, but it is, of course, the case here.

The third reason Haribhadra gives for the disparate order of terms in v. 1.17 is "for the sake of associating activity with the gnosis alone." This is related to the first reason above. According to Haribhadra, all of a Buddha's varied activities can only be based on his conventionally existent gnoses. The *svābhāvikakāya*, as emptiness, is a permanent, hence not a basis for conditioned activity. The *sāmbhogikakāya* and *nairmāṇikakāya* are manifestations that must be generated by something more basic. And that is the collection of gnoses, the undefiled dharmas. These comprise the fundamental, impermanent, and conditioned basis for all conditioned manifestations and enlightened activities, and as such are to be posited as a fourth *kāya*. Thus, in Haribhadra's view, gnosis and enlightened activity are closely associated in the *AA*, the conditioned gnosis being the primary cause of the activity, and the activity being the primary evidence for inferring such conditioned gnosis. For this reason, Haribhadra is saying, the terms *dharmakāya* (meaning gnosis) and *kāritra* (activity) were placed adjacent to each other in verse 1.17.

The first and the third of Haribhadra's reasons above are reiterations of his central concern to distinguish the conditioned basis of a Buddha's activity in the world from his unconditioned nature (in other words, to logically resolve the paradox of nonabiding nirvāṇa). His comments are remarkable for the succinctness with which they summarize his view of the logical relation between *AA* v. 1.17 and the entire structure of *AA* buddhology. In spite of its lucidity, however, Haribhadra's exposition of AA v. 1.17, is, technically speaking, not correct; it ignores many of the specific ways in which that verse is connected to the rest of the table of contents, the conclusion of the text, and its philological relations to other *trikāya* texts of its period. I refer the reader to our analysis of verse 1.17 in chapter 8, section 2, above.[71] Given the extensive evidence for a three-*kāya* interpretation presented there, it is clear that the objection that Haribhadra put into the mouth of the three *kāya* proponent above (that the *kāya* names would be out of order in v. 1.17 if it was read as a four-*kāya* expression) was about the weakest philological objection to his own interpretation of the *AA* that he could think of. Because his four-*kāya* interpretation is based so heavily on his own independent inference of what the *AA* should be saying, and is so little rooted in the expression of the text itself, he realized how vulnerable he was to objections on philological and textual grounds. So he tried to head them off by raising such an objection himself, albeit in the weakest form possible.

At the end of his remarks above, Haribhadra says: "Therefore [the *AA*] is consistent with all the statements in other quarters that the *kāyas* are fourfold." Later Indian commentators Ratnākaraśānti (ca. 1000 C.E.) and Abhayākaragupta (ca. 1100 C.E.) both assumed that by the expression "other quarters" *(pradeśāntara)* Haribhadra was referring to the tantric Buddhist traditions. Later Tibetan commentators shared this assumption.[72] In several of the Indian Buddhist tantras and their manuals for initiation rites, yogic practice, etc., four Buddha *kāyas* are specified. And Buddhist tantric practice was prominent in and outside of the major Buddhist monastic universities of North India in Haribhadra's time (the Pāla period). Haribhadra's remark, then, probably meant that his four-*kāya* interpretation of the *AA* (a nontantric Buddhist text) conformed, at least formally, to the four-*kāya* pattern established in the tantric tradition. And this may, in fact, have comprised an adjunct reason for his reading of four *kāyas* into the *AA*. Both Ratnākaraśānti and Abhayākaragupta, assuming this to be the case, criticized Haribhadra for inappropriately applying tantric categories to his interpretation of the *AA*, a nontantric text.

10.6
Reading Four *Kāyas* into the Rest of *Abhisamayālaṃkāra* Chapter 8

In the next portion of his *Sphuṭārthā*, Haribhadra quotes and comments upon *AA* vv. 8.7–8.8:

> That being so, in order to show the superiority of a Buddha's meditative power freeing from passions *(araṇā-samādhi)* over that of the disciples *(śrāvakas)*, etc., the following verse [*AA* v. 8.7] is said:
>
> "A disciple's meditative power freeing from passions is the avoidance of men's passions [arising] from seeing [that disciple]. The Victor's [Buddha's] meditative power freeing from passions is for cutting off the stream of their passions in towns, etc."

Having thought, "May there be no arising of passions in anyone because of seeing me," the arising of passions in people is avoided. [This is] the meditative power of the disciples *(śrāvakas)*, etc., that frees from passions. But the Tathāgata's meditative power freeing from passions eradicates the continua of passions of all beings in [entire] towns, etc.

In order to explain the superiority of a Buddha's gnosis [resulting from] resolve *(praṇidhijñāna)* over that of the disciples, etc., the following verse [*AA* v. 8.8] is said:

"It is accepted that the Buddha gnosis [resulting from] resolve is automatic, unattached, unobstructed, forever operative, and answers all questions."

Through its freedom from signs *(nimitta)*, it operates of its own accord. Because it does not adhere to things, it is free from attachment to forms, etc. Because it has abandoned the affective and cognitive obstructions *(kleśa-jñeya-āvaraṇa)* together with their propensities, it is unobstructed with reference to all objects of knowledge. Because it remains for as long as cyclic existence lasts *(saṃsāra)*, it is forever operative. Because it has obtained the analytical knowledges, it provides the answers for questions. Such is accepted for the Tathāgata's gnosis [resulting from] resolve. Since that of the disciples, etc., is just the reverse, it is not like [a Buddha's].[73]

Earlier it was mentioned that the gnoseology and buddhology of Indian Mahāyāna Buddhism had already outgrown the list of undefiled dharmas by the time the *AA* was composed. That list was woefully inadequate to communicate the all-encompassing gnostic qualities of a Buddha as they were already being articulated in many Mahāyāna sūtras and in treatises such as the *MSA*. But it was retained as a historical survival within Mahāyāna traditions and viewed as a valid description of Buddhahood from a phenomenal point of view (see chapter 4, section 2 above). The *AA*'s textual basis in the *PP* sūtra required that it give that list of undefiled dharmas a prominent place in its exposition of *svābhāvikakāya*. But its author, apparently sensing the need for some reinterpretation, singled out two of the undefiled dharmas—i.e., two of the gnoses of Buddhahood—in order to indicate the limitless capacities of a Buddha's gnosis according to contemporary Mahāyāna buddhology. The *AA* said the description of Buddha's gnosis resulting from resolve *(praṇidhijñāna)* as "automatic" (i.e., utterly spontaneous), "unobstructed" (i.e., all-pervasive), and "forever operative," and ascribed to Buddha's gnosis as a whole the powerful and all-encompassing properties ascribed to it in the Mahāyāna gnoseology of the time. In the corresponding portion of his *Āloka*, Haribhadra notes that a Buddha's meditative power freeing from passions *(araṇā-samādhi)* and gnosis resulting from resolve *(praṇidhijñāna)* were distinguished in *AA* 8 as paradigms for the ways in which all other Buddha dharma-gnoses are far superior to that of the disciples, etc.[74]

Haribhadra's commentary continues with explanation of *AA* vv. 8.9–8.11.

If [a Buddha] always abides as *dharmakāya* with a nature of great compassion, why isn't the welfare [of beings] always being accomplished? In order to respond to this, the following verse [(*AA* v. 8.9] is said:

"When the cause has reached fruition, whenever and for whomever there is benefit to be accomplished, then and there he appears."

With Buddha, etc., as a basis, through meeting one's spiritual guide, and so forth, the cause, i.e., the seed, the root of virtue planted in the past, reaches maturity. Then, any time the teaching of dharma, etc. would have long-term benefit for any such being, in order to benefit that being, the Bhagavan, through the fulfillment of his previous resolutions, accomplishes beneficial activity through a manifestation appropriate for that [very being at that very time]. So, even though he abides always nearby in the manner of a wish-fulfilling gem, [if] due to one's own karmic faults, the causes [for his manifestation to oneself] are incomplete, then [Buddha], who bestows their result, does not manifest. That is the purport [of the verse].

How is that so? An example is given by the following verse [*AA* v. 8.10]:

"But even when the god of rain pours down rain, an infertile seed does not sprout. So even when Buddhas arise, one who is unfit does not obtain the blessing."

Even when the king of gods is showering down rain, a seed such as a sesame that, being rotten, is infertile, does not sprout forth. Likewise, even when Buddhas arise who are expert at fulfilling all wishes, one without [karmic] fortune does not obtain the blessing, i.e., the hearing of the holy dharma, etc.

How can the *dharmakāya* consisting of gnosis *(jñānātmaka dharmakāya)* be called "pervasive" *(vyāpi)* and "permanent" *(nitya)* when it exists within the mental continuum of each yogi [Buddha] individually, and is produced *(utpadyamānaḥ)* moment by moment? [An answer is provided] by the following verse [*AA* v. 8.11]:

"Because of such extensiveness of activity, Buddha is declared to be pervasive. And because of his inexhaustibility *(akṣayatvāt)*, he is called permanent."

In the manner just indicated [in *AA* verses 8.8–8.10 above], Buddha is called "pervasive" *(vyāpi)* because of the extensiveness of the activity that he carries out through his universal manifestations, and he is called

> "permanent" *(nitya)* because the Bhagavan has no diminution, his continuity remaining for as long as cyclic existence lasts.[75]

From our historical-critical perspective on the *AA*, we would say that *AA* vv. 8.9–8.11 continue to update the description of Buddha's gnosis to contemporary Mahāyāna buddhology, in which *svābhāvikakāya/dharmakāya* is understood as all-encompassing and universally accessible. *AA* v. 8.11 refers back to vv. 8.8–8.10. Verse 8.8 described a Buddha's gnosis resulting from resolve as all-pervasive and forever operative. Verses 8.9–8.10 describe the pervasiveness of a Buddha's accessibility to every being and activity, based on such gnosis. Verse 8.11 reiterates those two themes: the pervasiveness and permanence (or eternality) of Buddhahood. In fact, v. 8.11 follows the Yogācāra pattern (discussed in chapter 5, sections 3–5, above) of characterizing the *svābhāvikakāya/dharmakāya* as pervasive, in its gnosis and manifestation, and permanent, in the general sense applicable both to the gnosis and to its manifestations (see chapter 5, section 5, above).[76]

Haribhadra, on the other hand, with his special mission to logically distinguish the unconditioned from the conditioned in Buddhahood, wants to interpret all verses from 8.2 through 8.11 to concern what he has identified as the "body of dharmas consisting of gnosis" *(jñānātmaka dharmakāya)* alone, the conventional, conditioned (and therefore impermanent) gnosis based upon which a Buddha's activity can be logically understood to enter into the conditioned world. Verse 8.8 described Buddha's gnosis as "forever operative" *(sadā sthitaṃ)*. Haribhadra plausibly glossed this as: "Because it remains for as long as cyclic existence lasts, it is forever operative." Such a gloss permits his understanding of the gnosis as conditioned and impermanent, while also permitting its description as "permanent" *(nitya)* in the sense of unceasing.

Above, Haribhadra says that verse 8.11, in part, serves as the *AA*'s answer to the question of how the *dharmakāya* consisting of gnosis *(jñānātmaka dharmakāya)* can be called "permanent" when it is changing moment by moment. This very question already imputes to the gnosis a conditioned and momentary nature, which is Haribhadra's rationale for positing it as a separate *kāya*. Then, in his comment on verse 8.11, he characterizes *dharmakāya* of gnosis in the following terms: "he is called 'permanent' because the Bhagavan has no diminution, his continuity remaining for as long as cyclic existence lasts." The expression "remaining for as long as cyclic existence lasts" echoes from his earlier comment on verse 8.8 and becomes a very specific tag for Buddha's gnosis, characterizing it (in its moment by moment impermanence) as never ceasing, and thus as the conditioned basis for never-ceasing activity. In this manner, Haribhadra interprets vv. 8.7 through 8.11 as a block to concern Buddha's gnosis and the way that it serves as a basis for activity. And this identifies vv. 8.2–8.11 together as a unified explication of *dharmakāya* of gnosis *(jñānātmaka dharmakāya)* that, according to Haribhadra, must be logically distinguished from *svābhāvikakāya* (a permanent) precisely because it serves as the conditioned, impermanent basis of a Buddha's conditioned activity.

Haribhadra next identifies the subject of *AA* v. 8.12 as *sāmbhogikakāya*, the third *kāya* of his four-*kāya* scheme.

Body of Communal Enjoyment *(Sāmbhogikakāya)*

> Having thus presented the second *kāya (jñānātmaka dharmakāya)*, the third *[kāya]* is taught, the body of communal enjoyment *(sāmbhogikakāya)*, which blazes with the marks and signs, and which is by nature a body of form:
>
> "This form of the Sage with thirty-two marks and eighty signs is to be understood as his embodiment in communal enjoyment *(sāmbhogikakāya)*, from its enjoyment of the great vehicle *(mahāyāna)*" (*AA* v. 8.12).
>
> Because it partakes in the pleasure and happiness of sharing the enjoyment of the impeccable Mahāyāna dharma in company with the great bodhisattvas who have entered into the ten stages *(bhūmis)*, it is the communal enjoyment body *(sāmbhogikakāya)* of the Buddha, the Bhagavan, whose nature is the thirty-two marks and eighty signs.[77]

This is self-explanatory. For discussion of the textual and historical significance of this verse, which, possibly for the first time in Indian Mahāyāna Buddhism, specifically assigns the marks and signs to the *sāmbhogikakāya* and makes them central to its definition, see chapter 8, section 4 of this book. Verses 8.13 through 8.32 (and Haribhadra's commentary on them) describe in detail all the marks and signs with some of their karmic causes; but this is not directly relevant to the present discussion.

We continue Haribhadra's commentary with his remarks on *AA* vv. 8.33–8.40 concerning *nairmāṇikakāya*, the fourth of his four *kāya*s. I will not translate all of his remarks, since most of them detail all twenty-seven types of Buddha activity, which, again, are not specifically relevant to this discussion. We will, however, translate his remarks on verse 8.33, his prologue to vv. 8.34–8.40, and his concluding remark on those verses. First, he separates verse 8.33 from all verses that follow it in order to comment on it individually as the *AA*'s definition of *nairmāṇikakāya*. Then, he gives a prologue to vv. 8.34–8.40 that explicitly ascribes all the activities listed in those verses to the *dharmakāya* consisting of gnosis (*not* to the *nairmāṇikakāya* of v. 8.33 per se). Next, he quotes vv. 8.34–8.40 and explains each of the twenty-seven types of activity. Finally, he concludes with a reaffirmation that all the Buddha activities just listed are to be ascribed to the *dharmakāya* consisting of gnosis *(jñānātmaka dharmakāya):*

Body of Manifestation(s) *(Nairmāṇikakāya)*

Having thus presented the third *kāya [sāmbhogikakāya],* the fourth *[kāya]* is taught, the body of manifestation(s) *(nairmāṇikakāya)*, which [appears] in common to all ordinary beings:

"The embodiment of the Sage in his manifestation(s) *(nairmāṇika-kāya)* is that through which he impartially carries out diverse benefits for the world. It is uninterrupted for as long as the existence [of the world]" (*AA* v. 8.33).

That which, through forms such as Śākyamuni's, carries out the desired benefit of beings in all realms of the universe equally for as long as cyclic existence *(saṃsāra)* lasts, is the manifestation body of the Buddha, the Bhagavan. It is uninterrupted because of its continuousness.[78]

All Activities Ascribed to the Body of Dharmas Consisting of Gnosis

Thus have the three [conventional] *kāya*s been presented, which are produced from the force of meditational practice, whose [ultimate] nature is the essence body *(svābhāvikakāya)*, and which, by being [different] cognitive objects for Buddhas, [bodhisattvas], *[śrāvaka*s*],* etc., are designated in dependence on [Buddha's] gnosis *(jñānam)*, etc. Conventionally the gnosis alone carries out the activities through its generation of manifestations as *sāmbhogikakāya*, etc. Thus, the activities for trainees through [those] manifestations, which occur based upon the power of that [gnosis], belong to the *dharmakāya* [consisting of gnosis]. With this sense, it is said [*AA* vv. 8.34–40]:

"Likewise, it is agreed, its activity *(karma)* is uninterrupted for as long as cyclic existence lasts: the activity that pacifies the states of rebirth, that establishes [beings] in the fourfold means of collecting [disciples], that establishes *(niveśanaṃ)* them in the comprehension of affliction and purification, in the proper nature of the welfare of beings, and in the six perfections, that establishes them in the Buddha path, in emptiness with respect to the primordial nature, in nonduality, in conventional symbolization *(saṃkete)*, in nonperception, and in the maturing of embodied beings, that establishes them in the bodhisattva path, in preventing adherence [to things], in the attainment of enlightenment *(bodhi)*, in the purity of a Buddha's realm, in definite destiny, that establishes them in the welfare of limitless beings, in the excellence of attending upon and devoting oneself to the Buddhas, in the limbs of enlightenment, in the nonwastefulness of deeds *(karma)*, and in the vision of the truths, that establishes them in the elimination of false views, in the method of [ascertaining] the baselessness of those [views], in purification and its accompanying accumulation, in the knowledge of nondistinction between conditioned and unconditioned, and that establishes them [finally] in nirvāṇa.

"This is regarded as the twenty-seven-fold activity of the *dharmakāya*."[79]

At this point, Haribhadra explains each of the twenty-seven types of activity listed in those verses. After explicating each of the twenty-seven types, he concludes his commentary on *AA* chapter 8 with the words:

> Thus, it is agreed, like the *dharmakāya* [consisting of gnosis], its twenty-seven-fold activity [operates] for as long as cyclic existence lasts.[80]

We noted in chapter 8 above that *AA* vv. 8.33–8.34, which lead into the rest of the verses, read straightforwardly in Sanskrit as a description of *nairmāṇikakāya* with its activity. If the verses are read together, which is of course how they appear in the *AA*, this is clear. Here they are together:

> [*AA* v. 8.33:] The embodiment of the Sage in his manifestation(s) *(nairmāṇikakāya)* is that through which he impartially carries out diverse benefits for the world. It is uninterrupted for as long as the existence [of the world].
>
> [*AA* v. 8.34:] Likewise, it is agreed, its activity *(karma)* is uninterrupted for as long as cyclic existence lasts: the activity that pacifies the states of rebirth, that establishes [beings] in the fourfold means of collecting [disciples].

The antecedent of "its activity" in v. 8.34 is clearly the *nairmāṇikakāya* of v. 8.33. Ārya Vimuktisena's (and our) three-*kāya* interpretation of *AA* 8 accords with this.[81] It was an established pattern in Yogācāra buddhology contemporaneous to the composition of the *AA* to identify a Buddha's extensive activity with *nairmāṇikakāya*,[82] and Ārya Vimuktisena, seeing *AA* 8 for the Yogācāra-*Prajñāpāramitāsūtra* mapping that it was, saw that Yogācāra pattern in them. He therefore accurately read *AA* vv. 8.1–8.11 as explication of *svābhāvikakāya*, vv. 8.12–8.32 as explication of *sāmbhogikakāya*, and vv. 8.33–8.40 as explication of *nairmāṇikakāya*. He saw how vv. 8.1, 8.12, and 8.33 linked the Yogācāra *svābhāvikakāya*, *sāmbhogikakāya*, and *nairmāṇikakāya* to their corresponding *Prajñāpāramitāsūtra* passages, and how the other verses delineated the content of those passages in relation to Yogācāra buddhology.

With respect to the section translated above, then, Ārya Vimuktisena recognized that *AA* verse 8.33 linked the Yogācāra *nairmāṇikakāya* to *PP*-sūtra passage 8.5's description of enlightened activities, and that vv. 8.34–8.40 delineated those very activities. He also saw accurately how the final half-verse of *AA* chapter 8, v. 8.40b, brings the entire chapter on Buddhahood to its conclusion by referring the reader back to its chapter title and overall subject matter: resultant *dharmakāya*. Verse 8.40b does this by ascribing the twenty-seven-fold activity of *nairmāṇikakāya* to the resultant *dharmakāya* in which it and all other topics of the chapter are situated. In Ārya Vimuktisena's accurate interpretation, then, *AA* vv. 8.34–8.40 inclusive were teaching the *nairmāṇikakāya*'s enlightened activity as agent of resultant *dharmakāya*. The *AA* was not (as Haribhadra claimed) newly positing a fourth *kāya*, a "body of dharmas consisting of gnosis" as a conditioned basis of activity. The concern to sort the unconditioned from the conditioned in Buddhahood, to solve the paradox of nonabiding nirvāṇa through logic, was Haribhadra's, not that of the *AA*'s author, and not Ārya Vimuktisena's.[83]

Haribhadra's logical project, then, dictated his new interpretation of those verses. Because he was primarily concerned to identify a distinct conditioned basis within Buddhahood for its conditioned activities and manifestations, he read that concern into the *AA*'s apposition of the terms *dharmakāya* and "activity" *(kāritra, karma)* in *AA* vv. 1.17 and 8.40. Wherever the phrase "*dharmakāya* with its activity" appeared, he wanted to interpret it as an ontological stipulation that the conditioned activity of the Buddha rests upon a conditioned basis within his attainment: a body of dharmas consisting of conditioned consciousnesses and mental factors: the very *dharmakāya* consisting of gnosis *(jñānātmaka dharmakāya)* that he read into *AA* 8 as a fourth *kāya*.

Again, if vv. 8.33 and 8.34 were read together as they appear in the *AA* (making *nairmāṇikakāya* in verse 8.33 the antecedent of "its activity" in verse 8.34 and hence all following verses), Ārya Vimuktisena's interpretation would appear obviously correct. Therefore, the first thing Haribhadra had to do was to separate those two verses, to make a distance between them in which to insert his perspective, in the hope that his readers would then project his perspective into the following verses. Therefore, immediately after his explanation of verse 8.33 above on *nairmāṇikakāya*, he presents again his rationale for positing a *dharmakāya* consisting of gnosis as the conditioned basis for enlightened activity:

> Thus have the three [conventional] *kāya*s been presented, which are produced from the force of meditational practice, whose [ultimate] nature is the essence body *(svābhāvikakāya)*, and which, by being [different] cognitive objects for Buddhas, [bodhisattvas], *[śrāvakas]*, etc., are designated in dependence on [Buddha's] gnosis *(jñānam)*, etc. Conventionally the gnosis alone carries out the activities through its generation of manifestations as *sāmbhogikakāya*, etc. Thus, the activities for trainees through [those] manifestations, which occur based upon the power of that [gnosis],

belong to the *dharmakāya* [consisting of gnosis]. With this sense, it is said [*AA* v. 8.34]:

"Likewise, it is agreed, its activity *(karma)* is uninterrupted for as long as cyclic existence lasts. . . . [84]

He reiterates that *svābhāvikakāya* is the ultimate nature of all other *kāyas*, their emptiness (which is unconditioned). The activities are carried out by conditioned manifestations. The source of the activity, then, must not be the manifestations themselves *(sāmbhogikakāya* and *nairmāṇikakāya)*, but the conditioned gnosis that must give rise to them: *jñānātmaka dharmakāya*. In other words, he repeats his earlier inference of a *kāya* logically separate from *svābhāvikakāya* (as conventional truth is distinct from ultimate truth), conditioned (while *svābhāvikakāya* is unconditioned), and causally and epistemologically distinct from *sāmbhogikakāya* and *nairmāṇikakāya* (being the conventional object only of Buddhas). Only then does he let the reader read verse 8.34: "Likewise, it is agreed, its activity is uninterrupted for as long as cyclic existence lasts. . . ." He has made the antecedent of the phrase "its activity" into the *dharmakāya* consisting of gnosis that he has just explained.

Haribhadra closes his remarks at the end of the chapter with the statement: "Thus, it is agreed, like the *dharmakāya*, its twenty-seven-fold activity [operates] for as long as cyclic existence lasts *(ā saṃsāram)*." This makes vv. 8.34–8.40 into a teaching on the activity of Buddhahood as it is based on the *dharmakāya* of gnosis. The phrase Haribhadra uses here, "for as long as cyclic existence lasts," echoes back from his comments on v. 8.11 above. There the phrase was specifically used to characterize Buddha's gnosis, even in its momentary nature, as unceasing, and hence, as the conditioned basis for unceasing, pervasive activity. Again, he has brilliantly woven his own logical construction into the verses of the *AA*.

10.7 Concluding Remarks

It is worth reviewing the historical circumstances which prepared the way for Haribhadra's buddhology. The *AA*'s eighth chapter, as we have seen, was a unique product created by mapping the three-*kāya* theory of Yogācāra onto the *Large PP Sūtra*. *AA* chapter 8, therefore, naturally became the basis of later controversy, for it could not be read easily as a simple expression of either of the traditions from which it was composed. It was constrained by its textual basis in the *PP* sūtra to characterize Buddhahood in ways never previously done in the Mahāyāna traditions of its time. In its definition of the *svābhāvikakāya*, for example, it gave the collection of undefiled dharmas a central position, which the Yogācāra tradition had not done. In its definition of *sāmbhogikakāya*, the marks and signs were given a new prominent position. And it made the extensive activities (described at great length in the *PP* sūtra) into one of four fundamental aspects of Buddhahood, also a new formulation.

Ārya Vimuktisena managed an accurate interpretation of the chapter by paying careful attention to both of the textual traditions out of which it had been composed. But from Haribhadra's eighth-century viewpoint, *AA* chapter 8's emphasis on the collection of undefiled dharmas and on activity as a primary category of Buddhahood was best understood through his new four-*kāya* analysis. This analysis was intended to logically sort out the conditioned aspects of Buddhahood (the undefiled dharmas, gnosis) from the unconditioned aspects (emptiness), and thereby to account for the activity of Buddhahood in the conditioned world. In other words, it was intended to make logical sense of the concept of nonabiding nirvāṇa, which had become normative for late Indian Mahāyāna, according to which Buddhahood was paradoxically both beyond the conditioned world (unconditioned) and active within it (conditioned). Since the *AA*'s unique mode of expression gave a prominent place both to the undefiled dharmas and to the activity of Buddhahood, it served as the perfect textual basis for Haribhadra's logical agenda.

Haribhadra's four-*kāya* interpretation of the *AA*, then, represented his application of the logic and Madhyamaka thought of his time to the textual material of the *AA*. As a product of late-eighth-century Buddhist logic and Madhyamaka analysis, it comprised a new theory of Buddhahood within the Indian Mahāyāna traditions of sūtra and śāstra. But, because his theory was embedded within his interpretation of the *AA*, some later Indian and Tibetan scholars saw the theory and the *AA* itself as one. Thus, those who later accepted his four-*kāya* theory in India and Tibet could not recognize it as a new historical development. In their view, Haribhadra's four-*kāya* analysis just represented an accurate interpretation of the *AA*, a text of the highest authority, authored by Maitreya himself. And an accurate interpretation of what Maitreya had said centuries earlier could not be understood to be a new theory.[85]

It appears, however, that it took some time before Haribhadra's interpretation of *AA* 8 became accepted in India. But because Haribhadra's *AA* commentaries (his *Āloka* and *Sphuṭārthā*) as a whole were so clear, in-depth, and masterful, he was soon generally acknowledged as the greatest Indian *AA* commentator, and his interpretations of the entire *AA*, including its eighth chapter, became increasingly influential in late Indian Buddhism and even more influential in Tibet. Eventually in Tibet, Haribhadra's *Sphuṭārthā* was accepted as the fundamental manual for study of the *AA*, and the most significant Tibetan *AA* commentators, even those who did not agree with all of Haribhadra's views, composed their treatises as subcommentaries to his *Sphuṭārthā*.[86]

11
Responses by Indian Scholars to Haribhadra's Four Buddha Bodies

It is not my purpose here to summarize the content of all other Indian commentaries on *Abhisamayālaṃkāra* chapter 8. Several of them deserve a careful study, and perhaps a monograph, in their own right. In this chapter I will briefly outline those Indian Buddhist reactions to Haribhadra's interpretation of *AA* 8 that became most important within late Indian and Tibetan Buddhism. Of all the *AA* commentaries mentioned below, only Ratnākaraśānti's *Sāratamā* is extant in Sanskrit. The other commentaries by Buddhajñānapāda, Dharmamitra, Prajñākaramati, Buddhaśrījñāna, Kumāraśrībhadra, Ratnākaraśānti, and Abhayākaragupta, although composed in Sanskrit, are presently extant only in their Tibetan translation in the Tibetan canon.

11.1 Buddhajñānapāda

The *Saṃcaya-gāthā-pañjikā*, a commentary on the *Abhisamayālaṃkāra*, is ascribed to a Buddhaśrījñāna and is extant only in the Tibetan canon (Pk 5196, Toh. 3798). The same author is identified by Tibetan historians Bu ston and 'Gos lo tsa ba as "Buddhajñānapāda," who is said to be an important disciple of Haribhadra's, which would date him to the late eighth century. Reputed to be the founder of the Jñānapāda lineage of the Guhyasamāja tradition, he was recognized in Tibet as a foremost Vajrayāna master.[1]

Buddhajñānapāda's commentary interprets the *Abhisamayālaṃkāra* by relating each of its sections to corresponding passages of the *Ratnaguṇa-saṃcaya-gāthā*, a versified version of the *Prajñāpāramitāsūtra* closely associated with the version in 8,000 verses. Although Haribhadra himself had also composed a commentary on the *Ratnaguṇa-saṃcaya-gāthā-sūtra* (Pk 5190), he did not relate that sūtra specifically to the *Abhisamayālaṃkāra*. If Buddhajñānapāda was indeed Haribhadra's student, it makes sense that he followed his teacher in attempting to relate the *Abhisamayālaṃkāra* to yet another version of the *Prajñāpāramitāsūtra*, other than the 25,000-verse version upon which it had been based, but closely associated with the version to which his teacher had related it (the version in 8,000 verses that is the basis for Haribhadra's *Abhisamayālaṃkāra-Āloka*). The section of Buddhajñānapāda's *Saṃcaya-gāthā-pañjikā* that corresponds to *AA* chapter 8 is of special interest to us. For if Buddhajñānapāda was Haribhadra's disciple, what he says about *AA* chapter 8 becomes historically significant. Does his own commentary accord with his reputed teacher's four-*kāya* formulation, or not?

Interestingly, it does not. In Buddhajñānapāda's interpretation of *AA* chapter 8, there are again three, not four *kāya*s. In addition, Buddhjñānapāda's understanding of those three *kāya*s draws directly upon the Yogācāra gnoseology and tripartite structure of soteriology originally formative of the three-*kāya* doctrine.

Buddhajñānapāda aligns the topics of *AA* chapter 8 line by line to a passage near the end of the *Ratnaguṇa-saṃcaya-gāthā-prajñāpāramitā-sūtra*. The sūtra passage in question follows a section that describes how a bodhisattva fulfills all six of the perfections that comprise the path to Buddhahood. Having completed the path, the bodhisattva attains its fruit, the attainment of a Buddha, described as follows:

1. He [as a Buddha] attains the purity of the field and the purity of [its] beings.
2. He also attains the lineage of the Buddha(s), the lineage of the Dharma,
3. And likewise the lineage of the Sangha.
4. He attains all dharmas.[2]

Although this *sūtra* passage has no actual historical-textual relation to the *Abhisamayālaṃkāra*, Buddhajñānapāda develops an ingenious way to relate it to the *AA*'s eighth chapter by referring back to the threefold Yogācāra structure of ultimate transformation into the three *kāya*s of Buddhahood. The basis of transformation comprises the eight Yogācāra consciousnesses, divided into three groups: (1) the substratum consciousness in which all karmic imprints are stored *(ālaya-vijñāna)*, (2) defiled consciousness *(kliṣṭa-manas,* the aspect of mind that fantasizes a self with subject-object dichotomy) together with mental consciousness *(manovijñāna)*, and (3) the other five sense-consciousnesses. The result of transformation consists of the four Buddha gnoses, also divided into three groups, which are then identified with the three *kāya*s in line with the Yogācāra system:

1. Ultimate transformation of the substratum consciousness = a Buddha's mirror gnosis *(ādarśa-jñāna)* = *svābhāvikakāya* (embodiment of Buddhahood in its essence).

2. Ultimate transformation of defiled and mental consciousnesses = a Buddha's gnoses of sameness and thorough inspection *(samatā-jñāna, pratyavekṣā-jñāna)* = *sāmbhogikakāya* (embodiment of Buddhahood in its communal enjoyment of the dharma).

3. Ultimate transformation of the other five sense consciousnesses = a Buddha's gnosis that accomplishes activities *(kṛtyānuṣṭhāna-jñāna)* = *nairmāṇikakāya* (embodiment of Buddhahood in its limitless manifestations).[3]

Let us look closely at Buddhajñānapāda's ingenious way of drawing direct correspondences between each of the three *kāya*s of *Abhisamayālaṃkāra* chapter 8, the lines of the sūtra passage quoted above, and the tripartite structure of the Yogācāra system of transformation.[4]

Buddhajñānapāda first identifies the subject matter of *Abhisamayālaṃkāra* chapter 8 as *dharmakāya*, the final result of the bodhisattva path, "whose identity is the fulfillment of perfect benefit for self and others." His use of *dharmakāya* carries its inclusive sense, encompassing all qualities of Buddhahood and all of its *kāyas*.[5] He then quotes the *AA*'s table of contents verse 1.17, which summarizes *AA* 8 by naming *dharmakāya* (in its inclusive sense) as the subject and title of the chapter and listing the three *kāya*s with enlightened activity as its four aspects.[6]

Next, he aligns the three *kāya*s, viewed as products of ultimate transformation, with lines of the sūtra passage quoted above. He begins by quoting the first line of the passage: "He [as a Buddha] attains the purity of the field and the purity of [its] beings."

This line, he says, expresses the *svābhāvikakāya* of a Buddha, which is to be understood as the outcome of ultimate transformation number (1) above. In this line, Buddhajñānapāda interprets "field" as the objective pole of cognition and "beings" as the subjective pole. Understanding both as dualistic appearances that emerge from the substratum consciousness *(ālayavijñāna)*, he interprets their "purity" as the ultimate transformation of that very consciousness. This, he says, is the mirror gnosis of the Buddhas *(ādarśa-jñāna);* and that (in line with the Yogācāra understanding) is *svābhāvikakāya.* He etymologizes the latter term accordingly: "[T]he embodiment [of Buddhahood] in its *essence (svābhāvikakāya)* is the nature of mirror gnosis, since that is ever the one nonconceptual *essence (svabhāva)* of the Bhagavans" (emphasis mine).

The second line of the sūtra passage says: "He also attains the lineage of the Buddha(s), the lineage of the dharma. . . ."

Buddhajñānapāda identifies "lineage of the Buddha(s)" as a reference to the Buddhas' gnosis of sameness *(samatā-jñāna)*, the result of ultimate transformation of the defiled consciousness *(kliṣṭa-manas)*, whose characteristic is great love and compassion. As the nature of method and wisdom, it is the substantial cause of all the Buddhas, hence "lineage of Buddha(s)." He identifies "lineage of the dharma" as a reference to the Buddhas' gnosis of thorough inspection *(pratyavekṣā-jñāna)*, the result of ultimate transformation of the mental, conceptualizing consciousness *(manovijñāna)*, possessed of unimaginable retained knowledge *(dhāraṇī)*. As the very nature of the scriptural teachings and their realization, it is the cause of dharma transmission, hence "lineage of dharma." He identifies the Buddha gnoses of sameness and thorough inspection together (in line with long-established Yogācāra understanding) as *sāmbhogikakāya*, etymologizing the latter term accordingly: "These two gnoses are the embodiment [of Buddhahood] in communal enjoyment *(sāmbhogikakāya)* because sameness and thorough inspection are the basis for enjoyment of dharma precisely as it has been realized." Thus, the sūtra line above, he says, expresses the *sāmbhogikakāya* of a Buddha understood as the outcome of ultimate transformation number (2) above.

Buddhajñānapāda interprets the next line of the sūtra as expression of *nairmāṇikakāya*, understood as the outcome of ultimate transformation number (3) above: "And likewise the lineage of the Sangha."

"Lineage of Sangha," he says, refers to the gnosis that accomplishes enlightened activity *(kṛtyānuṣṭhāna-jñāna)*, the result of ultimate transformation of the five external sense consciousnesses, which have become utterly purified by long practice of the perfection of enthusiastic perseverance. That gnosis, he says, is the substantial cause of all the enlightened activities of a Buddha, which thereby establishes the Sangha, the spiritual community, hence "lineage of Sangha." And because it is also the basis for all the varied manifestations that carry out a Buddha's activity, it is the "embodiment [of Buddhahood] in its manifestations *(nairmāṇikakāya)*."

Thus, Buddhajñānapāda's exegesis of *AA* 8 woven into the first three lines of the *Saṃcaya-gāthā sūtra* passage replicates the Yogācāra tripartite structure of transformation into the three *kāyas*.[7] Finally, he explains the fourth and final line of the passage so as to indicate how all three *kāyas* and their qualities are fully encompassed within Buddhahood (resultant *dharmakāya*) through one all-encompassing gnosis. The fourth line is: "He attains all dharmas."

Buddhajñānapāda explains it as follows: "Through the force of [the Buddha's] gnosis of the purified realm of universal thusness *(dharmadhātu-viśuddhi-jñāna)*, he comprehends all phenomena, both defiled and purified, in their undifferentiated nature."[8] This remark seems to express the nondual Yogācāra type of gnoseology that underlay the original formulation of three *kāyas*, and that was adopted by Ārya Vimuktisena and Candrakīrti in their delineations of three *kāyas*. Nondual awareness of the undifferentiated, ultimate nature of all phenomena, "knowledge of all in one taste," is itself the first of the three *kāyas*, *svābhāvikakāya/dharmakāya;* its all-pervasive engagement in the world takes expression in its manifestations as *sāmbhogikakāya* and *nairmāṇikakāya* .[9]

If Buddhajñānapāda was in fact Haribhadra's disciple, the fact that he relied upon the Yogācāra tripartite structure of ultimate transformation to reaffirm the prior three-*kāya* interpretation of *AA* 8, instead of following Haribhadra's four-*kāya* interpretation, might be significant. There would be two possibilities: either

Buddhajñānapāda composed his commentary prior to Haribhadra's composition of his main *AA* treatises (the *Sphuṭārthā* and the *Āloka*), or he composed it after them. If Buddhajñānapāda composed his commentary before Haribhadra's, it might indicate that the three-*kāya* interpretation of *AA* 8 that he followed was still the prevailing view right up to Haribhadra's time, further indicating that Haribhadra's four-*kāya* interpretation was indeed innovative. If Buddhajñānapāda composed his commentary after Haribhadra's main *AA* treatises (as seems most likely, the former being the reputed disciple of the latter), it may be even more significant. For it would mean that Haribhadra's own disciple parted company with him on his interpretation of *AA* chapter 8. And this could indicate that Haribhadra's interpretation of *AA* 8 was not immediately accepted among Indian scholars; that it took some time for it to become established and accepted. Further evidence for the latter possibility is provided by Dharmamitra's *AA* commentary, to which we now turn.[10]

11.2 Dharmamitra

Dharmamitra was the author of an important subcommentary on Haribhadra's *Sphuṭārthā* called the *Prasphuṭapadā* (Pk 5194). Dharmamitra's text is meant to serve as an explanation of Haribhadra's interpretations, to clarify Haribhadra's views, rather than as an independent treatise. He is thought to have lived in roughly the same period as Haribhadra (late eighth century to early ninth century), and this would mean that his *Prasphuṭapadā* may represent the first scholarly attempt in Indian Buddhism to comprehend and explain Haribhadra's new interpretation of *AA* 8.[11] For the most part, Dharmamitra did an incisive job. But his commentary is especially revealing in certain places where he completely misinterprets what Haribhadra had said. It seems that Haribhadra's interpretation of *AA* 8 was too novel for Dharmamitra to easily comprehend. And this gives further indication of the innovativeness of Haribhadra's views. Dharmamitra's remarks also give us an indication of how unsettled Mahāyāna buddhology was in the late eighth and early ninth centuries when he lived. Many different interpretations of *AA* 8 and the Buddha *kāyas* were evidently debated in his time, with Haribhadra's four-*kāya* explanation not immediately accepted.

Dharmamitra correctly identifies Haribhadra's primary distinction between the essence body *(svābhāvikakāya)* and the body of dharmas consisting of gnosis *(jñānātmaka dharmakāya)* to be a logical distinction between a thing (*dharmī,* the undefiled dharmas) and the essential quality of that thing (*dharmatā,* their emptiness). He also correctly points out that *jñānātmaka dharmakāya*, *sāmbhogikakāya*, and *nairmāṇikakāya* were distinguished by Haribhadra by reference to the types of persons for whom each conventionally appears: Buddhas, bodhisattvas, and the spiritually less mature respectively (although, unlike Haribhadra, Dharmamitra explicitly identifies *sāmbhogikakāya* as a conventional appearance for bodhisattvas of the tenth bodhisattva stage alone). Dharmamitra makes many interesting buddhological and gnoseological observations throughout his commentary that deserve careful study, but it is not our present purpose to discuss them at length.

In one particularly interesting portion of his commentary, Dharmamitra becomes utterly confused about Haribhadra's meaning. Haribhadra, in his *Sphuṭārthā*, after discussing the twenty-one types of undefiled dharmas that he identified as a fourth Buddha *kāya (jñānātmaka dharmakāya)* presented a hypothetical debate between himself and those who followed Ārya Vimuktisena's three-*kāya* interpretation of the *AA*. Haribhadra's argument runs as follows.

> 1. According to some, the body of dharmas [*dharmakāya* of verse 8.6] is explained to consist of all those [undefiled] dharmas, the factors fostering enlightenment, etc., the gnoses free from discursive conceptualization that are the transformed [result] of fundamental transformation *(āśrayaparāvṛtti)*.
>
> 2. But, others explain as follows:
>
> *AA* v. 8.1: "The essence body *(svābhāvika-kāya)* of the Sage: Its identity is the primordial nature *(prakṛti)* of the undefiled dharmas that are obtained in utter purity," literally means that, having accepted the supramundane undefiled dharmas [of the Buddha], the essence body's identity is their actual intrinsic nature *(prakṛti)*: nonarisingness *(anutpādatā)*. And that [essence body] is also *dharmatākāya* [body of reality], which is indicated by [the concluding word of v. 8.6]: *dharmakāya*, through the elision of the particle that indicates abstract nouns *(-tā)*.
>
> Then they [raise this hypothetical] question: "What are the undefiled [Buddha] dharmas, the intrinsic nature of which is the *dharma[tā]kāya*'s identity?" And they understand *[AA]* verses [8.2–8.6] [as the answer to that]: "The factors that foster enlightenment. . . ." etc.
>
> 3. Others [reply that] [Buddha's] nondual primary consciousnesses and mental factors *(citta-caittā)*, which are the transformed [result] of fundamental transformation *(āśrayaparāvṛtti)*, are what carry out [his] effective actions *(artha-kriyā)* of teaching the dharma, etc., by generating appearances that have specific purposes in conformance to the conventional [perspectives] of yogi [trainees]. How, according to those [whose assertion is immediately above], are those [primary consciousnesses and mental factors] that must surely be accepted, included [within the *kāyas*]?
>
> 4. Some, [criticizing] the four-*kāya* explanation, cite [*AA* v. 1.17, the table of contents for *AA* chapter 8]: "*svābhāvika*, *sasāmbhoga*, and *nairmāṇika* as well, / *dharmakāya*, with activity, is proclaimed as fourfold."

In [this] verse, [they claim,] since the word *dharmakāya* does not follow immediately after the word *svābhāvika*, there are only three *kāyas*.

5. But others [reply] that, on the strength of the intention just demonstrated, for felicity in the construction of the verse, and for the sake of associating activity with the gnosis alone, it was stated thusly. Therefore [the *AA*] is consistent with all the statements in other quarters *(pradeś-āntara)*[12] that the *kāyas* are fourfold.[13]

As explained in chapter 10, section 5 above, Haribhadra's own four-*kāya* view is expressed in paragraphs (1), (3), and (5) above, and the three-*kāya* view of Ārya Vimuktisena and his followers is expressed in paragraphs (2) and (4). In paragraph (1), Haribhadra states his own view that the collection of undefiled dharmas comprises what he has identified as the second of four *kāyas* taught in *AA* 8 *(jñānātmaka dharmakāya)*. In paragraph (2), Haribhadra paraphrases (and subtly misrepresents) Ārya Vimuktisena's commentary, where Ārya Vimuktisena includes the undefiled dharmas as Buddha's gnosis within the *svābhāvikakāya* itself. In paragraph (3), Haribhadra rebuts Ārya Vimuktisena (or rather his misrepresentation of Ārya Vimuktisena), by indicating that the undefiled dharmas as conditioned sense consciousnesses and mental factors can not be included in any of Ārya Vimuktisena's three *kāyas*. In paragraph (4), Haribhadra presents a hypothetical philological objection by a three-*kāya* proponent against his own four-*kāya* interpretation of the *AA*. And in paragraph (5), he defends his interpretation against the objection on both philological and logical grounds.[14]

Dharmamitra utterly misconstrued this key set of paragraphs. He did not realize that in them Haribhadra was presenting a debate, in the form of alternating arguments and responses by two parties. Dharmamitra mistakenly thought that four different interpretations of *AA* 8 (comprising four different theories of Buddhahood) were presented in those paragraphs. And he thought that Haribhadra set forth all four interpretations as equally valid, without rejecting any of them![15]

Dharmamitra, not recognizing that paragraph (1) in fact represents Haribhadra's own view, says that it represents the view of Jñānacandra and others who asserted the oneness and indivisibility of *svābhāvikakāya* and *dharmakāya*.[16] This is an astounding way to interpret that paragraph, which says nothing of the kind. Jñānacandra was the Yogācāra author of the *Kāyatrayāvatara-śāstra-vṛtti* (Pk 5291), a commentary on Nāgamitra's *Kāyatrayāvatāra-mukha-śāstra*, which teaches three *kāyas* in a traditional Yogācāra form.[17]

Even more astounding is Dharmamitra's interpretation of paragraph (2) above. Anyone who has read Ārya Vimuktisena's commentary on the *AA* can readily see that paragraph (2) represents Haribhadra's paraphrase of Ārya Vimuktisena. It appears that Dharmamitra never read Ārya Vimuktisena, for he completely misunderstands paragraph (2) to comprise a synopsis by Haribhadra of his own four-*kāya* explanation of the *AA*![18] Again, this is amazing, since the paragraph says nothing of the kind. Importantly, Dharmamitra at this point attributes Haribhadra's own four-*kāya* explanation of the *AA* not to Haribhadra himself, but to Haribhadra's teacher, Vairocana. Haribhadra himself never actually chose one interpretation over another, says Dharmamitra![19]

Dharmamitra's understanding of paragraph (3) above is equally inaccurate, but fascinating. He thinks a third interpretive position is being set forth, in which some scholar rejects the four-*kāya* explanation as it was presented in paragraph (2). According to this scholar (in Dharmamitra's explanation), the four-*kāya* explanation of the *AA* is wrong to identify *svābhāvikakāya* (i.e., the emptiness of the other three *kāyas*) as a separate *kāya* in itself. For then the body of dharma-gnoses *(jñānātmaka dharmakāya)*, being one entity with that unconditioned emptiness, would become unconditioned and could not be the basis of conditioned activity in the world. Or, if the body of dharma-gnoses *(jñānātmaka dharmakāya)* is accepted, the *svābhāvikakāya*, as one entity with it, would have to be conditioned, which is impossible since it is unconditioned emptiness. Therefore, this scholar concludes, there are only three *kāyas:* the *jñānātmaka dharmakāya*, the *sāmbhogikakāya*, and the *nairmāṇikakāya*. Ultimately, all three are nonarising, i.e., empty, but that emptiness is not to be identified as a separate *kāya.*[20] Again, this is a fantastic misrepresentation of what Haribhadra said in paragraph (3) above. But it is quite possible that it does represent the view of some early-ninth-century scholars with whom Dharmamitra was acquainted, and it is therefore of real historical interest.

His interpretation of paragraph (4) is equally fascinating. He believes that it represents a fourth interpretation of the *AA* and a fourth theory on Buddhahood. In paragraph (4), he says, another scholar is claiming that since *svābhāvikakāya* and *dharmakāya* in *AA* v. 1.17 (and vv. 8.1–8.6) are synonyms, there are only three *kāyas*. But this is to be understood in a special way. The *svābhāvikakāya/dharmakāya*, referred to as Samāntabhadra, is just the innate, pure luminosity of gnosis *(jñāna)* that conforms to the realm of dharma *(dharmadhātu*, universal thusness). It is beyond the perception and conceptualization of ordinary beings. But through the force of a Buddha's prayers prior to his enlightenment, Buddhahood communicates itself to trainees as possessed of the collection of undefiled dharmas (even though it is beyond any such conceptualization). Similarly, *sāmbhogikakāya* and *nairmāṇikakāya* appear to trainees through the force of previous prayers to help beings, but are also not the way Buddhahood actually exists. Therefore, in reality, a Buddha has only one *kāya*, pure luminosity—*dharmadhātu*, which is beyond the ken of non-Buddhas. But that one *kāya* is explained in Mahāyāna texts as three in order to make Buddhahood accessible to the conceptual categories of ordinary beings: *svābhāvikakāya/dharmakāya* being conceptualized by us in terms of the collection of undefiled dharmas, *sāmbhogikakāya* and *nairmāṇikakāya.*[21] Again, this is not what paragraph (4) says. But it may represent a particular way of articulating the three-*kāya* doctrine in Dharmamitra's place and time.

Paragraph (5) above, on the other hand, Dharmamitra gets right. He accurately understands it to be a reiteration of the four-*kāya* interpretation of *AA* 8.

Near the beginning of his commentary on *AA* 8, Dharmamitra makes interesting comments about the scholarly reaction in his time to Haribhadra's four-*kāya* explanation. Some scholars, says Dharmamitra, claimed that Haribhadra himself accepted just three *kāya*s (even though he taught four in his *Sphuṭārthā*) because, they said, he taught only three in another of his texts. Dharmamitra does not name that other text, but it was probably the revised version of the 25,000-verse *PP* sūtra, which is attributed to Haribhadra as editor in the colophon of its Tibetan translation.[22] Those scholars, says Dharmamitra, believed that Haribhadra taught four *kāyas* in his *Sphuṭārthā*, not as his own view, but as an expression of the view of his teacher, Vairocana. His own view was the teaching of three *kāyas*.[23] Dharmamitra gives a fascinating rebuttal to this. He refers to Haribhadra's comments in the five paragraphs of his *Sphuṭārthā* quoted above. He says that in those paragraphs, Haribhadra sets forth a number of different methods for dividing and enumerating the *kāya*s of Buddhahood, and that he rejects none of them. Therefore, concludes Dharmamitra, Haribhadra's own view is that all those different systems for enumerating the *kāya*s are acceptable. This means that, according to Dharmamitra, Haribhadra personally accepts every one of the positions which Dharmamitra read into paragraphs (1) through (5) above.

Since Dharmamitra is the first subcommentator on Haribhadra's *Sphuṭārthā* and lived close to the time of Haribhadra, his remarks are historically illuminating. According to Dharmamitra, at least some scholars of his time repudiated Haribhadra's four-*kāya* interpretation of *AA* 8. Some, in fact, apparently out of respect for Haribhadra, reaffirmed the traditional three-*kāya* interpretation by claiming that Haribhadra himself accepted it. Haribhadra's four-*kāya* explanations of the *AA*, they said, constituted a show of respect for his own teacher Vairocana, but did not represent his own views. This indicates that Haribhadra's new interpretation of *AA* 8 was unacceptable to some scholars who otherwise respected him and probably accepted his views on other matters. Haribhadra's interpretation of *AA* 8 was initially the source of real controversy.

It is also interesting that Dharmamitra understands Haribhadra to set forth four different multiple-*kāya* theories in his *Sphuṭārthā* paragraphs (1) through (5) above, and to accept them all equally. This could indicate that all four theories were alive in Indian Buddhism at the time, and that Dharmamitra found it inconceivable that Haribhadra would reject some of them. It appears that a plethora of buddhological theories abounded, and that Haribhadra's own four-*kāya* theory and interpretation of the *AA* initially appeared as just one more addition to the set of plausible theories. Dharmamitra's misinterpretation of the paragraphs above indicates that he did not even realize that Haribhadra's four-*kāya* interpretation involved a critique and refutation of earlier interpretations of the *AA*. It seems, then, that the initial reaction to Haribhadra's analysis of the *kāyas* was somewhat confused.

Unlike Dharmamitra, who lived so close to Haribhadra's time, several later Indian commentators understood Haribhadra, recognized his four-*kāya* analysis as logically superior to what had come before, and accepted his four-*kāya* interpretation of the *AA*. Among them were Prajñākaramati (ca. 950–1000 C.E.), Buddhaśrījñāna (ca. 1200 C.E., not to be confused with Buddhajñānapāda above), and Kumāraśrībhadra (date uncertain). It appears, then, that it took some time before Haribhadra's four-*kāya* theory and interpretation of the *AA* gained credibility and became somewhat established in late Indian Buddhism, but eventually it did.

11.3 Prajñākaramati, Buddhaśrijñāna, and Kumāraśrībhadra

Prajñākaramati's commentary on the *Abhisamayālaṃkāra* is the *Abhisamayālaṃkāra-vṛtti-piṇḍārtha* (Pk 5193). It is extremely brief, and, concerning *AA* 8, very incisive. Prajñākaramati summarizes Haribhadra's four-*kāya* interpretation of the chapter, and adds to it in an interesting way. He says that the subject matter of the *AA*'s eighth chapter is the resultant realization of enlightenment *(abhisamaya-phalam),* which is *dharmakāya* (i.e., the inclusive *dharmakāya*, which includes all *kāyas*). That realization of enlightenment has two aspects: benefit for oneself, and benefit for others.

Enlightened benefit for oneself, he says, includes both the ultimate truth *(paramārtha satya)* and the conventional truth *(saṃvṛti satya)* of Buddhahood. The ultimate truth of Buddhahood, its emptiness, is *svābhāvikakāya*. The conventional truth of Buddhahood is of three types, differentiated according to the three types of persons who conventionally perceive it: Buddhas, bodhisattvas, and *śrāvakas*, etc. This makes four *kāyas*, one of which is ultimate truth, and the other three of which are conventional truth.

Enlightened "benefit for others," on the other hand, is Buddhahood's salvific activity for other beings, which helps them reach enlightenment stage by stage.[24] Prajñākaramati's two-truth analysis issuing in four *kāyas* follows Haribhadra precisely. But his way of dividing the topics of *AA* 8 into "self-benefit" and "other-benefit," is, to my knowledge, unique.

Buddhaśrijñāna's *Abhisamayālaṃkāra* commentary is entitled *Prajñāpradipāvali* (Pk 5198). His comments on *AA* 8 comprise a brief, accurate summary of Haribhadra's interpretation, and, in one place, seem to echo Prajñākaramati's two-truth summary of the four *kāyas*.[25]

Kumāraśrībhadra's *Abhisamayālaṃkāra* commentary is entitled *Prajñāpāramitā-piṇḍārtha* (Pk 5195). Although Kumāraśrībhadra adopts Haribhadra's four-*kāya* interpretation of *AA* 8, he gives it a slightly different twist. Haribhadra had identified the collection of undefiled dharmas as a *kāya* distinct from the *svābhāvika-*

kāya. He had identified *svābhāvikakāya* as twofold: the innate purity (emptiness) of those dharmas and their adventitious purity (their freedom from mental obstructions). Kumāraśrībhadra identifies the *svābhāvikakāya* simply as the innate purity of Buddhahood, i.e., its emptiness alone. And he identifies the second *kāya*, which he calls *dharmakāya*, with the undefiled dharmas in their purity from adventitious stain. He agrees with Haribhadra, then, that the activity of Buddhahood is to be associated with the gnosis *dharmakāya* alone, conditioned gnosis being the source for enlightened activity in the conditioned world. Kumāraśrībhadra makes very clear Haribhadra's basic argument for positing a body of dharma-gnoses *(jñānātmaka dharmakāya)* distinct from *svābhāvikakāya*. He says that the *svābhāvikakāya* (as emptiness which is unconditioned) has no activity. Therefore, a fourth *kāya* must be posited to serve as the very source for conditioned activity, that being the body of dharma-gnoses *(jñānātmaka dharmakāya)*. And that means that *AA* 1.17, the table of contents for *AA* 8, does indeed teach four *kāya*s, with the words *dharmakāya* and "activity" intentionally connected in the verse as conditioned basis for activity and activity respectively.[26]

Later, in Tibet, the scholarly founder of the dGe lugs pa sect, Tsong kha pa blo bzang grags pa (1357-1419), followed in the footsteps of these late Indian scholars by adopting Haribhardra's four-*kāya* analysis of *AA* 8.

11.4 Ratnākaraśānti

In various Tibetan sources, Ratnākaraśānti (ca. 1000 C.E.) is reported to have been a student of Nāropā and a teacher of Atiśa and 'Brog mi, to have presided over Vikramaśila monastery, and also there to have been a contemporary of Jñānaśrīmitra, Ratnakīrti, Prajñākaramati, and Vāgīśvarakīrti.[27] He was certainly one of the preeminent teachers of late Indian Buddhism. In his writing, he relied predominantly upon Yogācāra texts, while viewing their ultimate import as harmonious with the Mādhyamika.[28]

Ratnākaraśānti wrote two commentaries on the *Abhisamayālaṃkāra*: the *Śuddhamatī* (Pk 5199, extant only in Tibetan translation) and the *Sāratamā* (Pk 5200, extant in Sanskrit and Tibetan). Of the two, the *Śuddhamatī* is most important for our purposes, for in its eighth chapter Ratnākaraśānti forcefully critiques and rejects Haribhadra's four-*kāya* theory and interpretation of *AA* 8, arguing for a return to the traditional three-*kāya* understanding in line with Ārya Vimuktisena's interpretation.

Why did Ratnākaraśānti feel compelled to forcefully reject Haribhadra's four-*kāya* interpretation of the *Abhisamayālaṃkāra*? What was the fundamental concern motivating his critique? Included among his criticisms are a call to return to Ārya Vimuktisena's three-*kāya* interpretation of key verses. Was his primary concern, then, philological, the accurate linguistic understanding of the verses of an inviolate, sacred text?

Ratnākaraśānti's fundamental concern was clearly not philological. There are several reasons for inferring this. First, both Ratnākaraśānti and his contemporary Ratnakīrti[29] inserted into their commentaries an altered version of a key *AA* verse so as to remove all linguistic grounds for Haribhadra's interpretation of it. The verse is *AA* 1.17, which Ārya Vimuktisena had understood to teach three *kāyas* and Haribhadra had reinterpreted to teach four. Ratnākaraśānti is known to have altered a number of other *AA* verses in his commentaries, making it likely, perhaps, that he was the one who made the change.[30] His critique of Haribhadra indicates that he was quite familiar with the commentaries of both Haribhadra and Ārya Vimuktisena, in which the original form of that verse appears.

This indicates that Ratnākaraśānti's principal concern was not philological accuracy per se. Rather, his concern was to return scholarly attention to the perspective on Buddhahood that he believed the *AA* to communicate. His intention was probably something like this: If a Sanskrit verse, in light of Haribhadra's reinterpretation, had come to be seen as plausibly ambiguous, then an altered form of it should be inserted to remove that ambiguity, in order to clarify anew the view of the original text that Ārya Vimuktisena had accurately captured and that Haribhadra's hermeneutic sleight of hand had now obscured.

In the case of Ratnākaraśānti, and Abhayākaragupta as well, this understanding of his intention is supported by the breadth of his critique. His arguments on the meaning of the *Abhisamayālaṃkāra* are not restricted to the meanings of individual verses. Rather, his arguments are made by reference to the textual tradition of Mahāyāna Buddhism taken as a whole, inclusive of the corpus of sūtras, tantras, and their commentaries. Ratnākaraśānti clearly interpreted the *Abhisamayālaṃkāra*'s chapter on Buddhahood not in philological isolation, but as one of many texts that express a perspective on Buddhahood that he viewed as fundamental to Mahāyāna Buddhism as a whole, a perspective that differed in some basic way from Haribhadra's as revealed in his comments on *AA* 8.

What was wrong with Haribhadra's perspective on Buddhahood, and what perspective did Ratnākaraśānti seek to defend against it? We noted in chapter 10 some of the concerns which Haribhadra had shared with other eighth-century Madhyamaka logicians. One such concern was to critique Yogācāra ontology from a Madhyamaka point of view. Another was to apply the analytic-inferential methods of Buddhist logic to old Buddhist problems. Several Mādhyamikas of the eighth century, such as Jñānagarbha and Śāntarakṣita, used the categories of Buddhist logic previously developed by Dharmakīrti to relativize and appropriate elements of Yogācāra tradition into a Madhyamaka system of thought and praxis. Haribhadra followed them in this, but went further in specifically targeting the Yogācāra ontology of Buddhahood itself for Madhyamaka critique, seeking thereby also to resolve the apparent paradox of nonabiding nirvāṇa that had been embedded in the Yogācāra *trikāya* model: Buddhahood as something transcendent, beyond conditions *(svābhāvikakāya)* yet active in the conditioned world *(sāmbhogikakāya, nairmāṇikakāya).*

A question that M. David Eckel raised may now help us to clarify the reason for Ratnākaraśānti's sharp response to Haribhadra. Eckel raised the question with reference to Jñānagarbha, a Mādhyamika logician of Haribhadra's period: "What we need is . . . a principle that will make clear how far Jñānagarbha can go in adopting Dharmakīrti's point of view without compromising the integrity of his own Madhyamaka method."[31] To paraphrase: In his use of logic, how might a Mādhyamika logician undermine the ultimate point of Mādhyamika, which is to deconstruct all appearances to emptiness, including all logical categories? Eckel does not mention any scholars after Jñānagarbha who may have criticized him for this. If we shift the attention to Haribhadra, however, Ratnākaraśānti seems to provide us with an example of just this kind of criticism.

However, Ratnākaraśānti, who relied heavily upon Yogācāra treatises and viewed them as ultimately consistent with Mādhyamika, would have rephrased Eckel's question in a more general form: "Has Haribhadra, in his application of logic and Abhidharma to Buddhahood, compromised the integrity of *Mahāyāna Buddhism as a whole* by assuming that human reason per se can understand an object that is far beyond its capacity to know?" Ratnākaraśānti's response to this question is an emphatic yes. Where then, in Ratnākaraśānti's view, did Haribhadra go wrong? In two interrelated ways: (1) In Ratnākaraśānti's view, Haribhadra tried to take human thought farther than it can go in comprehending Buddhahood. It is one thing to use logic to deconstruct the conceptual structures that hide reality and thereby obstruct attainment of Buddhahood. But it is another thing to use logic to try to infer the actual content of a Buddha's realization, something that is beyond the capacity of human thought to comprehend. Haribhadra, in doing the latter, subtly undercut the practice that actually leads to Buddhahood: entry into nondual, nonconceptual awareness. (2) In Ratnākaraśānti's view, then, Haribhadra did not understand the very status of the text he was interpreting. The *Abhisamayālaṃkāra*'s teaching on Buddhahood, like other authoritative teachings by Buddhas and great bodhisattvas, is not an expression of a system of human thought, but the revelation of a nondual awareness that transcends human thought. We will now examine Ratnākaraśānti's *AA* commentary, *Śuddhamatī*, on each of these points.

The *Śuddhamatī*'s eighth chapter concerns *AA* chapter 8 on *dharmakāya-phalaṃ*, Buddhahood as the result of the path in its totality. Ratnākaraśānti begins by citing *AA* v. 1.17 as the table of contents for the chapter. Because Haribhadra sought ambiguity in that verse to support his four-*kāya* interpretation, Ratnākaraśānti apparently rewrote the verse to make it less ambiguous than its original. The original verse of *AA* 1.17 in unaltered form, translated from the Sanskrit, reads as follows:

"In its essence, with its enjoyment, and in its manifestation(s) as well, / Embodiment of dharma *(dharmakāya)*, with its activity, is proclaimed as fourfold."

Haribhadra managed to impute enough ambiguity onto this verse to claim that it taught four *kāya*s, with the word *dharmakāya* referring to a fourth *kāya* (a body of dharma-gnoses) rather than to the title of the chapter (resultant *dharmakāya*; see chapter 8, section 2, above). In order to remove all such possible ambiguity, Ratnākaraśānti adopted an altered form of the verse of *AA* 1.17, translated as follows:

> In its essence, with its enjoyment, and in its manifestation(s) [it has] three aspects. With its activity, [then,] the embodiment of dharma *(dharmakāya)* is proclaimed as fourfold.[32]

This separates out the first three key terms as a set, a threefold embodiment of Buddhahood: in its own essence, in its enjoyment of dharma, and in its manifestations. Since, in this reading, it is Buddhahood itself that is designated (resultant) *dharmakāya*, any possibility of interpreting the latter term as a fourth *kāya*, as Haribhadra had done, has been precluded.

Ratnākaraśānti then quotes *AA* vv. 8.1–8.6, identifying them together as the *AA*'s teaching on the first of the three *kāya*s, *svābhāvikakāya*. (the embodiment of Buddhahood, resultant *dharmakāya*, in its essence). He defines *svābhāvikakāya*, drawing upon the language of the *AA*, as "the *dharmatā* essence *(svabhāva)* of the undefiled dharmas utterly pure." That *dharmatā* essence is the embodiment of Buddhahood in its essence *(svābhāvikakāya)*, says Ratnākaraśānti, because the undefiled dharma-gnoses, "by having become completely free of adventitious error, abide in their primordial nature *(rang bzhin, prakṛti)*." In support of this, Ratnākaraśānti quotes the *Mahāyānasūtrālaṃkāra* (*MSA* v. 9.2c–d):

> Purged of all obstructions, omniscience is attained.
> Like a chest of jewels thrown open is Buddhahood declared.[33]

By that description, and by choosing this particular metaphor of the *Mahāyānasūtrālaṃkāra* as an example, Ratnākaraśānti points to an important Yogācāra model of ultimate transformation: enlightenment as the manifestation of the mind's own innate purity *(citta-prakṛti-viśuddhi)*. According to this model, the minds of sentient beings are innately a luminous purity that is adventitiously covered by affective and cognitive obscurations, the obscurations of dualistic thought. The path to enlightenment is a process of purification, and enlightenment is fully attained by the elimination of those obscurations, revealing the primordial, luminous, and pure essence of mind that was always there. Then the mind "abides in its own primordial nature," and enlightenment is attained like "a chest of jewels thrown open," the jewel-like purity of mind, always present, now revealed.

Ratnākaraśānti then follows Ārya Vimuktisena's understanding on *AA* vv. 8.2–8.6, which list the undefiled dharmas and end "thus is *dharmakāya* denominated." Echoing Ārya Vimuktisena, Ratnākaraśānti etymologizes *dharmakāya* in verse 8.6 as *dharma[tā]kāya*, (embodiment of *dharmatā*, embodiment of the real nature of dharmas). This makes the entire set of *AA* vv. 8.1–8.6 an explanation of one Buddha *kāya*, called *svābhāvikakāya* (embodiment of Buddhahood in its essence) in verse 8.1 and *dharma[tā]kāya* (embodiment of the real nature of dharmas) in verse 8.6. Thus the Buddha dharmas listed in the verses are understood as a conceptually differentiated, phenomenal description of what in actuality is a Buddha's nondual awareness of the undifferentiated real nature of dharmas *(dharmatā)*. It does not, as Haribhadra would have it, constitute a separate component of Buddhahood, a fourth *kāya*. Whereas Haribhadra had called for a return to an Abhidharma-like understanding of *dharmakāya* in *AA* v. 8.6 (Buddha's realization as a collection of pure phenomena, a "body of dharmas"), Ratnākaraśānti, following upon Ārya Vimuktisena, calls for a return to the distinctly Mahāyāna understanding of *dharmakāya* formulated in *Prajñāpāramitā* sūtras: as "embodiment of *the real nature* of dharmas *(dharmatā)*" (not body, collection, of dharmas per se).[34]

Having previously cited a Yogācāra source *(Mahāyānasūtrālaṃkāra)* Ratnākaraśānti now quotes from the *Kāyatraya-stotra* (Praise to the three *kāya*s, Pk 2015), a text attributed to Nāgārjuna in the Tibetan canon, which describes *dharmakāya (= svābhāvikakāya)* as beyond singularity or multiplicity. The implication here is that *svābhāvikakāya/dharmakāya*, though sometimes designated in terms of a multiplicity of dharma qualities, is actually beyond any such multiplicity or conceptual differentiation. This replicates part of the pattern of Nāgārjuna's other hymns to Buddhahood *(Catuḥstava)*. And if the citation was intended as a Mādhyamika authority, authorization has now been provided from both principal schools of Mahāyāna for the perspective on Buddhahood that Ratnākaraśānti defends.[35]

Next, Ratnākaraśānti explicitly entertains Haribhadra's four-*kāya* interpretation of the *Abhisamayālaṃkāra*, in which the collection of undefiled dharmas is identified as a fourth *kāya*, a body of dharma-gnoses *(jñānātmaka dharmakāya)*. He also cites Haribhadra's remark that such a four-*kāya* interpretation of the *AA* accords with the four *kāya*s of "the other system."[36] Ratnākaraśānti assumes that Haribhadra means by "other system" the Mantranāya, the system of Buddhist practice based upon the tantras.[37] He then critiques and utterly rejects Haribhadra's theory and interpretation of the *AA*.

Importantly, Ratnākaraśānti's continuing critique does not center upon the words of the *Abhisamayālaṃkāra*, but portrays Haribhadra's four-*kāya* theory as an independent creation alien to the spirit of the entire Mahāyāna Buddhist tradition. He does so by asserting first that Haribhadra's four *kāya*s were never taught in any Mahāyāna sūtras, and then that Haribhadra's delineation of four *kāya*s is also alien to the tantric system (which teaches four *kāya*s but not in line with Haribhadra's understanding). This would mean that Haribhadra's perspective on Buddhahood has no place in either of the two systems of Mahāyāna Buddhist theory and practice (Pāramitāyāna, the Mahāyāna system based on sūtras and śāstras such as the *Abhisamayālaṃkāra*, and Mantranāya, the Mahāyāna system based on the tantras).

First, Ratnākaraśānti points out that three *kāyas*, and not four, are taught in the Mahāyāna sūtras. He says that the *Large Prajñāpāramitā Sūtra* teaches specifically three (not four) *kāyas* in its passages 8.1 through 8.3.[38] Ratnākaraśānti assumed that those three passages were common to the large recensions of the *Prajñāpāramitāsūtra*. In fact, they are found only in the revised version of the 25,000-verse *Prajñāpāramitā* sūtra *(rP)*, the version that contains topics of the *AA* inserted as titles for corresponding sūtra passages. The three passages to which he refers are *rP* 8.1–8.3, which are titled: "Svābhāvikakāya," "Sāmbhogikakāya," and "Nairmāṇikakāya," respectively.[39] In any case, the point Ratnākaraśānti is making is that while four *kāyas* are taught nowhere in the *Prajñāpāramitā* sūtras, three are explicitly taught in those *PP* passages. And, he says, only three (not four) *kāyas* are taught in other sūtras.[40] Ratnākaraśānti is saying that only three (not four) *kāyas* are taught in the Mahāyāna sūtras that form the sole scriptural basis for the system of Mahāyāna Buddhism (Pāramitāyāna) of which the *Abhisamayālaṃkāra* is a part.

Although, as noted earlier, Yogācāra treatises such as the *Mahāyānasūtrālaṃkāra (MSA)* first formalized the theory of three *kāyas* and denominated them, the basis for the *trikāya* concept certainly did lie in prior Mahāyāna sūtras: in their descriptions of the nonconceptual realization of *dharmakāya*, exalted Buddha forms of pure realms, and limitless manifestations of Buddhahood (see chapters 4 and 5 above). But by the time of Ratnākaraśānti (ca. 1000 C.E.), a number of later Mahāyāna sūtras (following the lead of treatises such as the *MSA)* did explicitly teach the three *kāyas* that the treatises had formalized: e.g., *rP* passages 8.1–8.3, the *Trikāyasūtra*, the *Suvarṇaprabhāsasūtra*, and the *Buddhabhūmisūtra*. Ratnākaraśānti, of course, did not have an historical-critical apparatus available to him, and therefore assumed that the three *kāyas* taught in texts such as the *Mahāyānasūtrālaṃkāra* (and *Abhisamayālaṃkāra*) were based upon a prior formalization of them in earlier sūtras. And since, in the traditional view, sūtras are the word of the Buddha, he quotes *rP* as the word of the Buddha without realizing that its passages on the three *kāyas* (8.1–8.3) were added many centuries after the historical Buddha (possibly based upon Ārya Vimuktisena's own *AA* commentary, see chapter 7 above).

Nevertheless, Ratnākaraśānti was correct that Haribhadra's understanding of four *kāyas* is foreign to the Mahāyāna sūtras. As noted in chapter 10, the very concept of four such *kāyas* was developed by Haribhadra based upon an eighth-century logical Mādhyamika agenda that was not operative in the composition of Mahāyāna sūtras of earlier periods. Therefore, in spite of his lack of historical-criticism, Ratnākaraśānti's basic claim that the perspective from which Haribhadra posited a four-*kāya* interpretation was not a part of Pāramitāyāna Buddhism until Haribhadra's period would appear to be correct.

Having established that Haribhadra's four-*kāya* understanding was not a part of nontantric Mahāyāna Buddhism, Ratnākaraśānti also rejects it as a part of the tantric system. Buddhist tantrism centers on the notion of the practitioners patterning their practice on the result that they are seeking to attain. In Buddhist tantric practice, then, the various components of the practitioner's psychophysical basis are brought into homologous alignment with components of Buddhahood, the ultimate result of the practice. Within tantric texts and commentaries, components of Buddhahood were schematically differentiated that would correspond on the result level (Buddhahood) to an equal number of psychophysical components of the basal level (the level of the not-yet-enlightened yogi/nī). This produced, in tantric systems, four- or fivefold patterns of Buddhahood, often described in terms of *kāya*s or gnoses *(jñānas)* that were aligned with four or five aspects of the basal level (e.g., the four or five principal subtle energy centers *(cakras)* of Indian physiology, the five *skandhas*, the fourfold basis of body, speech, mind and their unity, the five principal passions, etc.).[41]

As discussed in chapters 4 and 5 above, however, the three-*kāya* pattern of the early Yogācāra tradition (which surfaced in the *AA*'s eighth chapter) was formulated on a different basis. The three-*kāya* pattern represented an extrapolation from Yogācāra meditational practice and gnoseology to the concept of *svābhāvikakāya*, which was related to sūtra descriptions of *dharmakāya* (as nonconceptual gnosis), exalted Buddhas (identified as *sāmbhogikakāya*), and limitless manifestations (identified as *nairmāṇikakāya*).

Ratnākaraśānti's interpretation of *AA* chapter 8 agreed with Ārya Vimuktisena's. He understood the *AA* to be another three-*kāya* text that stood in the same (nontantric) tradition of yoga and gnoseology that had generated the three-*kāya* theory in texts such as the *Mahāyānasūtrālaṃkāra*. As a tantric scholar himself, he also recognized that the four *kāya*s taught in tantric texts derived from a very different theoretical and practical context than the three *kāya*s taught in the *Mahāyānasūtrālaṃkāra* or *Abhisamayālaṃkāra*. Therefore, Ratnākaraśānti criticizes Haribhadra for suggesting that his four-*kāya* understanding of the *AA* also conformed to tantric tradition. Ratnākaraśānti says that the four *kāya*s in tantra refer to the "body, speech and mind" of enlightenment, together with the "activity" *(karma)* or the "sameness" *(samatā)* of those three dimensions. This, he says, is a different theoretical formulation than Haribhadra's four-*kāya* reading of the *AA*, generated by a different context and purpose.[42] In Ratnākaraśānti's view, the teaching of three *kāya*s in the *AA* had its own special significance (related to the kind of yogic practice and gnoseology discussed in chapters 4 and 5 above), and this was only obfuscated by Haribhadra's attempt to read four *kāya*s into the text.[43]

Having finished giving his reasons that Haribhadra's perspective is not rooted in any part of the Mahāyāna textual tradition, Ratnākaraśānti turns next to Haribhadra's central inferential argument for positing four *kāyas*. Haribhadra, in his *Sphuṭārthā*, had asked how, if only three *kāyas* were accepted, are the consciousnesses and mental factors comprising a Buddha's undefiled dharmas to be included among those three *kāyas*? Haribhadra's interpretation of *svābhāvikakāya* made it just the emptiness of those dharmas, emptiness being permanent and unconditioned. Therefore, the Buddha dharmas themselves as impermanent, conditioned conventional existents could not be *svābhāvikakāya*. The Buddha dharmas could also not be identified with *sāmbhogikakāya* or *nairmāṇikakāya*, for, according to Haribhadra, they are the conditioned cause for such manifestations. Therefore, Haribhadra concluded, a fourth *kāya* consisting of the set of undefiled dharmas must be posited, and it is reasonable to understand the *AA* as teaching that fourth *kāya*.[44]

Ratnākaraśānti turns to this inferential argument of Haribhadra's: "In which of the [three] *kāyas*," Ratnākaraśānti asks, "are those [undefiled] dharmas to be included?" "In the *svābhāvika[kāya]*," he answers, "because they, by having become free of all error, are precisely the luminous quintessence, the *dharmatā*."[45] He continues: "The differentiation of their characteristics, being done in accord with the causal state, is conventional."[46]

Ratnākaraśānti is saying that, at the actual attainment of full enlightenment, a Buddha's awareness is no longer constructed of conditioned, conceptually differentiated dharmas, consciousnesses and mental factors. At Buddhahood, all dualistic conceptualization that had obscured the innate, luminous purity of the mind has been removed. What remains is the "luminous quintessence, the *dharmatā*"; nondual awareness of the real, undifferentiated nature of all phenomena, universal thusness, free from conceptual constructs of cognitive subject and cognitive object, free also from the conceptual construction of "undefiled dharmas." It is this nondual, nonconceptual gnosis of thusness, says Ratnākaraśānti, that is precisely *svābhāvikakāya*.[47]

The list of undefiled dharmas, then, says Ratnākaraśānti, is ascribed to a Buddha only conventionally, i.e., from a phenomenal point of view, based on the qualities a bodhisattva cultivates on the path prior to attainment of Buddhahood ("the causal state"). The qualities a bodhisattva cultivates provide the best conceptual understanding non-Buddhas might have of what Buddhahood might be like. For that reason, in scriptures and treatises such as the *Abhisamayālaṃkāra*, they provide a useful phenomenal description of Buddhahood, a description operative for non-Buddhas who are restricted to dualistic, conceptual understanding of something that they have not yet realized. But that description is not to be confused with a Buddha's own understanding. In reality, a Buddha's awareness is cognitively one with *dharmatā,* which is beyond all such conceptual differentiation.[48] The undefiled dharmas, then, are not a *kāya* distinct from *svābhāvikakāya*, as Haribhadra claimed. They are precisely *svābhāvikakāya* itself as it comes under the purview of ordinary beings and is designated for their phenomenal point of view.

We are now ready to return to the questions and points made at the beginning of this section. What perspective on Buddhahood was Ratnākaraśānti defending against Haribhadra's? Ratnākaraśānti wanted to return to the perspective on Buddhahood expressed in the seminal *trikāya* formulations of Yogācāra tradition (also upheld by several Mādhyamikas prior to Haribhadra), according to which Buddhahood in its own actual awareness *(svābhāvikakāya/dharmakāya)* can only be described in broad terms pointing to a nonduality beyond conceptual understanding, accurately comprehended only through its attainment by the nondual meditational praxis of Mahāyāna traditions. Haribhadra, as an eighth century Mādhyamika logician seeking new conceptual clarity on Buddhahood in its transcendent and immanent dimensions, believed he could infer the content of a Buddha's awareness through analogy to the cognitive makeup of non-Buddhas, based on Abhidharmic descriptions of the qualities of the path as reflected in the *Abhisamayālaṃkāra.* But in Ratnākaraśānti's view, the actual content of a Buddha's realization cannot be accurately comprehended through inference based on analogy to the cognitive makeup of non-Buddhas. And to believe otherwise is to overestimate the value and capacity of human reason vis-à-vis enlightenment. It is to value conceptual thought over nondual meditational praxis as the means to comprehend enlightenment.

Here lies, perhaps, the real point at issue. In Ratnākaraśānti's view, Haribhadra had mistaken the "finger pointing at the moon" for the moon. He had projected his own conceptual construction onto Buddhahood (the list of undefiled dharmas) and then, by positing that as a separate *kāya,* had mistaken it for the actual content of a Buddha's mind. But to overestimate the capacity of human reason to comprehend enlightenment in this way is to underestimate the real means to achieve it: entry into nonduality. The core realization of Buddhahood is a nondual gnosis, a direct yogic experience, not a conceptualization.

What function, then, do conceptualizations and descriptions of Buddhahood serve? If scholars are to discuss Buddhahood as the ultimate objective of a practice that people are actually trying to accomplish, how is it to be described so the practice to achieve it can be furthered rather than undercut? If scholars inadvertently mistake their own conceptualizations of Buddhahood for Buddhahood itself, and believe they have thereby comprehended it, they subtly point others away from the nonconceptual entry into nondual awareness that actually constitutes it. In Ratnākaraśānti's view, Haribhadra's analytic-inferential hermeneutic had not clarified the nature of enlightenment at all. It had just created a further obstacle to its actual realization.

Yogācāra formulations (adopted by some Mādhyamikas prior to Haribhadra) assumed that the proper position from which to understand Buddhahood was the position of nondual yogic experience itself. Authentic scriptures that expressed that authentic understanding were therefore to be given great weight. Here lies the reason for Ratnākaraśānti's prominent quotes from the *Prajñāpāramitā* sūtras, the *Mahāyānasūtrālaṃkāra*, and *Trikāyastotra* above. He believed that such authoritative scriptures and treatises, because they were taught by realized beings (Buddha, Maitreya, or prior great saints like Nāgārjuna), expressed the actual nondual essence of Buddhahood as well as it could be expressed in language. Logical inference alone, independent of yogic experience, could not. Thus, Ratnākaraśānti disagreed with Haribhadra too on the very status of the sacred text they were interpreting. For Ratnākaraśānti, the *Abhisamayālaṃkāra*'s teaching on Buddhahood, like other authoritative teachings by Buddhas and great bodhisattvas, is not an expression of a system of human thought, but the revelation of a nondual awareness that is beyond human thought. Enlightenment points to itself through the language of the text. Autonomous inference, such as Haribhadra's, about what enlightenment must be like from the perspective of human reason only further obscures what it can not comprehend.

Haribhadra's analysis commenced from a very different set of assumptions conditioned by his period in Indian Buddhist history. Eighth-century Buddhism was reveling in the power of logic to clarify and resolve problems that had previously seemed unsolvable. From Haribhadra's perspective, the ontological absolutism of the Yogācāra formulation of Buddhahood could be corrected through a Madhyamaka analysis that identified the essence of Buddhahood *(svābhāvikakāya)* precisely as its emptiness of ontological ultimacy. At the same time, he believed, by applying the Madhyamaka analysis of two truths, the paradox of nonabiding nirvāṇa could be clarified and resolved, and a firm philosophical foundation established for a Buddha's pervasive activity in the conditioned world.

In his analysis, however, Haribhadra distinguished the Buddha dharmas as a separate *kāya* from *svābhāvikakāya* precisely because of their supposed, distinct conventional appearance to Buddhas (while *sāmbhogikakāya* and *nairmāṇikakāya* were conventional appearances for non-Buddhas). This was no small matter. It implied that the set of undefiled dharmas literally constituted a Buddha's mind—that a Buddha conceptually distinguished that set as the content of his mind. According to Mahāyāna philosophy and yogic theory, conventional truth *(saṃvṛti satya)* comprises all phenomena that exist in a nexus of causal and conceptual construction, i.e., all things within the experiential world of ordinary beings (non-Buddhas). To ordinary beings, things appear to exist as though independent of such conceptual construction, as though self-existent. The yogis on Buddhist paths gradually learn to cognize all things within their experience as empty of such self-existence, as dependently originated *(pratītiya-samutpanna)*, arisen only in dependence on causes and conceptual construction. In Haribhadra's scheme, a Buddha's undefiled dharmas become a unique sort of conventional truth, for they would be the only conventional truth experienced directly by Buddhas alone. This would mean that, as conventional truth, they would have to be conceptually constructed by the Buddhas. But this runs counter to the entire earlier trend of Mahāyāna buddhology, according to which Buddhahood, in its own realization, has passed entirely beyond such conceptual construction.[49]

From Ratnākaraśānti's perspective, Haribhadra had become too mesmerized by his own logic. And Buddhahood was, in essence, a nondual yogic realization, not a logical construct. To mistake the actual nature of Buddhahood for one's concepts about it is to err grievously in the sacred purpose of scholarly exegesis. For it points sincere persons away from their goal, rather than toward it. The fierceness of Ratnākaraśānti's critique, I believe, stemmed from that very concern.[50]

11.5 Abhayākaragupta

Abhayākaragupta was a scholar at Vikramaśila monastery who lived about 1100 C.E. He is an important figure in late Indian Buddhism, in part because he wrote a masterful, encyclopedic treatise, called the *Munimatālaṃkāra* (extant only in Tibetan translation), in which he summarized the entire range of Mahāyāna praxis and buddhology through extensive reference to the traditions of *Prajñāpāramitā-Abhisamayālaṃkāra*, Mādhyamika and Yogācāra.[51] In the third chapter of this treatise, Abhayākaragupta explains the eight realizations *(abhisamayas)* of the *Abhisamayālaṃkāra*, and in one section, he focuses specifically on the eighth and final realization of the path, resultant *dharmakāya*, the subject matter of *AA* chapter 8.[52] It is this section to which we now turn.

Abhayākaragupta, in the beginning of his exposition on *AA* chapter 8, models his remarks on Ratnākaraśānti's *Śuddhamati*. Like Ratnākaraśānti, he quotes from a variety of sources within the sūtra/śāstra tradition of Mahāyāna Buddhism (Pāramitāyāna), to show that while three *kāyas* are taught in many scriptures of the highest authority, four *kāyas* are taught nowhere. Abhayākaragupta quotes from the revised version of the *Prajñāpāramitāsūtra* (passages 8.1–8.3 on the three *kāyas*), from the *Mahāyānasūtrālaṃkāra* (v. 9.65, which teaches three *kāyas* as the exhaustive expression of a Buddha's benefit for self and others), from the *Trikāyastotra* (which Abhayākaragupta ascribes to Nāgārjuna and which teaches the same three *kāyas* in a Mādhyamika mode of expression), and from Ārya Vimuktisena's *Abhisamayālaṃkāra-vṛtti* (which says *AA* chapter 8 is teaching the same three *kāyas*). Abhayākaragupta chooses a set of quotations which span the entire sūtra and śāstra tradition of nontantric Mahāyāna Buddhism: *Prajñāpāramitā-Abhisamayālaṃkāra*, Yogācāra, and Mādhyamika. Throughout, three (not four) *kāyas* are taught. He concludes that the four-*kāya* theory of Haribhadra (according to which the Buddha dharmas are distinguished from their emptiness and posited as a fourth *kāya*) was never a part of sūtra/śāstra (Pāramitāyāna) Buddhism until Haribhadra himself had imposed it. And as such, it is to be rejected.[53]

Having established that only three *kāyas* are taught in the *Pāramitāyāna* in general and the *Abhisamayālaṃkāra* in particular, he comments upon the first of those *kāyas*, the *svābhāvikakāya*. His remarks, again, are modeled in large part upon those of Ratnākaraśānti,[54] but carry a more specifically Madhyamaka mode of expression. Abhayākaragupta, explicating *AA* v. 8.1, says that the *svābhāvikakāya* is the nonarising and unconditioned essence of the undefiled dharmas obtained by the supramundane path; it is the lack of intrinsic existence of those dharmas freed from all conceptualization and discursive elaboration. Echoing both Ārya Vimuktisena and Ratnākaraśānti, he says the term *dharmakāya* of *AA* v. 8.6, means *dharma[tā]kāya* (embodiment of *dharmatā*), a synonym for the *svābhāvikakāya* of v. 8.1. In other words, *dharmakāya* of v. 8.6 does not, as Haribhadra had claimed, refer to a separate, fourth *kāya*. *Svābhāvikakāya (= dharma[tā]kāya)*, he says, by having passed beyond all conceptualization, thereby comprises a Buddha's personal nirvāṇa and supreme self-benefit. As the basis for manifestations of *sāmbhogikakāya* and *nairmāṇikakāya* that carry out vast activities for each being in accord with their precise karmic makeup, it is also pervasive.[55]

In this description, Abhayākaragupta uses Madhyamaka terminology to identify *svābhāvikakāya* more explicitly with emptiness *(śūnyatā)* than Ratnākaraśānti had done. He refers to it as the "the nonarising . . . essence," a common Madhyamaka expression for *śūnyatā*. Yet he also implies that *svābhāvikakāya* is gnosis as well, inclusive of the Buddha dharma-gnoses (in *AA* vv. 8.2–8.6) and the basis for pervasive activity. In fact Abhayākaragupta identifies *svābhāvikakāya* as both *śūnyatā* and gnosis together as one, and this becomes all the more explicit as he continues.

Like Ratnākaraśānti, Abhayākaragupta next poses the question central to Haribhadra's argument for four *kāyas*, in order to refute that argument: If only three *kāyas* are accepted, in which of them are the undefiled Buddha dharmas to be included? Responding to that question, Abhayākaragupta says:

> Precisely the *svābhāvika[kāya]*. For [the undefiled dharmas], by having become free of all cognitive obstructions and their propensities, are precisely the *dharmatā* possessed of the nature of non-self-existence.

He continues in Ratnākaraśānti's vein: "The differentiation of their characteristics, being done in accordance with the causal state, is conventional."[56]

Abhayākaragupta's first statement directly identifies the undefiled dharmas with *dharmatā*, the real nature of dharmas beyond all conceptual constructions of duality. The undefiled dharmas (gnosis), by having become fully purified of cognitive obstruction, *are dharmatā*, i.e., are indivisibly one with the real nature of things. By having become fully purified, gnosis is indivisible from emptiness within the perfected realization of ultimate truth *(paramārtha satya)*. Therefore, within the actual realization of a Buddha (which is *svābhāvikakāya*), no differentiation of dharmas and *dharmatā* is made. The list of undefiled dharmas, he says, is ascribed to a Buddha only conventionally, i.e., only from a phenomenal point of view, based on the different mental qualities that were possessed "in the causal state," the bodhisattva state prior to the attainment of Buddhahood.

Abhayākaragupta's message (similar to Ratnākaraśānti's) is that within a Buddha's own nondual realization (which is *svābhāvikakāya*) the undefiled dharmas are not distinguished in any way from their ultimate nature *(śūnyatā, dharmatā)*. Gnosis (undefiled dharmas) and emptiness are one. What then are a Buddha's undefiled dharmas? They are precisely the *svābhāvikakāya* as it is conceptualized and conventionally designated from the point of view of ordinary beings.

Abhayākaragupta then gives the quotations that Haribhadra had presented in his *Sphuṭārthā* and *Āloka* to support his theory of four *kāyas*. But Abhayākaragupta turns Haribhadra's own quotations against him:[57]

> Therefore it is said: "The nondistinction of what is discerned from the discernment is accepted," and "Precisely that which is a dependent arising you accept as emptiness." These serve as reasons to [establish] that *dharmāḥ* and [their] real nature *(dharmatā)* are not distinct from each other, which means *dharmāḥ* exist [only] conventionally. Therefore, it is by obtaining those [conventionally existent] illusion-like *dharmāḥ* that there does occur a comprehension, personally realized by the perfectly enlightened Buddhas alone, which is the *svābhāvikakāya*.[58]

Abhayākaragupta's point is close to that of Ratnākaraśānti, but his mode of expression here is more distinctively Madhyamaka. Like Ratnākaraśānti, Abhayākaragupta refutes Haribhadra's fourth *kāya* (consisting of the Buddha dharmas distinct from emptiness) by denying that any differentiation is made in a Buddha's own awareness between gnosis (the undefiled dharmas) and emptiness *(dharmatā)*. Ratnākaraśānti denied this differentiation based on the Yogācāra notion of the nonduality of subject and object, as it manifested in the revelation of the mind's innate luminosity at enlightenment. For Ratnākaraśānti, a Buddha's gnosis involved the full revelation of nonduality that no longer conceptually constructed "subject" versus "object," "gnosis" versus the *dharmatā*.

Abhayākaragupta's refutation of Haribhadra takes a more Madhyamaka mode of expression, focusing not just on the nondifference of subject and object *(grāhaka* and *grāhya)* but also on the nondifference of emptiness *(dharmatā)* and its conventionally existent locus *(dharma)*. Madhyamaka analysis focuses on a phenomenon and finds its emptiness of self-existence. The emptiness is referred to as *dharmatā*; the phenomenon that is the locus of that emptiness is referred to as *dharma* (or *dharmī*). Haribhadra had presented the quotes above ("The nondistinction . . ." and "Precisely that . . .") to show that although the undefiled dharmas and their emptiness *(dharmatā)* were the same in locus, they were distinguished conventionally, i.e., were separate for thought. Hence, the undefiled dharmas, as distinct from their emptiness, were to be posited as a separate, fourth *kāya*. Haribhadra intended his quotes to support that thesis.

Abhayākaragupta presents the same quotes to establish precisely the opposite thesis: that although ordinary beings distinguish the dharmas and *dharmatā* conventionally (by their conceptual thought), in reality they are one. Hence, a Buddha, whose realization is the perfect cognition of reality, knows them as one. Dharmas and *dharmatā* are only distinguished conventionally within the conceptual thought of non-Buddhas. Therefore, ordinary beings may understand the nondual realization of full enlightenment as the obtainment of the undefiled dharmas, and with reference to that, may conceptually distinguish a Buddha's gnosis from emptiness. But a Buddha's own realization conceptually constructs no such distinction.

Earlier, Abhayākaragupta had explicitly said (following Ārya Vimuktisena and Ratnākaraśānti) that the list of undefiled dharmas was a conventional (conceptual) differentiation of Buddhahood from a phenomenal point of view, which was based on the "causal state." At the end of the remarks above, he refers back to that, by indicating that a bodhisattva (in the causal state prior to Buddhahood) does indeed realize *svābhāvikakāya* by practicing and fully attaining the undefiled dharmas (as they are conventionally distinguished on the path to Buddhahood). But when the causal state, the path, has issued in the resultant state, the actual attainment of *svābhāvikakāya*, *dharmāḥ,* and their *dharmatā* are not differentiated. The *svābhāvikakāya* has left behind all such discursive conceptualization *(prapañca).*

Again, the basis upon which Haribhadra had distinguished a fourth *kāya* of dharma-gnoses *(jñānātmaka dharmakāya)* from *svābhāvikakāya* was the conventional appearance of the Buddhas dharmas, as distinct from their emptiness, to Buddha's own awareness. But such a distinction is a conceptual one, made precisely by ordinary beings, not by a Buddha. Hence, says Abhayākaragupta, *svābhāvikakāya/dharmakāya*, as it is realized by a Buddha (not by us), is undivided. To posit a fourth *kāya*, as Haribhadra did, is to assume that a Buddha conceptually distinguishes conventional from ultimate truth, and understands them separately much as we ordinary beings do. But our thought is not a Buddha's realization. Abhayākaragupta's point, like Ratnākaraśānti's, is that Haribhadra confused his own conception about Buddhahood for Buddhahood itself. While Ratnākaraśānti refuted Haribhadra's theory from a Yogācāra perspective, Abhayākaragupta made substantially the same refutation from a Madhyamaka perspective.

To provide authoritative Madhyamaka support for his view that Buddha's gnosis and emptiness are undifferentiated within his nondual realization, yet distinguished by us conventionally, Abhayākaragupta next paraphrases a portion of Candrakīrti's *Madhyamakāvatāra:*

> Likewise, it says in the *Madhyamakāvatāra*, "The nonarising [nature of phenomena] is thusness *(tathatā).* When the mind also becomes free from

> arising, it is as though it knows thusness, because it [the nonarising mind] depended upon its [thusness's] appearance *(ākāra)*. [In conventional understanding], when the mind takes on the appearance of some object, then it knows that object. Employing that conventional mode of expression, [we also say] it [the nonarising mind] knows [thusness]." Ācārya Candrakīrti taught this.[59]

The passage that Abhayākaragupta paraphrases here appears in Candrakīrti's explanation of Buddha's nondual gnosis. According to Candrakīrti, a Buddha's nonconceptual awareness consists of the "nonarising" of the mind as it conforms to "thatness" *(tattvam)*, the nonarising nature of things ("thatness" = "thusness," "emptiness"). Although traditionally it is said that a Buddha "knows" thatness, as if a Buddha's mind and its object were distinct, such a mode of expression is merely based upon conventional modes of thought and discourse. In ordinary discourse, says Candrakīrti, we say we know an object when our awareness appears in the image of that object. Similarly, a Buddha's mind, which has entered into the nonarising state conforming to the nonarising condition of thusness, is said by us to "know" thusness. But, says Candrakīrti, in reality, within a Buddha's realization of thusness, there is no knowing of anything, because both knower and known have become just "nonarisingness."[60]

Abhayākaragupta here draws support from Candrakīrti's gnoseology, according to which a Buddha's awareness is distinguished from thusness only within the conventional thought and discussion of ordinary beings, not within a Buddha's own realization. Abhayākaragupta's buddhology, like Candrakīrti's, conforms to the traditional three-*kāya* formulation that was centered on the *svābhāvikakāya/dharmakāya* as the undivided, nondual awareness of thusness. Though both Abhayākaragupta and Candrakīrti were Mādhyamikas, they saw nothing inconsistent in their buddhology conforming to the three-*kāya* structure as it was formulated in Yogācāra treatises. The ontological status of *svābhāvikakāya* was something some Mādhyamikas and Yogācāras might disagree upon. But the *svābhāvikakāya*'s own lack of conceptual differentiation into "gnosis" and "thusness" was something that, in the view of these scholars, was accepted by all Mahāyāna schools.[61]

It is for this reason, according to Abhayākaragupta, that a fourth *kāya* such as Haribhadra posited (consisting of Buddha dharma-gnoses distinct from thusness) was taught nowhere within sūtra/śāstra Mahāyāna Buddhism (Pāramitāyāna) until Haribhadra himself imposed it. Abhayākaragupta is in agreement with Ratnākaraśānti, then, that Haribhadra's fourth *kāya* was never a part of Pāramitāyāna.[62]

However, concerning the question of whether four *kāya*s similar to Haribhadra's were taught in tantric Buddhism (referred to as Mantranāya) Abhayākaragupta's position does not agree with Ratnākaraśānti's. Ratnākaraśānti had said that the four *kāya*s delineated by Haribhadra (posited by distinguishing gnosis from emptiness as a separate *kāya*) were not to be found in tantric Buddhism. The four *kāya*s of Mantranāya, said Ratnākaraśānti, were the body, speech, and mind of a Buddha together with their activity or their "sameness."[63]

Abhayākaragupta, on the other hand, affirms that a fourth *kāya* like Haribhadra's is indeed taught within tantric Buddhism. But, importantly, such a fourth *kāya* is posited in Mantranāya not (as Haribhadra had done) on the basis of a Buddha's *own* discrimination of gnosis from *dharmatā*, but on the basis of the tantric *trainees'* discrimination of gnosis from *dharmatā* for the purposes of their special practice. Abhayākaragupta says:

> Thus, a fourth *kāya*, a *kāya* [consisting] of [Buddha] dharmas, which conventionally appear out of the *dharmatā* while being one nature with it, referred to as *dharmakāya* and [posited by distinguishing] those *dharmāḥ* from the *dharmatā* that is their basis—[such a fourth *kāya*] is definitely not taught in the Pāramitāyāna.
>
> [However], in the Mantranāya [such a fourth *kāya*] is definitely taught as though it were separate from its *dharmatā*, because it is posited from the point of view of the trainees' discriminations. But in reality, there too [in Mantranāya] it is not separate. Therefore, sometimes [in the Mantranāya] *svābhāvikakāya* is expressed by the term *dharmakāya*, and sometimes *dharmakāya* is expressed by the term *svābhāvikakāya*. And sometimes the real nature of those two *kāyas* is expressed as the "union" *(yuganaddha)*, as the "embodiment of union" *(yuganaddhakāya)*, or as the "embodiment of the essence" *(svābhāvikakāya)*, since the pair of *dharma* and *dharmatā* are a unity: the latter being the very essence of the former and their actual nature being emptiness and compassion indivisible.[64]

Abhayākaragupta continues drawing distinctions between the *kāya* presentations of nontantric (Pāramitāyāna) and tantric Buddhism (Mantranāya), noting that tantric Buddhism conceptually divides Buddhahood again and again by reference to the perspective of trainees *(mos pa rnams)*, including schemes of five *kāyas*, etc.[65] He concludes by saying: "Therefore, Haribhadra's [interpretation of *AA* chapter 8] was a presentation of four *kāyas* drawn from other quarters [from the Mantranāya] which was out of context and inappropriate."[66]

Abhayākaragupta's understanding of what Haribhadra had done, therefore, significantly differs from Ratnākaraśānti's. In Ratnākaraśānti's view, Haribhadra had made up his theory of four *kāyas* himself and superimposed it upon the *Abhisamayālaṃkāra*. In Abhayākaragupta's view, Haribhadra had not made up his four-*kāya* theory independently. Rather, he had drawn that theory from tantric Buddhism, and then applied it inappropriately by reading it into the *Abhisamayālaṃkāra*, a nontantric text.

Such distinctions are made in the context of tantric practice so the trainees can imitate various aspects of Buddhahood as their practice. But those distinctions between gnosis and *dharmatā*, compassion and emptiness, etc. are made by tantric trainees who must conceptualize Buddhahood *prior* to achieving it. They are not made within a Buddha's own awareness. In fact, says Abhayākaragupta, in tantric theory too, upon the actual realization of Buddhahood, the conceptual distinction that trainees have drawn between gnosis (Buddha dharmas as a separate *dharmakāya*) and emptiness (*dharmatā* alone as a separate *svābhāvikakāya*) is erased. And this is expressed in tantric Buddhism precisely by the symbolization of resultant Buddhahood as a union *(yuganaddha)* in which all previously conceptualized distinctions between *dharma* and *dharmatā*, compassion and emptiness, saṃsāra and nirvāṇa, etc. are transcended.[67]

Thus, within the tantric system of Buddhism, says Abhayākaragupta, there is a purpose in provisionally distinguishing gnosis from *dharmatā* as part of the practice of trainees. This leads to four- and five-*kāya* schemes. But such schemes are not intended to serve as normative descriptions of Buddhahood in its own nondual realization, but as schemes for a tantric meditational practice that must conceptualize Buddhahood prior to achieving it.

Pāramitāyāna (the sūtra/śāstra system of Buddhism of which the *AA* is a part), unlike Mantranāya, is not centered on taking Buddhahood, as conceptualized by trainees, into the path of practice. The descriptions of Buddhahood per se found in Pāramitāyāna texts such as the *Mahāyānasūtrālaṃkāra*, *Mahāyānasaṃgraha*, and the *Abhisamayālaṃkāra* are themselves not schemes for yogic practice. They are normative descriptions of Buddhahood as the final outcome of such practice. They were intended to describe Buddhahood as personally realized by a Buddha *(svābhāvikakāya)*, and then as it manifests for non-Buddhas *(sāmbhogikakāya, nairmāṇikakāya)*. The three-*kāya* scheme of Pāramitāyāna centers on *svābhāvikakāya* as a realization that transcends all conceptual discrimination, including that which would separate gnosis from *dharmatā*, conventional from ultimate truth. This provides no basis within a Buddha's own awareness to distinguish a fourth *kāya* of gnosis separate from its emptiness. Hence, a theory of three *kāya*s was normative for Pāramitāyāna Buddhism (until Haribhadra saw fit to change it in the eighth century). In Mantranāya, too, Buddhahood in its own right is symbolized in terms of a union *(yuganaddha)* of conventional and ultimate truth, a unity of what used to be conceptually divided prior to enlightenment, but is no longer divided.

Thus, according to Abhayākaragupta, within both Pāramitāyāna and Mantranāya, the distinction between a Buddha's gnosis *(dharma)* and *dharmatā* (the real nature of things) is made only by persons who are not yet Buddhas. A Buddha's own awareness does not construct that distinction. And with that understanding, practitioners of Mantranāya conceptualize Buddhahood in four or more *kāya*s for purposes of their special practice, without mistaking that conceptualization for the actual realization of Buddhahood.

In Haribhadra's four-*kāya* theory and interpretation of *AA* 8, on the other hand, the fourth *kāya* is distinguished based upon a conceptual distinction between gnosis and *dharmatā* that is supposed to be made within a Buddha's own awareness.[68] This, in Abhayākaragupta's view, runs counter to both the Pāramitāyāna and Mantranāya traditions of Mahāyāna Buddhism.

According to Abhayākaragupta, therefore, Haribhadra took distinctions that were intended to be used only in the context of tantric practice, and applied them outside of that context to the normative descriptions of Buddhahood found within the Pāramitāyāna tradition. In Abhayākaragupta's view, Haribhadra had mistaken a conceptualization about Buddhahood used for practical purposes in tantric yoga for Buddhahood itself as it was actually realized by a Buddha. By taking a Mantranāya scheme out of its own context of praxis, Haribhadra had made a normative theory of Buddhahood that was acceptable neither to the Pāramitāyāna nor to the Mantranāya traditions of Mahāyāna Buddhism. Although Abhayākaragupta's reasons differ somewhat from Ratnākaraśānti's, in the end he reaches a similar conclusion: Haribhadra's four-*kāya* theory, as a normative theory of Buddhahood, is inconsistent with the entire Mahāyāna Buddhist tradition. Later, in Tibet, Go ram pa bsod nams seng ge (1429–89), one of the preeminent philosophers of the Sa skya sect, agreed with this conclusion.

12
The Controversy Continues in Tibet: Tsong kha pa and Go ram pa

12.1 Introduction

In Tibet, scholars chose either Ārya Vimuktisena's or Haribhadra's interpretation of *Abhisamayālaṃkāra* chapter 8, depending on what implications for buddhology they saw in their project of developing a systematic philosophy-theology out of the thousands of sūtras, tantras, and commentaries they had received from India. Within that project, Tibetans perceived a number of problems as interrelated: problems concerning the relation of the two truths, the perfect knowledge of them (which is enlightenment), and the description of that knowledge as "embodied" in Buddha *kāya*s. Tibetan scholars explored some of the implicit logical relations between Buddhist ontology (the two truths), epistemology (Buddha's gnosis) and theology (the Buddha *kāya*s) that earlier Indian scholars had not explicitly discussed. In doing so, they further deepened the debate over the *kāya*s that they had inherited from India. As in India, part of the debate centered on the eighth chapter of the *Abhisamayālaṃkāra*, but the interpretive choices made on that chapter were related to the systematic philosophies that Tibetans developed in their commentaries on other Indian texts as well, particularly texts such as Candrakīrti's *Madhyamakāvatāra,* whose last section (on the *buddhabhūmi*) explicates the nature of a Buddha's gnosis.

Of the many Tibetan scholars who commented upon the *Abhisamayālaṃkāra*, two are of special interest as we trace the three-*kāya* versus four-*kāya* debate into Tibet: Tsong kha pa blo bzang grags pa (1357–1419), the founder of the dGe lugs pa school of Tibetan Buddhism, and Go ram pa bsod nams seng ge (1429–89), one of the most influential scholars of the Sa skya school.

Tsong kha pa composed an extensive commentary on the *Abhisamayālaṃkāra* known as the *Legs bshad gser 'phreng* (Golden rosary of eloquence). It is of special interest to us for several reasons. Many of Tsong kha pa's decisions regarding the proper interpretation of Indian texts and schools became normative for the entire school that he founded. In many cases, dGe lugs commentators who came after him sought to fine-tune the doctrinal positions that Tsong kha pa had already established. Among Tsong kha pa's extensive collected works, *Legs bshad gser 'phreng* is one of the more controversial works. It is said to have been his first major scholarly composition. With that rationale, a few of its positions have not been followed by later dGe lugs commentators. It is believed that Tsong kha pa, in later life, passed on his more mature views of the *Abhisamayālaṃkāra* to one of his principal disciples, rGyal tshab dar ma rin chen.[1] Nevertheless, in the case of *AA* chapter 8, Tsong kha pa's basic interpretive decisions in *Legs bshad gser 'phreng* set the standard that rGyal tshab followed, thence the major commentators of the dGe lugs pa school who came after. Furthermore, Tsong kha pa's commentary surveys the views of Indian *AA* commentators, clearly specifying his rationale for adopting Haribhadra's interpretation of *AA* 8 over others'. It therefore sheds light on the original rationale for some of the basic buddhological positions that the dGe lugs pa school has followed to the present day.

The dGe lugs school that Tsong kha pa founded put great emphasis on the ethical foundations of Buddhist practice, monastic institutionalization, and study. Tsong kha pa's commentary provides an illustration of the way one extremely influential Tibetan scholar reconstructed the history of Indian Buddhist thought through Haribhadra's lens in such a way as to speak to the ethical, religious, and social institutional concerns he had in his own time and place.

The other Tibetan commentator we will focus on is the great Sa skya scholar Go ram pa bsod nams seng ge. Based on his own careful survey of the Indian texts, he too made the basic interpretive decisions on *AA* 8 that much of his school has followed up to the present day. He arrived at conclusions that were diametrically opposed to those of Tsong kha pa, and then argued articulately for his positions in explicit opposition to Tsong kha pa's. Go ram pa chose Ārya Vimuktisena's over Haribhadra's interpretation of *AA* 8, for reasons not unrelated to those of Ratnākaraśānti and Abhayākaragupta discussed in the previous chapter. In section 3 of this chapter, we will focus mainly on Go ram pa's most important *AA* commentary, the *sBas don zab mo'i gter* (Treasure of profound hidden meaning).

In Tsong kha pa and Go ram pa, then, we have two of the most influential Tibetan representatives of Haribhadra's and Ārya Vimuktisena's opposing buddhological positions. Their debate over the nature of enlightenment represents a historical continuation from India to Tibet of the controversy we have traced in the previous chapters, a controversy that quietly continues even up to the present day amongst dGe lugs and Sa skya scholars in Tibetan study centers of South Asia.

12.2
Tsong kha pa's Buddhology

In the eighth chapter of his *Abhisamayālaṃkāra* commentary, the *Legs bshad gser 'phreng*, Tsong kha pa surveys the views of the major Indian scholars we have discussed in the previous chapters, and chooses Haribhadra's interpretation of *AA* 8 over the others. Focusing especially on Ārya Vimuktisena, Ratnākaraśānti and Abhayākaragupta, he sets forth his reasons for rejecting their three-*kāya* interpretations of *AA* 8 and accepting Haribhadra's four-*kāya* interpretation instead.

First Tsong kha pa briefly summarizes Haribhadra's interpretation of *AA* 8 in terms of four *kāyas: svābhāvikakāya, jñāna-dharmakāya (ye shes chos sku*, an abbreviated Tibetan expression for Haribhadra's *jñānātmaka dharmakāya), sāmbhogikakāya*, and *nairmāṇikakāya.* He then takes special note of Dharmamitra. Dharmamitra, in his *Prasphuṭapadā,* claimed that some Indian scholars of his time thought Haribhadra accepted a three-*kāya* interpretation of the *AA*, but that he presented four *kāya*s in his *Āloka* and *Sphuṭārthā* merely as an expression of his teacher Vairocana's views. Dharmamitra himself reached the conclusion that Haribhadra personally accepted all the different ways of enumerating the *kāyas*.[2]

Tsong kha pa rebuts these contentions, arguing that the four-*kāya* presentations in the *Āloka* and *Sphuṭārthā* clearly represented Haribhadra's own view. He notes, however, that Haribhadra did express the aspiration to "attain the three *kāya*s" in the closing remarks of his *Āloka*, which would mean that, in some sense, Haribhadra did accept three *kāya*s. Tsong kha pa therefore concludes that Haribhadra's position is the following. Where a Buddha's dharma-gnoses are explicitly included within the first of three *kāya*s, i.e., where the first *kāya* is posited as a *dharmakāya* that includes gnosis, Haribhadra does accept three *kāya*s. But where the dharma-gnoses are not included in the first of three *kāya*s, i.e., where the first *kāya* is posited as *svābhāvikakāya* alone (distinct from gnosis), then Haribhadra cannot accept such a set of three *kāya*s as a normative description of Buddhahood. For this reason, Haribhadra rejected *svābhāvikakāya, sāmbhogikakāya, nairmāṇikakāya* as the set of *kāya*s taught in *AA* 8; in his view, Buddha's gnoses could not be identified with any one of those three *kāya*s. In Tsong kha pa's words: "Therefore, Ācārya [Haribhadra] accepts that *dharmakāya, sāmbhogikakāya*, and *nairmāṇikakāya* are correctly three *kāya*s. But he does not accept that *svābhāvikakāya, sāmbhogikakāya*, and *nairmāṇikakāya* are correctly three *kāya*s, because the consciousnesses and mental factors of the Buddha stage are not any of those *kāya*s."[3]

Already in these comments, it is clear Tsong kha pa viewed the *trikāya* formulation of Mahāyāna that preceded Haribhadra through Haribhadra's perspective. Tsong kha pa assumed that the traditional *trikāya* formulation of *svābhāvikakāya, sāmbhogikakāya*, and *nairmāṇikakāya* did not identify *svābhāvikakāya* with a Buddha's gnosis. Therefore, says Tsong kha pa, Haribhadra can accept three *kāyas* as descriptive of Buddhahood where the first is designated *dharmakāya* and inclusive of a Buddha's gnosis, but not where the first is designated *svābhāvikakāya* (which is supposed to exclude the gnosis).

Tsong kha pa may have been correct about this as the reason that Haribhadra could aspire to attain the three *kāya*s at the end of the very text in which he argues for four, without any sense of contradiction. But in this explanation, Tsong kha pa also reveals how his own understanding of key terms has been mediated by Haribhadra.

As chapters 4 and 5 above demonstrate, the original *trikāya* formulation of Mahāyāna Buddhism identified *svābhāvikakāya* precisely as a Buddha's nondual gnosis, with that gnosis understood as indistinguishable from its object: universal thusness. It was Haribhadra who logically separated the gnosis from the thusness of a Buddha's realization, then posited the gnosis as a separate (fourth) *kāya*. Thus, prior to Haribhadra, the term *svābhāvikakāya* did not designate thusness or *śūnyatā* alone, distinct from gnosis. Haribhadra himself reinterpreted the term to have that meaning. Tsong kha pa, seeing all this through Haribhadra's perspective, understood *svābhāvikakāya* through Haribhadra's reinterpretation of it, apparently unaware that the term had had another meaning prior to Haribhadra's time. As we also noted in chapter 4 section 5 above, *dharmakāya*, when used in its exclusive sense as the name for the first of the three *kāya*s, was simply equivalent to *svābhāvikakāya*.

Tsong kha pa next gives a brief summary of Ārya Vimuktisena's three-*kāya* interpretation of the *Abhisamayālaṃkāra* and discusses other Indian scholars who later followed it. He quotes Ārya Vimuktisena and explains his meaning:[4]

> [Ārya Vimuktisena's] *Abhisamayālaṃkāra-vṛtti* says: "Now [resultant] *dharmakāya* is to be explained. It should be known as threefold: *svābhāvikakāya* (essence body), *sāmbhogikakāya* (communal enjoyment body), and *nairmāṇikakāya* (manifestation body)."[5]
>
> In this system, [*svābhāvikakāya*, essence body] is the body that is the essence *(ngo bo)* of the Buddha dharmas purified of all defilement. [Ārya Vimuktisena] explains *[svābhāvikakāya]* as such with the understanding that the essence [comprising the *svābhāvikakāya*, the *dharmatā* of the *dharmāḥ*] together with the qualities that possess that essence [the *dharmāḥ* themselves] are undivided. [Bhadanta Vimuktisena's] *Abhisamayālaṃkāra-vārttika* agrees with [Ārya Vimuktisena's] *Abhisamayālaṃkāra-vṛtti*.

Here too, Tsong kha pa's understanding of Ārya Vimuktisena is mediated more by Haribhadra than he may have realized. As noted, Tsong kha pa understands *svābhāvikakāya* to refer not to Buddha's gnosis per se, but only to the "essence" of that gnosis, its emptiness and purity. Therefore, he says, Ārya Vimuktisena interpreted *AA* 8 to be teaching *svābhāvikakāya* as the essence (emptiness, *dharmatā*) of the gnosis with the implicit understanding that that essence and the thing whose essence it is (gnosis) are one locus (spatially undivided though separate for thought).[6] Tsong kha pa assumed that Ārya Vimuktisena distinguished *svābhāvikakāya* primarily through a logico-Mādhyamika analysis of *dharma* (conventional substratum, gnosis) and *dharmatā* (the emptiness of the substratum, the emptiness of the gnosis), where *svābhāvikakāya* is the latter as spatially undivided from the former. But this imputes to Ārya Vimuktisena a *dharma/dharmatā* framework for Buddha-*kāya* theory that Haribhadra himself had introduced long after Ārya Vimuktisena had lived.

As we have seen, prior to Haribhadra, the doctrine of *svābhāvikakāya* was not formulated in terms of a logical distinction between a substratum and its ultimate nature *(dharma* and *dharmatā)*, but yogically and gnoseologically as a nondual realization in which cognitive subject and object (gnosis and thusness) were not be distinguished; a nondual awareness in which all such conceptual distinctions have been entirely transcended. It is this formulation of *svābhāvikakāya* that Ārya Vimuktisena had followed, not Haribhadra's.[7]

Because Tsong kha pa understood the very term *svābhāvikakāya* through Haribhadra's late-eighth-century logical construction of it, he was apparently unaware the term had had another meaning prior to Haribhadra. Tsong kha pa therefore assumed that Ārya Vimuktisena, indeed all Indian scholars that had asserted three *kāya*s, had understood *svābhāvikakāya* as the logical construct that Haribhadra had made of it: emptiness, logically distinguished from gnosis. He was thus unaware that *svābhāvikakāya* had previously been formulated as a nondual attainment in which gnosis and emptiness are inseparable.

Tsong kha pa next quotes Ratnākaraśānti's and Abhayākaragupta's critique of Haribhadra and their reasons for following Ārya Vimuktisena on *AA* 8.[8] He also quotes from the eleventh-century scholar Ratnakīrti, whom he views as a minor *AA* commentator.[9] It is Ārya Vimuktisena, Ratnākaraśānti, and Abhayākaragupta upon whom Tsong kha pa focuses as the primary opposition to Haribhadra.

Having briefly summarized the opposing interpretations of *AA* 8, Tsong kha pa presents his own reasons for choosing Haribhadra's over the others. A translation of this portion of the *Legs bshad gser 'phreng* follows.[10] The paragraphs are numbered to show the correspondence between the sections of the translation below and my comments upon it which follow.

> 1. Which of these systems is to be accepted? As explained above, many Indian [scholars], and also many of us [Tibetans], have denounced Ācārya [Haribhadra's] position as wrong. Nevertheless, I think that it is the correct one. How so? Ratnākaraśānti's and Abhayākaragupta's ultimate criticism of it [boils down to this]: "The [Buddha dharmas consisting of] the factors which foster enlightenment, etc. were not taught as a fourth *kāya* in the Philosophical Vehicle.[11] And although [the *kāya*s] are

taught as four in the Mantranāya, the way in which they are posited in that system is different, since it represents a different vehicle." That is all.

2. The following response should be made to this. Upon examination, it does appear that the [undefiled] dharmas were actually taught as a fourth *kāya* in the Philosophical Vehicle. Doesn't the name of the fourth *kāya* [i.e., *dharmakāya*] appear clearly in the text of *Abhisamayālaṃkāra* [chapter 8] that begins [with v. 8.1]: "The *svābhāvikakāya* of the Sage" followed by [verses 8.2–8.6, which conclude by saying that the undefiled dharmas] "are called *dharmakāya*"? [Those who interpret the *AA* as a three-*kāya* text] argue that the expression *[dharmakāya]* refers to *dharmatākāya*, the suffix *-tā* having been elided. When one seeks for a [hidden] significance in the text, [one can find] a basis for arguing whether it teaches a *dharmatākāya* or a *dharmikāya*. But when the text is read literally, it does teach a separate [fourth] *kāya* [where v. 8.6 says the undefiled dharmas "are called *dharmakāya*"]. So what need is there to seek other significance [in the text]? For us the assertion [of a fourth *kāya*] is proven simply by the statement that is right there [in the text], while you [who interpret the *AA* as a three-*kāya* text] assert something that was not stated in the text at all!

3. Furthermore, the claim [by Ratnākaraśānti and Abhayākaragupta] that the [undefiled dharmas] were not taught separately in the Philosophical Vehicle as a body of gnoses *(jñānakāya)* needs to be examined.[12] Is this claim saying that the name ["body of gnoses," *jñānakāya*] was missing in [the sūtras and treatises of] the Philosophical Vehicle, or is it saying that what the name refers to was not taught?

4. If the former, then whenever a certain name is not clearly stated, the [thing the name refers to] is not being discussed. If that is the nature of the claim, then the ones who hold it must give up their own assertion that it is the *dharmatākāya* that is referred to [in *AA* v. 8.6 when it says that the Buddha dharmas] "are called *dharmakāya*." There are countless such [cases where something is affirmed without explicitly giving its name].

5. If the claim is making the latter point, [that what is referred to by the name "body of gnoses," *jñānakāya*, was not taught in the sūtras and treatises of the Philosophical Vehicle], then there are only two possibilities: either the undefiled dharmas are the two *rūpakāyas (sāmbhogikakāya* and *nairmāṇikakāya)*, or they are the *svābhāvikakāya*. If they are the *rūpakāyas*, wouldn't that contradict [Ratnākaraśānti's and Abhayākaragupta's] own position [that the dharmas are included in *svābhāvikakāya*]? Furthermore, the *rūpakāyas* also would not be separate *kāyas*, because they would be the nature of those undefiled dharmas, and [Ratnākaraśānti and

Abhayākaragupta] have themselves asserted that the undefiled dharmas are not a separate *kāya*.[13]

6. But if the undefiled dharmas are the *svābhāvikakāya*, are they unconditioned *(asaṃskṛta)* or conditioned *(saṃskṛta)?* If they are conditioned, it would contradict [Ratnākaraśānti's and Abhayākaragupta's] reliance for quotations upon Āryā Nāgārjuna and the *Mahāyānasūtrālaṃkāra*, since those two textual sources assert that the *svābhāvikakāya* is unconditioned and permanent by nature. This would damage the positions of both Ratnākaraśānti and his follower [Abhayākaragupta].[14] It would do [particular] damage to Abhayākaragupta's position, since he explained the *svābhāvikakāya* as unmade and without any creator (even the path) in accord with [Ārya Vimuktisena's explanation in the] *Abhisamayālaṃkāra-vṛtti*.[15] But if the undefiled dharmas were held to be unconditioned, then the two *rūpakāya*s would likewise be unconditioned, as there would be no difference in the reasoning.[16]

7. Furthermore, [those who claim that the undefiled dharmas were not taught separately in the Philosophical Vehicle as a body of gnoses, *jñānakāya*,] should explain how they do not contradict Vasubandhu's description of the *dharmakāya* as containing both conditioned and unconditioned components.[17]

8. [Supporters of Ārya Vimuktisena, Ratnākaraśānti, and Abhayākaragupta] could raise the following objection: "[Your four-*kāya* interpretation] of the *Abhisamayālaṃkāra* is not correct. For if it were correct, the *AA* would have to be expressing a [fourth] *kāya* when it uses the expression *dharmakāya* in [v. 1.17], the table of contents [for *AA* chapter 8]. But that is not so, because the [*AA*'s] table of contents [vv. 1.5–1.16] states the name of the realization *(abhisamaya)* that is the title for every one of the other seven chapters, e.g., "the Sage's total omniscience," etc. In the same way [when v. 1.17 of the table of contents says *dharmakāya*, it is stating the name of the realization which is the title of the eighth chapter, resultant Buddhahood as a whole, not the name of a fourth *kāya*.]

9. It may appear as though this objection were true. But within the body of *AA* chapter 8 [in v. 8.6], a *dharmakāya* is taught as a separate *kāya*. And when we make an inferential analysis of the sort presented above, [we do find that a separate *dharmakāya* consisting of a Buddha's undefiled dharmas] must be posited as a [fourth] *kāya*, because it can not be posited as any of the other three *kāya*s. Therefore, we must hold that the expression *dharmakāya* in [v. 1.17] of the table of contents teaches [two things at once]: the general realization [of resultant *dharmakāya*, resultant Buddhahood, as the title of *AA* chapter 8] and one out of four *kāya*s [the body of gnoses: *jñāna-dharmakāya*]. After all, what is achieved

by reasoning should not be overturned by words [alone], and it is evident that one word [can] express many meanings.

These are Tsong kha pa's reasons for choosing Haribhadra's four-*kāya* interpretation of the *Abhisamayālaṃkāra* over that of Ārya Vimuktisena and others.

Paragraph (1): First, Tsong kha pa says that Ratnākaraśānti's and Abhayākaragupta's objection to Haribhadra was based on a scriptural fundamentalism that was entirely philological, i.e., Haribhadra's fourth *kāya* of gnosis *(jñānakāya)* is not to be accepted because it was not explicitly taught in the scriptures and treatises of the "Philosophical Vehicle" (nontantric Mahāyāna Buddhism, Pāramitāyāna).

As discussed above in chapter 11, Ratnākaraśānti's principal objection to Haribhadra (taken up also by Abhayākaragupta) was not philological, but philosophical. Ratnākaraśānti believed that human thought and reason were far more limited in their capacity to comprehend the actual content of a Buddha's realization than Haribhadra believed. He criticized Haribhadra for thinking he could infer the content of a Buddha's awareness by analogy to the makeup of the mind of non-Buddhas on the path (as described in Abhidharma). As a corollary of that philosophical critique, Ratnākaraśānti differed fundamentally with Haribhadra on the status of scripture vis-à-vis Buddhahood. For Ratnākaraśānti (followed by Abhayākaragupta), when sacred text teaches the nature of Buddhahood, it reveals (as well as possible in language) what has been realized in nondual yoga. Because nondual yoga deconstructs some of the very presuppositions upon which dichotomous thought and language rest, some of what sacred text reveals about Buddhahood is necessarily incomprehensible to human thought alone. Thus, on the actual content of a Buddha's attainment, sacred text is to be received as revelation (until one realizes Buddhahood oneself through nondual praxis). Haribhadra, on the other hand, argued that where the *Abhisamayālaṃkāra* is plausibly ambiguous, its real meaning is inferable, because it surely seeks to express what is logical, i.e., reasonable for thought. Thus, when Ratnākaraśānti and Abhayākaragupta pointed out that a fourth *kāya* (that would entail conceptual differentiation within a Buddha's own attainment) was not taught in the whole corpus of Mahāyāna scriptures and treatises, they were trying to point to a philosophical meaning in that scriptural silence which Haribhadra had not recognized.

Tsong kha pa, not recognizing the philosophical substance of Ratnākaraśānti's and Abhayākaragupta's argument, reduced their objection to a trivial sort of scriptural fundamentalism: the claim that if something is not explicitly stated in the scriptures, it is not true. Tsong kha pa's reasons for supporting Haribhadra, then, take the form of a specific rebuttal to that fundamentalist objection.

Paragraph (2): Tsong kha pa must now confront the fact that there is very little (perhaps no) direct scriptural evidence that a Buddha's gnosis was ever explicitly taught as a distinct, fourth kāya in the Pāramitāyāna tradition prior to Haribhadra.

The only direct scriptural evidence Tsong kha pa can point to is verse 8.6 of the *Abhisamayālaṃkāra* itself. In the Tibetan translation of that verse, it appears to be saying that the undefiled dharmas (from the factors that foster enlightenment to total omniscience) "are called *dharmakāya*." This appears to identify the set of undefiled dharmas as a distinct, fourth *kāya* called *dharmakāya*. Tsong kha pa therefore claims that it is Haribhadra who read the *AA* literally and straightforwardly, and that interpreters such as Ārya Vimuktisena who etymologize *dharmakāya* as *dharmatākāya* (to equate it with *svābhāvikakāya*) were interpreting the *AA* loosely.

However, as we saw in chapter 8 section 3 above, the Sanskrit of *AA* verse 8.6 is less straightforward than it looked to Tsong kha pa in its Tibetan translation. Verses 8.2-8.6 in the Sanskrit list the twenty-one types of undefiled dharma and then conclude in verse 8.6: "thus is *dharmakāya* denominated." One possible meaning is that the *dharmakāya* (= the *svābhāvikakāya* of verse 8.1) is conceptualized and denominated as the collection of undefiled dharmas (but is not defined by that collection, having passed beyond all such conceptual differentiation). This, in fact, was Ārya Vimuktisena's interpretation of verse 8.6. It was also a natural one, because it conformed to the usage of the terms *svābhāvikakāya*, *dharmakāya*, and "undefiled dharmas" in the two main textual traditions out of which the *Abhisamayālaṃkāra* had been redacted: *Prajñāpāramitā* and Yogācāra. Tsong kha pa was also unaware that Ārya Vimuktisena's etymological explanation of *dharmakāya* as *dharmatākāya* conformed to *Prajñāpāramitāsūtra* passages that had provided that etymology to reinterpret *dharmakāya* in a distinctive Mahāyāna way: depicting Buddhahood as the real nature of dharmas *(dharmatā)* realized in nondual knowledge, not as a "body," a collection, of dharmas per se (see chapter 3 and chapter 9 section 3, above).

It is true that the Sanskrit of verse 8.6 is ambiguous enough to permit different interpretations (otherwise Haribhadra would have been unable to promulgate his interpretation at all). But Tsong kha pa's remarks indicate he was misled by the Tibetan translation into believing that Haribhadra's interpretation was the most literal and straightforward, when in fact, the Sanskrit indicates that Ārya Vimuktisena's is equally likely.[18] Beyond that, there are many other pieces of philological evidence that overwhelmingly support the conclusion that the *AA*'s eighth chapter teaches three *kāya*s (see chapter 8, sections 2–5, above). Some of that philological evidence appears clearly only in the Sanskrit original, not in the Tibetan translation, and was thus unavailable to Tsong kha pa.

Paragraphs (3)–(4): In fact, then, *AA* v. 8.6 provides no definite philological support for Haribhadra. But it was Tsong kha pa's only textual evidence to refute Ratnākaraśānti's and Abhayākaragupta's claim that Haribhadra's fourth *kāya* of gnosis had never been taught in Pāramitāyāna literature. Probably sensing how little textual evidence he had for his position, Tsong kha pa tries to establish that a fourth *kāya* of gnosis must have been implied in texts prior to Haribhadra even if it was never actually named. His method mirrors that of Haribhadra: logical inference dictates textual interpretation. Haribhadra believed that logic necessitated a fourth *kāya* of gnosis, from which he concluded that the *AA* had to have been teaching it. Tsong kha pa uses the same inference to posit the same fourth *kāya*, but concludes not only that it must have been taught in the *AA*, but that it must have been taught throughout Pāramitāyāna literature, even if it was not explicitly designated a *kāya*.

Tsong kha pa asks us to look closely at Ratnākaraśānti's and Abhayākaragupta's claim that a fourth *kāya* of gnosis was never taught in Pāramitāyāna literature before Haribhadra. He argues that even when a thing is not explicitly named, it may often be taught implicitly. Therefore, the fact that a name like *jñānakāya* (gnosis *kāya*) was not used prior to Haribhadra does not mean that what the name refers to was never taught.

This is certainly true. Still, it should give a scholar pause that, apparently, in the entire history of Pāramitāyāna (sūtra/śāstra) Mahāyāna Buddhism prior to Haribhadra, no one had thought to explicitly separate gnosis from emptiness as a separate *kāya* in its own right and designate it as such. A historical-critical scholar would naturally want to ask why. Tsong kha pa, however, never asked that question. He was looking at Indian intellectual history through Haribhadra's point of view. He therefore assumed that Haribhadra's logico-Mādhyamika assumptions and interests had always been operative throughout the history of Mahāyāna thought. Given that nonhistorical perspective, it seemed more reasonable to Tsong kha pa to argue that Haribhadra's four *kāya*s had always been implicitly taught than to seek the reason why they were never explicitly taught.

Paragraphs (5)–(7): Having established that a separate *kāya* of gnosis *could* have been taught implicitly in Pāramitāyāna without being named, Tsong kha pa now argues that it *had* to have been taught implicitly. And like Haribhadra, autonomous inference directs textual interpretation. He says that if the undefiled dharmas as gnosis were never taught (even implicitly) as a separate *kāya* prior to Haribhadra, then they would have to have been identified with one of the three *kāyas* that were taught. That would mean that the undefiled dharmas were either identified with the *rūpakāya*s *(sāmbhogikakāya* and/or *nairmāṇikakāya)* or with *svābhāvikakāya*. Ārya Vimuktisena, Ratnākaraśānti, and Abhayākaragupta all identified them with *svābhāvikakāya*.

But, Tsong kha pa's argument goes, the undefiled dharma-gnoses cannot be identified with *svābhāvikakāya*, because the former are conditioned and the latter is described in the various Mahāyāna textual sources as "uncreated," "permanent by nature," etc., which indicates it is unconditioned. In Tsong kha pa's view, in accord with logic one thing cannot be both conditioned and unconditioned. Therefore, the conditioned dharma-gnoses cannot be identified with *svābhāvikakāya,* which is unconditioned. If, on the other hand, it is said that the undefiled dharmas are unconditioned (because unconditioned *svābhāvikakāya*, as their emptiness, is their ultimate nature), then the *rūpakāyas* would have to be unconditioned for the same reason. This would be unacceptable to all parties, since *sāmbhogikakāya* manifests within conditions to teach great bodhisattvas, and *nairmāṇikakāyas* (such as Sākyamuni) are observed to arise and pass away. Tsong kha pa's use of inferential reasoning is modeled on Haribhadra's inference of a fourth *kāya*. As such, it replicates Haribhadra's attempt to do away with the apparent paradox of nonabiding nirvāṇa by logically distinguishing and separating unconditioned and conditioned components of Buddhahood (as explained in chapter 10).

But because he was trying to refute Ratnākaraśānti's and Abhayākaragupta's objection that the fourth *kāya* Haribhadra inferred was never taught in Pāramitāyāna texts, Tsong kha pa had to use Haribhadra's inference to support a wider hermeneutic claim than Haribhadra's. Whereas Haribhadra had explicitly applied the inference of a fourth *kāya* toward interpretation of the *AA* alone, Tsong kha pa used it to support the wider claim that such a fourth *kāya* had been implicitly taught throughout the Pāramitāyāna textual tradition. Therefore, Tsong kha pa, having posited Buddha's gnosis as a fourth *kāya* through reason, concludes that authoritative Mahāyāna sūtras and treatises had always taught such a fourth *kāya*. For, in Tsong kha pa's view, wherever those texts taught about a Buddha's gnosis, they were implicitly teaching all along about a fourth *kāya* consisting of that gnosis.

As previously noted, Haribhadra's inferential argument against Ārya Vimuktisena had involved two mistaken assumptions about Mahāyāna Buddhist understandings prior to his period. First, he assumed that Ārya Vimuktisena, like himself, had distinguished *svābhāvikakāya* logically as emptiness alone distinct from gnosis (i.e., that *svābhāvikakāya* was a logical construct, rather than an extrapolation from nondual yoga and gnoseology). This was not the case (see chapters 9 and 10 above). Secondly, he assumed that whoever accepted the existence of a Buddha's activity in the world had to agree that a Buddha possessed conditioned sense consciousnesses and mental factors *(citta-caitta)* necessary to generate such activity. This assumption, too, was incorrect (see chapter 10, section 5).

Tsong kha pa repeated Haribhadra's logical inference based on a similar set of mistaken assumptions about the perspectives of earlier Mahāyāna Buddhists. But because Tsong kha pa applied that inference toward a larger hermeneutic purpose than Haribhadra's (to prove that Haribhadra's fourth *kāya* had been taught, not only in the *AA*, but implicitly throughout Pāramitāyāna literature), the implications of those assumptions become broader.

First, Tsong kha pa, seeing the history of Buddhist thought through Haribhadra's eyes, also viewed *svābhāvikakāya* as a logical construct (rather than a direct extrapolation from nondual yoga and gnoseology). In conjunction with that, he assumed that although emptiness is unconditioned, a Buddha's gnosis was generally accepted in Pāramitāyāna to be conditioned (like any other form of consciousness). Given those assumptions, Tsong kha pa assumed that when texts such as *Mahāyānasūtrālaṃkāra* describe *svābhāvikakāya* as "permanent by nature," "unconditioned," etc., they are logically distinguishing *svābhāvikakāya* as emptiness alone from a Buddha's gnosis. Tsong kha pa also assumed that it was generally accepted in such texts that a Buddha's activities in the world had to be based upon sense consciousnesses and mental factors *(citta-caitta)*, which would mean that a Buddha's mind was a conditioned, conventional phenomenon. Therefore, a Buddha's realization must contain within it an unconditioned part (emptiness, ultimate truth) and a conditioned part (undefiled dharma-gnoses, conventional truth), distinguished as such within a Buddha's own awareness.

If these assumptions of Tsong kha pa's had been generally operative in the Mahāyāna textual traditions we explored in previous chapters (e.g., the *Prajñāpāramitā* and other Mahāyāna sūtras, the *Mahāyānasūtrālaṃkāra, Mahāyānasaṃgraha, Ratnagotravibhāga, Trikāyastotra*, etc.), then he certainly would have proved his point, because his assumptions already contain within them the substance of a four-*kāya* theory.

It is quite possible that Haribhadra's concern to logically distinguish the unconditioned and conditioned poles of Buddhahood as nonabiding nirvāṇa was a concern that developed gradually in Indian Buddhism, finally taking explicit form in Haribhadra's four-*kāya* interpretation of *AA* 8. Hsuan Tsang (the great Chinese scholar who studied at Nālandā in the seventh century), in his *Ch'eng wei-shih lun*, presents a theory of Buddhahood that makes a similar distinction between conditioned and unconditioned aspects of Buddhahood (although within the context of an overall three-*kāya* scheme).[19] And as Tsong kha pa noted, a passage paraphrased by Abhayākaragupta, ascribed by him to Vasubandhu, delineates a conditioned and an unconditioned aspect of *dharmakāya*. The text from which this passage was taken remains unidentified, but it may represent an attempt similar to Haribhadra's in later Indian Buddhism to sort out conditioned and unconditioned poles of nonabiding nirvāṇa in a way that separates gnosis from emptiness within a Buddha's realization (since Abhayākaragupta lived in the twelfth century, his ascription of the text to Vasubandhu does not carry much historical weight until we can identify the text). Dharmamitra's comments point to Haribhadra's teacher Vairocana as a formulator of four-*kāya* theory, which may also indicate a gradual development that culminated in Haribhadra's explicit expression of that theory in his interpretation of the *AA*.

However, Tsong kha pa intended his argument to prove that a separate gnosis *kāya* had been implicitly taught not just in a few later Indian texts leading up to Haribhadra's interpretation, but in Pāramitāyāna literature as a whole, including the texts explored in chapters 3 through 9 of this book (*Prajñāpāramitā* sūtras, *Buddhabhūmisūtra*, *MSA*, *Msg*, *RGV*, etc.). And these texts did not share some of the late-eighth-century logico-Mādhyamika assumptions that conditioned Tsong kha pa's view of them.

As explained in chapters 4 and 5 above, three-*kāya* texts like the *MSA*, *Msg*, etc. (in contradistinction to Haribhadra) did not construct *svābhāvikakāya* logically as emptiness logically distinguished from gnosis. To do so would have made no sense, since *svābhāvikakāya* was understood precisely as the nondual realization that is free of all such conceptually constructed dichotomies as "gnosis" and "emptiness." In these texts, abstract terms like *tathatāviśuddhi* and *nirvikalpajñāna* were common epithets for a Buddha's own attainment precisely because they pointed to a nondual comprehension in which thusness *(tathatā)* and gnosis *(jñāna)* were experientially indivisible (see chapter 4, section 6, above).

Thus, in traditions of Pāramitāyāna prior to Haribhadra, surveyed in chapters three through nine above, it was inconceivable to claim that a Buddha distinguished gnosis from emptiness as separate things within his own awareness. Since such a distinction could only be made conceptually, it would constitute precisely the kind of dichotomous conceptualization *(vikalpa, prapañca)* that a Buddha was said to have passed beyond. Rather, a Buddha's awareness of the phenomenal world was said to be based upon his nonconceptual gnosis of the *dharmadhātu* (universal emptiness). Texts acknowledged that such an awareness was impossible for us to comprehend. It was for precisely that reason that a Buddha's realization was so frequently described as literally inconceivable and beyond precise ascertainment through inference (see chapter 5, sections 2 through 4, above).

In addition, a Buddha's activities, based upon that nonconceptual gnosis (together with the force of prior vows, Buddha's sustaining power, and the karmic receptivity of trainees), were said to manifest spontaneously and uninterruptedly in accord with the capacities and needs of beings. As noted in chapter 5, section 3 above, Yogācāra commentaries specifically raised the question of how Buddhahood, consisting of nonconceptual gnosis, can carry out activities for beings when it is free of their conceptualizations. This is acknowledged to be a difficult question, not answerable by attempting a detailed analysis of a Buddha's awareness (which is beyond our comprehension). The answer many of these texts gave was *not* that a Buddha possesses the sense consciousnesses and mental factors *(citta-caitta)* necessary to generate activity. Rather, the answer was given in the form of analogies like that of the legendary wish-granting gem, which fulfills wishes without need of thinking. Like the wish-granting gem, it is said, a Buddha's activity is utterly automatic. As noted in chapter 10, section 5, above, Candrakīrti stated explicitly that a Buddha's awareness is free of sense consciousnesses and mental factors, having become cognitively one with thatness (*tattvam* = thusness, emptiness). For precisely that reason, in order to explain how a Buddha's nonconceptual gnosis can be the basis of universal activity, Candrakīrti relies on the familiar analogy of the wish-granting gem.[20]

And as explored in chapter 4 above, Yogācāra treatises (in harmony with related passages of *Prajñāpāramitā* sūtras) did not define a Buddha's own realization in terms of the list of undefiled dharmas. The collection of undefiled dharmas was understood to comprise a phenomenal description of a Buddha's awareness. A Buddha's own realization *(svābhāvikakāya)* was described just as the nondual gnosis of thusness that had passed beyond all such conceptualization. It was this nonconceptual attainment that was identified as *svābhāvikakāya/dharmakāya*, not the collection of conceptually differentiated dharmas (chapter 4, sections 2 and 3, above). Therefore, again, it made no sense from the perspective of earlier Pāramitāyāna traditions to posit the list of undefiled dharmas as a separate *kāya,* since that list just represented the way ordinary beings conceptualize *svābhāvikakāya*, not some distinct component of a Buddha's realization that is supposed to be separate from *svābhāvikakāya.*

Tsong kha pa assumed that where these texts describe *svābhāvikakāya* as "permanent by nature," "uncreated," or "unconditioned," they meant it in the strictly logical sense employed later by Haribhadra, which would imply that *svābhāvikakāya* is unconditioned emptiness distinct from gnosis. As discussed in chapter 5 (section 3), chapter 9 (section 3), and chapter 10 (section 3), *svābhāvikakāya/dharmakāya* prior to Haribhadra was routinely described as "permanent," "uncreated," or "unconditioned" in several broad senses, none of which implied that it was to be understood as emptiness logically distinct from gnosis. Thusness has always been; it is never newly created. Therefore *svābhāvikakāya,* as revelation of universal thusness, is obtained by the path of nondual yoga, but not created by it. Further, the Yogācāra doctrine of innate, pure luminous mind *(citta-prakṛti-viśuddhi)* also implied the uncreatedness of *svābhāvikakāya.* For *svābhāvikakāya* represents the removal of what had hidden the mind's intrinsic luminosity, not the creation of something new. None of these earlier ways to understand *svābhāvikakāya* as uncreated, permanent, or unconditioned assumed that it be understood as emptiness alone as logically separated from gnosis.[21]

Therefore, many of the key assumptions behind Tsong kha pa's argument run directly counter to those held by the authors of texts he characterizes, from the Mahāyāna sūtras themselves, through the *MSA*, *Msg*, *RGV*, and other formulative *trikāya* treatises to the commentaries of Ārya Vimuktisena, Candrakīrti, Ratnākaraśānti, and Abhayākaragupta.

Given this fact, of course, Tsong kha pa's argument fails to prove that the fourth *kāya* Haribhadra posited was implicitly taught throughout the Mahāyāna textual traditions prior to Haribhadra. Historically speaking, Tsong kha pa would have been better served by seeking to discover why textual traditions prior to Haribhadra had lacked such a distinction, rather than seeking to project that distinction onto those earlier traditions.

Paragraphs (8)–(9): Be that as it may, Tsong kha pa believed his arguments above to have proved Haribhadra's fourth *kāya* to have been taught generally throughout the Pāramitāyāna tradition at least implicitly, and in the *Abhisamayālaṃkāra* in particular. Like Haribhadra before him, Tsong kha pa realized how little direct textual support he had for all this. It behooved him to respond to a philological objection. Therefore, he next acknowledges a philological criticism by an opponent, who argues, based on the *AA*'s table of contents, that the *AA* teaches only three *kāyas*.

Abhisamayālaṃkāra verse 1.17 is the final verse of the *AA*'s table of contents, summarizing the content of its eighth chapter. It reads as follows:

> svābhāvikaḥ sasāmbhogo nairmāṇiko 'paras tathā
> dharmakāyaḥ sakāritraś caturdhā samudīritaḥ
>
> (*AA* 1.17)

> [In its essence, with its enjoyment, and in its manifestation(s) as well, *Dharmakāya*, with its activity, is proclaimed as fourfold.]

If the term *dharmakāya* in this verse does not refer to the overall subject matter and title of *AA* chapter 8 ("resultant *dharmakāya*," including all *kāyas* and all aspects of Buddhahood), then verse 1.17 would be the only part of the *AA*'s table of contents that leaves out the title of its corresponding chapter. Therefore, the objecter says, *dharmakāya* in the verse must refer to the title of *AA* chapter 8, not to a fourth *kāya* (Haribhadra's *[jñāna] dharmakāya)*. This means that verse 1.17 teaches just three *kāyas (svābhāvika*, *sasāmbhoga*, and *nairmāṇika)* with *dharmakāya* serving just as the title of chapter 8 (semantically inclusive of all three *kāyas*). Since verse 1.17 is the table of contents for *AA* chapter 8, the latter must be teaching three *kāyas*.[22]

To his credit, Tsong kha pa acknowledges the power of this argument. But relying heavily on his inferential argument above, combined with his understanding of *AA* verse 8.6's Tibetan translation (in which he understood the word *dharmakāya* to designate that fourth *kāya*), he concludes that the *AA* was indeed teaching four *kāyas*. Therefore, he decides, the term *dharmakāya* in v. 1.17 must refer simultaneously to the title of chapter 8 and to the *dharmakāya* of gnosis as a fourth *kāya* taught within chapter 8. As was the case with *AA* verse 8.6, Tsong kha pa read verse 1.17 in a Tibetan translation. The special adjectival morphologies of Sanskrit terms were lost in the Tibetan, giving Haribhadra's four-*kāya* reading of the verse more plausibility, perhaps, than it has in Sanskrit.[23]

But even reading the verse through Tibetan translation, Tsong kha pa should have asked himself this question: Precisely what does verse 1.17 proclaim "as fourfold"? If it is *dharmakāya*, and if, as Tsong kha pa claims, that term refers simultaneously to resultant *dharmakāya* (Buddhahood as a whole) and *jñānātmaka dharmakāya* (a fourth *kāya* of gnosis), then the verse proclaims *both* as fourfold. In that case, according to the verse, both have four aspects: designated *svābhāvika*, *sasāmbhoga*, *nairmāṇika,* and *kāritra* (= three *kāyas* plus enlightened activity). Then resultant *dharmakāya* would still be proclaimed to include just three *kāyas* plus activity (*jñānātmaka* is still not listed among its four aspects). And now, in addition, the supposed fourth *kāya* of gnosis would also be proclaimed to include those three *kāya*s plus activity! As explained in chapter 8 above, when all the evidence is in, Haribhadra's four-*kāya* interpretation of *AA* 8 is just not defensible.

As noted in chapter 10 above, Haribhadra's imputation of a fourth *kāya* upon the *AA* represented his unique application of late-eighth-century logic, Abhidharma and Mādhyamika analysis upon that unique text. Indeed, Ratnākaraśānti's and Abhayākaragupta's objection that Haribhadra's fourth *kāya* comprised a new perspective on Buddhahood foreign to the *AA* and to prior *Pāramitāyāna* understanding was essentially true. Thus, Tsong kha pa's attempt to refute that charge could not actually succeed. But, Tsong kha pa himself, through the school he founded, came to exert great influence on interpretation of Indian Buddhist thought in Tibet. And in his attempt to defend Haribhadra, Tsong kha pa artificially projected Haribhadra's perspective on key buddhological concepts back upon earlier Mahāyāna traditions whose thought was quite different. Through his defense of Haribhadra, then, Tsong kha pa reconstructed the history of the meanings of fundamental buddhological terms like *svābhāvikakāya* and *dharmakāya* for a great many Tibetan scholars later who were influenced by him.

Tsong kha pa's desire to defend Haribhadra must have stemmed from a concern of his own time and place within Tibet, just as Haribhadra's reinterpretation of the *AA* addressed a perceived need of his time in India.

The overall pattern of Tsong kha pa's activity in Tibet of the fifteenth century may provide clues to his fundamental concerns. He is renowned for having initiated a reform movement in Tibetan Buddhism, the dGe lugs school, a highly disciplined religious order that established numerous monastic institutions emphasizing monastic discipline, ethics, and rigorous study as essential foundations of practice, including tantric practice. The form of Buddhism that Tibet inherited was overwhelmingly tantric, and Tibetan chronicles and hagiographies tell many stories of Tibetans who fell into hedonism and black magic for personal gain through misinterpretation of tantric paradigms for taking sensory experience into the path. This was perceived as an ongoing danger in Tibet, since many transmitters of tantric practice were laymen and laywomen not subject to the social strictures of monastic institutions; and the teaching of tantrism was subject to gross misinterpretation outside its authentic channels of transmission. Much like the biblical mythos of the Hebrew people falling away again and again from their covenant with God, Tibetan stories often tell the tale of Tibetans who "broke their covenant" with the moral core of the Buddha's teaching by misinterpreting tantric practice apart from its moral foundations in Mahāyāna teaching.

Tsong kha pa's reform tradition and the monastic institutions it founded enjoyed significant support from nobility and the general populace even in his own time, undoubtedly in part because of the moral stature of Tsong kha pa himself. And this was surely due, in part, to the very real social concern noted above over the status of the Buddha dharma in Tibetan culture as a force for social well being and stability. In succeeding centuries, Tsong kha pa's reformed dGe lugs order gradually increased its social, political, and economic influence, acquiring central governmental control over Tibet in the person of the Fifth Dalai Lama by the mid-seventeenth century. It retained this control through succeeding Dalai Lamas and their regents until Chinese Communist annexation in the 1950s. While this is a complex historical development, at each stage the dGe lugs order has enjoyed support in part because of the continuing perception that, through its monastic institutions, it promulgates a moral ethos that helps rein in Tibetan tendencies toward anomie and promotes sociocultural stability and well being.

Related to this concern has been a concern on the part of many Tibetan scholastics to establish philosophical foundations for the full range of Mahāyāna practices; they were viewed as the moral and metaphysical foundation for the proper Buddhist use of tantrism. Indo-Tibetan scholastic schools established from the eleventh century onward, including Tsong kha pa's, retell the tale of a legendary debate in the eighth century during the first promulgation of Buddhism in Tibet between a Ch'an monk known as Ho-shang Mahāyāna and the Indian scholar Kamalaśīla. At this period, Ch'an traditions were exerting influence in Tibet, sometimes in competition with scholastic traditions from India. According to later Tibetan accounts, the Ch'an tradition represented by Ho-shang Mahāyāna rejected conceptual analysis and even moral virtue as a practice leading to enlightenment, on the grounds that such practices take place under categories of dichotomous conceptualization within conventional truth that only bind one further to saṃsāra. The emphasis, instead, according to these accounts, was on the teaching of enlightenment as innate (Buddha-nature) and on the Mahāyāna identification of saṃsāra with nirvāṇa understood in a radical and immediate way. Kamalaśīla, according to the story, argued for the full range of moral and analytical practices of Indian scholastic Buddhism as necessary both for the gradual realization of ultimate truth (emptiness) and to express that realization.

This story, as it was constructed centuries after the debate, probably serves more as a trope for later scholastic traditions than as an accurate description of what occurred. As such, it appears prominently in Tsong kha pa's voluminous summary of Mahāyāna thought and practice, the *Lam rim chen mo* (Great exposition of the stages of the path to enlightenment). In Tsong kha pa's account, because Ho-shang Mahāyāna went too far in his rejection of conventional truth, he rejected the systematic path of practice that actually leads to enlightenment; thereby leading his followers to disaster.

In Tsong kha pa's view, although the capacity to achieve enlightenment is innate, enlightenment itself is not. Like any other phenomenon, enlightenment is produced from its own proper causes, those causes being the practices that generate spiritual power (*puṇya*, karmic merit) and wisdom.[24] Those practices are based on firm moral discipline. And all such practice and discipline takes place within the realm of conventional truth. If, in a misdirected Buddhist zeal to affirm ultimate truth over conventional truth, the latter is accorded too little reality, there would be no basis to take spiritual discipline and practice seriously.

Thus, Tsong kha pa demonstrates both in his writing and in his social-institutional activity a strong concern to establish moral, metaphysical, and social-institutional foundations for systematic practice and gradual spiritual development. It was in this broader context of concern that many of Tsong kha pa's hermeneutical decisions on Indian Buddhist texts were made, including his decision to follow Haribhadra's interpretation of *AA* 8. Like Haribhadra, Tsong kha pa wanted to distinguish a conventional, conditioned aspect of Buddhahood from its unconditioned aspect, thereby to identify within a Buddha's realization a conventional, conditioned basis for its activity in the world. But Tsong kha pa's broader concern was to affirm the reality of conventional truth in general, to give conventional truth the ontological status necessary for Tibetan Buddhists to take moral discipline, graduated practice, and the social institutions that support such practice seriously.

Recall that Haribhadra's central argument for a fourth *kāya* of gnosis begins with the observation that a Buddha acts in the world through the manifestation of his *rūpakāya*s *(sāmbhogikakāya* and *nairmāṇikakāya).* The *rūpakāya*s, as phenomenal manifestations, are conditioned. Then they must have a conditioned cause within a Buddha's realization that generates them. And that cause would be a Buddha's undefiled dharmas, his gnosis, taken as a conditioned, conventional entity. Tsong kha pa, in defending Haribhadra, supports this reasoning. But to ask for the cause in Buddhahood of the *rūpakāya*s is already to assume that the *rūpakāya*s have enough reality, enough ontological status, to seek an underlying cause for them in a Buddha's own realization. At the core of Tsong kha pa's concern to defend Haribhadra is an ontological seriousness about the *rūpakāya*s, and by extension conventional truth in general, which was lacking in prior Mahāyāna buddhological traditions.

In *trikāya* formulations prior to Haribhadra, Buddha's nondual realization was said to be epistemologically one with the realm of ultimate truth, *dharmadhātu.* And that nondual gnosis of ultimate truth is what Buddhahood actually is: *svābhāvikakāya.* Based on that realization, and through the force of prior vows, the karmic readiness of trainees, pervasive manifestations miraculously appear in the phenomenal realm of conventional truth to carry out activities for beings; those manifestations are the *rūpakāya*s. But Buddhahood, ontologically speaking, is just *svābhāvikakāya.* The *rūpakāya*s are merely phenomenal appearances of Buddhahood as it is conceptually constructed by other beings. Causes for the *rūpakāya*s' manifestation in the phenomenal world are located in that world: in a Buddha's prior vows and merit as a bodhisattva on the path, the karmic purity of beings, etc. But precise causes for the *rūpakāya*s within a Buddha's own supramundane realization were never sought.[25]

Within *trikāya* traditions prior to Haribhadra, the question was never raised as to what comprised a conditioned cause of the *rūpakāya*s within a Buddha's own realization. Why not? Because in those traditions the *rūpakāya*s (and undefiled dharmas) were ontologically insignificant relative to the *svābhāvikakāya.*[26] In part, this stemmed from the meditational and gnoseological context in which the *trikāya* doctrine was formulated. This context granted conventional truth in general only a provisional ontological status that disappeared within the realization of ultimate truth. According to the Mahāyāna path system largely developed in Yogācāra traditions, when *ārya* bodhisattvas enter their meditative equipoise directly cognizing ultimate truth (emptiness), conventional truth longer appears. They have a nonconceptual gnosis of ultimate truth alone. Through the force of that, when they leave their meditative equipoise, their cognition of conventional truth is altered, so that the dualistic appearance of conventional phenomena seems like an illusion. *Ārya* bodhisattvas, then, alternate between their meditative equipoise on ultimate truth, in which conventional truth does not appear at all, and periods of activity in the phenomenal world, in which conventional truth does appear, though in an illusory manner. When ultimate truth is directly realized, conventional truth loses its provisional ontological status.[27]

But when *ārya* bodhisattvas finally achieve full enlightenment and become Buddhas, they no longer alternate between periods of meditation on ultimate truth and periods of activity in the world. The Buddhas' direct realization of ultimate truth, as their defining feature *(svābhāvikakāya)*, never ceases. The Buddhas never leave their "meditation" on ultimate truth. A Buddha's mind becomes epistemologically one with universal emptiness (the *dharmadhātu*) and all else that a Buddha knows or does is based upon that. Therefore, in Mahāyāna treatises previously discussed, a Buddha's knowledge of the phenomenal world (conventional truth) was not specified as an awareness of phenomena qua phenomena, but as an awareness of phenomena based on his awareness of ultimate truth. The Buddhas' knowledge of the phenomenal world was understood as an expression of their knowledge of the *dharmadhātu*, the latter knowledge being the fundamental one.[28]

Thus, gnoseologically, the Buddhas' awareness of the phenomenal world was only an expression of a more fundamental awareness, their nonconceptual gnosis of the ultimate nature of that world. And theologically, a Buddha's *rūpakāya*s that manifest in the world are just an appearance, conceptually constructed by the unenlightened, of the nonconceptual *svābhāvikakāya.*

But it appears that by Haribhadra's time, perhaps as part of a general logico-Mādhyamika concern to critique the Yogācāra ontology of Buddhahood, the *rūpakāya*s were accorded enough ontological status (at least in some Mādhyamika circles) for Haribhadra to plausibly ask for their cause within a Buddha's own realization. And similarly, the undefiled dharmas were accorded much greater ontological status as the actual content of a Buddha's gnosis, such that a Buddha perceived his own realization conventionally in terms of them.[29] In essence, Haribhadra tracked conventional truth itself right into the core of Buddhahood in a way that had not been done earlier.

Tsong kha pa, in supporting Haribhadra, also assumed that the *rūpakāyas* had enough ontological status to seek their cause within a Buddha's own realization. Following the thread of that concern, he (like Haribhadra) identified the undefiled dharmas as a conditioned, conventional component of a Buddha's own realization. The undefiled dharmas were distinguished (as conventional truth) from their *dharmatā* (as ultimate truth) precisely through their appearance as a conventional object to Buddha's own direct awareness.[30] This anchored conventional truth itself right in the core of a Buddha's own realization. In the *trikāya* traditions, Buddha's mind was inseparable from ultimate truth. In Tsong kha pa's scheme (following Haribhadra), Buddha's mind was now identified in its own right as a conventional, conditioned entity, distinct from ultimate truth, and suitable to be identified as a fourth *kāya*.

Furthermore, since, according to Tsong kha pa's scheme, a Buddha's omniscient awareness discursively distinguishes between the phenomenal and the ultimate aspects of its own realization, it would follow that it similarly distinguishes directly the phenomenal and ultimate aspects of all other things. In that case, a Buddha's awareness of the phenomenal world is no longer understood merely as an expression of his nondual gnosis of its thusness, but is on equal terms with it. A Buddha does not cognize phenomena through his gnosis of their thusness. He cognizes phenomena qua phenomena, just like he cognizes their thusness qua thusness. Then conventionalities (as dependent arisings, *pratītya-samutpāda*), like their thusness, are equally validated by a Buddha's direct cognition. And this would grant to conventionalities (as *pratītya-samutpāda*) an ontological status on a par with their thusness. Through all this, there is no implication that conventionalities exist independently as ultimate existents. But there is the implication that conventionalities, as dependent existents (empty of independent or ultimate existence), are validated by a Buddha's direct cognition just as much as their emptiness.

This is how Tsong kha pa's choice of Haribhadra's *AA* 8 interpretation fit into his overall concern to affirm the reality of conventional truth as the basis of spiritual practice. Haribhadra's theory granted the undefiled dharmas (as conventional truth) the ontological status conferred by a Buddha's direct cognition, and this, by implication, granted to conventional truth in general that same ontological status.

Tsong kha pa pursues this theme further in his commentary on Candrakīrti's *Madhyamakāvatāra*. In one portion of his comments on the "Buddhabhūmi" section of that text, Tsong kha pa speculates on the mechanism of a Buddha's awareness.[31] Significantly, for this purpose, he puts aside Candrakīrti's text for a little while to make primary reference instead to Jñānagarbha's *Satya-dvaya-vibhaṅga*. Jñānagarbha, as we have mentioned, was an eighth-century Indian Mādhyamika logician who was a formative influence on Haribhadra.[32] Based on a verse from Jñānagarbha's text, Tsong kha pa presents the theory that conventional truth, just as much as ultimate truth, is validated by a Buddha's direct cognition. According to Tsong kha pa, a Buddha's gnosis perceives all conventional phenomena and their emptiness (conventional truth and ultimate truth) equally at once. A Buddha cognizes all conventional phenomena dualistically (i.e., with cognitive subject and object appearing as separate), since in Tsong kha pa's interpretation of Prāsaṅgika Mādhyamika metaphysics, that is how conventionalities exist. But a Buddha cognizes ultimate truth (emptiness) nondualistically (with no separation between subject and object), since that is how it is directly realized in yogic cognition (in the direct realization of ultimate truth, gnosis enters its object indivisibly "like water poured into water"). This means that, according to Tsong kha pa, a Buddha cognizes conventional truth (dualistically) qua conventional truth, and ultimate truth (nondualistically) qua ultimate truth.[33]

Implicitly, then, Tsong kha pa grants to conventional truth an ontological status on a par with ultimate truth, since both are equally validated by Buddha's direct knowledge. While this does not imply that conventional truth is independently or ultimately existent, it does imply that conventional truth, in spite of its emptiness of ultimate existence, is quite real. And therefore to engage in immoral conduct, or to engage in spiritual discipline, has real consequences: a bad rebirth on the one hand, progress toward enlightenment on the other.[34]

It should be noted that Tsong kha pa's gnoseology, according to which the Buddhas' knowledge of conventional truth per se is as fundamental as their knowledge of ultimate truth, represents a departure from the gnoseology of *trikāya* Mahāyāna treatises (such as the *MSA*, *RGV*, *Msg*, *DDV*, etc.) which made the Buddhas' gnosis of ultimate truth their fundamental awareness.[35] It also departs from Candrakīrti's own text, which conforms significantly to other *trikāya* texts in its theory of a Buddha's gnosis.[36]

12.3
Go ram pa's Buddhology

Go ram pa bsod nams seng ge (1429–89) was one of the most influential scholars of the Sa skya order. He wrote two important commentaries on the *Abhisamayālaṃkāra*, known as the *Yum don rab gsal* and the *sBas don zab mo'i gter*. We will focus mainly on the latter commentary, as it is held to more properly represent Go ram pa's own mature views, and is written in a clear expository style. Rong ston shes bya kun rig (1367–1449), a teacher of Go ram pa, also ranks as one of the very great Sa skya scholars. A teacher of Rong ston's, gYag ston sangs rgyas dpal (1350?–1414), is regarded in Sa skya tradition as one of Tibet's most profound commentators on *Prajñāpāramitā* and the *Abhisamayālaṃkāra*. Go ram pa's views were undoubtedly influenced by both Rong ston and gYag ston. Another important Sa skya scholar, Ngag dbang chos grags (1572–1641), wrote subcommentaries on Go ram pa's major works, and is often referred to by Sa skyas in their study of Go ram pa's works.[37]

In the eighth chapter of his *sBas don zab mo'i gter*, Go ram pa presents his reasons for choosing the prior three-*kāya* interpretation of *AA* 8 over Haribhadra's four-*kāya* interpretation. Like Ratnākaraśānti and Abhayākaragupta before him, Go ram pa repudiates Haribhadra's four-*kāya* perspective both as alien to the Pāramitāyāna tradition in general, and as an inaccurate interpretation of the *AA* in particular.

His comments on *AA* chapter 8 begin with a brief overview of the different ways of enumerating Buddha *kāyas* in various Pāramitāyāna texts. Of particular interest are his comments on Buddhahood enumerated as just one *kāya* (a mode of presenting Buddhahood that Tsong kha pa had not discussed):[38]

> In the holy *Suvarṇaprabhāsa* [sūtra] it is said: "That which abides merely as thatness *(tattvam)* and the accurate gnosis [of it] *(samyag-jñāna)* is called *dharmakāya*, since it is free from all moral obstructions and has completed all virtuous qualities. The former two [*kāyas*, i.e., *sāmbhogika-kāya* and *nairmāṇikakāya*] are merely designated *(btags pa ba)* [as Buddha *kāyas*]. The *dharmakāya* is the actual one *(yang dag pa)*, because it serves as the basis of those [other] two *kāyas*. Why? Because apart from the thusness of phenomena *(dharma-tathatā)* and the nonconceptual gnosis [which realizes it] *(nirvikalpa-jñāna)*, there are no other qualities of the Buddhas."[39] In the [8,000-verse *Prajñāpāramitā*] sūtra, the section on the moderately weak aspiration for others' benefit, it is said: "Bhikṣus, do not adhere to this body as [my] actual body *(satkāya, sku dam pa)*. Bhikṣus, look upon me as the perfected *dharmakāya*." Some translations [of the same sūtra passage] have it: "Bhikṣus, without looking upon me as a body which is a perishing collection, look upon me as the perfected *dharmakāya*."[40] On the meaning of this, the *Āloka* says that [the Buddha's] admonition not to grasp his perishing collection, beautified by blazing marks and signs, as his body means that the two *rūpakāyas* are only nominal Buddha bodies *(btags pa ba)*, while the *dharmakāya* alone is the actual [Buddha] body *(mtshan nyid pa)*.[41]

Ngag dbang chos grag's comments on this discussion of Go ram pa's are significant:[42]

> Concerning the enumeration [of Buddhahood] in one *kāya*, from a Buddha's own point of view *(rang snang la)*, all Buddha bodies *(kāyas)* are just the *dharmakāya*. This is so because a Buddha, from his own point of view, perceives only the *dharmakāya*, not the bodies which are perishing collections (i.e., not the *rūpakāyas*). . . . [Ngag dbang chos grag quotes the *Suvarṇaprabhāsa* and 8,000-verse *PP* sūtra passages given by Go

> ram pa above, and then quotes the *Vajracchedikā- prajñāpāramitā-sūtra*:] As it says in the *Vajracchedikā:* "Whoever sees me as [my] form, whoever knows me as [my] voice, has entered a mistaken path. Those beings do not see me." But are the *rūpakāyas* then not bodies of Buddha? They are Buddha bodies, because they are the fruition of meditating on the four yogic practices *(catvāraḥ prayogāḥ)* and are thus [part of] resultant *dharmakāya* (Buddhahood). Nevertheless, the scriptural passages quoted above mean that from a Buddha's own point of view *(rang snang la)*, apart from the *dharmakāya* alone, there are no *rūpakāyas*.

Go ram pa, having explained Buddhahood as one *kāya* (just *dharmakāya*), then briefly summarizes its presentations as two *kāyas* and three *kāyas* in various Pāramitāyāna texts (the *Ratnagotravibhāga,* which presents Buddhahood both ways, and the *Mahāyānasūtrālaṃkāra, Mahāyānasaṃgraha,* and *Abhidharmasamuccaya,* which present three *kāyas*). Go ram pa says that most Pāramitāyāna texts (Mahāyāna sūtras and treatises) teach three *kāyas*. He then notes that some scholars (i.e., Haribhadra and his followers), in their comments on the *Abhisamayālaṃkāra*, divided Buddhahood into four *kāyas*, and that some later commentators, based upon that, further divided it into five (by dividing the *sāmbhogikakāya* or the *nairmāṇikakāya* into two types). Go ram pa says that such enumerations of Buddhahood in four or five bodies just involve "the expansion or contraction of one's conceptual categories," i.e., that such enumerations just represent further discursive elaboration on the part of scholars. He notes that the earlier great Sa skya master, bSod nams rtse mo (1142–82), refuted such scholars when he said that in the Pāramitāyāna four gnoses and three *kāyas* are taught, while it is a distinctive feature of the Vajrayāna (tantric Buddhism) alone to enumerate Buddhahood in terms of five gnoses and four *kāyas*.[43] This hearkens back to the criticisms by Ratnākaraśānti and Abhayākaragupta we noted in chapter 11.

A little later in his *sBas don zab mo'i gter,* Go ram pa further pursues the question of what it means for the *rūpakāyas* to be only "nominal" bodies of a Buddha *(btags pa ba)*, while the *dharmakāya* is the "actual" body of a Buddha *(yang dag pa, mtshan nyid pa)*, given the fact that many *trikāya* texts simply refer to all three *kāyas* as "bodies of Buddha":[44]

> Some textual traditions explain that the bodies *(kāyas)* of a Buddha are [actually] three; but some explain that the two *rūpakāyas* are only nominal bodies [of a Buddha, i.e., that there is only one actual Buddha body, the *dharmakāya*].
>
> How is this to be understood? The essential point is this. From a Buddha's own point of view *(rang snang la)*, he exists as *dharmakāya* alone, which is the realm of reality *(dbyings, dhātu)* and gnosis *(ye shes,*

jñāna) in one taste. This is so, because from his own point of view, he is fully enlightened with respect to all that is to be known as the realm of reality and gnosis in one taste which is *dharmakāya*.

With this meaning, the *Suvarṇaprabhāsa sūtra* explained the other two *kāya*s [the *rūpakāya*s] to be [merely] nominal *(btags pa ba)*. That sūtra also says: "The two *[rūpa]kāya*s are not to be referred to as 'nirvāṇa,' because there is no Buddha other than the *dharmakāya*. Why aren't the two *[rūpa]kāya*s to be referred to as 'nirvāṇa'? Those two *kāya*s are not the actual [Buddha] but merely nominally so; therefore every moment they arise and cease without existing as permanent." And the *Vajracchedikā* says: "The Bhagavan said: 'Subhuti, it is thus. Do not view the Tathāgata by reference to his excellent marks. Subhuti, if he was a Tathāgata by virtue of his excellent marks, a universal emperor [who also possesses such marks] would also be a Tathāgata. Therefore, do not view the Tathāgata by reference to his excellent marks." The *Vajracchedikā* then presents a verse on the meaning of that: "Whoever sees me as [my] form, whoever knows me as [my] voice, has entered a mistaken path. That being does not see me."

However, from the point of view of trainees *(gdul bya'i gzhan snang gi dbang du byas nas)*, even the two *rūpakāya*s are actual [not just nominal] Buddha bodies, because from within the trainees' perspective, there have to be actual *(mtshan nyid pa)* Buddha bodies carrying out the enlightened activities. And those, the trainees must postulate, are the two *rūpakāya*s that appear to their own minds. It is with this understanding that the *Ratnagotravibhāga* divides [Buddhahood] into the self-benefit ultimate body *(rang don don dam pa'i sku)* and the other-benefit conventional body *(gzhan don kun rdzob pa'i sku)*, where the activity carried out by the latter is posited as the activity of Buddha. Yet, the latter body is merely the reflection of the former body, the former body being the actual one. This is explained extensively there. . . .

Here in the *Abhisamayālaṃkāra*, the context is one in which the twenty-seven enlightened activities are related to the three *kāya*s. Therefore the text follows the point of view of the trainees in explaining even the two *rūpakāya*s as actual bodies of Buddha. This is because, [from the trainees' point of view,] apart from the two *rūpakāya*s, there is no other Buddha who is [observed to be] carrying out the activities.

In sum, when explaining a Buddha's own mode of existence, the *dharmakāya* alone is the only actual Buddha body, because in that context, even the *sāmbhogikakāya* and *nairmāṇikakāya* are posited as the three latter gnoses [of a Buddha, i.e., the gnosis of sameness, the gnosis that thoroughly inspects, and the gnosis that accomplishes activities], rather than as bodies of form adorned with marks and signs. But when explain-

> ing the way a Buddha carries out activity from the point of view of the trainees, the two bodies of form adorned with the marks and signs are also posited as actual Buddha bodies, because the context of discussion is [Buddha's] mode of appearance within the awareness of the trainees. And from the trainees' point of view, the two bodies of form appear to be Buddha.
>
> As it says in the *Āloka,* commenting on the section of the [8,000-verse *Prajñāpāramitā* sūtra] concerning the moderately weak aspiration for others' benefit: "The *rūpakāya* of the Tathāgata, seen by fortunate sentient beings blazing with the marks and signs, is not really the teacher, the *dharmakāya.* Nevertheless, by the power of the *dharmakāya,* which is endowed with a collection of limitless supreme stainless qualities, the [sentient beings'] own awareness appears in the form of such a *rūpakāya.*"[45] And in the *Suvarṇaprabhāsasūtra* it says: "For example, based upon the sky, lightning occurs. Based upon lightning, light occurs. Likewise, based upon the *dharmakāya,* the *sāmbhogikakāya* occurs. Based upon the *sāmbhogikakāya,* the *nairmāṇikakāya* appears."

Go ram pa's analysis of Buddhahood here hearkens back to the formulation of *dharmakāya* in *PP* sūtras and of *svābhāvikakāya/dharmakāya* in Yogācāra treatises. In both of these textual traditions (which are included in what late Indian Buddhists called Pāramitāyāna), Buddhahood was identified as ontologically one: simply *dharmakāya.* Ontologically, Buddhahood was understood as a nondual, undifferentiated realization of universal thusness. Though ordinary beings might conceptualize Buddhahood in terms of the list of undefiled dharmas or *rūpakāya*s, the actual realization of Buddhahood was known only to a Buddha. And that realization, having passed beyond all such conceptual differentiation, was referred to in *PP* sūtras as *dharmakāya.* Because that undivided gnosis of thusness itself comprised the essence *(svabhāva)* of Buddhahood, Yogācāra tradition referred to it also as *svābhāvikakāya,* "embodiment of Buddhahood in its essence." Other common terms for it in Yogācāra texts were *dharmakāya, anāsravadhātu, dharmadhātuviśuddhi, nirvikalpajñāna/tathatāviśuddhi,* etc. The basic *trikāya* structure of Yogācāra, later adopted by Mādhyamikas prior to Haribhadra, centered on the ontological oneness of Buddha's personal nondual realization: *svābhāvikakāya/dharmakāya.* Based upon that, the two *rūpakāya*s were delineated epistemologically, following their corresponding expressions in the Mahāyāna sūtras, according to two basic ways in which that one, unmanifest realization appeared to others (as a glorified Buddha form in a pure realm or as limitless manifestations in the worlds of beings; see chapters 3–5 above).

Go ram pa's quotes from the sūtras and treatises above are intended to remind us that, according to Pāramitāyāna traditions, Buddhahood is ontologically only one *kāya, dharmakāya* alone. And the *rūpakāyas* are merely the way that one *kāya* appears to non-Buddhas under their own conceptual categories. However, he uses the expressions *yang dag pa* and *tshan nyid pa* to refer to the *dharmakāya* as "actual," "real," and the expression *btags pa ba* to refer to the *rūpakāyas* as "nominal," "designated" to the real. This terminology appears to be derived from the *Suvarṇaprabhāsasūtra.*

The *Suvarṇaprabhāsasūtra* has one chapter devoted to the doctrine of three *kāyas* (*sKu gsum rnam par 'byed pa'i leu* in Tibetan translation). That chapter may be a late addition to the sūtra, since it is missing in the Sanskrit manuscript preserved in Nepal and in the earliest Chinese translation (Dharmakṣema's, ca. 414–33 C.E.), appearing only in Chinese translations from the sixth century C.E.[46] The chapter on the three *kāyas* appears in two of the three Tibetan translations of the sūtra. That chapter appears to have been composed based upon texts such as the *Mahāyānasūtrālaṃkāra* and *Mahāyānasaṃgraha*, since it goes into further detail on several of the buddhological issues that were more briefly raised in those texts. In the Tibetan translation that Go ram pa quotes, the explicit terms *btags pa tsam* (merely nominal, *prajñaptimātra*) and *yang dag par yod pa* (really or actually existent, *samyaksat*) are applied to the *rūpakāyas* and *dharmakāya* respectively. The sūtra goes on to say that the *dharmakāya* is the only actual *kāya*, because in reality, all of Buddhahood is included within the thusness and nonconceptual gnosis that comprises *dharmakāya.* Such explicit terminology as "actual" versus "nominal" did not appear in earlier Yogācāra *trikāya* literature (though, as Go ram pa notes, the *Ratnagotravibhāga* did use the analogous terms *paramārthakāya* [ultimate *kāya*] and *saṃvṛtikāya* [conventional *kāya*]), but the implication that Buddhahood was ontologically *dharmakāya* alone was clear, and the *trikāya* chapter of the *Suvarṇaprabhāsasūtra* makes that more explicit.[47]

Because Go ram pa has drawn the distinction between actual and nominal Buddha bodies with reference to the *Suvarṇaprabhāsasūtra* and certain passages in the *PP* sūtras, he must account for the fact that texts such as the *AA* (*Msg*, etc.) teach three *kāyas* without explicitly declaring one "actual" and the others "nominal." The *rūpakāya* (body of form), says Go ram pa, appears to be the actual Buddha from the point of view of the trainees who come into contact with it. Therefore, in texts that explain Buddhahood in a way that explicitly takes the trainees' point of view into account, the *rūpakāyas* are taught simply as Buddha bodies without declaring them as "merely nominal." This is particularly the case in the *AA*, where much emphasis is placed on a Buddha's activity that is carried out, from the perspective of trainees, entirely by the *rūpakāyas.* From the trainees' point of view *(gzhan snang)*, then, the *rūpakāya* is Buddha. From a Buddha's own point of view *(rang snang)*, his actual nature is beyond what trainees can comprehend, being *dharmakāya* alone.

Go ram pa never denies that the *dharmakāya* gives rise to the *rūpakāyas*, as his last quote from the *Suvarṇaprabhāsa* indicates ("Based upon the sky, lightning occurs," etc.). Therefore, he never denies that the *rūpakāyas*, based as they are upon the *dharmakāya*, are to be included within Buddhahood. But he does deny the *rūpakāya*s the ontological status of the *dharmakāya*. Ngag dbang chos grags comments quoted earlier were intended by him to clarify that point, because Go ram pa's mode of expression might otherwise leave him open to the charge that he denies the *rūpakāya*s are Buddha at all, in which case the sūtras taught by figures such as Śākyamuni would not be the word of Buddha. According to Ngag dbang chos grags, Go ram pa's point is that the *rūpakāya*s are nominal aspects of Buddhahood precisely because they are designated by trainees with the *dharmakāya* as basis, the *dharmakāya* being the only actual ontological material of Buddhahood.[48]

In the next to last paragraph of his remarks above, Go ram pa makes some interesting observations. Recall in chapter 5, section 4 above, we observed that the four gnoses taught in *Mahāyānasūtrālaṃkāra* v. 9.67–9.76 were identified by later commentators with the three *kāya*s. In particular, the gnosis of sameness *(samatājñāna)* and thorough investigation *(pratyavekṣājñāna)* were identified with the *sāmbhogikakāya*, while the gnosis that accomplishes activities (*kṛtyānuṣṭhānajñāna)* was identified with the *nairmāṇikakāya*. Go ram pa makes the interesting claim that this is done in order to explain a Buddha's own mode of existence. From a Buddha's own perspective, all aspects of himself are actually just aspects of his nondual gnosis. Texts that identify the Buddha gnoses above with the *rūpakāya*s, then, are emphasizing the fact that a Buddha, though conceptualized by non-Buddhas in terms of form *(rūpakāya*s*)*, is actually only nondual gnosis. In Go ram pa's view, then, other textual passages in which the *rūpakāya*s are presented as bodies of Buddha with the marks and signs, etc. (earlier in the *MSA*, *AA*, *Msg*, etc.) are assuming the perspective of the non-Buddhas. For unenlightened beings only know Buddhahood through the forms which appear to them, those forms being the way Buddhahood manifests to their own minds.

Go ram pa's comments above establish the framework in which his analysis of *AA* 8 will take place. In Go ram pa's view, the fundamental Mahāyāna textual traditions all identified Buddhahood ontologically as *dharmakāya* alone. Since from a Buddha's own point of view there is only one, indivisible *kāya (dharmakāya)*, and the two *rūpakāya*s are posited from the points of view of two types of trainees, those traditions taught three *kāyas* as the normative description of Buddhahood. Go ram pa saw the *AA* as one more expression of those textual traditions. And because the *AA* was in fact composed based upon those traditions (the *PP* sūtras and *trikāya* traditions of Yogācāra), he was predisposed toward an accurate analysis of it.

In Go ram pa's view, to divide the *dharmakāya* into two separate aspects (gnosis distinct from thusness) and posit them as two separate *kāya*s from a Buddha's own point of view (as Haribhadra and Tsong kha pa had done) was to run counter to the entire tradition of buddhology of which the *AA* was a part. It is for this reason that, prior to analyzing *AA* 8, Go ram pa put so much emphasis upon identifying *dharma-*

kāya as the one indivisible essence of Mahāyāna buddhology, the ontological core of Buddhahood that is undivided from a Buddha's own point of view.

Go ram pa now turns to the *Abhisamayālaṃkāra* proper. He presents Haribhadra's four-*kāya* interpretation of *AA* 8, rejects it, and argues for Ārya Vimuktisena's three-*kāya* interpretation. Go ram pa's criticisms of Haribhadra in the *sBas don zab mo'i gter* focus on Haribhadra's four-*kāya* interpretation of *AA* v. 1.17 (the table of contents for *AA* 8). According to Haribhadra, remember, the term *dharmakāya (chos sku)* in v. 1.17 designated a fourth *kāya* of gnosis rather than the title of *AA* chapter 8 (cf. chapter 8, section 2, and chapter 10, section 5, above):

> svābhāvikaḥ sasāmbhogo nairmāṇiko 'paras tathā
> dharmakāyaḥ sakāritraś caturdhā samudīritaḥ
>
> (Sanskrit *AA* 1.17)

> ngo bo nyid longs rdzogs bcas dang
> de bzhin gzhan pa sprul pa ni
> chos sku mdzad pa dang bcas pa
> rnam pa bzhir ni yang dag brjod.
>
> (Tibetan *AA* 1.17)

> [In its essence, with its enjoyment, and in its manifestation(s) as well, *Dharmakāya*, with its activity, is proclaimed as fourfold.]

Go ram pa points out the relationship between *AA* v. 1.4 (which names *AA* chapter 8 "Dharmakāya") and v. 1.17, noting that if *dharmakāya* in v. 1.17 is not the title of *AA* 8, it would be the only part of the *AA*'s table of contents not to name its chapter. Go ram pa argues that it makes no sense to say, as Haribhadra did, that *dharmakāya* appears last in verse 1.17 to associate Buddha's activity with his gnosis alone, since, by Haribhadra's own admission, the activities are carried out through the manifestation of *sāmbhogikakāya* and *nairmāṇikakāya* as well.[49] Go ram pa also notes that the particle *ni* in the Tibetan translation of v. 1.17 functions grammatically to identify the three-*kāya* terms *(svābhāvika, sasāmbhogaḥ, nairmāṇikaḥ)* as a set that is then equated with *dharmakāya*, which should mean that the latter term is used in its inclusive sense, designating Buddhahood as a whole, not a fourth *kāya*. Go ram pa then presents Ārya Vimuktisena's interpretation, which he accepts.[50]

In one section of his *Yum don rab gsal*, Go ram pa performs a masterful philological analysis in which he points out the relationships between the uses of the term *dharmakāya* throughout the entire *Abhisamayālaṃkāra*: *AA* vv. 1.4, 1.17, 8.6, 8.40, and 9.2. Since, as he demonstrates, the term *dharmakāya* is used in its inclusive sense in vv. 1.4, 1.17, 8.40, and 9.2 *(dharmakāya-phalam* inclusive of three *kāyas)*, and in its exclusive sense in v. 8.6 (as a synonym for *svābhāvikakāya*), the *AA* is indeed a three-*kāya* text. His analysis is based entirely on the Tibetan translation of the text, and therefore ignores evidence specific to Sanskrit morphologies discussed in chapter 8 above and the historical-critical considerations noted in chapter 7 above (which would further support his interpretation). Nevertheless, because he interprets key verses such as verse 1.17 and verse 8.6 in relation to the structure of the *AA* as a whole (not just through Haribhadra's peculiar readings taken in isolation from the rest of the text), he arrives at an accurate interpretation.[51]

In the prior section of this chapter, we saw how Tsong kha pa read *AA* 8 through Haribhadra's logico-Mādhyamika perspective, and then sought to justify that reading by projecting that perspective back into earlier textual traditions where it had not been operative. Go ram pa, on the other hand, read *AA* 8 through buddhological perspectives close to those operative in the texts from which it had been redacted, and then evaluated Haribhadra's and others' interpretations of it in that light. In this way, Go ram pa arrived at a more accurate analysis of its meaning than Tsong kha pa could.

Because Tsong kha pa followed Haribhadra in letting logical inference direct textual interpretation, his analysis of *AA* verses was predisposed toward Haribhadra's interpretations. As a result, he ignored most of the philological evidence which could have tipped him off to the fact that the *AA* was a three-*kāya* text. Go ram pa, analyzing *AA* 8 by reference to the entire structure of the text as a whole, unfettered by Haribhadra's peculiar interpretations, freely took note of the many pieces of evidence that support a three-*kāya* interpretation. In short, Go ram pa arrived at a more accurate interpretation of *AA* 8 than Tsong kha pa because his methods, at least in this particular case, were both historically and philologically sounder.

Go ram pa's buddhology, like that of earlier scholars we have discussed, is closely related to his gnoseology. As noted earlier, Tsong kha pa accepted four Buddha *kāya*s in part because he theorized that a Buddha's awareness simultaneously perceives and distinguishes conventional truth from ultimate truth. To Tsong kha pa, this logically implied a fourth kāya of gnosis, since a Buddha's dharmagnoses as conventional phenomena would be distinguished from their emptiness within a Buddha's own awareness, comprising a conventional *kāya* that is an object of Buddhas alone (while *sāmbhogikakāya* and *nairmāṇikakāya* are conventional objects of non-Buddhas). Go ram pa, on the other hand, strongly reaffirmed the *trikāya* buddhology of Mahāyāna Buddhism prior to Haribhadra, in part because his understanding of a Buddha's gnosis conformed more closely than Tsong kha pa's to that of earlier *trikāya* proponents such as Candrakīrti, Ārya Vimuktisena, and the authors of the *Mahāyānasūtrālaṃkāra*, *Mahāyānasaṃgraha*, *Ratnagotravibhāga,* etc., and their commentaries.

Like Tsong kha pa before him, Go ram pa discusses Buddha's gnosis mainly in his commentary on the "Buddhabhūmi" section of Candrakīrti's *Madhyamakāvatāra*. Go ram pa's commentary is called the *lTa ba ngan sel*. Whereas Tsong kha pa's theory of Buddha's gnosis owed much to his own logical inferences and prominent reference to Jñānagarbha's *Satya-dvaya-vibhaṅga*,[52] Go ram pa derived his gnoseology more directly from Candrakīrti's own text, understood in its literal sense.[53] As noted in chapter 9, section 2, above, Candrakīrti's *Madhyamakāvatāra* ("Buddhabhūmi" section, v. 2 and autocommentary) explains a Buddha's omniscience as a comprehension in which all phenomena are known "in one taste" through a Buddha's nondual gnosis of the one ultimate nature they all share, "thatness" (*tattvam, de kho na nyid* = thusness, emptiness). In other words, according to Candrakīrti, a Buddha's knowledge of the phenomenal world is all-encompassing precisely because it is an expression of his knowledge of the undivided and pervasive ultimate nature of that world. Candrakīrti's gnoseology of Buddhahood, like that of Ārya Vimuktisena and formulators of three-*kāya* doctrine, made a Buddha's nondual knowledge of ultimate truth his fundamental knowledge, upon which all his knowledge was based.[54]

Go ram pa follows Candrakīrti closely in this, and therefore criticizes Tsong kha pa's inferential theory of Buddha gnosis. According to Tsong kha pa's theory, a Buddha's knowledges of conventional truth and ultimate truth are both direct and equally fundamental. A Buddha's knowledge of conventional truth is not merely an expression of his knowledge of ultimate truth. A Buddha cognizes conventional truth dualistically (with cognitive subject and object appearing separate) and ultimate truth nondualistically (with no separation between cognitive subject and object). Thus, according to Tsong kha pa, a Buddha does not cognize conventional truth through his cognition of ultimate truth; rather he cognizes conventional truth qua conventional truth and ultimate truth qua ultimate truth, simultaneously and directly. As noted in the previous section, then, Tsong kha pa implicitly granted to conventional truth (as *pratītyasamutpāda*) an ontological status equal to ultimate truth, since both are equally validated by Buddha's direct knowledge, and a Buddha is understood to know all as it exists.[55]

Go ram pa's criticizes Tsong kha pa for having departed from Candrakīrti's text, and in such a way as to make a Buddha's gnosis into a contradiction. Go ram pa challenges Tsong kha pa as to how one mind (a Buddha's) can simultaneously see things both dualistically and nondualistically. If, says Go ram pa, as Tsong kha pa claims, a Buddha sees conventional truth as a separate entity from his own awareness, but sees ultimate truth as one entity with his own awareness, then he must see conventional truth as a separate entity from ultimate truth. In that case, ultimate truth would not be the ultimate nature of conventional truth, as Tsong kha pa accepts, but a separate entity altogether. Go ram pa raises many other arguments against Tsong kha pa's theory, but this is a particularly powerful one.[56]

Go ram pa attempts, in his theory of Buddha's gnosis, to follow Candrakīrti's text very closely. He interprets Candrakīrti as saying that a Buddha's knowledge comprehends all phenomena through the "one taste" of the *dharmadhātu*, i.e., through the one ultimate nature they all share. From the perspective of a Buddha's gnosis, ultimate truth, conventional truth, and the gnosis itself are all cognized nondually, inseparably, in one taste. It is only the discursive thought of trainees that divides a Buddha's gnosis into separate knowledges of ultimate and conventional truth. Thus, the entire phenomenal world conceptually constructed dualistically by sentient beings is fully known by a Buddha, but not in such a way that its dualistic appearance is validated as real within his own perspective. Rather, he knows it all through his nondual knowledge of the *dharmadhātu* (universal thusness) that pervades all. In Go ram pa's view, the dualistic conventional world of ordinary beings is the product of their own conceptual construction (based on their own *karma* and *kleśa*), not a Buddha's. A Buddha's knowledge of the dualistic world of ordinary beings must be through his knowledge of its ultimate nature, not through his own conceptual construction of such a world. Therefore, following Candrakīrti's expression, Go ram pa says that a Buddha's gnosis knows all conventional phenomena, but knows them in a nondualistic manner (with no separation between cognitive subject and object) and without any appearance of temporality, since he knows all through the nonarising and nonceasing *dharmadhātu*. Acknowledging that this is difficult to explain further, Gor ram pa concludes that, in the final analysis, Buddha's gnosis can only be described broadly (as he has) by relying upon the authoritative textual traditions that describe Buddhahood (the textual traditions of the "Maitreya" texts such as the *Mahāyānasūtrālaṃkāra*, *Ratnagotravibhāga*, etc., and the great Mādhyamikas such as Candrakīrti, which express what has been known directly through authentic yogic experience). Precisely how a Buddha cognizes cannot be determined by inferences such as Tsong kha pa's, which extrapolate from the logical and cognitive categories of non-Buddhas.[57]

Whereas a Buddha's gnosis knows all in one taste with the *dharmadhātu* (universal thusness), there can be no differentiation within a Buddha's own awareness per se. Buddha's indivisible gnostic realization, again, as the ontological essence of Buddhahood, can only be posited as one, undifferentiated *kāya: dharmakāya*, also called *svābhāvikakāya* as the embodiment of that essence. *Sāmbhogikakāya* and *nairmāṇikakāya* are the appearances it manifests to others. For Go ram pa, then, just as for Candrakīrti, Ārya Vimuktisena, Ratnākaraśānti, and Abhayākaragupta, the nondual gnoseology of Mahāyāna naturally issues in a *trikāya* scheme of buddhology that conforms to prior Yogācāra formulations.

Go ram pa's gnoseology and buddhology accorded better than Tsong kha pa's with buddhological traditions prior to Haribhadra. However, it left fundamental questions unanswered that Tsong kha pa had specifically tried to address. How can an unconditioned *svābhāvikakāya/dharmakāya* cause manifestation and activity in the conditioned world? And how can a Buddha cognize precisely and individually all conventional phenomena (which are conceptually constructed and differentiated by sentient beings) entirely through the "one taste" of the *dharmadhātu* (the emptiness of all such phenomena)? If this means (as Go ram pa claimed) that conventional phenomena qua phenomena do not appear to a Buddha (i.e., that all appears only in "one taste" with *dharmadhātu*), then in what sense does a Buddha know conventionalities at all? He would not see, for example, the house that we see, composed of different bricks and boards, since all he sees is one with the undifferentiated, the *dharmadhātu*. But if a Buddha does not even know the conventionalities we all see, it would make no sense for so many authoritative texts to call him "omniscient" *(sarvākarajña)*. Or, if a Buddha is held to be omniscient, the fact that he does not know the conventional world we inhabit would imply that it simply does not exist. Then there would be no ontological basis for moral conduct or spiritual practice of any kind, and Mahāyāna metaphysics would collapse into a form of nihilism. These are the sort of problems that Tsong kha pa had attempted to address.

In fairness to Go ram pa, however, these are not just problems raised by his theory, but problems inherent in Mahāyāna formulations prior to Haribhadra that Go ram pa defended. And it is questionable whether Tsong kha pa's attempt to solve such problems was successful. Go ram pa's criticism of Tsong kha pa above is powerful. And in Tsong kha pa's theory lies the implication (whether intended or not) that the dualistic conceptual construction of conventional truth, which traditional Mahāyāna metaphysics said a Buddha had passed beyond, now became a property of a Buddha's own realization.

As in India, we get the sense that these Tibetan scholars were wrestling with a deep tension in the heart of Mahāyāna systematic thought, a tension that creates a variety of interrelated philosophical difficulties in conceptualizing how Buddhahood simultaneously transcends the world and uninterruptedly engages it. The debate over Buddha *kāyas*, along with debates over the nature of a Buddha's awareness, the relation between enlightenment and the path that leads to it, and relations between enlightenment and the world, are all expressions of a deep structural tension in Mahāyāna thought inscribed in its doctrine of nonabiding nirvāṇa, the doctrine that a Buddha's attainment, inconceivably, bridges the poles of nirvāṇa and saṃsāra: the unconditioned and the conditioned, the ultimate and the relative, the infinite and the finite, the eternal and the temporal.

13
Sources of Controversy—Nonabiding Nirvāṇa and the Mahāyāna Quest for Authentic Reinterpretation of the Four Noble Truths

13.1 Introduction

A theme we have repeatedly returned to is the remarkable way logical tension in the doctrine of nonabiding nirvāṇa has quietly served as a driving force behind Mahāyāna doctrinal development around Buddhahood in India and Tibet. The long controversy over the *Abhisamayālaṃkāra* on Buddhahood may be viewed as one rather complex example of this phenomenon.

Ancient arguments over the nature and number of *kāya*s taught in the *AA* have puzzled traditional and contemporary scholars alike. If we engage only the surface level of discussion, we become puzzled not only by the purport of the disagreements, but more fundamentally, by the reasons for their significance to anyone at any time. Why was it important how many *kāya*s the *AA* taught? As we have seen, Haribhadra tried to resolve the tension in the Mahāyāna doctrine of nonabiding nirvāṇa, inscribed in the three-*kāya* model that the *Abhisamayālaṃkāra* had inherited from Yogācāra, by "updating" that model through the perspective of late-eighth-century Madhyamaka logic. But Haribhadra's new reading of the *Abhisamayālaṃkāra* had important implications for ontology, gnoseology, and soteriology that he may not have fully foreseen, and that forced later scholars to wrestle with the same underlying problem he had tried to address. Thus, it was the underlying logical tension in the doctrine of nonabiding nirvāṇa that implicitly organized the wide variety of concerns Indian and Tibetan exegetes brought to their readings of *AA* 8 on Buddha *kāya*s.

We argued in chapter 1 that the paradox of nonabiding nirvāṇa *(apratiṣṭhita nirvāṇa)* quietly fueled many areas of doctrinal tension in the development of

Indian and Tibetan Mahāyāna thought, and that our appreciation of its implicit role in the *AA* 8 controversy sensitizes us to its implicit role in those other areas: concerning topics of Buddhahood other than the *kāyas* and texts outside of the *Abhisamayālaṃkāra* corpus. The broader purpose of this book has been to show how tension generated by the leap from pre-Mahāyāna concepts of nirvāṇa to the Mahāyāna doctrine of nonabiding nirvāṇa has functioned as a far more significant force in the doctrinal development of Indian and Tibetan Mahāyāna as a whole than has generally been recognized. Our contextualization of the *AA* 8 controversy has traced that tension in Yogācāra and Madhyamaka texts as it surfaces in a wide range of interrelated doctrinal issues bearing upon Buddhahood: gnoseological, ontological, soteriological, and theological. That the doctrine of nonabiding nirvāṇa has been a source of so much systematic tension in Indian and Tibetan Mahāyāna, and that the tension has surfaced in a wide range of interrelated problems of Buddhahood, should now be clear.

This leaves us with a number of further questions. Why did the doctrine of nonabiding nirvāṇa come to be so widely accepted in Indian Mahāyāna Buddhism? What forces of doctrinal formation and praxis helped project that doctrine into the center of systematic Mahāyāna thought, and militate for its dominance in late Indian Buddhism and Tibet? And what role did those forces play in organizing the differing perspectives on Buddhahood of later Indian and Tibetan scholars?

Reflecting on these questions over the past few years, some possible answers have begun to suggest themselves to me. In the following sections of this chapter, I will voice these as hypotheses and present some of the textual evidence for them. These hypotheses cannot be adequately demonstrated in the space remaining, and may contain errors of judgment. But I do believe that at least the direction they chart has the potential to help clarify some apparently contradictory expressions of enlightenment in Mahāyāna texts that continue to cause confusion for scholars and practitioners, and also to shed some light on implicit principles around which differing perspectives on base, path, and fruit in India and Tibet have been organized. I suggest these hypotheses here as a charter for further research toward their correction or refinement, and for the critical responses that would be helpful toward that research.

In order to pursue the questions above, we need first to look more closely at the way in which the transition from pre-Mahāyāna to developed Mahāyāna thought created systematic doctrinal tension. I would suggest that the doctrine of nonabiding nirvāṇa gave rise to this tension by radically altering the normative formula at the heart of systematic Buddhist thought: the Four Noble Truths. To show how this is so, we will take another look at the Four Noble Truths formula as broadly understood in early Buddhist and Abhidharma thought, from which it was inherited by Mahāyāna.

According to early Buddhist and Sarvāstivāda Abhidharma formulations of the Four Noble Truths, the five *skandhas*, comprising the aggregates of materiality, consciousness, feeling tones, mental labelings, and volitional formations, include all psychophysical components of living beings, the entirety of their experienced worlds. The five aggregates are composite formations *(saṃskāra)*, impermanent, conditioned and permeated by clinging attachments to the ever-changing flow of experience. They therefore comprise a stream of subtle and intense forms of shifting dissatisfactions and sufferings, the three forms of *duḥkha* that comprise the First Noble Truth.

Since suffering is inherent to the conditioned formations of mind and body *(skandhas)*, whatever generates those formations is the fundamental cause of suffering. The Second Noble Truth identifies the causes of those formations as defiled actions of body, speech, and mind *(sāsrava karma)* and the defiled mental states that motivate them *(kleśa*s*)*, including at the most basic level: clinging attachment *(tṛṣṇā)* and ignorance of reality as it is *(avidyā)*.

The doctrine of twelve factors of dependent arising *(pratītya samutpāda)* delineates the process. Ignorance and attachment, through other *kleśa*s and defiled karma, give rise to the five aggregates which constitute the process of saṃsāra. To cut off ignorance and attachment by supramundane insight *(prajñā)*, then, is to end the suffering of saṃsāra, ultimately by bringing an end to the conditioned formations of body and mind per se, the inherent bases of suffering. Two types of nirvāṇa were then distinguished under the rubric of the Third Noble Truth *(duḥkha nirodha satya)*. The first type is nirvāṇa that retains the formations of body and mind that had been projected from prior kleśa and karma. It comprises an attainment of nirvāṇa "with residual conditioning" *(sopadhiśeṣa nirvāṇa)*. The second type of nirvāṇa occurs at an arhat or Buddha's physical death, at which time there is no further rebirth because the conditioned formations have come to an end. This is "final nirvāṇa" *(parinirvāṇa)*, also called "nirvāṇa without any further residual conditioning" *(nirupadhiśeṣa nirvāṇa)*, "final" because it involves the cessation of the formations of mind and body. Final nirvāṇa is the cessation of a Buddha's active presence or involvement in the defiled world.[1]

Notice, according to the first two Noble Truths, how ontology follows epistemology. The root cause of the conditioned formations of suffering *(skandha*s*)* is ignorance, described, for example, in terms of four basic misconceptions *(viparyāsa):* misconceiving permanence in the impermanent, pleasantness in the unpleasant, purity in the impure, and an autonomous self *(ātman)* in the formations of mind and body that have no self. According to such Abhidharma formulations of the Four Noble Truths, each living being's aggregates of body and mind *exist* because he or she has those misconceptions (which give rise to attachment, other passions, karma, and the twelve-link chain). And each person's aggregates, in the end, cease to exist when he or she fully attains the supramundane insight that cuts off those misconceptions and subsequent attachment. Thus, an ontological principle, conditioned existence, is causally related to an epistemological principle, ignorance, such that the cessation of ignorance brings about the cessation of conditioned existence.

It is worth reiterating that, according to this Four Noble Truth formula, removal of ignorance does not issue in a lasting, ignorance-free mode of participation in conditioned existence. An arhat or Buddha who has attained nirvāṇa does not, upon physical death, take form again in some manner that participates free of ignorance in the conditioned world. Rather, the final attainment of the unconditioned at physical death *(asaṃskṛta, parinirvāṇa)* is the total cessation of conditioned existence *(saṃskṛta saṃsāra)* for that individual.[2]

The Four Noble Truths had long been established as a central, normative doctrinal formula of Buddhism when Mahāyāna movements began to arise in ancient India and central Asia. To affirm the Four Noble Truths constituted part of the very identity of any learned follower of the Buddha. Mahāyāna Buddhists promulgated new sūtras as the Buddha's word with the understanding that they, like all sūtras, expressed the same Four Noble Truths, revealing them in their more profound and vast implications.

But Mahāyāna sūtras also gave a new, vivid expression to intuitions that projected an outcome for the bodhisattva path far more vast in its relation to the world than what had previously been inscribed in the Four Noble Truths. Several such basic intuitions of early Mahāyāna Buddhism, each an expression of praxis, fed an emerging notion in Mahāyāna sūtras that complete enlightenment *(samyaksaṃbodhi)* ought to keep a Buddha connected to the world in vast ways over space and time. This pushed up against the concept of nirvāṇa contained in the Third Noble Truth, which removed a Buddha from the world in a final nirvāṇa after only a few decades of activity. Early Mahāyāna intuitions were thus in tension with the Third Noble Truth as it had been received from prior tradition.

To give expression to these intuitions that the outcome of the bodhisattva path involves vast participation in saṃsāric space and time, Mahāyānists initially experimented with various ways to stretch the Third Noble Truth to have bodhisattvas or Buddhas put off or postpone their final nirvāṇa so as to remain active within saṃsāra to help beings in vast ways. But the Third Noble Truth could only be stretched so far to accommodate such intuitions.

As it became increasingly clear that early Mahāyāna intuitions of a Buddha's vast salvific connection to the world were simply not consistent with the received Third Noble Truth, Mahāyāna texts came to redefine a Buddha's nirvāṇa altogether as "nonabiding": liberated from personal bondage to the world yet eternally and pervasively engaged in the world for the sake of others. Giving a more authentic expression to these Mahāyāna intuitions, this doctrine was formalized in the writings of Nāgārjuna, and further developed in Yogācāra śāstras ascribed to Maitreya, Asanga, and Vasubandhu (such as those explored in chapter 5), becoming dominant in late Indian Mahāyāna.

But by radically redefining the Third Noble Truth without explicitly changing the first two Noble Truths upon which it had been based, this new doctrine generated logical tension at the heart of systematic Mahāyāna thought. It is this tension that lay behind so many interrelated problems of Buddhahood in later Indian Buddhism and Tibet. And Mahāyāna scholars, I would suggest, in seeking to resolve that tension by arguing for one model of Buddhahood over another, thereby actually sought an authentic Mahāyāna way to reinterpret the Four Noble Truths scheme as a whole, consistent with their intuitions of a Buddha's vast connection to living beings and to their world. Their differing perspectives on Buddhahood thus gave expression to deeper differences on the Four Noble Truths, all of which represented different ways of prioritizing and ordering the early Mahāyāna intuitions that had originally projected the doctrine of nonabiding nirvāṇa.

13.2
Mahāyāna Intuitions of a Buddha's Vast Connection to the World that Pushed up against the Third Noble Truth of Nirvāṇa

a. Nonabiding Nirvāṇa and Universal Emptiness

According to the dualistic pre-Mahāyāna formulation of saṃsāra and nirvāṇa sketched in section 1 above, yogic realization of the impermanent, selfless, and suffering nature of the psychophysical aggregates *(skandhas)* deconstructs the epistemological conditions for their being (ignorance and attachment), ultimately culminating in their cessation and the attainment of an unconditioned state *(nirvāṇa)* that stands apart from the conditioned worlds of living beings *(nirupadhiśesa nirvāṇa)*.

In contrast to this, the Mahāyāna's seminal intuition of emptiness *(śūnyatā)* generated a radically different model: the nonduality of saṃsāra and nirvāṇa. Taking the doctrine of dependent arising *(pratītya samutpada)* to its logical conclusion, Mahāyānists asserted that, despite the fact that each thing appears to possess its own autonomous existence apart from other things *(svabhāva)*, everything designated upon its causes, conditions, or parts exists only in dependence upon that nexus of causal and logical factors, and therefore, contrary to the appearance, does not exist autonomously.

As formulated in Madhyamaka and Yogācāra thought, the direct realization of emptiness does not realize something apart from dependently arisen phenomena. It realizes the emptiness of those phenomena, their own ultimate nature *(paramārtha)*. The Mahāyāna formulation of two truths thus locates ultimate truth (*paramārtha satya*, emptiness, thusness or suchness) within conventional truth (*saṃvṛti satya*, dependent phenomena).

This gradually helped project a new definition of a Buddha's final attainment, for a Buddha's nirvāṇa was no longer to be conceived as an unconditioned state that stands apart from the conditioned world *(nirupadhiśeṣa nirvāṇa)*, but as the perfect, nondual awareness of the ultimate nature *of* the world.[3] In other words, the centrality of perfection of wisdom *(prajñāpāramitā)* in Mahāyāna doctrinal formation helped project a doctrine of nonabiding nirvāṇa by indicating that a Buddha's nondual knowledge is to be localized *in* saṃsāra as the direct realization of the conditioned world's own ultimate nature (emptiness, suchness, the *dharmadhātu*). As Nāgārjuna's *Yuktiṣaṣṭikā*, verse 6, says:

> Existence and nirvāṇa: These two are not [really] to be found. [Instead,] nirvāṇa [may be] defined as the thorough knowledge of existence.[4]

But saṃsāra is often described as inconceivably vast, unlimited in terms of numbers of beings and the extent of their cosmos, while its ultimate nature (thusness, suchness, the *dharmadhātu*) is undivided, undifferentiated. Therefore, a Buddha's nondual awareness of the *dharmadhātu* is an inconceivably vast awareness, an awareness that also comprises, in some sense, a nondual communion with the entire cosmos through its one ultimate nature. A few sūtra quotes follow that exemplify this intuition of a Buddha's vast connection to the world and its beings through universal emptiness or suchness:

> The Tathagata cognizes the skandhas as identical with Suchness *(tathatā)*. . . . And just that Suchness of the skandhas, that is also the Suchness of the world. . . . Therefore then, Subhuti, that which is the Suchness of the skandhas, that is the Suchness of the world; that which is the Suchness of the world, that is the Suchness of all dharmas; that which is the Suchness of all dharmas, that is the Suchness of the fruit of a Streamwinner, and so on, up to: that is the Suchness of Pratyekabuddhahood, that is the Suchness of the Tathagata. In consequence all this Suchness. . . . is just one single Suchness, is without any trace of the variety of positivity and negativity, as being one, nondifferent, inextinguishable, unaffected, nondual, without cause for duality. That is this Suchness which the Tathagata has, thanks to the perfection of wisdom, fully known. . . . And thus a vision of this world takes place.[5]

> Where there arises an act of consciousness which has none of the skandhas for objective support, there the nonviewing of form, etc. takes place. But just this nonviewing of the skandhas is the viewing of the world. That is the way in which the world is viewed by the Tathagata.[6]

> Just as the suchness of the Tathagata, which is immutable and undifferentiated, is nowhere obstructed, so also the suchness of all dharmas, which is also immutable and undifferentiated. For the suchness of the Tathagata, and the suchness of all dharmas, they are both one single suchness, not two, not divided. . . . Just as the suchness of the Tathagata is undiscrim-

inated and undifferentiated, at all times and in all dharmas, so also the suchness of Subhuti. And for that reason, although we seem to have a duality when Subhuti has been conjured up from the suchness of the Tathagata, nevertheless nothing real has been lopped off that suchness, which remains unbroken, because one cannot apprehend an actually real agent that could break it apart.[7]

The Bodhisattva fully knows these things, but the Tathagatha is one who has fully known all dharmas through a wisdom which is conjoined with a single mark.[8]

Coursing in the baseless, he sees all dharmas as contained in this perfection of wisdom, and yet he does not apprehend those dharmas. And why? Because these dharmas on the one hand and that perfection of wisdom on the other are not two nor divided. And why? Because there is no differentiation between these dharmas. All dharmas are undifferentiated because they have been identified with the dharma-element *(dharmadhātu)*, with suchness *(tathatā)*, with the reality limit *(bhūtakoṭi)*.[9]

[Subhūti asked Mañjuśrī:] "Why are you a Worthy One, a Supremely Enlightened One?"

"Because I realize that all things are equal in the dharmadhātu."

Subhuti asked: "Mañjuśrī, in what stage do you really abide?"

"I abide in every stage. . . . As an illustration, consider the empty space in the ten directions. People speak of the eastern space, the southern space, the western space, the northern space, the four intermediate spaces, the space above, the space below, and so forth. Such distinctions are spoken of, although the empty space itself is devoid of distinctions. In like manner, virtuous one, the various stages are established in the ultimate emptiness of all things, although the emptiness itself is devoid of distinctions."[10]

The Buddhas' knowledge is free,
Unhindered in all times;
This realm of wisdom
Is equanimous as space.
The realms of beings of the cosmos
Ultimately have no distinction;
Thoroughly knowing all of them
Is the sphere of the enlightened ones. . . .
The minds of all sentient beings

In the past, present, and future,
The enlightened, in one instant,
Can thoroughly comprehend.[11]

How should great enlightening beings know the sphere of Buddha, who has realized thusness *(tathatā)* and is completely awake? Knowing the spheres of all worlds by means of unobstructed, unimpeded knowledge is the sphere of Buddha. Knowing the spheres of all times, all lands, all things, and all beings, the undifferentitated sphere of true thusness, the unobstructed sphere of the reality realm, the boundless sphere of absolute truth, the unquantified sphere of space, and the objectless sphere, is the sphere of Buddha. Just as the spheres of all times, and so on, up to the objectless sphere, are all infinite, so is the sphere of Buddha infinite.[12]

Buddha knows the thoughts and mental patterns of all sentient beings, their faculties, dispositions, inclinations, afflictions, obsessions, and habits; in sum, Buddha instantly knows all things in all times. . . . By knowing all things are natureless, a Buddha attains omniscience, and by great compassion continues to save sentient beings.[13]

As we saw in chapter 5, Yogācāra treatises gave these kinds of sūtra expressions an explicit doctrinal form in terms of nonabiding nirvāṇa inscribed in models of Buddha gnoses *(jñānas)* and Buddha *kāya*s. The *dharmakāya*'s nondual realization of thusness, free from the ignorance that binds beings to the world, is cognitively one with its undivided, ultimate nature (the *dharmadhātu*), which intimately connects it to the cosmos in all its vastness.

b. Nonabiding Nirvāṇa, *Bodhicitta*, and the Bodhisattva Path

Synergistic with the Mahāyāna intuition of a Buddha's vast connection to the world through its emptiness are early Mahāyāna intuitions of *bodhicitta* and the bodhisattva path, which also tended to connect a Buddha to the world in vast ways.

As illustrated above, to locate a Buddha's nondual knowledge in the world as the realization of its ultimate nature implies not only a depth to the knowledge but an inconceivable vastness to it: an unlimited realization of oneness with the nature of the entire universe, even further, of all universes over all time. Corresponding to this realization of oneness with the ultimate nature of all is a breakdown in the separation ordinary beings assume between "self" and other beings.

The Buddha asked Mañjuśrī, "Do you wish to treat the Tathāgata as a teacher of the Dharma who converts sentient beings?"

Mañjuśrī answered, "I do wish to treat the Tathāgata as a teacher of

> the Dharma who converts sentient beings, but the Dharma teacher and the listener are both inapprehensible. Why? Because they both abide in the dharmadhātu, and in the dharmadhātu sentient beings are not different from one another. . . ."[14]

Such an intuition is synergistic with the Buddha's frequent exhortation to his followers in Mahāyāna sūtras to generate an impulse for the liberation of all beings: *bodhicitta*. The cultivation of insight into emptiness can undercut the ontological separation ordinarily assumed between self and others, opening the bodhisattva's mind to the compassion of *bodhicitta* that seeks the well-being of infinite beings as "self." At the same time, a bodhisattva's cultivation of compassion and *bodhicitta* empowers her mind to open to the limitless realization of emptiness.

As noted in chapters 1 and 5, many Mahāyāna sūtras and śāstras declare the raison d'être of Mahāyāna thought and praxis as *bodhicitta*, the impulse to attain enlightenment for the sake of all living beings. The textual model of Mahāyāna practice (and the living model in present-day Tibetan practice) is not the arhat whose final liberation from the world severs all connection to it, but the bodhisattva who strives for a Buddha's awakening in order to guide all living beings to liberation. From the perspective of *bodhicitta*, the raison d'etre of the path is for oneself to be liberated into a scope of activity on behalf of beings so vast and of such profundity as to be inconceivable even to the arhats depicted in the Sūtra Pitaka. Thus the impulse of *bodhicitta* was another significant force behind Mahāyāna doctrinal formation in the direction of a Buddha's "nonabiding nirvāṇa" *(apratiṣṭhita nirvāṇa)*, a nirvāṇa that remains ever active in the world. In its *trikāya* formulation, that activity includes the uninterrupted teaching of the *sāmbhogikakāya*s and the repeated appearance of limitless varieties of *nairmāṇikakāya*.

According to the texts we studied in chapter 5, *bodhicitta* is expressed in formal vows to work for the liberation of beings and enacted through the skillful methods *(upāya)* that culminate at the completion of the bodhisattva path in a Buddha's spontaneous manifestations and activities. A bodhisattva's practice of "method" *(upāya)* involves aeons of practice of the perfections *(pāramitās):* giving in all forms, practices of virtue, patience, perseverance, and meditative concentration. Such practices generate a vast collection of karmic merit *(puṇya sambhara)* synergistic with the collection of wisdom *(prajñāpāramitā, jñāna sambhara)* through the structure of the fivefold bodhisattva path.

The doctrinal and practical elaboration of the bodhisattva path further impelled the doctrinal formation of a nonabiding nirvāṇa as its projected culmination. For Buddhahood as the fruition of the wisdom collection is unconditioned *(asaṃskṛta):* free from karmic conditioning and epistemologically one with the unconditioned nature of all phenomena *(dharmakāya)*. But Buddhahood as the momentum of *bodhicitta* previously enacted in the vast collection of merit on the path is the unceasing manifestation of diverse appearances *(rūpakāya)* to beings in their conditioned realms of experience *(saṃskṛta)* to guide them in accord with the purity of their own minds. It thus remains vastly connected to the world in space and time.

A passage from the *Avataṃsakasūtra*, a scripture important to Yogācāra formulators of Buddha-*kāya* and Buddha-*jñāna* theory, provides an eloquent expression of the Buddhas' unlimited connection to the world as the outcome of vast cultivation of prior causes on the path:

> Then the enlightening being Universally Good [the bodhisattva Samantabhadra] said to the great congregation of enlightening beings, "This matter is inconceivable. The Buddha, the one who realizes thusness, the worthy, the truly awake, becomes manifest by means of infinite phenomena. Why? It is not by one condition, by one phenomenon, that the manifestation of Buddha can be accomplished. It is accomplished by ten infinities of things. What are the ten? It is accomplished by the mind of enlightenment *(bodhicitta)* that took care of infinite sentient beings in the past. It is accomplished by the infinite supreme aspirations of the past. It is accomplished by great benevolence and compassion, which infinitely saved all sentient beings in the past. It is accomplished by infinite continuous commitments of the past. It is accomplished by infinite cultivation of virtues and knowledge tirelessly in the past. It is accomplished by infinite service of buddhas and education of sentient beings in the past. It is accomplished by infinite pure paths of wisdom and means in the past. It is accomplished by infinite pure virtues of the past. It is accomplished by infinite ways of adornment in the past. It is accomplished by infinite comprehensions of principles and meanings in the past. When these infinite, incalculable aspects of the teaching are fulfilled, one becomes a Buddha.[15]

In this text, Buddhahood is frequently depicted as infinite in scope both as the vast manifestation of infinite prior practices and in its nondual realization of the infinite *dharmadhātu*:

> When great enlightening beings know the manifestation of Buddha, they know it is infinite because they know it consummates infinite practices; then they know it is immensely vast because they know it pervades the ten directions; then they know it has no coming or going because they know it is apart from birth, subsistence, and extinction; then they know it has no action and nothing acted upon because they know it is beyond mind, intellect, and consciousness; then they know it is impartial because they know all sentient beings have no self; then they know it is endless

> because they know it pervades all lands without end; . . . then they know it is nondual because they know Buddha equally observes the conditioned and unconditioned; then they know all sentient beings gain benefit because the dedication of Buddha's original vows are freely fulfilled.[16]

A passage from the *Bodhicittavivaraṇa* ascribed to Nāgārjuna (verses 98–102) nicely expresses the interwoven nature of knowledge of emptiness and its compassionate expression in *bodhicitta* as bases for nonabiding nirvāṇa:

> The teachings of the world's Protectors accord with the [varying] capacities of living beings. The Buddhas employ a wealth of skillful means, which take many forms in the world.
>
> Teachings differ in being profound, or vast, or sometimes both at once. Yet all are invariably characterized by emptiness and nonduality.
>
> All *dhāraṇīs*, stages of path, and *pāramitās* of the Buddhas are expressions of *bodhicitta*, say the Omniscient ones.
>
> Those who thereby always work for beings in body, speech, and mind advocate the claims of emptiness *(śūnyatā)*, not the contentions of nihilism.
>
> Supreme beings do not abide in *nirvāṇa* or *saṃsāra*. Therefore Buddhas have spoken of it as "nonabiding *nirvāṇa*."
>
> The unique flavor of compassion is merit, [while] the taste of emptiness is supreme. Those who imbibe [them] to fulfil their own and others' welfare are the sons and daughters of the Buddha.[17]

c. Nonabiding Nirvāṇa, *Buddhānusmṛti*, and Devotional Practice

Many Mahāyāna sūtras express another practice that presumes a vast connection between Buddhas and beings, and was therefore fundamental to the emergence and doctrinal development of nonabiding nirvāṇa. That practice is *buddhānusmṛti*, the mindful recollection of Buddhas and their qualities, which becomes a vivid awareness of Buddhahood in the present. Notable examples of mindful recollection of Buddha as a practice that leads to direct encounters with Buddhas occur in the *Pratyutpanna-samādhi-sūtra*, where the practitioner comes face to face with Amitāyus and other Buddhas to receive their blessing and teachings, and the vivid envisioning of Amitāyus in the *Amitāyurbuddhānusmṛtisūtra*.[18] The "*Samādhi* of a Single Deed" described in the *Mahāratnakūtasūtra* collection and the *Saptaśatika-prajñāpāramitā-sūtra* provide another example:

> Mañjuśrī asked the Buddha, "World-Honored One, what should one do to acquire supreme enlightenment quickly?"
>
> The Buddha answered, "If one follows the teaching of the pāramitā

of wisdom, one can acquire supreme enlightenment quickly. Furthermore, there is the single deed samādhi: a good man or a good woman who cultivates this samādhi will also quickly acquire supreme enlightenment."

Mañjuśrī asked, "World-Honored One, what is the single deed samādhi?"

The Buddha answered, "To meditate exclusively on the oneness of the dharmadhātu is called the single deed samādhi. Those good men or good women who wish to enter this samādhi should first listen to discourses on the pāramitā of wisdom and cultivate it as taught. Then they can enter this samādhi, which, like the dharmadhātu, is nonregressive, indestructible, unobstructed, and signless.

Those good men or good women who wish to enter the single deed samādhi should live in seclusion, cast away discursive thoughts, not cling to the appearances of things, concentrate their minds on a Buddha, and recite his name single-mindedly. They should keep their bodies erect and, facing the direction of that Buddha, meditate upon him continuously. If they can maintain mindfulness of the Buddha without interruption from moment to moment, then they will be able to see all the Buddhas of the past, present, and future right in each moment. Why? Because the merits of being mindful of one Buddha are as innumerable and boundless as those of being mindful of countless Buddhas, for the inconceivable teachings of all Buddhas are identical and undifferentiated. All Buddhas achieve supreme enlightenment by the same suchness, and all are endowed with incalculable merits and immeasurable eloquence. Therefore, one who enters the single deed samādhi knows thoroughly that Buddhas as innumerable as the sands of the Ganges are indistinguishable in the dharmadhātu.[19]

Notice the relation in this passage between cultivating awareness of the Buddha in relative and ultimate senses. The practice is described as meditation upon "the oneness of the *dharmadhātu*," and the first task is to listen to and cultivate the teaching on the perfection of wisdom *(prajñāpāramitā)*: knowledge of emptiness, suchness. Then practitioners are to live in seclusion, develop detachment, concentrate on a Buddha and recite his name: relative practices. These practices give rise to a direct encounter with countless Buddhas, which is realized in its ultimate purport as an encounter with the undivided suchness that they all embody.

Mindful recollection of Buddhas is central to the *Samādhirājasūtra*, which again works with the interplay between ultimate and relative awareness of Buddhas within the "king of *samādhis*":

Since indeed this king of *samādhis* *(samādhirāja)* is the same as emptiness, it stands at the head of all pure moral practices. Dharmas are by nature always composed. The foolish, who apply their minds to what is inappropriate, do not understand this.

The Buddha is never absent for those who seek after this auspicious *samādhi*. They forever contemplate the most excellent of men once they have had recourse to this stage of peace.

One who recollects the Tathāgatas in all their aspects comes to be one whose mind and senses are calm. His thoughts will not be confused; he will forever be collected and he will become like an ocean, vast in learning and knowledge.

Moreover, after becoming established in this *samādhi* the bodhisattva who walks the promenade sees thousands of millions of Buddhas, more numerous even than the grains of sand in the Ganges.[20]

The interplay between relative and ultimate awareness in the mindful recollection of the Buddhas is a common theme in Mahāyāna sūtras. Another example from the *Avataṃsakasūtra*:

How should great enlightening beings see the body of Buddha? They should see the body of Buddha in infinite places. Why? They should not see Buddha in just one thing, one phenomenon, one body, one land, one being—they should see Buddha everywhere. Just as space is omnipresent, in all places, material or immaterial, yet without either arriving or not arriving there, because space is incorporeal, in the same way Buddha is omnipresent, in all places, in all beings, in all things, in all lands, yet neither arriving nor not arriving there, because Buddha's body is incorporeal, manifesting a body for the sake of sentient beings.[21]

In addition, there are many sūtra passages that describe a direct encounter with the Buddha, or with great numbers of Buddhas, as the outcome of purification of mind or devotion in a more general sense:

Buddha does not tell enlightening beings about the ultimate nirvana of Buddhas and does not show it to them. Why? Because Buddha wants to cause them to see all Buddhas always present before them, to see in one moment all the Buddhas of past and future, in their full splendor, just as if they were actually present, yet without entertaining any notions of duality or nonduality. . . .

For example, when the sun comes out and illumines the world, its image is reflected in all clean vessels of water, being in all places without coming or going. If one vessel breaks, then the reflection of the sun does not appear in it. Do you think it is the fault of the sun that its reflection does not appear there?

> No—it is just because the vessel is broken; it is not the fault of the sun.
>
> The knowledge of realization of thusness, Buddha knowledge, is also like this, appearing throughout the cosmos, without before or after: Buddha appears in the clean mind-vessels of all sentient beings. If the mind-vessel is always clean, the embodiment of Buddha is always seen; if the mind is polluted, the vessel breaks and the Buddha cannot be seen.[22]
>
> After great enlightening beings have heard this teaching [on the manifestation of Buddha], then they can know infinite things by knowledge of equality; . . . then they can see the Buddhas before them by means of supreme devotion; . . . then they can acquire all virtues by means of the power of knowledge and wisdom; then they can shed all worldly defilements by means of spontaneous knowledge; then they can enter the network of all ten directions by means of the will for enlightenment; then they can know the Buddhas of all times are of one and the same essence, by means of great observation. . . .[23]

In addition, and related to the practices of mindful recollection, devotion, purification, and ultimate awareness, many Mahāyāna sūtras make reference to samādhis (as in the *Samādhirājasūtra* quote above) or to high levels of attainment (as in the quote below) through which bodhisattvas make direct contact with numerous Buddhas, receive teachings, etc.

> Enlightening beings in this stage of Joy [the first *bhūmi*] get to see many Buddhas, by broad vision and by the power of vows seeing many hundreds of Buddhas, many thousands of Buddhas, many hundreds of thousands of Buddhas, many millions, many billions, many trillions of Buddhas. Having seen those Buddhas, those . . . enlightening beings honor and serve them with supreme zeal, presenting them with the necessities of life, such as food, clothing, drink, vessels, bedding, and medicines, and they also bring comforts for enlightening beings, and they also respect and support the religious community. These supreme roots of goodness the enlightening beings dedicate to consummate enlightenment.[24]

The Mahāyāna understanding that actual, direct contact with Buddhas is always possible, a natural outcome of the purification of one's mind through practice, has been an important presumption in devotional practice. Devotional practices characteristic of Mahāyāna include praying to and invoking Buddhas and bodhisattvas through their names or mantras, prostration, offering to them, confession before them, envisioning them and feeling their purifying presence and inspiration, supplications for their teaching and their continuing active presence in the world, receiving their teachings in dreams or visions, and nondual identification with them and their qualities.

Many modern scholars have characterized Buddhist devotional practices primarily as expressions of human religious need, e.g. a need for the Buddha "to be present, to console, clarify, teach, protect."[25] While this viewpoint has merit, it does not do full justice to many of the texts. The practice of envisioning the Buddha in the examples above is not merely an expression of a human need but the enactment of a deep intuition about the nature of reality. Reality discloses itself as a communicative and transformative power present to anyone whose vision becomes sufficiently purified through practice. For this reason "devotional" practices such as *buddhānusmṛti* were ensconced within collections of textual materials such as the *Ratnakuṭa, Prajñāpāramitā, Avataṃsaka, Samādhirāja* and *Pratyutpanna* sūtras as one element within a wide framework of Mahāyāna practice: cultivation of *bodhicitta* and compassion, ritual practices, perfection of insight into emptiness, practice of perfections, etc. As illustrated above, the texts often present these practices as interwoven, synergistic, and simultaneously operative. For this reason also, devotional practices take vivid expression in many of the most influential systematic treatises of Indian Mahāyāna, treatises ascribed not to sentimentalists but to the most accomplished scholar-adepts: Nāgārjuna, Maitreya, Asanga, Vasubandhu, Bhāvaviveka, Candrakīrti, Śāntideva, etc.

Thus, in the view of Mahāyāna sytematicians, "devotional" practices are not merely expressions of human need but the forms needed to elicit and express basic intuitions concerning the nature of reality itself. *Dharmakāya* pervades the universe with its communicative and transformative power. Its "presence" is more intimately accessed the more thorough one's deconstruction of the reifying concepts through which appearances present themselves—which is to say, the more thorough one's purification of mind by devotional practice, meditation on emptiness, and/or by reenvisioning insubstantial reality as the realm of purity that the *dharmakāya* knows it to be. An example of the latter practice from the *Amitāyurbuddhānusmṛtisūtra:*

> The Buddha told Ānanda and Vedehī, "After you have seen these things, you should then meditate on the Buddha. Why? Because all Buddhas and Tathāgatas are those whose body is *dharmadhātu,* the body of absolute reality which pervades the minds and thoughts of all sentient beings. Thus, when you think of the Buddha, your mind is identical with the thirty-two major and eighty minor signs of a Buddha. The mind that produces the Buddha is a mind that is the Buddha. The ocean of the true and universal knowledge of all Buddhas is born from the meditations of the mind. Therefore you should concentrate single-mindedly and visualize that Buddha, Tathāgata, Arhat, and Samyaksaṃbuddha."[26]

> When one has completed this meditation [envisioning Amitāyus and his pure realm], the practitioner should hear the sounds of the profound Dharma being proclaimed by the flowing water, the rays of light, the jewelled trees, and the wild ducks and geese. Whether one is coming out of a concentration or entering one, one will always hear the profound Dharma.[27]

The constellation of practices centered around *buddhānusmṛti*, by invoking the Buddhas and their spontaneous teaching as ever present and accessible, were likely also a major force in Mahāyāna doctrinal formulation of nonabiding nirvāṇa. For in such practices the Buddhas and their teachings are experienced as ever present and accessible, militating for a clear doctrinal formulation that the Buddhas' nirvāṇa remains ever active within our world, and pervasively so, for all who have the eyes to see them or the ears to hear them.

d. Nonabiding Nirvāṇa and Buddha-Nature

As suggested in portions of the prior quotations, some expressions of *buddhānusmṛti* ultimately point to a breakdown in the duality we usually assume between self and Buddha. And this dovetails with the insight of the *Prajñāpāramitā* sūtras that ultimately (as viewed by the Buddhas), there is no division between sentient beings and Buddhas, universal thusness being undivided.[28]

Dharmakāya, Buddhahood in its actual realization, is beyond "inner" or "outer," "self" or "other." Its qualities are found in a nondual, undivided awareness. Progress on the path correlates with vivid awareness of the qualities of the Buddhas opening toward a more and more total identification with them. In Indian Mahāyāna, the ultimate implication of *buddhānusmṛti* as nondual identification with Buddhahood, and of thusness as undivided, is the intuition that the minds of beings are already luminously pure in their very nature.

The latter intuition took explicit form in the teaching of *tathāgatagarbha*, Buddha-nature, the doctrine that all living beings, unbeknownst to themselves, already possess the nature of the Buddhas as the luminous pure nature of their own minds (*cittam prakṛti prabhāsvaram*, see chapter 5 section 3, above). It is an intuition that appears explicitly in several Mahāyāna sūtras and implicitly in many others, playing an important part in Yogācāra and late Mādhyamika doctrinal formation, feeding into the formation and development of the doctrine of nonabiding nirvāṇa as well. For if *dharmakāya* is omnipresent in nondual awareness of the nature of all beings and their realms of existence, and is thus to be found in the nondual pure substratum of beings' own minds, it is an intrinsic part of all beings, pervading them and their worlds, which would never disappear to the end of saṃsāra.

> The Buddha asked, "Mañjuśrī where should the state of Buddhahood be sought?"

> Mañjuśrī answered, "It should be sought right in the defilements of sentient beings. Why? Because by nature the defilements of sentient beings are inapprehensible."[29]

> There is nowhere the knowledge of Buddha does not reach. Why? There is not a single sentient being who is not fully endowed with the knowledge of Buddha; it is just that because of deluded notions, erroneous thinking, and attachments, they are unable to realize it. If they would get rid of deluded notions, then universal knowledge, spontaneous knowledge, and unobstructed knowledge would become manifest.[30]

> Just as water flows under the ground
> So those who seek it find it,
> [The water is] without thought, without end,
> Its effective power all-pervasive,
> Buddha knowledge is also like this,
> Being in all creatures' minds;
> If any work on it with diligence,
> They will soon find the light of knowledge.[31]

> Great enlightening beings should know that in each moment of thought of their own minds there are always Buddhas attaining true awakening. Why? Because the Buddhas do not attain true awakening apart from this mind. As this is true of one's own mind, so is it also true of the minds of all sentient beings—in all are Buddhas attaining true awakening, all-pervasive, existing everywhere, without separation or annihilation, without cease, entering the inconceivable doors or means of enlightenment. Great enlightening beings should know Buddha's attainment of enlightenment this way.[32]

Intimately connecting Buddhahood to all living beings, this teaching further supports the kind of interplay observed above between relative and ultimate awareness in the mindful recollection of the Buddhas. In relative, dualistic awareness, Buddhas are ever accessible to beings through practices of devotion, purification, and mindful recollection. In ultimate, nondual awareness, Buddhahood is experienced as the very nature of their own minds. Either perspective connects Buddhahood to all beings in inconceivably vast ways through space and time.

The teaching of Buddha-nature has been a central underpinning of tantric Buddhism in India and Tibet; it is understood as *phalayāna,* vehicle of the result, because it is a tradition of practice that draws upon one's own innate Buddhahood, the result of the path already present in obscured form, as the very path.

13.3
Postponement Models of Nirvāṇa as Doctrinal Experiments in the Direction of Nonabiding Nirvāṇa

Each of the Mahāyāna intuitions sketched in the previous section thus contributed to the notion that the ultimate outcome of Mahāyāna practice ought to remain ever connected to the world and in a vast way. But this pushed up against the Third Noble Truth of earlier tradition. In prior Abhidharma traditions, as noted, the Third Noble Truth functioned as the simple, total negation of the first two Noble Truths: To cut off one's ignorance and attachment (Second Truth) is to cut off the cause of conditioned existence (First Truth). The full attainment of the unconditioned, nirvāṇa, for Buddhas as for other arhats, was thus understood as the complete cessation of their own conditioned existence (Third Truth), i.e., the cessation of any further participation in the world upon physical death *(parinirvāṇa, nirupadhiśeṣanirvāṇa).*

The Mahāyāna intuitions of Buddhahood's vast participation in saṃsāric space and time sketched in the prior section thus came into severe tension with the Third Noble Truth. Initially, composers of some sūtras and śāstras experimented with ways of "stretching" the Third Truth to get it to accommodate a longer connection between Buddhas or bodhisattvas and saṃsāra. What I call "stretching" the Third Noble Truth is exemplified when texts declare that Buddhas or bodhisattvas avoid or postpone their entry into final nirvāṇa for long periods of time. In such passages, the pre-Mahāyāna understanding of the Third Truth is still assumed: Buddhas are still presumed to enter a final nirvāṇa that will entirely remove them from the world forever. But it had to be put off for long or indefinite periods of time in order to express Mahāyāna intuitions of Buddhas' vast participation in saṃsāric space and time discussed above.

Eventually such models of postponing nirvāṇa were found wanting. The assumption in postponement models that a Buddha eventually must leave the world permanently in a final nirvāṇa (pre-Mahāyāna understanding of the Third Noble Truth) was too constraining to give adequate expression to Mahāyāna intuitions of Buddhas' vast connection to the world. Eventually the assumption of an actual final nirvāṇa was abrogated as the new doctrine of nonabiding nirvāṇa became dominant. We might therefore view models of postponing nirvāṇa as doctrinal stepping-stones that contributed to the development and eventual normativity of the nonabiding nirvāṇa doctrine, by giving initial expression to Mahāyāna intuitions of Buddhas' vastness in tension with pre-Mahāyāna assumptions of nirvāṇa, a tension finally removed as the Third Truth came to be generally redefined as nonabiding nirvāṇa and the disappearance of Buddhas at their *parinirvāṇas* was then understood as apparent rather than real.[33]

Thus, texts that expressed postponement models, in their own way, were giving expression to intuitions of Buddhas' vast connection to the world. But such texts continued to be promulgated in Mahāyāna circles well after nonabiding nirvāṇa replaced postponement models as normative doctrine. And this has caused confusion for modern scholars, some of whom over the past century have bequeathed to us a definition of "bodhisattva" based on the postponement model which is quite at odds with what became normative after the doctrine of nonabiding nirvāṇa became widely accepted in India.

In his book *Mahāyāna Buddhism: The Doctrinal Foundations*, Paul Williams raises this problem as it has come to the attention of contemporary scholars:

> It is frequently said in textbooks that the compassion of the bodhisattva is so great that he postpones *nirvāṇa*, or turns back from *nirvāṇa*, in order to place all other sentient beings in *nirvāṇa* first. It seems to me, however, that caution and further research is required here. Such a teaching appears *prima facie* to be incoherent, and contains a claim that somehow a Buddha must be deficient in compassion when compared with a bodhisattva. If all other beings must be placed in *nirvāṇa* before a particular bodhisattva attains *nirvāṇa* himself there could obviously be only one bodhisattva. Alternatively, we have the absurd spectacle of a series of bodhisattvas each trying to hurry the others into *nirvāṇa* in order to preserve his or her vow! Moreover if sentient beings are infinite, a widely held view in the Mahāyāna , then the bodhisattva is setting himself an impossible task, and no bodhisattva could ever attain Buddhahood. . . . My purpose is simply to suggest sensitivity to the initial incoherence and textual uncertainty concerning the bodhisattva's claimed postponement of *nirvāṇa*, an assertion which appears to have become part of the lore of textbooks on Buddhism.[34]

When Williams says that a teaching of bodhisattvas postponing nirvāṇa "appears *prima facie* to be incoherent," he seems to be viewing it from an ahistorical perspective, as if the doctrine of nonabiding nirvāṇa long dominant in Indo-Tibetan traditions had always been fully established in all Mahāyāna movements from their inception. Expressions do occur in Mahāyāna sūtras of bodhisattvas and Buddhas avoiding or postponing their presumed final entry into nirvāṇa in order to continue working for beings. Such expressions contradict the later dominant doctrine of nonabiding nirvāṇa, according to which Buddhas (as *dharmakāya*) remain always active in the world. And when viewed from the perspective of that dominant doctrine, they do appear incoherent. But this is only when the historical perspective is lost. I would suggest that expressions of postponing nirvāṇa are better viewed as early Mahāyāna doctrinal experiments: attempts to stretch the Third Noble Truth prior to the development or broad acceptance of the nonabiding nirvāṇa doctrine that redefined the Third Noble Truth altogether. As such, where models of postponing nirvāṇa appear in texts sacred to traditions in which nonabiding nirvāṇa has long since become normative, they represent archaic remnants in tension with the model that superseded them.

One possible remnant of a "postponement of nirvāṇa" model appears in the *Mañjuśrī-buddhakṣetra-guṇavyūha-sūtra*, in which Mañjuśrī in a former life first generates *bodhicitta*, the impulse to liberate all beings:

> Now, in the presence of the entire assembly, I bring forth *bodhicitta* for the sake of all sentient beings. I vow to involve myself in *saṃsāra* countless times to bring great boons to living beings until the end of the future. . . . I shall not cherish the idea of attaining Buddhahood in haste, but until the end of the future I shall benefit all living beings and adorn and purify incalculable, inconceivable Buddha-lands.[35]

The desire not to attain "Buddhahood in haste" as an expression of concern for beings makes little sense from the perspective of a developed doctrine of nonabiding nirvāṇa, according to which a Buddha can do far more to help beings than any bodhisattva. It may represent a textual remnant from an earlier stage of doctrinal formation in which a Buddha's final nirvāṇa was still assumed to forever remove him from the world, so that Buddhahood itself had to be postponed by a bodhisattva who sought to continue to help beings. This passage stands in tension with other passages nearby that affirm and exalt Mañjuśrī's eventual attainment of Buddhahood. But such tensions within texts are not surprising from an historical-critical perspective. Alternative expressions are often uncritically retained in redacted texts from prior sources and practice milieus.

A related example of the "postponement" model for bodhisattvas occurs in explanations of *bodhicitta* in the *Lam Rim* literature of Tibet. Three types of *bodhicitta*, the motivation that defines a bodhisattva, are commonly distinguished: "kinglike," "boatmanlike," and "shepherdlike." Kinglike *bodhicitta* is the aspiration to first attain Buddhahood and then lead all other beings to it, like a prince who first becomes king and then looks after his kingdom. Boatmanlike *bodhicitta* is the aspiration to attain Buddhahood together with all beings, like a boatman who arrives on the other shore at the same time as his passengers. Shepherdlike *bodhicitta* is the aspiration to lead all beings to Buddhahood *before* achieving it for oneself, like a shepherd guiding his flock ahead of himself.[36] Shepherdlike *bodhicitta* is praised as the most courageous. Yet it makes no logical sense. How could one guide other beings to Buddhahood until one had attained it oneself? The doctrine of nonabiding nirvāṇa, normative in Tibet, declares the Buddhas best able to provide such guidance for the greatest number of beings until the end of time. One must seek to become a Buddha to lead others to that state. In Tibet, the bodhisattva Mañjuśrī is praised as an example of shepherdlike *bodhicitta*.[37] Perhaps the concept is drawn from the *Mañjuśrī-buddhakṣetra-guṇavyūha-sūtra*, comprising a remnant of an earlier "postponement" model still found inspirational, even if no longer entirely logical, in contemporary Tibetan practice.

Another vestige of a "postponement" model may appear in the *Lankāvatāra-sūtra*:

> [A]gain, Mahāmati, there are Bodhisattva Mahāsattvas who, on account of their original vows made for all beings, saying, "So long as they do not attain *nirvāṇa*, I will not attain it myself," keep themselves away from *nirvāṇa*. This Mahāmati, is the reason of their not entering into *nirvāṇa*, and because of this they go on the way of the Icchantika.[38]

According to this text, the *icchantika* is a type of being whose causes for liberation from saṃsāra have been cut, either through abandoning virtue by disparaging the bodhisattva vehicle, or, as in the case of the special type of bodhisattva described above, through the force of her vow to remain in saṃsāra for other beings. This particular expression is of special interest: "So long as they do not attain nirvāṇa, I will not attain it myself." This does not distinguish types of nirvāṇa, but seems to rule out the attainment of liberation for the individual in a totalistic way. This expression may represent a textual remnant from a model that assumed the end of the bodhisattva path, Buddhahood, to sever connection with the world forever at attainment of final nirvāṇa. Yet any such assumption comes into tension with the very next passage of the same text:

> Again, Mahāmati said, "Who, Blessed One, would never enter *nirvāṇa*?"
>
> The Blessed One replied: "Knowing that all things are in *nirvāṇa* itself from the very beginning, the Bodhisattva-Icchantika would never enter *nirvāṇa*."

This passage could be interpreted more directly in line with the Mahāyāna intuition of emptiness in nondual awareness that, as noted in section 2.a above, helped project the doctrine of nonabiding nirvāṇa: a person who becomes cognitively one with the emptiness of all things is inseparably connected to the world through that ultimate nature, apart from which there is no separate nirvāṇa to be "entered into." Again, the *Lankāvatārasūtra* is a text redacted from a diversity of sources, drawing upon models and practice intuitions that sometimes come into conflict. Here the model of postponing nirvāṇa is justaposed and reinterpreted through the nondual intuition of emptiness that would make the postponement model archaic by helping to project the new model: nonabiding nirvāṇa.

Other expressions that seem consistent with the "postponement of nirvāṇa" model may also represent textual remnants of doctrines that precede a fully developed doctrine of nonabiding nirvāṇa. In this regard, several passages are of interest from Bhāvaviveka's *Madhyamaka-hṛdaya-kārikā:*[39]

> [The Buddha] is called eternal for two reasons. He is eternally free from appearance and thus is completely free from concepts, and he eternally accomplishes what is good. (*MHK* 275)

The *Tarkajvālā*, ascribed by tradition to the same author, gives these comments on the verse:

> Mind and mental phenomena last only for a moment, and [moments] disappear into their beginning, middle, and ending parts. In the dharma element *(dharmadhātu)*, none of these things exists, so what can give rise to concepts? And if concepts do not arise, they also do not cease. This is one reason [the Buddha] is called eternal. [The Buddha] is also called eternal because he eternally accomplishes what is good for sentient beings. As it says in the sūtras, sentient beings are as limitless as space, karma and defilements are limitless, and saṃsāra is limitless. [The Buddha] is called eternal because he constantly accomplishes great vows and acts for the welfare of sentient beings as long as there is saṃsāra.

Here Bhāvaviveka (a sixth-century Mādhyamika) and the *Tarkajvālā* commentary present a developed classical description of nonabiding nirvāṇa broadly consistent with descriptions we saw in the *Abhisamayālaṃkāra*, *Mahāyānasūtrālaṃkāra*, and *Mahāyānasaṃgraha*. To attain Buddhahood is to attain a nirvāṇa that is free of the bondage of saṃsāra yet never leaves saṃsāra, through cognitive oneness with its nonconceptual nature *(dharmadhātu)* and through eternal enactment of the bodhisattva vow to liberate all beings.

Yet later the *Tarkajvālā* commentary expresses a different concept of nonabiding nirvāṇa, now ascribed to bodhisattvas, which seems to come into conflict with what was has just been said:

> *MHK* 294 a. [A bodhisattva] does not leave saṃsāra,
>
> Commentary: Because [a bodhisattva] has not removed defilements.
>
> *MHK* 294 b. But [a bodhisattva] is free from the harm of saṃsāra.
>
> Commentary: Because [a bodhisattva] does not create harmful *dharmas* and has overcome defilements.
>
> *MHK* 294c. [A bodhisattva] does not attain nirvāṇa,
>
> Commentary: Because [a bodhisattva] is concerned about sentient beings.
>
> *MHK* 294 d. But it is as if [a bodhisattva] were located in nirvāṇa.

> Commentary: Because [a bodhisattva] is capable of acting for others and for [the bodhisattva's own] self. . . .
>
> *MHK* 295 b. Even though [a bodhisattva] is defiled, [the Bodhisattva is defiled] in the way that space is [defiled].
>
> Commentary: [A bodhisattva] has some defilements to serve as the seed of saṃsāra, but [the bodhisattva] is not stained by them.

The commentary finishes the section with this interesting comment leading into *MHK* verse 296:

> Commentary: When [a bodhisattva] has attained extraordinary attainment and resides in nonabiding nirvāṇa *(apratiṣṭhita nirvāṇa)* but does not attain enlightenment,
>
> *MHK* 296. [The bodhisattva] has climbed the mountain peak of wisdom and is free from grief but looks with compassion on ordinary people who suffer and are burned by grief.

The *Tarkajvālā* commentary (though not the root text) labels the root verses above as a teaching of "nonabiding nirvāṇa" with reference specifically to bodhisattvas. It characterizes this "nonabiding nirvāṇa" as the condition of bodhisattvas who intentionally retain some measure of defilement without attaining enlightenment in order to retain their connection to saṃsāra, i.e. to continue to work for all saṃsāric beings. The root text need not be read precisely in this way. But the commentary's exegisis may be a textual remnant of a proto–"nonabiding nirvāṇa" model that preceded the later dominant model, one which retains the assumption from pre-Mahāyāna traditions that the final nirvāṇa of a Buddha would permanently remove him from the world, requiring bodhisattvas to retain defilement and postpone attaining Buddhahood in order to stay in saṃsāra.[40]

A passage in the *Ratnagotravibhāga* with its *vyākhyā* may bear some relation to this last quotation from the *Tarkajvālā*. The passage in question discusses the problem of how bodhisattvas cut the root of saṃsāra yet, through compassion, remain a part of saṃsāra for others. The RGV explains that ordinary birth, decay and death are generated by the forces of karma, *kleśa*, and ignorance (as erroneous thought: *ayoniśomanasikāra*) all of which are destroyed by bodhisattvas through realization of their essencelessness in the innate pure mind *(citta-prakṛti-viśuddhi)*. Nevertheless, bodhisattvas participate in the world through a mind-made body *(mano-māya-kāya)* that is connected to the world through the force of their roots of virtue, which are likened to *kleśa*s (defilements) and referred to metaphorically as such: *kuśalamūla-saṃprayuktā kleśāḥ* (defilements associated with the roots of virtue). The text makes clear that the bodhisattvas' roots of virtue, explained as types of enthusiastic perseverance, are not actually *kleśa*s, but are only designated as such because through them they are connected to the world that is the product of the *kleśas* of ordinary beings.[41] This seems both to invoke and to explain away a model of bodhisattvas' "retaining defilement" like that expressed in the *Tarkajvālā* just above, and may represent a refinement of some such model in the direction of the classical nonabiding-nirvāṇa doctrine that dominated late Indian Mahāyāna.

Along with differing formulations of a bodhisattva's relation to nirvāṇa and saṃsāra are alternative models of a Buddha's nirvāṇa. Like the alternative bodhisattva models above, these models give the appearance of doctrinal experiments, varied attempts to give expression to seminal Mahāyāna intuitions that come into more or less tension with the pre-Mahāyāna understanding of the Third Noble Truth prior to its redefinition in the classical doctrine of nonabiding nirvāṇa.

Perhaps the most common example of a "postponement" model of final nirvāṇa refers to Buddhas, and appears in one of the oldest and most continuously popular Mahāyāna ritual-meditation practices: the seven-limb offering ritual *(saptāngā pūjā)*. Core elements of this practice appear in Mahāyāna sūtras from the earliest emergence of Mahāyāna literature. The seven-limbed ritual became a performative element in many Mahāyāna śāstras and an important component of tantric *sādhanas*. It continues as a central part of Tibetan Buddhist ritual and meditational practice.[42] The seven parts of the ritual are: (1) prostration, (2) offering, (3) confession, (4) rejoicing in the merit of others, (5) asking the Buddhas to teach the Dharma, (6) requesting the Buddhas not to pass away into final nirvāṇa but to remain in the world for beings, and (7) dedicating the merit from these practices to the enlightenment of all beings.

The sixth "limb" is of special interest to us. There is an ancient legend preserved in the Pāli Vinaya that Ānanda, Śākyamuni Buddha's closest attendant and companion, neglected to request the Buddha to extend his life near his *parinirvāṇa*, for which he was censured by the first council of arhats.[43] Set within one of the Mahāyāna's very ancient ritual expressions, the sixth "limb" appears to put the Mahāyāna practitioner into Ānanda's place to correct his error. Taking Śāntideva's *Bodhicaryāvatāra* (composed in the late seventh century) as example, the corresponding verse (chapter 3 verse 6) says:

> With joined palms I implore
> The Jinas who wish to pass into nirvāṇa
> To please remain for countless aeons
> And not to leave the world in darkness.

The phrase "Jinas who wish to pass into nirvāṇa" is telling. "Jinas," meaning Victors, refers to the Buddhas (who have conquered all the defilements and obstructions to enlightenment). But here a pre-Mahāyāna assumption surfaces in an otherwise classical Mahāyāna treatise, the assumption that Buddhas reach a point in their teaching career when they are ready to enter a final nirvāṇa, which will take them forever away from the suffering world. This appears to represent an archaic remnant from an earlier period in doctrinal-*cum*-ritual development before the nonabiding-nirvāṇa doctrine became dominant (according to which a Buddha's nirvāṇa as *dharmakāya* is inseparable from the world and remains forever active within it). Yet Śāntideva's text is famous as one of the most powerful articulations in Mahāyāna literature of the aspiration to become a Buddha precisely in order to work through all of eternity for limitless beings, e.g.:

> What need be said then of one
> Who eternally bestows the peerless bliss of the Sugatas
> Upon limitless numbers of beings,
> Thereby fulfilling all their hopes?
>
> (*Bodhicaryāvatāra,* chap. 1, v. 33)

The sixth limb of the seven-limb ritual, as part of a ritual formula much older than the text in which it is set, comes into tension with other normative assumptions of this late-seventh-century text concerning the vast connection of Buddhahood to the world through space and time and the infinite implications of attaining Buddhahood for all beings.

The seven-limb offering ritual continues as a central practice in Tibetan Buddhism. The logical problem that the sixth limb poses long after the doctrine of nonabiding nirvāṇa became normative was noticed in Tibet, requiring explanation. Given the Tibetan assumption inherited from India that Buddhas as *dharmakāya* are eternal, that *sāmbhogikakāya*s never cease teaching, and that *nairmāṇikakāya*s of limitless variety manifest again and again in saṃsāra from the force of immeasurable compassion for beings, it makes little apparent sense to request Buddhas "who wish to enter nirvāṇa" not to do so, as if the ultimate aim of Buddhas was quiescence. Yet no one would want to delete part of the seven-limb ritual-meditation practice, which carries the blessing of thousands of years of practice experience. Therefore, the request that Buddhas remain in saṃsāra came to be explained as a karmic tool to extend one's own life, or to continue one's contact with manifestations and teachings of the Buddhas that pass away from us because of our own lack of merit.[44] The doctrinal framework has shifted from the earliest period of Mahāyāna, requiring new explanations to rationalize ancient practices that continue to be experienced as powerfully transformative.

A related model of a Buddha's nirvāṇa appears in a passage of the *Saddharmapuṇḍarīkasūtra*, in which a great stūpa manifests to praise the Buddha's teaching of that sūtra. Questioned about it, the Buddha declares that the stūpa contains the body of a previous Buddha, Prabhūtaratna. In a previous life Prabhūtaratna vowed that, following his final nirvāṇa, the stūpa containing his body would appear in any world-system where the *Saddharmapuṇḍarīkasūtra* is taught, to applaud its revelation. This passage is quoted and analyzed in relation to pre-Mahāyāna traditions in

M. David Eckel's *To See the Buddha.*[45] The text stretches previous understanding of the Third Noble Truth by asserting the power of a Buddha's prior vow of *bodhicitta* to project his forms into the world after his own final nirvāṇa. But it preserves the pre-Mahāyāna understanding of that Truth, that a Buddha does pass into a final nirvāṇa that forever removes him from any conscious awareness of the world.

Another model perhaps predating and contributing to the development of the classical nonabiding nirvāṇa model involves projecting the Buddha's life to a very long extension, so he may continue working for beings prior to his final departure from the world in a final nirvāṇa, which is still assumed. A well-known passage from the *Saddharmapuṇḍarīkasūtra* expresses this:

> Thus, since I attained Buddhahood, an extremely long period of time has passed. My life span is an immeasurable number of asamkhya kalpas, and during that time I have constantly abided here without ever entering extinction. Good men, originally I practiced the bodhisattva way, and the life span that I acquired then has yet to come to an end but will last twice the number of years that have already passed. Now, however, although in fact I do not actually enter extinction, I announce that I am going to adopt the course of extinction. This is an expedient means which the Thus Come One uses to teach and convert living beings.[46]

Here the pre-Mahāyāna understanding of the Third Noble Truth is still not questioned: A Buddha must eventually enter final nirvāṇa, forever leaving the world. But it is postponed for a very long time. Mahāyāna intuitions project a Buddha's long and extensive engagement in the world for beings, creating a tension with the received Third Noble Truth of nirvāṇa that require it to be put off for as long as possible.

In sum, early Mahāyāna intuitions tended to project a vast participation in saṃsāric space and time for the sake of living beings, which pushed up against the limitation of the pre-Mahāyāna Third Noble Truth that assumed a Buddha's absolute departure from the world after only a few decades of localized activity for beings. Textual and ritual remnants of early Mahāyāna models of nirvāṇa seem incoherent or confusing when they appear in texts and practice traditions after the doctrine of nonabiding nirvāṇa had become dominant. But they make sense when viewed historically as remnants of doctrinal experiments that preceded and, in their own tensions with the Third Noble Truth, contributed to the development and later normative acceptance of nonabiding nirvāṇa in Indian and Tibetan Buddhism.

In this regard, cults of high bodhisattvas such as Maitreya, Avalokiteśvara, Manjuśrī, etc., also become somewhat anomalous when viewed from the perspective of the nonabiding nirvāṇa doctrine that probably came to full maturity after the emergence of such cults. Cult practice, centered on bodhisattvas, reflected a stage of doctrinal development prior to the doctrine of nonabiding nirvāṇa that keeps Buddhas unceasingly in the world as its most powerful helpers.[47] As such, bodhisattva cult practices, including those centered upon the "future Buddha" Maitreya, represent an anomaly similar to that of the sixth limb of ritual offering. If Buddhas remain an active part of the world in the *dharmakāya*'s eternal manifestations, the significance of a "future Buddha" lessens, although the power of ritual and meditation practices centered on Maitreya may not. Perhaps in part because of the later dominance of the nonabiding-nirvāṇa doctrine, tantric traditions of India and Tibet tended to redefine high bodhisattvas as potent symbols or expressions of Buddhahood, as forms of *rūpakāya*. Yet the rich mythology of Tibetan traditions, retaining ancient expressions from different stages of Mahāyāna doctrinal development in Indo-Tibetan literature, continues to communicate ambiguity as to the exact status of figures such as Mañjuśrī, Avalokiteśvara, Tārā, and Maitreya.[48]

13.4
Tension Created by Redefining the Third Noble Truth as Nonabiding Nirvāṇa: The Mahāyāna Quest for Authentic Reinterpretation of the Four Noble Truths as a Whole

The Mahāyāna intuitions that pushed doctrinal development toward nonabiding nirvāṇa were themselves the expression and outcome of practices framed by the Four Noble Truths formula as it had been received from prior Buddhist traditions. From a Mahāyāna perspective, the teaching of the emptiness of all dharmas concerns the practice of *prajñā,* the heart of the Fourth Noble Truth, but understood in a way deeper than that communicated in prior Abhidharma traditions. The Mahāyāna teaching of emptiness was understood to express and inform the First, Second, and Third Noble Truths as well, by revealing the deepest structure of ignorance, the way in which dichotomous conceptualization constructs reality as a realm of clinging and hence suffering (First and Second Noble Truths), and by revealing how realization of emptiness alone eliminates those causes at their deepest level to attain nirvāṇa (Third Noble Truth). *Bodhicitta,* the aspiration to fully awaken for the sake of others, is an expression of compassion that follows directly from meditation on the First Noble Truth, understood as the suffering of all beings. And Mahāyāna devotional practices internalize and express the worldview of the Noble Truths: prostration and confession purify one's mental afflictions and karma (Second Noble Truth), while offering generates positive karma as fuel for progress on the path (Fourth Noble Truth), etc.

Mahāyānists thus viewed the intuitions summarized in section 2 as natural expressions of the Four Noble Truths in their actual practice and realization. Yet I suggest that the same intuitions set into motion a process of doctrinal development that eventually required Mahāyāna thinkers to find a uniquely Mahāyāna way of reinterpreting the Four Noble Truths formula as a whole.

As mentioned earlier, Mahāyāna intuitions of a Buddha's vast connectedness, having pushed up against the pre-Mahāyāna Third Truth in postponement moels of nirvāṇa, found fuller expression in a radically new Mahāyāna doctrine known as "nonabiding nirvāṇa." According to this doctrine, nirvāṇa and saṃsāra are inseparable. To fully attain the unconditioned *(nirvāṇa)* is not to leave the conditioned world *(saṃsāra)*, but to pervade it with one's nondual awareness and one's activity for beings. A Buddha's *parinirvāṇa* came to be viewed as merely the dissolution of one appearance of enlightenment, whose manifestations and activities are limitless in space and time and therefore inconceivable to us. This constituted a radical reformulation of the Third Noble Truth.[49]

But to so radically reinterpret the Third Noble Truth (now as nonabiding nirvāṇa) without also explicitly reinterpreting the first two Noble Truths to which it is connected created a doctrinal tension at the heart of Mahāyāna thought that would eventually push thinkers to find a uniquely Mahāyāna reinterpretation of the Four Noble Truths formula as a whole. The problem is this: The first two Noble Truths, left unaltered by the doctrine of nonabiding nirvāṇa, do not provide any clear epistemological or ontological basis for a Buddha's eternal, unlimited participation in the world, which that doctrine prescribes. They only provide the basis for the old, pre-Mahāyāna understanding of the Third Noble Truth. The old understanding had been that ignorance and attachment, *kleśas* and *karma* (Second Truth), were the epistemological-ontological causes of conditioned existence (First Truth). To remove those causes was, at physical death, to extinguish one's conditioned existence, hence to end forever one's participation in the world (Third Truth). The first two Noble Truths provide no basis for a continuous connection to the world after nirvāṇa, as required by a nonabiding-nirvāṇa doctrine. Yet Mahāyāna scholars, even as they formulated the latter doctrine, often continued to teach the first two Noble Truths in traditional form.[50]

The Buddhas, all Buddhists agreed, have eliminated whatever ignorance, *kleśa,* and defiled karma they had as sentient beings. According to the first two Noble Truths, these are the bases for each individual's experience of saṃsāra. Then, in the Mahāyāna reformulation of the Third Truth as nonabiding nirvāṇa, how are Buddhas to remain in saṃsāra, not for a few decades after enlightenment as the residual expression of their own past karma, but until all beings are liberated? In line with the Mahāyāna intuitions outlined in section 2 above, Buddhas are frequently described in Mahāyāna texts as omniscient, all-compassionate, universally available and active, etc. But what connects the Buddhas' *dharmakāya* to a conditioned world which is the fabrication of defiled mental factors that it does not possess?

In essence, the paradox created by the doctrine of nonabiding nirvāṇa is this: How can something *(dharmakāya)* be entirely free from the conditions out of which the phenomenal world is generated, and yet be pervasively operative in that world? This has been a seminal source of ongoing doctrinal tension over Buddhahood throughout the history of the Mahāyāna in India and Tibet. Yet that source of doctrinal tension, buried within the deep structure of Mahāyāna thought by the historical developments sketched above, is seldom openly identified.

A good example of this phenomenon not previously discussed occurs in the *Tarkajvālā* commentary upon Bhāvaviveka's *Madhyamakahṛdaya-vṛtti* of the sixth century. The *Tarkajvālā* seeks to address an objection raised by other Buddhists against the Mahāyāna concerning how a Buddha could be both eternal *(nitya)* and active in the temporal world *(anitya)*. M. David Eckel summarizes the opponent's argument:

> Bhāvaviveka tells us about an opponent who argues, "To teach that the Buddha is eternal *(nitya)* contradicts the scriptural statement that everything is impermanent." This seems to be the case, Bhāvaviveka says, because the teaching contradicts the doctrine of impermanence and because it violates the assumption that the peace of *nirvāṇa* is a definitive cessation of suffering. If the Buddha continues to be active, the Buddha must continue to change, and if the Buddha continues to change, the quest for enlightenment does not lead to a state of peace."[51]

Notice how the logical tension of nonabiding nirvāṇa lurks just below the surface of this discussion. Through that doctrine's implicit alteration of the Third Noble Truth, the Mahāyāna declares a Buddha to have fully attained the unconditioned (eternal, inactive), yet to continue unceasingly to work for beings in the world of change (impermanent, active). The non-Mahāyāna opponent objects from the perspective of the unmodified Third Noble Truth, the pre-Mahāyāna view: Nirvāṇa, fully attained, is the cessation of conditioned existence. It is just "peace": inactive, unconditioned. If someone continued to be ever active, it would mean he or she had not attained nirvāṇa. Because Mahāyāna texts never explicitly say that they have modified the Third Noble Truth in their doctrine of nonabiding nirvāṇa, the source of the tension underlying the surface argument is never explicitly pointed out.

As in that example, it is logical tension within the Four Noble Truths, created by redefining the Third Noble Truth in Mahāyāna as nonabiding nirvāṇa without altering the first two Noble Truths, that generated the host of interconnected epistemological, ontological, soteriological and theological problems of Buddhahood we examined in prior chapters. This is the tension that contributed to long disagreement over the *Abhisamayālaṃkāra* on Buddhahood, a disagreement initiated by Haribhadra's attempt to distinguish unconditioned and conditioned aspects of *dharmakāya* in order to show how it can be related to the conditioned world. The same underlying tension has contributed to disagreements in late Indian Buddhism and Tibet concerning (1) how a Buddha is aware of the world when the *dharmakāya* remains always in nondual equipoise on universal emptiness *(dharmadhātu)*, (2) how to account for the *dharmakāya*'s pervasive activity in the world (through *rūpakāyas*) given its nonconceptual nature, (3) whether a Buddha's awareness contains images of the world or not, (4) gradualist versus simultaneist models of awakening to Buddhahood, and (5) the centrality or marginality of Buddha-nature *(tathāgata-garbha)* in systematic thought.

The range of these problems and their underlying interconnectedness take vivid expression in the writings of several of the pioneers who first promulgated Buddhism in Tibet. I am thinking of King Khri Srong lde brtsan, the eighth-century Tibetan king and patron of Buddhism, to whom an important set of questions on Buddhahood is ascribed, and several very great scholars instrumental in the early or later spread of Tibetan Buddhism: Ye shes sde (a leading eighth-century Tibetan translator), Atiśa (eleventh-century Indian scholar and pioneer in the second promulgation of Buddhism in Tibet), Rong zom chos kyi gzang po (a great Tibetan rNying ma scholar of the eleventh century), and sGam po pa (twelfth century bKa' gdams pa master, foremost disciple of Milarepa, and father of the Tak po bKa rgyud lineages). These figures, in attempting to introduce their doctrinal inheritance from India to a new culture, were faced with the unresolved questions of Buddhahood we have explored in prior chapters. They recapitulate the questions in a succinct form that makes it easy to discern the underlying connection they share to the paradox of nonabiding nirvāṇa. The focus here shall be upon two pioneers of the early promulgation in Tibet: King Khri Srong lde brtsan and Ye shes sde.

King Khri Srong lde brtsan is renowned for his royal support of Buddhism in its early promulgation in eighth-century Tibet. He sent invitations to various foreign Buddhist teachers to come to Tibet, accompanied by lists of doctrinal and practical questions. David Snellgrove in his book Indo-Tibetan Buddhism, based on work by Daishun Ueyama, discusses a letter that an eighth-century Chinese monk at Tun-huang sent to King Khri Srong lde brtsan. According to the Chinese monk, the king had sent him a list of twenty-two questions for reply, several of which, we can now see, were elicited directly by the problem of nonabiding nirvāṇa:

> 1. What do these Bodhisattvas do when they have left the worldly shores and in order to save all living beings from the sufferings of afflictions *(kleśa)* do not interest themselves in the practices of the Early Disciples and Solitary Buddhas?
>
> 2. Furthermore in the case of those Bodhisattvas who have entered upon the practice of "no return," whatever they think internally, their bodies manifest this externally in Dharma (or: in the elemental particles, viz., *dharmas*). So when they are cultivating interiorly the Dharma of the supreme practice, what are their outward practices? What is the Dharma of the supreme practice?

> 6. Buddhas have three bodies *(kāya)*. The Dharma-body *(dharmakāya)* is coequal with the Dharma-sphere *(dharmadhātu)*. The Transformation-body *(nairmāṇikakāya)* exists individually in each Buddha. As for the Glorious-body *(sāmbhogikakāya),* is it one or differentiated?
>
> 7. Buddhas possess omniscience and that is why they practice quite freely the Six Perfections. But it [omniscience] has the pure and inactive nature of clear and tranquil water. So how are those two categories (viz., the inactivity of omniscience on the one side and the activity of the Perfections on the other)?
>
> 12. For Bodhisattvas *nirvāṇa* and *saṃsāra* are not distinguished at all? What is the meaning of that?[52]

Question 1 wrestles with the Mahāyāna redefinition of the Third Noble Truth: How is it that bodhisattvas attain the peace of nirvāṇa (having "left the worldly shores") yet still work to save all beings? Questions 2 and 12 are related. How does a bodhisattva realize the ultimate nature of things (the "supreme practice") while yet engaging saṃsāra? The king notes in his sixth question that the *dharmakāya* of the Buddhas and the *dharmadhātu* (universal unconditioned emptiness) are coequal. In the seventh question, he wonders how, given the inactive, unconditioned nature of omniscient *dharmakāya*, coequal with *dharmadhātu*, a Buddha can carry out his activities in the world. Again, it is the paradox of nonabiding nirvāṇa that underlies these concerns. What keeps bodhisattvas and Buddhas active in a world that is merely the construct of ignorance after they have broken through to its unconditioned, inactive, and empty nature?

Ye shes sde was a key Tibetan scholar-translator of King Khri Srong lde brtsan's period (second half of the eighth century), central to the early promulgation of Buddhism in Tibet. In addition to the vast corpus of Indian Buddhist texts that he helped translate, he wrote one of the first independent Tibetan treatises on Buddhist philosophy, the *lTa ba'i khyad par*. In it, he succinctly summarizes his understanding of all principal Mahāyāna doctrines of India as the framework for beginning the transmission of Buddha-dharma to his own culture.

Ye shes sde's *lTa ba'i khad par* summarizes trends he discerned in the wide range of Indian Buddhist texts available to him as one of the principal translators of the early Tibetan Buddhist promulgation.[53] In doing so, his text exposes the interrelated problems of Buddhahood that were generated in Indian Mahāyāna by the doctrine of nonabiding nirvāṇa, and reveals for us the relation between those problems and the problematic position of nonabiding nirvāṇa within the orthodox scheme of the Four Noble Truths. Furthermore, by reference to numerous Indian texts, Ye shes sde delineates an old Mahāyāna perspective on Buddhahood in a form it was taking in India prior to and during his period: a nondual yogic attainment perspective. And he shows us how that particular perspective, by the late eighth century in India, was coming to give a more and more central place to the doctrine of Buddha-nature, as the way to reinterpret the Four Noble Truths so as to accommodate Mahāyāna intuitions behind nonabiding nirvāṇa. This stands in vivid contrast to Haribhadra's perspective on Buddhahood, a logical, analytic-inferential perspective that was taking shape in the same period (late eighth to ninth centuries). A detailed look at several parts of Ye shes sde's text, therefore, helps us crystallize and vividly contrast certain Indo-Tibetan Buddhist perspectives and to put them in some historical context.

The *lTa ba'i khyad par* has a lengthy section on the Buddha *kāya*s, much of which is organized around problems created implicitly by the paradox of nonabiding nirvāṇa. At the place where the following quotation begins, Ye shes sde has just finished summarizing the extensive activities of the Buddha's *rūpakāya*s (Buddhahood embodied in manifest forms):

> Do the two *(rūpa) kāyas* possess conceptualization *(rtog pa)* or not [as would seem necessary to perform all their activities]? They do not conceptualize, because they arise out of the *dharmakāya* that has no dichotomizing conceptualization *(rnam par rtog pa)*. What [scriptural source] shows that? The *Ārya-suvarṇaprabhāsa-sūtra* says, "Although it seems as if they conceptualize, nevertheless, there is no conceptualization in thusness. And although the *(buddhakāya*s*)* are enumerated as three, in actuality, there is nothing as three." As [the Buddha] has taught in many sūtras, "The Tathāgatha is always in meditative equipoise [within thusness]."
>
> Then the following questions may occur: Does the Tathāgatha possess an awareness of the world per se that is pure *(dag pa 'jig rten pa'i ye shes)*, or not? Does his omniscience know the individual characteristics of things, or [just] their general characteristic [emptiness]?[54] Does it know through conceptualization, or free of conceptualization?"[55]

Ordinary beings, through a process of dichotomizing conceptualization (Tib., *rnam par rtog pa;* Skt., *vikalpa*) based upon ignorance, construct a world of dualism in which they intend and act (Second Noble Truth). To attain nirvāṇa is to cut off such dichotomizing conceptualization (Third Truth). In pre-Mahāyāna tradition, this would mean one ultimately left the world behind *(parinirvāṇa)*. But the *rūpakāya*s of Buddhas continue to act forever within the dualistic worlds of beings (Mahāyāna Third Truth as redefined by nonabiding nirvāṇa). Then do the Buddhas' actions express intentions of dichotomizing conceptualization? If so, Buddhas would not have removed their own causes for suffering. But if their actions involve no such conceptualization, on what basis are they cognitively connected to our dualistic world and active within it?

Ye shes sde in the quotation above, echoing Mahāyāna scriptures, reaffirms their message that Buddhas per se are *dharmakāya. Rūpakāya* forms are only expressions of *dharmakāya.* And *dharmakāya* is an uninterrupted, nonconceptual meditative awareness of thusness. Hence, it simply does not conceptualize. The Mahāyāna *dharmakāya* preserves a key feature of the pre-Mahāyāna concept of final nirvāṇa *(parinirvāṇa)*: It entirely transcends the world, in this case, by having entirely deconstructed it into emptiness.

This leads to further problems. In pre-Mahāyāna understanding of the Four Noble Truths, to cut off the conceptualizations of ignorance is to cut off the basis for one's place in a conditioned world: ultimately to leave the world behind in final nirvāṇa. But here where nonabiding nirvāṇa is assumed, there must be posited for Buddhas a continuing cognitive relation to the world, in spite of their having eliminated the world's cognitive source from their minds.

Then if a Buddha is utterly free from the conceptual construction of a dualistic world, does a Buddha know the world of our dualistic conceptualization, or not? In this regard, what does the traditional ascription of "omniscience" to a Buddha mean? Does a Buddha know the characteristics of individuated things, even while always in nonconceptual equipoise on emptiness? Or does "omniscience" just refer to a Buddha's awareness of the emptiness of all things, without awareness of individuated things?

Ye shes sde then responds to these questions as follows:

> A Tathāgata knows all things free from conceptualization: both their individual characteristics and their general characteristic [emptiness]. Prior [to attaining Buddhahood,] bodhisattvas' actions are not yet spontaneous, their obstructions are not yet fully purified, their power is not yet inconceivable. [They alternate between sessions of meditative equipoise and activity.] When they abide in meditative equipoise, they see emptiness, the general characteristic of all things, with nonconceptual awareness *(rnam par mi rtog pa'i ye shes).* When they arise from that equipoise [for postmeditation session activity], they know the individual characteristics [of things] to be merely an illusion, through their purified awareness of the world *(dag pa 'jig rten pa'i ye shes)* which is obtained subsequent to that [nonconceptual awareness].
>
> By proceeding to higher and higher levels through that training, [they attain] its fruit, the stage of Buddhahood where [all] conceptuality is cleared away and obstructions are [fully] purified. At that point meditative equipoise occurs of itself. Then, without ever arising from that equipoise, all the cognitive objects that exist are manifest at once.
>
> [Like bodhisattvas' knowledge of the world in postsession activity, Buddhas] know the individual characteristics [of things] to be mere illusion. But because [Buddhas] are free of conceptuality, they do not perceive

> things as entities nor do they grasp at their labels, and thus, [unlike bodhisattvas,] the fault of [conceptually splitting awareness into] cognitive subject and object does not occur.
>
> As it says in the *Buddha-avataṃsaka-sūtra*: "The mind of the Bhagavan Buddhas, having been purified through an inexpressible period of hundreds of billions of trillions of aeons, is free of obstruction. [It perceives] all realms of the cosmos without exception within its cognitive sphere. [It perceives] all of the *dharmadhātu* (universal emptiness) without exception within its cognitive sphere. It knows all with respect to past, present, and future, with one cognition *(dgongs pa gcig)*, free of obstruction. It possesses all in its comprehension." Such expressions are extensive in this sūtra.
>
> The *Āryasarvadharmasaṃgitisūtra* says: "For example a magician may [put on a show] of striving to liberate an illusory being. But he knew it would be an illusion from before [he conjured it up], so he has no attachment to it. Similarly, the three realms of beings are known by the fully enlightened sage to be like an illusion. He makes preparations for the sake of beings; but he has prior knowledge of them.[56]
>
> Therefore, at the level of a Buddha, there is no purified awareness of the world per se *(dag pa 'jig rten pa'i ye shes)*, [such as a bodhisattva possesses].[57]

Nonabiding nirvāṇa creates these problems of knowing, being, and acting in the world only for Buddhas. For it requires of Buddhas, and no one else, that they act within a dualistic, conceptually constructed world without ever emerging from meditative equipoise within nonconceptual, nondualistic awareness of its emptiness. Ye shes sde, recognizing this, seeks to resolve those problems by identifying what is unique about a Buddha's awareness of the world, and how it is to be distinguished from any other beings' awareness of the world, including that of high bodhisattvas prior to Buddhahood.

As he summarizes the matter, Mahāyāna śāstras most explicit on gnoseology say bodhisattvas prior to Buddhahood have not eliminated the cognitive obstruction *(jñeyāvarāṇa)* through which saṃsāra continues to appear to them in the dualistic form of subject and object.[58] For even high bodhisattvas, then, the Second Noble Truth still holds in the sense that they have not removed the cognitive basis for their finite existence within a dualistic appearance of saṃsāra. Their awareness is superior to that of ordinary beings because their meditative equipoise on emptiness profoundly effects the way things appear to them when they leave that meditation to act in the world. At that time the world looks far more illusory to them than to us, appearing to them as a mental fabrication, rather than as the solid, reified reality of our experience. Though different from our way of seeing the world, we can at least imagine how a bodhisattva might see it ("like a dream, a mirage, etc.").

But, Ye shes sde implies, we can not even imagine how a Buddha sees the world. A Buddha's knowledge of it has to be of a different order altogether. For a Buddha has removed all cognitive obstructions that prevent uninterrupted awareness of the world's emptiness. A Buddha, unlike anyone else, never leaves that nondual, nonconceptual awareness. So when Mahāyāna texts ascribe infinite knowledge of the world and unlimited activity to Buddhas, such things cannot be understood as expressions of a "worldly" awareness distinct from awareness of emptiness. They have to be understood as expressions of the awareness of emptiness itself. Ye shes sde cites the claim of Mahāyāna texts that Buddhas alone know all things in a single instant, precisely because they alone abide always in equipoise on universal emptiness: "At that point, meditative equipoise occurs of itself. Then, without ever arising from that equipoise, all the cognitive objects that exist are manifest at once."

Simultaneous cognition of the entire cosmos in past, present, and future cannot be accounted for, Ye shes sde implies, by adding up anyone's finite knowledge of the world, even that of high bodhisattvas. It can only be accounted for by a different kind of knowledge altogether: a knowledge that grasps the essential nature of everything at once *(dharmadhātu)*, without conceptual distinctions of time, space, subject, and object. Ye shes sde concludes: "Therefore, a Buddha does not possess purified awareness of the world per se [such as a bodhisattva possesses]."

Put another way, a Buddha, unlike a bodhisattva, is no longer a finite being. The *dharmadhātu* is infinite. A Buddha's mind, inseparable from it, is also infinite. According to the scriptures Ye shes sde cites, it is this infinite, nonconceptual awareness that breaks down the conceptual barriers of space and time that delimit the minds of all other beings, giving Buddhas alone knowledge of the entire cosmos at once. As noted in section 2.a above, such scriptural expressions fed into the doctrine of nonabiding nirvāṇa by epistemologically connecting *dharmakāya* to the entire world.[59]

As we have seen, Haribhadra reinterpreted *Abhisamayālaṃkāra* chapter 8 to try to solve the very same problems of nonabiding nirvāṇa that concerned Ye shes sde. He wrote in the same general period as Ye shes sde (late eighth century), but took an entirely different approach. Drawing upon Abhidharma as he perceived it reflected in the *Abhisamayālaṃkāra*, Haribhadra depicted a Buddha's *dharmakāya* awareness as a set of conditioned mental factors in continuity with those of the bodhisattva on the path to Buddhahood. He identified these conditioned mental factors as the basis for the *dharmakāya*'s connection to the world in knowledge, manifestation, and activity.

The contrast between the Indian Mahāyāna perspective that Ye shes sde discerned and the one Haribhadra was shaping in the same period is vivid. Based on his reading of the Indian texts, Ye shes sde assumed that the paradox of nonabiding nirvāṇa was unresolvable from the conventional perspective of non-Buddhas. Therefore, he seeks its solution in the uniqueness of a Buddha's realization. Haribhadra believed the paradox to be resolvable from a conventional perspective, assuming similarity between a Buddha's mind and the minds of non-Buddhas to infer a Buddha's connection to the world. In Ye shes sde's approach, a Buddha's *dharmakāya* bears similarity to the *parinirvāṇa* of pre-Mahāyāna tradition insofar as it utterly transcends the world (in Mahāyāna terms, by abiding forever in the emptiness of all reified appearances). Yet its transcendence goes further than that of *parinirvāṇa*, for it transcends even the duality of saṃsāra and nirvāṇa: the *dharmakāya* so fully breaks through the illusory world to its emptiness that it becomes eternally connected to the world in vast, intimate ways unfathomable to those still caught in delusion. Haribhadra connected the *dharmakāya* to the world by making it less transcendent, more similar to the conditioned content of a bodhisattva's mind, fathomable (so he thought) to a scholar of Abhidharma.

The comparison vividly illustrates the two perspectives on enlightenment in Indo-Tibetan thought, alluded to in chapter 1, that this book has been tracing: the nondual yogic attainment perspective and the analytic-inferential perspective. The former perspective understands *dharmakāya* primarily as a nondual, yogic attainment, obtained but not created by the path, literally beyond the grasp of human conceptuality or inference. The latter perspective, viewing *dharmakāya* more as the creation of the path, understands it through inference based upon analogy to the path.

As we have seen, the nondual yogic attainment perspective on Buddhahood has been dominant in the "Maitreya" texts and Yogācāra treatises referred to in chapter 5. Among the Mahāyāna intuitions described in section 2 of this chapter, this perspective takes the first intuition as fundamental: understanding Buddhahood as perfected nondual knowledge of the *dharmadhātu* (see 2.a above). As we have seen, this very intuition, expressed both in the *Prajñāpāramitā* sūtras' doctrine of nondual awareness as the defining principle of the Tathāgatha, and in the Yogācāra formulation of the first of three *kāya*s, was decisive in the *AA*'s teaching of *dharmakāya*. And in line with that, the nondual yogic attainment perspective on Buddhahood was upheld by Ārya Vimuktisena, Ratnākaraśānti, and Abhayākaragupta, and in Tibet by the Sa skya master Go ram pa (this perspective has been well represented not only in the Sa skya school, but also in bKa' brgyud and rNying ma schools). Ye shes sde discerned the same fundamental pattern of thought in his survey of the wide range of Indian Mahāyāna texts available to him in the latter half of the eighth century.

In contrast to this, the analytic-inferential perspective understands Buddhahood primarily through logical inference based upon analogy to Abhidharma descriptions of the path. As such, it bases itself mainly upon the second of the early Mahāyāna intuitions sketched in section 2 of this chapter: Buddhahood as the fruition of a vast collection of causes (see 2.b above). Although the roots of this perspective are therefore as ancient in Mahāyāna sources as that of nondual yoga, its explicit use of the tools of Buddhist logic with Abhidharma is a much later development in Mahāyāna, achieving one of its clearest expressions in Haribhadra's eighth-century commentaries on the *Abhisamayālaṃkāra* and becoming influential in Tibet through his later influence upon scholastic traditions, prominently that of the dGe lugs pa school of Tsong kha pa. Haribhadra, too, took the *Prajñāpāramitāsūtra* seriously in his reading of the *Abhisamayālaṃkāra*. But he read the sūtra (through the lens of *AA* 8) primarily as an Abhidharma-type summary of conventional factors of the path (definatory of Buddhahood), rather than as an expression of a nondual awareness that ultimately transcends all such factors.

We can further specify the contrast between the perspectives exemplified by Ye shes sde and Haribhadra. Ye shes sde's yogic attainment perspective relies primarily upon Mahāyāna traditions of nondual yogic praxis and gnoseology. Haribhadra, charting the inferential perspective, relies primarily upon codified Abhidharma descriptions of enlightenment and analytic methods of Buddhist logic. Ye shes sde accepts the logical tension of nonabiding nirvāṇa as a pointer to the transcendent uniqueness of a Buddha's mind, a nondual nature known adequately only through its yogic realization. Because of this, Ye shes sde uses sacred texts as revelation of a Buddha's perspective on nirvāṇa. Haribhadra views the logical tension in Buddha's nirvāṇa as a problem of human conceptualization, to be resolved through inference by analogy to what is known: the conditioned mental factors of the bodhisattva path. For this reason, he uses sacred text (*AA* 8) primarily as a point of departure for human systematic reflection on Buddha's nirvāṇa. Along the same lines, Ye shes sde finds the key to Buddhahood in a Buddha's realization of ultimate truth *(dharmadhātu)*. Haribhadra looks to conventional truth: inference by analogy to mental components of those who are on the path.

Our analysis of Mahāyāna tension in the Four Noble Truths can further clarify the contrast between these two perspectives. And it is here that Ye shes sde's treatise, contrasted with that of Haribhadra, sheds much light. The Second Noble Truth (ignorance, *kleśa,* and karma) is what situates living beings in the conditioned world by providing the causes of their minds and bodies, the *skandha*s. Since nirvāṇa in any form must involve freedom from the conditions that make the suffering world of beings, how is a Buddha's nonabiding nirvāṇa to be connected to that world? How are we to understand saṃsāra and nirvāṇa to be linked in Buddhahood? Since it was the redefinition of the Third Noble Truth as nonabiding nirvāṇa that created the problem, responses to it from either perspective have had implicitly to reevaluate the Four Noble Truths scheme as a whole.

In retrospect, we can now see that Haribhadra's approach links saṃsāra and nirvāṇa in Buddhahood by seeking a similitude of saṃsāra within nirvāṇa: a principle of conditionality within *dharmakāya* that would situate it in the conditioned world (like the Second Noble Truth situates living beings in the world through their conditioned formations). Haribhadra assumed a continuity between conditioned mental factors of the bodhisattva path and a Buddha's mind. Mental factors of the path, when fully purified and developed, become a Buddha's conditioned mental factors *(jñānātmaka dharmakāya)*. In essence, Haribhadra assumed that for nonabiding nirvāṇa to serve as a Mahāyāna Third Noble Truth linked to the world, it must be qualified by the impermanence and conditionality that the first two Noble Truths lend to the world.

Although Haribhadra's *Sphuṭārthā* commentary on *Abhisamayālaṃkāra* was translated into Tibetan during Ye shes sde's lifetime, Ye shes sde takes no notice of it in his treatise and may not have been familar with it. Ye shes sde would likely have been surprised by Haribhadra's approach to the problem. For according to the Second Noble Truth as Ye shes sde understood it, conditioned existence itself is a saṃsāric process that flows from ignorance. A Buddha, in his own core realization, must be presumed to be entirely free of the limitations of conditioned existence, including conditioned components of mind.[60]

For Ye shes sde, as for those who later criticized Haribhadra, to subject a Buddha's own awareness to conditionality and impermanence implies a finiteness that would negate a Buddha's attainment. A Buddha's mind, one with the *dharmadhātu*, is infinite and beyond conditioning. Infinite mind, through its oneness with the ultimate nature of all things, becomes omniscience. Infinite awareness cannot be generated by adding up finite conditions of the path. Rather, the path creates the conditions for a decisive break from finiteness and conditionality altogether.[61] Rather than extrapolating Buddhahood from an Abhidharmic account of the path, as Haribhadra had done, Ye shes sde relied primarily upon Mahāyāna sūtras connected to the three-*kāya* doctrine of the "Maitreya" texts that became the touchstone for Ārya Vimuktisena, Ratnākaraśānti, and Abhayākaragupta on *dharmakāya*.

But then how, without ascribing conditionality and finiteness to Buddhahood, did Ye shes sde respond to the problem of linking a Buddha's nirvāṇa to the saṃsāric world? If Haribhadra responded by seeking a similitude of saṃsāra within nirvāṇa, Ye shes sde did just the opposite. He identified a similitude of nirvāṇa within saṃsāra: Buddha-nature *(tathāgatagarbha)*. Having sorted through sūtras and commentaries formulative of the yogic attainment perspective on Buddhahood, Ye shes sde discerned the doctrine of Buddha-nature (implicit or explicit in many of those sources) as the authentic Mahāyāna way of reinterpreting the Four Noble Truths so as to connect saṃsāra and nirvāṇa within Buddhahood as nonabiding nirvāṇa.[62] The clues to his approach are his emphasis on purification, a Buddha's instantaneous awareness of all when all obstructions have been purified away (evident in the quotes above), and the key role of Buddha-nature *(tathāgatagarbha)* within several of the Mahāyāna topics he treats in the *lTa ba'i khyad par*.

Buddha-nature contributes significantly to Ye shes sde's understanding of the three vehicles *(triyāna)* taught in Mahāyāna texts. Ye shes sde's summary of the *śrāvaka* vehicle expresses the dualism of saṃsāra and nirvāṇa that had been inscribed in the pre-Mahāyāna formulation of the Four Noble Truths: The *śrāvaka* realizes the aggregates of mind and body to be suffering by nature, eliminates the *kleśa* and karma that are their causes, attains the cessation of the aggregates, and thereby separates from saṃsāra altogether at final nirvāṇa. "From among those two [saṃsāra and nirvāṇa], he realizes that one is to be abandoned, the other to be attained."[63] The *pratyekabuddha* vehicle does not alter this dualistic pattern. Ye shes sde defines the great vehicle (Mahāyāna), on the other hand, as that path and result which entails "the realization of the nonduality of saṃsāra and nirvāṇa," the realization of nonabiding nirvāṇa.[64] He glosses this in a traditional way: Due to wisdom *(prajñā)*, the bodhisattva sees the illusory nature of saṃsāra; due to compassion *(mahākaruṇā)*, he never abandons the beings who are caught in it.

But he also senses that for a nonduality of saṃsāra and nirvāṇa to make sense, another Mahāyāna principle needs to be invoked: Buddha-nature *(tathāgatagarbha)*, the doctrine that all living beings possess the essence *(garbha)* of a Buddha in obscured form and are therefore ultimately destined for Buddhahood. When concluding his discussion of the vehicles, therefore, Ye shes sde affirms the doctrine of Buddha-nature in support of his assertion that there can only be one final vehicle *(ekayāna)*:

> In many sūtras such as the *Ārya Samādhirāja* there are pronouncements that "all sentient beings possess the essence of the Tathāgatha" *(tathāgatagarbha)*, "all sentient beings shall become Buddhas; there are none who are not fitting receptacles," and so forth, which contradicts the notion [that any beings would never become Buddhas]. It is evident, then, that the other two vehicles, in the end, are to be included within the great vehicle (Mahāyāna), the one final vehicle."[65]

Mahāyāna alone is the ultimate goal of all three vehicles. And that means that the "nirvāṇas" of *śrāvakas* and *pratyekabuddhas* serve merely as "resting places" *(bsti ba'i gnas)* on the path to the nondual, nonabiding nirvāṇa of the Buddhas.

In other words, if saṃsāra and nirvāṇa are to be understood as nondual in Mahāyāna, the assumption of their duality in other vehicles could only be provisional, not final. And this means that the apparent duality between sentient beings and Buddhas must in some sense also be provisional, not final. A Buddha's nirvāṇa is not as separate from saṃsāra as it may seem to us (*dharmakāya* pervades all beings); and saṃsāra is not as separate from nirvāṇa as it may seem (beings are already receptacles of *dharmakāya* in a germinal or obscured form). Thus, in Ye shes sde's view, unless Buddha-nature *(tathāgatagarbha)* is assumed, the nondual paradigm of nonabiding nirvāṇa would not make sense.

Ye shes sde's concern to make sense of the nonduality of saṃsāra and nirvāṇa by affirming a basic nondifference between sentient beings and Buddhas appears again in his treatment of a Buddha's gnosis of sameness *(samatājñāna)*. A Buddha, he says, realizes thusness as the "one taste" of all phenomena. Because of this, a Buddha never constructs the distinction between "self" and "other" that other beings construct. This is a standard formulation of the gnosis of sameness (cf. chapter 5 section 4 above). In Ye shes sde's text, however, gnosis of sameness, Buddha-nature, and the nonduality of saṃsāra and nirvāṇa become mutually implicative. Since the Buddhas' awareness pervades all beings nondually in the one final nature they all share, saṃsāra already contains nirvāṇa in a way known only to the Buddhas.[66]

Buddha-nature is prominent in Ye shes sde's discussion of the *dharmakāya*, where he identifies Buddha-nature *(tathāgatagarbha)* not merely as a capacity to become a Buddha, but as the *dharmakāya* itself in obscured form. Quoting from one Mahāyāna sūtra, he says: "When Buddha nature *(tathāgatagarbha)* has not yet become clear, it is the foundation consciousness *(ālayavijñāna)*. But when it has become clear, it is *dharmakāya*."[67] Paraphrasing a śāstra, he says: "'*Dharmakāya* refers to Buddha nature as the primordial lineage of dharma. It is the very nature of all sentient beings. When it is covered over by erroneous patterns of thought, it is defiled. But when it has been purified by spiritual discipline, freed from error, it becomes what it actually is. And that is *dharmakāya*."[68]

Later, Ye shes sde gives a quote from the *Suvarnaprabhāsasūtra* that ascribes to *dharmakāya* four signature qualities of Buddha-nature: "Since the *dharmakāya* is based upon the true nature of self, it is called 'self,' and 'permanent.' Since it is based upon great concentration, it is called 'bliss.' Since it is based upon great gnosis, it is called 'pure'. . . ."[69] Ye shes sde then explains: "Since sentient beings are conditioned by karma and *kleśa*, [their aggregates are] impermanent, ungovernable, suffering, and impure. [The Tathāgata] teaches these [qualities of *dharmakāya*: permanence, self, bliss, and purity] as their antidotes." Having identified *dharmakāya* with Buddha-nature, Ye shes sde locates the pure awareness of nirvāṇa within saṃsāra, obscured from sentient beings by their defilements; an innate awareness made accessible to beings by the Buddha's teaching as their own intrinsic antidote to those defilements.[70]

Ye shes sde is now ready to respond to the problem of nonabiding nirvāṇa as it is situated within the Four Noble Truths. He does so in the conclusion of his text under his final topic: contemplation of the twelve factors of dependent arising in their reverse order. This is the standard formula, inherited from pre-Mahāyāna traditions, to chart the way to liberation through successive cessation of the conditions that construct saṃsāra:

> In reverse order, "by this ceasing, that ceases." In other words, by cessation of ignorance, conditioned formations, cease . . . up to: by birth ceasing, old age and death, etc. cease.[71]

This formula, which the Mahāyāna inherited as Buddhist orthodoxy, summarizes the pre-Mahāyāna understanding of the Four Noble Truths: by cutting off the causes of saṃsāra (Second Truth), one's existence in the world ceases (pre-Mahāyāna Third Truth). Ye shes sde, having summarized all traditional categories of Mahāyāna in his synoptic treatise, now faces the obvious problem of how to reconcile nonabiding nirvāṇa with this orthodox, pre-Mahāyāna formula in which attainment of nirvāṇa annihilates one's connection to saṃsāra. But based upon the linkage he has made in prior sections between Buddha-nature, *dharmakāya*, and the nonduality of saṃsāra and nirvāṇa, he is ready to respond:

> It is not the case that from cessation of ignorance there comes to be nothing at all. Nor does the [twelve-link chain of] dependent arising continue. Rather, when the defiled dimension ceases, one reverts to the pure dimension *(kun nas nyon mongs pa'i phyogs 'gags nas / rnam par byang ba'i phyogs su 'gyur te)*. For example, when [a sick person] has taken the appropriate medicine, then as his illnesses and [tendency for] short life disappear, he finds his health and [proclivity for] long life. Similarly, as obscured awareness ceases, unobscured awareness emerges *(ma rig pa 'gags te rig pa byung)*. From this, the fruits of *śrāvaka* and *pratyekabuddha* are accomplished. And by fulfilling all different kinds of collections of merit and wisdom which arise from that unobscured awareness *(rig pa las byung ba)*, the stages of the bodhisattva path are traversed to completion at the stage of Buddhahood. Then, having accomplished all, and having found all the magnificent qualities [of Buddhahood], one enters the nonabiding nirvāṇa which spontaneously carries out the welfare of all sentient beings for as long as saṃsāra lasts.[72]

Here Ye shes sde explicitly locates the source of doctrinal tension created by nonabiding nirvāṇa within the Four Noble Truths scheme, and resolves the problem by reformulating the Four Noble Truths so as to leave a principle of enlightenment that is vastly engaged in the world when the defiled causes of mind and body have ceased. He does this by subtly drawing upon the doctrines of Buddha-nature, *dharmakāya*, path as purification, and the nonduality of saṃsāra and nirvāṇa that were interwoven through his text.

His description of all the collections of the path as arisen from unobscured awareness dovetails with his simile of health and illness. Illness is not the entire nature of the body. The proclivity for health is even more basic, has always been there, and emerges naturally with the removal of illness. Similarly, the suffering of the aggregates and their causes are not the totality of a living being: the pure awareness dimension of their being is there, making itself known with the removal of the defilements that had obscured it. As his earlier discussions make clear, that intrinsic pure awareness is the *dharmakāya* itself, nondual and all-pervasive.[73]

This means that one whose defilements are completely removed, becoming a Buddha, would never thereby be removed from the world. Rather, one would become aware, in nondual fashion, of the intrinsic purity of all beings and the way in which their defilements obscure that purity. Ye shes sde has identified a principle (intrinsic pure awareness, intrinsic *dharmakāya*, Buddha-nature) through which *dharmakāya* can be understood as always connected to the world in a vast way, whether viewed in relation to those in which it is still obscured (sentient beings) or in relation to those in which it has been uncovered (Buddhas). Nirvāṇa, then, becomes not a disconnection from the world, but an awakening to one's pervasive connection to all beings in their underlying purity.

To sum up, Haribhadra, who was formulating a conceptual-analytical perspective on Buddhahood, and Ye shes sde, who upheld the prior nondual yogic attainment perspective, both faced the same problem in the eighth century: how to link saṃsāra and nirvāṇa within a Buddha's nondual attainment of nonabiding nirvāṇa. Haribhadra sought a saṃsāric principle (conditionality) within Buddhahood (conditioned mental factors, *jñānātmaka dharmakāya*). Ye shes sde, surveying the textual roots of the yogic attainment perspective he had inherited, discerned that it was the doctrine of Buddha-nature that made the proper connection: by locating a principle of nirvāṇa *(dharmakāya)* within saṃsāra (pervading all beings).

In both cases, the Four Noble Truths formula as a whole had to be reinterpreted in such a way as to accommodate the Mahāyāna doctrine of nonabiding nirvāṇa. But the form of that reinterpretation depended upon which of the Mahāyāna intuitions that had originally projected nonabiding nirvāṇa was viewed as central, and which as peripheral.

For Haribhadra, the Mahāyāna intuitions of *bodhicitta* and bodhisattva path were central: The long, patient collection of innumerable causes to create a state of Buddhahood that is connected to the world in a vast way for beings (section 2.b, above). Buddha's omniscience becomes the summation of knowledges of the path perfected, and his vast connection to the world becomes the vastness of his mind that the path has constructed *(jñānātmaka dharmakāya)*. Haribhadra reinterprets the Four Noble Truths to accommodate nonabiding nirvāṇa by inferring a similitude of saṃsāra in nirvāṇa: conditionality.

For Ye shes sde, Mahāyāna intuitions of nondual realization of *dharmadhātu* and Buddha-nature were crucial (sections 2.a and 2.d, above). A Buddha's omniscience is not a conditioned construct. It is the knowing of all through nondual awareness of the unconditioned, ultimate nature of all. Ye shes sde reinterprets the Four Noble Truths to accommodate nonabiding nirvāṇa by locating a similitude of nirvāṇa within saṃsāra: Buddha-nature. He identifies the pure, unconditioned nature usually associated with the Third Noble Truth *(nirvāṇa)* as a dimension of saṃsāra itself, lurking in the ontological background of the first two Noble Truths, revealed when the impurity of the first two Noble Truths is removed. Buddhas and living beings have never been separate in their true nature, the pure dimension of reality, though that fact is fully revealed only at Buddhahood. *Dharmakāya* is inseparable from the entire cosmos at Buddhahood because it has been inseparable from it all along.

But then what is the source of a Buddha's conditioned activities in the world? We have shown how the two formulations of Buddhahood above are each designed to accommodate nonabiding nirvāṇa to the Four Noble Truths. This can shed new light on the reason that total spontaneity has long been ascribed to a Buddha's activities in texts that have taken the nondual yogic attainment perspective. Ye shes sde illustrates this phenomenon. Immediately after the section, quoted earlier, in which he makes the claim that a Buddha knows all entirely free from conceptualization,[74] he raises the question that naturally follows:

> Then the following question may occur: "But how, from such nonconceptuality, can a [Buddha's] physical, verbal and mental creations arise [to manifest and act in the world]?[75]

How can the unconditioned and nonconceptual *dharmakāya* give rise to limitless activity for beings? Ye shes sde's answer, based on Mahāyāna sūtras, follows the yogic attainment perspective of the texts we examined in chapter 5, section 3. Buddhahood possesses limitless power for good as the natural outflow of the bodhisattva's long practice of the path *prior* to Buddhahood. Buddha activity is the automatic and spontaneous outflow of this power, which takes the form appropriate for trainees in accord with the relative purity of their minds. Ye shes sde employs the standard images of the wish-fulfilling jewel and wish-granting tree to illustrate the spontaneity and automaticity of Buddha activity, free from forethought or effort.[76]

Now we can see that nonabiding nirvāṇa, in tension with the Four Noble Truth formula, necessitated mechanical spontaneity for a Buddha's activity in the textual traditions Ye shes sde draws upon.[77] For Buddhahood requires total cessation of the first two Noble Truths, which from the nondual yogic-attainment perspective includes cessation of all the conditioned bases for intentional participation in the world. As such, and as the nondual realization of *dharmadhātu*, Buddhahood is unconditioned. But, as nonabiding nirvāṇa, it is supposed to give rise to conditioned manifestations and activities. Because conditioned things only derive from other conditioned things, the conditioned activities of nonabiding nirvāṇa had to be derived from conditions extrinsic to the core realization of Buddhahood: diachronically, past conditions preceding the attainment of Buddhahood (prior vows and merit of the bodhisattva path); synchronically, present conditions of sentient beings' minds (*rūpakāya* forms appear spontaneously to those purified enough to see them).[78]

Because Haribhadra (and Tsong kha pa) connected Buddhas to the world by ascribing conditionality to their minds, strictly speaking, they removed the doctrinal necessity of total spontaneity for the Buddhas' activity. But because the nondual yogic-attainment perspective dominated so much Mahāyāna literature on Buddhahood prior to the rise of the Buddhist logical tradition and Haribhadra, spontaneity had become ensconced as an orthodox presupposition, which Haribhadra and Tsong kha pa simply accepted, not noticing, perhaps, the doctrinal purpose it had served for a prior long-established perspective on Buddhahood that they did not hold.

13.5 Summary and Conclusions

a. Origins of the Tension in Mahāyāna Formulations of Buddhahood

Disagreements over *Abhisamayālaṃkāra* chapter 8 are the tip of a doctrinal iceberg. The concern underlying those disagreements originated with the very rise of the Mahāyāna, in the seminal intuitions of a Buddha's vast connection to the world that are expressed in its sūtras.

These include early Mahāyāna intuitions of Buddhahood as (1) a vast, nondual awareness of *dharmadhātu* (the ultimate nature of the entire cosmos), (2) a vast fruition of a long bodhisattva path, (3) a universally accessible source of blessing and teaching (through *buddhānusmṛti*, devotional practices, and higher samādhis), and (4) something ultimately inseparable from all living beings (the doctrine of Buddha-nature, *tathāgatagarbha*). Several or all of these intuitions became interwoven themes within Mahāyāna sūtras and śāstras, where each such intuition connected Buddhahood in a vast way to limitless beings and their cosmos through space and time.

These early Mahāyāna intuitions pushed up against the pre-Mahāyāna understanding of the Four Noble Truths, which had framed a duality between saṃsāra and nirvāṇa, such that the final attainment of nirvāṇa (Third Truth) cut one's connection to saṃsāra (First and Second Truths). Initially, some Mahāyāna texts stretched the Third Noble Truth to accommodate these intuitions through various models of postponing final nirvāṇa for Buddhas or bodhisattvas. But more Mahāyāna texts came to redefine the Third Truth altogether as nonabiding nirvāṇa: saṃsāra and nirvāṇa as nondual, Buddhahood as pervasively active within saṃsāra for limitless beings to the end of time. Perceived as the more authentic way of giving expression to early Mahāyāna intuitions of a Buddha's vast connection to beings, nonabiding nirvāṇa became normative for Indian Mahāyāna.

But having become normative, it presented a paradox at the very core of systematic Mahāyāna thought: How can something *(dharmakāya)* be entirely free from the conditions out of which the saṃsāric world is generated, yet remain pervasively engaged in that world to the end of time? How does a Buddha's attainment of nirvāṇa, which eliminates the first two Noble Truths as they apply to himself, leave him connected to the first two Noble Truths of other beings, active in their experiential worlds of defilement and suffering? In other words, how is the Mahāyāna to authentically reinterpret the Four Noble Truths consistent with its doctrine of Buddhahood as nonabiding nirvāṇa?

This is the core doctrinal problem that underlay disagreements over *Abhisamayālaṃkāra* 8 since the time of Haribhadra, and that also motivated a wide range of other interrelated disagreements on Buddhahood in late Indian and Tibetan Buddhism concerning a Buddha's awareness, modes of being, and participation in the world. The disagreements represent different ways of linking saṃsāra and nirvāṇa within Buddhahood by reinterpreting the Four Noble Truths scheme so as to resolve the logical tension of nonabiding nirvāṇa within it.[79]

b. Nondual Yogic-Attainment Perspective in Mahāyāna Doctrinal Formation

The paradox of nonabiding nirvāṇa was explicitly raised in some of the treatises most influential in formalizing the doctrine of nonabiding nirvāṇa for the Yogācāra school (namely, the "Maitreya" texts). The response of these treatises to the problem was that Buddhahood is a yogic attainment *(dharmakāya)* that is connected to the world in a vast way through its nondual awareness of the world's undivided, ultimate nature: the *dharmadhātu*. The *dharmakāya*'s infinitely vast connection to the world could not have been created out of the finite components of the path, but it is attained by the path. Because, in this view, the *dharmakāya* is an entirely nonconceptual yogic attainment, its activity through *rūpakāya*s had to be characterized as entirely spontaneous, free of forethought. And because *dharmakāya* is immovable, its activity in the conditioned world had to be accounted for through diachronic and synchronic conditions that are not part of the *dharmakāya*'s own core realization (collections of virtue from the bodhisattva path prior to Buddhahood, relative purity of the minds of sentient beings to whom the *rūpakāya*s can appear).

It is by ascribing nonconceptual spontaneity of action to the Buddhas that this nondual yogic attainment perspective includes the second of the Mahāyāna intuitions above (Buddhahood as a vast ouflow of long path practice) without contradicting the first intuition, which it takes as primary (Buddhahood as nondual realization of unconditioned *dharmadhātu*).

The nondual yogic attainment perspective on enlightenment sketched here, derived from the *Prajñāpāramitā* and other Mahāyāna sūtras' descriptions of nondual awareness *(prajñāpāramitā)* as the defining principle of the Tathāgatha, found expression in the doctrine of *svābhāvikakāya/dharmakāya* in the three-*kāya* model of Yogācāra, entered into the *Abhisamayālaṃkāra*'s eighth chapter in that form, and exerted strong influence upon later Indian writing on Buddhahood.

As we have seen, various doctrinal elements that contributed to the doctrine of Buddha-nature *(tathāgatagarbha)* also contributed to this nondual yogic perspective within these textual traditions (see chapter 5 section 3 above). In Yogācāra texts, the *svābhāvikakāya* was described as unconditioned, as something that is attained but not newly created, since it represents the coming to awareness of that which had always been present (thusness, *tathatā*). The core yogic practices that lead to its attainment were described as the disappearance of the illusory permitting the appearance of the real that had always been there. Expressions of the innate, luminous purity of mind also contributed to the notion of *svābhāvikakāya*. The doctrine of Buddha-nature, as we find it more fully developed in the *Ratnagotravibhāga* and several sūtras upon which it draws, teaches that all beings already possess the nature of the Buddha in an obscured form *(samalātathatā)*—enlightenment is attained, not created, by removing the obscurations to reveal the pure nature that had always been present *(vimalātathatā)*. The teaching of the *gotra* in the first chapter of *Abhisamayālaṃkāra*, identified with the undifferentiated *dharmadhātu* as the undivided basis of all vehicles and all bodhisattva practices, seems to resonate both with its teaching of *svābhāvikakāya* in chapter 8 and with this doctrine of Buddha-nature, the two coming to be aligned closely with it in Tibet.[80] But, as we saw in chapter 5, the doctrine of Buddha-nature *(tathāgatagarbha)* was not a highly developed or central doctrine in all of the textual traditions that contributed to the nondual yogic attainment perspective.

The nondual yogic attainment perspective sketched here therefore represents a perspective on Buddhahood of long continuity in the Mahāyāna even amidst great doctrinal development and change. It was upheld by Ārya Vimuktisena in his interpretation of the *AA*, identified by Ye shes sde in the eighth century as the normative Mahāyāna perspective, and invoked by Ratnākaraśānti and Abhayākaragupta in late Indian Buddhism and by Go ram pa in Tibet.

c. An Eighth-Century Analytic-Inferential Perspective

Haribhadra, reading portions of the *Prajñāpāramitāsūtra* through the lens of the *Abhisamayālaṃkāra* as an Abhidharma-like description of Buddhahood, and thereby understanding Buddhahood as the creation of the bodhisattva path, posited a conditioned content to a Buddha's attainment: pure conditioned consciousnesses and mental factors *(jñānātmaka dharmakāya)*. He thus accomodated nonabiding nirvāṇa to the Four Noble Truths by making nirvāṇa (Third Truth) more like saṃsāra (the first two Truths): possessed of a conditioned nature. In essence, he linked a Buddha's nirvāṇa to saṃsāra by identifying a similitude of saṃsāra (conditionality) in nirvāṇa.[81] Haribhadra's perspective was not initially accepted by all, but gradually came to exert much influence over late Indian scholastic Buddhism.

d. An Eighth-Century Nondual Yogic-Attainment Perspective

Ye shes sde, a principal figure in the early transmission of Buddhism to Tibet, shows us the increasingly central role that the doctrine of Buddha-nature (and cognate doctrines such as innate pure mind) had assumed by the eighth century within the Indian yogic attainment perspective on Buddhahood as it began to enter and influence Tibet. Ye shes sde, drawing upon many Indian Mahāyāna sūtras and śāstras, accommodates nonabiding nirvāṇa to the Four Noble Truths in a way opposite to that of Haribhadra, by identifying a similitude of nirvāṇa within saṃsāra: Buddha-nature. *Dharmakāya* can be understood to be connected to the world in a vast way because it always has been. As Buddha-nature, it pervades all living beings in an obscured form. It is because it has always pervaded all that, when the obscurations are removed by the path, it can be instantaneously aware of all. Ye shes sde discerned the important role of Buddha-nature within the nondual yogic-attainment perspective of the eighth century, which continued to be exemplified in the writings of Ratnākaraśānti (with his understanding of Buddhahood as manifestation of innate pure mind), Abhayākaragupta, Go ram pa, and others in India and Tibet.

e. Opposing Mahāyāna Ways to Reinterpret the Four Noble Truths

The nondual yogic-attainment and analytic-inferential perspectives of the eighth century represented opposing ways to reinterpret the Four Noble Truths so as to link saṃsāra to nirvāṇa in Buddhahood and thereby resolve the problem of nonabiding nirvāṇa. They differed according to which of the early Mahāyāna intuitions of a Buddha's vast connection to the world were identified as central, which as more peripheral. Of the four intuitions summarized in section 2 above, the yogic attainment perspective has viewed nondual realization of dharmadhātu as primary. And this came to be understood as mutually implicative with the intuition of Buddha-nature, which redefined the Four Noble Truths to join nirvāṇa and saṃsāra in nonabiding nirvāṇa. The analytic-inferential perspective of Haribhadra and his followers has viewed the intuition of vast path collections as primary, joining a Buddha's nirvāṇa to saṃsāra through a conditioned *dharmakāya (jñānātmaka dharmakāya)* understood as the creation of the path.

f. Historical, Sociological, and Practical Significance of these Two Perspectives on Buddhahood

What is the historical importance of each of these perspectives in Indian and Tibetan Buddhism? The nondual yogic-attainment perspective in India, with its increasing emphasis upon Buddha-nature (and cognate doctrines such as innate pure mind), was the primary organizing perspective of tantric practice traditions of late Indian and Tibetan Buddhism. First, resonant with the nondual yogic-attainment perspective traced above, and unlike the analytic-inferential perspective, tantric praxis takes the nondual perspective of Buddhahood (or at least a symbolic facsimile of it) as the point of view from which it is to be approached: nonduality of saṃsāra and nirvāṇa, appearance and emptiness, etc. Secondly, tantric praxis has involved, at its core, an immediacy of identification with Buddhahood made possible by the increasing centrality of the doctrine of Buddha-nature: One can identify immediately with *dharmakāya* only insofar as one understands it to be one's actual nature in the here and now. The legendary quickness of the tantric path (full enlightenment attainable even in one lifetime) has assumed this very understanding, permitting a rapid progression on the path by revealing the intrinsic purity of deity and maṇḍala as the actual, primordial nature of oneself and one's world. The yogic-attainment perspective has therefore been extremely influential upon Tibetan Buddhism, which is heavily tantric in all its praxis traditions, and particularly upon the bKa' brgyud, rNying ma, and Sa skya schools to the present day (Gorampa provided just one important example from the latter school).[82]

The analytic-inferential perspective exemplified by Haribhadra exerted its influence upon late Indian Buddhism and upon all scholastic traditions of Tibet through commentaries on the *Abhisamayālaṃkāra*. But it has had its greatest influence upon the dGe lugs school of Tsong kha pa, whose normative views of Buddhahood were organized through such a perspective, significantly affecting his interpretations of tantric practice as well. Thus, within Tsong kha pa's tradition, the immediate identification with Buddhahood at the heart of Indo-Tibetan tantric practice came to be interpreted as a dress rehearsal for enlightenment, an imitation of aspects of Buddhahood not presently possessed, and thereby a potent means for accumulating a vast collection of causes from which Buddhahood is to be created (not discovered).[83]

The problem of a Buddha's relation to the world has never been trivial to living Buddhist traditions, since one's understanding of Buddhahood is decisive for one's understanding of the path that attains it, which is decisive for one's spiritual practice. So for example, if specific forms of inferential understanding are most highly rated, both for inferring the nature of Buddhahood as the creation of the path and as the sole source of access to ultimate awareness, practice tends to center upon long periods of study combined with path accumulations, as in the dGe lugs tradition of Tibet (analytic-inferential approach). If, on the other hand, Buddhahood is understood as the present actual nature of living beings though obscured to them, a nondual attainment beyond conditions, hence obtained by the path but not made by it, other possibilities of access to ultimate awareness may be discerned, as in tantric Mahāsiddha traditions of late Indian Buddhism and Tibetan traditions of rDzogs chen, Mahāmudrā, and Lam 'bras, which are informed by them (nondual yogic-attainment approach).

The differing perspectives have some sociological implications as well. If ultimate awareness is believed to be accessed exclusively through analytic-inferential procedures accomplishable only after long periods of study, monastic study institutions become the sole mediators of enlightenment. If other possibilities of access to ultimate awareness are also permitted (e.g., immediate entry triggered by vivid encounter between master and disciple, by practices of guru yoga, or by forms of meditation that do not necessarily rest upon years of scholastic study), then nonmonastic social institutions, such as lay communities of disciples gathered around a tantric master in a village or mountain dwelling, may be viewed as equally significant or more central. Differing perspectives on Buddhahood inform and are informed by differing practice traditions and their social expressions.[84]

Finally, the long continuity of the yogic-attainment perspective as a factor in Mahāyāna doctrinal development sheds further light upon the growing centrality of the doctrine of Buddha-nature and cognate doctrines over the course of Indian Mahāyāna and Tibetan Buddhist history. First, Buddha-nature provided a way to heal the rift in the Four Noble Truths created by the emergence of Mahāyāna intuitions of enlightenment from pre-Mahāyāna traditions. It provided an authentic Mahāyāna reïnterpretation of the Four Truths, "authentic" because it could support the doctrine of nonabiding nirvāṇa without compromising the early Mahāyāna intuitions of nonduality and infinite scope that had originally projected it. Having provided such a powerful model for that purpose, Buddha-nature became a linchpin in the doctrinal development of Mahāyāna toward tantrism, the very heart of late Indian and Tibetan Buddhist praxis. The crucial role of Buddha-nature for an authentic Mahāyāna understanding of the Four Noble Truths took incisive expression in the *Śrīmālādevi-siṃhanāda-sūtra*, and we will close with it:

> World Honored One, the [real] Noble Truths are not truths belonging to Śrāvakas and Pratyekabuddhas, and are not merits belonging to them. The [real] Noble Truths are realized only by a Tathāgata, a Worthy One, a Perfectly Enlightened One, and afterwards revealed, demonstrated, and explained to sentient beings who are confined in shells of ignorance. . . .
>
> World Honored One, the [real] Noble Truths are very profound, subtle, difficult to perceive, hard to understand, and not to be discriminated; they are beyond the realm of thought and speculation, and transcend the credence of all the world. They are known only to Tathāgatas. . . . Why? These Truths explain the very profound Buddha nature *(tathāgatagarbha)*. . . . Since the Noble Truths are explained on the basis of Buddha nature, and since Buddha nature is profound and subtle, the Noble Truths are also profound and subtle, difficult to perceive, hard to understand, and not to be discriminated. . . .[85]

Notes

Chapter 1. Introduction

1. For some parallels between Mahāyāna Buddhist and Christian attempts to specify relations between transcendent and immanent aspects of Buddha or God, see Griffiths, *On Being Buddha*, pp. 76–77, 235–36 (with chapter 7, note 3).

2. The full name of the *Abhisamayālaṃkāra* is *Abhisamayālaṃkāra-prajñāpāramitā-upadeśa-śāstra* (The Ornament of realizations, a treatise of instruction on the perfection of wisdom). It will be abbreviated *AA*. The abbreviation here for the *Prajñāpāramitā* sūtras will be *PP*.

3. Haribhadra (c. 770–810 C.E.) was the first to ascribe the *Abhisamayālaṃkāra* (*AA*) to Maitreya. He did so in his two principal commentaries on the *AA*, the *Āloka* (ed. Wogihara, p. 1) and *Sphuṭārthā* (ed. Amano, 1975, p. 2). He claimed that Asanga and Vasubandhu wrote commentaries on the *AA*, although these have never been found. If true, the *AA* was composed by the fourth century C.E. The first commentary extant in any language is Ārya Vimuktisena's (ca. early sixth century). If this was the first commentary, it would put the *AA*'s terminus ad quem in the early sixth century. The textual history and date of the *AA* is discussed in more detail in chapter 7 below.

4. The content of the *Abhisamayālaṃkāra*, its structure, and its relation to the *Prajñāpāramitā* sūtras will be discussed in chapters 6 and 7 below. The *AA* is an extremely condensed text, purporting to summarize all the yogic practices and realizations of Buddhism, yet taking up only twenty-seven folio sides in the Tibetan Tripitaka (Pk 5184).

5. "Embodiment of dharma," *AA* vv. 1.4 and 1.17, or *dharmakāya-phalam* (resultant embodiment of dharma*)*, *AA* verse 9.2.

6. *AA* verse 9.2, the last verse of the text, names its final topic: *dharmakāyaphalam* (resultant *dharmakāya*), meaning the entire state of Buddhahood. In Ārya Vimuktisena's *AA Vṛtti* (Peking 5185, fols. 100-3-7) the *AA*'s final chapter is called: "chos kyi sku'i skabs bslab pa'i 'bras bu'i leu" (The *dharmakāya* section, the chapter on the result of the trainings).

In Haribhadra's *Sphuṭārthā* (ed. Amano, 1975, p. 262) the *AA*'s final chapter is called "Dharmakāya-Abhisambodha" (The complete realization of *dharmakāya*).

7. Haribhadra mentions commentaries by Asanga and Vasubandhu which are not extant in any language (*Āloka*, ed. Wogihara, p. 1), and there may have been others written later which were not preserved in the Tibetan canon. Extant commentaries on the *Abhisamayālaṃkāra* are discussed in chapters 6 and 11 below.

8. The *Abhisamayālaṃkāra*, as a verse text embedded within Haribhadra's *Sphuṭārthā*, was translated into Tibetan in the late eighth century C.E. by Vidyākaraprabhava and dPal brtsegs. It was then retranslated, both as embedded within the *Sphuṭārthā* and as a separate text, by Go mi 'chi med and bLo ldan shes rab in the eleventh century, according to the colophons of the Tibetan translations of the *Sphuṭārthā* (Pk 5191, fol. 300-4, lines 5–6), and the *Abhisamayālaṃkāra* (Pk 5184, fol. 8-3, line 3). The *Abhisamayālaṃkāra* was also translated into Tibetan (as embedded in Haribhadra's *Āloka*) by Subhaṣita, Rin chen bzang po, Atiśa, Dirapāla, and bLo ldan shes rab in the eleventh century (Pk 5189, fol. 234-4, lines 4–7).

9. The five basic areas of monastic study are *tshad ma*, Buddhist epistemology and logic (based upon the treatises of Dharmakīrti and Dignāga); *dbu ma*, Mādhyamika thought (based mainly upon the treatises of Nāgārjuna and Candrakīrti); *phar phyin*, the practices and realizations implicitly taught in the *Prajñāpāramitā* sūtras (based on Haribhadra's commentaries on the *Abhisamayālaṃkāra*); *mdzod*, Abhidharma (based mainly on Vasubandhu's *Abhidharmakośa*); and *'dul ba*, Vinaya (based on Gunaprabha's Vinaya commentary). The *Abhisamayālaṃkāra*, its commentaries, and the monastic manuals on them *(yig chas)* are the focus of the third area of study above.

10. All these Indian scholars and their commentaries will be discussed in chapters 9–11 below.

11. E.g., Conze, *Prajñāpāramitā Literature*, p. 103; Dutt, *Mahāyāna Buddhism*, p. 155; La Vallée Poussin, *Siddhi*, pp. 790–91; Obermiller, *Analysis of the Abhisamayālamkāra*, pp. 11–12.

12. Sakuma, "The Classification of the Dharmakāya Chapter of the *Abhisamālaṃkāra*," pp. 259–60. Pages 295–97 provide a bibliography of recent Japanese contributions to study of the *Abhisamayālamkāra*.

13. In this context, by "theological" questions I do not mean questions concerning the Jewish or Christian God, which has not been a central concern of Buddhist thinkers. Rather, I mean questions concerning ultimate reality, which transcends ordinary experience, and its embodiment in a Buddha's knowledge, compassion, and salvific activity for beings, which transcends our comprehension. For those interested in comparative theology, however, study of Buddhist understandings of *dharmakāya* could instigate rewarding new lines of inquiry into the nature of God; and I believe the reverse to be equally rewarding.

14. "New," at least, within our record of extant commentaries. As I mention below, the philosophical concerns Haribhadra expressed through his comments on *AA* 8 probably developed over the centuries between Ārya Vimuktisena and himself.

15. *Udāna* 80, quoted from Beyer, *The Buddhist Experience: Sources and Interpretations*.

16. The same fundamental doctrinal tension instantiates in other ways in many other specific, often seemingly unrelated, disagreements over Buddhahood in the history of Indian and Tibetan Mahāyāna thought. This is explored in chapter 13.

17. Nonabiding nirvāṇa is discussed in chapters 5 and 13.

18. In terms of developed Mahāyāna gnoseology, a Buddha has attained uninterrupted cognitive oneness with the unconditioned (the *dharmadhātu*), yet, simultaneously, is both cognizant of and pervasively active within the conditioned world on behalf of all beings.

19. Several such intuitions in relation to praxis are discussed in chapter 13, section 2.

20. Yogācāra doctrines informing and informed by the doctrine of nonabiding nirvāṇa are discussed in chapters 4 and 5, together with implications for Yogācāra gnoseology. Ārya Vimuktisena, through his comments on the *Abhisamayālaṃkāra*, reiterated many of these Yogācāra views (chapter 9). Candrakīrti's gnoseology is discussed in chapter 9, in comparison to Ārya Vimuktisena's. Reasons why the terms *dharmakāya* (embodiment of dharma) and *svābhāvikakāya* (embodiment of Buddhahood in its essence) became alternative terms for the Buddhas' own realization is discussed in chapter 4 section 5.

21. "Earlier traditions" refers here to the Yogācāra sources of *AA* 8, Yogācāra treatises based upon them (many of which are extant in the Tibetan canon), and extant *AA* commentaries prior to Haribhadra.

22. This is touched upon near the end of chapter 10.

23. Maitreya had emerged as primary exemplar and expositor of Mahāyāna in North India and Kashmir, and as a center of cult practices. On this, see Williams, *Mahāyāna Buddhism*, 229–30.

Chapter 2. The Buddha's Body of Dharmas *(Dharmakāya)* in Sarvāstivāda Abhidharma

1. La Vallée Poussin, "Documents d'Abhidharma: 2. La Doctrine des Refuges," p. 73.

2. Ibid., p. 75.

3. *Kośabhāṣya* 4.32.

4. Williams, *Mahāyāna Buddhism*, pp. 170–71 comes independently to the same interpretation of Sarvāstivāda understanding of *dharmakāya*.

5. *Kośabhāṣya* 6.67.

6. *Kośabhāṣya* 4.32, 7.28.

7. *Kośabhāṣya* 7.28.

8. La Vallée Poussin, "Documents d'Abhidharma: 2. La Doctrine des Refuges," pp. 75–76.

9. La Vallée Poussin, *L'Abhidharmakośa de Vasubandhu*, p. 297; idem, *Siddhi*, p. 767. On the five undefiled aggregates and their historical development in the Pali Canon and Abhidharmas, see Davidson, "Buddhist Systems, pp. 388–91.

10. Dutt, *Mahāyāna Buddhism*, pp. 148. Nagao, "On the Theory of the Buddha-Body," p. 27. On Harivarman, see Warder, *Indian Buddhism*, pp. 419–20. Candrakīrti lists the same five aggregates (*śīla, samādhi, prajñā, vimukti, vimuktijñānadarśana*) as factors that non-Mādhyamika opponents sometimes identified as the Tathāgata (*Prasannapadā* 22.1).

11. *Kośabhāṣya* 7.35ff.

12. See chapter 6 of the present work for translation of *AA* 8 vv. 2–6 in which the Buddha dharmas are listed. See Lamotte, *La Somme du Grand Vehicule d'Asanga (Mahā-*

yānasaṃgraha), pp. 51*–61*, and *Le Traité,* vol. 3, chaps. 31–42 for an extensive bibliography of Pali, Agama, and Sanskrit sources of the Buddha dharmas discussed here. As noted above, most of the Buddha dharmas that are listed in Mahāyāna texts such as the *Abhisamayālaṃkāra* were drawn from earlier pre-Mahāyāna sources: the Nikāyas, Agamas, and various proto-Abhidharma and Abhidharma traditions. A smaller subset of the dharmas are distinctively Mahāyāna, such as the four *sarvākārapariśuddhi, asaṃmoṣadharmatā,* and the Mahāyāna formulation of the eighteen *āveṇikadharmas* (cf. Lamotte, *Le Traité,* chap. 41). In Mahāyāna traditions, the entire set of Buddha dharmas (Buddha's mental qualities) were identified as *anāsrava* (undefiled), perhaps because all were understood to coexist with Buddha's gnosis of *śūnyatā,* which (according to Mahāyāna gnoseology) never ceases. In various Abhidharma traditions, not all of a Buddha's mental qualities were considered *anāsrava*, and this undoubtedly contributed to disagreements over precisely which qualities were to be identified as the Buddha refuge, *dharmakāya*, etc. See La Vallée Poussin, "Documents d'Abhidharma: 2. La Doctrine des Refuges," pp. 95ff. on the defiled dharmas of a Buddha, which include great compassion *(mahākaruṇā). Kośabhāṣya* 7.33 identifies great compassion as *laukika (sāṃvṛti)jñāna*, mundane knowledge, and *Kośabhāṣya* 7.2 identifies all *laukikajñāna* as defiled *(sāsrava).*

13. *Kośabhāṣya.* 7.34.

14. On nirvāṇa as conceived by the various Abhidharma schools including Sarvāstivāda, see Lamotte, *History of Indian Buddhism*, pp. 40–42, 609–11, and references; La Vallée Poussin, *Nirvāṇa*, pp. 148ff. on nirvāṇa as *amṛta* (immortal) and *asaṃskṛta* (unconditioned), pp. 168ff. on nirvāṇa with and without residual conditioning. Lamotte and La Vallée Poussin provide numerous references in the primary sources that need not be repeated here.

Chapter 3. The Buddhas' Embodiment of Dharma(tā) *(Dharmakāya)* in *Prajñāpāramitā* Sutras

1. For the list of *sarvadharmāḥ*, see, for example, Conze, *Mahāprajñāpāramitā Sūtra*, fol. P 165–69, sec. 1.5; Conze *Large Sutra*, pp. 120–23.

2. *Abhidharmakośa* 6.4.

3. Refer to the quotations from the *Jñānaprasthāna*, *Mahāvibhāṣā*, and *Kośabhāṣya* in the previous chapter.

4. E.g., Conze, *The Gilgit Manuscript of the Aṣṭādaśasāhasrikā-prajñāpāramitā* (the *PP* sūtra in 18,000 verses), fol. 276b, p. 35; Conze, *Mahāprajñāpāramitā* (the revised *PP* sūtra in 25,000 verses), fol. P 524: "Thus the bodhisattva *mahāsattva*, engaging in the perfection of wisdom *(prajñāpāramitā),* having stood in the two emptinesses: the boundless emptiness and the emptiness without beginning or end, teaches the dharma for living beings. [He tells them:] Everything in the three realms is empty. Here there is no form, feeling, recognition, mental formations, or consciousness. There are no aggregates, no elements, no sense fields. . . . Rather, all these dharmas are unreal. Their own-being is nonbeing. . . ."

5. Sometimes the word "essence" in Western literature connotes an ontological ultimate or absolute principle. The term is not used here with this sense. Throughout this book, the term "essence" refers simply to the defining principle(s) of a thing. The essence of a Buddha, in this sense, is what makes a Buddha a Buddha, or that without which he or she

would not be a Buddha. Because the *PP* sūtras deny independent or self-existence *(svabhāva)* to everything (including Buddhahood), its terms for the defining principle of a Buddha (including *dharmakāya, tathāgatakāya, dharmāṇāṃ tathatā*) do not refer to a self-existent thing. Rather they point to the emptiness of self-existence of things nondually known.

6. *Aṣṭasāhasrikā PP* as edited in Wogihara, *AA Āloka*, pp. 267–68. Conze's translation is in Conze, *The Perfection of Wisdom in Eight Thousand Lines*, p. 116. Compare to similar statements in the chapter 22 of the *Samādhirājasūtra*, ed. Regamey, pp. 49–59. I have taken cues from several portions of Paul Harrison's rendering of this passage ("Phantom Body" p. 56), for which I am grateful, while disagreeing with his understanding of *dharmakāya* in the passage.

On alternative interpretations of *prabhāvita*, see Harrison, "Phantom Body," p. 81 n. 50. For this passage, I choose the sense of being produced, manifested, or brought about, which would follow from the point of the previous sentence, which exhorts the monks toward their own realization of *dharmakāya* in order to see what a Buddha actually is. This would also be consistent with the following passages in the *PP* text, which repeatedly extol *prajñāpāramitā* for being what brings about a Buddha's cognition of things.

7. Harrison, "Phantom Body," pp. 52–53 for examples of similar expressions in pre-Mahāyāna sūtras.

8. See the continuation of the passage above in Conze, *Perfection of Wisdom in Eight Thousand Lines,* p. 117, where a broad causal relation between *prajñāpāramitā* and full enlightenment is elaborated: "Sakra: I would still choose just this perfection of wisdom [over relics], for the same reasons. For the relics of the Tathagata are true deposits of the cognition of all-knowing, but that cognition itself has come forth from the perfection of wisdom." For many references to causal and identity relations between *prajñāpāramitā* and enlightenment, see, for example, "All-knowledge", "Enlightenment," "Tathāgata," and "Dharmabody" listed in Conze's index to his *Perfection of Wisdom in Eight Thousand Lines*. The opening dialogue of the 25,000-verse *PP* sūtra (Conze, *Large Sutra*, pp. 45ff.) is between the Buddha and Śāriputra. The Buddha declares that the way to attain full enlightenment *(sarvākārajñatā)* is to train in *prajñāpāramitā* (perfection of wisdom), to which Śāriputra responds by asking how to so train. The teaching of the entire sūtra is occasioned by this interchange, which is also the likely beginning of the *PP* text basis for the *Abhisamayālaṃkāra*.

9. Another possibility within the wordplay: Tathāgata could conceivably be etymologized as "gone to thusness" or "come to thusness" *(tathatā-gata*, or *tathatā-āgata)*. But thusness *(tathatā)* is just the real nature of things *(dharmatā)*. Then Buddhahood can not involve the coming from or going to anything different from what is already the case. This kind of *PP* theme provides one doctrinal strand later woven into the tapestry of the Mahāyāna doctrine of Buddha-nature, *tathāgatagarbha*.

10. *Ashta,* in *AA Āloka*, ed. Wogihara, pp. 963–66. Cf. Conze, *Perfection of Wisdom in Eight Thousand Lines*, pp. 291–92.

11. On identification of the Buddha with thusness, see also *Ashta* 307 and Conze, *Perfection of Wisdom in Eight Thousand Lines*, pp. 193-94.

12. For my translation of the two *Ashta* passages quoted above and the *Vajracheddika* passage below, I am indebted to Paul Harrison for pointing out where the term *dharmakāya* is employed as a *bahuvrihi* adjective rather than a noun: "the Buddhas are those whose

body is dharma *(dharmakāyāḥ),*" or "the Buddhas have dharma as body." In line with the passage just quoted, I would add that the adjectival form of *dharmakāya* can also be interpreted as "having *dharmatā* as body," and where it appears as a substantive, may be interpreted as a *tatpuruṣa* (body of *dharmatā*, embodiment of *dharmatā*, embodiment in *dharmatā*) or as a *karmadhāraya* (embodiment as *dharmatā*), contra Harrison, "Phantom Body," p. 56 and note 48.

Harrison's article, however, pays little attention to the actual context of *dharmakāya* in the *PP* passages above and the surrounding passages. For example, his article misses all the following characteristics of the passage quoted above: (1) the punning wordplay that relates "Tathāgata" to *tathatā* in early paragraphs; (2) the identification of the Tathāgata with the real nature of dharmas *(dharmāṇāṃ-tathatā = dharmatā), not* with dharmas per se; (3) strong criticism of those who have not recognized the dreamlike nature of all dharmas and adhere to them as the real identity of the Tathāgata and imagine the Tathāgata to come and go as dharmas do; and (4) the wordplay in the later paragraphs that derives *dharmakāya* through the term *dharmatā* (*singular*, the real, undivided nature of dharmas known to the Tathāgata), not through the term *dharmāḥ* (*plural*, the miragelike phenomena to which foolish people cling).

It is worth noting here that Ārya Vimuktisena, consistent with this *PP* passage, identified *dharma[tā]kāya* as the proper etymology and principle meaning of *dharmakāya* in his commentary upon the *Large PP Sūtra* and *Abhisamayālaṃkāra* (see chapter 9).

Having missed all that, it doesn't occur to Harrison that by adopting the term *dharmakāya* from pre-Mahāyāna sources, the *PP* sūtra did not merely reiterate the prior meaning of *dharmakāya* from those sources ("collection of dharmas"), but reinterpreted it in line with the *PP*'s own central messages (*dharmakāya* = embodiment of *dharmatā* in perfect wisdom). As a result, his article mistakenly concludes that the first term in the nominal compound *dharmakāya* throughout the 8,000-verse *PP* sūtra is to be translated in the plural as dharmas (p. 58), rather than in the singular as indicating the real nature of dharmas. This would require us to understand the passages above to be identifying *dharmakāya*, the defining principle of a Buddha, as a collection of dreamlike dharmas that come and go, rather than as the real nature of those dharmas *(dharmatā),* which is free from coming or going! In his conclusion, Harrison even recommends that scholars of Mahāyāna texts henceforth generically translate the compound *dharmakāya* in line with that understanding—to mean body, collection of dharmas ("Phantom Body," pp. 74–75). His claim is based not on rigorous reading of the *PP* passages in their own context, but upon pre-Mahāyāna sources and extremely ambiguous usage of the term *fa-shen* in early Chinese translations (a term for *dharmakāya* that does not specify *dharma* as plural).

Harrison's thesis appears to be this: either the term *dharmakāya* in Mahāyāna passages such as those quoted above is to be uniformly interpreted in line with pre-Mahāyāna and Abhidharma understanding as "collection of qualities, etc.," or it will be wrongly interpreted as some kind of hypostatized "theistic principle," or "phantom body." This is a false dichotomy. It rules out a priori the very possibility that the meaning of *dharma* in the compound *dharmakāya* could have evolved, so that *dharmakāya* in the passages above refers *neither* to a collection of qualities ("dharmas," plural), *nor* to any hypostatized "phantom body," but to the emptiness of all phenomena nondually realized (*dharmatā*, singular). It forces him, therefore, to go to great lengths to ignore the meaning and the centrality of *prajñāpāramitā* itself in the *Prajñāpāramitā* sūtras.

Harrison's article was trying to make another point, however, which deserves serious attention, i.e., that we run the risk of subtly obfuscating the way *dharmakāya*, in texts like these, points to reality as empty, utterly insubstantial, when we translate the term as "Dharma body" or even as "Body of Dharma," as if it referred to some kind of hypostatized Cosmic Body or theistic absolute. I am therefore indebted to Harrison for convincing me that for many of the Mahāyāna texts I study, a better translation is "embodiment of dharma," (or "embodiment as dharma," or "in dharma," semantically subsuming *kāya* under *dharma,* not vice versa), though I would add that a central connotation of *dharma* in such texts is the real nature of things (*dharmatā*, their emptiness) known in ultimate awareness.

13. Conze, *Vajracchedikā-prajñāpāramitā-sūtra*, pp. 56–57, vv. 26a–b: "ye māṃ rūpeṇa ca-adrākṣur / ye māṃ ghoṣeṇa ca-anvayūḥ / mithyā prahāṇa prasṛtā / na māṃ drakṣyanti te janāḥ / dharmato buddhā drastavyā / dharmakāyā hi nāyakāḥ / dharmatā ca na vijñeyā / na sā śakyā vijānituṃ." Compare Schopen, "Manuscript of the *Vajracchedikā*," p. 105 (fols. 10b.6–11a1).

14. *Pañcaviṃśatisāhasrikā*, in Conze, *Mahāprajñāpāramitā*, fol. P78; cf. Conze, *Large Sutra*, p. 77.

15. *Pañcaviṃśatisāhasrikā*, in Conze, *Mahāprajñāpāramitā*, P 505b, cf. Conze, *Large Sutra*, pp. 551–52. This comprises a *Prajñāpāramitā* version of *buddhānusmṛti*, mindful recollection of the Buddha(s). Cf. Conze, *Large Sutra,* p. 556: "[H]e fully knows enlightenment without having apprehended the Buddha-dharmas." On expressions of *buddhānusmṛti* in several other Mahāyāna sūtras and their relation to Mahāyāna formulations of Buddhahood, see chapter 13 of the present book, section 2(c).

16. Translation by Conze, *Selected Sayings,* p. 117, #123, quoting from the *Saptaśatikā-prajñāpāramitā.*

17. *Pañcavimśati*, Conze, *Mahāprajñāpāramitā*, fol. P 484b–485b. Cf. *Large Sutra*, pp. 530–31.

18. Translation by Conze, *Selected Sayings,* p. 116, #122, quoting from the *Saptaśatikā-prajñāpāramitā.*

19. *Pañcavimsati*, in Conze, *Mahāprajñāpāramitā*, P 485a–486b. Cf. Conze, *Large Sutra*, p. 531. Along similar lines, see *Mahāprajñāpāramitā,* P 233, P 245b, P 505b, P 522; Conze, *Large Sutra*, pp. 231–32, 254, 552, 571–76.

20. My bases for discussion of the defining principle of Buddhahood are descriptions of it found in versions of the 8,000-, 18,000-, and 25,000-verse *PP* sūtras available in Sanskrit and Tibetan, and closely related descriptions in the *Vajracchedikā PP* and the *Saptaśatikā PP* (some of which are translated above).

The *Abhisamayālaṃkāra* was probably composed sometime between the fourth and the early sixth centuries C.E., and the primary *PP* text basis for it was the *PP* sūtra in 25,000 verses *(Pancavimśati)*. Hence, the *Abhisamayālaṃkāra*'s notions of what defines Buddhahood are connected to the latter text, and to those strata of the 8,000-verse *PP* sūtra and *Vajracheddikāsutra* that would have been available to the *Abhisamayālaṃkāra*'s author in his time.

According to Professor Lewis Lancaster's studies of the development of the 8,000-verse *PP* sūtras in Chinese translations, the accounts of *dharmakāya* I have quoted belong to the middle to later stages of the 8,000-verse *PP* sūtra, whose earliest Chinese translations were made in the early fifth and mid-seventh centuries (Rawlinson, "The Position of the *Aṣṭasāhasrikā Prajñāpāramitā* in the Development of early Mahāyāna," pp. 16, 30). The

Vajracchedikā PP was translated into Chinese at the beginning of the fifth century (Conze, *PP Literature*, p. 60). Obviously, these sūtras had a long period of development prior to their translation in China. A very similar account of *dharmakāya* versus *rūpakāya* is found in the *Samādhirājasūtra*, whose terminus ad quem has been put in the fourth century (Regamey, *Three Chapters from Samādhirājasūtra*, pp. 11–12). But see Schopen, "Notes on the Cult of the Book," pp. 153ff. and "Sukhāvatī," p. 204, where he notes that available evidence has pushed back estimations of the dates of the 8,000-verse *PP*, *Vajracchedikā PP*, and *Samādhirājasūtra*, dating the latter two to perhaps the second century C.E.

It appears to me, as to most contemporary scholars, that expressions of Buddha *kāyas* found in most *PP* sūtras precede the Yogācāra theory of three *kāyas*. The distinct three-*kāya* terminology of Yogācāra appears in the *Abhisamayālaṃkāra*. This provides a further indication that the *PP* conceptions of *dharmakāya* discussed in this chapter developed prior to the composition of the *Abhisamayālaṃkāra* (ca. the fourth century to the early sixth century), although expressions of them continued to be added to the *PP* sūtras in following centuries.

One point should be made parenthetically. Lancaster identified one mention of the word *dharmakāya* in a passage of the 8000-verse *PP* that seems to have the meaning "collection of dharma texts" rather than "ultimate defining principle of Buddhahood." The passage in question is likely part of the earliest stage of development of the 8000-verse *PP* text (Lancaster, "The Oldest Mahāyāna Sūtra," p. 36; cf. Harrison, "Phantom Body," p. 57). What I have focused on here are meanings of the word *dharmakāya* in the middle and later texts that became important to the Yogācāras and to the author of the *AA*, who drew both upon the Yogācāra and *PP* textual traditions of his time.

21. See, for example, Conze's *Large Sutra on Perfect Wisdom*, pp. 35–44, 175, 231, and 254, for various manifestations of the Buddha's physical form, designated as *rūpakāya* or *ātmabhāva*.

Chapter 4. Embodiment of Buddhahood in its Own Realization: Yogācāra *Svābhāvikakāya* as Projection of Praxis and Gnoseology

1. *Abhisamayālaṃkāra* v. 1.17, ed. Amano, 1975, p. 16. *AA* vv. 8.1, 8.6, 8.12, 8.33, 8.34, 9.2, ed. Amano, 1975, pp. 262, 264, 276, 290, 292. See chapter 6 of the present work for translation of all relevant sections of *AA* 8.

2. The *Abhisamayālaṃkāra* uses only the term *dharmakāya*. Haribhadra interprets its use in *AA* 8.6 to mean *jñānātmaka dharmakāya* (the *dharmakāya* consisting of gnosis). Later, Tibetan commentators rendered this *yeshe chos sku*, which in Sanskrit would be *jñāna-dharmakāya* (gnosis *dharmakāya*.) Here I enclose *jñānātmaka* in parentheses when it stands before *dharmakāya* to indicate that the term *jñānātmaka dharmakāya* does not appear in the *AA* itself but is of Haribhadra's making. *Sphuṭārthā*, ed. Amano, 1975, pp. 268, 274, 292; *Āloka*, ed. Wogihara, pp. 914, 915 line 21, 916 lines 18 and 22, 925.

3. *Abhisamayālaṃkāra-Sphuṭārthā*, ed. Amano, 1975, pp. 262, 290.

4. Ibid., p. 292.

5. One particular version of the *Large PP Sūtra*, which I refer to (following Conze) as the "revised *Pañcaviṃśatisāhasrikā Prajñāpāramitā*" (revised 25,000-verse *PP* sūtra),

mentions in one passage the names of the three *kāyas* found in the Yogācāra śāstras. However, much evidence will be presented later to show that this particular passage (and probably that whole version of the sūtra) was composed well after the composition of the *Abhisamayālaṃkāra*. No other version of any *PP* sūtra, to my knowledge, mentions the names of the three *kāyas*; though the *PP* sūtras do, of course, mention *dharmakāya* and *rūpakāya*.

6. Conze, *Prajñāpāramitā Literature,* pp. 102–4.

7. Obermiller, *Analysis of the Abhisamayālaṃkāra*, pp. 11–12; La Vallée Poussin, *Siddhi*, pp. 790–91; Dutt, *Mahāyāna Buddhism*, p. 155; Conze, *Prajñāpāramitā Literature*; p. 103.

8. Sūtras and collections of sūtras such as the *Prajñāpāramitā*, *Avataṃsaka*, *Akṣayamati*, *Sukhāvatīvyūha*, *Vimalakīrtinirdeśa*, and many others. In them, exalted Tathāgatas are described presiding over glorious realms of activity or pure realms: e.g. Śākyamuni and Akṣobhya of the *PP* sūtras, Vairocana of the *Avataṃsaka*, and Amitābha of the *Sukhāvatīvyūha*. And descriptions are given of Buddhas and bodhisattvas manifesting limitless arrays of forms to teach limitless beings in the ways appropriate to them.

9. Dutt, *Mahāyāna Buddhism*, pp. 136–70; Demieville, "Busshin"; La Vallée Poussin, *La Siddhi*, pp. 762–813.

10. This summarizes part of the description of these two *kāyas* found in Sthiramati's and Asvabhāva's commentaries on *MSA* 9.61 and in Vasubandhu's and Asvabhāva's commentaries on the *Msg* 10.30.

11. Four of these verses, 9.56–59, also appear at the end of the *Buddhabhūmisūtra,* ed. Nishio, pp. 72–73. I strongly suspect the *MSA* verse śāstra was composed prior to the *Buddhabhūmisūtra*. See John Keenan, "A Study of the *Buddhabhūmyupadeśa,*" pp. 336–54 for some good arguments for the *MSA*'s priority to the *Buddhabhūmisūtra*. He has since adopted the opposite view of the relative chronology of these texts, but I do not think he did so for good reasons ("Pure Land Systematics in India"; see also Paul Griffiths, "Buddha and God," p. 5 nn. 16 and 18). The *MSA* verse text often gives the appearance of a work in which seminal Yogācāra ideas, especially those concerning Buddhahood, are presented in a relatively brief and undeveloped form, while the *Buddhabhūmisūtra* (like Sthiramati's *MSA* commentary) gives a much more extensive and developed articulation of Buddhahood vis-à-vis *dharmadhātuviśuddhi* (purified realm of dharma) and the four *jñānas* (four aspects of a Buddha's gnosis). The four verses in question concern *dharmadhātuviśuddhi*, and it may be that they were composed prior to both texts, or, as I think more likely, that the *Buddhabhūmisūtra*, a prose text, borrowed them from the *MSA*, a verse text, as a verse basis for its prose discussion of *dharmadhātuviśuddhi.*

12. One verse apparently naming the three *kāyas* as functional modes of *dharmadhātuviśuddhi* appears in both the *MSA* (9.59) and in the *Buddhabhūmisūtra*, ed. Nishio, p. 23, but whereas the *MSA* further explains it in some detail in *MSA* 9.60–66 and its *bhāṣya*, the *Buddhabhūmisūtra* does not.

13. For example, the *Buddhabhūmivyākhyāna*'s explanation of the three *kāyas*, ed. Nishio, pp. 125–26, appears to draw heavily from the explanations found in the *MSA bhāṣya* (on *MSA* 9.60–66) and *Msg* chapter 10 (in Lamotte's edition, especially sections 10.1–10.3). The *Buddhabhumivyākhyāna* was written by Śīlabhadra, whose dates are thought to be 529–645 C.E. (ed. Nakamura, p. 281). The *MSA* is dated from approximately the third century to the fourth century C.E. (see below). The other texts listed here are probably all

later than the *MSA*. The *Ratnagotravibhāga (RGV)* is dated from approximately the fourth century to the fifth century C.E. (ed. Nakamura, p. 261) and quotes three times from the *MSA*'s ninth chapter on *bodhi* (Takasaki, *A Study*, p. 41). The *Kāyatrayastotra* is listed in the Tibetan Tripitaka as a work of Nāgārjuna (Pk 2015), but Taranātha identifies the author as Nāgāhvaya, whose date is not known but who is identified with the Vijñapti-Madhyamaka school (Ruegg, *Literature of the Madhyamaka School*, p. 56). I assume this text postdates the *MSA*, because the theory of three *kāyas* is so closely related to other Yogācāra models worked out in the *MSA* and later in the *Msg* (this will be discussed at length in this and the following chapter), while the *Kāyatrayastotra* appears to adopt the Yogācāra *kāya* model to a Madhyamaka mode of expression (Cf. Lindtner, *Nagarjuniana*, p. 16 n. 35 for a bibliography of modern editions of this text and further arguments that it is not by Nāgārjuna). The *Kāyatrayāvataramukhaśāstra* (Pk 5290) is listed in the Tibetan Tripitaka as a work by Nāgamitra, and its commentary, the *Kāyatrayavṛtti*, is ascribed to Jñānacandra, who is listed in the *Vijñaptimātratāsiddhi* as a (Yogācārin) disciple of Dharmapāla (sixth century). Both this śāstra and its *vṛtti* analyze the three *kāyas* in a much more highly developed form than the presentation found in the *MSA*. The *Abhisamayālaṃkāra* was probably composed sometime between the fourth century and the early sixth century C.E. (see chapter 6 below).

14. *MAVbhāṣya* 4.14. *DDV*, ed. sDe dge phi, fol. 47b4, 51b6. *RGV*, chapter 2, presents a three-*kāya* theory at some length. Because its focus is so squarely on the theory of *tathāgatagarbha*, it stands apart somewhat from the other texts mentioned here. However, it relates its basic model of enlightenment, *nirmala tathatā,* to the theory of three *kāyas* in much the same way that the *MSA*, *Msg*, and their commentaries relate *dharmadhātuviśuddhi* and *tathatāviśuddhi/nirvikalpajñāna* to the *kāyas*. It quotes from *MSA* 9, and in one portion of its second chapter it is clearly applying the *MSA*'s buddhology to its theory of *tathāgatagarbha*. See *RGV*, ed. Johnston pp. 85–88, Takasaki, *A Study,* p. 41.

15. A bibliography of speculations on the history of early Yogācāra can be found in Nakamura, *Indian Buddhism*, p. 263. Summaries are found in Ruegg, *La Theorie*, pp. 30–55; Davidson, "Buddhist Systems of Transformation," pp. 14–49, 126–49. Davidson reexamines the questions of authorship of all early Yogacara śāstras, and concludes that the authorship of the *MAV*, *DDV*, and *AA* is still unknown. I agree.

16. *AA-Āloka*, ed. Wogihara, pp. 914–25; *AA-Sphuṭārthā*, ed. Amano, 1975, pp. 262–92.

17. *MSA* 9.4 concerns Buddhahood's nondual character. *MSA* 9.5 concerns its power. Here *MSA* 9.4 and its *bhāṣya* are translated.

18. Levi, *MSA* and *bhāṣya*, 9.4: "sarvadharmāśca buddhatvaṃ dharmo naiva ca kaścana / śukladharmamayaṃ tattca na ca taistannirupyate / . . . sarvadharmāśca buddhatvaṃ tathatāyā abhinnatvāttadviśuddhiprabāvitatvāttca buddhatvasya na ca kaściddharmo 'sti parikalpitena dharmasvabhāvena śukladharmamayaṃ ca buddhatvaṃ pāramitādīnāṃ kuśalānāṃ tadbhāvena parivṛtteḥ / na ca taistannirdiśyate pāramitādīnāṃ pāramitādibhavenāparinispatteridamadvayalakṣanam." Thanks to Sara McClintock of Harvard for her helpful criticisms of my initial translation of this section.

19. The Tibetan translation of Sthiramati's commentary uses the word *sangs rgyas* (Buddha) where the Sanskrit and Tibetan translations of the *MSA* and *bhāṣya* use, respectively, *buddhatvam* and *sangs rgyas nyid* (Buddhahood).

20. The Tibetan translation of this quote differs significantly from the available Sanskrit texts. The *Vṛttibhāṣya*, quoting the *Vajracchedikā* as translated above, reads: "gang

zhig nga la gzugs su blta [lta in Peking ed.] / gang zhig nga la dgra [sgra in Peking ed.] ru rtogs / log par zhugs pa song bas te / skye bo de ni nga mi mthong // de bzhin nyid du sangs rgyas blta / 'dren pa rnams ni chos kyi sku / chos nyid shes par mi rung ste / de dag rnam par rig mi 'gyur" (sDe-dge mi, fol. 108a4–5). Conze's edition of the Sanskrit text reads: "ye māṃ rūpeṇa ca-adrākṣur / ye māṃ ghoṣeṇa ca-anvayuḥ / mithyā-prahāṇa-prasṛtā / na māṃ drakṣyanti te janāḥ // dharmato buddhā draṣṭavyā / dharmakāya hi nāyakāḥ / dharmatā ca na vijñeyā / na sā śakyā vijānituṃ" (Conze, *Vajracchedikā Prajñāpāramitā*, pp. 56–57). I translated Conze's Sanskrit text in the *Vajracchedikā* quote of the previous chapter. The Tibetan *Vṛttibhāṣya*'s quote is corrupt (e.g., the misspelling of *sgra* in the sDe-dge edition, and different spellings of *lta* in the sDe-dge and Peking editions), but it also differs in substance sufficiently from the available Sanskrit to indicate that Sthiramati may have been quoting from a different edition of the *Vajracchedikā*.

21. *Vṛttibhāṣya*, sDe-dge mi, fols. 107b6–108b4.

22. Compare *MAV* 1.1 and its *bhāṣya* (Nagao, *Madhyāntavibhāga-bhāṣya*, pp. 17–18):

> abūta parikalpo 'sti dvayan tatra na vidyate / śūnyatā vidyate tv atra tasyām api sa vidyate. *bhāṣya:* . . . evaṃ yad yatra nāsti tat tena śūnyam iti yathābhūtaṃ samanupaśyati yat punar atrāvaśiṣṭaṃ bhavati tat sad ihāstīti yathābhūtaṃ prajānātīty aviparītaṃ śūnyatā lakṣaṇam udbhāvitam bhavati.
>
> [The imagination of the unreal exists; duality is not found there. / But emptiness is found there; and in that {emptiness} also is that {imagination} found. *bhāṣya:* One correctly observes that that in which a thing does not exist is empty of that thing {i.e., imagination of the unreal is empty of real duality}. {And} one knows further that that which remains exists here truly {i.e., emptiness of duality exists truly}. Thus is the identity of emptiness made known unmistakenly.]

23. If all Sthiramati intends to say here is that all phenomena are Buddhahood because all phenomena are empty and Buddhahood is empty, then for him, *MSA* 9.4's first line could have said, "All phenomena are house," or "All phenomena are dog" with the same sense. Such a trivial interpretation of Sthiramati would have him read "all phenomena are *x*" to mean all phenomena have a nature of selflessness and so does *x,* where *x* stands for any phenomenon. Clearly Sthiramati wants to say more than this with reference to the *dharmakaya*.

24. This title in the Sanskrit *MSA bhāṣya* edited by S. Levi reads (p. 48): "Buddhatvopāyapraveśe" ([Concerning] entry into the method of Buddhahood). But the Tibetan translation of this differs slightly: "sangs rgyas nyid la 'jug pa'i thabs," "([Concerning] the method of entry into Buddhahood) (*MSA bhasya*, sDe-dge phi, fol. 161a6–7). The *Vṛttibhāṣya* agrees better with the Tibetan translation. It reads: "sangs rgyas su 'gyur ba'i thabs," [Concerning] the method of becoming Buddha" (sDe-dge mi, fol. 144a2). Asvabhāva's *MSA ṭikā* also agrees with the Tibetan translation, reading: "sangs rgyas nyid de la ji ltar 'jug pa de'i thabs kyi dbang du byas nas" (Concerning the method of how to enter into Buddhahood) (sDe-dge bi, fol. 75a6). The content of the four verses and their commentaries concern meditation on nonperception as a principal method by which bodhisattvas traverse the stages to Buddhahood and then attain it. It would appear, then, that the *MSA bhāṣya* manuscript

that was translated into Tibetan read: *buddhatvapraveśopāye.* The Sanskrit manuscript edited by Levi, having reversed the words *upāya* and *praveśa,* would appear to be mistaken.

25. *MSA* 78–79 and *bhāṣya,* ed. Levi: "buddhatvopāyapraveśe catvāraḥ ślokāḥ / yā 'vidyamānatā saiva paramā vidyamānatā / sarvathā 'nupalambhaśca upalambhaḥ paro mataḥ // yā parikalpitena svabhāvenāvidyamānatā saiva paramā vidyamānatā parinispannena svabhāvena / yaśca sarvathā 'anupalambhaḥ parikalpitasya svabhāvasya sa eva parama upalambhaḥ parinispannasvabhāvasya / bhāvanā paramā ceṣṭā bhāvanāmavipaśyatāṃ / pratilambhaḥ paraśceṣṭaḥ pratilambhaṃ na paśyatāṃ /saiva paramā bhāvanā yo bhāvanāyā anupalambhaḥ /sa eva paramaḥ pratilambho yaḥ pratilambhānupalambhaḥ."

26. *Vṛttibhāṣya*, sDe-dge mi, fol. 144a3-6.

27. *Vṛttibhāṣya*, sDe-dge mi, fol. 144a6-b1: "sgom pa dag ni mi mthong ste / sgom pa yi ni mchog tu 'dod / zhes bya ba la / sa gnyis nas sa bcu man chad kyi tshe gzung ba dang 'dzin pa dang nga dang bdag gir rtog pa spangs te / sgom par byed pa dang sgom par byed pa gnyis mi mthong bar sgom pa [gnyis]* sgom pa'i mchog tu 'dod de / ci'i phyir zhe na / dmigs su med pa'i mtshan nyid bsgom pa'i phyir // rnyed pa dag ni ma mthong na / rnyed pa yang ni mchog tu 'dod / ces bya ba la / sangs rgyas kyi sa'i dus na rdzogs longs spyod pa'i sku dang / sprul pa'i sku dang / stobs dang mi 'jigs pa la sogs pa'i chos rnyed par ma mthong ba nyid rnyed pa'i mchog ces bya ste / ci'i phyir zhes na / chos kun gyi mchog chos kyi sku rnyed pa'i mchog go." I read the starred word *gnyis* as a *nyid.* This accords with the exactly parallel constructions at mi 144a4 ("kun brtags pa dang por med par gyur pa de *nyid* yod pa'i mchog ces gdags te"), mi 144a5 ("mi dmigs te ma mthong ba *nyid* dmigs pa'i mchog ces bya"), and mi 144b1 ("chos rnyed par ma mthong ba *nyid* rnyed pa'i mchog ces bya ste"), and such scribal errors as *gnyis* for *nyid* are extremely common in Tibetan translations.

28. See, for example, *Msg* 10.3.1 with Asvabhāva's comments (Lamotte's numbering system); Asvabhāva's comments on *Msg* 9.1 (*Upanibandhana*, sDe-dge ri, fols. 273b3–274a3), and *Msg* 10.27 (*Upanibandhana*, sDe-dge ri, fols. 286a6–7); Sthiramati's *Triṃśikāvijñaptibhāṣyaṃ* (ed. Levi, commentary on vv. 28–30, pp. 43–44); Vasubandhu's *Trisvabhāvakārikā* vv. 36–38; Jñānacandra's *Kāyatrayavṛtti* (Pk 5291, Vol.101, fols. 122-4-6 to 122-5-1); *Buddhabhūmivyākhyāna* (ed. Nishio) pp. 59, 117–18, 122–23. Such passages describe Buddhahood or *dharmakāya* as the final yogic realization of *tathatā* by *nirvikalpajñāna*, the removal of *parikalpita* by *nirvikalpajñāna* to reveal *pariniṣpanna*, the indivisibility of *dharmadhātuviśuddhi* and *nirvikalpajñāna*, etc.

29. This special sixfold analysis of Buddhahood occurs in *MSA* and *bhāṣya* 9.56–59 and 21.60–61, the *Buddhabhūmisūtra* and its *vyākhyāna* by Śilabhadra (ed. Nishio, pp. 22–23 and 119–27), and *Msg* (10.27). The same sixfold analysis is also applied to meanings of terms in general in the *Abhidharmasamuccaya* (Griffiths, "Buddha and God," p. 4). All of these texts are Yogācāra. The application of this analysis to Buddhahood seems to be a distinctive feature of Yogācāra buddhology. The same analysis with the addition of four categories forms one of the primary methods of describing *tathāgatagarbha* in the *Ratnagotravibhāga* (vv. 1.29ff.) With the addition of two categories, the same sixfold scheme is the primary description of Buddhahood *(nirmalā tathatā)* in the same text (vv. 2.2ff.). This is one of the reasons why it appears that the *Ratnagotravibhāga* has close connections to doctrinal developments formative of the Yogācāra school (see Takasaki, *A Study*, pp. 400ff.).

30. *MSA* and *bhāṣya* 21.60–61, ed. Levi: "niṣpannaparamārtho 'si sarvabhūmiviniḥsṛtaḥ

/ sarvasatvāgratāṃ prāptaḥ sarvasatvavimocakaḥ // akṣayairasamairyukto guṇairlokeṣu dṛśyase / maṇḍaleṣvapyadṛśyaśca sarvathā devamānuśaiḥ // atra ṣaḍbhiḥ svabhāvahetuphalakarmayogavṛttyarthairbuddhalakṣaṇam paridīpitam / tatra viśuddhā tathatā niṣpannaḥ paramārthaḥ / sa ca buddhānām svabhāvaḥ / sarvabodhisatvabhūminiryātatvam hetuḥ / sarvasatvāgratām prāptatvam phalam/ sarvasatvavimocakatvam karma / akṣayāsamaguṇayuktatvam yogaḥ / nānālokadhātuṣu dṛśyamānatā nirmāṇakāyena parṣanmaṇḍaleṣvapi dṛśyamānatā sāṃbhogikena kāyena/sarvathā cādṛśyamānatā dharmakāyeneti trividhā prabhedavṛttiriti."

31. The terms *dharmadhātu-viśuddha* (purified dharma realm) and *dharmadhātu-viśuddhi* (purity of the dharma realm) are synonymous and interchangeable in the *MSA bhāṣya* and other commentaries on *Mahāyānasūtrālaṃkāra.*

32. *MSA* and *bhāṣya* 9.59, ed. Levi: "svabhāvadharmasaṃbhoganirmāṇairbhinnavṛttikaḥ / dharmadhāturviśuddho 'yaṃ buddānāṃ samudāhṛtaḥ // eṣa vṛttyarthamārabhya caturthaḥ ślokaḥ / svābhāvikasāṃbhogikanairmāṇikakāyavṛttyā bhinnavṛttikaḥ." Much more will be said about this verse in following section of this chapter.

33. *Msg,* ed. Lamotte, vol. 1, p. 90: "sangs rgyas rnams kyi chos kyi sku ni yon tan 'di dag dang ldan no // gzhan yang ngo bo nyid dang / rgyu dang / 'bras bu [dang] phrin las dang / ldan pa dang/ 'jug pa'i yon tan rnams dang yang ldan te / de lta bas na sangs rgyas rnams kyi yon tan bla na med par rig par bya'o."

34. *Msg upanibandhana,* sDe-dge ri, fols. 286a6–b1: "chos kyi sku ni gzhan yang ngo bo nyid dang zhes bya ba la sogs pa yon tan drug dang ldan no zhes bstan nas tsigs su bcad pa 'di dag gis 'chad do / kyod ni dam pa'i don grub ste / zhes bya ba ni rnam par dag pa'i de bzhin nyid kyis rab tu phye ba'i [Skt., prabhāvita] phyir ngo bo nyid kyis chos kyi sku yongs su grub pa'i phyir ro."

35. Usage of *svābhāvikakāya* and *dharmakāya* as synonyms will be further discussed in section 5 of this chapter.

36. The verses that appear as 9.56–9.59 in the *MSA* also appear at the end of the *Buddhabhūmisūtra,* where they are commented upon by Śīlabhadra in his *vyākhyāna* on that sūtra. We will refer both to the commentaries on the *MSA* and to Śīlabhadra's commentary on the *Buddhabhūmisūtra* in what follows.

37. *Vṛtti* is a primary (*kṛt*) derivative of the verbal root *vṛt,* whose most basic meaning is "to exist." *Vṛtti* has a wide range of meanings, a few of which are: "mode of life or conduct, course of action, behavior; mode of being, nature, kind, character, disposition; state, condition; activity, function" (Monier-Williams, *Sanskrit-English Dictionary,* s.v. "Vṛtti."). Takasaki translates *vṛtti* as "manifestation," the "manifestation" of the three *kāya*s (Takasaki, *A Study,* pp. 229ff., 324ff.). Though such a translation broadly applies to the two form *kāya*s (which manifest to great bodhisattvas and ordinary beings respectively) it does not apply to the *svābhāvikakāya,* which, as noted in the previous section, is "not visible to gods and men." I chose the translation "function" or "mode of function," because in this context *vṛtti* refers to the basic ways in which a Buddha's unobstructed realization of the thusness of all phenomena (*dharmadhātu-viśuddhi, MSA* v. 9.56) functions for himself and for others (v. 9.59).

38. According to the *bhāṣya* to *MSA* 9.60, the word *dharma* in the compound of verse 9.59 *(svabhāva[dharma]saṃbhoganirmānair)* is logically connected to the term *saṃbhoga* (*dharma-saṃbhogam* meaning "shared enjoyment of the dharma").

39. The secondary derivative morphology of a noun often lends an adjectival meaning to the term, broadly denoting a relation or connection to the meaning of the original noun. For example, the secondary derivative of *svabhāva* (essence) is *svābhāvika*, which often carries a range of adjectival meanings: e.g., "pertaining to," "belonging to," "with respect to" the "essence" of something (see Whitney, *Sanskrit Grammar*, secs. 1206, 1222; Monier-Williams, *Sanskrit-English Dictionary*, s.v. "Svābhāvika"). Based on the specific context of the passages under discussion here, I understand *svābhāvikakāya* to mean "embodiment" of the purified dharma realm "with respect to its own essence," or more simply, "in its own essence." The adjectival meanings of the first terms in the compound names *sāmbhogikakāya* and *nairmāṇikakāya* are similarly derived: "embodiment" of the purified dharma realm "with respect to communal enjoyment," and "embodiment" of the purified dharma realm "with respect to its manifestation(s)."

In the earliest treatises extant in Sanskrit that explained the *trikāya* theory in detail—the *MSA*, *Ratnagotravibhaga*, and *AA* (and those of their commentaries extant in Sanskrit)—the three terms under discussion most often appear in this secondary derivative, adjectival form *(svābhāvika, sāmbhogika, nairmāṇika)* not in the primary derivative forms *(svabhāva, sambhoga, nirmāna)*. See *MSA* vv. 60–66 and *bhāṣya; AA* chapter 8 vv. 1, 12, 33 and *AA-Āloka*, ed. Wogihara, pp. 914–24; *RGV-vyākhyāna*, p. 85. Sthiramati preserves the secondary derivative forms in his *Madhyāntavibhāgatīkā* (ed. Yamaguchi, p. 191). The secondary derivative forms are even reflected in the Tibetan translation of the *Buddhabhūmivyākhyāna*, ed. Nishio p. 125. The *Msg* is not extant in Sanskrit, but its exposition of three *kāya*s is based in large part on that of the *MSA*.

40. Cf. *PP* sūtra quotations from chapter 3 on thusness as undifferentiated.

41. This explanation is based on *MSA* 9.59-60 and *bhāṣya*. The *Buddhabhūmisūtra* verse equivalent to *MSA* 9.59 and its *vyākhyāna* give the equivalent explanation (ed. Nishio, pp. 125–26).

42. It has been most common in Western scholarship to translate the three Yogācāra *kāya*s as three "bodies." In past articles, I followed suit, but I now see this as a mistake. Questions raised about my translations by John Dunne at Harvard, and criticisms by Paul Harrison of the very notion of *dharmakāya* as a metaphysical "body" (cf. chapter 3, note 12 above), encouraged me to rethink the message of Yogācāra passages like those quoted here. For this I thank them.

Haribhadra, however, later resurrected Abhidharma understanding of *dharmakāya* as "body" (collection) of dharmas, and to align with that, his use of terms for *rūpakāya*s as well may be best translated as "bodies" ("communal enjoyment body, manifestation body"). Haribhadra returned these terms to a pre-Mahāyāna meaning (though understood now on a conventional level set within the Mādhyamika two-truth ontology). In chapter 10 on Haribhadra, this will be noted, and the reader will notice me alter my translation of *kāya* terms in line with him, or sometimes leave them untranslated.

43. This hearkens back to the *PP* sūtras' opposition of *dharmakāya* to *rūpakāya* that we saw earlier (the *dharmakāya* being what Buddha actually is; the *rūpakāya* being what ordinary people think he is). Typical in Yogācāra literature is the description of the *svābhāvikakāya* as *pratyātma-vedam* ("known only to oneself," to Buddha, not to others) and as *acintya* (beyond conception). Cf. comments on *MSA* 21.61 in section 3 above. See also *Msg* 10.3.5, 10.28.10; *Triṃśikāvijñaptibhāṣyaṃ*, ed. Levi, p. 44; *Buddhabhūmivyākhyāna*, ed. Nishio,

p. 125, *Kāyatrayastotra* v. 1; *Kāyatrayasūtra* Pk 949, vol. 37, fol. 108-3-2; *RGV* 2.42. *MSA* 9.62 describes the *svābhāvikakāya* as "subtle" *(sukṣma)*. Sthiramati explains this to mean that it is not a cognitive object for *śrāvaka*s or *pratyekabuddha*s (*vṛttibhāṣya,* sDe dge mi., fols. 166b5–6).

44. Sanskrit being a flexible language, the grammar does not by itself entirely rule out the possibility of interpreting the line as "the body of the Buddhas is threefold." I do want to suggest that, if the passage is read within its fuller context (delineated in sections 2–4 of this chapter), and with careful attention to each possible nuance of each form of expression, "threefold embodiment" is the simplest, most direct, and most likely interpretation.

45. *MSA* 9.65: "tribhiḥ kāyaistu vijñeyo buddhānaṃ kāyasaṃgrahaḥ / sāśrayaḥ svaparārtho yastribhiḥ kāyairnirdiśitaḥ."

46. *Buddhabhūmivyākhyāna,* ed. Nishio, pp. 125–26.

47. This will be discussed in chapter 8, section 2, of this book.

48. In line with *MSA* verse 9.56 on the "essence" *(svabhāva)* of the purified dharma realm and verses 9.59–9.60 on *svābhāvikakāya* as the functional embodiment of that essence within a Buddha's own awareness.

49. On this, see again the comments on *MSA* verse 9.4 presented in section 2 of this chapter.

50. The reason I use the phrase "communal enjoyment" in translating the terms *sambhoga* or *sāmbhogika* rather than "complete enjoyment" or "enjoyment" (currently common translations) will be explained in chapter 5, section 5, below.

51. Sections 2 and 3 of this chapter. On Buddhahood as a fundamentally indivisible nondual realization of emptiness/thusness, which takes expression in different ways for the different mentalities in which it is in contact, see also, e.g., *MSA* 9.60–62, *bhāṣya* and *vṛttibhāṣya*; *Msg* 7.11, 10.1, 10.3 *bhāṣya* and *upanibandhana*; *Buddhabhūmivyākhyāna* (ed. Nishio), pp. 125–26; *RGVV,* chap. 2 preamble and vv. 2.38-2.61; *Kāyatrayasūtra*; *Kāyatrayāvatāraśāstra*; the three-*kāya* chapter ("sku gsum rnam par 'byed pa") in later editions of the *Suvarṇaprabhāsasūtra.*

52. *MSA* chapter 9 may be the earliest systematic presentation of three *kāya*s in Yogācāra literature. It labels the first of the three *kāya*s: *svābhāvikakāya* (not *dharmakāya*). The next-earliest texts to teach three *kāya*s are probably *Msg* chapter 10 (based on *MSA* 9), *AA* 8, *Ratnagotravibhāga,* chapter 2 (see Davidson, "Buddhist Systems," pp. 132–44 for recent speculations on the chronology of the "Maitreya" corpus), and the *Buddhabhūmisūtra* (the four verses near the end of the sūtra on *dharmadhātu-viśuddhaḥ*). The relative dating of the *MSA* and *Buddhabhūmisūtra* is presently somewhat controversial, but that does not affect the argument here. As in *MSA* 9, the first *kāya* is called in all of these texts *svābhāvikakāya.* The *Dharmadharmatāvibhāga* refers to the first as *dharmakāya*. But this text mentions the three *kāya*s only in passing, and obviously drew the theory from other sources. It is in the commentaries and subcommentaries to these texts, ascribed to Vasubandhu, Asvabhāva, Sthiramati, etc., that the term *dharmakāya* begins regularly replacing the term *svābhāvikakāya* in the list of three *kāya*s. An example of this phenomena was provided toward the end of section 3 of this chapter: Asvabhāva's commentary on *MSG* 10.27. This becomes the norm in later texts such as the *Kāyatrayāvatāraśāstra*, *Kāyatrayasūtra*, *Kāyatrayastotra*, *Madhyamakāvatāra.*

53. *Msg* 9.1 identifies a Buddha's *dharmakāya* with *apratiṣṭhita-nirvāṇa* (nonabiding

nirvāṇa, the enlightenment of a Buddha as that which is neither bound to cyclic existence nor immersed in solitary quiescence), a seminal Mahāyāna concept of full enlightenment that will be discussed in chapter 5 below. *Apratiṣṭhita-nirvāṇa* is described there as the *āśrayaparāvṛtti* (fundamental transformation) of the bodhisattvas, in terms that refer to the entire resultant state of enlightenment (*āśrayaparāvṛtti* as a Mahāyāna model for full enlightenment will be discussed in detail in the following section). *Msg* 10.3 equates *dharmakāya* also with the entire state of enlightenment, by describing it in the same terms: as *āśrayaparāvṛtti*, meaning Buddhahood as a whole. *MSA* 9. 60 *bhāṣya* makes the same characterization. At 9.77 the *bhāṣya* closely relates *dharmakāya* with the *anāsravadhātu*, a *MSA* model of full enlightenment. Sthiramati's *vṛttibhāṣya* on *MSA* 9.60 and 9.66 identifies *dharmakāya* directly with *dharmadhātuviśuddhi*, another Yogācāra model of full enlightenment. The final verse of Vasubandhu's *Triṃśika* equates *dharmakāya* with Buddhahood as a whole: identifying it with *āśrayaparāvṛtti* and *anāsravadhātu* (*Vijñaptimātratāsiddhi*, ed. Levi, p. 43).

54. *Āśraya* = basis, foundation, fundament. *Parāvṛtti* (or its alternate form *parivṛtti*) = transformation. On the etymologies and general semantic equivalence of *āśraya-parāvṛtti* and *āśraya-parivṛtti* in classical Yogācāra texts, see Davidson, "Buddhist Systems," pp. 152–53.

55. *Msg* 9.1 (where the fundamental characteristic of *apratiṣṭhita-nirvāṇa* is *āśrayaparāvṛtti*), 10.1 (where like in *MSA* 9.60 *bhāṣya*, *svābhāvikakāya* is identified as the *dharmakāya*), 10.3.1 (where the first and primary characteristic of *dharmakāya/svābhāvika-kāya* is *āśrayaparāvṛtti*). Lamotte, *La Somme*, pp. 81, 84. *Apratiṣṭhita-nirvāṇa*, nonabiding nirvāṇa, is arguably the central concept of classical and late Indian Mahāyāna Buddhism. It will be discussed in the next chapter.

56. The *Buddhabhūmivyākhāyana* mirrors the explanation of the *MSA* 9.60 *bhāṣya*, i.e., *svābhāvikakāya* is identified with *dharmakāya* whose characteristic is *āśrayaparivṛtti* (ed. Nishio, p. 125).

57. I refer the reader to Ronald Davidson's excellent Ph.D. thesis for an in-depth explanation of *āśrayaparāvṛtti/parivṛtti* in Yogācāra literature. He traces the theory through the pre-Yogācāra and early and later Yogācāra texts, and separates out the different models for the basis and result of transformation (Davidson, "Buddhist Systems," pp. 160–259). Different models arose out of different milieus, textual traditions, etc. which fed into what eventually became known as Yogācāra, Cittamātra, or Vijñaptimātra tradition. He also points out stages in the literature where different models were consciously equated with each other through the use of *paryāya*, the notion of cognitive synonymy (pp. 116–25).
One important point here is that the Yogācāra understood its models of full enlightenment, including the three-*kāya* model, in terms of *āśrayaparāvṛtti*, i.e., as the completion of a process of yogic realization, not simply as objects of logical analysis.

58. *MSA* 9.12 and *bhāṣya*, ed. Levi, pp. 35–36.

59. *Vṛttibhāṣya*, sDe-dge mi, fol. 113b1–2: "da ni gnas yongs su gyur pa'i don bstan pa'i phyir tsigs su bcad pa drug rtsom mo zhe bya ba'i don to / de la gnas zhes bya ba ni gzugs kyi phung po nas rnam par shes pa'i bar du phung po lnga la bya ste / phung po de dag la yod pa'i nyon mongs pa dang shes bya'i sgrib pa spangs nas chos kyi dbyings rnam par dag par gyur pa dang / rnam par mi rtog pa'i ye shes su gyur pa la gnas gzhan du gyur pa zhes bya'o." Note how Sthiramati uses the terms *āśrayaparivṛtti (gnas yongs su gyur ba)* and *āśrayaparāvṛtti (gnas gzhan du gyur ba)* as synonyms.

60. *MAV* 1.14, ed. Nagao, p. 23: "tathatā bhūta-koṭiś cānimittaṃ paramārthatā / dharmma-dhātuś ca paryāyāḥ śūnyatāyāḥ samāsataḥ." The etymologies of each of these synonyms for *sūnyatā* is given in *MAV* 1.15 and *bhāṣya,* ed. Nagao, pp. 23–24.

61. See, for example, *MSA* 6.9 and *bhāṣya*; *MSA* 11.31 *bhāṣya*; *Msg* 8.18 with commentaries, ed. Lamotte, p. 247; *Msg* 9.1 and 10.3 with commentaries, ed. Lamotte, pp. 259–61, 268; *Buddhabhūmivyākhyāna,* ed. Nishio, pp. 21–22, 117–18, 58–59, 122–23. *MAV* 1.16 *ṭikā,* ed. Yamaguchi, p. 51; *DDV* 9, quoted in Davidson, "Buddhist Systems," pp. 289–92; *Kāyatrayavṛtti* fols. 122-4 to 5.

62. Recall section 2 above, Sthiramati on *MSA* 9.78: "Utter nonperception is the highest perception."

63. *MSA* 6.9 and *bhāṣya, MSA* 19.53–54 and *bhāṣya, MAV* 5.20 and commentaries, *DDV vṛtti,* sDe-dge bi, fol. 32b2–3. See also Ruegg, *La Théorie,* pp. 421ff. for an excellent summary of the *RGV*'s closely related theory of *samalā* and *nirmalā tathatā.*

64. *MSA* 6.9, *bhāṣya,* and *vṛttibhāṣya,* sDe-dge mi, fol. 80b2 where *nirvikalpajñāna* is defined as knowledge free of the conceptualization of subject and object. *MSA* 14.28 and *bhāṣya, MSA* 19.51–54 and *bhāṣya. Msg* 8.18 and *bhāṣya. Msg* chapter 8 with commentaries and the *DDV* with *vṛtti* give perhaps the fullest treatment of *nirvikalpajñāna* in Yogācāra literature. The *DDV*'s account of entry into *nirvikalpajñāna* will be discussed in detail below.

65. See also *Buddhabhūmivyākhyāna,* ed. Nishio, p. 66 where *dharmadhātuviśuddhi* is defined simply as *dharmakāya.*

66. Note that the *DDV vṛtti* specifically equates the terms *parivṛtti* and *parāvṛtti* within the compound *āśrayaparivṛtti/parāvṛtti,* both meaning "transformation." sDe-dge bi, fol. 38a3.

67. *DDV,* sDe-dge phi, fols. 51a6–51b2: "rnam pa drug gis chos nyid la / 'jug pa bla na med pa ste/ mtshan nyid kun tu gnas pa dang / nges par 'byed dang reg pa dang / rjes su dran dang de'i bdag nyid / nye bar son la 'jug pas so/ mtshan nyid mdo ni ji lta bzhin / gnas ni chos rnams thams cad dang / gsung rab mdo sde thams cad do/ de la nge par 'byed pa ni / theg pa chen po'i mdo sde la/ brten pa'i tshul bzhin yid byed pas / bsdus pa'i sbyor lam thams cad do / reg pa yang dag lta thob phyir/ mthong ba'i lam gyis mngon sum gyi / tshul du de bzhin nyid thob cing / nyams su myong ba gang yin pa'o / rjes su dran pa rig pas ni / mthong ba'i don la bsgom lam gyi / byang chub phogs kyis bsdus pa ste / de ni dri ma sel ba'i phyir / de la de yi bdag nyid du / nye bar son pa de bzhin nyid / dri ma med par gyur pa na / tham cad de bzhin nyid tsam du/ snang ba de yang gnas gyur pa/ grub pa yin no. . . ."

68. *DDV vṛtti,* sDe-dge bi, fol. 32a3–7.

69. *DDV,* sDe-dge phi, fol. 51b2–4.

70. *DDV vṛtti,* sDe-dge bi, fol. 32b2–3.

71. *MSA bhāsya,* ed. Levi, p. 170.

72. *DDV vṛtti,* sDe-dge bi, fol. 33a7–b1.

73. *DDV,* sDe-dge phi, fol. 52a3–4.

74. *DDV vṛtti,* sDe-dge bi, fol. 34a1–2.

75. *DDV,* sDe-dge phi, fol. 52b5–53a1.

76. *DDV vṛtti,* sDe-dge bi, 36a7–b2.

77. Ibid., 36b2–37a1.

78. *DDV,* sDe-dge phi, fol. 52a2–3. *DDV vṛtti,* sDe-dge bi, fol. 33b3–5.

79. See notes 60 and 61 above.

80. *MSA* 6.6–6.9, ed. Levi, pp. 23–24.

81. *MSA vṛttibhāṣya*, sDe-dge mi, fols. 79a5–80b7.

82. Common early and classical Yogācāra descriptions of Buddhahood as the fruition of yogic praxis are *tathatāviśuddhi* and *nirvikalpajñāna,* all other Buddha qualities being subsumed within those two. Other texts associated with Yogācāra thought extend this theme, characterizing Buddhahood as nothing but *tathatāviśuddhi* and *nirvikalpajñāna.* The latter comprise the *dharmakāya,* which is real *(samyak)* and ultimate *(paramārtha),* while the *rūpakāya*s, the Buddha dharmas, etc., are merely worldly designations *(prajñapti)* imputed to the *dharmakāya*. The *Suvarṇaprabhāsottamasūtra* (ca. Gupta period) says: "The former two *kāya*s [the *rūpakāya*s] are merely imputedly existent, whereas the third *kāya* [the *dharmakāya*] is really existent, since it is the source of the two [*rūpa*] *kāya*s. Why ? Because all Buddhas possess no other qualities apart from universal thusness *(chos kyi de bzhin nyid)* and nonconceptual gnosis *(rnam par mi rtog pa'i ye shes)*. . . . Universal thusness *(chos kyi de bzhin nyid)* and the gnosis of it *(de bzhin nyid kyi ye shes)* comprise all of a Buddha's qualities" (Tibetan edition, ed. Nobel, p. 43). The *Kāyatrayāvataramukhaśāstra* in the sTan 'gyur is ascribed to a Nāgamitra. Its commentary, the *Kāyatrayavṛtti*, is ascribed to Jñānacandra, who is listed in the *Vijāptimātratāsiddhi* as a disciple of Dharmapāla, an important sixth-century Yogācāra master (Brown, "Buddha Nature," p. 422). The sāstra says: "Except for stainless suchness and nonconceptual gnosis, the Buddhas have no other qualities." (Pk 5290, vol. 101, pp. 119-1-6 to 119-2-1). The *Kāyatrayavṛtti* comments on this: "Why is the *dharmakāya* alone ultimate [while the *rūpakāya*s are imputed]? To answer this, the root text says: 'Except for stainless thusness *(dri med de bzhin nyid)* and nonconceptual gnosis *(mi rtog ye shes)*. . . .' 'Stainless' means that thusness is free of adventitious stain. 'Nonconceptual gnosis' refers to the gnosis perceiving thusness in such a way that perceiver and perceived are the same.' . . . the Buddhas have no other qualities.' This means that apart from these two [stainless thusness and nonconceptual gnosis], there is nothing else. [At the Buddha stage] all things exist in the nature of these two, not in the nature of anything else. This is because all natures other [than these two] are objects of discursive fabrication *(spros pa'i yul)* and therefore false, and the Buddhas have no discursive fabrication." (Pk 5291, vol. 101, pp. 122-4-5 to 122-5-1).

Refer also to *PP* sūtra passages quoted in chapter 3 above and *Samādhirājasūtra* (e.g., *Samādhirājasūtra*, ed. Regamey, pp. 23–24, 49–59, 83–97) for similar emphases on the *dharmakāya* as the real *kāya;* hence complete identification of Buddhahood with thusness *(tathatā)* and its gnosis *(prajñāpāramitā)* alone.

83. I am indebted to the deceased Ven. Geshe Lobsang Namgyal for his pointing out to me the great importance of these four samādhis in the Yogācāra system of yogic praxis, and for enormously fruitful and enjoyable investigations together into various descriptions of them in Indian Yogācāra texts.

84. *MSA* 14.28 and *bhāṣya*, 14.29, ed. Levi, pp. 93–94.

85. Cf. *Vijñaptimātratāsiddhi*, trans. La Vallée Poussin, pp. 575–605. Ratnākaraśānti explains these four stages of yoga in his *Madhyamakālaṃkāravṛtti* (Ruegg, *Literature of the Madhyamaka School*, pp. 122–23). He understands them to describe the a fundamental meditation praxis in common between Yogācāra and Madhyamaka (p. 124). I shall publish an article on Ratnākaraśānti's writings soon in which this will be discussed.

86. *Msg* 3.12, ed. Lamotte, p. 53.

87. *Msg* 8.13, ed. Lamotte, p. 77.

88. *Msg bhāṣya* on 8.13, sDe-dge ri, fol.177a6-b1.

89. The *MSA* also explains *āśrayaparāvṛtti* in terms of the *trisvabhāva* theory in vv. 11.15–11.19 and 11.39–11.45. Different formulations of the *trisvabhāva* theory were coming to expression in third- to sixth-century Yogācāra, appearing in the *Saṃdhinirmocana* and *Lankāvatāra* sūtras, *Bodhisattvabhūmi*, *MSA*, *Msg* and commentaries, *Trisvabhāvakārikā*, *MAV bhāṣya*, and *Triṃśikā*. The *MSA*'s explanation of the theory differs in certain interesting respects from other texts', but not in ways that affect the discussion here.

90. My definitions for the three natures are given on a level of generality that I hope makes them fairly generally applicable to classical Yogācāra, in spite of the diversity of expressions mentioned in the preceding note. These definitions are based on the presentation of the three natures throughout the *Msg*, as well as their expression in *MAV* chapter 1, *MSA* chapter 11, and the *Trisvabhāvanirdeśa*. In the *Msg*, they are initially defined in passages 2.2–2.4, ed. Lamotte, pp. 24–26.

91. See *MAV* 3.10–3.13, 3.22, and commentaries on *pariniṣpannasvabhāva* as both *avikāra*, (immutable, *tathatā*) and *aviparyāsa* (unerring, *jñāna/marga*).

92. See *Msg*, ed. Lamotte, p. 18* for a bibliography of this and other such metaphors in early Yogācāra literature.

93. Ibid., p. 81.

94. *Msg Upanibandhana* on 9.1, sDe-dge ri, fols. 273b5–274a3.

95. See *Msg* 10.1.1, 10.3.1 on *svābhāvikakāya* = *dharmakāya* whose character is *āśrayaparāvṛtti*, explained as in *Msg* 9.1. See *Msg* 10.3.4 and 10.3.5, ed. Lamotte, pp. 83–85, on *dharmakāya* as *tathatāviśuddhi*.

96. *Nirvikalpajñāna* and *tathatāviśuddhi,* where *vyavadānabhāga paratantrasvabhāva* and *pariniṣpannasvabhāva* are *Msg* equivalents of *tathatāviśuddhi*. See also *Msg* 8.18 with commentaries on the inseparability of *nirvikalpajñāna* and *tathatā*.

97. *Msg* 9.2.4 and 9.3, ed. Lamotte, p. 82.

Chapter 5. Enlightenment's Paradox: Nondual Awareness of the Unconditioned *(Svābhāvikakāya)* Embodied in Conditioned Activity for Beings *(Sāmbhogikakāya, Nairmāṇikakāya)*

1. Sthiramati's comments on *Trimśikā* v. 30 offer insight into the general importance for Indian soteriology that the final goal of spiritual practice be unconditioned. *Trimśikā* v. 30 (ed. Levi, p. 43) describes full enlightenment or Buddhahood as follows: "sa evānāsravo dhātur acintyaḥ kuśalo dhruvaḥ / sukho vimuktikāyo 'sau dharmākhyo 'yaṃ mahāmuneḥ" [It is the undefiled realm, inconceivable, good, immutable, blissful, embodiment of liberation, called the *dharma{kāya}* of the great *muni*]. Sthiramati, (*Trimśikā bhāsya,* ed. Levi, p. 44) comments: "dhruvo nityatvāt / akṣayatayā / sukho nityatvādeva yadanityaṃ tadduḥkhaṃ ayaṃ ca nitya iti / asmāt sukhaḥ" [It is immutable because of its permanence and its inexhaustiblity. It is blissful precisely because of its permanence. For what is impermanent is suffering; but this is permanent, hence blissful].

2. The observations of this chapter concern classical Mahāyāna views of nirvāṇa at the stage of their development corresponding to the texts under discussion in chapter 4, i.e., from the third century to fourth century c.e. and thereafter (which covers the period of composition of the *Abhisamayālaṃkāra* and its commentaries). In chapter 13, we look at

alternative models of nirvāṇa in early Mahāyāna that competed for predominance among Mahāyāna thinkers before the doctrine of nonabiding nirvāṇa became widely accepted and then normative.

The term *kleśa* presents problems for translation. It refers to all emotions and reactions as they are infected by clinging attachment *(tṛṣṇā)* and nescience (or "ignorance," *avidyā*), where the latter is understood here as the false imputation of an unchanging or autonomous self upon the psychophysical aggregates of persons, and the false imputation of permanence, self-existence, intrinsic substantiality and duality upon all phenomena. With that understanding *kleśa* has been translated "mental afflictions," "deluded emotions," or occasionally "passions" (depending on context), or left untranslated. Together, *karma* and *kleśa* as controlling conditions of saṃsāra refer to deluded emotions, the mental, verbal, and physical actions they drive, and the vast effects of those actions on the experience of oneself and others.

3. On nonabiding nirvāṇa *(apratiṣṭhita nirvāṇa)* in texts under discussion, see, e.g., *Msg* 9.1 (quoted at the end of the previous chapter), *Msg* 10.3; *MSA* 9.14 *bhāṣya*, *MSA* 9.45, 9.70, 17.32, 17.42, 18.70, 19.62; and *MAV* 1.18. For other references throughout Mahāyāna literature, a good source is Lamotte, *La Somme*, pp. 47*–48*.

A variety of interrelated early Mahāyāna intuitions contributed to the formation of the doctrine of nonabiding nirvāṇa. This doctrine was the outcome of a long process of doctrinal trial and error as Mahāyānists sought ways to authentically express their distinctive intuitions of full enlightenment's vast scope within the constraints of doctrinal systems inherited from pre-Mahāyāna traditions. This is discussed at length in chapter 13 below.

4. "Form" *(rūpa)* is used very broadly in this context, i.e., to take form in the world in any way, to appear, to manifest. Scholastic literature identifies many types of manifestation of Buddhahood from the sūtras (nirmāṇa of body, speech, mind) that are included within a Buddha's "embodiment in forms" *(rūpakāya),* but that are neither physical nor visual phenomena, e.g., the power of Buddhahood to empower beings' minds to comprehend new aspects of dharma or to teach uncomprehended aspects to others, its power to communicate dharma through inanimate things, such as the sky, the wind, or the rivers, and so forth. Sthiramati's commentary on chapter 9 of *MSA* is a rich source of examples.

5. *Buddhabhūmivyākhyāna*, ed. Nishio, p. 125, lines 6–9.

6. *MSA* 9.66 and its commentaries explain the notion that all Buddha *kāya*s are the "same in basis" *(āśrayena samā),* meaning that there is no distinction in the *dharmadhātu*. As expressions of *dharmadhātuviśuddhi*, *dharmakāya*, etc., all *kāya*s are ontologically one.

7. *Ārya* bodhisattvas are bodhisattvas who have attained at least the path of direct seeing, which is also the first of the ten bodhisattva stages *(bhūmi*s*)* to full enlightenment.

8. *Buddhabhūmivyākhyāna*, ed. Nishio, pp. 125–26.

9. Sthiramati, *Vṛttibhāṣya*, sDe dge mi, fols. 136a2–b6. Along similar lines, the *Kāyatrayasūtra*, Pk vol. 37, #949 says: "chos kyi sku ni de bzhin gshegs pa'i ngo gang la blta bar bya'o / longs spyod rdzogs pa'i sku ni byang chub sems dpa'i ngo gang la blta bar bya'o / sprul pa'i sku ni mos pas spyod pa'i so so skye bo'i ngo gang la blta bar bya'o" [*Dharmakāya* is to be seen from the perspective of the Tathāgata. The *sāmbhogikakāya* is to be seen from the perspective of a bodhisattva. The *nairmāṇikakāya* is to be seen from the perspective of an ordinary being engaged in resolute practice]. Recall also section 2 of the previous chapter, where Sthiramati explained how Buddha dharmas and *rūpakāya*s describe Buddhahood from a phenomenal point of view but do not define it, since they are not its essence.

10. *MSA ṭikā*, sDe dge bi, 174a6–7.

11. *Buddhabhūmivyākhyāna*, ed. Nishio, p. 125, lines 14–17.

12. *Msg* 10.3.5, Lamotte, p. 85. On *dharmakāya (svābhāvikakāya)* as *acintya* and *pratyātmavedanīya*, see also *Triṃśikā* and *bhāṣya* by Sthiramati, ed. Levi, pp. 43–44; *RGV* and *vyākhyāna*, 1.5–1.8, 2.31–2.33, 2.38–2.48; Takasaki, *A Study*, pp. 156–60, 323, 325–28.

13. We saw in the previous chapter how the doctrine of *svābhāvikakāya* was an extrapolation from the yogic praxis and gnoseology of Yogācāra. But it was apparently considered sheer hubris to think that one could describe the precise content of the *svābhāvikakāya*'s awareness merely by extrapolation from the limited epistemological categories of ordinary beings, even ones who practice meditation. The leap from even the highest level of bodhisattva realization to a Buddha's realization is inconceivably vast. See, for example, section 4 of this chapter, and chapter 13, sections 2 and 4.

14. Cf. *Samādhirājasūtra*, chapter 22 vv. 50–52, ed. Regamey, pp. 58–59: "agrāhyaḥ sarvasatvehi / na pramāṇena gṛhyate / tathā hi kāyo budddhasya/ apramāṇo acintiyaḥ // apramāṇehi dharmehi / pramāṇaṃ tatra kalpate / akalpitehi dharmehi / buddho py evam akalpitaḥ // pramāṇaṃ kalpam ākhyāto / apramāṇaṃ akalpitam / akalpyaḥ kalpāpagatas / tena buddho acintiyaḥ."

15. One implication of this would be that the actual relation between ultimate and conventional truth, emptiness and conventional appearance, is never fully comprehensible to anyone but a Buddha. It cannot be properly and fully comprehended through conceptual thought, which always thinks of them as separate, or merely thinks the thought: "they are one," without knowing what that actually means in nondual experience.

16. Recall passages in the *PP* sūtras that identify Buddhahood with thusness, and therefore as immutable. *Aṣṭasāhasrikā PP*, fol. 513, in Conze's *Perfection of Wisdom in Eight Thousand Lines*, p. 291, says: "Tathagatas certainly do not come from anywhere, nor do they go anywhere. Because thusness does not move, and the Tathagata is thusness. . . . The thusness of these dharmas and the thusness of all dharmas, and the thusness of the Tathagata are simply this one single thusness." *Aṣṭasāhasrikā PP*, fol. 351, in Conze's *Perfection of Wisdom in Eight Thousand Lines*, p. 212, says: "Subhuti: 'What then is this supreme enlightenment?' The Lord: 'It is thusness. But thusness neither grows nor diminishes.'"

Msg 10.3.4, ed. Lamotte p. 85, 273–74, says: "It *[dharmakāya]* has the characteristic of permanence, because its characteristic is purified thusness *(tathatāviśuddhi)*. . . ." See also Asvabhāva's *Msg Upanibandhana*, sDe dge ri, fol. 277a2–3. *Msg* 10.29.2, ed. Lamotte, pp. 93, 315, says: "The *kāya* of the Tathāgatas is permanent *(nitya)* because the Tathāgatas are ever freed from stain." Asvabhāva comments that this means the *tathāgatakāya* is permanent because its essence is purified thusness *(tathatāviśuddhi)*. *Msg* 10.37, ed. Lamotte, pp. 98, 339–40, has: "Why is it said [in sūtras] 'the *kāya* of the Tathāgatas is permanent,' when the *sāmbhogikakāya* and the *nairmāṇikakāya* are both impermanent? Because the *niṣyandakāya* [i.e., the *sāmbhogikakāya*] and the *nairmāṇikakāya* are both based upon *dharmakāya* [which is permanent]. . . ." See also Asvabhāva's *Msg Upanibandhana*, sDe dge ri, fol. 295a3–5.

MSA 9.66b *bhāṣya*: "prakṛtyā nityatā svābhāvikasya svabhāvena nityatvāt" [The *svābhāvikakāya* is intrinsically permanent, because of its permanence by nature]. Sthiramati's commentary, sDe dge mi, fols. 138a7–b1: "rang bzhin rtag pa ni chos kyi sku ste / chos kyi sku ni rang bzhin gyis skye 'gag med pa'i rang bzhin yin pa'i phyir ro" [Intrinsic permanence {applies to} *dharmakāya*, because intrinsically *dharmakāya* is the nature of nonarising and nonceasing]. Cf. *MSA* 9.23 and *bhāṣya*; *RGV* 1.5–1.8 with commentary, *RGV* 2.18–2.28, 2.29–2.35, 2.44–2.46, 2.66–68.

17. Refer to quotes and references of the previous chapter. Cf. Ārya Vimuktisena's *Abhisamayālaṃkāra-vṛtti*, Pk 5185, fol. 92-4-8 to 5-2 (discussed in chapter 9, sec. 3 below): "chos kyi dbyings dang ldan par gyur pa zag pa med pa'i chos thams cad kyi rnam pa thams cad du rnam par dag pa'i rang bzhin te ngo bo nyid gang yin pa de ni bcos ma ma yin pa'i don gyis na / bcom ldan 'das kyi ngo bo nyid kyi sku yin par shes par bya ste / ngo bo nyid ces bya ba ni bcos ma ma yin pa zhes bya ba ni 'jig rten na grags pa yin no / 'jig rten las 'das pa'i lam ni de 'thob par byed pa yin gyi byed pa po ma yin no."

18. *Msg* 7.11.1–2, 9: "Permanent qualities *(dharmaḥ)* are Buddha qualities, because *dharmakāya* is permanent. Qualities of elimination are Buddha qualities, because the Buddha has eliminated all obstructions *(āvaraṇa)*. . . . Unstained qualities are Buddha qualities, because perfected thusness *(niṣpannā tathatā)* is unstained by any obstruction *(āvaraṇa)*." Asvabhāva's *Msg Upanibandhana*, sDe dge ri, fols. 265b2–3: "The *dharmakāya* has fundamental transformation *(āśrayaparāvṛtti)* as its characteristic. It is thusness *(tathatā)* free of all obstructions; permanent, because immutable. It *[dharmakāya]* is also supreme gnosis *(anuttara jñāna)*, which is unstained and unobstructed, because it is undefiled and is not a [karmic] maturation like the formless [realms]. That [supreme gnosis] is permanent *(nitya)*, because it is conjoined with thusness *(tathatāmiśra)*, and because it is unconditioned by the passions *(kleśa)* and their actions *(karma)*." *Viniścayasaṃgrahaṇī*, quoted in Davidson, "Buddhist Systems," p. 206: "Fundamental transformation *(āśrayaparāvṛtti)* is permanent *(nitya)* and nonappropriating *(anādāna)*, since it has been changed by the path focusing on thusness *(tathatālambanamārga)*." See also Davidson, "Buddhist Systems," pp. 210–12 paraphrasing the *Viniścayasaṃgrahaṇī* on liberated consciousness *(vimuktavijñāna)*, free of obstruction, being unconditioned. Cf. *Laṇkāvatāra Sūtra*, trans. D. T. Suzuki, p. 188: "However, Mahāmati, there is another sense in which the Tathagata can be said to be permanent. How? Because the knowledge arising from the attainment of enlightenment is of a permanent nature, the Tathagata is permanent. Mahāmati, this knowledge, as it is attained intuitively by the Tathagatas, Arhats, Fully-Enlightened Ones, is, indeed, permanent."

19. References to *cittam prakṛtiprabhāsvaraṃ*, primordial pure luminosity of mind, appear in the following texts we have been discussing and their commentaries: *MSA* 6.1 *(bhāṣya)*, 11.13ff., 11.41, 13.16–13.19, 18.43 *(bhāṣya)*; *MAV* 1.22, 5.22; *DDV*, sDe dge phi, fol. 49a4-5 (*DDV vṛtti*, sDe dge bi, fols. 38a3–b6); *RGV* 1.25, 1.49–1.50, 1.57–1.60, 1.63–1.68, 1.129, 2.8–2.9; *Buddhabhūmivyākhyāna*, ed. Nishio, pp. 65–67. Important discussions by modern scholars of *cittam prakṛtiprabhāsvaraṃ* in Mahāyāna and non-Mahāyāna sūtras and śāstras include: Ruegg, *La Théorie*, pp. 409–54; Takasaki, *A Study*, pp. 34–44; Regamey, *Three Chapters from Samādhirājasūtra*, pp. 25–26; Schayer, "Precanonical Buddhism," p. 131.

20. *DDV*, sDe dge phi, fol. 49a4–5.

21. *DDV vṛtti*, sDe dge bi, fol. 38a4–b4.

22. This will be discussed much more in chapter 13.

23. *MSA bhāṣya* 9.14, ed. Levi, p. 36.

24. "Quiescent state" meaning final nirvāṇa as conceived in non-Mahāyāna traditions, where saṃsāra and nirvāṇa are viewed as a mutual dichotomy. Cf. chapter 2.

25. *MSA* 9.51 and *bhāṣya*, ed. Levi, p.43. Sthiramati, *Vṛttibhāṣya*, sDe dge mi, fol. 131b3. Cf. *RGV* 2.18–2.20, ed. Johnston, pp. 82–83, Takasaki, *A Study*, pp. 319–20.

26. *Buddhabhūmisūtra*, ed. Nishio, 2.2.4, p. 5.

27. *Buddhabhūmivyākhyāna*, ed. Nishio, p. 71, lines 17–22.

28. *Buddhabhūmisūtra*, ed. Nishio, 2.2.6, p. 6.

29. Ibid., 2.2.1, p. 4. Cf. Conze, *Large Sutra*, p. 628. Candrakīrti's *Madhyamakāvatāra* has a passage very close in content to this. Like the *Buddhabhūmisūtra*, it uses the concept of *ekarasa* in comparing the way a Buddha's gnosis knows all things to the way undifferentiated space pervades all forms: "Just as space is not divided by the divisions of containers [that enclose it], so there is no division in reality made by phenomena. Through rightly comprehending with excellent knowledge that [all] is the same in one taste *(ekarasa),* you comprehend all things in one instant." *Madhyamakāvatāra*, ed. La Vallée Poussin, p. 356. A closely related concept in the *Abhisamayālaṃkāra* is that of *ekakṣaṇābhisambodha*, the single-moment comprehension of all phenomena. This is the subject matter of the *Abhisamayālaṃkāra*'s seventh chapter. With the realization of *ekakṣaṇābhisambodha*, all phenomena are known in an instant through knowing their single, ultimate nature, the *dharmadhātu*. Such a gnosis is described by some *AA* commentators as *ekarasa*, the gnosis of all things in "one taste." See chapter 9 below, section 2, on Ārya Vimuktisena's gnoseology. Also Ruegg, *Buddha-nature, Mind and the Problem of Gradualism*, pp. 156–58, 161; Conze, *Large Sutra*, pp. 556–72. Note also *Buddhabhūmisūtra*, ed. Nishio, pp. 21–22, where the gnoses of all bodhisattvas become undifferentiated, one taste *(ekarasa),* upon their entry into the *dharmadhātuviśuddhi* of the Tathāgatas. Cf. *MSA* 9.82–9.85.

30. *Msg Upanibandhana*, sDe dge ri, fol. 146b7.

31. *MSA* 9.6, ed. Levi, p. 34. *Vṛttibhāṣya*, sDe dge mi, 109a3–4 (should be read in conjunction with mi, 108a2–4). The *MSA* expresses this theme more characteristically in its explanation of the four gnoses *(jñānas)* of a Buddha, three of which "move" (operate in the conditioned world) while being based upon the one which is "unmoving" (fixed on the unconditioned *dharmadhātu*). This will be discussed below.

32. According to the *MSA*, *Msg,* and their commentaries, whereas *ārya* bodhisattvas alternate between periods of meditative equipoise on ultimate reality (in which they perceive thusness per se) and periods of activity (in which they perceive phenomena), Buddhas have the unique ability to perceive the ultimate and the phenomenal simultaneously (since only Buddhas have removed the obstructions to knowledge, *jñeyāvarāṇa*). The passages referred to above suggest one way in which this unique ability of the Buddhas was understood, i.e., that a Buddha perceives all phenomena *through* his perception of their thusness. Again, the precise mechanism of how a Buddha's gnosis functioned was not speculated upon. See also chapter 13, section 4, below.

33. *Vṛttibhāṣya*, sDe dge mi, fols. 117b7–118a1.

34. *Msg* 8.17, ed. Lamotte, p. 78.

35. *Msg Upanibandhana*, sDe dge ri, fols. 269a6–b2.

36. The capacity of the *dharmakāya* to give rise to activities appropriate to each being automatically, without any intentional thought, is one of the properties of Buddhahood explicitly designated "inconceivable" or "incomprehensible" *(acintya)* in *Ratnagotravibhāga* 1.25 and its commentary. *RGV* 1.25 and *RGVV*, ed. Johnston, pp. 21, 24; Takasaki, *A Study,* pp. 188, 192–94.

37. Cf. *MSA* 9.52 on Buddha's activity as automatic, free of premeditation. Cf. *Buddhabhūmisūtra* and *vyākhyāna*, 2.3, ed. Nishio, pp. 5, 68–70 where the *dharmadhātuviśuddhi*'s unpremeditated activity in the world is compared to the activities of beings that arise in

space without premeditation on space's part. Cf. *RGV* 1.6 and commentary, ed. Johnston, p. 8, where Buddhahood is described as spontaneous *(anābhoga)* because it is free of discursive proliferation *(prapañca)* and conceptualization *(vikalpa)*.

38. *Ratnagotravibhāga,* ed. Johnston, pp. 98–114; Takasaki, *A Study,* pp. 351–79.

39. What, if any, school of Buddhism the *RGV* is to be included within remains controversial. Some scholars have classified it as Yogācāra, some as Madhyamaka, and others see it as an expression of an independent *tathāgatagarbha* school of some kind (Ruegg, *La Théorie*, pp. 31–70). All can agree, I think, that many of the seminal ideas that fed into the Yogācāra tradition also contributed to the *RGV*'s theory of *tathāgatagarbha* (e.g., *cittaprakṛtiviśuddhi, nirmalā tathatā, gotra*, the six-category analysis of Buddhahood, *āśrayaparivṛtti*, and the three *kāya*s). To exclude the *RGV* from the present discussion on the grounds that its school is anomalous would be a mistake, since its buddhology is obviously closely related to that of the *MSA*, from whose ninth chapter on *bodhi* it quotes (Takasaki, *A Study,* pp. 40ff.).

40. *RGV* 1.145 and *RGVV*, ed. Johnston, pp. 70–71, Takasaki, *A Study,* pp. 284–86.

41. Cf. Sthiramati on *MSA* 9.62, explaining the *sāmbhogikakāya* as the natural outflow *(niṣyanda)* of the *svābhāvikakāya* (sDe dge mi, fol. 136b6-7). See also *Laṇkāvatara Sūtra*, chapter 15 (trans. Suzuki, p. 51), on Buddha as *dharmatā* (corresponding to *dharmakāya/svābhāvikakāya* of the Yogācāra śāstras), Buddha as *niṣyanda* (corresponding to *sāmbhogikakāya*) and Buddha as *nirmāṇa* (corresponding to *nairmāṇikakāya*), .

42. *Msg* 10.3.3.b, ed. Lamotte, p. 84. Besides the nonduality of being conditioned and unconditioned, *Msg* 10.3.3 lists two other ways in which the *dharmakāya* is understood to reconcile apparent opposites in its character of nonduality: its nonduality of being and nonbeing *(bhāvābhāvādvayalakṣaṇa)* and its nonduality of plurality and oneness *(nānātvaikatvādvayalakṣaṇa)*. Such qualities of the *dharmakāya* are all the more exalted for their apparent contradictoriness.

43. *Msg* 3.11–3.12, 4.9.6, 5.5.4, 8.8, 8.14–8.16 with commentaries, ed. Lamotte, pp. 53–54, 63, 67, 76–78; *MSA* 9.12, 11.31–11.33, 14.42–14.49, 16.41, 19.52 with commentaries.

44. *Msg* 10.28.10 and commentaries (read in conjunction with *Msg* chapter 8); *MSA* 9.56 and *bhāṣya;* Sthiramati on *MSA* 9.62; *DDV* 9.6.4 and 9.6.6.4, Davidson, "Buddhist Systems," pp. 290–91; *Buddhabhūmivyākhyāna*, ed. Nishio, p. 125; *RGV* 1.93, 2.7–2.8, 2.10–2.11, 2.18–2.20 with *vyākhyāna.* The statements of this and the following paragraph are based on these passages and the relevant portions of the previous section of this chapter.

45. *Msg* 10.28.10, ed. Lamotte, p. 92.

46. Asvabhāva, *Msg Upanibandhana*, sDe dge ri, fol. 288b4–7.

47. *MSA* 9.62 with *bhāṣya*, ed. Levi p. 45.

48. Sthiramati's *Vṛttibhāṣya*, sDe dge mi, fols. 136b6–137a1. Cf. Ratnakīrti's commentary on *Abhisamayālaṃkāra*, Pk #5197, vol. 91, fol. 183-2-7, in which he associates the twenty-one sets of undefiled Buddha dharmas with the *sāmbhogikakāya.* Most of the Buddha dharmas, as aspects of Buddha's mind cognizant of phenomena, would correspond to *pṛṣṭhalabdhajñāna.*

49. *Buddhabhūmivyākhyāna*, ed. Nishio, p. 125, lines 19–27.

50. *MSA* 14.42–14.49 with *bhāṣya*, ed. Levi, p. 96.

51. *RGV* and *vyākhyāna*, vv. 2.8, 2.10–2.11, 2.18–2.20, 3.1–3.3, 3.37–3.38, ed. Johnston, pp. 81–83, 91, 97.

52. *MSA* 9.67 and *bhāṣya*, ed. Levi, p. 46.

53. Sthiramati, *Vṛttibhāṣya*, sDe dge mi, fols. 138b6–139b7; Śīlabhadra, *Buddhabhūmi-vyākhyāna*, ed. Nishio, p. 85.

54. *Vṛttibhāṣya*, sDe dge mi, fol. 139b5–7. Cf. *Buddhabhūmisūtra* 2.3.5–6, ed. Nishio, pp. 9–10; *Buddhabhūmivyākhyāna*, ed. Nishio, pp. 89–92; Davidson, "Buddhist Systems," p. 315. Sthiramati on *MSA* 9.60, sDe dge mi, fol. 135b6, while identifying *adarśajñāna* with *dharmakāya*, refers to *adarśajñāna* as *dharmadhātvadarśajñāna*, a term that specifies *adarśajñāna*'s two functions of (1) nondually knowing the *dharmadhātu* and, through that, (2) nonjudgmentally reflecting all phenomena that are pervaded by the *dharmadhātu*. Later Indian Buddhism separated these two functions into two gnoses: *dharmadhātuviśuddhijñāna* and *adarśajñāna*, making five gnoses in all (as in Tantra). On this, see also Abhayākaragupta, *Munimatālaṃkāra,* sDe dge a, fol. 222a1.

55. *MSA* 9.67-9.69 and *bhāṣya*, ed. Levi, p. 46; Sthiramati on *MSA* 9.67-9.69, *Vṛtti-bhāṣya,* sDe dge mi, fols. 138b2–140a7.

56. Sthiramati on *MSA* 9.60, *Vṛttibhāṣya*, sDe dge mi, fol. 135b6. Śīlabhadra, *Buddha-bhūmivyākhyāna*, ed. Nishio, p. 59.

57. Sthiramati on *MSA* 9.70–9.71, *Vṛttibhāṣya*, sDe dge mi, fols. 140b1–141a4. Cf. M*SA* 14.30–14.31 and *bhāṣya*, ed. Levi, p. 94. The way in which realization of unbounded thusness is understood to generate compassion for limitless "others," and the compassion of limitless others is understood to further open one's capacity to realize unbounded thusness, is profound. It deserves careful study and contemplation far beyond what is presented here. See also MSA 14.30–14.31 and *bhāṣya.*

58. Sthiramati on *MSA* 9.60, *Vṛttibhāṣya*, sDe dge mi, fols. 135b7–136a1; Śīlabhadra, *Buddhabhūmivyākhyāna*, ed. Nishio, p. 59.

59. Sthiramati on *MSA* 9.60, *Vṛttibhāṣya*, sDe dge mi, fol. 136a1–a2; *Buddhabhūmi-vyākhyāna*, ed. Nishio, p. 59.

60. See chapter 4, note 8, above.

61. *Vṛttibhāṣya* sDe dge mi, 135b7–136a1; *Msg* 10.1.2 with Asvabhāva's commentary; *Buddhabhūmivyākhyāna*, ed. Nishio, p. 125; *RGV* 2.49. Cf. Ārya Vimuktisena's *Abhisamayā-laṃkāra* commentary, Pk 5185, vol. 88, fol. 96.2.6–7.

62. Monier-Williams, *Sanskrit-English Dictionary,* s.v. "Sam-."

63. The verbal root *sambhuj* connotes eating together, enjoying a feast together. The nominal form, *sambhoga,* in Indian literature commonly refers to mutual enjoyment of sensual pleasure, or specifies that pleasure as mutual enjoyment of sexual union. It is fascinating to consider possibilities of continuity in underlying connotations of the term *sām-bhogikakāya* (embodiment of mutual enjoyment), from classical Mahāyāna texts like the *Mahāyānasūtrālaṃkāra* through the rise of tantric Buddhism, where mutual enjoyment of sacramental feasts and sexual union become means to express and support deep blissful experiences of nondual awareness.

64. The first bodhisattva stage, *bhūmi*, corresponds to the path of direct seeing. The higher stages traverse the path of higher meditation to Buddhahood. These are elaborated in the *Daśabhūmikasūtra* (Scripture on the ten stages), which is part of the *Avataṃsakasūtra* collection.

65. Bu ston, *History of Buddhism*, trans. Obermiller, pp. 131–32.

66. *MSA* 9.61 and *bhāṣya*, ed. Levi, p. 45. *Vṛttibhāṣya,* sDe dge mi, fol. 136a6–b5. Cf.

Msg 10.35 and its commentaries, which describe the way *sāmbhogikakāyas* differ from each other in appearance and are surrounded by diverse retinues, consisting of bodhisattvas, *śrāvakas*, *devas*, etc.

67. In this case matching the Yogācāra *sāmbhogikakāya* with the marks and signs listed in the corresponding section of the *Large PP Sūtra*. This is discussed in chapter 8, section 4, below.

68. *MSA* 9.58–59, 9.63, 9.66, 9.74–75, 11.43 and *bhāṣya*, ed. Levi, pp. 44–47, 65. *MAV* 4.14 *bhāṣya*, ed. Nagao, p. 56. *DDV bhāṣya*, sDe dge bi, 33a1–3.

69. *MSA* 9.66 and *bhāṣya*, ed. Levi, p. 46; Sthiramati's *Vṛttibhāṣya*, sDe dge mi, fols. 138a2–b2.

70. *Msg* 10.37, ed. Lamotte, p. 98. Asvabhāva's *Msg Upanibandhana*, sDe dge ri, fol. 295a3–5.

Chapter 6. The *Abhisamayālaṃkāra* and its Eighth Chapter on Buddhahood

1. On the many different *Prajñāpāramitā* sūtras, see Conze, *PP Literature*, pp. 31–92. On the *Large Prajñāpāramitā Sūtra* existing in three versions, see ibid., p. 10. On the *Abhisamayālaṃkāra*, see ibid., pp. 101–20; Obermiller, "The Doctrine of *Prajñāpāramitā* as exposed in the *Abhisamayālaṃkāra* of Maitreya"; and idem, *Analysis of the Abhisamayālaṃkāra*.

2. Since the time of Ārya Vimuktisena, ca. sixth century C.E.

3. Conze, "Marginal Notes to the *Abhisamayālaṃkāra*," p. 21.

4. See Conze, *PP Literature*, pp. 102–4 for several examples of the *AA*'s superimposition of Yogācāra categories onto material from the *PP* sūtras. This will be further discussed in the next chapter.

5. On Maitreya as future Buddha, center of cult practice in Yogācāra milieus in Kashmir, and legendary teacher of Asanga, see Davidson, "Buddhist Systems," and Williams, *Mahāyāna Buddhism*, pp. 228ff.

6. *Abhisamayālaṃkāra-Āloka*, ed. Wogihara, p. 1; *Abhisamayālaṃkāra-Sphuṭārthā*, ed. Amano, 1975, p. 2.

7. *Abhisamayālaṃkāra-Āloka*, ed. Wogihara, p. 1; *Abhisamayālaṃkāra-Sphuṭārthā*, ed. Amano, 1975, p. 2..

8. Pensa's Sanskrit edition of *Abhisamayālaṃkāravṛtti*, chapter 1.

9. On the dates mentioned in this paragraph, see Nakamura, *Indian Buddhism*, pp. 253–74; Frauwellner, "Landmarks in the History of Indian Logic;" Davidson, "Buddhist Systems," pp. 14–49, 126–49; Ruegg, *La Théorie*, pp. 30–55, Ruegg, *Literature of the Madhyamaka School*, pp. 101–3. Alexander Naughton, in "The Buddhist Path to Omniscience," assigns the *AA* to the late sixth century with the assumption that Ārya Vimuktisena, his student Bhadanta Vimuktisena, and Haribhadra represent an unbroken lineage of the *AA;* Haribhadra's date is set in the eighth century (p. 112). However, the *AA* commentator Dharmamitra (ca. 800 C.E.), thought to be an immediate successor of Haribhadra (Ruegg, *Literature of the Madhyamaka School*, p. 102), mentions an "Upādhyāya Samyakvairocana" as Haribhadra's teacher for the *AA*, not Bhadanta Vimuktisena (*Prasphuṭapadā*, Pk 5194,

vol. 91, fol. 108-2-4). Haribhadra, in his *Āloka*, mentions his teacher as "guru Vairocana" (ed. Wogihara, p. 993), and in the Tibetan translation of his *Sphuṭārthā*, he bows to "The Upādhyāya Samyakvairocana" as his "excellent guru" (ed. Amano, 1975, p. 301). This means that there was at least one guru, and quite possibly several, in the lineage of the *AA* between Haribhadra and the Vimuktisenas. Nor is there any reason to rule out the possibility that Haribhadra, as he claimed, did know of commentaries on the *AA* by Asanga and Vasubandhu that are not now extant. However, since we have no extant *AA* commentaries prior to Ārya Vimuktisena's, we cannot rule out the very real possibility that Ārya Vimuktisena himself might have been the author of the *AA*. For this reason we can only say with some assurance that the *AA* was composed some time from the fourth century to the early sixth century C.E.

10. The twenty-one extant Indian commentaries on the *AA* are: The twelve commentaries that relate the *Abhisamayālaṃkāra* directly to different versions of the *Prajñāpāramitā* sūtras: (1) *Pañcaviṃśatisāhasrikā-prajñāpāramitopadeśa-śāstra-abhisamayālaṃkāra-vṛtti* by Ārya Vimuktisena (extant in Sanskrit, the first chapter of which is edited in Pensa's edition, Pk 5185 in the Tibetan canon); (2) *Abhisamayālaṃkārakārikā-vārttika* by Bhadanta Vimuktisena (Pk 5186); (3) the revised version of the *Pañcaviṃśatisāhasrikā-prajñāpāramitā* (Tib., *Leu brgyad ma*) ascribed to Haribhadra in the colophon of the Tibetan translation (a version of the 25,000-verse *PP* sūtra in which the subject and topic names of the *AA* have been inserted above corresponding sections of the sūtra; extant in Sanskrit and Tibetan, Pk 5188; (4) *Śuddhamatī* by Ratnākaraśānti (Pk 5199); (5) *Śatasāhasrikā-vivaraṇa* by Dharmaśrī (Pk 5203); (6) *Abhisamayālaṃkārāloka* by Haribhadra (Sanskrit editions by Wogihara and Tucci, Pk 5189); (7) *Sāratamā* by Ratnākaraśānti (Sanskrit edition by Jaini, Pk 5200); (8) *Marmakaumudī* by Abhayākaragupta (Pk 5202); (9) *Saṃcaya-gāthā-pañjikā-subhodinī* by Haribhadra (Pk 5190); (10) *Saṃcaya-gāthā-pañjikā* by Buddhajñāna(pāda) (Pk 5196); (11) *Prajñāpāramitā-kośa-tāla* by Dharmaśrī (Pk 5204); (12) *Aṣṭa-samāna-artha-śāsana* by Smṛtijñānakīrti (Pk 5187). The nine commentaries that explicate the *Abhisamayālaṃkāra* independently are (1) *Sphuṭārthā* by Haribhadra (Sanskrit edition reconstructed by Amano based on *Āloka* and Tibetan [1975], recent partial Sanskrit manuscript published by Amano [1983–87], Pk 5191); (2) *Prasphuṭapadā* by Dharmamitra (Pk 5194); (3) *Durbodha-āloka* by Dharmakīrtiśrī (Pk 5192); (4) *Abhisamayālaṃkāra-vṛtti-piṇḍārtha* by Prajñākaramati (Pk 5193); (5) *Prajñāpāramitā-piṇḍārtha* by Kumāriśrībhadra (Pk 5195); (6) *Prajñāpāramitā-piṇḍārtha-pradīpa* by Atiśa (Pk 5201); (7) *Prajñā-pradīpa-āvalī* by Buddhaśrījñāna (Pk 5198); (8) *Kīrtikalā* by Ratnakīrti (Pk 5197); (9) *Munimatālaṃkāra* by Abhayākaragupta (the third chapter of this work concerns the eight *abhisamayas* of the *AA*, Pk 5299). See Obermiller, "The Doctrine of *Prajñāpāramitā*," pp. 9–11; Conze, *PP Literature*, pp. 33, 36, 50, 51, 55, 112–15.

While most of the *AA* commentators were Mādhyamikas of one kind or another, some are difficult to classify in the schemes of later Tibetan doxography. It is not clear how to classify Ratnākaraśānti, who relied heavily on Yogācāra praxis and philosophy but considered Yogācāra and Madhyamaka doctrinally compatible (Ruegg, *Literature of the Madhyamaka School*, pp. 122–24). Nor is it clear how Ārya Vimuktisena should be classified, as his *AA* commentary freely uses Yogācāra categories like the three *svabhāvas* and eight *vijñānas* without ever explicitly identifying itself (at least to my eyes) as Mādhyamika. Yet, undoubtedly, it could be interpreted consistently as Yogācāra Mādhyamika if a doxologist seeks to do so. Dharmakīrtiśrī, a commentator on the *AA* famous in Tibet as Atiśa's teacher of *bodhicitta* practice, is reported to be Yogācāra, as is his disciple Ratnākīrti (Ruegg, *Literature of the Madhyamaka School*, pp. 109–10).

11. Interestingly, Buddhajñāna(pāda), who is widely believed in Tibet to have been a disciple of Haribhadra, in his *AA* commentary (the *Saṃcaya-gāthā-pañjikā*, Pk 5196, vol. 91) follows not Haribhadra but Ārya Vimuktisena in interpreting *AA* 8 to teach three *kāyas*. Furthermore, he does so with a decidedly Yogācāran mode of explanation, based on a correlation between the eight *vijñānas*, the four Buddha *jñānas*, and the three *kāyas* (Pk 5196, fols. 152-5-6 to 153-1-4). The commentators in India I am familiar with who explicitly accepted and followed Haribhadra's interpretation of four Buddha *kāyas* for *AA* 8 were Prajñākaramati (ca. 950–1000), Kumāraśrībhadra (date unknown to me), and Buddhaśrījñāna (ca. 1200), who composed the *Prajñāpradīpāvalī* on the *AA* (see Ruegg, *Literature of the Madhyamaka School*, pp. 102, 110, 116, 117 on all these figures). If Buddhajñāna(pāda) was indeed Haribhadra's disciple, as the Tibetan traditions believe, the fact that he did not follow Haribhadra's interpretation of *AA* 8 is significant. It may indicate that Haribhadra's interpretation was both new and controversial, and did not begin to receive ready acceptance in India for a century or more after his death. The commentary of Dharmamitra, who may have been an immediate successor of Haribhadra (Ruegg, *Literature of the Madhyamaka School*, p. 102), indicates that in his time there was real controversy surrounding Haribhadra's interpretation of four *kāyas* in *AA* 8 (Pk 5194, fols. 108-2-3ff.).

12. *Abhisamayālaṃkāra-Sphuṭārthā*, ed. Amano, 1975, pp. 14–16. Numbering of *AA* verses will follow Amano's 1975 edition. For what is still a good summary of the eight subjects and seventy topics of the *AA*, see Obermiller, "Doctrine of the *PP*," pp. 61–85. But be aware that Obermiller, because he relies on dGe lugs pa commentaries, is following Haribhadra's analysis of *AA* 8, not Ārya Vimuktisena's.

13. Ārya Vimuktisena, *Abhisamayālaṃkāra-vṛtti,* ed. Pensa, p. 14; Pk 5185 vol. 88, fols. 9-2-2 to 9-4-3.

14. *Abhisamayālaṃkāra-Sphuṭārthā*, ed. Amano, 1975, p. 14.

15. *AA* v. 9.2 is translated near the end of this chapter. Note the correspondence between the use of the term *dharmakāya* in *AA* 1.4 and 9.2, meaning Buddhahood as a whole *(dharmakāya-phalaṃ),* and the use of the term in *Abhidharmakośa* 7.34 and *bhāṣya: dharmakāya phalasaṃpad,* meaning *dharmakāya* as the entire result of the path (see chapter 2 above). Note also the correspondence to the Yogācāra use of the term *dharmakāya* when employed in its inclusive sense to refer to all of Buddhahood, including all three *kāyas*, all gnoses, etc. (chapter 4, section 5, above).

16. Obermiller, "Doctrine of the *PP*," pp. 61-85; Conze's English translation of the *Abhisamayālaṃkāra*, pp. 4–7.

17. *Abhisamayālaṃkāra-Sphuṭārthā*, ed. Amano, 1975, p. 16. The Tibetan for this controversial verse is: "ngo bo nyid longs rdzogs bcas dang / de bzhin gzhan pa sprul pa ni / chos sku mdzad pa dang bcas pa / rnam pa bzhir ni yang dag brjod" (*AA* 1.17). Because the Tibetan omits the second derivative morphology of the *kāya* names and the number of the verb (which appear clearly in the Sanskrit), later Tibetan interpretation of this verse has not had a full philological apparatus at its disposal. This will be discussed in chapter 8, section 6, below.

18. *Abhisamayālaṃkāra-vṛtti*, Pk 5185, 92-4-6 to 100-3-7.

19. *Abhisamayālaṃkāra-Sphuṭārthā*, ed. Amano, 1975 pp. 262–96; *Āloka*, ed. Wogihara, pp. 914–26. See chapter 4 of this book, note 2, on the term *(jñāna) dharmakāya.*

20. *Abhisamayālaṃkāra-Sphuṭārthā*, ed. Amano, 1975, p. 262.

21. Ibid., p. 264. Some of my translations of the terms for the twenty-one types of undefiled Buddha dharmas are interpretive, based on the Indian *AA* commentaries that explain the meanings of the terms, particularly the commentaries by Ārya Vimuktisena, Haribhadra, Dharmamitra, Dharmakīrtiśrī, Ratnākaraśānti, and Abhayākaragupta.

I leave the term *dharmakāya* untranslated for the time being in *AA* v. 8.6, because Ārya Vimuktisena and Haribhadra would have glossed the term very differently. In Ārya Vimuktisena's understanding, it meant "embodiment of dharma[tā]," embodiment of the real nature of things in nondual realization *(prajñāpāramitā)*. This is consistent with the *Prajñāpāramitāsūtra* usage described in chapter 3 above. In Haribhadra's view, *dharmakāya* in verse 8.6 meant "body of dharmas," i.e., the collection of a Buddha's pure dharmas or gnoses. This echoes Abhidharma understanding of *dharmakāya* set within the Mādhyamika context of *samvṛtisatya*. See chapter 2 above on Sarvāstivāda Abhidharma usage of *dharmakāya,* and chapter 10 below on Haribhadra's application of it within Madhyamaka.

22. *Abhisamayālamkāravṛtti*, Pk 5185, vol. 88, fols. 92-4-6 to 92-5-7. Sanskrit for the first chapter of this text has been edited by C. Pensa. Up to the present time, the rest of the text is available only in the Tibetan canon.

23. *Abhisamayālaṃkāra-Sphuṭārthā*, ed. Amano, 1975, pp. 262–70; *Āloka*, ed. Wogihara, pp. 914–17.

24. *Abhisamayālaṃkāra-Sphuṭārthā*, ed. Amano, 1975, p. 270.

25. For references on *araṇā* and *praṇidhijñāna* throughout Buddhist literature, see Lamotte's translation of *Msg*, "Notes et References," p. 53*.

26. *Āloka*, ed. Wogihara, p. 917, lines. 17–19. Haribhadra's explanation here is elegant.

27. On *araṇāsamādhi* and *praṇidhijñāna*: Ārya Vimuktisena's *Abhisamayālaṃkāra-vṛtti*, Pk 5185, 94-5-1 to 94-5-8; Haribhadra's *Abhisamayālaṃkāra-Sphuṭārthā*, ed. Amano, 1975, pp. 270–72; Ratnākarasānti's *Śuddhamatī*, Pk 5199, 281-5-6 to 282-1-3; Tsong kha pa's *Legs bshad gser 'phreng*, 478-6ff., 489-3ff. Also refer to all commentaries on M*SA* 21.45–21.46 and *Msg* 10.12–10.13, which correspond to *AA* 8.7–8.8.

28. *Abhisamayālaṃkāra-Sphuṭārthā*, ed. Amano, 1975, pp. 272–74.

29. Ibid. *Durbodha-āloka* by Dharmakīrtiśrī, Pk 5192, 49-3-4 to 49-5-8. On the Mahāyāna practice of *buddānusmṛti*, mindfulness of the Buddhas (which becomes a vivid awareness of Buddhahood present to oneself in dual or nondual form), see chapter 13, section 2c, below. Such practices may have contributed to the notion in *AA* verse 8.9 of Buddhahood's universal accessibility , and to the notion in verse 8.10 that Buddhahood only appears inaccessible until one's mind as been purified enough through long practice to become aware of its manifestations. All such notions contribute to the Mahāyāna doctrine of nonabiding nirvāṇa, discussed in chapter 13 below.

30. See chapter 5 of this book, sections 3 and 5, on descriptions in Mahāyāna sūtras and Yogācāra śāstras of Buddhahood as permanent. See also *Abhisamayālaṃkāra-vṛtti* of Ārya Vimuktisena, Pk 5185, 96-2-5.

31. *Abhisamayālaṃkāra-Sphuṭārthā*, ed. Amano, 1975, p. 274.

32. I refer the reader to chapter 5 of this book, section 3, on the pervasive activity of Buddhahood.

33. *Abhisamayālaṃkāra-Sphuṭārthā*, ed. Amano, 1975, p. 274, bottom. Haribhadra's comments here refer back to his comments on *AA* vv. 8.8 and 8.9 (ed. Amano, 1975 p. 272), where he also uses the phrases *pratibhāsa . . . kriyākarī (karaṇa)* and *ā saṃsāram avasthāna*, the former with reference to Buddha's capacity to act anywhere, any time (i.e., his pervasiveness, v. 8.9), the latter with reference to his gnosis *(jñāna)* being forever operative (*sadā sthitam*, i.e., permanent in the sense of eternality, v. 8.8).

34. *Abhisamayālaṃkāra-vṛtti*, Pk 5185, 96-2-5. After discussing *AA* verses 8.1–8.11, Ārya Vimuktisena says: "ngo bo nyid kyi sku bshad zin to" [the *svābhāvikakāya* has been explained].

35. *Abhisamayālaṃkāra-Sphuṭārthā*, ed. Amano, 1975, pp. 265–76; *Āloka*, ed. Wogihara, pp. 915–18. We might translate *jñānātmaka-dharmakāya* in line with Haribhadra's understanding as: "the body of dharmas consisting of gnosis," i.e., the collection of Buddha dharmas that comprise his gnoses. Notice how the meaning of *dharmakāya* here reverts to a form closer to the use of the term in Sarvāstivāda Abhidharma than in *Prajñāpāramitā* sūtras: *dharmakāya* as "body, collection of dharmas" rather than *dharmakāya* as "embodiment of dharma[tā]" (cf. chapters 2 and 3 above).

36. *Abhisamayālaṃkāra-Sphuṭārthā*, ed. Amano, 1975, p. 276.

37. Conze, *Large Sutra*, pp. 583–87, 657–65; *Gilgit Manuscript*, pp. 171–80. See also Alex Wayman, "Contributions," pp. 249–55, where Wayman notes that the eighty signs serve as a kind of commentary on the thirty-two marks according to Śākyamitra's commentary on the *Tattvasaṃgraha Tantra*. We may also note that Dharmamitra (ca. 800 C.E.), in his *Prasphuṭapadā* commentary on the *Abhisamayālaṃkāra*, identified the eighty signs as the retinue of the thirty-two marks. Dharmamitra specifically aligns subsets of the eighty signs as different retinues around each of the thirty-two marks (*Prasphuṭapadā*, Pk 5194, 11-4-4 to 112-1-6). Tsong kha pa quotes Dharmamitra on this in his *Legs bshad gser 'phreng*, pp. 497–6ff. Lamotte, in the appendix to his translation of *Msg*, pp. 54*–58*, gives a bibliography of the thirty-two marks and eighty signs throughout Buddhist literature.

38. *Abhisamayālaṃkāra*, ed. Amano, 1975, pp. 276–78; Conze, *Abhisamayālaṃkāra* (English translation), pp. 98–99; Conze, *Large Sutra*, pp. 657–59.

39. Conze, *Large Sutra*, pp. 658–61. Conze finds the passage identifying the virtuous causes for each of the thirty-two marks only in the Sanskrit manuscript of the revised version of the 25,000-verse *Prajñāpāramitā* sūtra, not in the Sanskrit manuscripts of the versions in 18,000 or 100,000 verses. The *Abhisamayālaṃkāra* says specifically in verse 8.20 that it drew its list of virtuous causes from the sūtra *(yathāsūtram)*, i.e., from the *Prajñāpāramitāsūtra*. Ārya Vimuktisena's commentary quotes from the 25,000-verse *Prajñāpāramitā* sūtra the passages on the virtuous causes of the thirty-two marks (*Abhisamayālaṃkāra-vṛtti*, Pk 5185, 96-5-8 to 97-4-4). His quotation differs in places from the revised version of the 25,000-verse *PP* sūtra extant in Sanskrit and Tibetan. This indicates that the version of the 25,000-verse *PP* available to him in his time (ca. early sixth century C.E.) contained the passage in question, although not in the exact form it came down to us in the later revised version of the sūtra. On the various versions of the 25,000-verse *PP* sūtra, see chapter 7 of this book.

40. *Abhisamayālaṃkāra* vv. 8.13–8.32 as embedded in the *Sphuṭārthā*, ed. Amano, 1975, pp. 276–84; English translation in Conze, *Abhisamayālaṃkāra*, pp. 98–102.

41. *Abhisamayālaṃkāra-Sphuṭārthā*, ed. Amano, 1975, pp. 290–92.

42. *Abhisamayālaṃkāra-vṛtti*, Pk 5185, 98-4-7, 98-5-1 to 98-5-2, 98-5-7, and 100-3-6.

At 98-4-7, Ārya Vimuktisena identifies the section of the *Large Prajñāpāramitā Sūtra* that explains the second of the twenty-seven activities as being "a teaching on the activity of the *nairmāṇikakāya.*" Within the context of his commentary, he thereby implies that all the activities are the *nairmāṇikakāya*'s. At 98-5-1 to 98-5-2, he identifies verses 8.33–8.34a taken together as concerning the activity of Buddhahood, the complete result of the path, and fundamental transformation *(āśrayaparivṛtti),* i.e., *dharmakāya* in the inclusive sense. But he also says that its activity is carried out by means of limitless manifestations *(nirmāṇa)* within the worlds of beings, i.e., by *nairmāṇikakāya.* For Ārya Vimuktisena, then, *nairmāṇikakāya* could also be glossed as "the *nirmāṇa*s of *dharmakāya,*" i.e., "the embodiment of dharma in its manifestations."

At 98-5-7, he refers to the twenty-seven activities as activities "of *dharmakāya.*" And at 100-3-6 he aligns *AA* verse 1.17a with verse 8.40b, saying: "'In its essence, with its communal enjoyment, and so also in its manifestation . . .' (*AA* 1.17a) shows three aspects [of resultant *dharmakāya*], and the teaching '. . . This is regarded as the twenty-sevenfold activity of *dharmakāya*' (*AA* 8.40b) is to be understood as explained [i.e., as the fourth aspect of resultant *dharmakāya*]." The "aspects" he refers to are the four topics of *AA* 8: three *kāya*s as functional modes of resultant *dharmakāya* and its activity. In other words, he takes the term *dharmakāya* as inclusive (referring to the resultant state of Buddhahood in its totality) both in verse 1.17 and in verse 8.40.

43. On exclusive and inclusive meanings of *dharmakāya* in Yogācāra literature, see chapter 4, section 5, above.

44. *Āloka,* ed. Wogihara, pp. 915 line 21, 916 lines 18 and 22, 918 line 12.

45. *Abhisamayālaṃkāra-Sphuṭārthā,* ed. Amano, 1975, pp. 290–96; *Āloka,* ed. Wogihara, pp. 923–25.

46. *Abhisamayālaṃkāra-Sphuṭārthā,* ed. Amano, 1975, p. 296, bottom; *Āloka,* ed. Wogihara, p. 925, lines 3–4. The only place I have found in his commentaries where Haribhadra employs the phrase ā *saṃsāram* to the *(jñānātmaka) dharmakāya* is in his remarks on v. 8.11 (*Abhisamayālaṃkāra-Sphuṭārthā,* ed. Amano, 1975, p. 274; *Āloka,* ed. Wogihara, p. 918 line 11).

47. *Abhisamayālaṃkāra-Sphuṭārthā,* ed. Amano, 1975, p. 298.

48. *Abhisamayālaṃkāra-vṛtti,* Pk 5185, 100-5-4 to 100-5-5; *Āloka,* ed. Wogihara, p. 992; *Abhisamayālaṃkāra-Sphuṭārthā,* ed. Amano, 1975, p. 301 (in Tibetan), ed. Amano, 1983, p. 15 (in Sanskrit). In his 1975 edition of the *Sphuṭārthā,* Amano (p. 300) reconstructs the Sanskrit for the *Sphuṭārthā*'s comments on *AA* 9.2 based on the *Āloka.* His 1983 edition (p. 15) presents the *Sphuṭārthā's* own Sanskrit, which corresponds to the Tibetan translation in *Sphuṭārthā,* ed. Amano 1975, p. 301. Ārya Vimuktisena and Haribhadra's *Āloka* identify the semantic antecedent of the term *hetuḥ* in *AA* v. 9.2 as *prayogaḥ,* while Haribhadra's *Sphuṭārthā* appears to identify it as *viṣayaḥ.*

Chapter 7. Literary-Critical Analysis of *Abhisamayālaṃkāra* Chapter 8: A Map that Projects the Three *Kāyas* of Yogācāra onto the *Large Prajñāpāramitā Sutra*

1. Conze, *Large Sūtra,* pp. 76–82.
2. *Abhisamayālaṃkāra-Sphuṭārthā,* ed. Amano, 1975, p. 26.

3. Conze, *Large Sūtra*, pp. 117ff. The correspondence between *AA* chapter 1, topic 4 *(gotra)*, and the 25,000-verse *PP* sūtra is established by Ārya Vimuktisena in his *Abhisamayālaṃkāra-vṛtti*, Pk 5185, 28-2-8 to 29-5-5. In fact, the correspondences between all seventy topics of the *AA* and the 25,000-verse *PP* sūtra were apparently first worked out by Ārya Vimuktisena, based upon whose work, in all likelihood, the revised 25,000-verse *PP* sūtra was redacted (see below).

4. Ruegg, *Literature of the Madhyamaka School*, pp. 86, 101.

5. The twenty-one extant Indian commentaries on the *AA* are:

The twelve commentaries that relate the *Abhisamayālaṃkāra* directly to different versions of the *Prajñāpāramitā* sūtras:

1. *Pañcaviṃśatisāhasrikā-prajñāpāramitopadeśa-śāstra-Abhisamayālaṃkāra-vṛtti* by Ārya Vimuktisena (extant in Sanskrit, the first chapter of which is edited in Pensa's edition, Pk 5185 in the Tibetan canon), which relates the *AA* to the 25,000-verse *PP* sūtra.
2. *Abhisamayālaṃkārakārikā-vārttika* by Bhadanta Vimuktisena (Pk 5186) which relates the *AA* to the 25,000-verse *PP*
3. The revised version of the *Pañcaviṃśatisāhasrikā-prajñāpāramitā*, abbreviated *rP* below (Tib., *Leu brgyad ma*) ascribed to Haribhadra in the colophon of the Tibetan translation, a version of the 25,000-verse *PP* sūtra in which the subject and topic names of the *AA* have been inserted above corresponding sections of the sūtra; extant in Sanskrit and Tibetan, Pk 5188
4. *Śuddhamatī* by Ratnākaraśānti (Pk 5199), which relates the *AA* to the 25,000-verse *PP*
5. *Śatasāhasrikā-vivaraṇa* by Dharmaśrī (Pk 5203), which relates the *AA* to the 100,000-verse *PP*
6. *Abhisamayālaṃkārāloka* by Haribhadra (Sanskrit edition by Wogihara and Tucci, Pk 5189), which relates the *AA* to the 8,000-verse *PP*
7. *Sāratamā* by Ratnākaraśānti (Sanskrit edition by Jaini, Pk 5200), which relates the *AA* to the 8,000-verse *PP*
8. *Marmakaumudī* by Abhayākaragupta (Pk 5202), which relates the *AA* to the 8,000-verse *PP*
9. *Saṃcaya-gāthā-pañjikā Subhodinī* by Haribhadra (Pk 5190), which relates the *AA* to the *Saṃcaya*
10. *Saṃcaya-gāthā-pañjikā* by Buddhajñāna(pāda) (Pk 5196), which relates the *AA* to the *Saṃcaya*
11. *Prajñāpāramitā-kośa-tāla* by Dharmaśrī (Pk 5204), which relates the *AA* to the *Saṃcaya*
12. *Aṣṭa-samāna-artha-śāsana* by Smṛtijñānakīrti (Pk 5187), which relates the *AA* to the 100,000-verse, the 25,000-verse, and the 18,000-verse *PP* sūtras

The nine commentaries that explicate the *Abhisamayālaṃkāra* independently, without specifically correlating it to any of the *Prajñāpāramitā* sūtras:

1. *Sphuṭārthā* by Haribhadra (Sanskrit edition reconstructed by Amano based on *Āloka* and Tibetan [1975], recent partial Sanskrit manuscript published by Amano [1983-87], Pk 5191)
2. *Prasphuṭapadā* by Dharmamitra (Pk 5194)

3. *Durbodha-āloka* by Dharmakīrtiśrī (Pk 5192)
4. *Abhisamayālaṃkāra-vṛtti-piṇḍārtha* by Prajñākaramati (Pk 5193)
5. *Prajñāpāramitāpiṇḍārtha* by Kumāriśrībhadra (Pk 5195)
6. *Prajñāpāramitāpiṇḍārthapradīpa* by Atiśa (Pk 5201)
7. *Prajñā-pradīpa-āvalī* by Buddhaśrījñāna (Pk 5198)
8. *Kīrtikalā* by Ratnakīrti (Pk 5197)
9. *Munimatālaṃkāra* by Abhayākaragupta (the third chapter of this work concerns the eight *abhisamaya*s of the *AA*, Pk 5299)

See Obermiller, "The Doctrine of *Prajñāpāramitā*," pp. 9–11; Conze, *PP Literature*, pp. 33, 36, 50, 51, 55, 112–15.

6. Conze, *PP Literature,* pp. 32–33.

7. It should also be noted that more Indian commentaries relate the *AA* to the 25,000-verse version of the *PP* sūtra than to any other version of the *Large PP Sūtra.*

8. Conze, *PP Literature,* p. 44.

9. Conze, *Large Sūtra,* pp. 549–656; Haribhadra, *Abhisamayālaṃkāra-Sphuṭārthā,* ed. Amano, 1975, pp. 252–97.

10. Conze, *Perfection of Wisdom in Eight Thousand Lines,* pp. 175–76.

11. For the *PP* textual basis of *AA* chapters 6–8 identified in the revised 25,000-verse *PP*, see the Sanskrit of that sūtra in Conze's *Mahāprajñāpāramitā Sūtra*, chapters 6 through 8. This can be compared to the same sections of the Tibetan translations of the unrevised and revised 25,000-verse *PP*, Pk 731 pp. 122-3-2ff. and Pk 5188 pp. 279-4-4ff., respectively. These texts are very close to the corresponding text of the Gilgit Sanskrit 18,000-verse *PP*, which, in the portions corresponding to *AA* chapters 6–8, is translated into English in Conze's *Large Sūtra*, pp. 549–656. The textual basis in the 8000-verse *PP* for *AA* chapters 6, 7, and 8 (as specified by Haribhadra) is less than one page of Conze's English translation of that sūtra. See Conze's *Perfection of Wisdom in Eight Thousand Lines,* pp. 275–76, beginning: "One should approach the resounding declarations of the perfection of wisdom through the [analogy of the] roaring of the lion's roar." The same 8,000-verse *PP* passages are found in Haribhadra's *Āloka*, ed. Wogihara, pp. 908–26, beginning: "siṃha nāda nadanatayā prajñāpāramitā nadanatā 'nugantavyā."

12. *Abhisamayālaṃkāra-Sphuṭārthā,* ed. Amano, 1975, p. 252.

13. Sanskrit of revised 25,000-verse *PP* in Conze's *Mahāprajñāpāramitā Sūtra*, sections 6.1–6.13. Ārya Vimuktisena's *Vṛtti*, Pk 5185, pp. 90-4-7ff. For the same passages in the 18,000-verse *PP*, Conze's *Large Sūtra*, pp. 549–56 gives the English translation, and Conze's *Gilgit Manuscript*, pp. 1–10 gives the Sanskrit.

14. *Abhisamayālaṃkāra-Āloka,* ed. Wogihara, p. 908.

15. Conze, *Perfection of Wisdom in Eight Thousand Lines,* p. 275.

16. *Abhisamayālaṃkāra-Āloka,* ed. Wogihara, p. 908.

17. Conze, *PP Literature*, pp. 36–40. Conze's typescript romanization of the Sanskrit is his *Mahā-prajñā-pāramitā-sūtra.* N. Dutt's edition of the Sanskrit is *The Pañcaviṃśati-sāhasrikā Prajñāpāramitā* (1934). The Tibetan translation is Pk 5188 in the bsTan 'gyur of the Tibetan canon.

18. Other reasons for my belief that the revised 25,000-verse *PP* sūtra was redacted some time after Ārya Vimuktisena are presented later in this chapter.

19. Conze, *Prajñāpāramitā Literature*, pp. 37–39; Lethcoe, "Some Notes," pp. 499–511.

For a description of extant *PP* sūtras, see Conze, *Prajñāpāramitā Literature*, pp. 31–74. The revised 25,000-verse *PP (rP)* is extant in eighteenth- and nineteenth-century Nepalese Sanskrit manuscripts, edited in Dutt, *The Pañcaviṃśatisahāsrikā Prajñāpāramitā* and Conze, *Mahāprajñāpāramitā Sūtra*, and is also extant in Tibetan translation in the Tibetan canon (Pk 5188). Nancy Lethcoe, using Chinese translations of the 25,000-verse *PP* sūtra, has charted the development of this sūtra over a period of several centuries and has clearly shown that its revised version *(rP),* extant only in Sanskrit and Tibetan, lies within that continuum of development. She noted that it is a late version of the 25,000-verse *PP* sūtra, revised by the insertion of *AA* topic names, and less obviously, by occasional transpositions and additions that bring the sūtra more closely into line with the *AA* (Lethcoe, "Some Notes," pp. 499–511).

20. Conze, *Mahāprajñāpāramitā Sūtra*, chapter 8, secs. 8.1–8.5; in Tibetan translation, Pk 5188, vol. 88: *rP* 8.1 is labeled at folio 3-5-1 "ngo bo nyid sku"; *rP* 8.2 is labeled at 3-5-5 "longs spyod rdzogs pa'i sku"; *rP* 8.3 is labeled at 3-5-8 "sprul pa'i sku"; *rP* 8.4 is labeled at 6-2-2 "sprul pa'i sku'i sgo nas chos kyi sku'i phrin las spyir bstan pa"; vol. 90, *rP* 8.5 is labeled at 61-2-2 "phrin las rnams"; and the title for *rP* chapter 8 (corresponding to *AA* chapter 8) is labeled at 61-2-2 "chos kyi sku'i mngon par rtogs pa."

For convenience, I am numbering sections of the *Large PP Sūtra* with an arabic numeral version of the numbering system employed by Conze in his editions of the *Large PP Sūtra* in Sanskrit and English translation (*Mahāprajñāpāramitā Sūtra,* secs. 8.1–8.5; *Large Sūtra,* pp. 572–643, 653–54; *Gilgit Manuscript,* pp. 164–243).

21. Ratnākaraśānti's *Śuddhamati*, Pk 5199, 281-5-2ff. and *Sāratamā*, Pk 5200, 92-4-4ff., ed. Jaini, p. 172; Abhayākaragupta's *Marmakaumudi,* Pk 5202, 198-5-6ff. and *Munimatālaṃkāra*, Pk 5299, 232-1-3ff. Dharmamitra and Dharmakīrtiśrī of Suvarnadvīpa, for the most part, did not quote the *PP* sūtra in their *AA* commentaries, because their texts are subcommentaries on Haribhadra's *Sphuṭārthā*, which comments on the *AA* independently of correlation to any particular *PP* sūtra. Dharmamitra and Dharmakīrtiśrī probably also assumed that their readers were familiar with Ārya Vimuktisena's commentary and/or r*P*. In their comments on *AA* 8, Ratnākaraśānti and Abhayākaragupta quote the *PP* sūtra and, in particular, *rP*, in order to show the sūtra basis for their disagreement with Haribhadra over the meaning of the *AA*. That disagreement is the subject of chapter 11 of this book.

22. Ratnākaraśānti's *Śuddhamati*, Pk 5199, 281-5-2ff. and *Sāratamā*, Pk 5200, 92-4-4ff., ed. Jaini, p. 172; Abhayākaragupta's *Marmakaumudi,* Pk 5202, 198-5-6ff. and *Munimatālaṃkāra*, Pk 5299, 232-1-3ff.

23. Bu ston's *Lung gi snye ma*, vol. 2, pp. 204ff.; gYag ston's *Rin po che'i phreng ba blo gsal mgul rgyan*, vol. 4, pp. 382ff.; Rong ston's *Tshig don rab gsal*, 554-1ff.; Tsong kha pa's *Legs bshad gser phreng*, vol. 2, 465-4ff.; rGyal tshab's r*Nam bshad snying po'i rgyan*, pp. 549ff; Sera rje btsun chos kyi rgyal mtshan's *Chos sku spyi don*, 14b3 to 15b7. *rP* 8.1–8.3. comprises sections 8.1.–8.3. of Conze's *Mahā-Prajñāpāramitā Sūtra*; in Tibetan translation: Pk 5188, 3-4-1 to 3-5-8.

24. *AA* 8 verses 1–33 on the Buddha *kāyas*. See chapter 6 translation above.

25. Sanskrit of *rP* 8.1.–8.3: *Mahāprajñāpāramitā Sūtra*, sections 8.1.–8.3.; Tibetan: Pk 5188, 3-4-1 to 3-5-8; cf. Conze's English translation: *Large Sūtra*, pp. 653–54.

26. The titles: "svābhāvikaḥ kāyaḥ," "sāmbhogikaḥ kāyaḥ," and "nairmāṇikaḥ kāyaḥ" appear in the revised 25,00-verse *PP* as the titles of their respective passages (Conze, *Mahā-Prajñāpāramitā Sūtra*, fols. P523a8–523b5). Ratnākaraśānti and Abhayākaragupta quoted

these passages as the *PP* textual basis for *AA* 8, and as evidence that the *AA* teaches three Buddha *kāyas* (*Sāratamā*, ed. Jaini, p. 172; *Marmakaumudi*, Pk 5202, 198-5-6 to 199-1-1). This is discussed in chapter 11 of this book.

27. Compare this passage of *rP* to *AA* verses 8.1–8.6 as translated in chapter 6 of this book. The correspondence is clear. It is no surprise that late Indian and Tibetan commentators identified *rP* 8.1 as the textual basis for *AA* vv. 8.1–8.6. The same observation holds true for *rP* 8.2 and 8.3 and their corresponding verses in the *AA* (vv. 8.12 and 8.33 on *sāmbhogikakāya* and *nairmāṇikakāya,* respectively).

28. Tibetan, Pk 5188, 3-5-2 to 3-5-5, reads a little differently: "[T]he body of the Tathāgatas, Arhats, fully enlightened Buddhas always and everywhere adorned with the thirty-two marks of the great being and the eighty associated signs, demonstrates to the bodhisattvas, the great beings, pleasure and satisfaction, joy and happiness in the unsurpassed enjoyment of the supreme Mahāyāna dharma." Compare to *Sāratamā*, ed. Jaini, p. 172.

29. Tibetan, Pk 5188, 3-5-6 to 3-5-8, says: "[W]hen . . . he has realized highest, complete enlightenment, he carries out the benefit of all beings by means of a cloud of multiform manifestations of the body of the Tathāgata, the Arhat, the Fully Enlightened One, in the ten directions, in endless and boundless world systems, during the whole of time." This could be rephrased: "[W]hen . . . he has realized highest, complete enlightenment, the Tathāgata, the Arhat, the Fully Enlightened One carries out the benefit of all beings by means of a cloud of multiform manifestations of his body, in the ten directions, in endless and boundless world systems, during the whole of time."

30. Ratnākaraśānti in *Śuddhamatī* and *Sāratamā*, Abhayākaragupta in *Munimatālaṃkāra* and *Marmakaumudī*, Go ram pa bsod nams senge ge in *sBas don zab mo'i gter*.

31. See chapter 4, section 4, above on the derivation of the three *kāya* names.

32. For Haribhadra's reading of *AA* vv. 8.1–8.6 according to the *Sphuṭārthā,* see *Abhisamayālaṃkāra-Sphuṭārthā,* ed. Amano, 1975, pp. 262–70, and according to the *Āloka*, ed. Wogihara, pp. 914–17 (Sanskrit). For translations of his Sphuṭārthā commentary on these verses, see chapter 10 of this book.

33. Bu ston's *Lung gi snye ma*, vol. 2, pp. 206ff.; gYag ston's *Rin po che'i phreng ba blo gsal mgul rgyan*, vol. 4, p. 387-6ff.; Tsong kha pa's *Legs bshad gser phreng*, vol. 2, 469-5 to 470-4; Sera rje btsun pa's *Chos sku spyi don*, 15a4–15b7.

34. I label the two parts of *rP* 8.1, corresponding to Haribhadra's *svābhāvikakāya* and *jñānātmaka dharmakāya*, "*rP* 8.1a" and "*rP* 8.1b," respectively.

35. E. Obermiller's groundbreaking study of the *AA* analyzed the *AA* by referring to Haribhadra's *Āloka* and *Sphuṭārthā*, and by relying heavily on several major Tibetan *AA* commentaries (*Analysis of the Abhisamayālaṃkāra*, pp. vii–viii). His report that *AA* 8 taught four Buddha *kāyas* was based on these sources. But the Tibetan commentators upon which he relied (Bu ston, Tsong kha pa, rGyal tshab, 'Jam dbyang bshad pa) all identified revised 25,000-verse *PP* passages 8.1–8.3 (quoted above) as the sūtra basis for *AA* 8's Buddha-*kāya* teaching (Bu ston's *Lung gi snye ma*, vol. 2, pp. 204ff.; Tsong kha pa's *Legs bshad gser phreng*, vol. 2, 465-4ff.; rGyal tshab's *rNam bshad snying po'i rgyan*, pp. 549ff). A number of scholars since Obermiller followed his lead, based on similar sources, reporting simply that *AA* 8 teaches four *kāyas* (Conze, *Prajñāpāramitā Literature*, p. 103; Dutt, *Mahāyāna Buddhism*, p. 155; La Vallée Poussin, *Siddhi*, pp. 790–91; cf. Obermiller, *Analysis of the Abhisamayālaṃkāra*, pp. 11–12).

In order to arrive at a proper interpretation of *AA* 8, it is important first to identify its actual textual basis in the *PP* sūtra, and then to see how this sheds light on its teaching of the Buddha *kāyas*. Because this had not previously been done, there has been a tendency to repeat what scholars such as Obermiller have said without realizing that the Tibetan sources upon which he relied had misidentified the *PP*-sūtra basis of *AA* 8, and that this has a bearing on the interpretation of *AA* 8.

36. Lethcoe, "Some Notes," pp. 499–511.

37. Ibid., pp. 500–504.

38. Ibid., p. 504.

39. Ibid., pp. 503–5.

40. Ibid., 504.

41. Conze, *PP Literature,* p. 21.

42. Lethcoe, "Some Notes," p. 499 n. 3.

43. Conze, *Selected Sayings*, p. 12.

44. The 100,000-verse *PP* is extant in a number of Sanskrit manuscripts, and in Tibetan translation in the bKa' 'gyur (Pk 730; see Conze's *PP Literature*). The unrevised 25,000-verse *PP* is not entirely extant in Sanskrit. The first three-fifths of the sūtra are preserved in Sanskrit in the Gilgit Manuscript of the *Large PP Sūtra* (Conze, *Prajñāpāramitā Literature,* p. 35; Vira and Chandra, *Gilgit Buddhist Manuscripts*). But the latter portions of the sūtra are missing. The latter portions are relevant here since they are the ones that correspond to chapters 6 through 8 of the *AA*. The unrevised 25,000-verse *PP* is, however, fully extant in Tibetan translation (Pk 731). The first three-fifths of the 18,000-verse *PP* sūtra are not extant in Sanskrit, but the last two-fifths, corresponding to chapter 6 through 8 of the *AA*, are preserved in Sanskrit in the Gilgit Manuscript (Conze, *PP Literature,* p. 40; Vira and Chandra, *Gilgit Buddhist Manuscripts*.). The 18,000-verse *PP* is fully extant in Tibetan translation (Pk 732).

45. Conze, *PP Literature*, pp. 37, 44.

46. Pk 730. These passages are missing at the beginning of chapter 63, fol. 213-5-1.

47. Pk 731. The passages are missing at the beginning of chapter 62, fol. 134-5-3. The Sanskrit for this part of the sūtra is not extant.

48. Conze, *The Gilgit Manuscript,* p. 35. The passages are missing at the beginning of *parivarta* 73.

49. Pk 732, they are missing at the beginning of chapter 73, fol. 146-1-7.

50. Conze, *PP Literature*, pp. 31–41. Conze and the rNyingma edition of the bKa' 'gyur list Ye shes sde with a question mark as translator for the 25,000-verse *PP* sūtra. If true, this would put the translation in the late eighth century.

51. See Snellgrove and Richardson, *Cultural History of Tibet*, p. 78 for dates of Khri srong lde brtsan. For lDan kar listing, see *Journal Asiatique* 241 (1953): 319. For discussion of problems posed by eighth-century Indian expressions of Buddhahood for King Khri srong lde brtsan and Ye shes sde in their concern to introduce Buddhism into Tibetan culture, see chapter 13 of this book, section 4.

52. See also Conze, *Gilgit Manuscript*, p. 64, where he notes: "VIII 1–3 are found in [r]P only, but not in Ad [18,000], S [100,000] or the unrevised P [25,000]."

53. Tshul khrims rgyal ba cotranslated a Vinaya text with Atiśa (Roerich, *Blue Annals*, p. 86), placing him in the eleventh century (Atiśa died in 1054). Śāntibhadra is listed in the *Blue Annals* (p. 360), along with Atiśa, as an Indian teacher of the *Guhyasamāja Tantra* to 'Gos lhas btsas, an eleventh-century disciple of 'Brog mi (992–1072 C.E.).

54. Basing himself on a report by the Tibetan scholar Taranatha (sixteenth to seventeenth centuries) that said that Ārya Vimuktisena (ca. early sixth century) consulted a revised version of the *PP*, Conze surmised that the version of *rP* extant in nineteenth-century Nepalese Sanskrit manuscripts belonged to the fifth century (*PP Literature*, p. 37), while the version in the Tibetan canon whose postscript identifies Haribhadra as redactor was a further revision by Haribhadra in the late eighth century. However, *rP* passages 8.1–8.3 are found equally in the extant Nepalese Sanskrit manuscripts of *rP* and in the Tibetan translation of *rP*. The evidence presented here tends to indicate that *rP*, in all its extant editions, was redacted in the late eighth century at the earliest, which would support its attribution to Haribhadra. Evidence presented below will demonstrate that *rP* passages 8.1–8.3 postdate Ārya Vimuktisena. And since all extant editions of *rP* contain passages 8.1–8.3, all editions in Sanskrit and Tibetan postdate Ārya Vimuktisena, which means that there was no edition of *rP* in the fifth century as proposed by Conze. We will also present evidence below that Haribhadra himself referred to *rP* and probably redacted it. The remark by Taranatha that Conze relies upon was made a thousand years after Ārya Vimuktisena and carries little weight in comparison to the textual evidence discussed here and below.

55. Ratnākaraśānti's *Śuddhamati*, Pk 5199, 281-5-2ff. and *Sāratamā*, Pk 5200, 92-4-4ff., Jaini's Sanskrit edition, p. 172; Abhayākaragupta's *Marmakaumudi*, Pk 5202, 198-5-6ff. and *Munimatālaṃkāra*, Pk 5299, 232-1-3ff.

56. Pensa, *L'Abhisamayālaṃkāravṛtti di Ārya-Vimuktisena*, 1967.

57. *Abhisamayālaṃkāra-vṛtti*, Pk 5185, vol. 88, pp. 92–100. At 92-4-6ff. Ārya Vimuktisena identifies the three *kāyas* as the first three topics of *AA* chapter 8. At 98-4-7 and 98-5-1 to 98-5-3, he explicitly identifies the fourth topic of *AA* chapter 8 as *sprul pa'i sku'i phrin las* (the activity of the *nairmāṇikakāya*.) On *AA* 8 and its contents, see chapter 6 of this book.

58. *Abhisamayālaṃkāra-vṛtti*, Pk 5185, 92-4-7 to 92-5-7 on *svābhāvikakāya*, and 96-2-5 to 96-2-8 on *sāmbhogikakāya*.

59. *Abhisamayālaṃkāra-vṛtti*, Pk 5185, 98-5-3 to 98-5-7.

60. *Abhisamayālaṃkāra-vṛtti*, Pk 5185, 98-5-3 to 98-5-7; Conze, *Mahāprajñāpāramitā Sūtra*, section 8.4; Conze, *Gilgit Manuscript*, p. 164; *Large Sūtra*, p. 573.

In Conze's translation, *PP* passage 8.4 begins: "How, O Lord, when all dharmas are like a dream, nonentities, with nonexistence for their own-being and empty of own-marks, can there be a definite distinction between them . . . ?"

61. *Abhisamayālaṃkāra-vṛtti*, Pk 5185, 99-1-5ff.; Conze, *Mahāprajñāpāramitā Sūtra*, sec. 8.5; Conze, *Gilgit Manuscript*, p. 167; idem, *Large Sūtra*, p. 576.

In Conze's translation, *PP* passage 8.5 begins: "Here, surveying the world with my Buddha-eye, I have seen in the Eastern direction, in world systems countless like the sands of the Ganges, bodhisattvas who have deliberately hurled themselves into the great hells. . . ."

62. See translation of *AA* vv. 8.1–8.6 in chapter 6 of this book (with a brief sketch of Ārya Vimuktisena's interpretation). A fuller treatment occurs in chapter 9 below.

63. *Abhisamayālaṃkāra-vṛtti*, Pk 5185, 92-5-8 to 96-2-1. On Abhidharma sources for Ārya Vimuktisena's and others' discussions of some of the *anāsrava* dharmas, see Sera rje btsun chos kyi rgyal mtshan's *Chos sku spyi don*, pp. 29a-1 to 33a-4.

64. *Abhisamayālaṃkāra-vṛtti*, Pk 5185, 96-1-7 to 96-1-8: "rab 'byor rnam pa thams cad mkhyen pa nyid kyi dmigs pa ni dngos po med pa'o / bdag po ni dran pa'o / rnam pa ni zhi ba ste mtshan nyid med pa'o / zhes gsungs so."

65. The *PP* passage in the previous note occurs in the unrevised 25,000-verse *PP*, Tibetan translation, Pk 731, fol. 143-2-1. On the Chinese translations, see Lethcoe, "Some Notes," p. 504, table 2, #67. The passage Ārya Vimuktisena quotes (in the previous note) is also found in the Tibetan translations of the 100,000-verse *PP*, 18,000-verse *PP*, and *rP*. It is not found in the Gilgit Manuscript of the 18,000-verse *PP*, nor in the Sanskrit manuscripts of *rP*. For this reason Conze does not include it in his *Large Sūtra* (see sec. 8.5, p. 583), nor in its Appendix I, p. 656.

66. *Abhisamayālaṃkāra-vṛtti*, Pk 5185, 96-5-8. The *PP* passage Ārya Vimuktisena quotes on the causes of the thirty-two marks is found in the unrevised 25,000-verse *PP* in Tibetan translation, Pk 731, fols. 143-5-1 to 144-2-6 as well as in *rP*. From *rP* it is translated in Conze's *Large Sūtra*, pp. 659–61.

67. *Abhisamayālaṃkāra-vṛtti*, Pk 5185, fols. 97-4-5ff. Ārya Vimuktisena indicates he is quoting the *PP* sūtra with the expressions: *āha* (*gsungs pa ni* in Tibetan), and *sūtrasya vacana* (*mdo'i tshig* in Tibetan). The *PP* passage he quotes is in the unrevised 25,000-verse *PP*, Pk 731, fols. 144-2-6 to 145-4-1 as well as *rP*. It is translated in Conze's *Large Sūtra*, pp. 586–87.

68. *Abhisamayālaṃkāra-vṛtti*, Pk 5185, fols. 98-4-6 to 98-4-7. The Tibetan reads: " 'di gnyis kyi bshad pa ni sprul pa'i sku'i phrin las ston pa'i mdo las 'jig rten las 'das pa'i chos kyi sbyin pa'i bsdu ba'i dngos po nyid kyis ston par 'gyur te des na dang po ma gsungs so."

69. Unrevised 25,000-verse *PP*, Pk 731, fols. 140-1-8 to 145-4-1; translated from *rP* in Conze's *Large Sūtra*, pp. 580–87.

70. *Abhisamayālaṃkāra-vṛtti*, Pk 5185, 98-5-3 to 98-5-4. *rP* 8.4 is translated in Conze, *Large Sūtra*, pp. 573ff. See chapter 6 of this book for my translation of *AA* 8 vv. 33-34a.

71. *Abhisamayālaṃkāra-vṛtti*, Pk 5185, pp. 98-4-7 to 100-3-4. *rP* 8.5 is translated in Conze, *Large Sūtra*, pp. 576–643.

72. *Abhisamayālaṃkāra-vṛtti*, Pk 5185, 98-4-7. At fol. 98-4-7, Ārya Vimuktisena identifies the activity of *PP* passage 8.5 as *sprul pa'i sku'i phrin las* (the activity of the *nairmāṇikakāya*). At fol. 98-5-7, he identifies the same activity as *chos kyi sku'i phrin las* (the activity of the *dharmakāya*). There is no contradiction. At fol. 98-5-1, he explains that the *nairmāṇikakāya* is the means through which *dharmakāya-phalaṃ*, i.e., Buddhahood, acts. He understands the term *dharmakāya* in verse 8.40 to carry its inclusive sense, referring to Buddhahood as a whole. See chapter 5, section 5, of this book on exclusive and inclusive meanings of *dharmakāya* in Yogācāra. Also see my remarks on Ārya Vimuktisena's interpretation of *AA* vv. 8.33–8.34a in chapter 6 above.

73. Actually, as mentioned in chapter 6 above, I do not rule out the very real possibility that Ārya Vimuktisena himself was the author of the *Abhisamayālaṃkāra*, and that his *vṛtti*, therefore, comprises his own commentary upon it: a passage-by-passage clarification of the entire 25,000-verse *Prajñāpāramitā* sūtra as he himself had versified it in the *Abhisamayālaṃkāra*. The *Abhisamayālaṃkāra*, after all, first appears in the extant written record embedded within Ārya Vimuktisena's commentary upon it. This, of course, would only further support the argument being made here.

74. For scholars who would like to see this demonstrated in detail, comparing passage for passage Ārya Vimuktisena's comments with *rP* passages 8.1–8.3, see Makransky, "Controversy over Dharmakāya in India and Tibet," p. 48n.

75. *Abhisamayālaṃkāra-Sphuṭarthā*, ed. Amano, 1975, pp. 262–97. See Conze's English translation of the *Abhisamayālaṃkāra*, pp. 96–105, or my translation of *AA* chapter 8

in chapter 6 of this book, and compare to *PP*-sūtra passages 8.4–8.5 as translated in Conze, *Large Sūtra*, pp. 573–643.

76. Dutt, Conze, and Lethcoe have all noted how the revised 25,000-verse *PP* sūtra recast the 25,000-verse *PP* sūtra by inserting the section headings of the *AA* into the corresponding sections of the sūtra. In addition, Conze and Lethcoe noted that the sūtra in its revised edition was altered in certain places (by additions and transpositions) to bring it more closely into line with the *AA*. (Dutt, *Pañcaviṃśatisāhasrikā Prajñāpāramitā*, pp. v–xiii; Conze, *Prajñāpāramitā Literature*, pp. 37–39; Lethcoe, "Some Notes," pp. 500ff.) With reference to rP passages 8.1–8.3, Conze, noting that these passages are missing in the Gilgit Manuscript of the 18,000-verse *PP*, believed they were later additions to the *PP* sūtra (Conze, *Gilgit Manuscript*, p. xvii). Elsewhere, however, based on the report of Taranatha, Conze surmised that the revised 25,000-verse *PP* belonged to the fifth century, and that Ārya Vimuktisena consulted the revised *PP* before writing his own commentary on the *AA* (*PP Literature*, p. 37). Lethcoe ("Some Notes," p. 504) found that revised *PP* passages 8.1–8.3 were missing in all Chinese translations of the 25,000-verse *PP*. Up to the present time, however, no one had noticed the evidence of Ārya Vimuktisena's commentary, which proves that *PP* passages 8.1–8.3 were added after Ārya Vimuktisena (and were likely composed taking his remarks as basis). Nor had anyone noticed the implications of this for the interpretation of *AA* 8.

77. Lethcoe, "Some Notes," pp. 499–511; see especially her conclusions on pp. 510–11.

78. Ibid., pp. 503–4. See Conze, *Large Sūtra*, for the English translation of the *Large PP Sūtra* with *AA* subtopic headings 1.1e.7–10, 1.10.8.c–d, 3.1–3, 3.5, and 8.1–8.3 inserted in the sūtra, in accord with *rP*, on pp. 48, 199–200, 298–99, 653–54. The sūtra passages corresponding to all those *AA* subtopics are found in *rP* and are missing in all Chinese translations of the 25,000-verse *PP* sūtra.

79. The unrevised 25,000-verse *PP* sūtra is extant in its entirety only in Chinese and Tibetan translation, not in Sanskrit. Hence the importance of determining whether the passages missing in all Chinese translations are also missing in the Tibetan translation or not.

80. Again, *PP* passages 8.1–8.3 are missing in all versions of the 25,000-verse *PP* sūtra except *rP*, but are found in all extant editions of *rP* in Sanskrit and Tibetan translation.

81. Pk 5188, fols. 61-3-1 to 61-3-2.

82. Conze, *PP Literature*, p. 37.

83. "ca-śabdopāttā mārgajñatādayo 'pi prāg uktāḥ," in *Abhisamayālaṃkāra-vṛtti*, ed. Amano, 1983, p. 4 near bottom. For Tibetan, see *Abhisamayālaṃkāra-Sphuṭārthā*, ed. Amano, 1975, p. 267 bottom.

84. The Sanskrit term that usually does the duty Haribhadra wants *ca* to do is *ādi*, meaning "etc." If the *AA*'s author had meant to say what Haribhadra interprets him as saying, he would more likely have used *ādi:* making *sarvākārajñatādi* or some equivalent.

85. Conze, *Large Sūtra,* pp. 121–23, 152–60, 315–17, 580–83, 654–56.

86. "Saptatriṃśadbodhipakṣā (etc. to)... sarvākārajñatā mārgajñatā sarvajñatā vā ime khalu subhute anāsravāḥ sarvadharmā. . . ." Conze, *Mahāprajñāpāramitā Sūtra*, sec. 8.1.; translated in Conze, *Large Sūtra*, p. 653 and by me in section 2.a above.

87. Ruegg, *Literature of the Madhyamaka School*, p. 102.

88. Dharmamitra, *Prasphuṭapadā*, Pk 5194, fols. 108-2-3 to 108-2-4.

89. The prayer at the end of the *Āloka* appears in *Abhisamayālaṃkāra-Āloka,* ed. Wogihara, p. 994; Haribhadra's explication of four *kāya*s in the same text appears at pp. 914–26.

90. *Abhisamayālaṃkāra-Sphuṭārthā,* ed. Amano, 1975, pp. 262–97; *Saṃcaya-gāthā-pañjikā subhodini,* Pk 5190, 269-3-3. Dharmamitra's own *AA* commentary will be discussed in chapter 11 below.

91. Passages *rP* 8.1–8.3 were added to the *PP* sūtra, we believe, no earlier than the late eighth century, quite possibly by Haribhadra himself, while the *AA* was composed sometime between the fourth and the early sixth centuries.

92. Conze, *Mahāprajñāpāramitā Sūtra,* sec. 8.4. For Conze's English translation of the passage, see Conze, *Large Sūtra,* pp. 573–76; idem, *Gilgit Manuscript,* pp. 164–67; Tibetan translation in *rP,* Pk 731, fols. 134-5-3 to 137-2-4.

93. Conze, *Mahāprajñāpāramitā Sūtra,* sec. 8.5; idem, *Large Sūtra,* pp. 576–643, esp. pp. 578–87; idem, *Gilgit Manuscript,* pp. 167–243; Tibetan: Pk 731, pp. 137-2-4 to 187-3-3, especially pp. 139-1-1 to 145-5-5.

94. Conze, *Large Sūtra,* pp. 578ff.

95. Ibid., pp. 580–87.

96. See chapter 3 of this book above, and section 2.b.5 of this chapter on lists of Buddha dharmas in various versions of the *Large PP Sūtra.*

97. Conze, *Large Sūtra,* pp. 583–87.

98. Ibid., pp. 576ff., in which the Buddha surveys the universe and describes his observation of countless bodhisattvas going out in all directions and entering into all realms of beings to carry out activities for their benefit. The *AA*'s author, interpreting the textual material in *PP* passage 8.5 as a basis for the Yogācāra concept of *nairmāṇikakāya,* appears to have designated the activities of the bodhisattvas in passage 8.5 as activities of manifestations of Buddhahood (*nirmāṇa, AA* v. 8.33).

99. The reader may wish at this point to review the translation of *AA* 8 verses in chapter 6 of this book, to see the pattern described here in the *AA* verses translated there.

100. *PP* passages 8.4–8.5: Conze, *Large Sutra,* pp. 573–643. The *AA*'s internal structure, and its pattern of aligning Yogācāra concepts to *PP* passages will be further detailed in the next chapter.

101. As noted at the beginning of this chapter, the *AA* sometimes superimposed schema for the Buddhist path onto the *PP,* schema that must have been an accepted part of Mahāyāna thought during the period of the *AA*'s composition, but may not have been prominent in the earlier period when its *PP* sūtra text basis was formed. Some of these schema are clearly Yogācāra. For example, the similes for the twenty-two types of *bodhicitta* are not mentioned within the *PP* sūtra. *AA* verses 1.18–1.20 superimpose them over the *PP* (Conze, *Large Sūtra,* pp. 46–53), and a similar list is found in the *MSA* (verses 4.14–4.20), a Yogācāra work. Conze has noted other places in the *AA* where Yogācāra ideas are superimposed over the *PP* material (*PP Literature,* pp. 102–4). But nowhere is this more evident than in *AA* chapter 8.

102. Conze, *PP Literature,* p. 103; Dutt, *Mahāyāna Buddhism,* p. 155; La Vallée Poussin, *Siddhi,* pp. 790–91; Obermiller, *Analysis of the Abhisamayālaṃkāra,* pp. 11–12.

103. If the *AA* did teach four *kāyas* as Haribhadra understood them, then its author would have been significantly reinterpreting the term *svābhāvikakāya* in particular, giving it a meaning different from that found in Yogācāra texts. See chapters 4 and 5 of this book on *svābhāvikakāya* in Yogācāra, and chapter 10 below on Haribhadra's interpretation.

104. *Abhisamayālaṃkāra-vṛtti,* Pk 5185, on the *PP* textual basis of *svābhāvikakāya*:

fols. 92-5-6ff., 98-4-6 to 98-4-7, on *sāmbhogikakāya*: fols. 96-2-5ff., 97-4-5ff., and 98-4-6 to 98-4-7, on *nairmāṇikakāya* and *karma:* fols. 98-5-1ff., 99-1-4ff. See also remarks in sections 2.b.3 and 2.b.4 above on Ārya Vimuktisena's identification of *PP* passage 8.5 as the source of the *AA*'s teaching on *svābhāvikakāya* and *sāmbhogikakāya*. In fols. 98-5-1ff., Ārya Vimuktisena explains first that *nairmāṇikakāya* is the infinite assemblage of manifestations by *dharmakaya-phalaṃ* (resultant *dharmakāya*, Buddhahood) to work for beings in the ten directions. Then he quotes and paraphrases *PP* passages 8.4 and 8.5 to show that the bodhisattvas described in those passages are such manifestations, and that their activities are therefore the activities of *dharmakaya-phalaṃ*, Buddhahood, carried out by its embodiment in manifestations *(nairmāṇikakāya)*. All of this will be discussed in greater detail in chapter 9 of this book.

105. As far as we know, Haribhadra was the first to revise this interpretation by newly proposing that the *AA* taught not three but four *kāyas*.

Chapter 8. Internal Evidence that *Abhisamayālaṃkāra* Chapter 8 Teaches the Three Yogācāra *Kāyas*

1. Conze, *Large Sutra,* pp. 573–643. Conze gave numbers to each of the sections of the *Large PP Sūtra* in correspondence with each of the topics of the *Abhisamayālaṃkāra.* He did this based upon the *AA* topic headings as they were inserted into the revised 25,000-verse *PP* sūtra *(rP)*. As concluded in the previous chapter, based on the textual evidence, *rP* was not composed until after the *AA*. And *rP* passages 8.1–8.3, which were not part of the *PP* sūtra when the *AA* was composed, cannot be the textual bases for the *AA*'s eighth chapter. So we are left with the *PP* passages now inappropriately numbered "8.4" and "8.5" as the actual scriptural basis for *AA* chapter 8. Had Conze known all this, he probably would have just designated those two passages together as "8," i.e., as the complete *PP* basis of *AA* chapter 8.

2. On this, see chapter 3 of this book.

3. Conze, *Large Sutra*, pp. 580–83, 654–56. See also chapter 7 of this book, sections 2.b.5–6.

4. See, for example, Conze, *Large Sutra,* pp. 37–44. See also pp. 1–5.

5. Ibid., pp. 583–87, 657–65.

6. Ibid., pp. 576ff.

7. As opposed to the primary derivative forms frequently used by Western scholars in discussing the *trikāya* doctrine: *svabhāva(kāya), sambhoga(kāya), nirmāṇa(kāya)*. On this, see chapter 4, section 4, above.

8. *Abhisamayālaṃkāra-Sphuṭārthā,* ed. Amano, 1975, p. 16; *Abhisamayālaṃkāra-Sphuṭārthā,* ed. Amano, 1983, p. 5. I refer the reader also to chapter 6 of this book, where *AA* chapter 8 and related verses are presented and translated.

9. In the analysis of the grammar of *AA* v. 1.17 that follows, I was helped immeasurably by Ven. Ngawang Samten of the Tibetan Institute in Sarnath, Varanasi, who gave me much insightful feedback. In the analyses of the Sanskrit of the *AA* throughout this chapter, I was also greatly helped through conversations with Ven. Ngawang Samten, Professor Ram Śaṅkar Tripāṭhī of Varanasi Sanskrit University, and Professor Sempa Dorje of the

Tibetan Institute, through whom I developed much love for Sanskrit, and much appreciation for its complications. If there are any errors in my analysis of Sanskrit verses, they are certainly my own. If there is any wisdom, it is undoubtedly owed to these great scholars.

10. *Vṛttibhāṣya,* sDe dge mi, fol. 136a1.

11. Pk 5290, 118-1-3 to 4. *The Kāyatrayāvatāra-śāstra-vṛtti,* a commentary on *Nāgamitra's text,* is also extant in the Tibetan canon (Pk 5291). It is ascribed to Jñānacandra, a Yogācāra disciple of Dharmapāla, ca. 530–61 C.E. See Ruegg, *History of Madhyamaka Literature,* p. 56; and the appendix to Brown, "Buddha Nature," which lists Jñānacandra among the lineage of Yogācāra masters according to Hsuan Tsang.

12. *Abhisamayālaṃkāra-Sphuṭārthā,* ed. Amano, 1975, pp. 268–70; Āloka, ed. Wogihara, pp. 20–21, 914–16. Haribhadra's interpretation of *AA* 1.17 and chapter 8 will discussed in more detail in chapter 10 of this book. A brief summary of his interpretation of *AA* v. 1.17 is provided here for purposes of comparison in establishing the correct interpretation.

13. *Abhisamayālaṃkāra-Sphuṭārthā,* ed. Amano, 1975, p. 14.

14. Ibid., pp. 14–16. AA vv. 1.5–1.16 list the topics for each of the eight substantive chapters, and then present the title of the chapter at or near the end of each corresponding verse. AA v. 1.6 gives "Sarvākārajñatā" as the title of chapter 1, v. 1.9 gives "Mārgajñatā" as the title of chapter 2, v. 1.11 gives "Sarvajñatā" as the title of chapter 3, v. 1.13 gives "Sarvākārābhisambodha" as the title for chapter 4, v. 1.15 gives "Mūrdhābhisamaya," "Anupūrvika[abhisamaya]," and "Ekakṣaṇābhisambodha" as the titles of chapters 5, 6, and 7 respectively. All these terms correspond to the names of chapters as given in AA vv. 1.3–1.4. Then, in v. 1.17, the term *dharmakāya* appears, which corresponds to the title for chapter 8 as given in v. 1.4. According to our three-*kāya* understanding of v. 1.17, "Dharmakāya" is in fact the title of chapter 8, referring to resultant *dharmakāya (*Buddhahood as a whole), which comprises the three *kāyas* plus enlightened activity *(kāritra).* According to Haribhadra's four-*kāya* interpretation of v. 1.17, the title of chapter 8 would be the only chapter title missing in vv. 1.5–1.17, the entire table of contents for the *AA.*

15. *Abhisamayālaṃkāra-Sphuṭārthā,* ed. Amano, 1975, pp. 14–16.

16. Ibid., p. 298.

17. Cf. gYag ston, *bLo gsal mgul rgyan,* fols. 1303b3–1304a1; Go ram pa bsod nams seng ge, *Yum don rab gsal,* fols. 309a2–b4. These great Tibetan scholars noticed this very pattern.

18. *Abhisamayālaṃkāra-Sphuṭārthā,* ed. Amano, 1975, p. 262.

19. Ibid., p. 264. I leave *dharmakāya* untranslated for the time being in *AA* v. 8.6, because Ārya Vimuktisena and Haribhadra would have glossed the term very differently. In Ārya Vimuktisena's understanding, it meant "embodiment of dharma[tā]," embodiment of reality in nondual realization *(prajñāpāramitā).* This is consistent with *Prajñāpāramitāsūtra* understanding, as we discussed in chapter 3 above. Ārya Vimuktisena's comments will be discussed in chapter 9 below. In Haribhadra's view, *dharmakāya* in verse 8.6 meant "body of dharmas," i.e., the collection of a Buddha's pure dharmas or gnoses per se, echoing Abhidharma descriptions of *dharmakāya* (cf. chapter 2 above) but adapted by Haribhadra to a Mādhyamika ontology of *samvṛtisatya.* This is discussed in chapter 10 below.

20. On this, see chapter 4, sections 2 and 3, above.

21. See Conze, *Large Sutra,* pp. 580–83, 654–56 for Conze's translation of the section of passage 8.5 in the 18,000-verse and 25,000-verse *PP* sūtras; it presents the list of Buddha dharmas upon which the list in *AA* vv. 8.2-8.6 is based. Such lists of undefiled Buddha dharmas

are common throughout the *Large PP Sūtra* (as discussed in chapter 7, section 2.b.5 of this book).

22. There is an intriguing passage in the *Mahāyānasamgraha, Msg* 10.3, which contains a phrase quite close in expression to *AA* 8.1 (ed. Lamotte, p. 84 Tib., p. 269 French). This section of the *Msg* discusses five special characteristics *(lakṣaṇas)* of the *dharmakāya*. The second characteristic of *dharmakāya* (*Msg* 10.3.2) is called *dkar po'i chos kyi rang bzhin gyi mtshan nyid* (the characteristic of being the nature of virtuous dharmas). The Tibetan term *rang bzhin* could have been a translation of either the Sanskrit term *svabhāva* (as Lamotte gives on p. 269), or, equally possible, the Sanskrit term *prakṛti.* If the original was *prakṛti,* the expression in *Msg* 10.3.2 could be reconstructed as: *śukladharma prakṛti-lakṣaṇa,* which is semantically close to the expression in *AA* v. 8.1 defining *svābhāvikakāya* as *dharmāḥ nirāsravāḥ . . . teṣāṃ prakṛti-lakṣanaḥ*. This expression in *Msg* 10.3.2 is not the primary definition of *svābhāvikakāya* in that text, but as part of a discussion on various characteristics of dharmakāya, it indicates how the *svābhāvikakāya/dharmakāya* is to be related to the undefiled dharmas phenomenally ascribed to Buddhahood. It is possible that the author of the *AA* modeled his v. 8.1 on *Msg* 10.3.2, or vice versa, or both drew from a similar pool of ideas. In any case, the *AA* author's project of relating *svābhāvikakāya* to the list of undefiled dharmas mentioned in *PP* passage 8.5 required him to make those dharmas part of the primary definition of *svābhāvikakāya,* apparently for the first time in Indian Buddhist literature.

23. *MSA* 9.60 *bhāṣya,* ed. Levi, p. 45; *Msg,* 10.1.1, ed. Lamotte, pp. 83 (Tib.), 266 (French); *Buddhabhūmivyākhyāna,* ed. Nishio, p. 125. See chapter 4, section 5, on inclusive and exclusive senses of *dharmakāya.* The inclusive sense refers to Buddhahood in its totality with all discernible aspects: all three *kāya*s, etc. The exclusive sense refers to just the first of the three *kāya*s, referred to in Yogācāra texts alternatively as *svābhāvikakāya* and *dharmakāya.*

24. *Abhisamayālaṃkāra-vṛtti,* Pk 5185, fols. 92-5-2 to 92-5-7. On Ārya Vimuktisena's interpretation of *AA* verses 8.1-8.6, see chapter 9 below.

25. *Abhisamayālaṃkāra-Sphuṭārthā,* ed. Amano, 1975, pp. 264–70; *Āloka,* ed. Wogihara, pp. 914–16. See also chapter 10 of this book.

26. Careful note must be made of the location of *iti* in *AA* verse 8.6 if verses 8.2–8.6 as a set are to be properly interpreted. In interpreting *AA* chapter 8, we rely primarily upon the Sanskrit text of the *AA,* not its Tibetan translation. For in some cases the Tibetan translation introduces its own special problems.

The Tibetan translation of *AA* verse 8.6, for example, misplaces the term *zhes* (Tibetan for *iti*) by putting it after, rather than before, *chos kyi sku* (Tibetan for *dharmakāya*). By doing so, the meaning in the Tibetan is shifted closer to the meaning which Haribhadra imputed to the verse. The final half of *AA verse 8.6 in Sanskrit reads: sarvākārajñatā ceti dharmakāyo 'bhidhīyate (iti* precedes *dharmakāyaḥ),* which can be glossed: "[the set of undefiled dharmas ending with] total omniscience: thus is *dharmakāya* denominated." As noted above, the Sanskrit says that *dharmakāya* is denominated in terms of the list of undefiled dharmas (total omniscience being the final item of the list). It does not say that *dharmakāya is* the set of conceptually differentiated dharmas.

The Tibetan translation, however, reads: "rnam pa thams cad mkhyen nyid dang / chos kyi sku zhes brjod pa yin" *(zhes* follows *chos kyi sku).* See *Abhisamayālaṃkāra-Sphuṭārthā,* ed. Amano, 1975, p. 265. This could be glossed: "[the set of undefiled dharmas ending with] total omniscience are called *dharmakāya.*" The Tibetan translation, then, seems to say that *dharmakāya* is the name for the set of undefiled dharmas! The Tibetan reformulates the syntax of the verse in such a way as to lend greater support to Haribhadra's interpretation of it, according to which the term *dharmakāya* refers to a fourth Buddha *kāya* consisting of the undefiled dharmas. Strictly speaking, however, the misplacement of *zhes* in the Tibetan constitutes a subtle mistranslation of the Sanskrit.

The *AA* was first translated into Tibetan by Vidyākaraprabhava and dPal brtsegs (eighth century C.E.) as a root text embedded within Haribhadra's *Sphuṭārthā.* The Tibetan translation of verse 8.6, then, may have been affected by Haribhadra's interpretation of that verse. On the problematics presented by the Tibetan translation of *AA* verse 8.6, see Makransky, "Controversy over Dharmakāya in Indo-Tibetan Buddhism," pp. 351–58, and chapter 12, section 2, of this book.

27. *Mahāyānasūtrālaṃkāra* verse 21.45 *bhāṣya,* ed. Levi, p. 184. *Mahāyānasaṃgraha-upanibandhana,* sDe dge ri, fol. 282b1-b5.

28. *Mahāyānasaṃgraha,* ed. Lamotte, pp. 36, 39. *Mahāyānasūtrālaṃkāra,* verse 21.46, ed. Levi, p. 184. For other references on *araṇā* and *praṇidhijñāna* throughout Buddhist literature, see Lamotte's French translation of *Mahāyānasaṃgraha,* p. 53*.

29. *Mahāyānasūtrālaṃkāra,* ed. Levi pp. 36, 39; *Ratnagotravibhāga,* verses 4.42–4.52, ed. Johnston, pp. 104–6; Takasaki, *A Study,* pp. 364–67.

30. *Mahāyānasūtrālaṃkāra,* ed. Levi, pp. 36–37, 46; *Mahāyānasaṃgraha,* ed. Lamotte, pp. 273–74. Cf. Conze, *Prajñāpāramitā Literature,* pp. 102–3.

31. *Abhisamayālaṃkāra-Sphuṭārthā,* ed. Amano, 1975, p. 276.

32. On this, see the final section of chapter 3 above.

33. *Mahāyānasūtrālaṃkāra,* ed. Levi, p. 185.

34. The verse is: "satpauruṣyaṃ prapadyante tvāṃ dṛṣṭvā sarvadehinaḥ / dṛṣṭamātrāt-prasādasya vidhāyaka namo 'stu te." *MSA* 21.49, ed. Levi, p. 185; quoted in *Mahāyānasaṃgraha,* ed. Lamotte, p. 295; commented upon in *Mahāyānasaṃgraha-upanibandhana,* sDe dge ri, fol. 283b3–5.

35. *Ratnagotravibhāga* verses 3.1–3.3, ed. Johnston, p. 91; Takasaki, *A Study,* pp. 336–37. For the *Ratnagotravibhāga*'s explication of *sāmbhogikakāya* and *nairmāṇikakāya,* see *RGV,* ed. Johnston, pp. 79–90, and Takasaki, *A Study,* pp. 324ff.

36. *RGV,* ed. Johnston, p. 97: "dvātriṃśallakṣaṇāḥ kāye darśanāhlādakā guṇāḥ / nirmāṇa-dharmasaṃbhogarūpakāyadvayāśritāḥ." Takasaki, *A Study,* p. 349. In this particular verse, the term *rūpakāya,* standing in *tatpuruṣa* relation to *nirmāṇa* and *dharmasaṃbhoga* dictates that the latter two terms be in *kṛt* rather than *taddhita* form.

37. With the important exception of the *Abhisamayālaṃkāra,* formulative explanations of *sāmbhogikakāya* in Yogācāra literature follow the pattern set by the *Mahāyānasūtrālaṃkāra* and its *bhāṣya* on verse 9.60, which was quoted earlier: The *sāmbhogikakāya* is the embodiment of the Buddhas that appears in a pure realm before the circles of assembly to share its enjoyment of dharma. Upon introducing *sāmbhogikakāya* and defining it, no mention of marks and signs is ever made. Cf. *Mahāyānasūtrālaṃkāra* 9.60–9.66 and commentaries; *Mahāyānasaṃgraha* 10.2 and commentaries; *Buddhabhumisūtra* and *vyākhyāna,* ed. Nishio, pp. 125–26; *Ratnagotravibhāga,* chapter 2, verses 38–61, with the *vyākhyāna* introducing the verses.

38. As mentioned in chapter 3 of this book. The list of thirty-two marks and eighty

signs in PP 8.5 appears in Conze, *Gilgit Manuscript,* pp. 49–53, 176–80; idem, *Large* Sutra, pp. 583–87, 657–65. The equivalent list, with some variations, is presented in passage 8.5 of all editions of the *Large PP Sūtra* available in Sanskrit and Tibetan.

39. Cf. *Mahāyānasūtrālaṃkāra* verse 9.60 with *bhāṣya; Mahāyānasaṃgraha* 10.1.2.

40. *Abhisamayālaṃkāra-Sphuṭārthā,* ed. Amano, 1975, pp. 276–84. For English translation, see Conze, *Abhisamayālaṃkāra,* pp. 98–102.

41. *Vṛttibhāṣya,* sDe dge mi, fol. 136b4–b5.

42. See chapter 6 of this book for summary of *AA* vv. 8.13–8.32.

43. Conze, *Mahāprajñāpāramitā Sūtra,* secs. 8.4 and 8.5. *Large Sutra,* pp. 573–76 for passage 8.4, pp. 576–652 for passage 8.5. Although not identical in every term or, where there are lists of dharma terms, in the precise order of the terms, substantially equivalent passages for 8.4 and 8.5 occur in all editions of the *Large PP Sūtra* available to me in Sanskrit and Tibetan (see chapter 7, section 2.b.4 above). The same can be said of all sections of *PP* passages referred to below.

44. Conze, *Mahāprajñāpāramitā Sūtra,* section 8.5.2; idem, *Large Sutra,* pp. 580–87.

45. Conze, *Mahāprajñāpāramitā Sūtra,* sections 8.5.3–8.5.27; idem, *Large Sutra,* pp. 587–643.

46. *Abhisamayālaṃkāra-Sphuṭārthā,* ed. Amano, 1975, pp. 290–92.

47. This needs to be pointed out, because Haribhadra, unlike Ārya Vimuktisena, ascribed *AA* v. 8.33 alone to *nairmāṇikakāya,* and vv. 8.34–8.40 to a fourth *kāya* that he called "gnosis *dharmakāya*" *(jñānātmaka dharmakāya),* making different subjects of vv. 8.33 and 8.34. This is mentioned below. The Sanskrit does not support Haribhadra.

48. The distinctive Yogācāra sixfold analysis of Buddhahood is discussed in chapter 4, section 3, of this book.

49. That the first of these six categories is associated with both the concept and the name of *svābhāvikakāya* in Yogācāra literature is argued in chapter 4, section 3, above.

50. Chapter 4, section 4, above.

51. See, for example, Conze, *Large Sutra,* pp. 37–44.

52. Haribhadra's interpretation of these verses has been summarized in the last section of chapter 6 of this book.

53. It is my hope that this book may finally put an official end to this controversy in favor of Ārya Vimuktisena. The controversy over interpretation of *AA* 8 began with Haribhadra's alternative interpretation of the text approximately twelve hundred years ago.

54. Differing perspectives on those key verses have been presented briefly in chapters 6 and portions of this chapter. They will be further discussed in chapters 10–12.

55. Tibetan exegetes of AA 8 were faced with special hermeneutic problems created by the Tibetan translation of the text. This is discussed in Makransky, "Controversy over Dharmakāya in Indo-Tibetan Buddhism," pp. 351–58 and below in chapter 12, section 2.

Chapter 9. Ārya Vimuktisena on Gnoseology and Buddhology in the *Abhisamayālaṃkāra*

1. The first chapter of the *Abhisamayālaṃkāra-vṛtti* was published in an edited Sanskrit edition by C. Pensa, *L'Abhisamayālaṃkāra-vṛtti di Ārya-Vimuktisena* (Rome: Is.M.E.O.,

1967). The rest of the Sanskrit manuscript has not been made available. Chapters 2 through 8 are available only in Tibetan translation, on the basis of which my analysis of chapters 7 and 8 below are made. I have consulted both the Peking and sDe dge editions.

2. Ruegg, "Ārya and Bhadanta Vimuktisena," pp. 306–7; Ruegg, *Literature of the Madhyamaka School,* p. 86.

3. *Abhisamayālaṃkāra-Āloka,* ed. Wogihara, p. 1.

4. *AA* v. 1.16, ed. Amano, 1975, p. 16; *Sphuṭārthā,* ed. Amano, 1985, p. 138; *Āloka,* ed. Wogihara, pp. 909–11; *Abhisamayālaṃkāra-vṛtti,* Pk 5185, fol. 91-5-1 to 92-4-5.

5. Obermiller, "The Doctrine of *Prajñā-pāramitā,*" p. 71; Conze, *Prajñāpāramitā Literature,* p. 106; Galloway, "Sudden Enlightenment in the *Abhisamayālaṃkāra,* the *Lalitavistara,* and the *Śikṣāsamuccaya,*" pp. 140–46. Galloway's paper treats *AA* chapter 7 on *ekakṣaṇa abhisambodha* (one-moment comprehension) as a "small treatise on sudden enlightenment." Since a Buddha is already enlightened, Galloway seems to be assuming, in accord with Haribhadra, that the *ekakṣaṇa abhisambodha* is the realization of a bodhisattva just prior to Buddhahood.

6. *Abhisamayālaṃkāra-vṛtti,* Pk 5185, fols. 91-5-3, 92-1-5 to 92-1-6, 92-2-2, and 92-3-2.

7. Quote from *PP* sūtra: Conze, *Mahāprajñāpāramitā Sūtra,* beginning of section 7.1; idem, *Gilgit Manuscript,* p. 11; idem, *Large Sutra,* p. 556.

8. *Abhisamayālaṃkāra-Sphuṭārthā,* ed. Amano, 1975, p. 254.

9. *Abhisamayālaṃkāra-vṛtti,* Pk 5185, fols. 91-5-1 to 91-5-7.

10. Cf. Conze, *Large Sutra,* p. 557: "Having made that gift common to all beings, he dedicates it to the supreme enlightenment. But he dedicates it in such a way that, when dedicating, he does not review a sign, i.e. 'this is the gift, to him I give, (by) that I give, or who is it that gives'. . . . And why? Because all such entities are empty. . . ."

11. *Abhisamayālaṃkāra-Sphuṭārthā,* ed. Amano, 1975, p. 256.

12. *Abhisamayālaṃkāra-vṛtti,* Pk 5185, fols. 92-1-3 to 92-1-5.

13. *Abhisamayālaṃkāra-Sphuṭārthā,* ed. Amano, 1975, p. 256.

14. Ibid., p. 258.

15. *Abhisamayālaṃkāra-vṛtti,* Pk 5185, fols. 92-2-2 to 92-2-5.

16. See Conze, *Large Sutra,* pp. 565–71.

17. *Abhisamayālaṃkāra-vṛtti,* Pk 5185, fol. 92-2-6 to 92-2-8.

18. *Gilgit Manuscript,* p. 24: "yasya svabhāva nāsti tasya lakṣaṇaṃ nāsti, yasya lakṣaṇaṃ nāsti tad ekalakṣaṇaṃ yaduta- alakṣaṇaṃ" [That which has no self-existence has no identity. That which has no identity has just one identity, i.e. no identity]. Corresponds to Conze, *Large Sutra,* p. 565, par. 2.

19. Conze, *Mahāprajñāpāramitā Sūtra,* section 7.4; idem, *Gilgit Manuscript,* p. 33; idem, *Large Sutra,* p. 571.

20. *Abhisamayālaṃkāra-vṛtti,* 5185, fol. 92-3-6 to 92-4-2.

21. Conze, *Mahāprajñāpāramitā Sūtra,* end of section 7.4; idem, *Gilgit Manuscript,* p. 33 (Sanskrit), p. 163 (English); idem, *Large Sutra,* pp. 571–72.

22. Apparently, then, Ārya Vimuktisena understood the *PP* sūtra passages that correspond to single-moment comprehension (*AA* 7) to be describing bodhisattvas who have completed the path, and are therefore Buddhas or manifestations of Buddhahood. Indeed, the sūtra passages in question concern how a bodhisattva "fulfills" all the perfections and

qualities of a Buddha through his or her perfection of wisdom. They could plausibly be read either as a description of a Buddha's knowledge (as Ārya Vimuktisena did) or as a description of a bodhisattva's knowledge near the end of the path (as Haribhadra did). The *Abhisamayālaṃkāra*'s seventh chapter, which corresponds to those sūtra passages, may however not be so ambiguous. Its first verse opens with a key phrase: "It should be known that the comprehension of the Sage is of a single moment. . . ." Throughout *AA* chapter 8 on resultant *dharmakāya,* "Sage" (muni) in each key verse explicitly designates the Buddha (vv. 8.1, 8.12, 8.33). Ārya Vimuktisena, aware of that pattern, read *AA* chapters 7 and 8 together as discussions of a Buddha's gnosis and embodiment, respectively.

The *PP* passages that are the basis for *AA* chapter 8, like those for *AA* chapter 7, appear to be talking about bodhisattvas and their activities. The *AA*'s author in chapter 8 also blurs the distinction between Buddha and bodhisattva, understanding bodhisattva activities in *PP* 8.5ff. as manifestations of Buddhahood *(nairmāṇikakāya).* On this, see chapter 8, section 5, of this book.

23. See chapter 5, section 3, above.

24. See chapters 4 and 5, above.

25. *Abhisamayālaṃkāra-Sphuṭārthā,* ed. Amano, 1975, pp. 2–3.

26. On the "Yogācāra-Mādhyamika" classification of late Indian Buddhist scholars by Tibetans, see chapter 10, section 1, below.

27. "Khyod kyis skad cig gis ni shes bya thugs su chud." Candrakīrti, *Madhyamakāvatāra,* ed. La Vallée Poussin, p. 356. The autocommentary specifies the knowledge as knowledge of all *(thams cad mkhyen pa'i ye shes).*

28. He does so based upon his reading of the *Daśabhūmikasūtra,* a portion of the Avatamsaka literature central to Yogācāra formulations of Buddhahood discussed in chapters 4 and 5, above.

29. The *PP* sūtra quote appears in Conze, *Mahāprajñāpāramitā Sūtra,* section 1.2.3; idem, *Large Sutra,* p. 63. Ārya Vimuktisena's comment is *Abhisamayālaṃkāra-vṛtti,* Pk 5185, fol. 16-3-4 to 16-3-5.

30. *Abhisamayālaṃkāra-vṛtti,* Pk 5185, fol. 91-1-4 to 91-2-4, corresponding to Conze, *Large Sutra,* pp. 551–52. On *buddhānusmṛti* in the *PP* and several other Mahāyāna sūtras, and its implications for Mahāyāna formulations of Buddhahood, see chapter 3, note 15, above, and chapter 13, section 2.c, below.

31. On all this, see chapter 4, sections 2–4, above.

32. *Abhisamayālaṃkāra-vṛtti,* Pk 5185, fols. 92-4-6, together with 100-3-7.

33. Cf. Conze, *Large Sutra,* pp. 580–87; idem, *Gilgit Manuscript,* pp. 46ff., 172ff.

34. *Abhisamayālaṃkāra-vṛtti,* Pk 5185, fols. 92-4-8 to 92-5-2.

35. On "essence" *(svabhāva),* meaning purified thusness/nonconceptual gnosis, as the first of the six Yogācāra categories of Buddhahood, see chapter 4, section 3, above.

36. On this, see chapter 5, section 3. Ārya Vimuktisena's parallels to Yogācāra commentators get quite specific. His etymology for *svabhāva* of *svābhāvikakāya—svabhāva* (essence) is that which is not made (Tib., *bcos ma ma yin pa;* Skt., *akṛtima*)—is the same expression used by the Yogācāra commentator Asvabhāva (ca. sixth century) in his etymological explanation of *svābhāvikakāya* as taught in *Mahāyānasaṃgraha* 10.1 (a principal early source of three-*kāya* theory: *Msg upanibandhana,* sDe dge ri, fol. 275a3). Cf. gYag ston, *bLo gsal mgul rgyan,* fol. 1274b2-4.

37. *Abhisamayālaṃkāra-vṛtti,* Pk 5185, fols. 92-5-2 to 92-5-6

38. Ibid., fols. 92-5-6 to 92-5-7. The Tibetan reads: "rkyen phyis pas chos nyid kyi sku zhes bya ste / gzhan du chos rnams kyi sku ni chos kyi sku zhes bya ba yin pa'i phyir ngo bo nyid bdag par 'gyur ba [sDe dge: ngo bo nyid bkag par 'gyur ba] dang / sphyod pa'i don yin pa'i phyir 'dus byas su 'gyur ba'i nyes pa yod do / de la sku zhes bjrod pa ni sngon gyi gnas skabs gyi rjes su 'brangs nas nye bar btags pa yin par bya'o." "Dag par 'gyur ba" in the Peking edition is most probably a scribal error. I chose the sDe dge reading "bkag par 'gyur ba" in the translation above, because it makes sense (whereas the Peking reading does not), and because "bkag par 'gyur ba" is what appears in Bhadanta Vimuktisena's commentary (also only available in Tibetan translation, Pk 5186, fol. 178-2-2). Major Tibetan commentators such as gYag ston and Tsong kha pa also used that reading.

39. *Abhisamayālaṃkāra-Sphuṭārthā,* ed. Amano, 1975, p. 256.

40. Recall passages from the 8,000-verse *PP* sūtra quoted above in chapter 3 of this book, which semantically connect the terms *dharmatā* and *dharmakāya,* the latter being the nondual knowledge of a Buddha that sees through dharmas to their real nature *(dharmatā).* "The Bhagavan has said that all dharmas are like a dream. And those who do not know all dharmas to be like a dream as explained by the Tathāgata, they adhere to the Tathāgatas through [their] nominal body *(nāmakāya)* or physical body *(rupakāya),* and imagine there is a coming or going of the Tathāgatas. . . . But those who know all dharmas to be like a dream as they really are, as explained by the Tathāgata, they do not imagine a coming or going of any dharma, . . . they know the Tathāgata by means of his real nature *(dharmatayā).* . . . Those who know the real nature *(dharmatā)* of the Tathāgata, they practice close to full enlightenment; they practice the perfection of wisdom." And: "The Tathāgatas are *dharmakāya,* and the real nature of dharmas *(dharmatā)* does not come or go. Precisely so, there is no coming or going of the Tathāgatas." And the *Vajracchedikā:* "Those who saw me by my form, those who followed me by my voice, have been engaged in wrong practice: me those beings will not see. From the dharma are Buddhas seen. Indeed the Guides are *dharmakāya.* But the real nature of things *(dharmatā)* cannot be discriminated, and so must not be discriminated."

41. I take Tibetan *spyod pa'i don* here as translation for *caryārtha. Carya* derives from the verbal root *car,* which carries primary meanings of to move, go, walk, roam about, etc., and a host of secondary meanings derived from them: to behave, act, be engaged in, practice, etc. (Monier-Williams, *Sanskrit-English Dictionary,* s.v. *"Car"*). The primary meanings make most sense in this context. Ārya Vimuktisena is saying that if *svābhāvikakāya/dharmakāya* were to be defined simply as the collection of impermanent dharmas listed in verses 8.2–8.5, it would become a moving, shifting, fluctuating collection of phenomena—not the core realization of Buddhahood as *PP* and Yogācāra traditions understood it. The dharmas listed in vv. 8.2–8.5 are to be understood as a phenomenal description of a Buddha's realization, not its defining essence.

42. In Indian commentaries on the *AA* (those by Ārya Vimuktisena, Bhadanta Vimuktisena, Dharmamitra, Ratnākaraśānti, Abhayākaragupta), the word *kāya* in *dharmakāya* is etymologized in one or more of three ways: *kāya* = *āśraya:* support, basis (*dharmakāya* = the support of all excellent qualities, dharmas); kāya = *śarīra:* body *(dharmakāya* = embodiment of *dharmatā); or kāya* = *saṃcaya:* collection or accumulation (*dharmakāya* = collection of excellent qualities, dharmas). The term *kāya* in *rūpakāya,* in both pre-Mahāyāna and Mahāyāna texts, has generally meant *śarīra,* "body" or "physical manifestation."

43. See chapter 5, sections 3 and 4, for discussion of "moving" and "unmoving" knowledge in Yogācāra texts.

44. In contradistinction to Ārya Vimuktisena, I believe texts like the *Prajñāpāramitā* sūtras quoted in chapter 3 above, by reinterpreting *dharmakāya* as *dharmatākāya,* implicitly reinterpreted the meaning of *kāya* as well, from "body" in the sense of "collection," to "body" in the sense of "embodiment." For that reason, I believe *dharmakāya* in such texts is well translated as "embodiment of *dharmatā*" or "embodiment of dharma" (where "dharma" refers to nondual realization of *dharmatā*). On this, see chapter 3, above, especially note 12.

45. Cf. Conze, *Large Sutra,* p. 575: "Here the Bodhisattva who practices the perfection of wisdom gives gifts . . . ; to all he gives gifts after he has formed the notion of nondifferentiation. And why? Because he has cognized all dharmas as being just one undifferentiatedness. Having given gifts without differentiating, he becomes the recipient of an undifferentiated dharma, i.e. omniscience [of a Buddha]." Conze, *Gilgit Manuscript,* p. 38 with note 4-4 on the Tibetan.

46. *Śuddhamati,* Pk 5199, fol. 281.5.2: "de dag mtshan nyid kyi dbye ba ni rgyu'i gnas skabs kyi rjes su 'brangs nas kun rdzob yin no / spros pas mchog go [sDe dge: chog go]." Referring to the collection of undefiled dharmas, Ratnākaraśānti says: "The differentiation of their characteristics, done in accord with the causal state [of the bodhisattva], is conventional." The list of undefiled dharmas does not capture the undifferentiated nature of a Buddha's ultimate awareness, but it provides a means of limited comprehension for those limited to conventional truth, modeled on the mental factors of the bodhisattva path that lead to its attainment.

47. There is further specific correspondence between Ārya Vimuktisena's comments on dharmakāya and Yogācāra tradition. The etymology which Ārya Vimuktisena presents for *dharmakāya* (dharma understood as an abbreviation for *dharmatā*), is not only a *Prajñāpāramitā* derivation but a popular mode of explanation in the Yogācāra tradition as well. This etymology was used by Yogācāra commentators to show how the term *dharmakāya* in its exclusive sense is a synonym for *svābhāvikakāya,* since *dharmatā* and *svabhāva* both connote the unconditioned, final nature of things. Asvabhāva, the sixth-century Yogācāra scholar, presents the *dharma-dharmatā* etymology for *dharmakāya* in order to explain why *Msg* 10.1 identifies *svābhāvikakāya* (immediately upon introducing it) as *dharmakāya.* In fact, Asvabhāva's comments on this etymology are so close to Ārya Vimuktisena's that it is likely that either one of the commentators modeled his remarks on the other or each drew from a common textual basis (*Msg Upanibandhana,* sDe dge ri, fol. 275a3). The *Kāyatraya-vṛtti* by Jñānacandra (ca. late sixth century), also presents the *dharmatā* etymology for *dharmakāya* early in its exposition (Pk 5291, fol. 122-1-1). The same etymology appears in Sthiramati's commentary on the *Madhyāntavibhāga,* v. 4.14, ed. Yamaguchi, p. 191.

48. *Abhisamayālaṃkāra-vṛtti,* Pk 5185, fols. 92-5-7 to 96-2-1. Tsong kha pa (Legs bshad gser 'phreng, fols. 233b6 to 239a5), points out the portions of *AA* commentaries where some of the twenty-one undefiled dharmas were discussed prior to chapter 8 (principally under the first topic of *AA* chapter 4, "Ākāra"). He also shows the relation between Haribhadra's commentary on several of the undefiled dharmas (which parallels Ārya Vimuktisena's comments) and their descriptions in the *Abhidharmakośa* and *Abhidharmasamuccaya.*

49. Cf. Conze, *Large Sutra,* pp. 596, 575.

50. *Abhisamayālaṃkāra-vṛtti,* Pk 5185, fol. 96-1-2 to 96-1-7.

51. See chapter 5, section 3, above.

52. See chapter 4, section 6, above for explanation of these terms.

53. Ārya Vimuktisena quotes the *PP* text basis for *sarvākārajñatā* at Pk 5185, fol. 96-1-6. His quote corresponds to part of *PP* passage 8.5.2 in the unrevised 25,000-verse *PP* sūtra, Pk 731, fol. 143-2-2; revised 25,000-verse *PP* sūtra (*rP*), Pk 5188, fol. 11-5-1; 18,000-verse *PP* sūtra, Pk 732, fol. 151; and 100,000-verse *PP* sūtra, Pk 730, fol. 230-2-2.

54. On this, see chapter 7, section 2.b.3, of this book.

55. *Abhisamayālaṃkāra-vṛtti,* Pk 5185, fols. 94-5-1ff., 94-5-3ff., 96-2-1 to 96-2-5.

56. Ibid., fol. 96-2-5 to 96-2-6: "sku des sangs rgyas bchom ldan 'das byang chub sems dpa' chen pos chen po la zhugs pa rnams dang thabs cig tu kha na ma tho ba med pa theg pa chen po'i chos kyi longs spyod kyi dga' ba dang bde ba so sor myong bar mdzad pa yin no." On definitions of *sāmbhogikakāya* in Yogācāra texts, see chapter 4, section 4, and chapter 5, section 2, above.

57. Ibid., Pk 5185, fols. 96-2-8 to 98-4-6. Ārya Vimuktisena's quotes and paraphrases are all drawn from *PP* passage 8.5.2: Conze, *Mahāprajñāpāramitā Sūtra,* section 8.5.2; idem, *Gilgit Manuscript,* pp. 46–53; idem, *Large Sutra*, pp. 580–87.

58. *Abhisamayālaṃkāra-vṛtti,* fol. 98-4-6 to 98-4-7.

59. For further discussion of this, see chapter 7, section 2.b.3 above.

60. The reader may want to refer to chapter 6 of this book in conjunction with the remarks below. Ārya Vimuktisena's understanding of *AA* vv. 8.33–8.40 on the activity of *nairmāṇikakāya* is in line with our own, presented in chapter 8, section 5, of this book.

61. *Abhisamayālaṃkāra-vṛtti,* Pk 5185, 98-5-1 to 98-5-2.

62. Ibid., fol. 98-5-1 to 98-5-7; for translation of *AA* vv. 8.33–8.40, see chapter 6, above.

63. *Abhisamayālaṃkāra-vṛtti,* Pk 5185, fols. 98-5-3 to 98-5-5, 99-1-4 to 100-3-4.

64. Ārya Vimuktisena (*Abhisamayālaṃkāra-vṛtti,* Pk 5185, fol. 98-4-7) identifies *PP* passage 8.5 (which describes extensive activities done by bodhisattvas throughout the realms of beings) as "the portion of sūtra that teaches the activity of *nairmāṇikakāya*." At fols. 98-5-1 to 98-5-2, he defines *nairmāṇikakāya* as the manifestations *(nirmāṇāḥ)* into all realms of beings by which the resultant *dharmakāya* (Buddhahood) carries out its activities. At fol. 98-5-7 he says *AA* vv. 34–40 are taught to answer the question: "How many kinds of activity has the [resultant] *dharmakāya?*" In sum, he interprets *AA* vv. 33–40 together as a teaching on the activities of resultant *dharmakāya* (*dharmakāya* in the inclusive sense) carried out by means of its limitless manifestations: *nairmāṇikakāya.*

65. Here is verse 1.17 as it appears in the first chapter of Ārya Vimuktisena's commentary: "ngo bo nyid longs rdzogs bcas dang / de bzhin gzhan pa sprul pa ni / chos sku mdzad pa dang bcas pa / rnam pa bzhir ni yang dag brjod." At the end of his comments on *AA* 8 (Pk 5185, fols. 100-3-5 to 100-3-6), Ārya Vimuktisena explicitly identifies *dharmakāya (chos sku)* of *AA* v. 1.17 line 3 above with *dharmakāya* of v. 8.40, line 3, both understood as resultant *dharmakāya* (inclusive of all three *kāyas*): "ngo bo nyid longs spyod bcas dang / de bzhin gzhan pa sprul pa ni [*AA* v. 1.17a] / zhes bya ba **rnam pa gsum dang** / chos kyi sku yi phrin las 'di / rnam pa nyi shu bdun du bzhed [*AA* v. 8.40b] / ces bstan pa yin pa de bshad par rig par bya'o."

In a recent article ("Classification of the *Dharmakāya* Chapter," pp. 287–90), Hidenori Sakuma noticed that Bhadanta Vimuktisena, the *AA* commentator immediately following Ārya Vimuktisena, altered *AA* v. 1.17 in the first chapter of his commentary as follows (probably to remove any ambiguity that it teaches three *kāyas*): "ngo bo nyid longs rdzogs bcas dang / sprul pa dang ni de ltar gsum / mdzad pa dang bcas bshi ru brjod." Many centuries later, three supporters of Ārya Vimuktisena's three-*kāya* interpretation also provided a modified version of *AA* 1.17 that supports a three-*kāya* reading: Ratnākaraśānti (ca. eleventh century), Ratnakīrti (ca. eleventh century), Abhayākaragupta (ca. twelfth century). Sakuma assumed their version was based upon Bhadanta Vimuktasena's modification of the same verse, but actually it appears to have been based upon Ārya Vimuktisena's comment as quoted just above. Taking Ratnākaraśānti's Śuddhamati as example, *AA* v. 1.17 reads: "ngo bo nyid longs rdzogs bcas dang / de bshin sprul dang **rnam gsum dang** / chos sku mdzad par bcas pa ste/ rnam pa bshir ni yang dag brjod." This version, in exactly the same way as Ratnakīrti's and Abhayākaragupta's versions, links the first two lines that name the three *kāya*s to the term *dharmakāya* of the third line *(chos sku)* by the phrase *rnams gsum dang,* implying that those three *kāya*s as a set comprise what is meant by *dharmakāya,* thus supporting a three-*kāya* reading of the verse. But this way of linking the first two lines of v. 1.17 to the term *dharmakāya* of the third line follows Ārya Vimuktisena's comments at the end of *AA* 8 quoted just above, where he uses the very same phrase *(rnams gsum dang)* to point out how the three *kāya*s of v. 1.17's first two lines should be understood equally to comprise the *dharmakāya* of v. 1.17 line 3 and of v. 8.40 line 3.

This made no difference to the controversy over *AA* 8 in India and Tibet, however. Since Haribhadra introduced an alternative reading of *AA* 8 in the eighth century, philology has not been the real point of controversy over its interpretation. Rather, philology has been employed to authenticate philosophical positions by ascribing them to a received text of traditional authority. This is clear in Haribhadra's work, to which we turn in the next chapter. Thus, those who supported a three-*kāya* or four-*kāya* interpretation after Haribhadra's time did so based not primarily upon philological concerns but upon the differing perspectives on enlightenment which they brought to the text. Those who followed Ārya Vimuktisena viewed Buddhahood through a nondual yogic attainment perspective, sketched in this chapter, and could easily interpret the *AA*'s verses in line with that. Those who followed Haribhadra's reading viewed Buddhahood through an analytic-inferential, Abhidharmic perspective, to be discussed in the next chapter, and found it possible to interpret the *AA*'s verses in line with that.

Of course, from a strictly philological standpoint, Ārya Vimuktisena's interpretation of *AA* 8 was correct, because his perspective on *AA* 8 was based upon the literary traditions from which it had been redacted: *PP* and Yogācāra.

At fol. 100-5-4, Ārya Vimuktisena also identifies the *dharmakāya* of v. 8.40 (associated with the twenty-seven types of activity) as the *dharmakāya-phalam* of v. 9.2 with its activity. According to him, then, the term dharmakāya in *AA* vv. 1.17, 8.40, and 9.2 carries its inclusive sense as *dharmakāya-phalam,* and the term *dharmakāya* in v. 8.6 carries its exclusive sense as a synonym for *svābhāvikakāya.* See chapter 8 above for translation and analysis of *AA* vv. 1.17, 8.40, and 9.2; and section 3 of this chapter for Ārya Vimuktisena's interpretation of v. 8.6.

66. On this, see also the analysis of vv. 8.33–8.40 in chapter 8, section 5, above.

Chapter 10. Haribhadra's Analytic-Inferential Perspective on Buddhahood: Buddha Dharmas as Fourth "Body"

1. Jñānagarbha is to be included with Śāntarakṣita, Kamalaśīla, and Haribhadra in their general pattern of critiquing, relativizing, and reappropriating elements of Yogācāra

from a Madhyamaka point of view. But he is closer to Bhāvaviveka in his ontology, accepting external objects on the conventional level. Hence, he was classified by Bu ston as "Sautrāntika-Mādhyamika"; Eckel, *Jñānagarbha's Commentary,* pp. 19–23.

2. See chapters 4 and 5 above for discussion of all these topics within Yogācāra.

3. M. David Eckel's identification of philosophical currents formative of eighth century Mādhyamikas such as Jñānagarbha also applies to Haribhadra: "Jñānagarbha stood at a point in the history of Madhyamaka when Madhyamaka authors were asked to respond to Yogācāra critics while making a subtle accommodation to the style of the Buddhist logicians. And all this had to be done in a form consistent with the convictions of the Madhyamaka tradition itself." Eckel, *Jñānagarbha's Commentary,* p. 5. For the influence of prior Mādhyamikas and the logician Dharmakīrti upon Jñānagarbha, and by extension, other eighth-century scholars such as Haribhadra, see ibid., chapters 1 and 4.

4. On possible historical connections, and more certain philosophical connections, between the eighth-century Mādhyamikas Śrīgupta, Jñānagarbha, Śāntarakṣita, and Haribhadra, see ibid., pp. 15–23.

5. The quotation appears on ibid., p. 54. The element of Dharmakīrti's system under discussion is "effective functionality" *(artha-kriyā)* as the criterion of the ultimately real. Jñānagarbha denies effective functionality as the criterion for ultimate reality, but reaffirms it as the criterion of conventional reality, thereby reappropriating the concept for Mādhyamika use. Haribhadra, as we shall see below, applies the concept to the components of a Buddha's awareness in ways that ran counter to earlier understandings of Buddhahood.

6. On Yogācāra epistemology *cum* meditational praxis, see chapter 4, section 6, of this book.

7. *Madhyamakālaṃkāra,* quoted in Eckel, *Jñānagarbha's Commentary,* p. 22. Phenomena appear as self-existent wholes, but upon analysis the "whole" is found to be a conceptual designation upon "parts," each of which also appears as a self-existent whole that, in turn, cannot bear analysis, until the conceptual edifice of self-existent appearance collapses into emptiness. This form of analysis, which appears in Vasubandhu's *Viṃśatikā,* was apparently adopted for Mādhyamika use by Srīgupta and Śāntarakṣita. See Eckel, *Jñānagarbha's Commentary,* p. 22.

8. *Madhyāntavibhāga* 1.1 *ṭikā,* ed. Yamaguchi, p. 10: "abhūtaparikalpo 'sti': svabhāvata iti vākyaśeṣaḥ."

9. Ruegg, *Literature of the Madhyamaka School,* pp. 90–92; Kajiyama, "Later Mādhyamikas on Epistemology and Meditation," pp. 114–43 on Śāntarakṣita's *Madhyamakālaṃkāra.*

10. Ruegg, *Literature of the Madhyamaka School,* pp. 88–89, 102.

11. Ibid., p. 93. Ruegg notes that Haribhadra quotes from Śāntarakṣita's *Madhyamakālaṃkāra* in his *Abhisamayālaṃkāra-Āloka.* Haribhadra also quotes a number of verses from Jñānagarbha's *Satyadvayavibhaṇga* in his *Āloka* (Eckel, *Jñānagarbha's Commentary,* p. 23). Jñānagarbha is reported to have been a teacher of Śāntarakṣita's (ibid., p. 15; Ruegg, *Literature of the Madhyamaka School,* pp. 69, 89).

12. In his *Āloka,* Haribhadra quotes from the works of Dignāga and other commentators of the logico-epistemological school, Vasubandhu, the *Abhidharmakośa,* and the *Abhidharmasamuccaya,* as well as from the works of Nāgārjuna, Aryadeva, and other Mādhyamikas (see Wogihara's index to the *Āloka,* pp. 11–14).

13. One theme Haribhadra repeatedly explicates in his commentary on *AA* 8 is the importance of clearly distinguishing the ultimate or unconditioned aspect of a Buddha's

awareness, on the one hand, from the conventional, conditioned aspect of it, on the other, to show particularly how the latter aspect serves as the basis for a Buddha's conventional appearances and activities in the conditioned world. He expresses this fundamental concern in differing ways five times over the course of the chapter. See sections 3–6 of this chapter.

14. Yogācāra understanding of all this has been discussed in chapter 5, section 3, of this book.

15. Haribhadra refers to Ārya Vimuktisena as a Mādhyamika in the introduction to his *Abhisamayālaṃkāra-Sphuṭārthā*, ed. Amano, 1975, pp. 2–3.

16. Eckel, *To See the Buddha,* p. 170.

17. The "Buddhabhūmi" chapter of the *Madhyamakāvatāra* describes *dharmakāya* and its gnosis in terms very much like those of Ārya Vimuktisena (as noted in chapter 9, section 1, above) and of Yogācāra texts (chapters 4 and 5, above). As in Yogācāra texts previously discussed, Candrakīrti's "Buddhabhūmi" chapter centers its three-*kāya* doctrine on the nondual gnosis of ultimate reality, which is the first *kāya (dharmakāya)*. According to him, all phenomena share the ultimate nature of "thatness" (*tattvam* = *tathatā,* thusness). Thus, a Buddha's nondual cognition of the thatness of all phenomena comprises a knowing of all things in one moment *(ekakṣaṇa)* and in one taste *(ekarasa):* "Just as space is not divided by the divisions of containers [that enclose it], so there is no division in reality made by phenomena. Through rightly comprehending with excellent knowledge that [all] is the same in one taste *(ekarasa),* you comprehend all things in one instant." See La Vallée Poussin's Tibetan edition for the autocommentary, pp. 356ff; Huntington's *Emptiness of Emptiness,* p. 190, for translation of root text..

18. Ruegg, *Literature of the Madhyamaka School,* p. 56 n. 163. The *Trikāyastotra* is ascribed to Nāgārjuna by late Indian scholars like Dharmamitra (ca. 800 C.E., *Prasphuṭapadā,* Pk 5194, fol. 109-2-3) and Abhayākaragupta (ca. 1100 C.E., *Munimatālaṃkāra,* sDe dge A, fol. 217b2). But such ascription comes many centuries after Nāgārjuna lived. Since Nāgārjuna mentions only two *kāya*s in other of his texts, and since the development of the three-*kāya* theory in Yogācāra circles seems well established, it is likely that someone else wrote the *Trikāyastotra.* Tāranātha ascribes the text to a Nāgāhvaya (Ruegg, *Literature of the Madhyamaka School,* p. 56). In any case, apart from the names of the three *kāya*s, it uses no specifically Yogācāra terminology and its description of the first *kāya, dharmakāya,* is distinctly reminiscent of Nāgārjuna's praise to Buddhahood as *śūnyatā* in portions of his *Catuḥstava.* It looks like a Mādhyamika appropriation of the *trikāya* doctrine.

19. Dharmamitra, a commentator on Haribhadra's *Sphuṭārthā* who probably wrote close to Haribhadra's time, said that some Indian scholars of his time ascribed Haribhadra's four-*kāya* interpretation of the *AA* to Haribhadra's teacher Vairocana. This will be discussed in chapter 11, section 2, below.

20. The translation is based on Amano's 1983 Sanskrit edition of *Sphuṭārthā* chapter 8, together with his 1975 edition and the corresponding passages from Wogihara's Sanskrit edition of the *Āloka* (see the bibliography for references). I also checked the Sanskrit editions against the Tibetan critical edition provided in Amano's 1975 work (which he based upon the Dergye, Peking, and Narthang recensions).

21. In chapters 3–5 above, I translated *kāya* names as, e.g., *dharmakāya:* "embodiment of dharma-[tā];" *svābhāvikakāya:* "embodiment [of Buddhahood] in its essence;" *sāmbhogikakāya:* "embodiment [of Buddhahood] in communal enjoyment;" *nairmāṇikakāya:* "embodiment of [Buddhahood] in limitless manifestations." Those translations express meanings

developed in the *Prajñāpāramitā* and Yogācāra literature analyzed in those chapters. In this chapter, when translating Haribhadra, I gloss the terms differently to accord with Haribhadra's different understanding. For Haribhadra, *svābhāvikakāya,* for example, is not to be understood as the defining essence *(svabhāva)* of Buddhahood in the Yogācāra sense (purified thusness and nonconceptual gnosis indivisible, as explained in chapter 4, section 3, above). For him, *svābhāvikakāya* is primarily the emptiness of Buddhahood, its intrinsic unconditioned, "nonarising" nature *(svabhāva),* distinct from the gnosis which he characterizes as conditioned (discussed in section 3 below). Also, for Haribhadra, *dharmakāya* of verse 8.6 reverts back to its Abhidharma connotation, "body of [Buddha] dharmas," understood here as the collection of Buddha gnoses (discussed in section 4, below). Indeed, the term *kāya* for Haribhadra tends to retain its older senses of "body" or "collection" rather than "embodiment" (the sense conforming more directly to *Prajñāpāramitā* and Yogācāra literature). Therefore, I do not translate *svābhāvikakāya* here as "embodiment of Buddhahood in its essence" (Yogācāra connotation), but as "essence body." And *dharmakāya,* which meant "embodiment of dharma[-tā]" in *PP* literature, reverts back to its Abhidharma sense "body of [Buddha] dharmas" (for *AA* verse 8.6), though qualified by Haribhadra's Mādhyamika understanding of those dharmas as phenomenal qualities of Buddhahood (conventional truth, not ultimate truth). Similarly, in what follows, I translate Haribhadra's *sāmbhogikakāya* and *nairmāṇikakāya* as "bodies" of communal enjoyment and manifestation respectively. All this is explained in the following sections of this chapter.

22. *Abhisamayālaṃkāra-Sphuṭārthā,* ed. Amano, 1983, p. 3, fol. 24b1–b3.

23. Ibid., fol. 24b3–b4.

24. Ibid., pp. 3–4, fol. 24b4.

25. Ibid., p. 5, fol. 25a4–a6.

26. Haribhadra's argument revolves around the apparent ambiguity of the key terms in this verse. Therefore, I must leave the key terms untranslated here to permit his argument to unfold. My own translation of the verse appears in chapter 8 of this book, section 2. Haribhadra's point here is explained in the following sections of this chapter.

27. *Abhisamayālaṃkāra-Sphuṭārthā,* ed. Amano, 1983, has *praśāntara. Sphuṭārthā,* ed. Amano, 1975, p. 270, *Āloka,* ed. Wogihara, p. 916, and Tibetan have *pradeśāntara (phyogs gzhan),* which makes more sense.

28. *Abhisamayālaṃkāra-Sphuṭārthā,* ed. Amano, 1983, p. 5, fol. 25a6–a7.

29. Ibid., pp. 5–7, fol. 25a8–b6.

30. Ibid., fol. 25b3 has *buddhādyālambanena. Sphuṭārthā,* ed. Amano, 1975, p. 272, has *buddhādyālambane.* Tibetan puts the expression in the genitive and links it to *hetu: sangs rgyas la sogs pa la dmigs pa'i rgyu* [the cause for perceiving Buddha, etc.]. Dharmamitra's subcommentary on the *Sphuṭārthā,* the *Prasphuṭapadā,* does not comment on this verse. But Dharmakīrtiśrī's subcommentary, the *Durbodhāloka,* glosses the expression as *sangs rgyas la dmigs pa la sogs pa 'tshang rgya ba nyid kyi rgyu.* Dharmakīrtiśrī (ca. 1000 C.E.) explains Haribhadra's meaning as follows: "By making contact with one's guru and preceptor, then based upon their teaching, one visualizes Buddha, etc., i.e. [sitting] in the *vajrāsana* posture and so forth, one visualizes the Buddhas, bodhisattvas, etc. That comprises the cause. Then by training on the paths, etc., it becomes mature, and the cause for the manifestation of [Buddha] ,who bestows the [final] result of enlightenment, is obtained" (*Durbodhāloka,* Pk 5192, fols. 49-3-7 to 49-4-1). Dharmakīrtiśrī appears to identify the

"cause" referred to in *AA* v. 8.9 (and in Haribhadra's comments) primarily as the refuge cum *buddhānusmṛti* practice in Indo-Tibetan Buddhism, which involves visualizing Buddhas, bodhisattvas, etc. And the result of this, he says, is both the future manifestation of Buddha to the yogi and the yogi's own attainment of enlightenment as Buddha through that. Dharmakīrtiśrī (of Suvarṇadvīpa) is reputedly the famous Indonesian guru of Atiśa (Ruegg, *Literature of Madhyamaka School,* p. 110), who passed on to Atiśa his special practices for the development of compassion and bodhicitta. It is intriguing to see Dharmakīrtiśrī make apparent reference in his commentary to practices that he himself may have passed on to Tibet through his famous disciple, and that continue to the present day.

31. *Abhisamayālaṃkāra-Sphuṭārthā,* ed. Amano, 1983, p. 6, fol. 25b2–25b4.

32. Ibid., p. 7, fol. 25b7. I leave out Haribhadra's comments on *AA* vv. 8.13–8.32, concerning details of the Buddha's thirty-two physical marks and signs with their karmic causes.

33. Ibid., pp. 12–13, fol. 27b3–b4.

34. Ibid., fol. 27b4–b7.

35. Ibid., p. 14, fol. 28a4. I leave out Haribhadra's comments on *AA* vv. 8.34b–39 above, which delineate how the twenty-seven Buddha activities lead trainees onto higher and higher stages of the path to full enlightenment.

36. Ibid., p. 3, fol. 24b1–b3.

37. Monier-Williams, *Sanskrit-English Dictionary,* s.v. *"vivikta."*

38. *Abhisamayālaṃkāra-vṛtti,* Pk 5185, 92-5-1 to 2. See chapter 9, section 3, above.

39. On the unconditioned nature and permanence of Buddhahood, see chapter 5, sections 3 and 5, above.

40. See chapter 4, sections 3 and 6, and chapter 5, sections 3 and 4, above for analysis of Yogācāra texts on these themes.

41. Given Haribhadra's concern for the innate purity of mind that becomes *svābhāvikakāya* as described above, it is indeed quite possible that his theory of *svābhāvikakāya* coordinates with his theory of gotra. This was suggested to me by the Venerable Samdhong Rinpoche, director of the Central Institute of Higher Tibetan Studies. It deserves further research.

42. The expression *mayopamādvayajñāna* (nondual gnosis of [all] as an illusion), as a reference to the perfection of wisdom *(prajñāpāramitā),* is commonly found in Haribhadra's *Āloka.* But the expression *mayopamavijñānasarvadharmapratipatti* is not so common. Hence, my speculation that it may constitute a subtle swipe at the Yogācāras. Tibetan translates the latter: "rnam par shes pa sgyu ma lta bus chos thams cad rtogs pas" [{obtained through} the realization of all dharmas by consciousness which is like an illusion]. The Sanskrit reads more easily as presented in the translation above. But Dharmamitra, who wrote the first subcommentary on Haribhadra's *Sphuṭārthā,* the *Prasphuṭapadā,* glosses the expression in accordance with the Tibetan translation (Pk 5194, fols. 108-3-8ff.).

43. *Abhisamayālaṃkāra-Sphuṭārthā,* ed. Amano, p. 3, fol. 24b3–b4.

44. Ichigo, "Śāntarakṣita's *Madhyamakālaṃkāra,*" p. 160. Cf. Eckel, *Jñānagarbha's Commentary,* pp. 54-55 on *tathya-samvṛti.*

45. Triratnadāsa's commentary is called *Prajñāpāramitā-saṃgraha-vivaraṇa,* and is only extant in Tibetan (Pk 5208) and Chinese (Taisho, no. 1517).

46. Triratnadāsa, *Prajñāpāramitā-samgraha-vivaraṇa,* Pk 5208, fols. 2-3-8 to 2-4-2.

47. On the *dharmi-dharmatā* structure of Haribhadra's analysis of the *kāyas*, see Dharmamitra's subcommentary on the *Sphuṭārthā:* the *Prasphuṭapadā,* Pk 5194, pp. 108–9; and *Abhayākaragupta* (discussed in chapter 11, sec. 5, below).

48. *Sphuṭārthā,* ed. Amano, 1983, pp. 3–4, fols. 24b4–25a4.

49. Ibid., fol. 24b3–b4.

50. See chapter 5, sections 3 and 4, above on Yogācāra gnoseology; chapter 9, section 2, on Ārya Vimuktisena's and Candrakīrti's gnoseologies. As noted previously, according to the "Buddhabhūmi" chapter of Candrakīrti's *Madhyamakāvatāra* with *bhāṣya,* all phenomena share the ultimate nature of "thatness" *(tattvam).* A Buddha cognizes all phenomena through his perfected, nondual cognition of their thatness. Therefore, he knows all phenomena "in one taste" *(ekarasa).* See La Vallée Poussin's Tibetan edition, pp. 356ff. This will come up again in discussions below.

51. This took expression in the Ratnagotravibhāga's special terminology for the *kāyas*: *paramārtha kāya,* meaning "*kāya* of ultimate truth" (= *svābhāvikakāya/dharmakāya)* and *saṃvṛti kāya,* meaning "*kāya* of conventional truth" (corresponding to *sāmbhogikakāya* and *nairmāṇikakāya*); *RGV,* chapter 3.

52. In his *Sphuṭārthā,* Haribhadra distinguished the *dharmakāya* consisting of gnosis *(jñānātmaka dharmakāya)* from his other two conventional *kāyas (sāmbhogikakāya* and *nairmāṇikakāya)* epistemologically, according to the types of person for whom each is a cognitive object (ed. Amano, 1983, fols. 24b3–b4, above). Buddhas, he said, conventionally cognize the set of undefiled dharmas *(= jñānātmaka dharmakāya),* while bodhisattvas and lesser beings cognize the *sāmbhogikakāya* and *nairmāṇikakāya,* respectively. This entails that Buddhas themselves distinguish the undefiled dharmas conventionally, through their own discursive conceptualization. Haribhadra may not have intended this outcome, but it is implied by his buddhology.

If, in giving his epistemological criterion for distinguishing the undefiled dharmas as a separate kāya, Haribhadra had only meant that sentient beings conceptually construct the undefiled dharmas and then impute them onto Buddhahood, he would have had no reason to distinguish them as a separate *kāya.* For his three conventional *kāyas* are distinguished precisely according to whom they appear, and *nairmāṇikakāya* is already identified as that aspect of Buddhahood distinguished by its appearance to ordinary beings. If Haribhadra had been fully consistent with earlier Mahāyāna buddhology, according to which Buddhas experience their own gnostic realization entirely free of conceptual differentiation, he could not have distinguished *svābhāvikakāya* from *jñānātmaka dharmakāya,* since the latter is only distinguished from the former conceptually, and is only experienced directly by Buddhas.

53. Contrast this with the gnoseologies explored in chapters 3, 4, and 5 above, which make nondual cognition of emptiness the primary cognition of a Buddha, and *dharmakāya* a Buddha's primary mode of knowing and being, while awareness of the world and manifestations within it are characterized as secondary expressions of that primary mode.

54. See also, below, our discussion of Haribhadra's comments in his *Abhisamayālaṃkāra-Sphuṭārthā* (ed. Amano, 1983, fols. 25a4-a6) where he ascribes primary sense consciousnesses and mental factors *(citta-caitta)* to a Buddha's gnosis, which also runs counter to earlier buddhological traditions.

55. Haribhadra, *Āloka,* ed. Wogihara, p. 993.

56. The *AA* commentaries by Bhadanta Vimuktisena, Dharmamitra, Dharmakīrtiśrī, Ratnākaraśānti, Abhayākaragupta, etc. also explicate the list of undefiled dharmas at vary-

ing lengths. Tsong kha pa's *Legs bshad gser 'phreng* has extensive discussion of the undefiled dharmas, relating several of Haribhadra's descriptions to those in the *Abhidharmakośa* and *Abhidharmasamuccaya* (*Legs bshad gser 'phreng,* fols. 233a–239a). gYag ston sangs rgyas dpal's *Rin po che'i phreng ba blo gsal mgul rgyan* also has detailed discussion of them. For a bibliography of descriptions of the undefiled dharmas in Indian Buddhist literature, see *Msg*, ed. Lamotte, pp. 51*–61*. See also Lamotte's *Le Traité de la Grande Vertu de Sagesse* for detailed descriptions.

57. The various indices and bibliographies of Tibetan literature indicate that, although Yogācāra texts such as the *Mahāyānasūtrālaṃkāra* were popular bases for commentary in eleventh- and twelfth-century Tibet, such commentaries became rare in later centuries, while commentaries on the *AA* became increasingly common. The *AA* became one of the five principal fields of study in Tibetan monasteries (along with Abhidharma, Mādhyamika, Vinaya, and epistemology/logic). It became a primary basis for study of Mahāyāna practices, paths, and stages to enlightenment, while other "texts of Maitreya," such as the *MSA* (whose explanation of Mahāyāna practice is much more extensive and readable than the *AA*'s) became less studied.

58. *Abhisamayālaṃkāra-Sphuṭārthā,* ed. Amano, 1983, p. 5, fol. 25a4–a6.

59. *Abhisamayālaṃkāra-vṛtti,* Pk 5185, fols. 92-4-8 to 92-5-2. See chapter 9, section 3, above.

60. Haribhadra makes this attribution at the beginning of his *Abhisamayālaṃkāra-Sphuṭārthā,* ed. Amano, 1975, p. 3.

61. Cf. This book chapter 3, chapter 4 section 2 and chapter 9 sections 2 and 3 on treatment of the Buddha dharmas in *Prajñāpāramitā,* Yogācāra, and Ārya Vimuktisena's writing, respectively.

62. *Abhisamayālaṃkāra-Āloka,* ed. Wogihara, pp. 20–21 (where Haribhadra distinguishes four *kāya*s in *AA* v. 1.17 in these terms), 914 (glossing v. 8.1), 916 (on vv. 8.2–8.6 debating with Ārya Vimuktisena), and 925 (where he explains Buddha's activity through the manifestation of *rūpakāya*s generated by conditioned gnosis). Parallel passages in the *Sphuṭārthā* occur in the 1975 Amano edition, pp. 262, 268, 270, 290–92; and the 1983 Amano edition, fols. 24b3–b4, 25a4–a6, 25a6–a7, 27b3–b7. These are pointed out and discussed below.

63. Haribhadra ascribes the *AA* to Maitreya at the beginning of his commentaries: *Abhisamayālaṃkāra-Āloka,* ed. Wogihara, p. 1; *Abhisamayālaṃkāra-Sphuṭārthā,* ed. Amano, 1975, p. 2.

64. *Madhyamakāvatāra,* ed. La Vallée Poussin, pp. 358–62.

65. On this, recall Haribhadra's comment above in his *Abhisamayālaṃkāra-Sphuṭārthā* (ed. Amano 1983, fol. 24b3): "Differentiated in accordance with [different] mentalities, they [the three conventional *kāya*s] are established by being the cognitive objects for Buddhas, bodhisattvas, and *śrāvaka*s, etc." This means *jñānātmaka dharmakāya* appears conventionally and directly only to a Buddha's awareness (just as *sāmbhogikakāya* appears directly to *ārya* bodhisattvas and *nairmāṇikakāya* to lesser beings), and is to be distinguished conventionally as a separate *kāya* for that reason.

At this point in his Āloka, though not in his *Sphuṭārthā,* Haribhadra presents another hypothetical objection by a three-*kāya* proponent, and his own rebuttal (*Abhisamayālaṃkāra-Āloka,* ed. Wogihara, p. 916, lines 18–22). He has the three-*kāya* proponent paraphrase a half-verse from Nāgārjuna's *Madhyamakakārikās* (v. 24.18), in which it is said: "Precisely that which is a dependent arising *(pratītyasamutpādaḥ)* you accept as emptiness *(śūnyatā).*" He then says that a three-*kāya* proponent might claim, based on that half-verse, that the *dharmakāya* consisting of gnosis *(jñānātmaka dharmakāya)* was implicitly presented (in the *AA*) in its teaching of the *dharmatākāya* (i.e., the *svābhāvikakāya*), since the *dharmakāya* consisting of gnosis is a dependent arising, which has been included as such with its emptiness, *svābhāvikakāya,* in the presentation of the three *kāyas*. Haribhadra rebuts this by saying that, based on the very same reason, the *sāmbhogikakāya* and *nairmāṇikakāya* should also not have been taught separately (in the *AA*), since their emptiness is equally the *svābhāvikakāya.* Then, he says, the opponent might reply that the *sāmbhogikakāya* and *nairmāṇikakāya* were specified separately (in the *AA*) because they are mentioned in scripture (*pravacana,* traditional texts) and are posited through their conventional appearance to yogis. For the very same reason, he replies, the *dharmakāya* consisting of gnosis is also to be specified separately. Again, he makes several bad assumptions in this line of argument. First, neither Ārya Vimuktisena nor the three-*kāya* texts of the *AA*'s period logically separated emptiness from gnosis to identify *svābhāvikakāya* as emptiness alone (as Haribhadra has his opponents do). It is possible that some Mādhyamika scholars in Haribhadra's time propounded a three-*kāya* interpretation of *AA* 8 based on a Mādhyamika identification of *svābhāvikakāya* as emptiness alone. If so, Haribhadra's rebuttal could apply to them, but not to Ārya Vimuktisena, whose interpretation is surely the one to be reckoned with. Secondly, Haribhadra's final remark indicates he assumed that the collection of undefiled dharmas *(jñānātmaka dharmakāya)* appears conventionally as a collection of differentiated dharmas to a Buddha's own awareness, i.e., that a Buddha cognizes conventionalities qua conventionalities, not through the nondual cognition of their thusness. This was not the position of those who formulated the theory of three *kāyas*, Ārya Vimuktisena, or Candrakīrti. Finally, Haribhadra's final remark also appears to have been based on the assumption that, like the *sāmbhogikakāya* and *nairmāṇikakāya,* the collection of undefiled dharmas were identified as *dharmakāya* in traditional Buddhist scriptures. They were identified as such in Sarvāstivāda Abhidharma (see chapter 2 above), but not in the *PP* sūtras upon which the *AA* is based, nor in the Yogācāra texts that first formalized the three-*kāya* doctrine (see chapters 3–5 above).

66. See chapter 8 above, where philological and structural analysis of the *AA* establishes it as a three-*kāya* text.

67. I quote *AA* v. 1.17 with the four key terms left in Sanskrit, so as to permit the kind of semantic ambiguity that Haribhadra read into the verse, without which his four-*kāya* interpretation of it could not be seriously entertained. A precise English translation of the verse would read: "In its essence, with its enjoyment, and in its emanation as well, *dharmakāya,* with its activity, is proclaimed as fourfold" (i.e., the verse expresses just three *kāyas*, together with enlightened activity, as four aspects of Buddhahood, referred to as [resultant] *dharmakāya*). If such a translation were presented here, however, it would not leave Haribhadra the room he needs to argue that the verse teaches four *kāyas*. To accommodate him for now, I have tried to provide him the ambiguity in the translation that he needs.

68. *Abhisamayālaṃkāra-Sphuṭārthā,* ed. Amano, 1983, p. 5, fol. 25a6–a7.

69. For detailed analysis of this key verse, see chapter 8 of this book, section 2.

70. Tsong kha pa's analysis of Haribhadra's three reasons for the order of *kāya* terms in *AA* 1.17 appears in *Legs bshad gser 'phreng,* 242a6 to 242b5. After much reflection, I believe Tsong kha pa's understanding of the three reasons to be correct. And without seeing

Tsong kha pa's commentary, it surely would never have dawned on me how much meaning Haribhadra had put into his very condensed expression.

71. One of the many arguments we gave in chapter 8 above for a three-*kāya* reading of *AA* v. 1.17 was the fact that the term *dharmakāya* serves as the title of *AA* chapter 8 in vv. 1.4 and 9.2, and that, in Haribhadra's interpretation, verse 1.17 would become the only verse in the entire *AA* table of contents that does not give the title of its chapter (since Haribhadra interprets the term as a fourth *kāya,* not the as the subject title for the chapter). One Tibetan scholar, who followed Haribhadra's interpretation of the *AA*, when faced with the evidence presented above that v. 1.17's *dharmakāya* must refer to the title of *AA* 8 *(dharmakāya-phalam),* and that v. 1.17 therefore teaches three *kāyas,* suggested an alternative to me. Defending Haribhadra, he said that the term *dharmakāya* in v. 1.17 must refer simultaneously to both a fourth *kāya—jñānātmaka dharmakāya* (as Haribhadra claimed)—and to the *dharmakāya-phalam,* which includes all four *kāya*s (which my evidence proved; Tsong kha pa makes the same move in his *Legs bshad gser 'phreng,* fols. 226b3–b5; see chapter 12 below). If that is the case, then *dharmakāya* in both senses is "proclaimed as fourfold" in v. 1.17. That would mean v. 1.17 is proclaiming both *dharmakāya phalam* and *jñānātmaka dharmakāya* to have the four aspects indicated by the adjectival forms in the verse: *svābhāvika, sasāmbhoga, nairmāṇika,* and *sakāritra.* Then *dharmakāya phalam* would still be proclaimed in the verse to include just three *kāya*s plus activity (*jñānātmaka* is still not listed among its four aspects). And in addition, *jñānātmaka dharmakāya* would also be proclaimed to include three *kāya*s plus activity. The problems with Haribhadra's interpretation just proliferate the more one tries to defend it.

72. Ratnākaraśānti, *Śuddhamati,* Pk 5199, fol. 281-4-7 to 281-5-1; Abhayākaragupta, *Munimatālaṃkāra,* Pk 5299, fol. 232-5-5 to 232-5-6; cf. Tsong kha pa, *Legs bshad gser 'phreng,* fol. 224b2, 227a2–a3.

73. *Abhisamayālaṃkāra-Sphuṭārthā,* ed. Amano, 1983, pp. 5–7, fol. 25a8–b6.

74. *Abhisamayālaṃkāra-Āloka,* ed. Wogihara, p. 917, lines 17–19.

75. *Abhisamayālaṃkāra-Sphuṭārthā,* ed. Amano, 1983, p. 6, fol. 25b2–b4.

76. In chapter 5, section 5 above, we noted the way in which Yogācāra treatises ascribed permanence to Buddhahood as a whole, where *svābhāvikakāya/dharmakāya* itself was understood to be permanent "by nature," while its manifestation as *sāmbhogikakāya* and the continuity of its manifestations as *nairmāṇikakāya* were understood to be permanent in the sense of never ceasing.

77. *Abhisamayālaṃkāra-Sphuṭārthā,* ed. Amano, 1983, p. 7, fol. 25b7.

78. Ibid., pp. 12–13, fol. 27b3–b4.

79. Ibid., fol. 27b4–b7.

80. Ibid., p. 14, fol. 28a4.

81. See chapter 8, section 5 above.

82. See chapter 5, section 5 above.

83. See chapter 6 and chapter 8 on *AA* vv. 8.34-8.40 and chapter 9, section 4, above for Ārya Vimuktisena's and our analyses of the same verses as sketched here.

84. *Abhisamayālaṃkāra-Sphuṭārthā,* ed. Amano, 1983, fol. 27b4–b7.

85. Some later Tibetan scholars endorsed Haribhadra's four-*kāya* interpretation of *AA* 8 (because they accepted his inferential arguments), and then projected his four-*kāya* view back into all earlier Mahāyāna traditions. Such scholars did not notice that Haribhadra had

misrepresented Ārya Vimuktisena's position, because they perceived Ārya Vimuktisena and the entire corpus of three-*kāya* discussion prior to Haribhadra through Haribhadra's representation of them. In accord with Haribhadra's account, they believed that Ārya Vimuktisena had identified *svābhāvikakāya* as emptiness alone (distinct from gnosis), and since it made no logical sense to insist that the gnosis (as a separate *kāya,* conventional truth) should not be logically distinguished from its emptiness (ultimate truth), they concluded that Ārya Vimuktisena must also have privately accepted the four-*kāya* formulation of Buddhahood. They therefore claimed that Haribhadra's and Ārya Vimuktisena's disagreement over *AA* 8 only concerned the wording of the *AA*: i.e., whether its verses explicitly teach four *kāya*s or explicitly teach three *kāya*s. According to this view, Ārya Vimuktisena had argued only that the *AA* taught three *kāya*s explicitly, while privately accepting that it taught four implicitly (Se ra rje btsun chos gyi rgyal mtshan, *Chos sku phyi don,* fols. 35a4ff.; earlier Tibetan followers of Haribhadra, such as Tsong kha pa and rGyal tsab dar ma rin chen, never made that specific claim). Such a claim issues from a perspective that sees the entire history of Mahāyāna buddhology through Haribhadra's late-eighth-century point of view. Actually, Mahāyāna buddhological traditions prior to and contemporaneous with the *AA* had never separated Buddha's gnosis from the thusness it nondually cognized in order to formulate a separate *dharmakāya* consisting of gnosis alone, and Ārya Vimuktisena followed those traditions.

86. E.g., Bu ston rin chen grub, gYag ston sangs rgyas dpal, Rong ston shes bya kun rig, Tsong kha pa blo bzang grags pa, Go ram pa bsod nams seng ge, rGyal tshab dar ma rin chen, Karmapa Mi bskyod rdo rje, Śākya mchog ldan, and many others.

Chapter 11. Responses by Indian Scholars to Haribhadra's Four Buddha Bodies

1. Ruegg, *Literature of the Madhyamaka School*, p. 102. Another Indian scholar, also designated "Buddhaśrījñāna" in the Tibetan canon, dated ca. 1200, wrote a different commentary on the *Abhisamayālaṃkāra* called the *Prajñā-pradipāvali.* So as not to confuse the two, I use the name "Buddhajñānapāda" for the late-eighth-century scholar who is under discussion in this section.

2. *Prajñāpāramitā-saṃcaya-gāthā*, sDe dge Ka 19b-5. Conze, *Perfection of Wisdom in Eight Thousand Lines*, p. 71, par. 5.

3. On the threefold Yogācāra scheme of ultimate transformation *(āsrayaparāvṛtti),* with the four Buddha gnoses, divided into three groups, aligned with the three *kāya*s, see chapter 5 section 4 of this book.

4. The following analysis follows Buddhajñānapāda's *Saṃcayagāthāpañjika*, Peking 5196, 152-5-3 to 153-1-6 (= Toh. 3798, sDe dge Nya 188a1 to 189a4).

5. Of the three *kāya*s, *svābhāvikakāya/dharmakāya* was identified in the *MSA* and other Yogācāra treatises as the fulfillment of benefit for oneself, *sāmbhogikakāya* and *nairmāṇikakāya* as fulfillment of benefit for others. See chapter 5 of this book.

6. See chapter 8, section 2, of this book for analysis of verse *AA* 1.17 in line with literary analysis and Ārya Vimuktisena.

7. See note 3 above.

8. *Saṃcayagāthāpañjika*, Peking edition, fol. 153-1-5 to 6.

9. On the relation between nondual gnoseology and the three-*kāya* doctrine, see chapter 4 above; chapter 5, sec. 4; and chapter 9, sec. 2.

The expression that Buddhajñānapāda uses for Buddha's gnosis here *(dharmadhātu-viśuddhi-jñāna)* seems to resonate simultaneously with Yogācāra and with a Vajrayāna gnoseology that may have been emerging in his period. On the one hand, Yogācāra texts identified *svābhāvikakāya/dharmakāya* with a nondual, nonconceptual gnosis of *dharmadhātu* that is also referred to as *dharmadhātuviśuddhi* (purified realm of dharma) and *tathatāviśuddhi* (purified thusness), pointing to the inseparability of cognitive "subject" and "object" in nondual knowledge (see chapters 4 and 5 above). On the other hand, Vajrayānists later added one gnosis to the four-gnosis scheme of Yogācāra, calling the fifth gnosis *dharmadhātu-viśuddhi-jñāna*, the very expression Buddhajñānapāda uses in this passage. Buddhajñānapāda is careful first to replicate the long-established tripartite scheme of Yogācāra, relating the three *kāya*s to the four gnoses of Yogācāra in three groups. After that discussion, in his final remark on *dharmadhātu-viśuddhi -jñāna*, he appears to hearken back to the nondual Yogācāra gnoseology that underlay the three-*kāya* scheme, while also possibly alluding to an emergent Vajrayāna gnoseology. His remarks seem to chart a course that draws skillfully from long-established Yogācāra formulations while alluding to a newly emerging Vajrayāna one, without contradicting either.

10. In a recent article, Hidenori Sakuma imputes a four-*kāya* interpretation of *AA* 8 to Buddhajñānapāda. I have to disagree with that part of his article for the following reasons: (1) It ignores Buddhajñānapāda's own detailed remarks delineating three *kāya*s which are summarized above. (2) Sakuma's interpretation therefore ignores Buddhajñānapāda's replication of the threefold Yogācāra scheme of ultimate transformation. Apparently unfamiliar with the long-established Yogācāra custom, which Buddhajñānapāda follows, of including nondual *jñāna* within *svābhāvikakāya*, Sakuma mistakenly assumes that to do so must indicate an "esoteric" approach (Vajrayāna), which he assumes must be a four-*kāya* approach and which he then imputes to Buddhajñānapāda. (3) As noted in chapter 9, note 65, above, Bhadanta Vimuktisena reconstructed *AA* v. 1.17 to support the three-*kāya* interpretation of the *AA*, and three scholars from the eleventh to twelfth centuries (Ratnakīrti, Ratnākaraśānti, and Abhayākaragupta) did so a different way, apparently based upon Ārya Vimuktisena's commentary. Sakuma argues that Buddhajñānapāda, in the late eighth century, could not have interpreted *AA* 8 as a three-*kāya* teaching, because he did not use one of those modified versions of that verse (in spite of the fact that Buddhajñānapāda clearly teaches three *kāya*s in his own remarks). And he believes that the Tibetan translators' use of *dang* in their translation of *AA* 1.17 establishes their four-*kāya* interpretation of the verse, hence also Buddhajñānapāda's. Actually, usage of *dang* in translated verse is ambiguous; it can easily substitute for *ni* or *ste* (See, for example, the closing portion of Bhadanta Vimuktisena's own commentary, where he follows Ārya Vimuktisena in summing up *AA* 8 as a three-*kāya* text by splicing the first half of *AA* 1.17 to the last half of verse 8.40, with *dang* appearing in the very place Sakuma mistakes as an implication of a fourth *kāya:* Pk 5186 185-5-3 to 4. Compare to Ārya Vimuktisena, Pk 5185 100-3-5 to 6.) In any case, it is illogical to ignore a commentator's own remarks in the text to impute a view to him that he does not there espouse, based on speculations about what the Tibetan translators may have thought. Indeed, I see no reason why the various modifications of v. 1.17 should be anything but a

footnote to the entire controversy. They determined no commentator's understanding of the text, since those who wanted to read four *kāyas* into it could (and did) draw from the original version both Ārya Vimuktisena and Haribhadra used, and those who wished to read three *kāyas* into it could use either the original or modified versions (*AA* verse 1.17 prior to its modification by Bhadanta Vimuktisena, after all, did teach three *kāyas*, just as Ārya Vimuktisena had read it: see chapter 8, section 2, above and this chapter, section 4).

While appreciating many other features of Sakuma's article, I would argue that a better understanding of Buddhajñānapāda's buddhology comes from taking more seriously what he states directly.

11. On Dharmamitra's probable date, see Ruegg, *Literature of the Madhyamaka School*, p. 102.

12. *Abhisamayālaṃkāra-Sphuṭārthā,* ed. Amano, 1983, p. 270, has *praśāntara. Sphuṭārthā,* ed. Amano, 1975, p. 270, *Āloka,* ed. Wogihara, p. 916, and Tibetan have *pradeśāntara* (Tib., *phyogs gzhan*), which makes more sense.

13. In *Abhisamayālaṃkāra-Sphuṭārthā,* ed. Amano, 1983, the debate runs from fol. 25a4 to 25a7, as presented in chapter 10, sections 2 and 5, above.

14. See chapter 10, section 5, above for detailed explanation of Haribhadra's Abhidharmic reading of *AA* 8 and his eighth-century logico-Mādhyamika construction of his opponents.

15. On this, see also Tsong kha pa, *Legs bshad gser 'phreng*, fol. 223a4-b6.

16. Dharmamitra, *Abhisamayālaṃkāra-Prasphuṭapadā*, Pk 5194, fol. 110-5-4 to 5-5.

17. See chapter 8, section 2, above for reference to these two texts.

18. *Prasphuṭapadā*, Pk 5194, fol. 110-5-6. See *Legs bshad gser 'phreng*, fol. 241a1–a2 where Tsong kha pa says that Dharmamitra's misconstrual of paragraph (2) as Haribhadra's own position is "a basis for thunderous laughter."

19. Dharmamitra, *Abhisamayālaṃkāra-Prasphuṭapadā*, Pk 5194, fols. 108-2-3 to 2-5, 110-5-6.

20. Ibid., fols. 110-5-7 to 111-1-2.

21. Ibid., fols. 111-1-3 to 2-2.

22. See chapter 7, section 2.b.5, above.

23. Dharmamitra, *Abhisamayālaṃkāra-Prasphuṭapadā*, Pk 5194, fol. 108-2-3 to 2- 5.

24. *Abhisamayālaṃkāra-vṛtti-piṇḍārtha*, Pk 5193, fol. 62-2-5 to 3-2.

25. *Prajñāpradīpāvali*, Pk 5198, fols. 220-4-8 to 224-4-7. Fol. 224-1-3 to 1-5 briefly summarizes the four *kāyas* with reference to the two truths, similar to the way Prajñākaramati did. In one brief remark, Buddhaśrījñāna allows also for the three-*kāya* theory by including gnosis and *dharmatā* in one *kāya*.

26. *Prajñāpāramitāpiṇḍārtha*, Pk 5195, fols. 118-1 to 2. sDe dge, Nya, fols. 115b4–116a1. On *AA* v. 1.17, the table of contents for *AA* 8, see this book, chapter 8, section 2; for Haribhadra's interpretation, see chapter 10, section 5.

27. Ruegg, *Literature of the Madhyamaka School*, pp. 111, 122 (n. 405); *Sāratamā*, ed. Jaini, p. 3; Mimaki, "The Intellectual Sequence," pp. 297–303. For an overview of Ratnākaraśānti's writings, see Ruegg, *Literature of the Madhyamaka School*, pp. 122–24.

28. Ruegg, *Literature of the Madhyamaka School*, p. 124. Mimaki, "The Intellectual Sequence," p. 298 n. 1. See Katsura's elegant outline of Ratnākaraśānti's *Prajñāpāramitopadeśa* as example of his numerous references to classical Yogācāra texts (*MSA, MAV,*

Trimśikā, etc.), viewed as harmonious with the real import of the Mādhyamika (in, e.g., Nāgārjuna's *Yuktiṣaṣṭikā*).

29. Ratnakīrti, a contemporary of Ratnākaraśānti, also rejected Haribhadra's interpretation of *AA* 8 in his *AA* commentary, the *Kīrtikala* (Pk 5197). Because I believe the *AA* commentaries of Ratnākaraśānti and Abhayākaragupta to shed more light upon fundamental doctrinal tensions in late Indian and Tibetan Buddhism, they are the focus of this and the following section.

30. *Sāratamā*, ed. Jaini, pp. 7–13. Ratnākaraśānti's altered version of *AA* 1.17 appears in both the first and eighth chapters of his *AA* commentary *Śuddhamatī*, and in the eighth chapter of the Sanskrit text of *Sāratamā*. The same altered version (with only minor differences) appears in Ratnakīrti's *AA* commentary *Kīrtikalā*, chapter 1, though the unaltered version reappears in his eighth chapter (Sakuma, "Classification of the Dharmakāya Chapter," pp. 284–86). Ratnākaraśānti's altered version of 1.17 is discussed just below. See also this chapter's note 10 and chapter 9, note 65.

31. Eckel's question and its relevance to Haribhadra is noted above in chapter 10, sec. 1.

32. "ngo bo nyid longs rdzogs bcas dang / de bzhin sprul dang rnam gsum dang / mdzad dang bcas pa chos sku ste / rnam pa bzhir ni yang dag brjod." *Śuddhamatī*, Pk 5199, fol. 281-2-8 to 3-1. A Sanskrit altered verse close to the Tibetan appears in *Sāratamā*, chapter 8: "svābhāvikaḥ sasāmbhogo nairmāṇika iti tridhā / dharmakāyaḥ sakāritraś caturdhā samudīritaḥ." Ratnākaraśānti apparently borrowed the phrase that sets off the three *kāya*s as a complete set (Tib., *rnam gsum dang*) from the end of Ārya Vimuktisena's commentary, where Ārya Vimuktisena uses the phrase to semantically link the first two lines of *AA* verse 1.17 to the last two lines of verse 8.40. See chapter 9 n. 65.

33. *Śuddhamatī*, Pk 5199, fol. 281-3-6 to 3-8: "zag pa med pa'i chos rnams rnam pa thams cad rnam par dag pa chos nyid kyis [sDe dge: kyi] ngo bo nyid gang yin pa de ni sangs rgyas bcom ldan 'das kyi ngo bo nyid kyi sku ste / glo bur gyi 'khrul ba thams cad dang bral bas rang bzhin du gnas pa'i phir ro // de skad du yang / sgrib pa kun gyi dri med dang / rnam pa thams cad mkhyen nyid thob / rin chen snod ni phye ba ltar / sangs rgyas nyid ni yang dag bstan zhes bya ba gsungs so."

34. For Ārya Vimuktisena's interpretation, which Ratnākaraśānti here reiterates, see chapter 9, section 3, above. For the etymology of *dharmakāya* as embodiment of *dharmatā* in *Prajñāpāramitā* sūtras, see chapter 3 above.

35. *Śuddhamatī*, Pk 5199, fols. 281-4-5 to 4-6. Although unlikely that the *Kāyatraya-stotra* was actually composed by Nāgārjuna, since the formalized three-*kāya* doctrine likely postdates him, the text may well have been recognized as Madhyamaka in Ratnākaraśānti's time. See chapter 10, note 18.

36. *Abhisamayālaṃkāra-Sphuṭārthā*, ed. Amano, 1983, fol. 25a7; chapter 10, sections 2 and 5. Ratnākaraśānti paraphrases "other quarters" as "other system" *(tshul gzhan)*.

37. Ibid., fols. 281-4-6 to 4-7.

38. In the *Śuddhamatī*, he refers to *PP* passages 8.1–8.3 as "the three passages in the *Bhagavatī (Prajñāpāramitā)* which begin with the word 'Moreover, . . .' and which teach just three *kāya*s." In the *Sāratamā*, he quotes them directly: *Śuddhamatī*, Pk 5199, fol. 281-4-7, 281-5-2; *Sāratamā*, ed. Jaini, p. 172.

39. See chapter 7, section 2.a. above for discussion of the importance of these passages in late Indo-Tibetan Buddhism and for a translation of them.

40. *Śuddhamatī*, Pk 5199, fols. 281-4-7 to 4-8.

41. For detailed discussion of such schemes of homology, see Snellgrove, *Indo-Tibetan Buddhism*, section 2.

42. *Śuddhamatī*, Pk 5199, fols. 281-4-6 to 281-5-1.

43. Abhayākaragupta, another late Indian scholar steeped in the traditions of Pāramitāyāna and Mantranāya, differed from Ratnākaraśānti. He believed that a four-*kāya* description of Buddhahood like Haribhadra's was indeed a part of tantric tradition. And he thought Haribhadra had borrowed his four-*kāya* theory from tantric Buddhism and applied it inappropriately by reading it into the *AA* (a Pāramitāyāna text; *Munimatālaṃkāra*, Pk 5299, fol. 232-5-5 to 232-5-6). Abhayākaragupta's views are taken up in the following section.

44. As discussed in chapter 10, section 5, above on *Abhisamayālaṃkāra-Sphuṭārthā*, ed. Amano, 1983, fols. 25a4–a6.

45. *Śuddhamatī*, Pk 5199, fols. 281-5-1 to 5-2: "de ltar na ni chos de dag sku gang (sDe dge adds "gyis") yin bsdus bar 'gyur zhe na / ngo bo nyid kyis te / de dag ni 'khrul ba thams cad dang bral bas gsal ba'i bdag nyid chos nyid tsam yin pa'i phir ro."

46. Ibid., fol. 281-5-2: "de dag mtshan nyid kyi dbye ba ni rgyu'i gnas skabs kyi rjes su 'brangs nas kun rdzob yin no."

47. Ratnākaraśānti gives a clear presentation of his gnoseology in his *Prajñāpāramitopadeśa*. One interesting passage is quoted in Kajiyama, *Introduction to Buddhist Philosophy*, p. 156, where Ratnākaraśānti identifies *prakāśamātra* (pure luminosity), *lokottarajñāna* (supramundane gnosis), and *pariniṣpannasvabhāva* (the perfected nature) as the true knowledge of reality *(saṃyag-jñāna)*, free from conceptual construction of cognitive subject and object: "de bas na chos thams cad sems tsam dang rnam par shes pa tsam dang gsal ba tsam yin pas rnam par rig pa'i gzung ba phyi rol gyi don yod pa ma yin pas / rnam par rig pa rnams kyang 'dzin pa'i rang bzhin du yod pa ma yin te / 'di gnyis ni yid kyi mngon par brjod pa'i phyir chos thams cad kyi kun brtags pa'i rang bzhin yin no / gang la brtags she na / don med par yang kun tu brtags pa'i ngo bo nyid la mngon par zhen pa'i bag chags las skyes pa'i don du snang ba'i yang dag pa ma yin pa'i kun tu rtog pa'o / yang dag pa ma yin pa'i kun tu rtog pa de ni chos rnams kyi gzhan gyi dbang gi ngo bo nyid dang 'khrul pa dang phyin ci log dang log pa'i shes pa yang yin no / 'di ltar de'i gzung ba dang 'dzin pa'i rnam pa ni 'khrul pa dang bslad pa'i dbang 'bah zhig gis snang bas brdsun pa'i phyir yang dag pa ma yin pa'i kun tu rtog pa de la de skad ces bya ste / de'i rang bzhin de ni yang dag pa ma yin pa'o / yang dag pa nyid gang yin zhe na / gsal ba tsam mo / de nyid kyis na rnam pa de ni 'khrul pa'i mtshan ma dang spros pa'i mtshan ma zhes bya bar brjod de / 'khrul pa'i dmigs pa yin pa'i phyir ro / gnyis kyi mtshan zhes kyang bya ste / gnis ltar snang ba'i phyir ro / spros pa'i mtshan med [read: ma] thams cad 'jig rten las 'das pa'i ye shes la 'gag par 'gyur la / des na de ni ma 'khrul pa dang yang dag pa'i ye shes su yang dag brjod do / de nyid kyi phyir de yang yongs su grub pa'i ngo bo nyid yin te."

See also *Sāratamā*, ed. Jaini, pp. 172–73, where Ratnākaraśānti explicitly equates *svābhāvikakāya* (of *AA* vv. 8.1–8.6) with the *dharmadhātuviśuddhi* of Yogācāra tradition.

48. Ārya Vimuktisena had employed a similar argument to refute the Abhidharma contention that the *dharmakāya* consisted of the collection of undefiled dharmas (*Abhisamayālaṃkāra-vṛtti*, Pk 5185, fols. 92-5-6 to 5-7). Ārya Vimuktisena said that the term *kāya* in *dharmakāya* (meaning "collection") was merely designated to the *dharmakāya (= svābhāvikakāya)* "in accord with the previous state" (i.e., in accord with the state prior to Buddha-

hood when the bodhisattva's mind was differentiated as distinct, conditioned dharmas). But the *svābhāvikakāya/dharmakāya* is not itself any such collection, because it is beyond such differentiation, and unconditioned (see chapter 9, sec. 3 above). Ratnākaraśānti's argument here (*Śuddhamatī*, Pk 5199, fol. 281-5-2) bases itself on Ārya Vimuktisena's. But whereas Ārya Vimuktisena used it to criticize the Abhidharma position on *dharmakāya*, Ratnākaraśānti uses it to criticize Haribhadra. This is appropriate, because, as we have seen, Haribhadra's eighth-century four-*kāya* perspective resurrected the Abhidharma view of *dharmakāya*, although updating it to a Madhyamaka analysis of ultimate and conventional truth. In Sarvāstivāda Abhidharma, *dharmakāya* was, simply, the collection of Buddha dharmas. In Haribhadra's scheme, *jñānātmaka dharmakāya*, as that collection of dharmas, is the nature of a Buddha's mind on the level of conventional truth, while the emptiness of that collection, *svābhāvikakāya*, is its nature on the level of ultimate truth (see chapter 10, sec. 5, above).

49. On this, see chapter 10, note 37.

50. In several other of Ratnākaraśānti's writings, he contextualizes for us the broader perspective on praxis and Buddhahood from which he criticized Haribhadra in his *Śuddhamatī*. These include the *Prajñāpāramitopadeśa*, *Mādhyamikālaṃkāravṛtti*, and *Mādhyamikālaṃkāropadeśa*. In these texts, he draws frequently upon the Yogācāra model of innate luminous purity of mind to explain the ultimate awareness of enlightenment *(paramārtha saṃyag-jñāna)* that reveals itself when the yogic deconstruction of cognitive subject and object has been fully achieved. Toward this, he describes in detail the stages of deconstructive, nondual yoga that reveal the innate, primordial awareness that, when fully manifest, constitutes Buddhahood in its own realization *(svābhāvikakāya/dharmakāya)*. I will publish an article on this in the near future.

51. I would like to acknowledge here the series of excellent, groundbreaking lectures on Abhayākaragupta's work that Matthew Kapstein presented as a visiting lecturer at the University of Wisconsin-Madison in February 1988. The portions of Abhayākaragupta's *Munimatālaṃkāra* that I discuss below were not covered in Professor Kapstein's lectures, and any errors in what follows are my own.

52. *Munimatālaṃkāra*, Pk 5299, fols. 231-5-8 to 236-5-6.

53. Ibid., fols. 232-1-3 to 232-2-7.

54. *Śuddhamatī*, Pk 5199, fols. 281-4 to 5; *Sāratamā*, ed. Jaini, pp. 172–73.

55. *Munimatālaṃkāra*, Pk 5299, fols. 232-3-6 to 4-1: "de ltar ni byang chub kyi phyogs la sogs pa'i chos rnams kyi ngo bo skye ba med pa ma bcos pa 'dus ma byas pa 'jig rten las 'das pa'i lam gyis thob par bya ba spros pa'i sgro 'dogs pa mtha' dag ldog pa rang bzhin med pa nyid ni ngo bo nyid kyi sku ste / ngo bo'i rkyen phyis pas bstan pa'i phyir chos nyid kyi sku yin pas chos kyi sku yang ngo / 'dir rnam par rtog pa thams cad nges par 'da'o zhes mya ngan las 'das pa dang rang gi don phun sum tshogs pa dang / gzugs sku gnyis kyi rten nyid kyis skal pa ji lta bar phan pa sna tshogs pa'i mdzad pa rgya che ba nyid kyi phyir khyab pa'o."

Later in his commentary, Abhayākaragupta quotes the same passage from the *Vajracchedikā-prajñāpāramitā-sūtra* analyzed in chapter 3 above, which implicitly etymologizes *dharmakāya* through the term *dharmatā* (*Munimatālaṃkāra*, fols. 234-1-8 to 3-2; see chapter 3, above; and chapter 9, section 3). Like Ārya Vimuktisena and Ratnākaraśānti before him, Abhayākaragupta reaffirmed the Mahāyāna reinterpretation of *dharmakāya* as "embodiment of the real nature of dharmas" *(dharmatākāya),* against the Abhidharmic understanding that Haribhadra had resurrected of "body (i.e., collection) of dharmas."

Following that, Abhayākaragupta proceeds to etymologize "Tathāgata" (Buddha as the "thus gone" or "thus come") to mean the Buddha's nondual realization of that which is to be realized (thusness), the realization in which no dharmas are seen and there is no actual coming or going with respect to them (fols. 234-3-1 to 3-6). This echoes the passage from the 8,000-verse *PP* sūtra also analyzed in chapter 3 above.

56. *Munimatālaṃkāra*, Pk 5299, fols. 232-4-1 to 4-5: ". . . sangs rgyas kyi chos de rnams sku chis bsdus she na/ ngo bo nyid kho nas te / bag chags dang bcas pa'i sgrib pa ma lus pas dben pas rang bzhin med pa nyid kyi bdag nyid chan gyi chos nyid tsam yin pa nyid kyi phyir la / de rnams kyi mtshan nyid tha dad pa ni de rnams kyi rgyu'i gnas skabs kyi rjes su 'brang bas kun rdzob pa'o."

57. The first quotation is given by Haribhadra in his *Sphuṭārthā*, ed. Amano, 1983, fols. 24b3–b4 (chapter 10 above, section 3). The second occurs in Haribhadra's *Āloka*, ed. Wogihara, p. 916 (see chapter 10, note 65).

58. *Munimatālaṃkāra*, Pk 5299, fols. 232-4-5 to 4-7: "de nyid kyi phyir / gang phyir dben pa dben gyur las / tha mi dad pa nyid du 'dod / ces pa dang / gang zhig rten ching 'brel 'byung ba / de nyid kyod ni stong par bzhed / ces pa'i rigs pas chos dang chos nyid la tha dad med pa'i phyir / chos de rnams kyang kun rdzob tu yod pa rnams so / de nyid kyi phyir sgyu ma'i rang zhin can gyi chos de rnams rtogs pas kong du chud pa / yang dag par rdzogs pa'i sang rgyas kho na'i so so rang gis rig par bya ba ni ngo bo nyid kyi sku'o."

59. Ibid., fols. 232-4-7 to 5-2: "de bzhin du dbu ma la 'jug par / skye med de bzhin nyid do gang tshe blo yang skye ba dang bral ba / de'i tshe de yis de bzhin nyid rtogs bzhin te de'i rnam par sten pa'i phyir / ji ltar sems ni gang gi rnam par 'byung ba de ni des ni [sDe dge: na] yul / yongs su shes ltar de'i tha snyad nye bar blangs nas rig par gyur pa'o zhes slob dpon zla ba grags pas gsungs so."

60. *Madhyamakāvatāra*, "Buddhabhūmi" section, ed. La Vallée Poussin, pp. 357–58. ". . . de'i phyir rtog pa las de kho na nyid rtogs so zhes rnam par bzhag gi dngos su na 'ga' zhig 'ga' zhig gi shes pa ni ma yin te/ shes pa dang shes bya gnyi ga yang ma skyes pa nyid kyi phyir ro."

61. Since Abhayākaragupta's reference to Candrakīrti's gnoseology occurs within his comments on *AA* 8 that have also referred back to Ārya Vimuktisena's commentary, it appears that Abhayākaragupta noticed the similarity between the gnoseologies of Ārya Vimuktisena and Candrakīrti pointed out above in chapter 9, section 2, with their implications for support of a three-*kāya* model of Buddhahood.

Let us pursue, for a moment, the buddhological section of Candrakīrti's *Madhyamakāvatāra* to which Abhayākaragupta refers. Given Candrakīrti's gnoseology above, the question naturally arises as to how a Buddha can teach the world about ultimate reality (thatness, thusness) when, in actuality, there is no "knower" of it. Candrakīrti says that the teaching of thatness manifests in the world through the words of *rūpakāya*s and miraculously generated sounds, based upon aeons of a Buddha's prior merit, his blessing, and the suitability of trainees. He then goes on to explain the utter spontaneity of a Buddha's teaching and activity. A Buddha, utterly free of conceptualization, his gnosis fixed in the *dharmadhātu* (universal thusness) without moving from it for even a moment, carries out works for the benefit of sentient beings like a wish-fulfilling gem (i.e., without need of thought or reflection, free of *citta-caittāḥ*). He does so through the force of prior prayers made as a bodhisattva (before full enlightenment) and based upon the karmic maturity of trainees (*Madhyamakāvatāra*, ed. La Vallée Poussin, pp. 358–61).

Candrakīrti's discussion here is reminiscent of similar discussions in Yogācāra texts that first formulated the doctrine of three *kāya*s, texts that centered their buddhology upon *svābhāvikakāya/dharmakāya* both as the nondual gnosis of universal thusness and as the source of spontaneous, pervasive activity in the world (see chapter 5, secs. 3 and 4 above). Abhayākaragupta's buddhology is in substantial agreement with Candrakīrti's. Both commentators propound a three-*kāya* model that conforms structurally to the original Yogācāra conception, without thereby accepting the ontological substantialism affirmed by some Yogācāras concerning the ultimate existence of awareness itself.

Jayānanda, who lived in the second half of the eleventh century, wrote an extensive commentary on Candrakīrti's *Madhyamakāvatāra*. In it, he specifies how a Buddha's nondual attainment, which is nonarising and beyond all conceptual differentiation, is divided into different types of gnosis according to function by reference to the conceptual point of view of trainees. He specifies this both with reference to the scheme of five gnoses of his time (the four gnoses of Yogācāra plus *dharmadhātu-viśuddhi-jñāna*) and with reference to the list of dharma gnoses such as that found in the *Abhisamayālaṃkāra* (*Madhyamakāvatāra-ṭikā*, sDe dge ra 325b–326b5, 327a8–b4). I thank John Dunne for drawing my attention to Jayānanda.

62. *Munimatālaṃkāra*, Pk 5299, 232-5-4 to 5-5.

63. See previous section.

64. *Munimatālaṃkāra*, Pk 5299, 232-5-4 to 5-8: "de ltar na rten chos nyid dang chos rnams ni kun rdzob tu de las byung ba rnams dang de'i bdag nyid kyis so zhes pas ni chos rnams kyi sku gang yin pa ni chos kyi sku'o / zhes sku bzhi pa ni pha rol tu phyin pa'i tshul la nges par bstan pa med do / sngags kyi tshul las ni gdul bya'i khyad par gyi ngor chos nyid logs pa bzhin du rnam par bzhag pas nges par bstan to / dngos por na der yang logs par gyur pa med do / de nyid kyi phyir 'ga' zhig tu chos kyi sku'i sgras ngo bo nyid kyi sku brjod par bya la / 'ga' zhig tu ngo bo nyid kyi sku'i sgras chos kyi sku'o / kha cig tu ang sku gnyis kyi rang bzhin chos dang chos nyid zung ni de'i bdag nyid kyis 'brel pa'i phyir dang / stong pa nyid dang snying rje dbyer med pa'i [sDe dge adds "rang"] gi ngo bo nyid kyis 'brel pa zhes zung 'jug dang zung 'jug gi sku dang ngo bo nyid kyi skur yang ngo."

65. Ibid., 233-1-1 to 1-5.

66. Ibid., 233-1-5 to 1-6: "de'i phyir skabs su ma bab cing mi 'thad pa phyogs gzhan nas gsungs pa'i sku bzhi rnam par bzhag pa ni seng ge bzang po'i'o zhes gnas so."

67. On the concept of transcendent-immanent unity *(yuganaddha)* as the outcome of the tantric Buddhist path, see Snellgrove, *Indo-Tibetan Buddhism,* pp. 281ff.

68. See chapter 10, sec. 3 above, where Haribhadra distinguishes *jñānātmaka dharmakāya* as a separate *kāya* because of its distinct, conventional appearance to Buddhas per se. Abhayākaragupta, having repeatedly characterized the nature of a Buddha's attainment as nondual realization of thusness beyond any such conceptual differentiation, later echoes Haribhadra's description of the Buddha dharma-gnoses as an appearance for Buddhas, though without specifying them as a fourth *kāya*. He appears here, then, to be describing aspects of a Buddha's awareness as trainees conceptualize them, since a few lines later he again reaffirms that all such aspects are not to be mistaken for *dharmakāya* per se, quoting the familiar

Vajracchedikāsūtra passage: "Those who saw me by my form, those who followed me by my voice, have been engaged in wrong practice, me those beings will not see. . . ." i.e., *dharmakāya* = *dharmatā* in nondual knowledge; not forms, sounds, or any set of dharmas per se (*Munimatālaṃkāra*, Pk 5299, 233-5-5 to 234-1-2 , 234-1-8 to 3-2).

Chapter 12. The Controversy Continues in Tibet: Tsong kha pa and Go ram pa

1. For this reason rGyal tshab's *Abhisamayālaṃkāra* commentary, *rNam bshad snying po'i rgyan* (Quintessential ornament of explanation) is probably the most widely referred to by later dGe lugs pa commentators.

2. Chapter 11, section 2, above.

3. *Legs bshad gser 'phreng*, fol. 223a3–b5. Later in his *Legs bshad gser 'phreng* (fol. 228a3–a5), Tsong kha pa identifies *svābhāvikakāya* as generally understood in the Mahāyāna with the thusness (emptiness, *dharmatā*) of a Buddha's mind, distinct from gnosis.

4. Ibid., fol. 224a1–a3.

5. *Abhisamayālaṃkāra-vṛtti*, Pk 5185, fols. 92-4-6 to 4-7. Because Tsong kha pa's buddhology is refracted through Haribhadra's lens, I translate the *kāya* terms when quoting Tsong kha pa in conformance with the way I translated them for Haribhadra. On this, see chapter 10, note 20. I do this even when Tsong kha pa cites Ārya Vimuktisena, because his reading of the terms in every such text was already affected by Haribhadra.

6. Tsong kha pa reiterates this understanding of Ārya Vimuktisena later in his *Legs bshad gser 'phreng* at fol. 239b1–b6.

7. On Haribhadra's substitution of a Madhyamaka logical distinction of *dharmī* (conventional substratum) and *dharmatā* (emptiness, the ultimate nature of the substratum) for the Yogācāra formulation of nonduality between *grāhya* (cognitive object) and *grāhaka* (cognitive subject), see chapter 10, above (end of section 3). On Haribhadra's distortion of Ārya Vimuktisena's position in his rebuttal of him, see chapter 10, section 5.

8. *Legs bshad gser 'phreng*, fols. 224a3–225a6. Cf. chapter 11 above, sections 4 and 5.

9. Ibid., fol. 225a6–b4.

10. Ibid., fols. 225b5–226b6.

11. "Philosophical Vehicle" (Tib., *mTshan nyid theg pa;* Skt., *Lakṣaṇayāna*), a synonym for "Pāramitāyāna," referring to nontantric Mahāyāna Buddhist thought of the sūtras and śāstras, including the *Abhisamayālaṃkāra*.

12. Tsong kha pa's expression *jñānakāya* (Tib., *yeshe kyi sku*) is an abbreviation for Haribhadra's *jñānātmaka dharmakāya*, his fourth *kāya* of dharma-gnoses, which he distinguished from *svābhāvikakāya* as their emptiness.

13. Ratnākaraśānti and Abhayākaragupta had said that the undefiled dharmas were not to be distinguished as separate from *svābhāvikakāya* (chapter 11, sections 4 and 5). Tsong kha pa is saying that in that case, if the undefiled dharmas were identified with the *rūpakāyas*, then the *rūpakāyas* too could no longer be distinguished as separate from *svābhāvikakāya*. This argument is just for the purpose of covering all logical options, since neither Ratnākaraśānti nor Abhayākaragupta identified the undefiled dharmas with the *rūpakāyas*. Ratnakīrti did, but Tsong kha pa's argument here does not speak to him, since Ratnakīrti, by including

the undefiled dharmas in the *sāmbhogikakāya*, did logically separate them from *svābhāvikakāya* (*Abhisamayālaṃkāra-vṛtti kīrtikalā*, Pk 5197, fol. 183-2-7 to 2-8).

14. Both Ratnākaraśānti and Abhayākaragupta quoted the *Trikāyastotra* (ascribed to Nāgārjuna) and the *MSA* in order to show that only three (never four) Buddha *kāyas* were taught throughout Pāramitāyāna (nontantric) Mahāyāna Buddhist literature. Tsong kha pa is saying that these texts teach the *svābhāvikakāya* as unconditioned and permanent by nature, which for him implies that it is just emptiness distinct from gnosis. See below.

15. This is probably a reference to Abhayākaragupta's definition of *svābhāvikakāya* in his *Munimatālaṃkāra* (Pk 5299, fols. 232-3-6 to 3-7) which is modeled on Ārya Vimuktisena's explanation of *svābhāvikakāya* as uncreated and obtained by the bodhisattva path but not made by it (Pk 5185, fols. 92-4-8 to 5-2). On Ārya Vimuktisena's explanation, see chapter 9, section 3, above.

16. Tsong kha pa understands *svābhāvikakāya* (as Haribhadra defined it) to be the *dharmatā* unconditioned nature of the undefiled dharmas (Buddha's gnosis) and of the *rūpakāyas* (which are generated by that gnosis). Tsong kha pa is saying that three-*kāya* interpreters of the *AA* such as Ratnākaraśānti and Abhayākaragupta identify the undefiled dharmas with the *svābhāvika-kāya* because it is their *dharmatā* (their emptiness). But then by the same logic, the *rūpakāyas* must also be identified with the *svābhāvikakāya*, since the latter is also their *dharmatā*. But then if the undefiled dharmas are said to be unconditioned because they are one with the *svābhāvikakāya*, the *rūpakāyas* would have to be unconditioned for the same reason.

17. Tsong kha pa refers here to a passage ascribed to Vasubandhu by Abhayākaragupta in his *Munimatālaṃkāra* (Pk 5299, fol. 232-2-7 to 3-4). Abhayākaragupta noted that some scholars referred to a passage ascribed to Vasubandhu in their support of Haribhadra's positing four *kāyas*. Abhayākaragupta paraphrases Vasubandhu as having said the following. A Buddha possesses just three *kāyas*: *dharmakāya*, *sāmbhogikakāya*, and *nairmāṇikakāya*. But the *dharmakāya* has an unconditioned and a conditioned aspect. The unconditioned aspect is purified thusness *(tathatāviśuddhi)*, and it is that alone which is ultimately realized as a Buddha's nature. The conditioned aspect comprises the conditioned dharmas (the ten powers, etc.) through which a Buddha obtained Buddhahood in the pure realm of *Akaniṣṭha* (*Legs bshad gser 'phreng*, fol. 225a2 to a6).

Later supporters of Haribhadra contend that this passage implicitly teaches four *kāyas*, since the *dharmakāya* is divided into an unconditioned and a conditioned aspect. But Abhayākaragupta says that the conditioned aspect was meant to be included within the unconditioned aspect of *dharmakāya*, and that even in this passage only three *kāyas* are taught. For according to Abhayākaragupta's remarks later in the *Munimatālaṃkāra*, the differentiation of undefiled dharmas is just a conventional designation upon *svābhāvikakāya* for comprehension by non-Buddhas, a designation based upon the conditioned mental qualities a bodhisattva used to have on the path prior to attaining Buddhahood. And according to the passage ascribed to Vasubandhu above, the "conditioned" aspect of *dharmakāya*, comprising the undefiled dharmas, consists of those dharmas through which Buddhahood was obtained, but is not the actual nature of a Buddha once enlightenment (as *tathatāviśuddhi*) has been obtained.

Ratnākaraśānti and Abhayākaragupta claimed that the undefiled dharmas were taught nowhere in Pāramitāyāna literature as a fourth *kāya* until Haribhadra introduced that theory.

Abhayākaragupta's paraphrase of Vasubandhu above is the only textual evidence Tsong kha pa presents for a four-*kāya* theory in *Pāramitāyāna* other than his earlier quote of *AA* v. 8.6.

Tsong kha pa's argument would be weightier if somebody could find the text by Vasubandhu in which the passage is supposed to exist, and if a direct quotation more directly supported Haribhadra's position. No one, to my knowledge, has been able to identify that text. The fact that Tsong kha pa points only to this arcane text (which comes down to us through a paraphrase of Abhayākaragupta's) may well indicate that he could find no other sūtra or treatise in the entire Pāramitāyāna tradition prior to Haribhadra that explicitly teaches a fourth *kāya*. That would further support the claim of Ratnākaraśānti and Abhayākaragupta that no such fourth *kāya* was ever taught in Pāramitāyāna. Of course, Tsong kha pa's main reasons for supporting Haribhadra's four-*kāya* theory (like Haribhadra's reasons) were inferential, not textual. Still, he couldn't resist pointing to Abhayākaragupta's paraphrase of Vasubandhu as textual support. And this shows us how little textual support he really had. See below.

18. *AA* vv. 8.2–8.6, recall, list the twenty-one Buddha dharmas and then relate them to the term *dharmakāya*. Here is the Sanskrit (abbreviated) with English translation:

> bodhipakṣāpramāṇāni vimokṣā anupūrvaśaḥ / . . . sarvākārajñatā ceti dharmakāyo 'bhidhiyate
> [The factors that foster enlightenment, the measureless thoughts, the liberations, . . . and total omniscience": thus is *dharmakāya* denominated.]

Here is the Tibetan with an English translation that conforms specifically to the Tibetan:

> byang chub phyogs mthun tshad med dang / rnam par thar dang mthar gyis ni /
> . . . rnam pa thams cad mkhyen nyid dang / chos kyi sku shes brjod pa yin
> [The factors that foster enlightenment, the measureless thoughts, the liberations,
> . . . and total omniscience are called *dharmakāya*.]

Notice the apparent subtle shift in meaning from the Sanskrit to the Tibetan. In the Sanskrit, the particle *iti* placed after the list of dharmas and before *dharmakāya* marks off that list as a set of terms by which *dharmakāya* is designated, conforming to *Prajñāpāramitāsūtra* and Yogācāra models of *dharmakāya* as a realization beyond conceptual differentiation that is merely designated in terms of dharmas for the comprehension of non-Buddhas. The Tibetan places the term *zhes* (corresponding to *iti*) not after the list of dharmas (as in the Sanskrit) but after the Tibetan word for *dharmakāya*, which, read most directly, would connote the opposite of the Sanskrit: The undefiled dharmas are called *dharmakāya*, as if the dharmas per se are what is meant by *dharmakāya*. Therefore, if read literally from Tibetan alone, the verses appear to identify a fourth *kāya* that is not just designated in terms of the dharmas, but is the dharmas, and therefore to be distinguished from the *svābhāvikakāya* of v. 8.1, which is their nature. This is what misled Tsong kha pa. The Tibetan translation of the *AA* may have already been influenced by Haribhadra's commentary in which it is embedded. On hermeneutic problems created for Tibetan scholars by the *Abhisamayālaṃkāra*'s Tibetan translation, see Makransky, "Controversy over Dharmakāya in Indo-Tibetan Buddhism," pp. 351–58.

19. *Vijñaptimatratāsiddhi*, ed. La Vallée Poussin, pp. 704–6, 790–91.

20. *Madhyamakāvatāra*, ed. La Vallée Poussin, pp. 357–63.

21. On this, cf. gYag ston, *bLo gsal mgul rgyan*, fol. 1274b, lines 2-4.

22. See chapter 8, section 2, above for a detailed grammatical analysis of this verse. The very argument presented above is one of many raised in that section to establish that *AA* v. 1.17 teaches just three *kāyas*.

23. The Tibetan translation Tsong kha pa used looks like this: "ngo bo nyid longs rdzogs bcas dang / de bzhin gzhan pa sprul pa ni / chos sku mdzad pa dang bcas pa / rnam pa bzhir ni yang dag brjod" (Tibetan *AA* 1.17). See note 18 above, and Makransky, "Controversy over Dharmakāya in Indo-Tibetan Buddhism," pp. 351ff., for a fuller discussion of the hermeneutical problems created by Tibetan translation of key verses in the *AA*.

24. This perspective comes into tension, in India and Tibet, with a stronger interpretation of enlightenment as innate that underlay much Indo-Tibetan tantric thought and practice. This is discussed below in chapter 13, sections 4 and 5.

25. See chapter 5, sections 2-4, above.

26. See chapter 4, section 2, above.

27. See chapter 5, section 4, above.

28. On this, see especially chapter 5, section 4, and chapter 9, section 2, above.

29. See chapter 10, sections 1 and 5, and chapter 11, section 4, above.

30. *Legs bshad gser 'phreng*, 232b1–b6.

31. *dGongs pa rab gsal*, pp. 458–61.

32. See chapter 10, section 1.

33. *dGongs pa rab gsal*, pp. 458–59: "bden gnyis rang 'grel las / mkhyen pa'i skad cig gcig gis ni / shes bya'i dkyil 'kkhor kun khyab can / zhes gsungs pa ltar yin pas mnyam gzhag gi ye shes de las ngo bo tha dad pa'i ji snyed pa mkhyen pa'i rjes thob kyi yeshes med pai' phyir na/ ye shes gcig gis bden pa gnyis kyi shes bya thams cad mkhyen par 'dod dgos so / gang gi tshe chos nyid la ltos te ji lta ba mkhyen pa'i ye shes su song ba de'i tshe blo de'i ngor gnyis su snang ba thams cad nye bar zhi bas ye shes de chu la chu bzhag pa bzhin du ro gcig tu zhugs pa yin la / gang gi tshe chos can la ltos te ji snyed pa mkhyen par song ba de'i tshe / yul yul can so sor snang ba'i gnyis snang yod kyang / gnyis snang 'khrul pa'i bag chags drungs phyung pas snang yul la ma 'khrul pa'i gnyis snang yin gyi 'khrul pa'i gnyis snang min te. . . ."

34. The social-institutional implications of Tsong kha pa's and other Tibetan scholars' views on Buddhahood are further explored in chapter 13, section 5.f.

35. As noted just previously and in chapter 5, section 4.

36. On Candrakīrti's gnoseology, see chapter 9, section 2; chapter 10, section 5; and chapter 11, section 5, above.

37. The information in this paragraph was culled from discussions with Khenpo Mig mar Tse ring at the Tibetan Institute, Sarnath, India; from reading the commentaries of Rong ston and gYag ston on *AA* 8, whose themes Go ram pa takes up in his commentaries; and from Gene Smith's prefaces to *Abhisamayālaṃkāra* commentaries of gYag ston and Rong ston: *gYag ston sher phyin mngon rtogs rgyan 'grel bzhugs so*, vol. 2 (New Delhi, Ngawang Topgay, 1973), p. 1; *Roṅ-ston śes-bya-kun-rig*'s *Study of the Abhisamayālaṅkāra* (New Delhi, Ngawang Topgay, 1972), preface.

38. *sBas don zab mo'i gter*, fols. 215a6–b4.

39. Nobel, *Suvarṇaprabhāsottamasūtra*, p. 43, lines 22–29. Go ram pa's quote is close, but not identical, in wording to Nobel's critical edition of the Tibetan translation. He may have been using a different translation.

40. This quote occurs in the 8,000-*PP* sūtra, ed. Wogihara, p. 268, translated in Conze, *The Perfection of Wisdom in Eight Thousand Lines*, p. 116.

41. Go ram pa appears to be paraphrasing Haribhadra's comment in *Āloka*, ed. Wogihara, p. 270, lines 1–3. He quotes Haribhadra's comment directly below when discussing the distinction between the *rūpakāya*s as nominal Buddha *kāya*s and the *dharmakāya* as the only actual Buddha *kāya*.

42. *Kun mkhyen bla ma'i dgongs don rab gsal* (Ngag dbang chos grags's subcommentary on Go ram pa's *sBas don zab mo'i gter*), fols. 171b6–172a5.

43. *sBas don zab mo'i gter*, fols. 215b4–216a5. Go ram pa is referring to bSod nams rtse mo's *rGyud sde sphyi'i rnam gzhag*.

44. *sBas don zab mo'i gter*, fols. 216a6–217b3.

45. *Abhisamayālaṃkāra-Āloka*, ed. Wogihara, p. 270, lines 1–3.

46. Demieville, "Busshin," p. 180. The Tibetan translations are Pk 174–76.

47. Nobel, *Suvarṇaprabhāsottamasūtra*, p. 43. This discussion in the sūtra appears to be closely related to similar discussions in the *Kāyatrayāvatāramukhaśāstra* by Nāgamitra (Pk 5290) and *Kāyatrayavṛtti* by Jñānacandra (Pk 5291), where it is also said that apart from *tathatāviśuddhi* and *nirvikalpajñāna* (which comprise *dharmakāya*) there are no other qualities of the Buddhas, for which reason the *rūpakāya*s are merely nominally existent *(btags pa'i yod)* while the *dharmakāya* is ultimate and real *(don dam pa)*, Pk 5290, fol. 119-1-4 to 6.

48. See Ngag dbang chos grags, *Kun mkhyen bla ma'i dgongs don rab gsal*, fols. 173a6–174b6.

49. Chapter 10, section 5 .

50. *sBas don zab mo'i gter*, fols. 218a2–219b5. Cf. chapter 9, section 3, above.

51. *Yum don rab gsal*, especially fol. 309a2–b4. Go ram pa incisively points out the logical relationships between *AA* vv. 1.4, 1.17, 8.6, 8.40, and 9.2, which were discussed in chapter 8 above. He also points out an important pattern I did not note in chapter 8 above. Each of the verses in *AA* chapter 8 that introduces a Buddha *kāya* characteristically identifies it as the "*kāya* of the *muni*" (embodiment of the Sage). Thus *AA* v. 8.1 describes what it calls the "*svābhāvikakāya* of the *muni*," v. 8.12 describes the "*sāmbhogikakāya* of the *muni*," and v. 8.33 describes the "*nairmāṇikakāya* of the *muni*." If v. 8.6's mention of *dharmakāya* was intended to name a fourth *kāya*, it should have followed the same pattern and referred to that fourth *kāya* as the "*dharmakāya* of the *muni*."

52. *dGongs pa rab gsal,* pp. 458–61.

53. *lTa ba ngan sel,* fols. 109a6–110b3.

54. On Yogācāra *trikāya* gnoseoleogy, see chapter 5, section 4. On Candrakīrti's gnoseology, see chapter 9, section 2; chapter 10, section 5; and chapter 11, section 5.

55, *dGongs pa rab gsal,* pp. 458–61.

56. *lTa ba ngan sel*, fols. 107a6-109a1.

57. Ibid., fols. 109a6–110b3: "gzhung 'dir [Candrakīrti's *Madhyamakāvatāra, Poussin,* p. 356] / ro mnyam nyid du yang dag thugs su chud par mdzad gyur nas / mkhyen bzang khyod kyis skad cig gis ni shes bya thugs su chud/ /ces te / shes bya'i sgrib pa phra zhing

phra ba spangs pa'i skad cig ma gcig la ye shes skad cig ma gcig gis chos thams cad chos kyi dbyings su ro gcig par rtogs pa'i tshe ye she de'i ngor ji lta ba dang / ji snyed pa dang / yul can ye shes gsum po ngo bo tha dad du mi snang la / de'i rjes su mnyam bzhag de las langs pa yang mi srid de / thugs mnyam par ma bzhag pa mi mnga ba sangs rgyas kyi thun mong ma yin pa'i yon tan du gsungs pa'i phyir dang / de nas bzung ste ye she de'i ngor dus snga phyi'i dbye ba yang med pa'i phyir te skye 'gag mi snang ba'i phyir ro / de gsum dbyer med ro gcig tu rtogs pa la gdul bya'i ngor ldog pa'i sgo nas cha shas phye na ji lta ba rtogs pa'i cha nas mnyam bzhag dang / ji snyed pa rtogs pa'i cha nas rjes thob dang / ye shes de nyid rtogs pa'i cha nas so so rang rig pa zhes pa'i tha snyad 'jog la / ngo bo tha dad pa med par ma zad rtogs tshul tha dad pa tsam yang med do / des na chos nyid ji lta ba rtogs kyang chos can ji snyed pa'i dbye ba ma 'dres pa so sor rtog pa'i cha nas 'phags pa 'og ma'i mnyam bzhag las khyad par 'phags / chos can ji snyed pa snang yang skye 'gag tu mi snang ba dang / gnyis snang med pa'i cha nas 'phags pa 'og ma'i rjes thob las khyad par du 'phags te / gzhung lugs tshad ldan gyi bshad tshul la brten nas / 'di tsam zhig smra bar nus kyi des yul rtogs tshul ji lta ba zhin so so skye bos bsam par ga la nus. . . ."

Chapter 13. Sources of Controversy—Nonabiding Nirvāṇa and the Mahāyāna Quest for Authentic Reinterpretation of the Four Noble Truths

1. See chapter 2 for references. It is necessary here to give more specific detail on pre-Mahāyāna concepts of the Four Noble Truths formula in order to specify the systematic problem that the Mahāyāna doctrine of nonabiding nirvāṇa created by implicitly altering that formula.

2. See Lamotte, *History,* pp. 40–42 for a summary with canonical references.

3. Emptiness, suchness, or the *dharmadhātu,*is often described as unconditioned *(asaṃskṛta),* since the emptiness of phenomena itself is always the case, never changes, and does not depend on any further conditions.

4. Lindtner, *Master of Wisdom*, pp. 74–75.

5. *Aṣṭasāhasrikā-prajñāpāramitā-sūtra*, in Conze, *Perfection of Wisdom in Eight Thousand Lines*, pp. 176–77.

6. Ibid. p. 179.

7. Ibid., pp. 193–94. *Prajñāpāramitā*, nondual knowledge of undivided suchness, does not impute ontological ultimacy upon distinct persons or phenomena ("although we seem to have a duality when Subhuti has been conjured up . . . , nothing real has been lopped off that suchness"). As such, it is an unobstructed awareness of the one, ultimate nature of all things at once. Cf. following quotes.

8. *Pancaviṃśatisāhasrikā-prajñāpāramitā-sūtra*, in Conze, *Large Sutra*, p. 628; idem, *Gilgit Manuscript,* p. 116. The "single mark," *ekalakṣaṇa*, is emptiness, suchness, the one ultimate identity of all things.

9. Conze, *Large Sutra* p. 571; idem, *Gilgit Manuscript,* p. 33. See also *Large Sutra,* pp. 638–40 on the sameness of all beings, all dharmas, and the Tathāgata within a Buddha's awareness; and *Saṃdhinirmocanasūtra*, chapter 4, "Questions of Subhuti," in Powers, *Wisdom of the Buddha,* pp. 51–65 on the ultimate sameness of all phenomena.

10. *Mahāratnakūṭa sūtra*, in Chang, *Treasury of Mahāyāna Sūtras*, p. 31.

11. *Avataṃsakasūtra*, in Cleary, *Flower Ornament Scripture*, pp. 310–11.
12. Ibid., pp. 1005–6.
13. Ibid., pp. 1009–10.
14. *Mahāratnakūṭasūtra*, in Chang, *Treasury of Mahāyāna Sūtras*, p. 106 See note 8.
15. *Avataṃsakasūtra*, in Cleary, *Flower Ornament Scripture*, p. 974.
16. Ibid. p. 979.
17. Lindtner, *Master of Wisdom*, pp. 64–67. Based on the Tibetan he provides there, I have altered his translation in a few places.
18. See Williams, *Mahāyāna Buddhism*, 220ff., and Harrison, "Buddhānusmṛti."
19. *Mahāratnakūṭa sūtra*, in Chang, *Treasury of Mahāyāna Sūtras*, pp. 109–10; also quoted in Williams, *Mahāyāna Buddhism*, p. 220. Compare this "single-deed samādhi" to the *pratyutpanna samādhi* from the *Pratyutpannasūtra* and the "samādhi of the vision of the Buddhas of the ten directions" in early Chinese translations of the *Aṣṭasāhastrikā-prajñā-pāramitā-sūtra*, summarized in Harrison, "Buddhānusmṛti." Another sūtra within the *Mahāratnakūta* collection quotes the Buddha as follows: "Moreover, there are four things that can cause a Bodhisattva to meet Buddhas. What are the four? To be mindful of Buddhas constantly and single-mindedly. To praise the merits of the Tathāgatas. To be completely flawless in observing the precepts that have been taken. And, to make great vows with supreme aspiration. . . ." Chang, *Treasury of Mahāyāna Sūtras*, p. 16.
20. *Samādhirājasūtra*, in Gomez and Silk, *Study in the Literature of the Great Vehicle*, p. 77.
21. *Avataṃsakasūtra*, in Cleary, *Flower Ornament Scripture*, p. 983.
22. Ibid., p. 1014.
23. Ibid., p. 1018.
24. Ibid., pp. 708-9.
25. Williams, *Mahāyāna Buddhism*, p. 219. Cf. Rahula, *What the Buddha Taught*, p. 50.
26. Grossnick, "Readings in Mahāyāna Buddhism," p. 97.
27. Ibid., p. 99.
28. As in the *Prajñāpāramitāsūtra* quotations of section 2.a, above.
29. *Mahāratnakūṭa sūtra*, in Chang, *Treasury of Mahāyāna Sūtras*, p. 28. This is one example of how *Prajñāpāramitā* thought has fed into the doctrine of Buddha-nature *(tathāgatagarbha)*, contributing to tantric thought as well.
30. *Avataṃsakasūtra*, in Cleary, *Flower Ornament Scripture*, p. 1002.
31. Ibid., p. 1004.
32. Ibid., p. 1011.
33. Since in the nonabiding-nirvāṇa model, the *dharmakāya*, which is the formless basis for repeated, countless manifestations, never disappears.
34. Williams, *Mahāyāna Buddhism*, p. 52.
35. *Mahāratnakūṭasūtra*, in Chang, *Treasury of Mahāyāna Sutras*, p. 175. Paul Williams pointed out this passage in his rich textual resource *Mahāyāna Buddhism* (p. 239), although he did not notice its possible relation to the discussion much earlier in his book concerning bodhisattvas postponing nirvāṇa.
36. See for example, Paltrul Rinpoche, *Words of My Perfect Teacher*, p. 218.
37. Ibid.

38. Suzuki, *Lankāvatāra Sūtra*, p. 59.

39. This and the following passages from the *Madhyamaka-hṛdaya-kārikā* and *Tarkajvālā* are quoted from Eckel, *To See the Buddha,* pp. 162–63, 173–74. I changed his translation of *apratiṣṭhita nirvāṇa* from "nirvana-without-foundation" to "nonabiding nirvāṇa" to make the terminology consistent with this book.

40. Cf. Eckel, *To See the Buddha*, pp. 237–38 n. 56: Lamotte's observations on the need for bodhisattvas to retain a vestige of defilement to remain on the path and connected to the world.

41. *Ratnagotravibhāga* 1.68 and *vyākhyā*. Takasaki, *A Study,* pp. 243–46. I thank John Dunne at Harvard for pointing out this passage to me.

42. Elements of this practice occur in the *Triskhandhakasūtra*, one of the earliest Mahāyāna sūtras and practice manuals (Hirakawa, *History of Indian Buddhism*, p. 252). Fuller expressions appear in the *Bhadracaripraṇidhāna-gāthā,* which is part of the *Avataṃsaka-sūtra* (see Nakamura, *Indian Buddhism* p. 196), the *Dharmasaṃgraha*, the *Ratnāvalī* of Nāgārjuna, *Prāṇidhānā-saptati-nāma-gāthā* of Ārya Śūra, and the *Bodhicāryāvatāra* of Śāntideva. On Tibetan practice, see Makransky, "Offering *(mChod pa)* in Tibetan Ritual Literature."

43. See Lamotte, *History of Indian Buddhism*, pp. 125–26.

44. See, for example, Paltrul Rinpoche, *The Words of My Perfect Teacher*, p. 325, with notes 245 and 246.

45. Eckel, *To See the Buddha,* pp. 81–83.

46. Watson, *Lotus Sutra*, p. 227. Along similar lines, see the projection of Buddhas' lives to thousands of billions of years in the *Samādhirājasūtra*, in Gomez and Silk, *Studies in the Literature of the Great Vehicle*, pp. 63ff.

47. Bhāvaviveka includes in his list of objections by non-Mahāyāna Buddhists against the Mahāyāna that it praises bodhisattvas even more highly than the Buddha: *Tarkajvālā*, Toh. 3856, sDe dge Dza 156a 3–4.

48. See Williams, *Mahāyāna Buddhism*, chapter 10, for a summary of the most popular bodhisattvas' mythologies.

49. Cf. reference to nonabiding nirvāṇa in *Abhisamayālaṃkāra* verses 8.9–8.11 and 8.33–8.34a in chapter 6, above, and in the texts under discussion in chapter 5.

50. See, for example, Nāgārjuna's *Ratnāvalī* vv. 1.29–1.30 (my translation and emphasis): "The skandhas arise from conceptualization of a self whose object is false. How can there be an arising in truth of something whose seed is false? To perceive the skandhas as untrue removes the conceptualization of self. And from that, the skandhas arise no more." In other words, by removing mistaken conceptualization, the root cause of suffering (Second Noble Truth), one eliminates the basis for conditioned existence (the skandhas, First Noble Truth).

Nāgārjuna's *Yuktiśaṣṭikā*, vv. 37–38, in Lindtner, *Master of Wisdom* p. 85: "Since the Buddhas have stated that the world is conditioned by ignorance, does it not stand to reason that this world is [a result of] discrimination? When ignorance ceases, how can it not be clear that what ceases was imagined by ignorance?" Similarly, see Nāgārjuna's *Mulamadhyamakakarikas* 18.5a with Candrakīrti's *Prasannapadā* comments: "'From the wasting away of the afflictions and karmic action there is freedom.' [*MMK* 18.5a]. Possessive attachment having wasted away, birth into personal existence, which depends on it, is no more. When personal existence has come to an end, how can there be the cycle of birth, old age and death?" Sprung, *Lucid Exposition of the Middle Way*, pp. 171–73.

In all such passages, the cessation of ignorance, passions, etc., entails the simple cessation of conditioned existence, echoing the pre-Mahāyāna understanding of the first two Noble Truths in their relation to the Third Noble Truth. Yet the same authors teach Buddhahood as nonabiding nirvāṇa, limitless *rūpakāyas* continuing to appear from *dharmakāya* within the conditioned world (as in *Ratnāvalī* v. 212, 461–64, 485–87, *Bodhicittavivaraṇa* vv. 98–102, *Madhyamakāvatāra,* "Buddhabhūmi" section).

51. Eckel, *To See the Buddha,* pp. 109–10; *Tarkajvālā*, sDe dge Dza 156a 1–3.

52. Snellgrove, *Indo-Tibetan Buddhism*, pp. 436–38.

53. Ye shes sde's *lTa ba'i khyad par* summarizes the tenets of four Buddhist doctrinal schools (including Hīnayāna, Cittamātra, Yogācāra-Madhyamaka, and Sautrāntika Madhyamaka), the three vehicles *(yāna)*, the four Buddha gnoses *(jñāna)*, the eight consciousnesses *(vijñāna)*, the two truths, the two kinds of no-self, the three natures *(trisvabhāva)*, the three *kāya*s, and the twelve factors of dependent origination.

Among the sūtras and śāstras Ye shes sde cites in that text are the *Avataṃsaka, Ghanavyūha, Daśabhūmika, Dharmasaṃgiti, Prajñāpāramitā, Buddhabhūmi, Lankāvatāra, Lokottaraparivarta, Vibhiṣaṇa-vyākaraṇa, Samādhirāja,* and *Suvarṇaprabhāsa* sūtras, and the *Mūlamadhyamakakārika* of Nāgārjuna, *Prajñāpradīpa* and *Madhyamakahṛdayakārikā* of Bhāvaviveka, *Madhyamakālaṃkāra* of Śāntarakṣita, *Madhyamakāloka* of Kamalaśīla, *Yogācāra-ṭīkā, Mahāyānasūtrālaṃkāra* and *tīkā, Madhyāntavibhāga-ṭīkā, Mahāyānasaṃgraha* of Asanga, and the *Buddhabhūmisūtra-ṭīkā* of Śīlabhadra (Ruegg, "Le *lTa-ba'i khayd-par* de Ye-shes-sde," *Journal Asiatique*, 1981, pp. 226–27).

On Ye shes sde and his *lTa ba'i khyad par*, see Snellgrove, *Indo-Tibetan Buddhism*, pp. 439ff., and Ruegg, "Le *lTa-ba'i khayd-par* de Ye-shes-sde," pp. 207–29.

54. Ye shes sde specifies in the passage quoted below that in this particular context, "general characteristic" means emptiness.

55. *lTa ba'i khad par*, Pk 5847: 106-1-1 to 1-4; sDe dge Jo 219b4–6.

56. A Buddha's "prior knowing" *(snga nas shes)* of illusory beings may refer to his knowing of their nonarising nature, their emptiness. At least that appears to be Ye shes sde's understanding in line with the "magician" analogy.

57. *lTa ba'i khyad par*, Pk 5847: 106-1-5 to 2-5; sDe dge Jo 219b6–220a6.

58. See chapter 5, notes 43 and 44.

59. Like Ye shes sde of the early promulgation (late eighth century), several pioneers in the later promulgation of Buddhism to Tibet (eleventh to twelfth centuries) felt it necessary to raise and respond to epistemological problems of Buddhahood which derive from nonabiding nirvāṇa. Like Ye shes sde, Atiśa explicitly rejected the idea that a Buddha possesses a direct awareness of the conventional world distinguishable from his nonconceptual awareness of emptiness. He states in his *Madhyamaka-upadeśa* and its commentary (Toh. #3929, 3930; sDe dge Ki 96a4ff., 110a1ff.) that while bodhisattvas possess knowledge of illusory relative phenomena subsequent to their meditative equipoise on the *dharmadhātu (pṛṣṭhalabdhajñāna),* Buddhas do not, for Buddhas never leave meditative equipoise on the *dharmadhātu.* In answering the objection that, in that case, Buddhas would be unable to work for the liberation of beings, Atiśa argues that in a Buddha's realization, even the discursive category "nonconceptual awareness" is to be rejected, how much more so "awareness of

the world subsequent to it" *(pṛṣṭhalabdhajñāna).* sGam po pa, in his famous compendium of Mahāyāna thought, *Thar pa rin po che'i rgyan*, summarizes disagreements by earlier Tibetan scholars as to whether a Buddha can have direct knowledge of the conventional world per se, since that world is constructed by the dichotomizing thought processes of beings that a Buddha no longer possesses. In the end, sGam po pa voices agreement with his Ka dam pa teachers (in line with Atiśa perhaps) that Buddhahood in itself is just *dharmakāya*, which is unborn and beyond all conceptual categories *(skye med, spros bral)*, even categories such as "awareness" *(jñāna, ye shes)* (Mi rigs dpe skrun khang 1989, pp. 332–38). Rong zom chos kyi bzang po, in his treatise *Man ngag lta ba'i phreng ba*, summarizes *sākara* and *nirākara* views of late Indian scholars: disagreements over whether a Buddha's awareness can contain images of the world or not (*Selected Writings*, pp. 73–74). I will discuss these writings as Indo-Tibetan responses to the paradox of nonabiding nirvāṇa in future writing.

60. Ye shes sde makes this explicit at Pk fol. 109-1-1 to 1-4, where he specifies that nirvāṇa (including a Buddha's nirvāṇa) shares with thusness the characteristic of freedom from birth, decay, and all conditionality, and is therefore referred to as "immutable, thoroughly established" *(avikāra-pariniṣpanna)* within the *trisvabhāva* scheme.

61. Recall Ārya Vimuktisena's oft-quoted explanation of *AA* 8.1 on *svābhāvikakāya/dharmakāya:* "The supramundane path obtains *[svābhāvikakāya/dharmakāya],* it is not its creator." Ye shes sde conformed with this. Haribhadra, on the contrary, viewed the path as the creator of Buddhahood in its conditioned nature *(jñānātmaka dharmakāya).*

It becomes clear that the nondual yogic-attainment perspective we have been tracing permits, although it need not necessitate, a doctrine of sudden and simultaneist enlightenment: a sudden breakthrough to all-knowledge through knowledge of the single principle that encompasses all (the *dharmadhātu*). For from this perspective, the path merely creates the conditions for a decisive break from conditionality at Buddhahood; it does not create Buddhahood. This can be understood as consistent with either gradualist or simultaneist understandings of the path: a gradual collection of the conditions for that decisive break, or an immediate entry into it triggered by, e.g., the gesture or word of a teacher. And it has supported the full range of such understandings in India and Tibet. Nevertheless, because the nondual yogic attainment perspective *permits* a sudden and simultaneist perspective on the path, whereas the analytic-inferential perspective (which views Buddhahood as the *creation* of the gradual collections of the path) does not, many of the contrasts we have drawn here between Haribhadra and Ye shes sde appear during the same period in disagreements between Kamalaśīla and Vimalamitra on "sudden" *(cig car ba)* versus "gradual" *(rim gyis pa)* enlightenment. See Gomez, *Early Ch'an*, pp. 401–7.

62. In chapter 5 above, we traced several Mahāyāna themes which contributed to the concept of *dharmakāya* as unconditioned. The same themes contributed to the formulation of *tathāgatagarbha* (Buddha-nature) in texts centered on that doctrine: enlightenment as nondual identification with thusness where thusness is undivided among sentient beings and Buddhas; enlightenment as purification of the adventitious defilement that has covered ever-present thusness; enlightenment as the removal of that which obstructs the innate purity of mind (*citta-prakṛti-viśuddi*). *Svābhāvikakāya/dharmakāya* is often characterized in Mahāyāna texts as unconditioned, permanent, etc. when viewed not as the creation of something new but as the realization or recognition of something that has always been the case.

See chapter 5, section 3 above. On Ratnākaraśānti's emphasis upon innate purity of mind as a touchstone of his nondual yogic-attainment perspective on Buddhahood, see chapter 11, section 4.

63. *lTa ba'i khyad par*, Pk 104-1-1; sDe dge Jo 215a 3–7.

64. "'khor ba dang mya ngan las 'das pa gnyis su med par rtogs pa." In ibid., sDe dge Jo 216b6.

65. Ibid., sDe dge Jo 217b4–6.

66. Ibid. sDe dge Jo 218a1–2,

67. Ibid., sDe dge Jo 218b4. Ye shes sde names this sūtra "'phags pa dung phreng gi mdo." I am unable to identify it.

68. Ibid., sDe dge Jo 218b6–7. He names the śāstra "don bsdus pa zhes bya ba'i bstan bcos," which I have not been able to identify as well.

69. Ibid., sDe dge Jo 222a 4.

70. Cf. *Śrīmālādevisiṃhanādasūtra*, a foundational scripture on Buddha-nature *(tathāgatagarbha)* that identifies it with *dharmakāya:* "World-Honored One, concerning the five aggregates, deluded sentient beings consider the impermanent to be permanent, suffering to be joy, nonself to be self, and the impure to be pure. The *Śrāvakas* and *Pratyekabuddhas,* with all their pure wisdom, never glimpse the Buddha's *dharmakāya* or the state of the Tathāgata. If a sentient being, out of faith in the Tathāgata, regards the Tathāgata as permanent, joyous, pure, and possessing a self, he does not see the [Tathāgata] wrongly; he sees him correctly. Why? Because the *dharmakāya* of the Tathāgata is the perfection of permanence, the perfection of joy, the perfection of self, and the perfection of purity" (Chang, *Treasury of Mahāyāna Sūtras*, p. 379. See Williams, *Mahāyāna Buddhism*, pp. 99–102 for corresponding expressions in the *Mahāparinirvāṇa* and *Śrīmālādevī* sūtras, both of which contributed the same fourfold description of *tathāgatagarbha/dharmakāya* (permanence, joy, self, purity) to the *Ratnagotravibhāga* (vv. 1.35–1.39 with *vyākhyā*).

71. *lTa ba'i khyad par*, sDe dge Jo 228a3–4. The full formula may be paraphrased as follows: By ignorance ceasing, conditioned formations cease; through that, consciousness ceases; through that, name and form (the aggregates of mind and body) cease; through that the sense bases cease; through that sense contact ceases; through that feeling ceases; through that attachment ceases; through that grasping ceases; through that becoming (leading into the next rebirth) ceases; through that birth ceases; and through that, old age, death, and sufferings cease.

72. Ibid., sDe dge Jo 228a4–7.

73. Ye shes sde's choice of expression in this passage invokes the underlying purity which he referred to in earlier passages on Buddha-nature, *dharmakāya*, and Mahāyāna nirvāṇa. In this passage, "When the defiled dimension ceases, it reverts to the pure dimension," together with "as obscured awareness *(ma rig pa)* ceases, unobscured awareness *(rig pa)* emerges," parallels the discussion quoted just above: "When it [*dharmakāya* as Buddha-nature] is covered over by erroneous patterns of thought, it is defiled. But when it has been purified by spiritual discipline, freed from error, it becomes what it actually is. And that is *dharmakāya*." Also parallel are his previous discussions on purification of foundation consciousness, *dharmakāya*, and Mahāyāna nirvāṇa: "When Buddha-nature (*tathāgatagarbha*) has not yet become clear, it is the foundation consciousness *(ālayavijñāna)*. But when it has become clear, it is *dharmakāya*." "Nirvāṇa is utterly purified thusness, whose

characteristic is fundamental transformation. Through purification of the foundation consciousness, it is free from the harm of birth, destruction or conditionality." (sDe dge Jo 226a4–5).

74. The second of Ye shes sde's quotations presented above, which begins: "A Tathāgata knows all things free from conceptualization."

75. *lTa ba'i khyad par,* sDe dge Jo 220a6.

76. Ibid., sDe dge Jo 220a6–b3.

77. Ye shes sde's treatise draws from a number of the "Maitreya" texts and Yogācāra treatises we examined in chapter 5, section 3, above, and sūtras related to them (see note 53 above). The same basic account of Buddha activity as spontaneous reflex is also standard in Mādhyamika texts by Śāntideva (*Bodhicaryāvatāra* vv. 9.33–9.37) Candrakīrti (*Madhyamakāvatāra*, "Buddhabhūmi" section) and others.

78. Eckel, *To See the Buddha,* chapters 4 and five give an elegant summary of diachronic and synchronic doctrinal formulations of Buddhahood. What I am adding here is an analysis of how nonabiding nirvāṇa, because of tension it creates within the inherited formula of the Four Noble Truths, helped shape those formulations.

79. Paul Griffiths points out a tension in classical Mahāyāna treatises between the unconditioned, transcendent aspect of Buddhahood *(dharmakāya)* and the conditioned immanent aspect (embodied in *sāmbhogikakāya* and *nairmāṇikakāya*). He argues: "[I]t is difficult not to conclude that the digests [treatises], while they do provide a defensible intellectual resolution of this tension, do not make a proper marriage between this resolution and the structure . . . of the systems they use to express and argue for their buddhology." He concludes that Indian Mahāyāna doctrines of buddhahood entail a direct identification of all beings with Buddhahood, which would do away with the Mahāyāna's own "*diagnostic* and *prescriptive* soteriological commitments" (Griffiths, *On Being Buddha*, chapter 7; emphasis mine).

The tension Griffiths notes, I believe, is precisely the tension of nonabiding nirvāṇa as a doctrine which redefined the Third Noble Truth (nirvāṇa) without formally redefining the first two Noble Truths (suffering and its causes, saṃsāra). The first two Noble Truths are the Buddha's "diagnosis." By not formally redefining them, the doctrine of nonabiding nirvāṇa leaves the status of the Fourth Noble Truth (path, "prescription") ambiguous, since the path is the means through which saṃsāra and nirvāṇa (the first two Noble Truths and the Third Noble Truth) are to be integrated at attainment of Buddhahood (see note 61). I differ from Griffiths in focusing more upon foundations (in both doctrine and praxis) for that tension and upon the ways Buddhist scholars themselves have engaged that tension through differing perspectives.

Griffiths's treatment of Buddhist doctrines as a set of propositions divorced from their contexts of practice has provided some good insights, but I am doubtful it will issue in an understanding of Buddhahood close to what Mahāyānists themselves have had, because what the doctrines might mean in their deepest senses is left unengaged. This is especially true with respect to the doctrine/awareness of emptiness in its relation to all other aspects of systematic thought and practice. It is for this reason that I want to look further in future work at Mahāyāna intuitions (such as those sketched in section 2 above) that projected new doctrines of nirvāṇa in part as the outflow of practice, not as the outcome of speculative thought alone.

According to a good many Yogācāra and Mādhyamika writings already noted, perhaps the single most important quality of Buddhahood is its mysteriousness: our inability to capture it in finite thought. Does this fit into Griffiths's scheme of maximal greatness? Perhaps. But this quality has a unique heuristic function of challenging not only how we tend to think of Buddhahood but also how we tend to think of ourselves and everything else. Underlying the debates of Buddhist scholars discussed in this book has been an implicit question: In seeking to "understand" Buddha, what are we willing to let happen? Will only a propositional knowledge be permitted, which fits comfortably into our most cherished preconceived categories of self-understanding? Or will a profound challenge to those preconceived categories be permitted? If the former, say many of these scholars, what we always arrive at in "Buddha" is a projection of our own unanalyzed frames of reference (an idol). If the latter, actual knowledge of Buddha will not leave our "selves" unscathed. Substitute the word "God" here for Buddha, and it is not hard to identify Buddhist and Christian scholars who, on this issue, have had more in common with each other than with some other members of their own religious communities.

80. Cf. Ruegg, "Ārya and Bhadanta Vimuktisena," p. 317.

81. Although Haribhadra followed and further developed Ārya Vimuktisena's interpretations of *gotra* in the *AA*'s first chapter, the resonance of that concept with Buddha nature apparently had little effect on Haribhadra's overall thought on how to link saṃsāra and nirvāṇa in *dharmakāya*.

82. On the centrality of the doctrine of Buddha-nature for Indian tantric thought and praxis in general, see Snellgrove, *Indo-Tibetan Buddhism*, pp. 111ff., 220ff. Snellgrove gives an apt quote from the *Hevajra Tantra* (1.9.2–4) on p. 125: "This self-experiencing, this supreme bliss, arises from the pure condition of the sense-spheres. Form and so on, and whatever other sense-spheres there are, all these appear to the yogin in their purified condition, for of Buddha-nature is this world." Along similar lines, see Farrow and Menon, *Hevajra Tantra*, 1.9.20–21, 2.2.30 (with *Yogaratnamālā* commentary), 2.2.39-40, 2.2.44. On tantric praxis as immediate identification with Buddhahood itself as the primordial, pure nature of beings and their universe, see e.g., Matsunaga, "Tantric Buddhism and Shingon Buddhism," pp. 7–14; Tucci, *Theory and Practice of the Maṇḍala;* Guenther, *Ecstatic Spontaneity*, chapter 2, with Saraha's *King Dohā*, vv. 3, 6, 13, 18, 32, 33, 36; Kvaerne, "On the Concept of Sahaja in Indian Buddhist Tantric Literature," pp. 124–34. For examples of the same structure of thought in contemporary practice traditions of rNying ma, bKa' brgyud and Sa skya, see, e.g., Dudjom Rinpoche, *Nying ma School,* pp. 243–51, 263–67; Nyoshul Khenpo Rinpoche, *Natural Great Perfection*, pp. 69–82; Khenpo Konchog rGyaltsan, *Garland of Mahamudra Practices,* pp. 14, 54, 56, 58; Kalu Rinpoche, *Secret Buddhism*, pp. 37, 48–52; Thrangu Rinpoche, *King of Samadhi*, pp. 154–55; Deshung Rinpoche, *Three Levels of Spiritual Perception*, pp. 461–63.

83. For contemporary expressions of this, see, e.g., H.H. the Dalai Lama Tenzin Gyatso, *Tantra in Tibet* pp. 60–62, Geshe Lhundup Sopa, "Excursus on the Subtle Body in Tantric Buddhism," pp. 50–51; Geshe Kelsang Gyatso, *Tantric Grounds and Paths*, p. 17; Cozort, *Highest Yoga Tantra,* pp. 26–28, 41–42, 58.

The argument here is not that an innatist view of Buddhahood has excluded the rhetoric of path collections, nor that a view of Buddhahood as creation of path has excluded the rhetoric of innate purity. Rather, the concern is to compare between traditions the principles identified as primary (organizing the whole scheme of thought and practice) and the principles identified as secondary (interpreted in terms of the primary principles). Broadly speaking, for traditions organized through the nondual yogic-attainment perspective of Buddhahood, intrinsic purity has been primary; path collections are interpreted in such a way as to support the manifestation of an intrinsic purity already present (whether that manifestation is gradual or sudden). For traditions organized through the analytic-inferential perspective, path collections have been primary; intrinsic purity being interpreted as an open potential within beings to accumulate the vast causes that create Buddhahood.

84. Any statement purporting to draw absolute distinctions between entire traditions of practice is overly generalized. These two paragraphs are no exception. There is a great deal of diversity within each of the Tibetan schools on social-institutional contexts of practice. On the other hand, anyone who has been in contact with Tibetan traditions will recognize the broad patterns of difference I am trying to point out, and may benefit from the attempt here to specify some relations between those patterns of difference and perspectives on Buddhahood presently under discussion.

85. *Śrīmālādevīsiṃhanādasūtra*, in Chang, *Treasury of Mahāyāna Sūtras*, p. 377.

Selected Bibliography

Indic Materials

Abhidharmakośabhāṣya, by Vasubandhu. In *Abhidharmakośa and Bhāṣya of Ācārya Vasubandhu with Sphuṭārthā Commentary of Ācārya Yaśomitra,* edited by Swami Dwarikadas Shastri. Bauddha Bhāratī Series, no. 5. Vārāṇasī: Bauddha Bhāratī, 1971.

Abhisamayālaṃkāra-Āloka, by Haribhadra. In *Abhisamayālaṃkār'ālokā Prajñā-pāramitāvyākhyā,* edited by U. Wogihara. Tokyo: Toyo Bunko, 1934.

Abhisamayālaṃkāra-Durbodha-Āloka, by Dharmakīrtiśrī. Pk 5192, vol. 91.

Abhisamayālaṃkāra-Prasphuṭapadā, by Dharmamitra. Pk 5194, vol. 91.

Abhisamayālaṃkāra-Sphuṭārthā, by Haribhadra. In *A Study on the Abhisamaya-alaṃkāra-kārikā-śāstra-vṛtti,* by Hirofusa Amano. Tokyo: Japan Science Press, 1975. Sanskrit reconstruction based on *Āloka* and Tibetan translation.

Abhisamayālaṃkāra-Sphuṭārthā by Haribhadra. Edited Sanskrit manuscript: Hirofusa Amano, "Sanskrit Manuscript of the *Abhisamayālaṃkāra-vṛtti,* (1)," *Bulletin of Hijiyama Women's Junior College* 17 (1983): 1–15; idem, "Sanskrit Manuscript of the *Abhisamayālaṃkāra-vṛtti,* (2)," *Bulletin of the Faculty of Education of Shimane University* 19 (1985): 124–38; idem, "Sanskrit Manuscript of the *Abhisamayālaṃkāra-vṛtti,* (3)," *Bulletin of the Faculty of Education of Shimane University* 20 (1986): 67–86; "Sanskrit Manuscript of the *Abhisamayālaṃkāra-vṛtti,* (4)," *Bulletin of the Faculty of Education of Shimane University* 21 (1987): 39–51. Pk 5191, vol. 90.

Abhisamayālaṃkāra-Śuddhamati, by Ratnākaraśānti. Pk 5199, vol. 91.

Abhisamayālaṃkāra-vārttika, by Bhadanta Vimuktisena. Pk 5186, vol. 88

Abhisamayālaṃkāra-vṛtti, by Ārya Vimuktisena. Pk 5185, vol. 88. Edited by C. Pensa, Serie Orientale Roma 37. Rome: Is.M.E.O., 1967. Chapter1 alone is edited in Sanskrit.

Aṣṭasāhasrikā-prajñāpāramitā-sūtra (= 8,000-verse *PP* sūtra). Pk 734, vol. 21. In *Abhisamayālaṃkār'ālokā Prajñāpāramitāvyākhyā,* edited by U. Wogihara. Tokyo: Toyo Bunko, 1934.

Aṣṭādaśasāhasrikā-prajñāpāramitā-sūtra (= 18,000-verse *PP* sūtra). Pk 732, vols. 19–20. In *The Gilgit Manuscript of the Aṣṭādśasāhasrikāprajñāpāramitā: Chapters 70 to 82, Corresponding to the 6th, 7th and 8th Abhisamayas,* edited and translated by Edward Conze. Rome: Is.M.E.O., 1974.

Bodhicaryāvatāra, by Śāntideva and *Bodhicaryāvatāra-pañjikā,* by Prajñākaramati. Edited by P. L. Vaidya. Darbhanga: Mithila Institute, 1960.

Bodhicittavivaraṇa, ascribed to Nāgārjuna. Pk 5470. In *Master of Wisdom: Writings of the Buddhist Master Nāgājuna,* edited and translated by Christian Lindtner. Oakland, Calif.: Dharma Publishing, 1986.

Buddhabhūmi-sūtra. In *The Buddhabhūmi-sūtra and the Buddhabhūmi-vyākhyāna of Śīlabhadra,* edited by Kyoo Nishio. Tokyo: Kokusho Kankokai, 1982.

Buddhabhūmi-vyākhyāna, by Śīlabhadra. In *The Buddhabhūmi-sūtra and the Buddhabhūmi-vyākhyāna of Śīlabhadra,* edited by Kyoo Nishio. Tokyo: Kokusho Kankokai, 1982.

Dharmadharmatāvibhāga. Pk 5523, 5524. sDe dge 4022, 4023, sems tsam phi, fols. 46b1–49a6, 50b1–53a7.

Dharmadharmatāvibhāga-vṛtti. Pk 5529. sDe dge 4028, sems tsam bi, fols. 27b1–38b6.

Hevajra Tantra. In *The Hevajra Tantra: A Critical Study,* edited and translated by David Snellgrove. New York: Oxford University Press, 1959.

Hevajra Tantra and the *Yogaratnamālā.* In *Yogaratnamālā: The Concealed Essence of the Hevajra Tantra,* edited and translated by G. W. Farrow and I. Menon. Delhi: Motilal Banarsidass, 1992.

Kāyatrayastotra. Pk 2015, vol. 46. Sanskrit text in George N. Roerich, *The Blue Annals* (Delhi: Motilal Banarsidass, 1979), p. 1, quoting the *Sekkodeśaṭikā* of Naḍapāda.

Kāyatrayasūtra. Pk 949, vol. 37.

Kāyatrayāvatāramukhaśāstra, by Nāgamitra. Pk 5290, vol. 101.

Kāyatrayavṛtti, by Jñānacandra. Pk 5291, vol. 101.

Madhyamaka-hṛdaya-kārikā, by Bhāvaviveka. Pk 5255, vol. 96.

Madhyamaka-hṛdaya-vṛtti-tarkajvālā, ascribed to Bhāvaviveka. Pk 5256, vol. 96.

Madhyamakālaṃkāra-vṛtti-madhyamaka-pratipadā, by Ratnākaraśānti. Pk 5573, vol. 114.

Madhyamakāvatāra, by Candrakīrti. In *Madhyamakāvatāra par Candrakīrti*, edited by Louis de La Vallée Poussin. Bibliotheca Buddhica, vol. 9. St. Petersburg: L'Academie Imperiale des Sciences, 1912.

Madhyamakopadeśa, by Atiśa (Dīpaṃkaraśrījñāna). Pk 5324, vol. 102; Toh. 3929.

Madhyāntavibhāga. Edited by Gadjin M. Nagao. Tokyo: Suzuki Research Foundation, 1964.

Madhyāntavibhāgabhāṣya, by Vasubandhu. Edited by Gadjin M. Nagao, with *Kārikā.*

Madhyāntavibhāgaṭikā, by Sthiramati. Edited by Sylvain M. Levi and Susumu Yamaguchi. Nagoya: Nakaku, 1934.

Mahāyānasaṃgraha, by Asanga. In *La Somme du Grand Vehicule d'Asanga*, edited and translated by Etienne Lamotte. Publications de l'Institut Orientaliste de Louvain, no. 8. Louvain: Institut Orientaliste, 1973.

Mahāyānasaṃgrahabhāṣya, by Vasubandhu. Pk 5551, vol. 112. sDe dge 4050, sem tsam ri, fols. 121b1–190a7.

Mahāyānasaṃgrahopanibandhana, by Asvabhāva. Pk 5552, vol. 113. sDe dge 4051, sem tsam ri, fols. 190b1–296a7.

Mahāyānasūtrālaṃkāra. In book 1 of *Mahāyāna-Sūtrālaṃkāra: Exposé de la Doctrine du Grand Vehicule*, edited by Sylvain Levi. Bibliotheque de l'Ecole des Hautes Etudes, fasc. 159. Paris: Librairie Honoré Champion, 1907.

Mahāyānasūtrālaṃkārabhāṣya, by Vasubandhu. In book 1 of *Mahāyāna-Sūtrālaṃkāra: Exposé de la Doctrine du Grand Vehicule*, edited by Sylvain Levi. Bibliotheque de l'Ecole des Hautes Etudes, fasc. 159. Paris: Librairie Honoré Champion, 1907.

Mahāyānasūtrālaṃkāraṭikā, by Asvabhāva. Pk 5530, vol. 108. sDe dge 4029, sem tsam bi, fols. 38b6–174a7.

Marmakaumudi, by Abhayākaragupta. Pk 5202, vol. 92.

Munimatālaṃkāra, by Abhayākaragupta. Pk 5299, vol. 101.

Mūlamadhyamaka-vṛtti-prasannapadā by Candrakīrti. Pk5260, vol. 98. In *Madhyamakavṛttiḥ: Mūlamadhyamakakārikās de Nāgārjuna avec le Prasannapadā, commentaire de Candrakīrti*, edited by Louis de La Vallée Poussin. Bibliotheca buddhica, vol. 4. St. Petersburg: Academie Imperiale des Sciences, 1913.

Pañcaviṃśatisāhasrikā-prajñāpāramitā-sūtra (= 25,000-verse *PP* sūtra). Revised. In *Mahā-Prajñāpāramitā Sūtra,* edited by Edward Conze. Ann Arbor, Mich: University Microfilms. Conze's typescript romanization of the Sanskrit.

Pañcaviṃśatisāhasrikā-prajñāpāramitā-sūtra. Pk 5188, vols. 88–90. In *The Pañcaviṃśatisāhasrikā Prajñāpāramitā, Edited with Critical Notes and Introduction*, edited by Nalinaksha Dutt. London: Luzac & Co., 1934. Edited edition of *rP*, first chapter only.

Pañcaviṃśatisāhasrikā-prajñāpāramitā-sūtra. Unrevised. Pk 731, vols. 1819. In

Gilgit Buddhist Manuscripts, edited by R. Vira and L. Chandra. Śatapitaka, vol. 10:3–5. New Delhi: International Academy of Indian Culture, 1966–70.

Prajñāpāramitā-bhāvanopadeśa, by Ratnākaraśānti. Pk 5580, vol. 114.

Prajñāpāramitopadeśa, by Ratnākaraśānti. Pk 5579, vol. 114.

Ratnagotravibhāga and *Ratnagotravibhāga-vyākhyāna*. Edited by E. H. Johnston. Patna: The Bihar Research Society, 1950.

Ratnakaraṇḍodghāṭanāma-Madhyamakopadeśa, by Atiśa (Dīpaṃkaraśrījñāna). Pk 5325, vol. 102; Toh. 3930.

Ratnāvalī, by Nāgārjuna. Pk 5658, vol. 129. In *Nāgārjuna's Ratnāvalī,* vol. 1: *The Basic Texts (Sanskrit, Tibetan, Chinese)*, edited by Michael Hahn. Bonn: Indica et Tibetica, 1982.

Samādhirājasūtra. In *Three Chapters from the Samādhirājasūtra*, edited and translated by K. Regamey. Warsaw: The Warsaw Society of Sciences and Letters, 1938. A translation of chapters 8, 19, and 22.

Saṃdhinirmocanasūtra. In *Saṃdhinirmocana Sūtra: l'Explication des Mystères*, edited and translated by Etienne Lamotte. Louvain: Bibliotheque de l'Université, 1935.

Saṃdhinirmocanasūtra. In *Wisdom of Buddha: The Saṃdhinirmocana Sūtra,* edited and translated by John Powers. Berkeley, Calif.: Dharma Publishing, 1995.

Satyadvayavibhanga, by Jñānagarbha. In *Jñānagarbha's Commentary on the Distinction Between the Two Truths,* by Malcolm David Eckel. Albany: State University of New York Press, 1986.

Sāratamā, by Ratnākaraśānti. Pk 5200, vol. 92. Edited by P. Jaini. Tibetan Sanskrit Works, no. 18. Patna: K. P. Jayaswal Research Institute, 1979.

Śatasāhasrikā-prajñāpāramitā-sūtra (= 100,000-verse *PP* sūtra). Pk 730, vols. 12–18 (complete). Edited by P. Ghosha. Bibl. Ind. 1, nos. 146–48. Calcutta: Asiatic Society of Bengal, 1902–13. Contains only chapters 1–12.

Sikṣāsamuccaya, by Śāntideva. Edited by P. L. Vaidya. Darbhanga: Mithila Institute, 1961.

Sūtrālaṃkāravṛttibhāṣya, by Sthiramati. Pk 5531, vol. 108. sDe dge 4034, sems tsam, fols. mi 1b1-283a7, tsi 1b1-266a7.

Suvarṇaprabhāsottama-sūtra. Edited by Johannes Nobel. Leiden: E. J. Brill, 1958.

Triṃśikā, by Vasubandhu, with the *Triṃśikāvijñaptibhāṣya* of Sthiramati. In *Vijñaptimātratāsiddhi*: *Deux Traités de Vasubandhu*, edited by Sylvain Levi. Paris: Librairie Ancienne Honoré Champion, 1925.

Vajracchedikā Prajñāpāramitā. Edited and translated by Edward Conze. Rome: Is.M.E.O., 1957.

Vajracchedikā Prajñāpāramitā. Translated in Gregory Schopen, "The Manuscript of the *Vajracchedikā* Found at Gilgit," in *Studies in the Literature of the Great Vehicle*, edited by Luis Gomez and Jonathan Silk, 89–140. Ann Arbor: University of Michigan Center for South and Southeast Asian Studies, 1989.

Vijñapti-mātratā-siddhi, by Ratnākaraśānti. Pk 5756, vol. 138.
Yuktiṣāṣṭikā, by Nāgārjuna. P 5225, vol. 95.

Tibetan Writings

Bu-ston rin-chen-grub. *Sher 'grel rgya cher bshad pa lung gi snye ma.* Vārāṇasī: Pleasure of Elegant Sayings, 1979.

sGam-po-pa bSod-nams-rin-chen. *Thar pa rin po che'i rgyan.* Lhasa: Mi rigs dpe skrun khang, 1989.

Go-ram-pa bsod-nams seng-ge. *sBas don zab mo'i gter gyi kha 'byed.* No. 50, fols. 245-1-1 to 358-1-3 in vol. 13 of the *Sa skya pa'i bka' 'bum,* Tokyo: Toyo Bunko, 1969.

———. *lTa ba ngan sel.* No. 48, fols. 24-3-1 to 84-3-6 in vol. 13 of the *Sa skya pa'i bka' 'bum.* Tokyo: Toyo Bunko, 1969.

———. *lTa ba'i shan 'byed theg mchog gnad kyi zla zer.* No. 47, fols. 1-1-1 to 24-2-6 in vol. 13 of the *Sa skya pa'i bka' 'bum.* Tokyo: Toyo Bunko, 1969.

———. *Yum don rab gsal.* No. 49, fols. 85-1-1 to 244-3-6 in vol. 13 of the *Sa skya pa'i bka' 'bum.* Tokyo: Toyo Bunko, 1969.

rGyal-tshab dar-ma-rinchen. *rNam bshad snying po'i rgyan.* Vārāṇasī: Pleasure of Elegant Sayings, 1980.

———. *Theg pa chen po rgyud bla ma'i ṭikā.* Delhi: Ngawang Gelek, n.d.

Ngag-dbang chos-grags. *Kun mkhyen bla ma'i dgongs don rab gsal.* New Delhi: Ngawang Tobgye, 1985. A subcommentary on Go-ram-pa's *sBas don zab mo'i gter.*

Rong-ston shes-bya-kun-rig. *Tshig don rab tu gsal ba.* In *Roṅ-ston śes-bya-kun-rig's Study of the Abhisamayālaṃkāra.* New Delhi: Ngawang Topgay, 1972.

Rong-zom Chos-kyi-bzang-po. *Man ngag lta ba'i phreng ba.* In *Selected Writings (gsuṇ thor bu) of Roṇ-zom Chos-kyi-bzaṇ-po.* Smanrtsis Shesrig Spendzod Series, vol. 73. Leh: S.W. Tashigangpa, 1974.

Sera rje-btsun cho-gyi-rgyal-mtshan. *Chos sku phyi don.* Bylakuppe, India: Sera Je Monastery, n.d.

———. *dNgos brgyad don bdun cu nges par 'byed pa'i thabs dam pa.* Bylakuppe, India: Sera Monastery, n.d.

———. *sKal bzang klu dbang gi rol mtsho zhes bya ba las skabs brgyad pa'i sphyi don.* Bylakuppe, India: Sera Je Monastery, n.d.

Śākya mchog-ldan. *Lung rigs rol mtsho.* In *The Complete Works of gSer-mdog Paṇ-chen Śākya-mchog-ldan,* vols. 1 and 2. Thimphu, Bhutan: Kunzang Tobgey, 1975.

Tsong-kha-pa. *dBu ma dgongs pa rab gsal.* Vārāṇasī: dGe ldan spyi las khang, 1984.

——— *Legs bshad gser phreng.* Dharamsala, India: Shes rig dpar khang, 1985.

gYag-ston sangs-rgyas-dpal. *Rin po che'i bang mdzod. gYag ston sher phyin mngon rtogs rgyan 'grel bzhugs so* New Delhi: Ngawang Topgay, 1973.

———. *Rin po che'i phreng ba blo gsal mgul rgyan.* Rajpur, India: Sa skya College, n.d.

Ye shes sde. *lTa ba'i khyad par.* Pk 5847, vol. 145. Toh. 4360.

Works in European Languages

Akanuma, Chizen. "The Triple Body of the Buddha." *Eastern Buddhist* 2 (1922): 1–29.

Brown, Brian E. "The Buddha Nature: A Study of the Tathāgatagarbha and Ālayavijñāna." Ph.D. diss., Fordham University, 1981.

Buswell, Robert E., and and Robert M. Gimello, eds. *Paths to Liberation: The Mārga and its Transformations in Buddhist Thought.* Honolulu: University of Hawaii Press, 1992.

Cabezón, José I. "The Canonization of Philosophy and the Rhetoric of Siddhānta in Tibetan Buddhism." In *Buddha Nature*, edited by Paul Griffiths and John Keenan, 7–26. Los Angeles: Buddhist Books International, 1990.

Chandra, Lokesh. *Materials for a History of Tibetan Literature.* Part 3. New Delhi: International Academy of Indian Culture, 1963.

Chang, Garma C. C. *A Treasury of Mahāyāna Sūtras.* Translated by the Buddhist Association of the United States. University Park: Pennsylvania State University Press, 1983. Translation of selected sūtras from the *Mahāratnakūṭa* collection.

Cleary, Thomas. *The Flower Ornament Scripture.* Berkeley, Calif.: Shambhala, 1987. Translation of the *Avataṃsakasūtra.*

Conze, Edward. *Abhisamayālaṃkāra.* Rome: Is.M. E. O., 1954.

———. "The Composition of the Aṣṭasāhasrikā Prajñāpāramitā." Reprinted in *Thirty Years of Buddhist Studies.* Oxford: Bruno Cassirer, 1967.

———. *The Large Sutra on Perfect Wisdom.* Delhi: Motilal Banarsidass, 1979. Translation of the revised *Pañcaviṃśatisāhasrikā-prajñāpāramitā* combined with portions of the *Śata.* and *Aṣṭādaśa PP* sūtras.

———. "Marginal Notes to the Abhisamayālaṃkāra." In *Liebenthal Festschrift*, edited by Kshitis Roy. Visvabharati: Santiniketan, 1957.

———. *Materials for a Dictionary of the Prajñāpāramitā Literature.* Tokyo: Suzuki Research Foundation, 1967.

———. *The Prajñāpāramitā Literature.* 2d ed. Tokyo: Reiyukai, 1978.

———. *The Perfection of Wisdom in Eight Thousand Lines & Its Verse Summary.* Bolinas, Calif.: Four Seasons Foundation, 1975. Translation of the *Aṣṭasāhasrikā-prajñāpāramitā.*

———. *Selected Sayings from the Perfection of Wisdom*. London: The Buddhist Society, 1955.

———, ed. and trans. *The Gilgit Manuscript of the Aśṭādaśasāgasrujā-prajñā-pāramitā*. Rome: Is.M.E.O., 1974.

Cozort, Daniel. *Highest Yoga Tantra*. Ithaca: Snow Lion, 1986.

Dalai Lama, His Holiness the Fourteenth. *Tantra in Tibet: The Great Exposition of Secret Mantra by Tsong kha pa*. London: Allen & Unwin, 1977.

Davidson, Ronald Mark. "Buddhist Systems of Transformation: *Āśraya-parivṛtti-parāvṛtti* Among the Yogācāra." Ph.D. diss., University of California, Berkeley,1985.

Demieville, P. "Busshin." In *Hobogirin: Dictionnaire Encyclopédique du Bouddhisme d'après les Sources Chinoise et Japonaises*. Tokyo: Maison Franco-Japonais, 1931.

Deshung Rinpoche. *The Three Levels of Spiritual Perception: An Oral Commentary on the Three Visions (Nang Sum) of Ngorchen Konchog Lhundrub*. Translated by Jared Rhoton. Boston: Wisdom, 1995

Dudjom Rinpoche, Jikdrel Yeshe Dorje. *The Nyingma School of Tibetan Buddhism: Its Fundamentals and History*. Translated by Gyurme Dorje with the collaboration of Matthew Kapstein. Boston: Wisdom, 1991.

Dutt, Nalinaksha. *Mahāyāna Buddhism*. Delhi: Motilal Banarsidass, 1978.

Eckel, Malcolm David. *Jñānagarbha's Commentary on the Distinction Between the Two Truths*. Albany: State University of New York Press, 1986.

———. *To See the Buddha*. New York: Harper Collins, 1992.

Edgerton, Franklin. *Buddhist Hybrid Sanskrit Grammar and Dictionary*. New Haven: Yale University Press, 1953.

Emmerick, R. E., trans. *The Sūtra of Golden Light: Being a Translation of the "Suvarṇabhāsottamasūtra."* London: Luzac, 1970.

Frauwallner, Erich. "Landmarks in the History of Indian Logic." *Weiner Zeitschrift für die Kunde Sud- und Ostasiens* 5 (1961): 125–48.

———. *On the Date of the Buddhist Master of the Law Vasubandhu*. Rome: Is.M.E.O., 1951.

Galloway, Brian. "Sudden Enlightenment in the *Abhisamayālaṃkāra,* the *Lalitavistara,* and the *Śikṣāsamuccaya.*" *Weiner Zeitschrift für die Kunde Sud- und Ostasiens* 32 (1988): 141–47.

Gomez, Luis. "The Direct and Gradual Approaches of Zen Master Mahāyāna: Fragments of the Teachings of Mo-ho-yen." In *Studies in Ch'an and Hua-yen,* edited by Robert Gimello and Peter Gregory, pp. 69–167. Honolulu: University of Hawaii Press, 1983.

———. "Indian Materials on the Doctrine of Sudden Enlightenment." In *Early Ch'an in China and Tibet*, edited by Whalen Lai and Lewis Lancaster, 393–434. Berkeley, Calif.: Asian Humanities Press, 1983.

Gomez, Luis O., and Jonathan A. Silk, eds. *Studies in the Literature of the Great Vehicle*. Ann Arbor: University of Michigan Center for South and Southeast Asian Studies, 1989.

———. "The Sūtra of the King of Samādhis: Chapters I–IV." In *Studies in the Literature of the Great Vehicle*, team translation edited by Luis Gomez and Jonathan Silk, 1–88. Ann Arbor: University of Michigan Center for South and Southeast Asian Studies, 1989.

Gregory, Peter N., ed. *Sudden and Gradual: Approaches to Enlightenment in Chinese Thought*. Honolulu: University of Hawaii Press, 1987.

Griffiths, Paul J. "Buddha and God: A Contrastive Study in Ideas about Maximal Greatness." *The Journal of Religion* 69, no. 4 (October 1989): 502–29.

———. *On Being Buddha: Maximal Greatness and the Doctrine of Buddhahood in Classical India*. Albany: State University of New Press, 1994.

Griffiths, Paul J., Noriaki Hakamaya, John P. Keenan, and Paul L. Swanson. *The Realm of Awakening: A Translation and Study of the Tenth Chapter of Asanga's "Mahāyānasaṃgraha."* New York: Oxford University Press, 1989.

Grossnick, William. "Readings in Mahāyāna Buddhism." Unpublished manuscript.

Guenther, Herbert V. *Ecstatic Spontaneity: Saraha's Three Cycles of Dohā*. Berkeley, Calif.: Asian Humanities Press, 1993.

———. *The Jewel Ornament of Liberation by sGam-po-pa*. Berkeley, Calif.: Shambala, 1971.

Gyaltsen, Khenpo Konchog. *The Garland of Mahamudra Practices*. Ithaca: Snow Lion, 1986.

Gyatso, Geshe Kelsang. *Tantric Grounds and Paths: How to Begin, Progress On, and Complete the Vajrayana Path*. London: Tharpa, 1994.

Hanson, Mervin Viggo. "The *Trikāya:* A Study of the Buddhology of the Early Vijñānavāda School of Indian Buddhism." Ph.D. diss., University of British Columbia, 1980.

Harris, Ian Charles. *The Continuity of Madhyamaka and Yogācāra in Indian Mahāyāna Buddhism*. New York: E. J. Brill, 1991.

Harrison, Paul. "Buddhānusmṛti in the *Pratyutpanna-Buddha-Saṃmukhāvasthita-Samādhi-Sūtra*." *Journal of Indian Philosophy* 6 (1978): 35–57.

———. "Is the Dharma-kāya the Real 'Phantom Body' of the Buddha?" *Journal of the International Association of Buddhist Studies* 15, no. 1 (1992): 44–94.

Hirakawa, Akira. *A History of Indian Buddhism from Śākyamuni to Early Mahāyāna*. Translated by Paul Groner. Honolulu: University of Hawaii Press, 1990.

Hookham, S. K. *The Buddha Within: Tathagatagarbha Doctrine According to the Shentong Interpretation of the "Ratnagotravibhaga."* Albany: State University of New York Press, 1991.

Huntingdon, C. W., and Geshe Namgyal Wangchen, trans. *The Emptiness of Emptiness: An Introduction to Early Indian Mādhyamika*. Honolulu: University of Hawaii Press, 1989.

Ichigo, Masamichi. "Śāntarakṣita's *Madhyamakālaṃkāra.*" In *Studies in the Literature of the Great Vehicle*, edited by Luis Gomez and Jonathan Silk, 141–240. Ann Arbor: University of Michigan Center for South and Southeast Asian Studies, 1989.

Jackson, Roger. *Is Enlightenment Possible?* Ithaca: Snow Lion, 1993.

Jaini, Padmanabh S. "The *Ālokā* of Haribhadra and the *Sāratamā* of Ratnākaraśānti: A Comparative Study of the Two Commentaries of the *Aṣṭasāhasrikā.*" *Bulletin of the School of Oriental and African Studies* 35 (1972): 271–84.

Kajiyama, Yuichi. *An Introduction to Buddhist Philosophy: An Annotated Translation of the "Tarkabhāṣa" of Mokṣākaragupta.* Kyoto: Kyoto University, 1966.

———. "Later Mādhyamikas on Epistemology and Meditation." In *Mahāyāna Buddhist Meditation*, edited by Minoru Kiyota. Honolulu: University of Hawaii Press, 1978.

———. "Stūpas, the Mother of Buddhas, and Dharma-body." In *New Paths in Buddhist Research*, edited by A. K. Warder. Durham, N.C.: Acorn Press, 1985.

Katsura, Shoryu. "A Synopsis of the *Prajñāpāramitopadeśa* of Ratnākaraśānti." *Journal of Indian and Buddhist Studies* 25, no. 1 (1976): 487–84.

Kawamura, Leslie, ed. *The Bodhisattva Doctrine in Buddhism.* Waterloo, Ont.: Wilfred Laurier University Press, 1981.

Keenan, John P. "Pure Land Systematics in India: The *Buddhabhūmisūtra* and the *Trikāya* Doctrine." *The Pacific World*, no. 3, fall 1987, 29–35.

———. "A Study of the *Buddhabhūmyupadeśa:* The Doctrinal Development of the Notion of Wisdom in Yogācāra Thought." Ph.D. diss., University of Wisconsin-Madison, 1980.

Kiyota, Minoru, ed. *Mahāyāna Buddhist Meditation: Theory and Practice.* Honolulu: University of Hawaii Press, 1978.

Kvaerne Per. "On the Concept of Sahaja in Indian Buddhist Tantric Literature." *Temenos* 11 (1975): 88–135.

Lai, Whalen, and Lewis Lancaster, eds. *Early Ch'an in China and Tibet.* Berkeley: Asian Humanities Press, 1983.

Lamotte, Etienne. *History of Indian Buddhism from the Origins to the Śaka Era.* Translated by Sara Webb-Boin. Louvain: Institut Orientaliste Louvain-la-Neuve, 1988.

———. *Le Traité de la Grande Vertu de Sagesse.* Tomes 1–4. Louvain: Institut Orientaliste, 1949–76.

———, ed. *La Somme du Grand Vehicule d'Asanga.* Translated by Etienne Lamotte. Publications de l'Institut Orientaliste de Louvain, no. 8. Louvain: Institut Orientaliste, 1973.

Lancaster, Lewis R. "An Early Mahayana Sermon About the Body of the Buddha and the Making of Images." *Artibus Asiae* 36 (1974): 287–91.

———. "The Oldest Mahāyāna Sūtra: Its Significance for the Study of Buddhist Development." *Eastern Buddhist* 8, no. 1 (1975): 30–41.

———, ed. *Prajñāpāramitā and Related Systems*. Berkeley: University of California Press, 1977.

La Vallée Poussin, Louis de. *L'Abhidharmakośa de Vasubandhu: Traduction et Annotations*. Paris: Paul Geuthner, 1924.

———. "Documents d'Abhidharma 1. Textes Relatifs au Nirvāṇa et aux Asaṃskṛtas en General." *Bulletin de l'Ecole Française d'Extreme-Orient*, 30 (1930): 1-28.

———. "Documents d'Abhidharma 2. La Doctrine des Refuges." *Melanges Chinois et Bouddhiques* 1 (1931–32): 65–109.

———. *Nirvāṇa*. Etudes sur L'Histoire des Religions, 4. Paris: Gabriel Beauchesne, 1925.

———. "Studies in Buddhist Dogma: The Three Bodies of a Buddha *(Trikāya)*." *Journal of the Royal Asiatic Society*, 1906, 943–77.

———. *Vijñaptimātratāsiddhi: La Siddhi de Hiuan-tsang*. Paris: Paul Geuthner, 1928–29.

Lethcoe, Nancy R. "Some Notes on the Relationship between the *Abhisamayālaṃkāra*, the revised *Pañcavimśatisāhasrikā*, and the Chinese translations of the unrevised *Pañcavimśatisāhasrikā*." *Journal of the American Oriental Society* 96, no. 4 (1976): 499–511.

Lindtner, Christian. *Master of Wisdom: Writings of the Buddhist Master Nāgārjuna*. Oakland, Calif.: Dharma Publishing, 1986

———. *Nāgārjuniana*. Copenhagen: Akademisk Forlag, 1982.

Lopez, Donald S. *A Study of Svātantrika*. Ithaca: Snow Lion, 1987.

Makransky, John J. "Controversy over Dharmakāya in India and Tibet: A Reappraisal of its Basis, *Abhisamayālaṃkāra* Chapter 8." *Journal of the International Association of Buddhist Studies* 12, no. 2 (1989): 45–78.

——— "Controversy over Dharmakāya in Indo-Tibetan Buddhism: An Historical-Critical Analysis of *Abhisamayālaṃkāra* Chapter 8 and its Commentaries in Relation to the *Large Prajñāpāramitā Sūtra* and the Yogācāra Tradition." Ph.D. diss., University of Wisconsin-Madison, 1990.

———. "Offering (mchodpa) in Tibetan Ritual Literature." In *Tibetan Literature: Studies in Genre,* edited by José Cabezon and Roger Jackson, pp. 312–30. Ithaca, N.Y.: Snow Lion, 1996.

———. "Proposal of a Modern Solution to an Ancient Problem: Literary-Historical Evidence that the *Abhisamayālaṃkāra* Teaches Three Buddha *Kāyas*." *Journal of Indian Philosophy* 20 (1992): 149–90.

Malalasekera, G. P. *Encyclopaedia of Buddhism*. Sri Lanka: Government of Sri Lanka, 1973.

Masson-Oursel, M. P. "Les Trois Corps du Bouddha." *Journal Asiatique,* ser. 2, 1 (1913): 581–618.

Matsunaga, Yūkei. "Tantric Buddhism and Shingon Buddhism." *Eastern Buddhist* 2, no. 2 (November 1969): 1–14.

Mimaki, Katsumi. "The Intellectual Sequence of Ratnākaraśanti, Jñānaśrimitra, and Ratnakīrti." *Asiatische Studien Etudes Asiatiques* 46, no. 1 (1992): 297–306.

Monier-Williams, Monier. *A Sanskrit-English Dictionary*. Oxford: Oxford University Press, 1899.

Nagao, Gadjin. *Index to the Mahāyāna-sūtrālaṃkāra*. 2 vols. Tokyo: Nihon Gakujuten Shinkokai, 1958–61.

———. "On the Theory of Buddha-Body *(Buddha-kāya)*." Translated by Hirano Umeyo. *Eastern Buddhist* 6, no. 1 (May 1973): 25–53.

Nakamura, Hajime. *Indian Buddhism: A Survey with Bibliographical Notes*. Osaka: KUFS Publications, 1980.

Naughton, Alexander T. "The Buddhist Path to Omniscience." Ph.D. diss., University of Wisconsin-Madison, 1989.

Nyoshul Khen Rinpoche. *Natural Great Perfection*. Edited and translated by Lama Surya Das. Ithaca: Snow Lion, 1995.

Obermiller, E. *Analysis of the Abhisamayālaṃkāra*. London: Luzac, 1933.

———. "The Doctrine of Prajñā-pāramitā as exposed in the *Abhisamayālaṃkāra* of Maitreya." *Acta Orientalia* 11 (1933): 1–133.

———. *History of Buddhism* by Bu ston. Translated by E. Obermiller. Heidelberg: Otto Harrassowitz, 1931.

Paltrul Rinpoche. *The Words of My Perfect Teacher*. Translated by the Padmakara Translation Group. San Francisco, Calif.: Harper Collins, 1994.

Powers, John. *The Yogācāra School of Buddhism: A Bibliography*. Metuchen, N.J.: Scarecrow Press, 1991.

Rahula, Walpola. *What the Buddha Taught*. New York: Grove Press, 1959.

Rawlinson, Andrew. "The Position of the *Aṣṭasāhasrikā Prajñāpāramitā* in the Development of Early Mahāyāna." In *Prajñāpāramitā and Related Systems: Studies in Honor of Edward Conze*, edited by Lewis Lancaster. Berkeley, Calif.: Berkeley Buddhist Studies Series, 1977.

Regamey, K. *Three Chapters from the Samādhirājasūtra*. Warsaw: The Warsaw Society of Sciences and Letters, 1938.

Renou, Louis, and Jean Filliozat. *L'Inde Classique: Manuel des Etudes Indiennes*. Tome 1. Paris: Payot, 1947–49.

———. *L'Inde Classique: Manuel des Etudes Indiennes*. Tome 2. Paris: Ecole Française d''Extreme-Orient, 1953.

Reynolds, Frank E. "The Several Bodies of Buddha: Reflections on a Neglected Aspect of Theravada Tradition." *History of Religions* 16, no. 4 (May 1977): 374–89.

Roerich, George N. *The Blue Annals*. Delhi: Motilal Banarsidass, 1976.

Ruegg, David Seyfort. "Ārya and Bhadanta Vimuktisena on the Gotra-Theory of the Prajñāpāramitā." *Weiner Zeitschrift für die Kunde Sud- und Ostasiens* 12–13 (1966–68): 303–17.

———. "Autour du *lTa ba'i khyad par* de Ye śes sde (version de Touen-Houang, Pelliot Tibetain 814)." *Journal Asiatique,* 1981, 208–29. Also listed as "Le *lTa-ba'i khad-par* de Ye-shes-sde".

———. *Buddha-nature, Mind, and the Problem of Gradualism in a Comparative Perspective*. London: SOAS, University of London, 1989.

———. "The Jo naṅ pas: A School of Buddhist Ontologists According to the *Grub mtha śel gyi me loṅ*." *Journal of the American Oriental Society* 83 (1963): 73–91.

———. *The Literature of the Madhyamaka School of Philosophy in India*. Wiesbaden: Otto Harrassowitz, 1981.

———. *La Théorie du Tathagatagarbha et du Gotra: Etude sur la Soteriologie et la Gnoseologie du Bouddhisme*. Publications de l'Ecole Française d'Extreme-Orient, vol. 70. Paris: E.F.E.O., 1969

———. *Le Traité du Tathāgatagarbha de Bu ston Rin chen grub*. Paris: Ecole Française D'Extreme-Orient, 1973.

Sakuma, Hindenori S. "The Classification of the Dharmakāya Chapter of the *Abhisamayālaṃkāra* by Indian Commentators: The Threefold and the Fourfold Buddhakāya Theories." *Journal of Indian Philosophy* 22 (1994): 259–97.

Schayer, St. *Mahāyāna Doctrines of Salvation*. London: Probsthain and Co., 1923.

———. "Precanonical Buddhism." *Archiv Orientalni* 7 (1935), 121–32.

Schopen, Gregory. "The Phrase '*sa pṛthivīpradeśaś caityabhūto bhavet*' in the *Vajracchedikā:* Notes on the Cult of the Book in Mahāyāna." *Indo-Iranian Journal* 17 (1975): 147–81.

———. "Sukhāvatī as a Generalized Religious Goal in Sanskrit Mahāyāna Sūtra Literature." *Indo-Iranian Journal* 19 (1977): 177–210.

Snellgrove, David. *Indo-Tibetan Buddhism: Indian Buddhists and their Tibetan Successors*. Boston: Shambhala, 1987.

Snellgrove, David, and Hugh Richardson. *A Cultural History of Tibet*. Boston: Shambhala, 1986.

Sopa, Geshe Lhundup. "An Excursus on the Subtle Body in Tantric Buddhism (Notes Contextualizing the Kalacakra)." *Journal of the International Association of Buddhist Studies* 6, no. 2 (1983): 48–66.

Sprung, Mervyn, trans. *Lucid Exposition of the Middle Way: The Essential Chapters from the "Prasannapadā" of Candrakīrti*. London: Routledge & Kegan Paul, 1979.

Stcherbatsky, Theodore. *The Conception of Buddhist Nirvāṇa*. Delhi: Motilal Banarsidass, 1977.

Stein, Otto. "Notes on the Trikaya-Doctrine." In *Jha Commemoration Volume*, pp. 389–98. Poona Oriental Series, no. 39. Poona: Oriental Book Agency, 1937.

Suzuki, Daisetz Teitaro, trans. *The Lankavatara Sutra*. Boulder, Colo.: Prajñā Press, 1978.

———. *Studies in the Laṅkāvatāra Sūtra.* London: Routledge & Kegan Paul, 1930.

Takasaki, Jikido. *A Study on the Ratnagotravibhāga.* Serie Orientale Roma, vol. 33. Rome: Is.M.E.O., 1966.

———. "The *Tathāgatotpattisaṃbhava-nirdeśa* of the *Avataṃsaka* and the *Ratnagotravibhāga.*" *Journal of Indian and Buddhist Studies* 7, no. 1 (1958): 48–53.

Thrangu Rinpoche. *King of Samadhi: Commentaries on the "Samadhi Raja Sutra" and the "Song of Lodro Thaye."* Translated by Erik Pema Kunsang. Hong Kong: Rangjung Yeshe, 1994.

Thurman, Robert A. F., ed. "Maitreyanātha's *Ornament of the Scriptures of the Universal Vehicle.*" English translation of the *Mahāyānasūtrālaṃkāra* and *bhāṣya*, translated by Losang Jamspal, Michael Sweet, Robert Thurman, Joseph Williams, and Leonard Zwilling. Unpublished. 1979.

———, trans. *The Holy Teaching of Vimalakīrti.* University Park: Pennsylvania State University Press, 1976.

Tola, Fernando, and Dragonetti, Carmen. "The *Trisvabhāvakārikā* of Vasubandhu." *Journal of Indian Philosophy* 11 (1983): 225–66.

Tucci, Giuseppi. "Ratnākaraśānti on Āśraya-parāvṛtti." *Asiatica*, 1954, 765–67. Festschrift for Friedrich Weller.

Warder, A. K. *Indian Buddhism.* Delhi: Motilal Banarsidass, 1980.

Watson, Burton. *The Lotus Sutra.* New York: Columbia University Press, 1993.

Wayman, Alex. "Contributions Regarding the Thirty-Two Characteristics of the Great Person." In *Liebenthal Festschrift*, edited by Kshitis Roy. Visvabharati: Santiniketan,1957.

Williams, Paul. *Mahāyāna Buddhism: The Doctrinal Foundations.* New York: Routledge, 1989.

———. "Some Aspects of Language and Construction in the Madhyamaka." *Journal of Indian Philosophy* 8 (1980): 1–45.

Willis, Janice Dean, trans. *On Knowing Reality: The Tattvārtha chapter of Asanga's "Bodhisattvabhūmi."* New York: Columbia University Press, 1979.

Wood, Thomas E. *Mind Only: A Philosophical and Doctrinal Analysis of the Vijñānavāda.* Honolulu: University of Hawaii Press, 1991.

Index